Theories of Political Protest and Social Movements

Political protest and social movements are ubiquitous phenomena. This book focuses on the current theoretical approaches that aim at explaining them: the theory of collective action, the resource mobilization perspective, political opportunity structure theory, the identity approach, the framing perspective, and the dynamics of contention approach. The book has three objectives: (1) Many basic concepts like political opportunities or identity are not clearly defined. It is further often a matter of interpretation as to what factors are supposed to affect which phenomena. The first aim is therefore to provide a detailed introduction to, and a clear restatement of, the theories. Only then is it possible to assess and improve them. (2) For each theory the major strengths and weaknesses are discussed, and various modifications and extensions are suggested. (3) Building on these analyses, it is shown how the theories can be integrated into a single theoretical paradigm: the structural-cognitive model.

Karl-Dieter Opp is Professor at the University of Leipzig, Germany, and Affiliate Professor at the University of Washington, Seattle. His areas of interest include collective action and political protest, rational choice theory, philosophy of the social sciences and the emergence and effects of norms and institutions. He is the author of *The Rationality of Political Protest* (1989), coauthor of *The Origins of a Spontaneous Revolution: East Germany, 1989* (1995) and editor (with M. Hechter) of *Social Norms* (2001).

Theories of Political Protest and Social Movements

A multidisciplinary introduction, critique, and synthesis

Karl-Dieter Opp

Routledge
Taylor & Francis Group

LONDON AND NEW YORK

First published 2009
by Routledge
2 Park Square, Milton Park, Abingdon, Oxon, OX14 4RN

Simultaneously published in the USA and Canada
by Routledge
270 Madison Avenue, New York, NY 10016

*Routledge is an imprint of the Taylor & Francis Group,
an informa business*

© 2009 Karl-Dieter Opp

Typeset in Times New Roman by Swales & Willis Ltd
Printed and bound in Great Britain by
Antony Rowe, Chippenham

British Library Cataloguing in Publication Data
A catalogue record for this book is available from the British Library

Library of Congress Cataloging in Publication Data
A catalog record for this book has been requested

ISBN 10: 0–415–48388–3 (hbk)
ISBN 10: 0–415–48389–6 (pbk)
ISBN 10: 0–203–88384–5 (ebk)

ISBN 13: 978–0–415–48388–9 (hbk)
ISBN 13: 978–0–415–48389–6 (pbk)
ISBN 13: 978–0–203–88384–6 (ebk)

Contents

List of figures

List of tables

Preface

Political protest has become a legitimate way and is widely used to influence the decisions of governments and other organizations. Organizers of protests are a large spectrum of groups like social movements, unions, and citizen initiatives. It is therefore not surprising that social scientists have tried to explain the origins of protest and social movements. Nonetheless, extant theories do not yet provide satisfactory answers to why protest and social movements rise and decline. Existing theoretical paradigms still struggle to explain various puzzles. One is why so few people participate in protest events, although the protesters have the same goals as many others who are silent. Another puzzle is that even if severe repression is to be expected many people take to the streets, as the east European protests in 1989 and 1990 testify. What motivates people to take to the streets if it is likely that this has very harmful consequences? Another puzzle is the form of protest that is chosen. Why are protests sometimes violent and sometimes peaceful? For example, why were the large-scale protests against a planned change of the French labor law in March 2006 violent, whereas the protests in East Germany in 1989 against the communist regime – after decades of intense deprivation – were peaceful?

This book focuses on the theoretical perspectives that aim at explaining such events and, in general, provide explanations of the rise and decline of protest, social movements, and other challenging groups. The first objective is to propose a *restatement and clarification of the major theoretical perspectives*. Although most of them have existed for decades the clarity of their basic concepts like political opportunities or identity leaves still much to be desired. It is further often a matter of interpretation what the factors are that are supposed to explain a certain class of phenomena. Only if the concepts and propositions of the theories are clear is it possible to discover their strengths and weaknesses and to improve them.

This is the second aim of the book: it provides a *detailed critical analysis of each perspective*. For this purpose, a guideline is developed in chapter 1 that sets out criteria for evaluating the theories. But the book is not only destructive. A further aim is to improve the theories by suggesting various *modifications and extensions*.

These analyses set the stage for the major concern of the book: it is a *synthesis of the perspectives*. Building on the initial restatement, critical analyses, and suggested modifications of the theories, it is shown how they can be integrated into a single theoretical framework which is called the *structural-cognitive model*. One achievement of this model is that it shows in detail how the different theoretical approaches are related.

Let us look at the contents of the book in more detail. As was said before, in discussing a theoretical perspective we start with its reconstruction. Which texts should be the basis of such a reconstruction? For each perspective, there exists a founding paper or book. For example, the article by J. D. McCarthy and M. N. Zald from 1977 is the founding article of the resource mobilization perspective. This article sets the stage for the further development of the perspective. In general, thus, a useful procedure for reconstructing the propositions of a perspective is to analyze in detail those basic texts. Surprisingly, this has never been done. To be sure, these texts are cited time and again, but we do not find any thorough discussion that restates them in a clear way and analyzes in detail their strengths and weaknesses. This is the procedure applied in this book: each of the chapters concerned with a theoretical perspective starts with the basic text. The advantage is that it can be clearly seen what the further development of the perspective is and to what extent subsequent work solves the old problems, breaks new ground or generates new problems.

After the restatement of the propositions of the founding article or book a detailed discussion follows. Then subsequent developments are analyzed. Furthermore, each chapter suggests new propositions that modify the respective perspective.

In discussing the strengths and weaknesses of a perspective it must be decided which criteria are to be applied. In contrast to most critiques, we analyze the *explanatory power* of each perspective: does it explain the *form* of political action or the *kind* of challenging groups? E.g. does a perspective explain when groups or individuals choose violent action and when they stick to conventional tactics? It goes without saying, that we further discuss in detail the *empirical validity* of the perspectives.

The theories have so far not been assessed in regard to their *hidden agenda*. This means that advocates of a perspective might pursue a research program without ever acknowledging it explicitly and without being aware of it. This hidden agenda that the present book unveils is one of the major arguments for the proposed structural-cognitive model and the suggested thrust of future theory and research. To be sure, some of the approaches are mainly structural (i.e. their propositions are referring to the macro level), others are mainly individualistic (i.e. their propositions refer to the micro level). However, all provide some rudimentary linkage of both levels. That is to say, all perspectives actually engage in micro-macro explanations, but this is never done in an explicit, systematic, and clear way. The book takes up this hidden agenda. If all perspectives actually engage in micro-macro explanation, why not do this in an explicit and systematic way? This is the major thrust of the book and of the structural-cognitive model: engaging in micro-macro explanations that involve macro theories, a micro theory, and "bridge assumptions" that connect both levels (see chapter 1 for a detailed discussion).

Because of the importance of this explanatory strategy for the argument of the book we will briefly illustrate it. Assume a macro proposition (i.e. a statement about collectivities) reads that open political opportunities lead to collective protest. Why? The answer could be that opportunities (a macro factor) change individual costs and benefits (micro factors); these then influence individual behavior (a micro factor) which, in turn, makes up collective action (a macro factor). Thus, macro variables (opportunities) affect micro variables (costs and benefits) which ultimately lead to collective protest (macro variable). This argument includes a macro proposition, a micro proposition, and "bridge assumptions": there is a macro-to-micro ("top-down") and micro-to-macro ("bottom-up") relation. Thus, a *mechanism* is specified that explains the macro proposition. The question is: why does an open opportunity structure lead to protest? The answer is: because opportunities alter certain individual incentives to political action which make up collective forms of protest behavior. The book shows in detail that such micro-macro explanations are a major requirement for a satisfactory explanation of protest phenomena.

This kind of explanation is rather uncommon in the social movement literature. But, it is shown in each chapter concerned with one of the existing perspectives, that this is its hidden agenda. Therefore, we ask for each theoretical perspective: (a) Does it implicitly apply a *general theory of action* (i.e. a *micro theory*)? (b) Does it implicitly pursue *micro-macro explanations*? As our detailed analyses of existing theories show, both questions are to be answered affirmatively for each perspective.

Let us look in more detail at the contents of the chapters. Chapter 1 (What kind of theory do we need and what is a good theory?) provides a guideline for criticizing the theories in the field. It further introduces some general theories of action that are – most of the time implicitly – applied in the perspectives discussed. It is further explained what a micro-macro approach is and what its advantages are. Chapter 2 (Protest, social movements, and collective action: conceptual clarifications and the subject of the book) discusses the basic concepts in the field and suggests how they could be defined in a clear and theoretically fruitful way.

Chapters 3 to 8 and chapter 10 focus on the extant theoretical perspectives: the theory of collective action (chapter 3) and its application to protest and social movements (chapter 4), the resource mobilization perspective (chapter 5), political opportunity structure theory (chapter 6), identity theory (chapter 7) and the framing perspective (chapter 8). The most recent dynamics of contention approach is the subject of chapter 10. Chapter 9 does not present a theoretical perspective but suggests new propositions that focus on framing and identity. To generate these proposition the social psychological balance theory is applied.

Chapter 11 suggests a synthesis of the existing approaches, the "structural-cognitive model." This is the core chapter of the book: based on the discussion of the previous chapters, we propose a unified theory that explains movement related phenomena. We further discuss briefly four case studies and suggest possibilities to apply the structural-cognitive model. If the book is used in classes – see below, these case studies could be used as a starting point for elaborating the structural-cognitive model and for a comparative discussion of the model and the other theories.

The final chapter, chapter 12, is a summary and general discussion of the major arguments provided in the book. We further provide some guidelines for future theory and research.

The book is about protest and social movements. These are the terms that are most of the time used to describe the field of study. However, the definitions of these terms in the literature vary widely. In this book these terms are defined in a very wide sense (chapter 2): "protest" involves any collective action aimed at influencing the decisions of others. This is actually the theme of the book. To be sure, this includes the activities one typically has in mind when one speaks about protest such as participating in demonstrations or signing petitions. However, the definition covers a much wider array of activities that are used in order to influence others' decisions such as negotiating or enhancing one's resources or taking legal action. Similarly, we focus on protest groups which are defined as any collectivity of actors who want to achieve their shared goals by influencing decisions of a target. This includes "social movements" such as the peace or civil rights movement, but many other groups as well. Thus, the subject of the book is rather wide.

The book is not written in social science jargon and should thus be understandable at the level of undergraduate students. The detailed exposition and critique of the basic theoretical perspectives is the subject of any course on political protest and social movements in sociology, political science and political psychology. It is thus eligible as a *textbook* in those classes. I believe that instructors as well as students will like the book because teachers and students alike are not only interested in who says what in the literature, but want to look at problems, at the differences between the perspectives and in particular at the possibilities for integrating them. These are exactly the themes addressed in the book, and no other book provides such discussions.

But the book is by no means only a textbook. Its aim is also to contribute to the development of theory in the field. A major readership is thus academics of various social science disciplines, mainly sociology, political science, and political psychology.

Acknowledgments

The plan to write this book and the first pages of a manuscript go back to 1991. But somehow other projects were more attractive. The events that led me to begin with the book in its present form were the classes about social movements and political protest that I held – after my retirement – at the Department of Sociology of the University of Leipzig (Germany) and the Department of Sociology at the University of Washington (Seattle). The basic idea of the book, to begin the discussion of each theoretical approach with its founding paper or book, then provide a detailed critical analysis of this and the later work, and, finally, propose a synthesis, was developed over the years and tried out in my classes. I am indebted to the students who helped me through their vivid participation which showed me where presentations and arguments had to be improved and where new arguments had to be provided. I would further like to thank in particular the graduate students and colleagues at the University of Washington who provided valuable suggestions and critique. They are, in alphabetical order: Michael Hechter (now university of Arizona), Edgar Kiser, Margaret Levi, Steven Pfaff, Erin Powell, and Kate Stovel. I am further indebted to my colleagues and graduate students from the Department of Sociology at the University of Washington where I have been visiting regularly since 2003. I am very grateful for the support of the department and the University. The truly academic atmosphere in the department was (and still is) a very stimulating environment for writing such a book.

Peter Abell (London School of Economics) gave me valuable suggestions for chapter 9 (Identity, framing, and cognitive balance: toward a new theory of identity and framing). I would also like to thank "my" editor at Routledge, Gerhard Boomgaarden, for his valuable suggestions.

1 What kind of theory do we need and what is a good theory?

This chapter sets the stage for the substantive discussions in the following chapters. In order to understand what this chapter is about it is necessary to briefly sketch the research program suggested in this book. The starting point is that each theoretical perspective[1] in the social movement literature deals with micro-macro relationships.[2] This will be shown in detail in the following chapters. For example, in the literature on political opportunities an assumption is that changing opportunities (macro factors) affect certain individual incentives (micro factors). Furthermore, each theoretical perspective applies some general (social psychological) theory of individual behavior, i.e. a micro theory. For example, if it is assumed that political opportunities affect individual incentives to protest, it is implicitly held that incentives affect protest behavior. Otherwise, changing political opportunities would not change collective political action. The problem of the vast social movement literature is that this theoretical structure is never spelled out in detail: neither micro-macro relationships nor micro theories are clearly specified. The message of this book is that this is a failure and that a reorientation of theory and research to engage in such micro-macro modeling is necessary.[3] The present chapter will discuss some components of this research program.

In regard to applying general theories about individual behavior (i.e. micro theories), several question arise: Which theories might be taken into consideration? How can these theories be applied to explain specific phenomena and what are these theories good for? Sections 1 to 3 address these questions.

Since micro-macro modeling is the exception rather than the rule in the social movement literature, the question arises as to what the arguments are for pursuing this explanatory strategy explicitly and systematically. Section 4 provides the major arguments. Section 5 discusses a possible alternative that is largely pursued in the literature: the procedure is just to combine the factors which the perspectives focus on as additive independent variables.

Sections 6 and 7 are concerned with issues of theory construction and concept formation.[4] At first sight, this seems rather superfluous. Does not even an undergraduate student know what a good theory looks like? If this is true we would expect that theories in the social sciences and especially in the social movement literature are less often flawed, and we would not expect that even renowned scholars make simple methodological mistakes. For example, definitions and empirical hypotheses are often mixed up, and it seems unclear to some authors what a "tautology" is and what the difference between a tautology and circular reasoning is. Therefore, it seems advisable to provide a short discussion of issues of theory construction and in particular of the question of how to criticize a theory.

Similarly, there are misconceptions in regard to concept formation. For example, it is held that wide concepts are to be avoided. This and other issues of concept formation are discussed in section 8.

1. General social psychological theories for social movement research

Theories of protest and social movements are theories of the middle range.[5] These are theories that explain specific kinds of phenomena such as protest participation, crime or divorce. If scholars want to explain specific phenomena, a common strategy is to search for conditions that are causes for these phenomena.

Another strategy is to apply a general theory that includes the phenomena to be explained as a specific class of explananda. For example, in order to explain protest behavior one might apply a general theory of action that comprises protest behavior as a special form of action. This strategy of applying a general theory is typically employed by advocates of the theory of collective action: the general theory is a theory of action and the phenomena to be explained are a specific kind of action, namely collective action.

It is very rare that a general theory is explicitly and systematically applied by the proponents of the other perspectives in the social movements literature. However, the analyses in this book clearly show that the proponents of these other perspectives *implicitly* apply a general theory of action. We will argue later in this chapter, that the application of general theories is to be strongly recommended. This raises the question of which general theories seem most appropriate to the field of social movements and protest. This section provides a brief outline of these theories.

The theory of rational action

The theory of *collective* action is one of the theoretical perspectives in the field of social movements and protest. It is based on Olson's seminal work (Olson 1965) and will be discussed in detail in chapter 3 of this book. This perspective is the only one that uses explicitly rational choice theory (RCT) to generate hypotheses that explain specific social phenomena. In this subsection the basic propositions of this theory are presented – they will be called the "general model." Next, two important versions of the theory are distinguished: the narrow and wide version. Finally we look at a widely accepted critique of the theory, namely the tautology charge.

The general model

The first proposition of RCT[6] is that *preferences* (i.e. the goals or motives or desires) of individual actors are conditions for their behavior. In other words, individual behavior is goal-oriented or, put differently, an individual's interests are a determinant of his or her behavior. The second proposition reads that behavior depends on the *constraints* or, equivalently, behavioral opportunities the individual is faced with. "Constraints" are any phenomena that impede the individual's goal attainment, whereas "opportunities" are any phenomena that promote the individual's goal attainment. For example, if individuals wish to express their discontent against a government, the expected negative sanctions would be a type of constraint (i.e. an event that impedes the realization of individual goals). The third proposition is that individuals choose between the behavioral alternatives open to them by maximizing their utility. In other words, individuals do what they think is best for them. Thus, RCT consists of the *preference proposition*, the *constraints proposition* and the *utility-maximization proposition*.

The narrow and the wide version

For the theoretical discussions in this book it is important that there are two versions of RCT. The version which social movement scholars usually have in mind and criticize is the *narrow version* that is mainly used in neo-classical economics.[7] In addition to the propositions of the general model, assumptions are, e.g. that reality is perceived correctly, that only material incentives matter, that individuals explicitly calculate the costs and benefits of their action,[8] that individuals are fully informed, and that individuals maximize their objective utility from the viewpoint of an observer. This narrow version is only a caricature of a *wide version* which assumes "bounded rationality." The wide version is used by most sociologists of the rational choice tradition and is increasingly becoming accepted by economists as well.[9] Basic assumptions of the wide model are that beliefs (which includes perceptions) and all sorts of costs and benefits (including soft incentives such as norms or informal sanctions) may be determinants of behavior. Another assumption is that persons "satisfice," that is, do what they think is best for them and not what objectively (i.e. from the viewpoint of a third omniscient person) yields the highest possible benefits.

This wide version can be applied to explain various phenomena which social movement scholars are interested in. Examples are individual protest behavior, the decision to mobilize resources, and decisions of authorities about how to deal with protests.

Including non-economic incentives and beliefs (that may be at odds with reality) in an explanation of collective action and protest behavior has the consequence that RCT can be applied to a vast variety of situations. For example, the great number of spontaneous political protests during the East European revolutions cannot be explained by economic incentives alone. Empirical research suggests that perceptions of repression, social rewards and the belief that personal participation in collective action matters (i.e. that perceived personal influence is high) are important determinants of participation. There are many situations where it seems that individuals cooperate without any incentives (or, more precisely, without any palpable incentives). An example is contributing to the Wikipedia Encyclopedia or the *Oxford English Dictionary*, which seems to lack any external remuneration.

Authors are not even mentioned. Experimental results in the dictator and ultimatum games are stunning as well. Assume a dictator disposes of a sum of, say, $100 and may offer you any percentage of this money. If you reject, nobody receives anything. If you agree, each gets the respective amount. Assume the dictator offers you one cent. Would you accept? One could argue that even with one cent you are better off than before and you will accept. But most subjects reject such an offer. In general, offers of about 50 percent are accepted. This is the ultimatum game. In the dictator game a person – the dictator – only decides what amount another person gets. Again, the dictators may keep all the money, but that does not happen: most dictators give substantial amounts.[10] Why? It seems that a fairness norm works: one has a good conscience if one sticks to certain rules of distributing some assets. Thus, "soft" incentives and not material rewards are essential in these situations.

The tautology charge

Social movements scholars who criticize RCT most of the time attack the narrow version (see, e.g., Fireman and Gamson 1979; see also Koopmans 2005: 20, 28). But often they reject a wide version as well. A major argument against the wide version – but also often against the narrow version – is that it is *tautological* or, equivalently, *analytically true* (see, e.g., Fireman and Gamson 1979: 20; Ferree and Miller 1985: 40; Ferree 1992: 30 argues that the whole rational choice approach is tautological).[11] It is striking that the authors who raise this critique do not provide a detailed analysis of the theory showing why it is supposed to be tautological. In order to examine whether this charge is correct, it is first necessary to clarify what it means that a statement is tautological (or analytically true).

A sentence is "tautological" (or, more precisely, "analytically true") if its truth can be determined by analyzing the meaning of its terms. For example, the sentence "all bachelors are unmarried" is in this sense tautological (or analytically true) because when we analyze the meaning of the terms "bachelor" and "unmarried" we find that a bachelor is, by definition, a person who is unmarried. The sentence thus says "unmarried persons are unmarried," which is certainly a true sentence.[12] Thus, finding out whether a statement is tautological requires one to analyze the meaning of its terms. If it turns out that this is sufficient to determine its truth, the statement is tautologically.

Is the wide version of RCT tautological? This would be the case if the truth of the theory could be determined by analyzing the meaning of its terms. It can easily be seen that this is not sufficient to determine its truth: the dependent variable is some behavior, whereas the independent variables refer to motivations and beliefs. Knowing what the meaning of "behavior," "preferences," and "beliefs" is, does not give us any information about the truth or falsity of RCT. Instead, we have to look at reality in order to determine whether preferences and beliefs really lead to behavior, i.e. whether the theory fits the facts. The theory is thus clearly not tautological or analytically true.

But perhaps Fireman and Gamson do not mean "tautological" in the strict logical sense, when they raise the tautology charge.[13] They have probably in mind that including "soft" incentives may enable the researchers to invoke any incentives *ad hoc* without providing empirical evidence. For example, one may consider a behavior that provides some service to a person as an indicator that this behavior has been driven by a moral norm or altruism. This procedure would correspond to an example given by Karl R. Popper: there was a thunderstorm and person A maintained that the cause was that Zeus (the king of the gods in Greek mythology) was angry. Another person B asked how A knows that. A answered: don't you see that there is a thunderstorm? The sentence in question is not a tautology because an analysis of the meaning of the terms of "there is a thunderstorm because Zeus is angry" cannot give us any hint about its truth. What Fireman and Gamson apparently mean with "tautology" is that RCT is *circular*. Roughly, that means that the dependent variable is seen as a sufficient reason to assume that independent variables have certain values. Thus, the existence of a behavior that benefits others is seen as a sufficient reason to assume that there was an altruistic motivation. This procedure has nothing to do with a tautology.

It goes without saying that circular reasoning is not acceptable in science. This implies that an assumption that a behavior is caused by a norm, by sanctioning or altruism has to be tested in a way that the variables are measured independently of each other. This is stuff of the first classes in the methods of empirical research. The question is whether this procedure is part of the wide version of RCT. Of course, circular reasoning is *not* part of the theory – see the previous presentation.

However, proponents of RCT *could* apply circular reasoning. This can be done for every theory, including the theories that Fireman and Gamson and other critics of RCT favor. The common procedure in RCT is to try to provide empirical evidence for the validity of rational choice explanations by applying the methods of empirical research. Thus, "altruism" will not only be assumed but one will try to find out empirically whether benefitting others is really based on altruistic motivations. If a circular procedure is applied, then this is a fault of the scientists who apply the theory. A theory is usually not circular, only scientists who violate the rules of proper scientific procedure apply circular reasoning. Thus, the argument that the wide version is tautological (or analytically true) or circular is absolutely untenable. The only interesting point in this critique is that such an obviously false allegation is held by so many critics.

It is awkward that Fireman and Gamson themselves use non-economic incentives in their alleged alternative to Olson's theory. Thus, they invoke norms, etc. as factors in explaining protest behavior, but without applying any theory explicitly. This procedure raises two problems. One is, how the authors know that these factors are relevant – see our discussion of the role of theories below. The other problem is that the authors' argument implies the following: if norms, beliefs, etc. are invoked as factors without (explicitly) applying a theory, then no tautology or circularity is involved. But if one adduces a theory that implies that norms, beliefs, etc. are explanatory factors, tautological or circular reasoning is involved. This is certainly absurd.

In the social movement literature it is not only the theory of rational action which is considered tautological. This objection is raised against other theories as well.

For example, Goodwin and Jasper (1999) assert that the political opportunity structure proposition (see chapter 6 in this book) is tautological if "political opportunities" are defined in a broad way (30, 31, 36). Again, a detailed argument for this claim is missing. We will show below that this claim is plainly wrong (see p. 25: "A note on broad and narrow concepts").

Value expectancy theory

This theory (VET) is a version of the theory of rational action.[14] The theory assumes that individuals perceive certain behavioral alternatives (such as demonstrating or working for a protest group). The decision to choose one of these alternatives depends on the perceived behavioral consequences (such as a cleaner environment or receiving approval from members of a protest group). For each behavioral consequence, its utility (or valuation) and its subjective expected probability that the consequence occurs are multiplied. For example, for the behavioral alternative "demonstrating" the utility and likelihood of getting approval from important others are multiplied.[15] A high value of the product of the utility and probability of a given consequence means that the consequence is valued by the individual very positively and expected with high certainty. The greater the number and values of such products for a given behavioral alternative are, the higher is, by definition, the net utility of a given behavioral alternative. The theory states that the behavioral alternative with the highest net utility is performed.

How do the general models of RCT and VET differ? Both explain actions; the explanatory variables are preferences (utilities or values) as well as perceived constraints (subjective probabilities, i.e. beliefs). The assumption that individuals choose the alternative with the highest net utility is equivalent to utility maximization (i.e. doing what one thinks is best).

The difference between the two theories is that VET is more informative: it tells us exactly how preferences and constraints influence behavior: we have to ascertain empirically the behavioral consequences for each perceived behavioral alternative, and we have to multiply the utilities and probabilities. Since VET is more specific than the general model, it seems preferable to apply it in empirical research.

It has been argued that VET (and the general model as well) can also be applied to explain preferences and beliefs. The idea is that a preference forms if its existence has many benefits for a person that are expected with a high subjective probability. This idea is contained in the theory of attitude formation, in dissonance and balance theory that will be discussed later in this section – we will briefly address this idea when we discuss these theories. In a similar vein, holding or acquiring a belief is also based on costs and benefits.

Attitude theory

Rational choice and value expectancy theory are often criticized because they do not explain their independent variables. The theory developed by Martin Fishbein and Icek Ajzen[16] explains, among other things, attitudes toward an attitude object.

The theory posits that persons value an object (a social movement, a political candidate, a leader of a movement, representatives of the state, the police) if this object is associated with many features that are valued positively and that are ascribed to the object with a high subjective probability. For example, assume a political candidate is divorced, has a criminal record and is alcoholic. If people believe that a candidate has these properties and if they value these properties negatively, these valuations are transferred to the whole person (i.e. the attitude object): people will dislike the candidate to a great extent. Similarly, the single features of a social movement will add up to generate a general valuation of the movement.

Dissonance and balance theory

Dissonance theory and balance theory are focusing on the relations between cognitive elements which are constituents of a mental model or, equivalently, cognitive structure.[17] The question the theories address is which changes of certain cognitive elements will change other cognitive elements. The reason for change is that certain configurations of cognitive elements are dissonant or imbalanced (i.e. costly). An example which is mentioned by Festinger (1957) is a person who smokes, knows that smoking causes cancer and values a long life. This cognitive configuration is apparently psychologically uncomfortable and, thus, dissonant. Such a situation is, in terms of the theory of rational action, costly. Therefore, it is likely that actors change a dissonant situation. The theories state conditions specifying when which types of changes are likely.

The question of when cognitive elements change is exactly the question the framing perspective focuses on (see chapter 8). Although dissonance and balance theory are highly relevant for the questions the framing approach tries to tackle, neither dissonance nor balance theory have been applied. We will show in chapter 9 how hypotheses being addressed by the framing and identity perspectives can be generated by applying these two social psychological theories.

Social Identity Theory

Another theory that has rarely been applied in the field of social movements[18] is social identity theory (SIT), based on the work of Henri Tajfel and associates (see in particular Tajfel and Turner 1979, 1986).[19] The theory assumes that individuals compare the groups they are members of (their ingroups) with other groups (the outgroups). If it turns out that the ingroups have a lower (perceived) social status, i.e. possess a relatively large number of important negative features, the individual's social identity is diminished (see, e.g., Tajfel and Turner 1979: 43). "Social identity" refers to "the part of an individual's self-concept which derives from his knowledge of his membership of a social group (or groups) together with the value and emotional significance attached to that membership" (Tajfel 1978: 63). The individual's self-concept (or, equivalently, self-image) is his or her self-evaluation. The social status of the ingroups one is attached to, compared to other (out-) groups, thus contributes to the individual's self-concept. Why is this important? The answer is: "Individuals strive to achieve or to maintain positive social identity" (Tajfel and Turner 1986: 16). In terms of the theory of rational action, a negative or a low social identity is a cost.

Accordingly, one would expect that individuals try to change a situation in which their ingroups have a low social status and, thus, in which their social identity is low or negative. This is exactly the hypothesis of SIT: "When social identity is unsatisfactory, individuals will strive either to leave their existing groups and join some more positively distinct group and/or make their group more positively distinct" (Tajfel and Turner 1986: 16).

These possible reactions are then further classified in the literature. Making a group "more positively distinct" may be achieved by "redefining or altering the elements of the comparative situation" (ibid., 19–20). For example, an individual may seek new features of the ingroup so that a comparison with outgroups becomes more favorable. Apart from this cognitive restructuring "social competition" may be an option, i.e. actions that aim at raising the status of the ingroup. This includes protest behavior. Thus, the theory may be applied to explain participation in protest behavior.

The literature abounds with classifications of the reactions to a low ingroup status. Tajfel and his associates as well as later work further suggest various conditions for choosing a particular option in a situation of unsatisfactory social identity. One of the major problems of SIT is that there is so far no satisfactory theory that specifies exactly under which conditions which alternative is chosen.

Nonetheless, it seems promising to apply the theory to explain social movement phenomena. Although cognitive restructuring has been addressed by the framing perspective, clear and testable propositions are missing (see chapter 8). SIT may provide some suggestions for conditions that affect framing. An attractive feature of SIT is that it considers not only protest (or social competition) as an option in a problematic situation, but many other possible reactions as well.

Are there better theories?

Each theory in the social sciences is controversial. The theories we have just discussed are no exception. Rational choice theory and, thus the theory of collective action, have aroused a particularly sharp and in part emotional criticism. It is not possible and not necessary either to discuss these criticisms in detail. When we discuss the micro model for political protest in chapter 4 we will address some basic arguments against the rational actor model. In this section, we will only emphasize two points.

(1) It is not sufficient reason for discarding a theory, i.e. not further using it, if it proves problematic. If all theories with some problem would be abandoned not a single theory in the social sciences would be left. This includes the theoretical perspectives in the field of social movements. As we will see in later chapters, each of these perspectives is burdened with various problems.

The basic criterion for dismissing a theory is that there is a better one. There can be no doubt that the theories mentioned before have been applied successfully to various explanatory problems and that no clearly superior theories are available. It is thus a useful strategy to apply the theories presented before to explain social movement phenomena.

(2) Critics of rational choice theory would reject this claim. For example, Ferree and Miller (1985) argue that the "obscurantism of incentive formulations can best be seen by contrast to the approaches to group interests found, for example, in Mead ... and Marx" (41).[20] What the authors then present as an alternative are at best orienting hypotheses (for the exact meaning of this term see below) and not informative propositions. For example, the authors claim that "individuals derive their interests through their memberships in groups" or that "social organizations shape individual interests by defining events in different ways as well as by providing a 'schedule of preferences,' or values, to attach to the events thus defined" (41). First of all, an interest cannot be "derived" in a strict logical sense from group memberships, only sentences can be derived from other sentences – this is a basic and in general well-known fact of formal logic. But maybe the authors use the word "derive" not in its technical sense but in the sense that individuals' interests "are determined" by group memberships. This would be only an informative hypothesis if it is specified what kinds of "interest" are brought about by what kinds of group memberships. The second hypothesis – organizations "shape" interests – does not tell us what kinds of interests are brought about by what kinds of organizations. These examples illustrate that there are many orienting hypotheses around but they need extensive elaboration to arrive at an informative theory. The authors do not provide such propositions and they are not found in the literature as well. Thus, the kind of critique illustrated by Ferree and Miller does not provide an alternative to the theories presented before.

2. The application of theories: a first look at how to explain macro events by micro theories

A theory can be applied in two ways. One is to derive general propositions. For example, the theory of rational action is the "background theory" of the theory of collective action. In other words, general propositions about collective action – e.g. the larger a group, the less likely is the provision of a public good – are derived from the theory of rational action. In this section, we focus on the application of a theory to explain *singular events* such as the origins of the civil rights movement or the protests around Three Mile Island after the nuclear accident on March 28, 1979. These explanations thus address phenomena that take place at certain times and places.

Let us begin with an illustration which is summarized in Figure 1.1. In the fall of 1989 protests in Leipzig and in East Germany in general increased dramatically and finally led to the collapse of the communist regime. This is the *explanandum*, i.e. the event to be explained.[21] There are numerous factors that could be and are proposed in the media and in scientific treatises as causes for the protests. Is, for example, the increased discontent of the population before the fall of 1989 a causal factor? Or was the structure of the city with a big square at the center that is well suited as a

An Example

Theoretical propositions

(1) Rational choice theory: Individuals choose the action that is least costly and most beneficial for them.

(2) Assumptions about relevant incentives to participate:

Protest $= a + b_1$ (Discontent $\times$ Perceived Influence) $+ b_2$ Moral Incentives $+$
$+ b_3$ Social Incentives $- b_4$ (Severity $\times$ Probability of Repression).

Incentives are interdependent: high discontent and influence raise moral and social incentives.

Initial conditions

(1) Changes of incentives:

- $\rightarrow$ increase of discontent
- $\rightarrow$ increase of perceived influence
- $\rightarrow$ increase of moral incentives
- $\rightarrow$ increase of social incentives
- $\rightarrow$ repression does not change
- $\rightarrow$ increasing discontent and influence raised moral and social incentives.
- $\rightarrow$ incentives to joint action: people knew where to meet other dissatisfied people.

(2) Effects of internal and external events (Gorbachev's reforms, the liberalization in Poland and Hungary) on changes of incentives

Other assumption

Definitional assumption: A demonstration consists of the joint protests of individuals at a certain location.

Explanandum: Increase of the protests in Leipzig in the fall of 1989 (between September 25 and end of November 1989).

The structure of the explanation

explanans
law/theory
initial conditions

---

explanandum

Figure 1.1 Explaining the relationship between external events and an increase of the East German protests in 1989

demonstration site important in contributing to the origin of demonstrations? It is typical for the literature on the East German revolution that a vast array of factors are regarded as causes. These are specific events that have occurred before the protests. These causes are the *initial conditions* in an explanation (see Figure 1.1).

How do we know which factors have actually been causes of the protests? The statements referring to causes are *singular causal statements* such as "the discontent of the population led to protest." How do we know that these statements are true? "Plausibility" of the statement or an "understanding" of the situation are unreliable: people's feelings of plausibility and understanding differ. We need more objective criteria for ascertaining whether certain factors are causes. This is exactly the role of theories. As the previous section shows, theories provide general information about the *kinds* of factors that are causes for certain types of phenomena. For example, rational choice theory calls our attention to costs and benefits and political opportunity theory to political opportunities as causes. This *general* information about factors can be utilized in *specific* situations. For example, if a theory stipulates that in general increasing political opportunities raise protest, we may use this information to find out in specific situations whether opportunities had increased before protest rose. Thus, theories function as spotlights that shed light on the factors that are causes for the phenomena to be explained.

This illustrates the importance of theories in explanations. There is no other reliable way to select the relevant causal factors. Even if our theories are problematic, they are better then just selecting factors arbitrarily or on the basis of subjective criteria.

To select the relevant factors in our example we apply rational choice theory (RCT). We formulate it in the following way: individuals choose the action that is least costly and most beneficial for them. "Political protest" is an action. Therefore, in order to explain protest RCT prompts us to search for those costs and benefits that might instigate people to participate in protests.

What are these costs and benefits? As we will see in more detail in chapters 3 and 4 (section 4), the following kinds of costs and benefits, i.e. *incentives*, have been shown to be important in various empirical studies. Two major factors are the intensity of *political discontent* and the individuals' *perceived personal influence*. This is the extent to which an individual thinks her or his protest makes a difference. These variables interact, i.e. the effect of discontent depends on the extent to which individuals consider themselves influential. The effect of discontent is high if influence is strong and vice versa.

Two other factors are important: a shared feeling that there is an obligation to participate under certain conditions (moral incentives), and the extent to which protest yields social rewards from important others (social incentives). The major cost of participating in the East German revolution was the expected state *repression*: participation becomes unlikely if the severity and probability of repression are high. To summarize:

$$\text{Protest} = a + b_1 (\text{Discontent} \times \text{Perceived Influence}) + b_2 \text{ Moral Incentives} + b_3 \text{ Social Incentives} - b_4 (\text{Severity} \times \text{Probability of Repression}).$$

This is a proposition – we call it the *protest model* – that is based on RCT because it consists of costs and benefits. RCT is thus used as a guide to find types of factors that seem important. These are incentives and not the age, gender, or the genes of actors. But the *specific* kinds of costs and benefits are not implied by RCT. The researcher has to formulate hypotheses about these incentives and test them empirically.[22]

The protest model implies that an increase of the positive incentives – given the negative incentives (repression) – must precede an increase in protest behavior. Whether this is the case must be determined empirically. Let us assume that empirical data confirm the increase of the positive incentives and the stability of repression (for details see the references in note 21).

The explanation does not yet address the question of why the incentives led to *joint* protests at certain places. This can only be explained if there are additional incentives that prompt individuals to convene in a certain place at a certain time. It is argued (for details see the literature cited before) that discontented citizens expected that other discontented citizens will convene in the center of the city on Mondays due to the peace prayers. There was thus an incentive to gather in certain places at certain times.

This explanation is not yet satisfactory. It is certainly interesting to know that the incentives changed in the way described before. But we would also like to know why the incentives changed during 1989. It has been argued that the protests in East Germany had been instigated by various *external and internal events* such as the new liberal policies of the Soviet Union under Gorbachev in 1985, by the liberalization of Poland and Hungary, and by certain decisions of the East German government (such as approving of the crackdown of the Chinese student movement in June 1989). It is important to note that these are *macro factors,* i.e. properties of collective actors like the Russian government. Again, the question is: How do we know that these events were causes of the protests?

If the protest model is correct then this depicts the immediate causes of the protests, i.e. the individual incentives to protest. If external and internal events are causal factors as well, then they should have had a causal impact on the incentives. Thus, the basic idea is that the external and internal events have changed the incentives in particular ways. This is thus an effect of macro factors on micro factors – the latter are the independent variables of the protest model, i.e. of a micro theory. To establish these *top-down* (i.e. macro-to-micro) relationships between the external events and the incentives is the second step in the explanation. For example, the liberalization in Poland and Hungary on the one hand and the immobility and intransigence of the East German regime on the other, increased *discontent* and *perceived influence.* In regard to the latter, our data indicate (see note 21) that East German citizens thought their protests would increase the likelihood that the regime will initiate political reforms and that their *personal* participation would make a difference. The external events further increased moral indignation, i.e. *moral incentives* rose: citizens were upset that the East German government did not react to widespread discontent, in contrast to Hungary, Poland, and the Soviet Union under Gorbachev.

Hypotheses about the effects of external and internal events on incentives are again singular causal statements. In our research we tried to find out by various interview questions what the effects of these events were. For example, respondents were asked what they thought when they learned that their government had approved of the crackdown against the Chinese students (a macro event). For example, did they expect that the authorities would now sanction protesters in their own country more severely? Another procedure is to apply theories where the external and internal events are initial conditions and the incentives dependent variables.

Figure 1.1 summarizes the explanation. The procedure is the Hempel-Oppenheim scheme of explanation.[23] The initial question in our example was how a series of protest events is to be explained – this is the explanandum. This is derived from the sentences above the line which symbolizes a logical implication, i.e. the statement below the line is derived from the statements above the line. The statements above the line are called "explanans" (i.e. the statements which provide the explanation). Thus, the explanandum can be derived from the explanans. This structure is again depicted in the lowest panel of the figure. An explanation can thus be expressed in the following way: Why does the explanandum occur? Because the initial conditions obtained *and* because the law/theory holds that provides the general information, that the initial conditions are among the factors that generate the explanandum.

Explanations may be more or less satisfactory. A first condition for a satisfactory explanation is that the law or theory must have empirical content. Thus, a tautology such as "if political opportunities increase, protests will increase or not increase" cannot be applied to explain concrete empirical phenomena.

Furthermore, the law, the initial conditions and the explanandum must be true. Since we can never determine the truth of a statement, the practical substitute is that law, initial conditions, and explanandum must be well confirmed by empirical research. Finally, the explanandum must logically follow from the explanans.

These demands also imply that the circularity argument is not tenable. The reason is that the initial conditions in an explanation – such as norms and beliefs – must be determined empirically. An explanation that does not provide empirical evidence for the existence of the initial conditions is not satisfactory according to the Hempel-Oppenheim scheme.

The most important feature of this explanatory scheme is that without applying a theory, an explanation fails to provide any argument for the selection of the initial conditions. The "explanation" is then only a singular causal statement, such as Gorbachev's policies were a cause for the East German revolution. This is unsatisfactory because the theory is missing – see the Hempel-Oppenheim scheme: the question is not answered as to why other causes are not relevant.

The Hempel-Oppenheim scheme is controversial and has been criticized on many counts. The major argument for the scheme is that there is no other way to provide good reasons for the selection of the phenomena that are supposed to be causes for an explanandum.

Another argument in favor of the scheme is that those who reject it implicitly apply it. To illustrate, let us look at a bizarre explanation. The only time German tennis players Steffi Graf and Boris Becker won the tennis championships at Wimbledon was in July 1989. Assume that this is invoked as the cause for the revolution in East Germany. What could those who reject the Hempel-Oppenheim scheme object to in this argument? Plausibility? If so, why is the Graf/Becker win implausible as a cause of the East German revolution? Plausibility judgments can vary. If so how does one choose between the judgments? The argument for why the previous explanation is unacceptable would probably be that it is well known that sports events do not cause revolutions. But this is a law (or theory) that excludes certain events as causes.

One of the few writings where micro-macro explanations are explicitly addressed is McAdam, McCarthy, and Zald's review of the field (1988). Although they explicitly endorse the importance of links between macro and micro level[24] (709) they want to concentrate on a "third level, intermediate between the individual and the broad macro contexts in which they are embedded" (709) because "real action takes place" on this "third level" (709). On this third level are "micro-mobilization contexts" which are "defined as any small group setting in which processes of collective attribution are combined with rudimentary forms of organization to produce mobilization for collective action" (709). The authors mention examples such as subgroups within a union, various non-political groups and friendship networks. There can be no question that these contexts are important for collective action – which is completely consistent with a micro-macro approach. In contrast to the authors, however, an explanation of collective action must explore how such micro-mobilization contexts change the incentives of individual actors. Micro-mobilization attempts may fail when the incentives provided are not sufficient. The authors undergird this argument when they write that "in these collective settings are to be found the established structure of solidary incentives on which most social behavior depends" (710). Thus, the immediate determinants of political action are the incentives individuals are faced with.

3. Advantages of applying a general theory of action

Why is it useful to apply a general theory and not be content with formulating theories of the middle range? There is no detailed discussion of this question in the social movement literature. The macro orientation of many scholars may suggest that it is perhaps taken for granted that the application of general theories about individual behavior is not necessary and even not desirable. However, it is claimed time and again that applying social psychological theories could improve explanations of social movement phenomena. For example, W. Gamson emphasized already early on (Gamson, Fireman, and Rytina 1982) that the resource mobilization perspective "has not been particularly strong on the role of ideas" (8) and that it "needs its own, more appropriate social psychology, focusing less on sources of frustration and more on the cognitive and face-to-face interaction processes involved in mobilizing for collective action" (9; see also Gamson 1992). Unfortunately, it is not clear which theories or findings of social psychology these authors have in mind. Only one thing is clear: they do not refer to general informative theories and in particular not to the theories presented before. This holds also for Snow and Oliver (1995) who devote a whole chapter to "social psychological dimensions and considerations" of social movements and only mention rational choice theory. So it seems useful to discuss in detail some of the major reasons that speak in favor of applying general theories about individual action to explain social movement phenomena.

(1) The most convincing argument for applying a general theory is that the proponents of all theoretical perspectives in the social movement literature actually apply a general theory. But this happens implicitly – with the exception of the theory of collective action. We will show this in detail in each of the following chapters. If the proponents of all these perspectives actually apply a general theory, the question arises as to why they don't do this explicitly. This would have the advantage that the theoretical arguments that are provided would be more transparent and, thus, be open to criticism.

(2) Another argument for applying general theories is that they may provide additional evidence for and thus *confirm* theories (or hypotheses) of the middle range. If a general theory is confirmed and it can be shown that a more specific theory or hypothesis can be derived from the general theory, this is a confirmation of the specific theory. The reason is that it is not possible to derive a wrong statement from a set of true statements (or from a true theory). Thus, the truth value of the general theory is transmitted to the derived theoretical propositions.

(3) It often happens that the application of a general theory *modifies* a special theory. Applying a general theory thus provides a strategy of finding weaknesses of a special theory. For example, McAdam's "political process model" (see chapter 6 in this book) – a version of the political opportunity structure perspective and, thus, a middle range theory – claims that "cognitive liberation" is a factor for political action (McAdam 1982: chapter 3). It seems that this term means, in plain English, perceived efficacy of political action (see p. 50). In this case, value expectancy theory implies that this is indeed a relevant variable: it is the subjective probability that certain desired consequences such as the provision of public goods will occur if persons choose to become politically active. This part of McAdam's model is thus confirmed by applying a general theory. But if it is meant that the chances of joint action to provide the desired goods increase (i.e. the success of collective action increases), this is not a relevant factor: the free rider problem might become particularly salient here, if the individual reasons that the others will provide the good without his or her help, the individual might refrain from participating (Finkel, Muller, and Opp 1989). Group success will only affect collective action under certain conditions (chapter 4, section 4). Thus, it is likely that applying a general theory modifies more specific theories.

(4) Application of a general theory may not only be applied to *given* middle range propositions. It is possible to generate *new* propositions. For example, in order to explain why citizens protest against an authoritarian regime despite severe repression, a general theory could be applied that explains behavior in repressive situations. It is thus not necessary to begin from scratch when the issue is to explain certain new phenomena.

(5) There is another advantage of applying a general theory. Theories of the middle range are often not very informative. They explain only very broad types of phenomena. For example, some hypotheses accounting for protest behavior explain only when individuals choose to protest in some way, but they fail to explain the form of protest from a given repertoire of action. For example, when will individuals choose to block streets or to kill a politician or to stage a demonstration? The general theories sketched in the previous section are in general much more informative. Value expectancy theory, for example, can explain very specific kinds of behavior. When we know the perceived behavioral alternatives, the perceived consequences and their utilities and subjective probabilities, we can exactly predict the kind of behavior actors will choose.

The general conclusion is that the application of general theories of action is a highly useful strategy to improve explanations. Renouncing this strategy would mean that a possibility to improve our theoretical knowledge is forgone.

4. The importance of a microfoundation of macro explanations

One might admit that the general theories outlined in the previous section have some value in explaining individual behavior. However, it might be argued that social movement scholars are mostly interested in macro theory. Therefore, micro level propositions are only of secondary importance. Efforts at improving theory in the field of social movements should thus be concentrated on the refinement of macro theories. Is this argument tenable? The answer is clearly "no." There are three major arguments.

The implicit micro-macro explanations in social movement theory

Assume that proponents of the macro perspectives like the political opportunity structure approach argue that micro-macro explanations are not necessary. Let us ignore for a moment the previous arguments against such a claim. Assume now that proponents of the macro perspectives themselves apply a micro-macro approach, although it is never formulated explicitly and never applied systematically. If advocates of a perspective violate their own methodological creed, then the approach would further lose credibility.

We will show in detail in the later chapters that proponents of the macro approaches (resource mobilization and political opportunity perspectives) as well as those who focus on micro models (identity and framing approaches) propose models that include macro as well as micro hypotheses. The problem is that we do not know what exactly the relationships between the micro and macro level are and what exactly the micro model is that has been applied. This is even the case in the theory of collective action (see chapter 3): although M. Olson (1965) specifies a macro-micro model, it is not clearly spelled out. The basic theoretical model that social movement scholars implicitly accept is that changes on the macro level have an impact on individual incentives (or on factors which are properties of individual actors) which, in turn, change their protest behavior. These individual actions, then, translate into macro phenomena such as collective action or protest events. Sidney Tarrow, a major proponent of the political opportunity structure perspective, proposes such a model:

> I argue in this book that contentious politics is triggered when changing political opportunities and constraints create incentives for social actors who lack resources on their own. They contend through known repertoires of contention and expand them by creating innovations at the margin. When backed by dense social networks and galvanized by cultural resonant, action oriented symbols, contentious politics leads to sustained interaction with opponents. The result is the social movement. (Tarrow 1998: 2)

The first proposition is that political opportunities and constraints – which are factors on the macro level – have a causal impact ("create") on incentives of "social actors." These include individuals and not yet social movements because, as the last sentence states, they have not yet originated. Thus, the quotation begins with a macro-to-micro proposition: changes of political opportunities and constraints lead to changes of incentives of individual actors. Beside opportunities and constraints other macro factors are mentioned: "dense social networks" and "cultural resonant, action oriented symbols." Arrow 1 in Figure 1.2 symbolizes this relationship.

A micro-macro model does not imply that macro factors affect all incentives on the individual level. For example, assume that developments in communication technology make communication less costly. This may then lower the costs of mobilization, but grievances or moral incentives may remain stable.

The previous argument further suggests that the macro-to-micro relationship is causal and, thus, empirical. As we will see in chapter 3, such relationships may also be analytical (or tautological). What is the difference? Assume that a micro-model explains individual voting behavior and the macro model's dependent variable is the voter turnout (see relationship 3 in the figure). This is an analytical relationship, i.e. a logical truth: the voter turnout is just an aggregation of the individuals' voting behavior, referring to the percentage of the population with a right to vote. In general, a relationship is analytical if one needs to analyze only the meaning of the

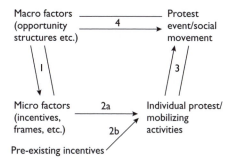

Figure 1.2 The basic structure of theories of social movements and protest

expressions in the statement in order to establish its truth (see the discussion of the tautology charge against rational choice theory earlier). An empirical link could be an effect of the previous repression of protests on the subjective probability of repression in coming protest events.

Let us return to the relationship between political opportunities and changes of incentives (relationship 1 in the figure). It seems that this is an empirical relationship. But could it also be analytical? For example, assume that the influence of a single individual actor in a group is equal to 1 divided by the group size. The influence of an individual in a group of 1,000 members would then be 1/1000. In this case, the macro-to-micro relationship would be analytical (or tautological), i.e. one needs only to look at the meaning of the terms in order to recognize that the statement is true.

It is further clear from the quotation that the individual incentives have effects on the behavior of the individuals – see arrows 2a and 2b. It is important to note that incentives may affect behavior that are not affected by macro events. These are "pre-existing" incentives. For example, there may exist strong obligations to protest that are activated by a critical event, but the felt obligation itself is not changed. Two questions are not answered by Tarrow and they are not answered in his book either: (1) What exactly are the incentives that determine individual action? (2) What are the individual behaviors that are caused by which incentives?

The outcome of the process is, according to the previous quotation, "the social movement." This is the dependent macro variable. It seems that the macro relationship is causal – see the arrow between the macro variables (relationship 4 in Figure 1.2). Could the relationship also be a correlation (see the line in the figure)? This is not clear and it is not spelled out in Tarrow's book either. We suspect that the macro relationship is a correlation. The reason is that the relationship is explained by the whole process that runs via the micro level. In other words, opportunity structures (and other macro variables) bring about social movements *because* the former change the incentives of individual actors which motivate the actors to form social movements. Thus, the micro variables are intervening variables that mediate between the independent and dependent variable(s) at the macro level and thus explain the macro relationships.

When the outcome of the process is a social movement, the question arises of how the individual behaviors that are determined by incentives generate the movement. There must be some coordination of individual behavior so that, by definition, there is a social movement. So the question is whether the transition from "individual behavior" (like individual protest or mobilizing action) to "social movement" is an analytical or empirical relationship – see arrow or line 3 of Figure 1.2.

The argument provided by Tarrow is typical for the literature. Micro-macro models are proposed or at least their importance is emphasized, but most of the time they are only insinuated and not clearly formulated.[25] In other words, the literature largely provides *explanation sketches* and not clear and full-fledged explanations: important ingredients of the explanation are missing, as the previous example demonstrates: it is not clear what factors influence which other factors, and which relationships are causal or analytical. This makes the explanation untestable.

It is important to note that the model in Figure 1.2 is only a basic heuristic device. Models that describe actual processes of movement formation or the development of protest over time are more complicated. For example, certain macro events may change various incentives of individuals in different directions. If the outcome is collective protest, this may change decisions of the target (a macro variable) which, in turn, again influence incentives such as perceived influence on the micro level. These changes of incentives may instigate new protest events, etc. There are thus various transitions from the macro to the micro level. The literature on social movements is far away from specifying such complex micro-macro models.

This section has argued that social movement scholars implicitly use micro-macro arguments in their writings, but they do not propose detailed micro-macro explanations. We will see this in great detail throughout this book. This implicit agenda suggests the importance of micro-macro modeling. A still more convincing argument for micro-macro modeling would be when leading scholars in the field explicitly *demand* such modeling and criticize existing macro approaches like the resource mobilization and political opportunity perspectives for not engaging in this kind of theory construction, i.e. for ignoring "agency." Indeed, McAdam, McCarthy and Zald do exactly this: in their review of the field (1988) they claim that resource mobilization and political opportunity structure perspectives "must take into account processes and variables operating at the *macro* and *micro* levels of analysis" (697, italics in the original). They further complain about the "macro bias" in the field (698). It is striking that this has largely remained only a programmatic statement, as the following chapters will show in detail.

To summarize, the point of this section is that the propagation and implicit application of micro-macro explanations suggest that this kind of explanation is a fruitful theoretical strategy.

The black-box argument

Why do proponents of macro approaches always refer to the micro-level? Omitting the micro-level leaves us uninformed about the processes or mechanisms that bring about macro phenomena or macro relationships. For example, assume that after the formation of a new coalition government with left-wing parties the amount of protests in a country increases. We will not be satisfied in knowing this relationship. The reason is that we would like to know how this relationship has originated. Why did so many people take to the streets when the new government was formed? A satisfactory answer would be when we know what incentives motivated people to protest. In other words, macro relationships are comparable to *black boxes*: we do not know what is in the box, i.e. between the independent and dependent macro variables. Put differently, knowing what the *mechanisms* are that explain a macro phenomenon (such as the demonstrations in Leipzig) or macro relationships (such as the relationship between changing political opportunities and changing collective political action) provides *depth* to an explanation.

The following example is perhaps an even more convincing illustration of this argument. It has been found that sometimes an increase in state repression raises protest and thus has a radicalization effect. This is counter-intuitive because we would expect that repression has a deterrence effect. We certainly want to know what motivates people, i.e. individual actors, to express their discontent when repression becomes more severe. How else can we explain why there is no deterrence effect, i.e. a decrease of protest after repression has increased, if not by looking at the motivations and reactions of individual actors? This example also indicates that the claim just to be satisfied with having found that repression has aroused protest is not convincing. Only a specification of a macro-micro model satisfies our need for a full and deep explanation.

Conditions for the validity of macro propositions

Let us look again at the previous quotation from Tarrow's book above. His claim is that political opportunities and other macro phenomena create incentives. Is this always the case? As we will see in chapter 6, changing political opportunities often do not change political action. The explanation is that changing opportunities do not always create sufficiently strong incentives to generate political action. Thus, changing opportunities affect political action *only if the incentives change to a certain extent.*

This example suggests two important points. The first is that macro propositions are often – or perhaps always – invalid. This holds not only in the field of social movements but in general. So far macro laws have not been discovered. The second point is, as the previous examples suggests, that general theories about individuals state the conditions under which macro propositions hold. There will be ample evidence for this in the coming chapters. To anticipate some of this discussion, Mancur Olson's (1965) hypothesis that increasing group size makes the provision of public goods unlikely is no law, i.e. it is often wrong (see chapter 3). Why? Olson argues that group size is linked to disincentives to contribute to the provision of public goods. But it often happens that this alleged macro-to-micro link between group size and incentives does not hold. This is another illustration for the previous point: the group size proposition is no social scientific law; a theory about individual behavior (again rational choice or value expectancy theory) states the conditions for the validity of the hypothesis.

This is perhaps the most important argument for working on micro-macro explanations: to state it cautiously, when we have a chance to find the conditions for the validity of macro propositions by providing micro-macro explanations, there is every reason to pursue this explanatory strategy.

The previous argument implies that a micro-macro approach advanced here will not provide any macro laws. The only lawful statement in a micro-macro explanation is the micro theory.

Another implication of a micro-macro approach is this. Skocpol (1995: 42) argues that "it seems unlikely that micro level models will ever completely displace historical-institutional analysis of macroscopic patterns of political conflict and change." This is again a misunderstanding of a micro-macro approach. It is obvious that the micro theory alone can never provide any "historical-institutional analysis." But a micro-macro model can provide *explanations* of historical-institutional macroscopic patterns.

Conclusion

The previous arguments indicate that the application of theories about individual behavior are of utmost importance if the focus is on exploring macro relationships. If micro theories are necessary, then the previous argument requires to use *general* theories and not only theories of the middle range. Furthermore, these theories of individual behavior have to be embedded in the way described earlier in micro-macro explanations.

This methodological strategy is controversial. A new approach which focuses on the dynamics of contention and that will be presented and discussed in detail in chapter 10 largely abandons theory and instead intends to specify mechanisms. The latter aim, i.e. looking at processes of contention, is certainly welcome, but the arguments presented before suggest that abandoning theory is absolutely not an acceptable strategy. To reiterate, the basic problem that is unsolved is how to select the explanatory factors involved in mechanisms. Explanations by mechanisms also suggest that certain factors are involved in processes of contention. How are they selected? There is no alternative to apply theories. Thus, the basic flaw of the new perspective is that explanations by laws and mechanisms are seen as incompatible alternatives. As we will see in chapter 10, this is not tenable. Providing explanations by mechanism is a fruitful strategy, but they have to be founded on theories.

5. Factor explanations as a synthesis of social movement perspectives: an alternative to applying theories?

Proponents of the identity and framing approach argue that the resource mobilization and political opportunity perspectives are incomplete. Identity and framing must be added to explain social movement activities. Culture is another factor that has to be considered. This critique has been generally accepted (see, e.g., Zald and McCarthy 2002). The basic idea thus is that each theoretical perspective captures important aspects of reality that influence protest and social movements. The next obvious step is, so it seems, to combine the variables. In other words, if protest or social movements are to be explained, consider resources, opportunities, identity, and framing. A typical example is the causal diagram by McAdam, Tarrow, and Tilly (2001: 17) that combines the key variables of the existing theoretical perspectives aimed at explaining social movement phenomena: "mobilizing structures," "opportunity and threat," and "framing processes" all affect "repertoires of contention." The authors also suggest causal relationships between these factors. To complete the schema, "identity" could be added. Thus, the rule seems to be: in order to explain social movement activities one should employ political opportunities, resources, identities, and frames and, in addition, culture as independent variables. Empirical research then may decide which of the factors is more important in specific settings. This procedure may be called a *factor explanation*. It means that every independent variable that might be relevant is to be included in an explanation.[26]

If this procedure is accepted one wonders why not a multitude of other factors are included to explain social movement phenomena. For example, why not include demographic variables, nationality, or personality characteristics as well? That is to say, in designing an empirical study that is intended to find the "right" independent variables, begin with whatever seems relevant and then decide after having performed multivariate analyses what is relevant.

The first major problem of factor explanations is that they do not yield predictions about what forms of phenomena are brought about. For example, if resources and opportunities increase, does violent protest rise or do legal demonstrations increase? Thus, the dependent variables consist of a wide array of political actions or other phenomena. More formally, factor explanations predict: phenomenon a or b or c or d ... or ... is to be expected. Such explanations explain little. This is often disguised when the researcher chooses a given dependent variable such as a violent protest because he or she is interested in its explanation. Then the influence of independent variables is explored. The flaw in this procedure is that it is completely *ad hoc*: the independent variables do not imply that the phenomena to be explained are to be expected. In other words, there is no theory that leads us to expect that the phenomena to be explained will arise.

The second problem is that the researcher has no clear guideline that determines which independent variable should be included in the explanation. The selection criterion is completely *ad hoc*. For example, how does a researcher decide what kinds of resources, opportunities, identities, etc. are relevant for the origin of a certain protest event such as demonstrations against the Iraq war?[27] Thus, everything is open in a factor explanation: it is not clear what exactly the explanatory factors are – they are selected *ad hoc*, and it is not clear what phenomena can be explained – again, they are determined *ad hoc*.

The difference between theoretical and factor explanations becomes still clearer when we assume that instead of a factor explanation we apply one of the theories outlined in the previous sections. As was said before, the theories explain specific kinds of behavior or attitudes depending on the kinds of incentives. Furthermore, the theories are a guideline which leads us to select specific explanatory phenomena. In regard to the theory of rational action, these are incentives.

The conclusion is that one needs a *theory* that integrates the different factors. It is definitely not satisfactory to put the independent variables all together in a basket and select *ad hoc* those that best fit a given dependent variable that is selected *ad hoc* as well. This differs from the application of a theory, that guides us in selecting the independent as well as the dependent variables.

Factor explanations are regarded as a *synthesis* of the different theoretical perspectives. They are a "synthesis" in the sense that several variables from different approaches are combined – like throwing different kinds of vegetables in a basket. It is not a *theoretical* synthesis in the sense that a theory is provided that shows which effects the factors have on which phenomena. Such a theoretical syntheses will be suggested later (see chapter 11).

6. Three features of a good theory

The following chapters will show that propositions about social movements and political protest are often deficient in several respects. For example, the concepts are vague; it is not clear what the dependent and independent variables are and how they are related, and the explanatory power of the perspectives leaves much to be desired. A book that focuses on detailed critical analyses of theoretical perspectives should lay down the criteria that are applied to evaluate the perspectives. This is the major concern of this section.

The precision of a theory: its structure and concepts

"Clarity" first refers to the *structure of a theory*. That is to say, it should be clear what the independent and dependent variables of a theory are. In addition, it would be desirable to tell the reader what relationships are supposed to obtain between the variables. For example, does an independent variable have a positive or negative effect on dependent variables? Is the effect linear? Are there interaction effects of independent variables?

To answer these questions it is advisable to display a theory as a *causal diagram* where the variables are connected with arrows symbolizing causal relationships and lines or arches referring to correlations. Trying to represent a theory as a causal diagram is also a good strategy to find out to what extent the structure of a theory is clear. We will make ample use of causal diagrams in this book. Our discussion of the theories will show that their structure is often far from clear.

Not only the structure of a theory, but its *concepts* should be clear or precise as well. This is a necessary condition for the fruitfulness of a concept. What other properties a concept must have will be discussed in the next section.

Validity

Ideally, a theory should be true. But since theories are general statements not confined to certain times and places their truth can never be determined. What scientists can do and actually do is to test a theory as rigorously as possible. As long as there are no falsifications the theory can be regarded as true or valid. This seems generally accepted. The problems begin when we look at how social movement scholars test theoretical propositions. Many empirical studies are not really tests of a theory in the sense that there is a chance that the theory will be falsified. For example, adherents of a perspective often list various cases that are in line with its basic propositions. Did the scholar really search cases that are *not* in line with his or her theory? A test must be an attempt to falsify a hypothesis because in the social sciences it is easy to find confirming evidence for almost every hypothesis. The question then is whether scholars who list confirming evidence really tried hard to find disconfirming data. This question must in particularly be posed for case studies.

Which of the hypotheses about protest and social movements are valid? This question cannot be answered at present. There is so far no systematic in-depth *meta-analysis* of the extent to which the hypotheses of the various perspectives have been empirically confirmed and to which extent the tests are more or less rigorous. Such a meta-analysis should apply or develop criteria of the rigor of empirical tests and should indicate to what extent theories or propositions are falsified or confirmed. We surmise that such an analysis would reveal deficits in the procedure of testing the various theories. A serious obstacle to such a meta-analysis is that the theories are not very clear, as will be seen in the following chapters, so that it will be difficult or impossible to decide whether a theory is really tested by an investigation.

Explanatory power

The third criterion that is usually applied to evaluate a theory is its explanatory power. What exactly does this mean? The explanatory power of a theory is high if it provides relatively specific explanations, i.e. if it is incompatible with a great many empirical phenomena.[28] In order to apply this criterion more easily, it is useful to break it down into several sub-criteria.

The range and specificity of the phenomena to be explained

The first sub-criterion refers to the *class of phenomena that can be explained*: a theory should be capable of explaining a relatively broad range of phenomena. For example, a theory that explains protest is preferable to a theory that explains student protest. Furthermore, a theory should explain which *specific phenomenon* from a given class of phenomena obtains. For example, a theory should not only explain protest but which specific form of protest is to be expected: when do individuals choose to participate in a legal demonstration and when do they decide to attack politicians? Thus, it is not enough if a theory refers to a broad class of phenomena such as crime or social movements. If the theory can not predict which kind of crime or social movement occurs its explanatory power is low. A theory of protest then only states that

> protest of kind A *or* protest of kind B *or* protest of kind C *or* Protest of kind D ...

is to be expected. This is hardly very informative: we do not learn which of these forms of protest will occur. Every form of protest is possible. It is much more informative when the theory states that

> protest of kind A *and not* protest of kind B *and not* protest of kind C *and not* protest of kind D ...

obtains.

A weakness of many theories about protest and social movements is that the theories are not very specific: they explain when social movements emerge but they do not inform us about exactly what kind movement it is that will originate.

Let us look at another example for a theory that is not informative at all. We often find hypotheses claiming that a condition C *can* lead to an effect E. Such can-propositions imply that if C obtains then E may occur; but it is not excluded that E may not occur. Can-statements thus amount to

condition C brings about or does not bring about E.

This is a classical *tautological statement* with no informative value at all: the class of phenomena to be explained is utterly unspecific. Actually, everything is left open. It may be that authors who offer such can-propositions mean that C leads to E with a certain positive probability. For example, the hypothesis "increasing opportunities can lead to an increase in protests" may mean that there is some positive probability that increasing opportunities lead to protests. But taken literally, can-statements are tautologies.

But there are can-statements that do exclude some social phenomena. For example, Benford writes: "While frame disputes can foster the extinction of some movement groups, these contests can also promote the formation of new ones" (Benford 1993: 695). Is anything excluded? The hypothesis does not mention the possibility that movement groups further exist unchanged. Thus, frame disputes do not have the effect that movement groups remain stable. So Benford's hypothesis is not a tautology but nevertheless a statement that is rather unspecific (i.e. has low explanatory power).

Applied to social movements and protest, theories should be capable of explaining specific forms of protest and social movements. For example, a hypothesis "a general increase of societal resources leads to the origin of new social movements" has only a low explanatory power: it is left open what the form of movement is that comes into being: What are the goals of the movements? What is their size? How are they organized?

The range of application of a theory

The second sub-criterion of the explanatory power of a theory is its *range of application*. The broader the range of application, the more informative is the theory. A theory that can only be applied to western types of democracy cannot inform us, for example about the conditions for protests in authoritarian regimes like the East European communist dictatorships in 1989–1990.

To be more specific, theories should not be formulated for specific groups or types of individuals. If this is the case we do not learn anything about other groups or individuals.

A note on broad and narrow concepts

Theories are often criticized because their concepts are too "broad." For example, Goodwin and Jasper (1999) argue in their discussion of the political opportunity structure hypothesis: "The broadest definition makes the thesis tautological" (30). It is therefore important to avoid an "expansive definition" (36). In a similar vein, McAdam (1996) complains about the "conceptual plasticity" of the concept of political opportunities. This concept is all-encompassing and therefore loses its analytic power (25). Furthermore, McAdam argues that an "overly inclusive definition of political opportunities is dangerous" (1996: 26). Marwell and Oliver (1984: 5–6) complain that "the concept of collective action is intrinsically too broad: it captures actions toward public goods that are not social change goals, and it lumps together actions of widely different scope."

It is typical that the authors do not provide a detailed justification for their claims. For example, Goodwin and Jasper do not explain why a broad concept makes a hypothesis tautological. As was said before, a sentence is "tautological" (or analytically true) if its truth can be determined by analyzing the meaning of its terms. What is the relationship between a tautology and a more or less broad concept? The answer is that there is no such relationship. Whether a statement is tautological depends on the meaning of the terms of the statement, not upon its "conceptual plasticity." For example, a theory about "political opportunities" and "social movements" is tautological if, for example, the meanings of the first and second expression are equivalent. But it is irrelevant whether the concepts are broad or narrow.

If only narrow concepts have "analytic power" we would conclude that general behavioral theories such as the theories of learning, which explain in detail when individuals acquire which kind of behavior, do not have any "analytic power." Of course, the opposite is true: the theories cannot only explain a broad class of phenomena; in addition, they explain which specific form of the behavior will originate. Further, the range of application of these theories is not constrained in any way. According to the previous sub-criterion of "explanatory power" such theories have a high explanatory power.

This will be illustrated with the two graphs of Figure 1.3. Assume first that there is a proposition about the effects of protest so that protest is the independent variable. If protest is defined broadly (see the outer circle of the first graph of Figure 1.3), the proposition stipulates for many kinds of behavior what their consequences are. If protest is defined narrowly (see the inner circle of the figure), we know only for a relatively small class of behavior what happens if they are performed. Thus, broad concepts that refer to conditions for the occurrence of explananda are highly desirable.

Now assume that there is a very broad class of phenomena to be explained (see the second graph of Figure 1.3). When we define "protest" very broadly, a

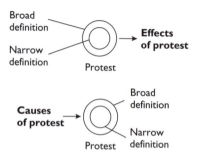

Figure 1.3 The explanatory value of theories with broad and narrow concepts

theory of protest would have the potential to explain a relatively large class of behavior. But if protest is defined narrowly, only little can be explained. But, as we saw before, if a theory only explains a broad class of phenomena, but not when specific kinds of these phenomena are brought about, its explanatory power is low. Thus, it is not sufficient if theories refer to a broad class of phenomena as dependent variable; in addition, they must be capable of explaining specific kinds of these phenomena.

The weakness of orienting hypotheses

A specific class of relatively uninformative propositions are orienting hypotheses (Merton 1957: 88). Let us look at an example. McCarthy and Zald (1977) write: "The resource mobilization approach emphasizes both societal support and constraint of social movement phenomena ..." (1213). This is not an informative proposition that specifies which variables have which effects. It is said that societal support and constraint are important factors – but what kind of societal support and constraint? The effects are also only very broadly specified: they refer to "social movement phenomena." What are these phenomena? It seems that the authors refer to aspects of social movements, but which aspects are meant is left open. These propositions are orienting statements (or general orientations) that point to classes of variables that should be considered in explanations, but it is not specified what exactly is to be explained and what the relationships between the variables are (Merton 1957: 88).

Although orienting hypotheses are not informative, they are useful as a first step for finding more informative hypotheses: they point to classes of possibly relevant factors for certain kinds of explananda. They guide theorists to look at certain kinds of phenomena. The task of the theorist then is to transform the orienting propositions into full-fledged theories.

7. Basics of concept formation

The literature about social movements and political protest is replete with definitions. As we will see in chapter 2, there are numerous definitions of "protest," "social movement," and related terms. These definitions raise several questions. Why do scholars define so many different concepts – and why do they define concepts at all? Is there a "best" definition? In general, which criteria must a "good" definition meet? The present section focuses on these questions.[29]

A necessary condition: useful concepts must be precise

There is one condition that every concept must fulfill: a concept must be precise. What does this mean? A concept is, by definition, precise if it can be decided for any phenomenon whether the concept designates it or not. Take as an example the term "group." For some phenomena it is clear that they are groups – examples are a family or a some friends who meet regularly for many years. Is an organization or a country a group? Sometimes "group" refers to any set of persons with a common property (such as the passengers in a train compartment, or women), sometimes a "group" is only given if there is some durable interaction between a collectivity of persons. This example indicates that it is sometimes no problem to decide that certain phenomena are to be subsumed under a concept – a family is certainly a group; sometimes an unequivocal assignment is not possible – it cannot be decided whether a category of individuals or countries is a group. This indicates that precision or clarity is a matter of degree.

It is desirable that the area of uncertainty or imprecision is as small as possible: the more phenomena or classes of phenomena there are that cannot be assigned to an expression or a concept, the less precise and, thus, the less useful the concept is. If a relatively vague concept is the dependent variable of a theory, it is not clear for many phenomena whether the theory is capable to explain them or not. To illustrate, if a theory explains the emergence of "groups" without any definition of this concept, there are many phenomena where the theory cannot make any predictions because it is not known whether the phenomena fall under the theory or not. If a vague concept is an independent variable, there are many situations where the theory cannot be applied either. For example, if a theory holds for "groups" and if this concept is not clear, there are many collectivities of individuals where it cannot be decided whether the theory can be applied or not. It is thus useful to try to formulate the concepts of a theory as clearly as possible.

To illustrate, McAdam (1995: 224) provides the following definition of "expanding political opportunities": "By expanding political opportunities I mean *changes in either the institutional features or informal political alignments of a given political system that significantly reduce the power disparity between a given challenging group and the state*" (the definition is printed in italics in the original). Thus, in order to determine whether there is an "expanding political opportunity" one must determine whether there is a "significant" reduction of the "power disparity" between a group and the state. First it is unclear what exactly a "power disparity" is: already the concept of "power" is a vague concept and should thus be defined. It is further unclear what a "significant" disparity is. Assume there is a quantitative measure of "power disparity" ranging from 0 to 10. Which value or value range is "significant"?

The practical procedure of determining the precision of a concept is to list various phenomena or situations that might be subsumed under a concept. For example, does the "power" of a country depend on the number of wars won in the past, on the gross national product, on the geographical size, on the size of the population? If it is not possible to tell for given phenomena whether they can be subsumed under a concept, a definition or specification of the meaning of the term is necessary.

Why are concepts defined as they are defined? The theoretical import of a concept

What are the criteria for a useful concept? It is striking that social movement scholars almost never provide any detailed argument about the reasons for choosing the definition they suggest. Even in detailed discussions of conceptual issues the question is usually not addressed as to what the criteria are for a fruitful definition (see, e.g., Diani 1992). At best, there is some assertion that a definition is fruitful or useful, but a detailed justification for such a claim is missing. For example, Marwell and Oliver (1984) introduce the new term "collective campaign" (13). This expression is supposed to "group collective events into meaningful units that are useful for research" (12). Do many other similar concepts in the literature not group events into meaningful units as well? Why are these classifications not "meaningful"? The authors do not answer these questions.

One criterion authors might have in mind when they think a concept is "useful" or "fruitful" is that the concept is a component of a fruitful theory (i.e. a valid theory with a high explanatory content). This is a basic requirement for a theoretically fruitful concept.

When does a concept have "theoretical import"? A first step to tackle this question is to perform a thought experiment. For a given theory one should try out different concepts. Take the proposition that a rise of political opportunities raises protest. How should "protest" be defined? We could look at various situations and ponder for which kinds of behavior this proposition might hold true. For example, is the proposition valid for individual behavior or only for collective behavior (i.e. actions of groups such as social movements) or for both? Is the proposition probably true if the action has some unconventional feature in the sense that it is against the law or other generally accepted rules? If such considerations suggest that the rise of political opportunities leads to an increase of individual as well as collective action and that it is irrelevant whether the action violates some rules, then it is theoretically not useful to restrict the definition of protest so that it only refers to joint or unconventional behavior.

If such thought experiments are inconclusive a useful strategy is to employ a rather *wide concept*. This enables us to formulate an informative theory, as we saw before.

The thought experiment is only a first step to generate some ideas about how a theoretically fruitful concept might look like. Only an empirical test of a theory can provide evidence about the theoretical import of a concept. One could then think of the following research design to test the results of the thought experiment. A given theory could be tested by using different concepts of protest or social movement as the dependent or independent variable. One could then analyze for which concept the theory fares better.

It would be desirable if scholars who introduce a new concept discuss in much more detail why they choose the definition they suggest. For example, why do McCarthy and Zald (1977) define "social movement" as opinions and beliefs of a population? So far, "social movement" was defined as a certain kind of group. A group or organization is now termed "social movement organization." Why? Is this definition theoretically fruitful?

Everyday meaning

It often seems that scholars try to provide a definition that captures the everyday meaning of a concept. For example, H. Tajfel discussing social movements from the perspective of Social Identity Theory explains that "social movements can be roughly described as presenting three inherent and defining characteristics: a certain duration; the participation of a significant number of people from one or more social groups; and a shared system of beliefs" (Tajfel 1981: 291). It seems that Tajfel tries to characterize how the term "social movements" is used in everyday language. But why should the definition of a concept match everyday meanings? Concepts of the natural sciences like "force" differ from everyday language. In the social movements literature, McCarthy and Zald's (1977) concept of social movements which was mentioned already clearly deviates from everyday usage and is nonetheless adopted by many social movement scholars. Should a scientific concept be consistent with its everyday meaning?

The major criterion for the fruitfulness of a definition is its theoretical importance. Concepts taken from a natural language need not be theoretically fruitful. Furthermore, these concepts are often vague or have different meanings. For example, what is the everyday meaning of "protest" and "social movement"? This is not clear at all, and probably these concepts will be used differently by different people. Thus, even if one would claim that definitions in the social sciences should conform to their everyday meaning, it would not be possible in many cases to achieve such a match.

But if a definition is suggested and there is an expression in the natural language that comes close to the definition, it is useful to use this expression. Assume one defines "attitude" as "a behavior that is aimed at introducing social change by influencing the decisions of authorities." The word whose meaning comes close to this definition is "protest." Using "attitude" is not wrong, but not useful because "attitude" has a clearly different meaning in everyday language. Using "attitude" to denote the behavior described will probably lead to misunderstandings.

Definitions as abbreviations and descriptions of the subject of studies

Definitions may have a very simple objective: replacing a long sentence with a short term. For example, McCarthy and Zald's (1977) definition of "social movement" might have been introduced as an abbreviation of "opinions and beliefs of a population." Thus, instead of always writing "opinions and beliefs of a population" the shorthand term "social movement" can be used. But then the question is whether a term should be introduced that has an everyday meaning that clearly differs from the definition. In everyday language, "social movement" refers to a group or organization and not to opinions or beliefs. It would have been preferable to use a term that has a similar meaning as "opinions and beliefs of a population" – such as ideology or beliefs.

The goal of abbreviations may also be to describe phenomena by a shorthand term that is intended to describe phenomena to be studied. For example, scholars may be interested in explaining when states collapse, i.e. when their elites change and when new institutional rules are created. These situations may be defined as "revolutions." It goes without saying that these are legitimate purposes for introducing definitions.

Propositions as part of definitions

Although it is clear that a definition is a specification of the meaning of a term that can thus not be true or false it often happens that propositions, i.e. causal statements, are part of definitions. For example, Eisinger (1973) defines "political opportunities" as the likelihood that changes in the political environment raise the "chances of success of citizen political activities" (11). Thus, in order to determine whether a change in the political environment is a "political opportunity" one must examine whether this change has a causal effect on the (objective) probability that the "chances of success" of political action of certain groups increase. Only if this causal statement can be confirmed there exists, by definition, an increase in political opportunities. Similar definitions are provided by other proponents of the political opportunity perspective (see chapter 6).

In general, there is no principal objection to include causal statements in definitions. But the problem is that in order to determine whether certain phenomena can be subsumed under a definition one must perform empirical research to test the respective causal statement. In regard to political opportunities, it is very difficult and probably in most cases impossible to determine to what extent a change in the political environment of a group changes the objective probability that the group will reach its goals (i.e. increases a group's chances of success). A consequence of this difficulty is that proponents of the political opportunity structure approach never engage in such research. Instead, they assume *ad hoc* that political opportunities increase or decrease.

To avoid such difficulties it is preferable to avoid causal statements in definitions. But if there is clear evidence that such definitions are theoretically fruitful, such "complex" definitions are useful. In the political opportunity structure literature, however, such evidence does not exist, as we will see in chapter 6: there is no disadvantage to eliminate the causal statement from the definition.

8. Summary and conclusions

This chapter has discussed various problems concerning the research program proposed in this book and the critical analyses of the major theoretical perspectives explaining social movement phenomena that will be presented in the following chapters. The starting point was that social movement scholars time and again demand the application of social psychological theories in explanations of macro phenomena, but that they do not apply such theories explicitly and systematically. The basic message of this book is to pursue such micro-macro explanations systematically. One question in carrying out this research program is what the micro theories are that could be applied to explain social movement related phenomena. We further discuss the procedure of applying these theories.

If it is granted that the application of theories about individuals is fruitful, the question arises whether one should apply *general* theories about human action or more *specific* theories, i.e. theories of the middle range. Our discussion provides arguments in favor of applying general theories.

It might be argued that the application of individual level (i.e. micro) theories may be important for many explanatory issues, but why should they be applied to explain macro phenomena? We provide the major arguments for the importance of a micro foundations of explanations on the macro level. One is that social movement scholars themselves actually suggest micro-macro explanations, but they usually provide only explanation sketches. So why not formulate these explanations explicitly? Another argument is that a pure macro explanation is a black box: it does not inform us about what happens on the individual level, i.e. what mechanisms bring about macro phenomena. A pure macro explanation thus lacks depth. The third – and perhaps most important argument – is that macro explanations are often wrong and that micro theories help to specify the conditions for their validity.

An alternative to applying theories is to provide factor explanations: just combine all the variables that have been suggested by the major perspectives in the field of social movements – opportunities, resources, frames, identities – as independent variables and let empirical research decide which of them are relevant. It is shown why this procedure is not acceptable: it is not clear what kinds of opportunities, etc. generate what kinds of protest, social movement, etc., i.e. the dependent variables are not clear.

A book that focuses on a critical analysis of theories should lay down the criteria that are to be applied to judge theories. We briefly discuss three criteria that a good theory must fulfill: a theory should be clear, it should have explanatory power, and it should be true (i.e. it should have been tested and should be consistent with the existing empirical evidence). We surmise that these criteria are not controversial. If this is true it is astounding that they are not applied systematically in major works of social movement theory. It therefore seems useful to discuss them in the initial chapter.

Another question that is discussed is when definitions of concepts are fruitful. One major criterion is "theoretical importance," i.e. concepts must be components of informative and valid theories. A necessary condition for a fruitful concept is that it must be precise.

Methodological discussions are not very popular among sociologists and in particular not among social movement scholars. Unfortunately, the state of social movement theory indicates that more knowledge about the basics of theory and concept formation in the social sciences would be one strategy of avoiding many mistakes and improve existing theory and research in the field.

2 Protest, social movements, and collective action

Conceptual clarifications and the subject of the book

A book that addresses the major theoretical perspectives in the field of social movements and political protest should begin by defining these terms because they are used in different and often ambiguous ways. The present chapter addresses these conceptual issues. We provide a critical analysis of extant definitions in the literature and propose definitions that encompass a rather wide range of phenomena.

1. Examples: What is a "protest" and a "social movement"?

Let us begin with the concept of protest. All definitions agree that "protest" refers to a behavior. But there is disagreement about the kind of behavior that is to be called "protest." Let us start with some examples. There are activities that everyone would classify as protest action and that are studied by social movement scholars: demonstrations like those against the Iraq war especially in Europe in 2003, or against changes to the labor law in France in 2006, initiating a petition or signing it in order to prevent or demand a government action, and boycotts that are intended to prevent or demand some action of a government or an organization. Sit-ins, street blockades, and occupying sites are other examples that are in general classified as protest actions.

Readers will probably disagree whether the following activities are "protest" as well: terrorist acts, complaints of a group of students about the syllabus of a professor, reports of a group of employees to the management of a firm about the discriminatory behavior of the head of a department, a tenant's objection to a rent increase, citizens' request to the government for a subsidy of a kindergarten, a letter of an interest group to the members of a parliament requesting tax exemption, or telling a waiter that the meal was not good.

The following actions are clearly not protests: ordering a meal, making an appointment with a friend, asking for a credit at a bank, criticizing one's partner for his or her behavior toward somebody else, voting, joining an automobile club, moving to another apartment, or joint jogging of a group of friends.

Thus, there is a range of phenomena for which it cannot be decided whether they fall under the concept or not. In other words, the concept is ambiguous. The same holds for the concept of "social movement." This term refers to groups – but what kind of groups? Let us again look at some examples.

It is clear that large groups or organizations whose goal is to prevent the utilization of nuclear energy, to bring about equal rights for white and black Americans, to prevent war, or to protect the environment are "social movements." These groups are also called "movements": the anti-nuclear movement, the civil rights movement, the peace movement, and the environmental movement.

Are the following groups "social movements"? A citizen group in a residential area that wants to improve the quality of life in the area, develops some plans about how that could be accomplished and then wants to talk to the government; neighbors of a residential area who set up a schedule to watch their houses in order to prevent crime; a group of families who pool a certain percentage of their net income to set up a kindergarten. Are these "social movements"? At least for some of those groups there is no clear answer.

It is clear that the following groups are not social movements: interest groups such as unions, employer organizations, student organizations, sports clubs, firms, and parliaments.

So far we drew on the everyday meaning of "protest" and "social movement." The question is what the meaning of these terms in the social movement literature is and whether there is a range of indetermination as well.

2. Definitions from the literature

There is a vast number of definitions of "protest," "social movements," and related terms such "challenging group" or "social movement organization" in the literature. Often different terms have the same or a very similar meaning, and the same term has different meanings. Table 2.1 gives some examples of definitions that are typical for the plethora of definitions in the literature in several respects: (1) The definitions are often not clear, i.e. we do not know for many behaviors or groups whether they fall under a given definition or not. (2) The definitions refer to different phenomena. Let us look at some of those definitions.

Protest behavior

The first two definitions in Table 2.1 share the following definitional criteria with many other definitions. (1) Protest is an *action* or a behavior. This is a common element in all definitions. Most social movement scholars conceive protest as a *joint action*. Thus, it is not a protest if a single citizen writes a harsh letter to a politician demanding withdrawal of a decision. But if a group of individuals sign the letter this counts as an act of protest. (2) The actors *object to one or more decisions of a target* (or several targets), as definition 1 says. This implies that actors have at least one common goal. When protest is defined as an action that "expresses a grievance, a conviction of wrong or injustice" (definition 2) this implies that actors' goals are not achieved. (3) The *actors are unable to achieve their goals by their own efforts*; instead, they put pressure on third parties or antagonists, i.e. targets. Both definitions 1 and 2 in the table include this criterion. (4) The behavior is *not regular*. Definition 1 refers to the "unconventional" nature of an activity to be called a protest, whereas definition 2 mentions single actions which, thus, lack regularity. An action may be "unconventional" or "irregular" if there are no institutional rules prescribing that it is repeated over time. Thus, party conventions, meetings of a parliament, or elections are conventional, in contrast to demonstrations or street blockades.

Table 2.1 Protest, social movements, and other concepts: definitions from the literature

(1) "... *protest activity* is defined as a mode of political action oriented toward objection to one or more policies or conditions, characterized by showmanship or display of an unconventional nature, and undertaken to obtain rewards from political or economic systems while working within the system" (Lipsky 1968, italics not in the in the original).

(2) "An *act of protest* includes the following elements: the action expresses a grievance, a conviction of wrong or injustice; the protestors are unable to correct the condition directly by their own efforts; the action is intended to draw attention to the grievances; the action is further meant to provoke ameliorative steps by some target group; and the protestors depend upon some combination of sympathy and fear to move the target group in their behalf" (Turner 1969, italics not in the original).

(3) A *challenging group* "meets two central criteria": "it must be seeking the mobilization of an unmobilized constituency," "its antagonist lies outside of its constituency" (Gamson 1990: 14–17).

(4) A "*social movement*" is "a set of opinions and beliefs in a population which represents preferences for changing some elements of the social structure and/or reward distribution of a society" (McCarthy and Zald 1977).

(5) "A *social movement organization* is a complex, or formal organization which identifies its goals with the preferences of a social movement or a countermovement and attempts to implement those goals" (McCarthy and Zald 1977, italics not in the original).

(6) "A *social movement* is a purposive and collective attempt of a number of people to change individuals or societal institutions and structures" (Zald and Ash 1966, italics not in the original.)

(7) *Social movements* are "effort[s] by a large number of people to solve collectively a problem that they feel they have in common" (Toch 1965: 5).

(8) "*Social movements* are voluntary collectivities that people support in order to effect changes in society. Using the broadest and most inclusive definition, a social movement includes all who in any form support the general ideas of the movement. Social movements contain social movement organization, the carrier organizations that consciously attempt to coordinate and mobilize supporters" (McCarthy and Zald 1973, italics not in the original).

(9) [The term] *Social movement* "I reserve for those sequences of contentious politics that are based on underlying social networks and resonant collective action frames and which develop the capacity to maintain sustained challenges against powerful opponents" (Tarrow 1998: 2).

(10) *Social movements* "are better defined as collective challenges, based on common purposes and social solidarities, in sustained interaction with elites, opponents, and authorities" (Tarrow 1998: 4).

(11) "By *contentious politics* we mean: episodic, public, collective interaction among makers of claims and their objects when (a) at least one government is a claimant, an object of claims, or a party to the claims and (b) the claims would, if realized, affect the interests of at least one of the claimants. Roughly translated, the definition refers to collective political struggle" (McAdam, Tarrow, and Tilly 2001: 5, italics not in the original).

(12) "Social movements have traditionally been defined as organized efforts to bring about social change" (Jenkins and Form 2005).

These criteria capture the phenomena that are studied in the social movement literature: the subject is joint action of individuals that does not take place regularly, whose aim is to achieve goals by putting pressure on third parties.

The two definitions further have one feature in common with most – or perhaps all – other definitions of protest: they lack precision. For example, what is a "political" in contrast to a non-political action (definition 1)? When does an action "express" a grievance (definition 2) – maybe the author means that the actors (not the action) express their goal to redress a grievance and that they try to achieve this goal through certain behaviors?

Definitions 1 and 2 also include different dimensions. For example, definition 1 says, in contrast to definition 2, that the action must be "political." Only definition 2 includes a causal statement: "the protestors depend upon some combination of sympathy and fear to move the target in their behalf."

Social movements

There seem to be more efforts to define "social movement" than "protest." Accordingly, we included more definitions of "social movement" than of "protest" in Table 2.1. What do the definitions have in common and how do they differ?[1]

There is one definition that differs from all the others: McCarthy and Zald (1977 – see definition 4 in Table 2.1) define a "social movement" as a certain "set of opinions and beliefs." All other authors define "social movement" as a collectivity of individuals. This is, according to McCarthy and Zald, a "social movement organization" (SMO). Many scholars have followed this usage.

Let us look at the other definitions in our list. Although all definitions agree (except McCarthy and Zald) that a "social movement" is a collectivity of individuals, they refer to different kinds of collectivities. Many scholars define a social movement as an *organization*. Others simply see a social movement as a *number of people* (definitions 6, 7, 8). In definition 9 "social movement" refers, among other things, to "sequences of contentious politics." This implies that *groups* – of whatever kind – are involved in such sequences. Definition 3 also mentions groups. "Organized efforts" in definition 12 refers to groups as well.

Most of the definitions include *goals* as a definitional criterion. For some authors any common goals (definitions 3, 5, 6, 7, 10) are sufficient. Other definitions restrict the kind of goals. In definition 3, the goal is to seek mobilization. The goal to effect change is part of definitions 6, 8 and 12. Definition 7 just posits that a social movement is given if a group tries to solve a problem. "Solving a problem" means that there is at least one goal that is not realized. This definition thus is equivalent to definitions that require some common goal for a social movement to exist.

Another component of definitions of "social movement" is that there is an *antagonist*. This implies that members of the group do not want to or cannot achieve their goals on their own but want to influence the decisions of others. In definition 3, the antagonist must be outside the constituency, whereas other definitions do not specify characteristics of the antagonist (such as definition 3).

Finally, a social movement is given if there is not only a collectivity of individuals but there must be *joint* (i.e. coordinated) *action*: there must be an "effort" (definition 7) or an "attempt" (definition 6) to implement goals or an "organized effort" (definition 12). When Tarrow specifies that there must be "interaction" (definition 10) with "elites, opponents, and authorities" this also implies that individuals jointly act to achieve their goals. According to these definitions, a social movement is only given if its members are active. A group that only discusses political issues or what a "good society" should look like is not a social movement.

There are other criteria in our list and in the literature as well. Some definitions include causal statements. For example, for Tarrow a "social movement" is given only if "sequences of contentious politics" are "based on underlying social networks" and other factors.

Our list further includes a definition of "contentious politics" (definition 11) that is used in a new approach to social movements and political protest (see chapter 10 of this book). Although the definition does not mention the terms "protest" or "social movement," it actually captures phenomena that the definitions in our list and in the literature refer to. "Makers of claims" are, among other things, "social movements"; the definition further refers to antagonists and to goals ("claims").

The definitions in Table 2.1 have one other dimension in common: most of them are surprisingly unclear. For example, "formal organization" is defined in various ways in the literature: What exactly do authors mean when they define a social movement as an "organization"? Is it a collectivity with a hierarchical structure? This would be a high degree of formal organization. Or is it sufficient if there is some coordination of activities of various groups with a common goal? Thus, the "peace movement" may consist of various loosely-structured groups at the local level whose activities are coordinated by a committee. This would be a low degree of formal organization.

Our list includes only a selection of the many definitions in the literature. Diani (1992) and Snow and Oliver (1995: 571–572) also discussed various definitions of "social movement." Snow and Oliver (1995: 571) concluded that "most conceptualizations include the following elements: change-oriented goals; some degree of organization; some degree of temporal continuity; and some extra-institutional (e.g. protesting in the streets) and institutional (e.g. political lobbying) activity." These dimensions – with the exception of "political lobbying" – are also present in the definitions that have been reviewed before. "Some degree" of temporal continuity is implied even for short-term movements, founded for a certain purpose such as preventing a transport of nuclear waste through a village. The finding of Snow and Oliver implies and thus concurs with our previous analysis that there are some common dimensions in the definitions, but that there is also much heterogeneity in regard to the degrees of organization, etc. that must be present for a social movement to exist.

3. Suggestions for defining "protest" and "social movement"

The previous section provides a descriptive analysis: we looked at existing definitions of "protest" and "social movement" and analyzed to what extent they share certain dimensions. This analysis does not answer a basic question: What is an appropriate or fruitful definition of those terms? In this book, the issue is theory construction. Therefore, the criterion for a "good" definition is its theoretical fruitfulness (for details see chapter 1). What do fruitful definitions for "protest" and "social movements" look like? This section suggests an answer to this question.

Protest behavior

The present state of theory and research in the field of protest and social movements does not allow us to judge definitions by their theoretical fruitfulness. In other words, we can't tell which of the definitions (e.g. those listed in Table 2.1) makes a given theory more or less valid if it is included in the theory. Perhaps a new definition is theoretically more fruitful than any of the existing ones? If it is presently not possible to judge which definition is best, one should choose a wide definition. As we saw in chapter 1, only wide definitions can lead to theories with high explanatory power.

There are many possible wide definitions of protest behavior. As we saw in chapter 1, one possibility is to choose a definition that addresses the object of study, i.e. that describes all the phenomena social movement scholars have been interested in. This would be a working definition whose fruitfulness has to be tested. What are these kinds of behavior?

First of all, social movement scholars are concerned with *joint or, equivalently, collective action*. The term "joint" or "collective" first refers to coordinated actions of several individuals such as a planned demonstration. It may further designate any unorganized action of individuals. In this wide sense spontaneous collective action such as the Monday demonstrations in Leipzig in 1989 which were not organized are an example of "collective" action. In this book, "collective" action comprises organized as well as spontaneous joint behavior. There can be no question that both kinds of behavior have been of interest to social movement scholars. "Joint action" or, equivalently, "collective" action is thus understood as action of several individuals regardless of whether there is coordination or not.

The social movements literature further focuses on individuals who *cannot achieve their goals by themselves*. Instead, they put pressure on third parties, i.e. on antagonists or targets, to influence their decisions. Thus, social movements cannot by themselves prevent wars, close down nuclear power stations or create equal rights for different groups.

We thus arrive at the following definition:

> *Protest* is defined as joint (i.e. collective) action of individuals aimed at achieving their goal or goals by influencing decisions of a target.

Protest actions may have many other features: they may be more or less organized, they may be more or less regular, they may be legal or illegal, more or less legitimate, violent and so on. It does not seem fruitful to include such features in a definition. Scholars who are interested in these and other features may treat them as separate dependent or independent variables. For example, a question could be when protest (in the above sense) turns violent. In order to answer these questions the dimensions of interest need not be included in a definition.

Let us look at implications of this definition. When groups want to influence the decisions of a target actor they engage in various kinds of activities. For example, they may try to meet with representatives of the target and negotiate; they may engage in legal action against the target; they may try to solicit ("mobilize") resources such as new members, support by other groups, and money; they may organize a formerly loosely-structured group by setting up a statute specifying positions and procedures for election and for meetings. Our case study (chapter 4, section 2) of a Spanish mining village where protests emerged against the plan of a company to build a new pit showed that a wide variety of actions were chosen including violent protests and negotiations. This is typical for social movements.[2] All these activities are joint actions in order to influence the decision of a target. They are thus to be subsumed under "protest." This concept thus differs from a narrow definition where only direct confrontations with a target (like engaging in demonstrations) are called "protest." This wide definition is certainly useful. It allows the researcher to explain the wide array of activities that collectivities of actors perform in order to achieve their goals. Even if the main interest is in explaining only protest in a narrow sense, a full explanation also requires to explain the behavioral alternatives open to groups. One question is why some groups choose protest in a problematic situation, whereas other groups choose other options such as negotiation or file a suit.

Social movement scholars typically address situations where the actors put pressure on a target to make a certain decision. The reason may be that actors *cannot* achieve their goals on their own. There are other situations where actors are able but *do not want* to achieve their goal on their own. To be sure, the government may be requested to provide more police protection to reduce crime, but the citizens could themselves act to reduce crime or at least contribute to its reduction by organizing a neighborhood watch. Environmental protection can be achieved by protests that put pressure on the government to make new laws, but citizens may also contribute to a clean environment on their own in various ways. In a similar vein, one may demand laws against discrimination, but demonstrations may also aim at alerting citizens themselves not to discriminate minorities. Our previous definition includes such cases where actors can achieve their goals on their own but don't want to: the definition says that protest is given when the actors "want to achieve their goal or goals by influencing decisions of a target."

The definition does not require that the activities are unconventional. If this means that protests don't take place regularly, we can imagine actions that would usually count as protest and that are regular. For example, it could have become a custom that on the first Monday of each month there is a demonstration at the Augustus Square in Leipzig – in memory of the Monday demonstrations in 1989–1990 – where different speakers discuss some political issues or express their concerns. Studying this kind of action which is regular or institutionalized is certainly of interest to social movement scholars.

There can be no question that the previous definition also comprises behavior that usually would not be subsumed under the term "protest." Assume that father A and his son object to the decision of the father's wife and daughter to buy European wine. This is protest according to the previous definition: there is joint action of father and son; the actors want to achieve their goal by influencing the decision of a target (mother and daughter). Social movement scholars are probably not interested in such family conflicts. Thus, it may be suggested to exclude such cases by adding additional dimensions. For example, one might require that actions must be "political" (see the term in the first definition above) so that conflicts within families are no longer protest. One problem of adding other dimensions will be that it probably increases the ambiguity of the term "protest" – as would be the case by requiring that "protest" is a "political" activity.

Before one tries to restrict the definition so that it includes only behaviors social movement scholars are interested in, one should ask why this is necessary. Does it really hurt if a definition refers, among other things, to cases that are not of interest? One may simply ignore such cases. It is more important that a definition includes cases that are of interest. Furthermore, it may turn out in the future that all of a sudden some of these "strange" cases raise interest. It often happens that the range of phenomena to be explained widens.

This argument seems to be in line with the actual procedures of social movement scholars. It is strange that definitions of protest usually do not provide a detailed analysis of the kind of cases that are covered by a definition. For example, it seems that our strange case above is also implied by definitions 6 and 12 in Table 2.1. Apparently, those implications seem to be irrelevant, otherwise they would be discussed. Or, perhaps, nobody was interested in analyzing the implications of those definitions.

Social movement

The criteria for a fruitful definition of "protest" were that it encompasses a rather wide variety of phenomena and captures those activities social movement scholars are interested in. These criteria hold for a fruitful definition of "social movement" as well. A plausible starting point is the previous definition of "protest." Why not call a group of actors who pursue their goal(s) by putting pressure on a target a "social movement"? The definition thus could read: A *social movement* is defined as a collectivity of actors who want to achieve their goal or goals by influencing the decisions of a target.

This definition refers to the phenomena that are studied by social movement scholars. Examples are collectivities like the peace, environmental, anti-nuclear and civil rights movement. However, the definition also designates groups that one would usually not call "social movements." One example is unions: these are collectivities that put pressure on employers to increase wages or improve working conditions; they are thus social movements according to the previous definition. A small citizen initiative requesting that a government prevents the construction of a highway through their residential area would be a social movement. The father and the son – see the previous example – would count as a social movement as well: they are a collectivity of actors with the goal to influence the decisions of a target (mother and daughter).

The previous definition thus comprises some "strange" cases as the definition of "protest." The argument in regard to our definition of protest can be applied here as well: it does not hurt if a definition refers to a broad class of phenomena social movements scholars are not interested in. They may simply ignore those phenomena.

Nonetheless, the above definition will probably raise strong objections by social movement scholars because the difference to its everyday meaning is too strong – whatever this meaning exactly is. To be sure, a scientific term does not need to be consistent with its everyday meaning, but it makes communication easier if it comes close to it. Nonetheless, as we saw, the phenomena the definition refers to are of interest in the social movement literature. But the term – social movement – does not fit. An expression that comes closer to the definition is *protest group* – one could also speak of a "challenging group" (see definition 3 above). Thus, we suggest the following definition:

> A *protest group* is, by definition, a collectivity of actors who want to achieve their shared goal or goals by influencing decisions of a target.

A "social movement" is a certain kind of a "protest group." But what are the special features of a social movement? Two dimensions are frequently mentioned in the literature, as has been mentioned already: one is *some degree of formal organization.* It was said already that this dimension is not clear. When we use the "formal organization" as a criterion to demarcate social movements from other groups the question arises of what the degree of formal organization is that makes a group a social movement.

Another feature that is often associated with the term "social movement" is *size.* Typical social movements such as the peace movement are relatively large groups. But what is the size where a social movement begins – is it 50, 100, 200, or 1,000 members?

Such quantitative dimensions lose their precision when they are used to define categorical variables such as a "large" or "small" group. The reason is that they must be dichotomized. For example, if a social movement is defined as a "large" group with a "high degree of formal organization," the variables "size" and "degree of formal organization" must be dichotomized. This means that it must be decided where the cutting point is. Specifying such cutting points is arbitrary. For example, when is a group "large"?

The difficulty of demarcating a social movement from a protest group can be solved by introducing a *quantitative concept of social movement*: a group may be more or less like a social movement. The larger the protest group is and the more formal its organization is, the closer it comes to a social movement. "Longevity" is another dimension. Again, we could stipulate: the longer a protest group exists, the closer it comes to a social movement. Thus, if a group reaches for all dimensions the maximum value, it comes closest to a social movement.

Introducing a quantitative concept of social movement is not as far away from everyday usage as it seems at first sight. We often describe groups by saying that it is more or less similar to a certain type of group. For example, assume a group of about 100 people lives in a remote area and is self-sufficient. One might say that this comes very close to a society.

A problem is that the quantification becomes complicated when the number of quantitative dimensions becomes larger. It may then happen that a protest group has high values on some dimensions, medium values on others and low values on still other dimensions. In this case, we must specify a function that relates the dimensions to the quantitative social movement concept.

A second procedure for differentiating between protest groups and social movements is preferable. When social movement scholars are interested in the degree of formal organization, the size and other properties of groups, *these dimensions can be introduced as additional independent or dependent variables*. For example, an explanatory problem could be when different degrees or kinds of organization develop or when groups grow or shrink. The suggestion thus is this: we start with the previous definition of "protest group." The scholar can then select the groups he or she is interested in. For example, a social movement scholar will not deal with requests of a group of tenants to a landlord to lower rents, but is interested in groups that demand certain decisions from a government. The explanatory question is how such groups come into being and how certain properties of these groups can be explained. Among these properties are degree of organization and size.

This procedure avoids complex and vague definitions like those listed in Table 2.1. It further allows the scholar to be rather free in choosing the groups he or she wants to study. In general, thus, the question is – in regard to protest – why one should pack all the interesting features of groups in a definition. It is preferable to keep a definition simple and treat interesting features not included in the definition as dependent or independent variables.

Throughout this book, we will speak of "social movements" because this is the terminology in the field of social movement research. We thus use current language. But we actually refer to "protest groups" in the above sense. The reader should thus be alerted that "social movement" means a special kind of protest group, but that it is not clear what this kind of group actually is. In order to avoid confusion, it is best to have in mind the groups that are typically called social movements like the peace, environmental, civil rights, or women's movements. However – to reiterate – the subject are protest groups and the task is to explain various features of these groups.

4. What do social movement theories explain?

If the previous definitions of "protest" and "protest group" are theoretically fruitful this implies that the existing theoretical perspectives can explain these phenomena. Thus, the perspectives should explain joint action intended to change decisions of targets and the formation of collectivities of actors who want to achieve their shared goal or goals by influencing the decisions of a target. Are the existing perspectives really capable of explaining this wide range of phenomena?

The answer is that this is not clear. The theories do not specify in detail the forms of behavior or kinds of groups they are supposed to explain. The typical procedure is to apply the perspectives to phenomena a researcher is interested in. If there is disconfirming evidence, it is in general not clear whether the class of phenomena to be explained must be changed or whether the independent variables are wrong. However, it seems plausible that at least some of the existing perspectives are capable of explaining the phenomena our definitions refer to. This is most plausible for the theory of collective action (see chapter 3): it is claimed that incentives are relevant for behavior. This implies that those behaviors are chosen for which incentives are strongest. These behaviors may range from negotiating and demonstrating to setting up large groups with hierarchical organizations.

It seems further plausible that resource mobilization and political opportunity perspectives encompass a wide array of behaviors that can be explained. For example, assume that opportunities increase (for example, a rightist government is replaced by a leftist one) or that resources of groups increase (for example, a social movement is supported by a powerful actor such as a union). Why should the groups or their representatives only consider to stage protests in a narrow sense or set up a social movement in the sense of a large organization? What the options are that are chosen depends on various conditions, and these conditions may lead to various kinds of behaviors and groups. Many case studies show indeed that social movements in a narrow sense also try various options. Furthermore, framing and identity hypotheses are not only referring to protest and social movements in a narrow sense, although the cases adduced to illustrate the hypotheses often suggest this. For example, if it is held that collective identity leads to action to support the group, this holds for all kinds of groups, including "protest groups."

At this point, the claim that existing theories of protest and social movements actually address "protest" and "protest groups" as defined above is largely speculative. But as a preliminary working hypothesis it is useful to assume for the time being that the perspectives can in principle explain "protest" and "protest groups" as defined above. If it turns out that this is not possible, the definition can be changed.

The previous argument assumes that the theoretical perspectives mentioned are clearly formulated and testable. As we will see this is not the case. This makes it very difficult if not impossible to test the theoretical import of the previous definitions. They thus will remain working definitions for the time being.

5. Summary and conclusions

This chapter addresses the basic concepts that are used in the theoretical perspectives which are analyzed in this book, namely protest and social movement. The first part of the chapter looked at examples from everyday language and at definitions from the literature on social movements and political protest. One major problem with these definitions is that it is not clear why authors choose the definition they suggest. When explanation is at issue the major criterion applied to judge a definition is its theoretical fruitfulness. This implies, among other things, that a definition should capture a rather wide class of phenomena. So the respective theory can in principle explain a large class of very specific explananda. Another criterion is that a definition should refer to the phenomena that are of interest to social movement scholars.

Consistent with these criteria we suggest to define *protest* as joint (i.e. collective) action of individuals aimed at achieving their goal or goals by influencing decisions of a target. A *protest group* is defined as a collectivity of actors who want to achieve their shared goal or goals by influencing decisions of a target. A "social movement" is a type of protest group with several distinguishing characteristics such as size and degree of organization. It is suggested to address protest groups and explain characteristics (i.e. variables) that are often used to demarcate social movements and other groups. Examples are size and degree of organization. The chapter further discusses the merits and problems of these definitions. It is argued that the theoretical perspectives discussed in this book actually can explain protest and protest groups, as defined above. "Protest" and "protest groups" as defined above are thus subject of this book. In order to stick with the language used in the field of social movement research, we will nonetheless use the term "social movement" instead of "protest group." As specific examples the reader may wish to refer to the typical activities (such as demonstrations) and groups (such as the peace or civil rights "movements") when the theoretical perspectives will be discussed in the following chapters.

3 Group size, selective incentives, and collective action

The basic work of the theory of collective action is Mancur Olson's *The Logic of Collective Action* (1965).[1] Immediately after its publication, it became one of the most discussed and most criticized theories in the social sciences.[2] The theory does not address social movement phenomena directly. The question the theory addresses is when people act jointly to achieve some common goal. This is a broader question than explaining why people participate in protest or social movement activities or why social movements originate. But because these phenomena are forms of joint action in order to accomplish some common goals, the theory of collective action can be applied to explain social movement phenomena. Indeed, there is an extensive literature that explains social movement phenomena with the theory of collective action.

Before applying this theory to social movement phenomena it is useful to present and discuss it in detail. This makes it possible to recognize its strengths and weaknesses and, thus, possible limitations as a theoretical foundation for the field of social movements. Another reason for a detailed discussion is that the theoretical approach this book advances is based on the *approach* of the theory of collective action: this theory integrates a macro proposition, a micro theory and suggests various micro-to-macro (bottom-up) and macro-to-micro (top-down) assumptions. In other words, the theory sets forth a micro-macro approach. This is done in a much more explicit way than in the other theoretical perspectives discussed in this book. This is not to say that we adopt the theory in its present form. As this chapter shows, the theory has many weaknesses. Nonetheless, much of it can be retained as a foundation for an integrated approach to social movements and political protest.

The most important contributions of this chapter are, first of all, a reconstruction of Olson's micro-macro theory: it is shown in detail how the group size proposition is rooted in assumptions about the effects of group size (macro level) on individual incentives. Second, we discuss in detail a micro model of contributions to the public good and particularly the interdependence of incentives that has been addressed rarely in the literature. We further discuss various extensions of Olson's theory.

1. Mancur Olson's *Logic of Collective Action*

It is common that those who publish a new theory first tell the reader what the deficiencies of preceding theories are and how the new theory remedies these problems. Olson is no exception. The theories he criticizes all posit that in general individuals with common interests tend to act to realize their interests.[3] Olson maintains the opposite. He lists various examples which are in line with his proposition. In addition, he buttresses his hypothesis by a general theory of action: he claims that "rational" and "self-interested" (for the meaning of these terms see below) individuals will not – contrary to what some theorists assert – contribute to attain their common goals. Let us now look at Olson's theoretical argument in more detail.

The background theory: rationality and self-interest

Olson assumes that individuals are "rational" and "self-interested." What do these terms mean? Olson's theoretical basis is the theory of rational action or, equivalently, the economic model of man. We have expounded the theory in chapter 1, section 1. Although the term "rational" is used in various meanings in the literature, in this context *rational* means that individuals' behavior is governed by its costs and benefits and that individuals do what is best for them. In other words, individuals maximize their utility. To illustrate, if Olson writes that it is "rational" not to contribute to achieve the common goal (i.e. not to contribute to the provision of a public good – this term is explained below) in a large group, this means, that the costs of contributing are higher than the benefits.

Self-interest refers to "egoism" – one should better use the term "selfishness." A person with a highly egoistic preference is, by definition, mainly concerned with his or her own well-being. A highly altruistic person has an intrinsic interest in the welfare of others. It is important to note that it is perfectly compatible with rational choice theory that altruistic preferences may influence behavior. An altruistic preference is a special sort of a preference and is thus a factor that may affect behavior. For example, a mother has in general an intrinsic interest in the welfare of her child and is thus highly altruistic. This preference will affect her behavior toward the child.

It is important to distinguish utility-maximization on the one hand and self-interest on the other. Highly self-interested (i.e. egoistic) as well as highly altruistic individuals maximize their utility. The altruist finds satisfaction (i.e. utility) in serving other people and, thus in increasing their well-being. Examples are monks who devote their life to help others. In doing so they maximize their own utility. Rationality and self-interest (i.e. selfishness) are often confused in the literature.

The subject of the theory: common interests, public goods, and collective action

The theory of collective action is concerned with a collectivity of individual actors who have a *common interest*. An example is the interest of the residents of a community to reduce pollution. If the interest is realized this means that a *good* is provided such as a reduction in pollution. In economics, a good is defined as everything that has (positive or negative) utility. If the collective interest is achieved the good is of a special kind: it is a *public good*. Olson defines this term in the following way:

A common, collective, or public good is here defined as any good such that, if any person X_i in a group X_1, ..., X_i, ..., X_n consumes it, it cannot feasibly be withheld from others in that group. (14)

This definition has several implications.

Non-exclusion. The definition implies that a public good exists, by definition, if nobody can be excluded if it is provided. For example, the cleanliness of a shared apartment is "consumed" by each person who lives in the apartment. Further, nobody can be excluded from enjoying a clean (or dirty) or suffering from a dirty (or clean) apartment. Each has a right to stay in the apartment and thus enjoy (or suffer from) the public good. Another example: police protection provides the public good "security against crime." This is available for every member of a state and no member can be excluded from enjoying it. For example, the state cannot provide a list of people who have not paid taxes and exclude them from protection.

Feasibility of exclusion. In those examples, it may in principle or physically be possible to exclude individuals from enjoying the public good. For example, tenants can physically prevent other tenants from staying in the apartment; in the middle ages, a person could be declared as an outlaw and was not protected by the state. But law would prohibit this procedure in modern states. In these examples, exclusion is not "feasible." What does this mean?

It is sometimes in principle possible to exclude members of a group from the consumption of the public good, but – as Olson puts it – it is nonetheless not "feasible." This means that the costs of excluding a person from the consumption of a good are high. Since these costs vary a great deal in different situations, "exclusion" is in fact a *quantitative variable*, and one should thus distinguish between *degrees of the feasibility of exclusion*.

Free riding. The criterion of non-exclusion applies also for those who did or do not contribute to the provision of the good. For example, those tenants who share the apartment and do not participate in cleaning it will nevertheless enjoy the results of the efforts of other members. Those who consume the public good without contributing to its provision are called *free riders*.

Jointness of supply and rivalness of consumption. "Jointness" of supply means that if the good is available to one member of a group, it is available to all members. Nonetheless, the utility of the good for one person may depend on the number of other persons in a group. In this case, there is *rivalness of consumption*. For example, in a public park the degree to which a person enjoys the park will normally depend on the number of individuals who are in the park. There is thus rivalness of consumption.

Group specificity. It is important to note that a public good is always group specific. External security is a public good only for a given state. Cleanliness of an apartment is a public good only for the tenants who share the apartment.

Collective action. Any contribution to the provision of a public good is, by definition, "collective action." The term "collective" suggests that the action must be carried out by several (i.e. at least two) actors. However, Olson also discusses the special case where only one individual produces the collective good for a group. In the apartment, e.g. only one person may clean it. But this is an extreme case. In general, "collective" refers to contributions of several actors.[4]

"Collective action" is what the theory tries to explain. The *question* thus is: *When do individuals act jointly to contribute to and, thus, provide the public good?* Put differently, it is explained when individuals with a common goal act to realize their goal. A *group* is defined as a collectivity of individuals with a common goal or, equivalently, with a common interest.

It is important to note that the theory addresses the behavior of individual actors, i.e. their *contribution* to the provision of the public good. These contributions then add up to the provision of the public good or to a certain quantity of the public good. For example, the fewer individuals refrain from polluting, the more of the public good "clean environment" is produced. There is thus a relationship from the *micro level* (individual contribution) to the *macro level* (production of the public good). We will return to this relationship later in this chapter.

A first illustration of the theory: firms in a competitive market

Before Olson presents his theory in detail, he illustrates basic points of his argument with the following example (9–12). If the reader has difficulty in understanding it, this section might be skipped. The theory is exposed in detail after this example.

Assume there is a market with perfect competition, i.e. there are many small firms and no firm can influence the market price. Each firm wants to get the highest possible profit. It is assumed that each firm acts rationally in the above sense, and acts out of self-interest, i.e. the welfare of other firms is not of intrinsic interest. A further assumption is that the marginal costs of a firm – that is the costs of each additional product – first decrease and then increase. In other words, when a firm increases its production from a very few to many products, additional products cost first less and then more. The respective curve is thus u-shaped (the x-axis represents the number of products, the y-axis the marginal costs).[5]

Now assume that there is a situation in which the marginal costs (MC) of a firm are lower than the market price (P). Remember that each firm wants to maximize its profit. This is accomplished when the MC of a firm are equal to the price P: as long as the additional costs (MC) for a product are lower than P, it pays to increase production. The consequence is that there is a general increase in supply: all firms have the same goal, namely to increase their profit, and, thus, extend production. A general increase in supply leads to a decrease of the price. That is to say, the firms supply now more than the consumers buy for the given price. In order to sell their products, firms lower their price or go bankrupt. As a consequence, the profits of the firms decrease.[6]

What has this situation to do with collective action and collective goods? The common or collective interest of the firms is a high price. This is the common or collective good. How could the firm contribute to provide the collective good or higher amounts of the collective good? The decline in revenues came about because the firms increased production. Accordingly, if all firms would restrict their production, the price would increase or remain high. A contribution of a single firm to a price rise is thus to restrict production. But this would be highly costly. The firm would lower its profits further and the restricted production of a single firm would not have any *noticeable* – a term that Olson uses time and again – effect on the general price level. Thus, no firm has any incentive to contribute to the production of the collective good.

This example illustrates Olson's theory very well.[7] Note that the situation described has the following features: (1) There is a large group with a collective interest, namely a high price level. (2) A contribution of a single individual to bring about a higher price of the good is to curtail output; but this will not in any way further the provision of the good. That is to say, a contribution of a single firm would not be – to use Olson's term – noticeable. (3) There are no special incentives that obtain if a firm contributes (i.e. restricts output) or defects (i.e. increases production). As we will see, these special incentives are called "selective incentives." It is difficult to imagine what such incentives could be in this situation and who would be motivated to provide them. A single firm would not be motivated to provide those specific incentives because this would again have only a negligible effect on the provision of the public good and would be costly. There is thus not only the problem of providing the first-order public good, i.e. a higher price level, but also to provide selective incentives. These are "second-order public goods" in the sense that they are instrumental for providing the first-order public good. The problems of providing the first-order public good thus hold for the second-order public good as well. We will now present the theory in more detail and will take up all the questions discussed in this section.

The theory of collective action: a reconstruction of Olson's implicit micro-macro theory

Olson summarizes his basic proposition right at the beginning of his book: "Indeed, unless the number of individuals in a group is quite small, or unless there is coercion or some other special device to make individuals act in their common interest, *rational, self-interested individuals will not act to achieve their common or group interest*" (2, italics in the original). This quotation consists of several propositions which will be discussed in detail in the following sections.

The macro proposition: group size and public goods production

The above quotation first suggests a macro proposition. This is the most controversial proposition in Olson's theory. It reads:

> *Group size proposition:* The larger a group is, the less likely it is that a public good is provided.[8]

The units of analysis of this propositions are *groups*. These are a collection of individual actors with a common goal (8).

The micro model: conditions for individual participation

The above quotation further involves conditions for *individual* behavior. It is assumed that rational and self-interested individuals do not act in their common interest. In other words, they do not *contribute* to achieve their goals (or common interest) – unless there is coercion or some other special device. Such special devices are kinds of costs and benefits and are called *selective incentives* (51). "Selective" means that the respective incentives are contingent on the behavior, whereas the public good is available to every member of a group, even if he or she has not contributed. For example, "force" or punishment only occurs when individuals do not contribute to the public good. In this sense, "force" is a negative selective incentive. Positive selective incentives are rewards and are offered to those who contribute. What matters at this point is that selective incentives refer to incentives obtained by individual actors when they contribute or do not contribute. In other words:

> *Selective incentives proposition:* The stronger the positive selective incentives for contributing and the stronger the negative selective incentives for not contributing, the more likely individuals contribute to the provision of the public good.

This is a micro proposition referring to the behavior of individual actors.

Contributions are costly. The production of the public good requires, for example, time and other resources, i.e. opportunity costs (which refer to the utility forgone when one contributes to the provision of the public good). Thus:

> *Costs proposition:* The higher the costs of contributing to the provision of the public good, the less likely is contribution.

When Olson discusses contributions in small groups he hypothesizes that the *intensity of the interest* in the collective good is an incentive to contribute. For example, assume that one common goal of, say, five students who share an apartment is to keep the apartment clean. Since the apartment is small each member's cleaning activity has a visible effect. In the extreme case, one member alone could provide the public good. Furthermore, when we assume that the apartment is small, the costs of cleaning are not high. It is therefore likely that each member will participate in cleaning activities. Now assume that the tenants differ in the extent to which they have an interest in a clean apartment. Those with a very high interest will most likely contribute. They may even clean the apartment on their own if the others do not want to contribute. This example illustrates that two factors are important for participating in the provision of a public good: the first is the *public goods motivation* (or the intensity of preference for the public good); the second is the extent to which an individual's contribution is *noticeable* (Olson's term) or efficacious, i.e. the extent to which an individual's contribution makes a difference in regard to the provision of the public good. In other words:

Public goods motivation proposition: The more intense the goal of providing the public good is, the more likely individuals will contribute.

Efficacy proposition: The higher the influence of an individual's contribution on the provision of a public good is, the more likely an individual will contribute.

These two factors have a *multiplicative* (or interaction) *effect* and not an additive effect. An additive effect would obtain if an increase in the public goods motivation would always raise the contribution to the public good, regardless of the efficacy of the contribution. But this is not plausible because even an intense interest in the public good will not lead to a contribution if there is no noticeable effect of one's contribution. This means that the effect of the intensity of the motivation to provide the public good depends on the extent to which the contribution makes a difference and vice versa. This is, by definition, an interaction effect in the statistical sense.

This completes the micro model explaining the participation in the provision of public goods. We will now show how this model is related to the group size proposition.

The structure of the theory: the basic model

So far we discussed two types of propositions: one is a macro proposition claiming a relationship between group size and the provision of a public good. The other is a micro proposition stating conditions for individual participation in providing the public good. The question arises: How are these hypotheses and these two levels related? It is unfortunate that Olson does not systematically develop his theory along these lines. We must carefully look at the text to find out how the micro-macro relationships are conceived.[9] So what is the relationship between the group size proposition and the micro model explaining individual public goods participation?

A clue to answer this question is a hypothesis that Olson repeats on almost every page: in a large group the individual contribution is not noticeable. This hypothesis asserts a relationship between a macro variable, namely group size, and a variable of the micro model, namely efficacy: the larger the group is, the less efficacious are individual contributions to the public good. Olson thus assumes a *top-down effect* (or, equivalently, macro-to-micro proposition) from group size (macro level) to efficacy (micro level). If – on the micro level – efficacy decreases, individual contribution becomes less likely. This is a hypothesis on the micro level. Since this hypothesis holds for every member of a group, the consequence is that the likelihood that the public good is produced decreases. This is a *bottom-up effect* (or, equivalently, micro-to-macro effect) from the micro level (individual contribution) to the macro model (provision of the public good): individual contributions add up to the provision of the public good.

This argument illustrates the structure of Olson's theory: it is a micro-macro model. Before we reconstruct and discuss this model in detail let us look at its structure which is displayed in Figure 3.1.[10] Note that this model is consistent with the basic model for a micro-macro model in chapter 1, section 4 (see Figure 1.2). The macro proposition of Olson's theory – see arrow 3 in Figure 3.1 – asserts, as we saw before, that there is a negative relationship between group size and public good provision. Is this a causal effect or simply a correlation? This question is never addressed by Olson and neither in the literature. We posit that it is a correlation – which is symbolized by the line. The reason is that this relationship is explained: the micro-macro model shows why or under what conditions group size is related to public goods production: the causal process runs from group size to the individual level – first to the incentives and then to individual action – and from there back to the collective level. The model thus implies under what conditions group size does and does not affect public goods production. In other words, the relationship between group size and public goods provision is negative *because* group size brings about disincentives for individual contributions to the public good which, in turn, impede the provision of the good. This implies that only the incentives are relevant for the production of the public good; group size has no additional separate causal effect on public good provision. Otherwise, there should be an arrow from "group size" to "individual contribution to the public good."

There is another important implication of the model. The negative correlation obtains *only if* group size generates negative incentives to contributing to the provision of the public good. But whether this is always the case is, as we will see, doubtful. Thus, the top-down relationships are crucial for the group size proposition to hold true. If these relationships change or are not valid, there will be no or even a positive correlation between group size and public goods provision.

The macro relationship between group size and public goods production obtains, among other things, because in a large group the individual contribution is negligible. Is the relationship between "group size" and "efficacy" empirical or analytical?[11] Olson does not discuss this question. "Noticeability" in Olson's theory is an objective measure, i.e. an individual's actual influence or efficacy: it is 1 divided by the number of group members (or the number of contributors). For example, if the group has, say, 10,000 members an individual has, by definition, a lower influence (namely 1/10,000) in bringing about the public good than if the group size is 10 (influence here is 1/10). Thus, the relationship is analytical (see line 1 in Figure 3.1). This is symbolized by the line between the respective variables. However, when Olson speaks of a "noticeable" or "perceptible" contribution he may refer to the individual's beliefs or perceptions. In this case, the macro-to-micro hypothesis is empirical: if a group is large then the effect is that individuals perceive a low

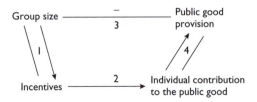

Figure 3.1 The structure of the micro-macro model of the theory of collective action

influence. But Olson is an economist and in economics the common assumption is that perceptions match reality. Therefore, we assume that the relationship between group size and efficacy is analytical. But, as we will see later, there are also empirical relationships between group size and variables on the micro level. Relationships of type 1 in Figure 3.1 may thus be both: empirical as well as analytical.

What about the relationship between the individual contributions to the public good (the micro variable) and the provision of the public good (the macro variable) – see relationship 4 in Figure 3.1? For many public goods, this relationship is analytical. For example, the fewer individuals pollute a river (i.e. the fewer individuals contribute to the public good "clean river"), the lower is the pollution of the river (i.e. the less of the public good is provided). This is similar to the relationship between the number of individual crimes in a neighborhood and the crime rate: the latter is, by definition, equal to the number of individual crimes, divided by population size. We will return to this micro-to-macro relationships between individual contributions and the overall public good later.

But there are also empirical bottom-up relationships. For example, assume that individuals want to bring about a norm demanding not to pollute the local river. They sanction others which is a contribution to the emergence of the norm. But whether the norm comes about is an empirical matter. The sanctions may not be effective, i.e. they may not lead to the internalization of or conformity to the norm. Thus, relationships between individual contributions and public goods provision may be analytical as well as empirical, depending on the kind of the public good that is at issue.

The basic structure of the theory of collective action is thus a micro-macro model: there is a macro-proposition, namely the group size proposition. There is further a micro-proposition which claims that individual incentives (i.e. interest in the public good, efficacy, costs, and selective incentives) affect contributions to the public good. This micro model is the only relationship that is always empirical and causal: incentives have empirical and causal effects on behavior. The third type of relationships are *bridge assumptions*. One consists of propositions about top-down (i.e. macro-to-micro) relationships: group size is supposed to be related to various incentives. The other type of bridge assumption consists of propositions about bottom-up (micro-to-macro) relationships. In the theory of collective action, these are relationships between the individual contributions and the provision of the public good. Let us now turn to Olson's micro-macro model in more detail.

The macro-micro model in detail: a reconstruction of Olson's theory

Figure 3.2 summarizes Olson's micro-macro theory. Let us first look at the micro model. It is first assumed, as we saw before, that the interest in (i.e. preference for) the public good is an incentive for contributing to the public good. This implies that – given the preference for a public good – the *share of the public good* individuals receive when they are active is an incentive for participation. This is the variable

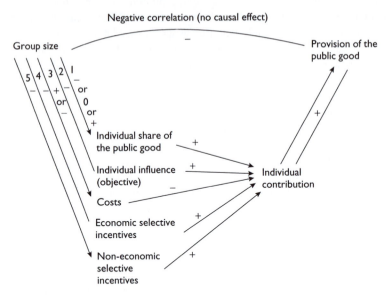

1   pp. 23, 28, 34; non-market groups: non-rivalness exists pp. 37–38, 48.
2   pp. 12, 16, 43, 44, 45, 53.
3   p. 37 for market groups; non-market groups: size is related to *low* costs;
    p. 46: costs per person include organization costs.
4, 5 pp. 60–62 referring to small groups; but if the likelihood of providing a public
    good in large groups is very small then the selective incentives should be
    scarce in large groups.

Figure 3.2 A reconstruction of M. Olson's micro-macro model (based on Olson 1965/1971)

Olson mentions when he discusses the relationships between group size and public
goods provision. Is group size related to the individual's share of the public good?
Olson posits that members of small groups get a higher share of the public good
than members of large groups (see arrow 1 of Figure 3.2). The assumption here is
that the public good shows rivalness of consumption, i.e. the utility of a good for a
member depends on the number of group members. In this case, indeed, members
of large groups get a lower share of the public good than members of smaller
groups. There is thus a negative relationship between group size and the individual
share of the public good.

However, rivalness of consumption is not the assumption made throughout
Olson's book. When he distinguishes between market and non-market groups, he
argues that market groups are interested in keeping the group as small as possible
until only one firm is left that can dictate the price. Here rivalness obtains. Non-
market groups, however, are interested in many members so that a high amount of
the public good is provided (like exemption from tax or subsidies). This seems to
imply: the larger the group the higher is the individual share of the public good.
There is thus no rivalness of consumption. Otherwise non-market groups would be

interested in keeping the group small. This seems plausible when Olson writes that in a non-market lobbying organization a high number of members does not "necessarily" reduce the benefits for others (37). Thus, if there is rivalness of consumption, group size correlates negatively with the individual share of the public good. But there may be "positive rivalness" in the sense that a large number of members increases the individual's share of the public good. If there is no rivalness, no correlation obtains. The relationship between group size and the share of the public good an individual receives thus depends on the situation.

Is the relationship between group size and share of the public good empirical or analytical? Do we need to carry out an empirical study to find out whether individuals get more or less of the public good if size varies? For example, how can we determine whether a public park is a collective good with rivalness? Apparently, we must find out how individuals feel when the number of visitors of a park varies. In regard to a non-market group, how does Olson know that many members are advantageous for a member of the group? It seems that an empirical assumption is involved that a large number of members have effects on the willingness of a government to provide a public good. Thus, the relationship between group size and the individual share of the public good seems to be empirical.

Figure 3.2 next includes the relationship between group size and (actual) *individual influence* which has been discussed in the previous section (see arrow 2): we saw that this is a negative analytical relationship.

The micro model further includes the individual's *costs* of contributing to the provision of a public good. According to Olson, these costs also depend on group size (see arrow 3). In his discussion of non-market groups, Olson argues that an increase in the number of members lowers the costs for those in the group (37). Thus, there is a negative correlation between group size and the individual costs of a contribution: the larger the group, the lower are individual costs. However, Olson also points out that the costs of providing the good include costs of organization and communication which are relatively high if the group is large (47). For each single member, this means that there are high costs if the group is large. There is thus a positive effect: the larger the group, the higher the costs per member. It is not clear under which conditions what effect obtains.

The two final macro-to-micro (i.e. top-down) links are relationships between group size and selective incentives (60–62, see arrows 4 and 5). In general, it is more likely that positive selective incentives that instigate contributions to the public good are provided in relatively small groups because there are only, Olson argues, face-to-face interactions (62). This holds for economic as well as for non-economic incentives such as social rewards.

To be sure, Olson introduces beside group size other macro-properties like the *inequality* of a group in regard to the interest in the public good. But these additional factors are not discussed in detail and they do not, according to Olson, invalidate the group size proposition, they are only additional variables. We will therefore not deal with these other factors at this point.

We can now see clearly why and under what conditions group size is supposed to correlate negatively with public goods provision: in general, group size diminishes economic and non-economic selective incentives to contribute and influence. If we assume that these are the variables with the strongest effects on individual contributions, it follows that there is a negative correlation of group size and public goods provision. This is the case when the other variables do not matter much. If we do not want to make this assumption, a negative correlation of group size and public goods production will obtain if group size correlates negatively with the individual share of the public good and with influence, and if the costs are high when the group is large.

So far we have reconstructed Olson's theory and not discussed any problems. But the reader may have noticed already why the group size proposition is so controversial. Its validity hinges upon the assumptions, in particular on the bridge assumptions (i.e. micro-to-macro and macro-micro links). And they have been criticized extensively. One problem is whether there are always the negative correlations symbolized by arrows 2, 4 and 5. Are these lawful statements? What is the empirical evidence for their validity? Another problem is that relationships 1 and 3 are indeterminate: there may be positive or negative effects, and in regard to relationship 1 there may be no effect at all. The implication is that there will not always be a negative correlation between group size and public goods provision. We will expect to find sometimes no correlations and sometimes positive correlations. The question then is under what conditions group size has which effects on the incentives to contribute. We will return to these issues in the section "Macro-to-micro relationships: the validity of the group size proposition." We will now turn to the critique of Olson's theory.

2. Critique of the theory

The voluminous literature that criticizes Olson's theory is not only destructive, Olson's theory has also led to new theoretical developments and to a many empirical investigations. In what follows we will first discuss some of the critique that seems most important. The next section (section 3) focuses on major developments of the theory.

The range of application

Many critics complain that the theory holds only under certain conditions. This is correct, as we will see shortly. But this should not be used as an argument to discard the theory. If one would eliminate every theory which holds only under certain conditions, no theory would be left, especially in the social movement field. For example, major propositions of the resource mobilization perspective hold only in a democratic society where social movement organizations can compete for resources (see chapter 5). If a theory holds under certain conditions, the next step should be to drop the conditions and suggest hypotheses about the effects that obtain when the conditions are not given. In this particular context, the question arises as to what the conditions are for the validity of the theory of collective action.

The units of analysis: organizations or groups?

It has been argued that Olson's theory can only be applied to economic interest groups (see, e.g., Udéhn 1993: 240). In contrast, Olson notes that his theory "can be extended to cover communal, religious, and philanthropic organizations, but the theory is not particularly useful in studying such groups" (6, see also, e.g., 61–62). The reason is, it seems, that non-economic incentives prevail in these groups which Olson does not want to address (see below). But if we include these incentives in the theory, it is no longer necessary to restrict the range of application of the theory to economic interest groups. As we will see later, we argue that the restriction to economic incentives is absolutely unnecessary and that Olson's arguments for this claim are flawed.

Olson's focus in his book is on organizations (6). Other types of groups are not addressed (note 6). But this does not imply that the theory can only be applied to organizations. To be sure, the case studies Olson presents to illustrate his theory refer to organizations. But if one looks at the formulation of his theory, the range of application is much wider: *any collectivity of actors with a common goal is the subject of the theory*. This becomes clear when Olson formulates the basic question he addresses – see, for example, the first few sentences of the introduction to his book: When do individuals act jointly in order to achieve their common goal? Individuals who act jointly may be any collectivity of individuals with a common goal.

The assumption of consensus

When the theory applies to any collectivity of individuals with a common interest then this implies that there is consensus at least in regard to this common interest. Olson notes that this is indeed an "unrealistic assumption" (60). Accordingly, Olson does not deal with the consequences of a conflict of interest.

The micro model revisited

Misperception: perceived and actual influence

A central variable in Olson's micro model is the extent to which the individual's contribution to the public good is "noticeable," i.e. to which extent the individual's contribution results in a greater amount of the public good. Olson refers to the individual's actual influence, i.e. to his or her influence from the viewpoint of an observer. Olson certainly would not deny that perceived and not actual influence is important. But as an economist he makes the assumption common in economics that in general individuals perceive reality as it is. There may be occasional discrepancies between reality and beliefs, but misperceptions will adapt because it is costly to hold wrong beliefs in the long run.

This is a plausible assumption in many situations. For example, when a thief underestimates the likelihood of being detected, he or she will certainly adapt his or her subjective probability when he or she gets arrested. But what happens if the thief overestimates the likelihood of being caught and does not commit any crime?

There is not necessarily a perceived cost of believing that "crime does not pay" when actually it will pay.[12]

The assumption of a general match of actual and perceived influence is certainly not correct in the field of collective action. In regard to political participation, i.e. a particular kind of collective action, numerous empirical studies show that perceived political influence in large groups is in general not zero and varies across members of the group (see Finkel, Muller, and Opp 1989; Finkel and Muller 1998; Gibson 1991; Klandermans 1984; Moe 1980; Muller and Opp 1986; Opp 1988, 1989). In general, people overestimate their political influence. This is not implausible. First of all, actual influence of an individual actor in regard to political participation is difficult to assess. It is easy to convince oneself and others that protests had or will have some effect. There is an incentive to do so because when one has participated it is dissonant to believe that the investment has been futile. Therefore, dissonance is reduced if people overestimate their personal influence. The same holds if there is a strong motivation to participate. One would in this situation like to be influential. Since actual influence cannot be gauged it is likely that one overestimates his or her influence. Whatever the explanation of the frequent overestimation of perceived influence may be, the important point for the theory of collective action is that perceived influence often does not match actual influence and that individuals overestimate their influence. Thus, the micro model must include "perceived influence" and not "actual influence."

In applying the theory it is thus necessary to determine empirically what the individual beliefs about political influence are. This is necessary because we cannot make general assumptions about how influential people think they are. The effect of "group size" and the new micro variable "perceived influence" is thus empirical and no longer analytical.

When is the interest in public goods important in large groups?

We saw that public goods preferences and efficacy have an interaction effect on the contribution to the public good. That is to say, the effect of the interest in the public good depends on the extent to which one thinks one is influential and vice versa. Public goods preferences do not have effects on contributions in large groups if Olson's assumption is correct that individual contributions are not "noticeable." The reason is that then influence is practically zero. If we modify this assumption and assume, based on many empirical studies, that influence is in general not zero and varies, then the interest in the public good matters also in large groups. Olson's assumption that public goods are provided in large groups only due to selective incentives is thus not correct.

The role of expected group success

It is often argued that not or not only perceived *personal* influence is an important factor for contributing to the provision of a public good. Another factor mentioned in the literature is the extent to which individuals think that the *group*, i.e. joint action, is successful. To what extent is this assumption correct? In order to answer this question let us first formulate the micro model in a more precise way. The effects of personal influence (p_i), of the influence of the group, i.e. the effect of joint action on the provision of a public good (p_g), of V (the value of the public good) on the behavioral alternatives "contribution" (C) or "defection" (D, i.e. not contributing) can be expressed by the following equations:[13]

$$E(C) = (p_g + p_i)V - C_c \qquad (1a)$$
$$E(D) = p_g V \qquad (1b)$$

$E(C)$ = expected utility of performing C (contribution to the public good);
$E(D)$ = expected utility of defecting (i.e. not contributing to the provision of the public good);
p_g = subjective probability that the good is provided by the other members of the group, if the individual does not contribute (group efficacy);
p_i = subjective probability that the individual contribution makes a difference to the provision of the public good (individual efficacy or individual influence);
V = value of the public good to the individual;
C_c = costs of the contribution to the individual.

This model is incomplete because selective incentives are missing. The reason is that at this point we are not interested in the effects of selective incentives.

It is important to note that the expected success of the group (p_g) is included in both equations. The reason is that the other actors' contribution has the same effect whether the individual contributes or defects. Group success is thus irrelevant for the individual decision to contribute. But the individual's influence matters: whether his or her contribution makes a difference is captured by p_i. If this term is positive then the individual's contribution becomes more likely because the expected utility of cooperation becomes higher. However, there is still the cost C_c. If this is relatively large individuals will not contribute (see equation 1a).

Olson's assumption for large groups is that p_i is zero, i.e. the individual's contribution is not "noticeable." The above equation then reduces to:

$$E(C) = p_g V - C_c \qquad (2a)$$
$$E(D) = p_g V \qquad (2b)$$

In other words, the individual will not contribute: E(C) is always smaller than E(D) because a contribution is always costly so that C_c is in general positive and must be subtracted in equation 2a from the public goods term (that is identical in both equations 2a and 2b). Again, the influence of the others (p_g) – whatever its size – is the same whether the individual contributes or defects and does thus not affect the individual's contribution or defection.

The major conclusion from the model in regard to group success thus is that it does not have any direct effect on the individual's decision to contribute or defect.

So far the model makes an implicit assumption: individual influence and group influence are independent of each other. This implies, for example, that the individual's influence does not change when the influence of the group increases or decreases. Is this a plausible hypothesis? Assume that group success is the number of units of a public good that is provided by a government, and that group success is a function of the size of a group. Let the function look like the accelerating curve 4 in Figure 3.4. Thus, when the number of group members is small and increases, public goods provision increases only very slowly up to a certain point. After that increases group size is increasingly successful. Does the influence of a single group member increases with increasing group success? Assume that the curve holds for a group where individual I is not a member. Now assume that individual I joins the group. In real life, cases where interest groups or social movements are the groups, the curves with and without I will hardly differ. It is true, that I gets more of the public good if the group grows and more of the public good is provided, but the difference I makes if the group is more or less successful is, as Olson would say, not "noticeable."

But assume that p_i correlates with p_g (see equations 1a and 1b above). What would be the outcome in the previous equations? For C and D p_g would be equal. Thus, p_g would not affect contributions to the public good. Only p_i would vary according to group efficacy. A consequence could then be that Olson's assumption that p_i is zero in large groups would be false. But group success would still not have any effect on C or D.

Including actual group success, i.e. the objective probability that the group obtains the public good, causes two problems. One is that it is very difficult to measure actual group success, and there is no attempt in the literature to develop an objective measure. The second problem is that for the behavior that is to be explained, not objective but perceived group success is relevant.

Let us thus therefore look at *perceived* individual influence and *perceived* group success. We saw in the previous section that one reason why individuals overestimate their influence is that actual influence is difficult to gauge from an individual's point of view. Perceived group success is a highly elusive phenomenon as well. It is very difficult for a group member to assess the objective probability of group success. This assessment is thus subject to biases in the same way as perceived personal influence.

The question then arises as to what the relationship is between *perceived* group success and *perceived* personal influence. It is plausible that a mismatch between individual and group influence causes cognitive dissonance: it seems "odd" to assume on the one hand that joint action will be successful, but reason on the other hand that the own contribution is negligible or not necessary. Cognitive consonance is achieved when group and individual expected success are matched.

If a situation is dissonant there are most of the time several possibilities to restore consonance. For example, if there is a discrepancy between group efficacy and individual influence, an individual may change his or her perception of group influence. But this seems unlikely: the belief that a group will be successful is socially reinforced: it is, for example, one of the major strategies of social movement leaders to make the constituency believe that the movement will succeed. It is further a socially accepted pattern that successes of groups are ascribed to individuals. For example, when a team wins an Olympic medal each member is the winner and receives a medal. Thus, it is more likely that personal influence will rise and tend to match group efficacy.

We thus assume that the direction of the causal effect is from "group influence" to "individual influence": the higher perceived group influence, the higher will be perceived personal influence. To be sure, people have some general sense of efficacy ("internal control") but they adapt it to the specific situation. When they join a group they make some judgment about the chances of success of joint action and then adapt their own feeling of influence.

The group success proposition may hold only under certain conditions. One is a relatively strong personal interest in the public good. The other is that there are relatively strong incentives to participate. Both conditions do often not obtain for interest groups. For example, even if drivers think that the AAA is a successful interest group, members as well as non-members will probably think that their personal membership will not make a difference for the success of the politics of the AAA. Dissonance will not be large because the policy goals of automobile clubs are not an essential part of the members' life and the incentives to participate are only weak.

Group success could influence contributions to the public good not only by increasing perceived personal influence, *group success may further activate a norm to participate.* The reason is that the norm of cooperation seems to be conditional. Cooperation is not a "must" in every situation. For example, if the public good is not regarded as very important, one will not regard it as a duty to cooperate. If there is some likelihood that the group will succeed, there is a duty to support the group.[14] In this situation, friends will encourage participation and invoke a duty to contribute. If expected group success is very low, it is less likely that a norm to contribute will be activated.

There is perhaps an *inverted u-curve*: assume the x-axis represents expected group success (from low to high), the y-axis symbolizes the obligation to contribute (again from low to high). The curve will then resemble an inverted u: if perceived group success is low and increases the obligation to protest will increase as well – up to a certain point. If the group is supposed to be rather successful the individual will "relax," i.e. the public good will be provided anyway so why should the individual participate. Thus, the obligation to protest decreases. However, it is also plausible that there is a linear positive relationship: increasing group success raises the perceived obligation to protest (and other incentives – see the next paragraph). Further research is needed to explore this relationships.

Expected group success has a third effect. If members of a group expect that joint action will be successful, they will try to get friends and acquaintances to participate. Thus, they will express their appreciation of participating. In other words, expected group success strengthens incentives to participate. To summarize:

> *Group success proposition:* The higher the expected success of joint action to provide a public good, the higher is perceived personal influence on the

provision of the public good, the more likely a norm to participate is activated, and the more likely social rewards for participating are provided.

Thus, expected group success has no direct effect on participation.

The group success proposition also modifies the hypothesis that group success aggravates the free rider problem. First of all, not actual but perceived group success is important. Assuming that group success does not influence incentives it is plausible that high expectations of group success lets the individual think: why should I participate if the others produce the public good? But assuming that perceived group success affects perceived individual influence, activates a protest norms and generates social rewards for participation, group success makes the free rider problem less salient because it increases direct incentives to participate. Thus, group success may have a strong *indirect* effect on participation – via the incentives mentioned.

How do individuals assess whether their joint action will be successful? A variable that is sometimes used in empirical work on political participation is *past group success* (Muller 1972, 1979; Finkel, Muller, and Opp 1989). For example, in assessing the probable success of sit-ins at the beginning of the civil rights movement, students might look at what happened in previous sit-ins (see, e.g., Andrews and Biggs 2007, with further references). We thus suggest:

> *Past group success proposition*: The more similar past collective action is to planned collective action in the present, and the more successful past collective action has been, the higher is present expected group success.

The expected number of participants

It is argued that the *expected number of participants* in collective action has an effect on participation in collective action events.[15] Why should this variable be relevant? A participant may use the expected number of participants as a *signal* for estimating his or her personal influence and the likelihood of group success. It is plausible that one of the hypotheses of everyday knowledge is that a large group is more successful to provide a public good than a small group. Thus, if the expected number of participants is large, individuals infer that group success will be likely. According to the group success proposition, this will enhance personal influence.

The norm of participation is conditional, as was seen before. One condition is the expected personal and collective influence of collective action. Perhaps another condition is that it is not right to let the others do the work. This would suggest that a large expected number of participants activates a norm of cooperation. This, again, leads to social incentives.

One incentive to participate in a large group is that the costs of participating become relatively low. Negative sanctions of friends or acquaintances are probably higher if only few others participate. But if the group is large, costs are lower. This holds in particular for repression. The perceived likelihood that an individual will be a victim of repression becomes lower if the number of participants is large.

Thus:

> *Effects of the number of contributors:* The larger the expected number of par-
> ticipants in collective action, the higher is perceived personal influence, the
> higher is expected group success, the more likely a norm of participation is acti-
> vated, and the lower are the costs of repression and other costs of participation.

Again, the number of participants has no direct effect on contributions to the public
good.

The relationship between group success, number of participants, and personal
influence may be modeled in a different way. Klandermans (1984) and later Finkel,
Muller, and Opp (1989) assume that these variables interact with each other and
have a direct (interaction) effect on the dependent variable. Klandermans and
Finkel *et al.* provide some empirical evidence for these alternative propositions. In
our own later research, however, measures of group success did not have the
expected effect (Opp and Gern 1993: 667). Perceived personal influence was
always the variable with the clearest direct effect on protest behavior. In addition,
we find the model with indirect effects more plausible. Further research is needed
to test alternative models.

The importance of non-economic incentives

In applying the theory of collective action it is important to determine empirically
what the specific incentives are that have brought about collective action or prevented individuals from acting to accomplish their collective interests. As was said
before (see chapter 1), the incentives that are present in specific situations cannot
be part of the theory. Olson lists various economic (or monetary) incentives such as
material benefits or punishment by the state in case of tax evasion. Furthermore,
people are, Olson writes, motivated by "a desire to win prestige, respect, friendship,
and other social and psychological objectives" (60). These are "social incentives"
(60). Olson further mentions "erotic," "psychological," and "moral" incentives
(61, footnote 17) and internalized norms ("moral attitudes," ibid.) where defection
leads to guilt or shame, and cooperation to a good conscience. All these incentives
are selective because, as Olson argues, the respective benefits obtain only if individuals contribute, whereas the costs occur when defection is chosen.

It seems at this point that Olson applies a wide version of rational choice theory
that also includes "soft" incentives. However, when he defines "rational" as a
behavior that is "pursued by means that are efficient and effective" (65) for achieving the actor's goals, this is not an assumption of a wide version because it means
that individuals have complete and correct information and that there is no
misperception.

It is in line with this narrow version when Olson does not want to include moral
incentives (61, footnote 17). But his arguments against using these incentives hold
for other "soft" incentives as well. What are the arguments for not including
soft incentives in explanations of collective action? (1) It is "not possible to get
empirical proof of the motivation behind any person's action" (61, footnote 17).

Therefore, the theory would become untestable if one relies on "moral explanations." In other words, soft incentives cannot be measured. This argument is flawed for several reasons.[16] First of all, it implies that Olson's own theory would not be testable either. He assumes self-interest (i.e. egoism), and this is a motivation "behind any person's action." Second, the decision to exclude a variable from a theory must not depend on the possibility of measuring it but on its explanatory importance. It often happens in the natural sciences that a theory is proposed but that the measuring instruments required to test the theory have not yet been developed. Nobody would argue to do away with the theory because measurement is not yet possible. Instead, natural scientists try to develop the measurement instruments and then test the theory. In regard to non-economic incentives, the question thus is not whether these incentives can be measured but whether they can explain behavior. If an incentive cannot be measured for the time being one has to wait until the respective measurement instruments have been developed. Third, it is not true that moral motivations and other "soft" incentives cannot be measured. Sociologists have developed an extensive methodology to measure all sorts of motivations, including the internalization of moral norms. Further, such instruments exist and have been applied in explanations of collective action, e.g. in research on social movements, as we shall see later.

(2) Olson's second argument is that for the groups considered no such explanation is needed (61, footnote 17). Even if that is conceded, the question is whether the same holds for other groups which are not addressed in Olson's book. That has to be examined by empirical research. As we will see later, non-material incentives are of utmost importance for many groups such as social movements.

(3) Olson further argues that most organized pressure groups work for their own gain, and for such groups it is hardly plausible that moral codes play a role (61, footnote 17). First of all, why should a member of a union or another pressure group not feel obliged to contribute to the public good the group tries to provide? Why should there not be social incentives which encourage participation? One would like to see empirical evidence for this claim that non-economic incentives are entirely irrelevant for organized pressure groups.

(4) According to Olson, social pressure and social incentives work only in groups of smaller size where members have face-to-face contact (62). It seems that this is by definition true because a "social incentive," like a social sanction, is a face-to-face interaction. But this may occur in any group. For example, in the large-scale demonstrations in 1989 against the communist regime in Leipzig (East Germany) participants constrained each other to use violence. Thus, it is again an empirical question in what kind of groups non-economic incentives prevail.

(5) An argument against the wide version of the theory of rational action involving a wide array of incentives as possible causes of collective action is not raised by Olson but by many other theorists: it reads that this would make the theory *tautological* (see, e.g., Fireman and Gamson 1979). We have discussed this argument already in chapter 1, section 1, when we presented the theory of rational action. It was shown that this argument is clearly flawed.

It is certainly a major weakness of Olson's micro-model that it does not include all kinds of incentives as possible motivations for collective action. This is also one of the major lines of critique of Olson's theory from the social movements camp (see, e.g., Fireman and Gamson 1979; Jenkins 1983). But it is a simple decision to extend Olson's micro model by allowing not only "hard" but all sorts of "soft" incentives. This is one of the messages of this chapter and the entire book.

Collective action as a determinant of incentives

So far it was assumed that the causal direction is from incentives to action. But it is plausible that sometimes behavior affects incentives which, in turn, change the respective behavior. For example, it has been claimed that activists "develop certain identities for themselves. This is the identity-construction approach to political activism" (Teske 1997: 121). The claim is that activism leads to fundamental changes in the beliefs, values, norms, and attitudes of the activists (see Teske 1997: chapter 4). Another plausible hypothesis is that frequent protest participation leads to contacts with other activists and, as a consequence, to involvement in protest encouraging networks. So far the vast literature on protest and social movements is largely silent on the effects of protest behavior on the incentives. It is common that orienting statements are provided like the one quoted above: what are "fundamental changes" and which "beliefs, values, norms and attitudes" of activists change under which conditions? It is also common that there is no clear specification of conditions when protest affects incentives. It is plausible, for example, that long-term protest participation will more likely change incentives than occasional participation. It is further plausible that it depends on various conditions which effects protest will have. For example, becoming a movement member depends on the efforts of a movement to recruit new members, and then adopting new beliefs depends on the already existing beliefs and attitudes of a person.

We will not discuss possible effects of protest on the incentives in this book. In explaining protest action we will adopt the strategy of looking at given and changing incentives of individual actors. We will leave it open whether a person's incentives changed due to the person's action. We further assume that the major causal effect is from incentives to protest and that a feedback effect only obtains under very special conditions. We are aware that these are problematic assumptions. But other scholars have made such assumptions as well because of a lack of hypotheses on the feedback effects of protest on incentives.

Another procedure would be to apply general propositions. For example, if the question is whether protest participation has changed beliefs or attitudes, one could apply general hypotheses about belief and attitude change to explain changes. But this will not be done here either.

The causal interdependence of incentives

The assumption in Olson's micro model is that there are no causal relationships between the independent variables. Our discussion of the effects of group success

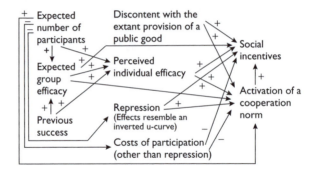

Figure 3.3 The interdependence of incentives to collective action

and individual influence is not in line with this assumption. We also posited that there is a relationship between group efficacy and the activation of a norm to cooperate. In this section, we will look at other interdependencies. The resulting causal model depicting all interdependencies between the independent variables is summarized in Figure 3.3.[17]

Assume that there is an intense preference for a public good or, put differently, great discontent with the extent to which a public good is provided. The strong grievances in former communist countries in 1989–1990 are an example for such a situation. These grievances will first activate a cooperation norm. Norms are conditional, as was said before. Among other things, a cooperation norm (and in particular a norm to participate in protest action) demands, among other things, that one should participate if discontent is high (Jasso and Opp 1997; Opp, Voss, and Gern 1995: chapter 5). In other words, grievances lead to moral indignation. It is thus to be expected that high discontent activates a norm to participate.

Another effect of grievances is that participation will be encouraged by friends and acquaintances. Thus, grievances trigger social incentives to participate. This will only be the case if grievances are not regarded as justified. But this will almost always be the case.

We further suggest that high perceived influence has a positive effect on social incentives and activates a norm of participation. If people think that their protest will have a strong impact, they will feel obliged to participate. If there is no chance that a contribution to a public good matters, participation is not considered a duty.

The effects of state repression are quite diverse. In general, repression is a cost and will thus deter the punished behavior. But this holds ceteris paribus, i.e. when other costs and benefits of the punished behavior do not change if repression obtains. But the ceteris paribus clause is often not met: if repression is regarded as illegitimate and if it is not too strong, it will raise incentives to contribute to the provision of the public good.[18] In particular, if repression is low and increases, then mutual encouragement and appeals to the obligation to protest will rise. If repression is very strong, it will no longer activate a cooperation norm and social incentives. The effects of repression on social incentives and on the activation of a cooperation norm thus resemble an inverted u-curve, where the x-axis refers to repression and the y-axis to protest.

It seems further plausible that the high costs of protest – apart from repression – provide an excuse not to protest: that is, social encouragement will be low and there is no obligation to protest. For example, when a student might miss an exam, he or she is excused from attending a demonstration that takes place at the same time.

Further research is needed to test and expand the previous hypotheses about the interdependence of incentives. Whatever the results of such research are, there can be no question that there are such interdependencies. It is surprising that there is so little theory and research on this topic.

Why are hypotheses about the interdependence of incentives important? Even if personal influence in a large group is zero and, thus, public goods preferences don't have a direct effect on cooperation or protest behavior in particular, these variables may nevertheless have an *indirect effect* on contributions to the public good – via social incentives and a norm of cooperation. It is further important, that repression may instigate cooperation and protest in particular indirectly by affecting the positive incentives to protest. The *interdependence of incentives thus contributes to the solution of the free rider problem.*

Does interdependence among actors invalidate the micro model?

It is a truism by now that collective action is a dynamic process where actors are interdependent, i.e. the actions of one actor have an impact on the costs and benefits of other actors. This means that behavior of a certain group of actors influences the behavior of other actors or other groups of actors. We will look at these processes in more detail below. The question at this point is whether the micro model discussed above is appropriate to analyze the often complex dynamics of collective action. Does the micro model not assume that actors act independently of each other? The answer is clearly "no." The micro model – and the theory of rational action in general – assumes that each individual makes his or her own decision. But this does not imply that actors decide in social isolation. Actors may and most of the time will take into account the reactions of other actors as behavioral consequences. Furthermore, other actors may be constraints that influence decisions. The previous micro model even takes some features of the situation explicitly into account, namely social incentives.

The relevance of other actors is explicitly taken account of in threshold models (see, e.g., the now classic work of M. Granovetter such as 1978). A hypothesis is that the number of actors who perform a given action change the costs and benefits of other actors for this action. This will under certain conditions instigate a cascade of protests. We will discuss these processes later in more detail. At this point it is important to emphasize that the micro model – and the theory of rational action in general – can be applied to explain social processes and processes of collective action in particular.

Can the form of collective action be explained?

Much theory in the field of social movements explains when protest originates but it is left open as to what form of protest is chosen by the actors. For example, do individuals block streets, participate in legal demonstrations, or in terrorist acts if political opportunities change? We will see in later chapters that current approaches have problems in explaining the form of collective political action. The micro model outlined above posits that the form of action which is chosen depends on the kind of incentives. For example, when actors think that their influence is highest when they choose generally accepted or legal strategies and when they have internalized a norm not to use any violent action, it is likely that some "normal" protest behavior is chosen. But if individuals accept justifications for violence and think that their influence is highest by choosing violent forms of protest, violence is most likely. Social incentives matter as well: when the important others reward only conventional types of protest, it is likely that individuals refrain from violence. Thus, the micro model can be applied to explain any specific form of collective action. We will return to the explanation of the form of protest in the next chapter (see the section: What is to be explained? The "repertoire of contention").

Micro-to-macro relationships: Is the public good an empirical or analytical function of individual contributions?

The theory of collective action explains under which conditions individuals jointly act in order to provide a public good. It is a common implicit assumption that there is an analytic relationship between the amount of contributions and the amount of the public good provided. If, for example, individuals drive less frequently, there is less pollution. The amount of pollution of the individuals aggregates to overall pollution, like individual crimes add to the crime rate. This is not an empirical relationship: we know without conducting empirical studies that driving less is "good" for our environment. There is thus an analytic relationship between contributions to a public good and the degree to which the public good is produced.

This is not the case if the public good is provided by third parties. Protesters try to put pressure on third parties such as a government, and these third parties provide the good, such as less utilization of nuclear energy or more civil rights. Another example are norms. Assume individuals sanction smokers in order to contribute to the emergence of a general non-smoking norm. Sanctioning would thus be a contribution to a public good in the form of a general norm. But sanctioning may not be successful: it may not be strong enough to raise the costs for smoking to a degree that smokers stop smoking. There is thus an empirical relationship between sanctioning (as a contribution to a public good) and a non-smoking norm (the public good).

The important point is that Olson's theory and much subsequent theorizing on collective action implicitly assume that there is an analytical relationship between contribution to and the production of public goods. But, as the previous examples illustrate, there are public goods for which this relationship is empirical. If this is the case, additional theory is needed to explain when the third parties provide the public good. The contributions of the actors is certainly an important variable to bring about the public good, but it is not the only variable.

Macro-to-micro relationships: the validity of the group size proposition

The proposed negative relationship between group size and public goods provision is probably the most criticized part of Olson's theory. Indeed, this hypothesis is really its weak point.[19] First of all, the group size proposition has been falsified. An early example is the study by Tillock and Morrison (1979). McCarthy *et al.* (1988) report the following finding of their research on drunk driving: "The larger the population of a community, the more likely any kind of organization [against drunk driving – KDO] should be to form ..." (74). Olson's hypothesis would lead us to expect the opposite, i.e. that we find few (and not many) organizations in large communities. But there is also supportive evidence (Isaac and Walker 1988; Alencar, de Oliveira Siqueira, and Yamamoto 2008; see further the evidence Olson himself provides for his proposition). If a proposition sometimes holds and sometimes doesn't, the question is under what conditions group size has which effects.

When we look at our reconstruction of the micro-macro model proposed by Olson, we get some first clues about the reasons why the group size proposition does not hold and what the conditions are when it does hold. One of the assumptions is that the individual's share of the public good depends on the size of the group. It was already noted that this proposition is wrong because it assumes that there is always rivalness of consumption. This means, as was noted above, that the individual's utility of consuming a unit of the public good declines if additional individuals join the group. Thus, if there is no rivalness, there is no negative relationship at all between group size and the individual share of the public good.

Another questionable assumption is that individual influence is low or negligible in large groups. As was said before, it is important how individuals *perceive* their personal influence. It was argued before that the expected success of large groups leads to high personal influence. Thus, perceived personal influence – which matters for explaining participation – may be high in large groups. But even if the reader doubts the previous proposition there is no evidence that in general perceived influence in large groups is low. On the contrary, many empirical studies show that people overestimate their influence, that influence which is by no means zero and varies across individuals in large groups.

The assumption that the individual costs of contribution to the provision of public goods are always high if the group is large is incorrect as well. There are many examples where individual actors can provide a public good to a very large group at low costs. Marwell and Oliver (1993: 44) provide an example: the authors had to buy a compiler for their research. The license allowed it to place the compiler in a public access file so that it was available to any computer user. Thus, the costs of the provision of a public good did not depend on the size of the audience. We will see later that there are several processes where large-scale spontaneous contributions to public goods emerge and where individual costs are very low and even decline with the size of the group.

Similar arguments hold for the relationships between group size and economic or non-economic selective incentives. For example, the activation of a fairness norm is more likely the larger a group is. People will think that they have to contribute when so many others contribute or when so many others are in need of a public good. In this instance, there is a positive relationship between group size and normative incentives. Nonetheless, there are also situations where Olson is right: informal "solidary" selective incentives are more prevalent in smaller groups. If a large group is a crowd such as a big demonstration, there is in general little mutual encouragement or positive sanctioning. However, large groups are often composed of small friendship groups. For example, demonstrations do not consist of isolated individuals. Many participants arrive with their friends. Thus, even if Olson is right that selective incentive occur more often in smaller groups, they add up in a large group when it consists of many small groups.

To summarize, the group size proposition holds only under certain conditions. The micro theory applied is capable of contributing to the formulation of hypotheses that specify these conditions.

Can there be selective incentives? A wrong implication of the theory

A further critique of Olson's theory is that he does not answer the question of where the selective incentives come from. Olson could respond to this critique as follows: the theory posits that a public good is produced in a large group *if* there are selective incentives. This is a testable hypothesis: if there is collective action in a large group and if there are no selective incentives, the theory is falsified. Thus, it could be argued, it is not necessary to explain how selective incentives come about. These are independent variables, and no theory needs to explain its independent variables. It would certainly be interesting to explain the provision of selective incentives or why preferences for public goods originate. But this is a next step in theory construction. Other theories, including the theoretical perspectives in the social movement literature, also assume that certain variables such as political opportunities or resources are given, i.e. they are not explained.

However, the theory of collective action would run into difficulties if it implies that there can't be selective incentives in a large group. If this is an implication of the theory and if we find large groups where selective incentives are provided, the theory would be falsified.

Indeed, the theory implies that selective incentives will not be provided in large groups. The argument is this: assume that individuals do not have an incentive to contribute *directly* to the provision of the public good such as spending some money to set up an army. Likewise, there would be no incentive for an *indirect* (or instrumental) contribution such as sanctioning other persons to spend money for the army either. To illustrate, assume that you, the reader, and I, the author, know that voting in a national election does not have any impact. Thus, our perceived personal influence is literally zero. Our preference for one of the party programs would thus not instigate us to vote. This is the situation Olson describes. What would be my incentive to prompt you to participate? I know that your participation would not change the situation, and you know this too. You would probably sanction me negatively: you would think that I am crazy to get you to do things that are futile.

The implication thus is that no selective incentives will ever be provided in a large group. Nonetheless, we find that there are many large groups where selective incentives are provided. This is thus a falsification of the theory.

This argument can be formulated in terms of the theory of collective action. Setting up a system of selective incentives is in itself a public good. Because providing selective incentives is instrumental to providing the primary or *first-order public good*, it is called a *second-order public good* (Oliver 1980; Heckathorn 1989). For example, national defense is a primary public good. Setting up an army is instrumental for achieving the primary goal, namely protection against foreign attacks.

Since Olson's argument implies that large groups will not provide any public good, this holds for first-order as well as for second-order public goods. The free rider problem thus holds for selective incentives as well. Thus, Olson's theory implies that there can be no selective incentives in large groups. However, we find many large groups where selective incentives are provided. This falsifies the theory. We will take up this issue later and will show how this problem of the theory can be solved.

Missing macro-to-micro relationships

Olson focuses on group size. But this is not the only macro property that might be relevant for the provision of a public good. Another macro variable is *group heterogeneity* in regard to resources or, in general, in regard to the incentives of the micro model. Although Olson mentions heterogeneity, its effects are not analyzed in detail. But it is a very important group property (see the Heckathorn 1993; Marwell and Oliver 1993). For example, if a group consists of a subgroup with particularly high resources, this group could provide the public on its own or mobilize others to contribute. Thus, if resources are heterogeneous, public goods production will be more likely. But heterogeneity in public goods preferences could paralyze public goods production due to conflicts of interest. This suggests that the heterogeneity of the incentives to contribute or, in general, the *distribution of incentives in a group* is important for the production of a public good.

There are other macro factors that sociologists would call social structures that may affect public goods contributions. *Social networks* are an example. In other words, individuals are interdependent (see, e.g., the critique of Marwell and Oliver 1993: chapter 1). This might be relevant for the provision of selective incentives such as social rewards, as we will see later: when people know or like each other, rewards for participation will be more likely than in groups consisting of isolated individuals.

3. Production functions, critical mass, thresholds, and the free rider problem: new contributions to the theory of collective action

In this section we will present several innovative extensions of the theory of collective action that we deem particularly important. These extensions address certain assumptions of Olson's theory. It is discussed what happens when these assumptions are relaxed or modified.

Production functions: the group size proposition revisited

The group size proposition assumes a negative effect of group size on the likelihood of the provision of a public good. In reality, the relationship between group size and public goods production is very different. There are cases where the activities of large groups have little impact. For example, the large-scale demonstrations against the Iraq war all over the world did not prevent the war. There are other cases, however, where joint action of large groups contributed to change history. An example are the large-scale demonstrations against the communist regimes in 1989–1990 which contributed to the collapse of the authoritarian governments and to the emergence of a new political and economic order. Marwell and Oliver (1993: chapter 4)[20] and Heckathorn (1989; 1996, but see already Frohlich *et al.* 1975) have discussed in detail various functions between the number (or proportion) of contributors to the public good (x-axis) and the amount or proportion of the public good produced (y-axis). Some of these functions which are called *production functions* are displayed in Figure 3.4.

Let us start with the simplest *linear function* (line 1 in Figure 3.4): each additional individual's contribution adds the same additional amount of the public

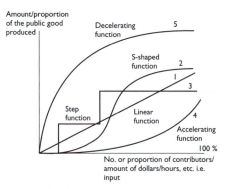

1 Linear function.
2 S-shaped curve; begins with low returns (start-up costs), then period of higher returns, then saturation effect with lower returns.
3 Step function.
4 Decelerating; low start-up costs; returns high for initial contributors and then decline.
5 Accelerating: high start-up costs and long initial period of small returns.

This figure is based on Marwell and Oliver 1993: chapter 4; and Heckathorn 1996.

Figure 3.4 Possible production functions of public goods

good, regardless of how many individuals have already contributed and regardless of the amount of the public good that has already been provided.

The *S-shaped function* (curve 2 in the figure) is more realistic or perhaps even typical (Oberschall 1980: 48–49; Heckathorn 1996: 273). In the initial phase the contribution of each individual has a very small effect. We have drawn the first section of the curve very flat and identical with the x-axis so that there will be some provision of the public good only if at least a certain number of actors contribute. There are thus high start-up costs. But in the middle phase the marginal contribution of each (additional) actor is relatively high. In the final phase when the public good is produced to a high extent, additional contributions will have only small effects.

The *step function* (see function 3 in the figure) shows some similarity to the S-shaped function: in the first phase individual contributions do not have any effect at all. But then, all of a sudden, the next individual provides an explosive increase of the amount of the public good. Then, quite a number of contributors are necessary until the next one again brings about a sharp increase in public goods provision.

The first section of the *accelerating function* (curve 4) resembles the first phase of the S-shaped function, but the first phase is flatter; furthermore, the slope increases over the whole range of the curve. In general, a relatively large number of contributors is needed until a substantial amount of the public good is provided. There are thus high start-up costs. But if these are overcome, additional contributors' support for the public good leads to a substantial increase of public goods production. There is "positive interdependence: each contribution makes the next one more worthwhile and, thus, more likely" (Marwell and Oliver 1993: 63).

The *decelerating function* (curve 5) with a decreasing slope resembles the second phase of the S-shaped curve, but extends over the whole range of the x-axis. It means that the initial contributors' contributions have a very large effect. When the number of contributors increase, the additional amounts of the public good produced decline. This means that there is "negative interdependence: each contribution makes others' subsequent contribution less worthwhile, and thus less likely" (Marwell and Oliver 1993: 61).

Many other functions can be drawn. For example, the step function in the figure consists of two steps. There may be step functions consisting of three or more steps. We will not describe more possible production functions. Instead, we will discuss several questions related to these functions.

Two types of functions: production functions and mobilization functions

If the relationship between individual contributions and the public good is analytical, there is no problem in establishing the micro-to-macro (i.e. bottom-up) relationship: when we have explained individual contributions we arrive at the amount to which the public good is provided by simply aggregating individual contributions. But assume that the relationship is not analytic. Take the case of protest as a contribution to the public good where the public good is delivered by third parties such as governments. In this case, there are two phenomena that have to be explained: the amount of individual contributions (like participation in protest activities) and the extent to which the public good is provided (like taking measures to curb pollution).

How are both variables related? In general, it is assumed that if there is a large number or proportion of contributors, it is likely that the public good is provided by third parties. But there are cases where this generalization does not hold, as the extensive literature in political science and in particular in public choice theory shows. The example mentioned is the large-scale protests against the Iraq war. Thus, not only the number of participants matter. Whether third parties meet the demands of a group depends, for example, on the status of the contributors. If a group of homeless people demand a service from the government it is less likely that they are heard than if a group of university professors or medical doctors ask the government for a service. The motivation of the members of the government to yield to the demands depends, for example, on the extent of support in the population or on the date of the next election. If this is close and if there is a neck-and-neck race, the government will be more willing to provide some amount of the public good than if the expected support by voters is high and if elections take place in four years. In explaining the provision of a public good that is provided by third parties it is thus important to look at two phenomena: one is the extent to which participation of a certain proportion of a group leads to the cooperation of other members of the group. This is the *mobilization function*. The second phenomenon is the extent to which the proportion of cooperators brings about the provision of the public good. This is the *production function*.

Both curves may differ. Figure 3.5 exhibits two examples. The first is the accelerating curve we discussed before (see Figure 3.4, curve 4). Again, the horizontal axis depicts the proportion of the group members who contribute. If the contributors cannot provide the public good themselves, what could be the meaning of the vertical axis? The "production" of the contributors could consist of the number of other group members that are mobilized, i.e. for whom those, who have contributed, provide incentives that lead to new contributions. For example, if

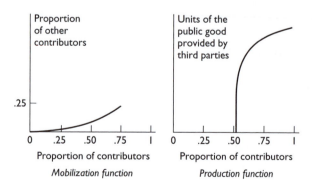

Figure 3.5 Two types of production functions: mobilization and public goods production functions

25 percent of the group members participate in a demonstration, this might have the effect that the next demonstration will be attended by another 5 percent of the members. If 75 percent of the group members demonstrate then on the next occasion all members may become active (i.e. the other 25 percent left).

The second figure on the right is a production function. The dependent variable on the y-axis is the amount of the public good provided, but this time those who provide the good are third parties. The curve indicates that a relatively high proportion of contributors is required, namely more than half, before a relatively great amount of the public good is provided. If the proportion of contributors further increases, more units of the public good are provided, but at a decreasing extent.

When we compare both curves we see that there is no nice coincidence of the mobilization and the public goods provision curve. When the number of contributors increases, there is an increase in the mobilization of others, but only if more than 50 percent of the members of a group are active, a great amount of the public good is provided. We can even imagine that a great number of members of a group is mobilized but that the public good is not provided at all. The anti-Iraq demonstrations are an example.

The distinction between mobilization and production functions is not only of academic interest. In modern societies many public goods are no longer provided on a voluntary basis by the groups who demand the good. Especially in modern welfare states it is quite common that state authorities or bureaucracies provide the good. In these cases, if a relatively large group demands more of a public good, the first step is mobilization. But this is only the first step of a production process. The next step in the process of the provision of the good is the decision of those who are in charge of providing it. There is thus a *two-step process* in the provision of a public good. This is especially important in the field of protest and social movements, as will be seen in the next chapter.

Explaining production functions

Production functions assert: *if* a certain number (or proportion) of individuals contribute, then a certain amount of the public good is produced.[21] One question of interest is to specify production functions in various situations. It is further interesting to explain what form production functions will have under what conditions. How can the form of a production function be explained?

A production function is, like the group size proposition, a macro proposition. When we want to explain a given production function the procedure should thus be the same as in the explanation of the group size proposition (see Figure 3.2). Similarly, increase, decrease, or no change of the slope of a production function should coincide with the increase, decrease, or stability of incentives to participate in the production of the public good.[22] There may be different processes or mechanisms[23] that bring about a given production function.

One possible mechanism is described by Oberschall (1980: 49–51) for the S-shaped curve (see Figure 3.4). In order to get the production process started, a certain number of participants must contribute. These are the activists or, put differently, the political entrepreneurs. Their incentives to participate are very high. They anticipate that their initiative will set in motion further mobilization and, thus, the provision of the public good. If the slope of the curve begins to increase, each additional participant's contribution brings about an additional amount of the public good. A consequence may be that perceived personal influence increases. But at the beginning, many individuals must be mobilized in order for the public good to be provided to a higher extent. The more participants contribute, the lower will become the individual costs of participation; positive incentives to participate increase as well such as "personal rewards for participating with like-minded others in a cause, the conviction of doing the right thing, the earned esteem of group members" (49). Thus, the curve becomes relatively steep. After some time, most of the potential participants have been mobilized and the additional amount of the public good provided decreases and thus also the additional benefits. The curve flattens.

This is only one possible process that leads to the S-shaped curve. Another process is spontaneous coordination. How can the process start if there are no political entrepreneurs? Assume some members of a community believe that if a certain number of individuals convene at a square it is likely that the government perceives this as a signal for general discontent and for subsequent loss of support. This belief in group success activates various incentives for this group (see Figure 3.3). Assume that these incentives are so strong that several people convene. Now let the government meet part of the demands of the group. This raises the belief in group success for another group of community members. Again this activates other positive incentives (see the model in Figure 3.3) so that next time this group will go to the square. This process continues. Finally, there are individuals whose incentives to attend the meetings are so low that they actually will stay home. The participants may become more and more satisfied so that the government is not willing to provide more of the public good. The curve thus flattens.

It has been argued that some functions such as decelerative functions ease public goods production, whereas others such as accelerating functions make public goods production difficult. The reason is that for the decelerating function fewer people must be mobilized in order to get a substantial part of the public good. Since few additional people are sufficient to get a substantial additional amount, it is likely that the required group size will come about. For an accelerating function, the situation is different: many people must participate in order to get a relatively small amount of the public good.

Table 3.1 Group size, percentage and number of individuals to be mobilized for the provision of one unit of the public good

Size of the group	Percentage of individuals who must participate for providing 1 unit of the public good	Number of individuals who must participate
10	10 %	1
10,000	10 %	1,000
100,000	10 %	10,000

This argument holds only if we assume that group size (and probably other parameters) are given. Let us look at a simple example – see Table 3.1. Let us assume that a decelerating function obtains. Assume further that 10 percent of the members of a group must contribute in order to receive 1 unit of the public good. In a group of 10 members it is then sufficient that one member contributes. Now let the group consist of 10,000 members. Again, 10 percent of the group must contribute in order to produce 1 unit of the public good. In other words, 1,000 people must become active. Imagine a third group that consists of 100,000 members. Here 10,000 members must contribute for 1 unit of the public good. In general, if the group is large it will be more difficult to get enough individuals to participate in the production of a public good.

This example indicates that for a given form of production function incentives to provide the public good will be very different. One important variable is, as our example suggests, the size of a group. Another may be group heterogeneity. Given the size of a group "heterogeneity" refers to certain distributions of incentives. Thus, the previous argument holds only for a given size of a group.

Can production functions help to explain or predict public goods provision?

Assume we can identify types of situations in which certain production functions hold. For example, assume we know which function holds when students demand additional funds for their universities from a government. Assume further that the function is s-shaped. Could we use this knowledge for predictive or explanatory purposes? We could only make a conditional prediction such as: *if*, say, 10 percent of the students participate, the government will provide 1 percent more funds per year. Thus, the production function does not tell how many group members will participate in which situations. Assume, for example, students wish that their universities get more funds. What will be the participation rate? We do not know, and the production function does not provide an answer to this question. Only a detailed analysis of the incentive structure can provide information on possible participation.

The previous argument presupposes that we have some firm knowledge of the form of production functions for different situations. However, this is not the case. Perhaps we can generate production functions when we have detailed information about a series of past collective action events where the number of participants varies over time and where we can observe what amount of a public good has been provided and how many people participated. The civil rights movement in the USA could be such an example. But so far there has been no attempt to specify empirical production functions for different types of situations. For social movements where public goods are provided by third parties, it will probably be difficult to find such functions. The reason is, as has been said before, that the success of a given number of participants depends on the decisions of others. For them, numbers are not the only incentive to make a decision.

We can conclude that our knowledge about the existence of different production functions is important because it shows that there is no simple relationship between group size and public goods production. But systematic attempts at identifying production functions for different types of situations are so far missing.

Mechanisms to solve the first- and second-order free rider problem

Olson's solution of the free rider problem is simple: there must be selective incentives. The vast number of contributions to the further development of the theory shows the great variety of possibilities of how members of a group can be motivated to contribute to the provision of a public good. In this section we will highlight some of these mechanisms.[24]

Is the free rider problem a problem at all? Social movement scholar have objected that collective action theory is obsessed by the free rider problem because it is assumed that human beings are essentially asocial. This assumption, it is argued, is highly problematic from a feminist and social constructionist perspective (Ferree 1992: 36). Here the "first and most fundamental human relationships are those of trust and dependence" which exist already in infants (ibid.). This speaks "against the theoretical significance of free riding" (Ferree 1992: 38).[25] Whatever the natural endowment of persons is, the observation is that in real life situations the vast majority of those interested in the provision of a public good do not contribute in most cases. A striking example is Edward J. Walsh's data about the nuclear accident at Three Mile Island in 1979 (Walsh 1988). Two years after the accident, the anti-nuclear activists' organizations had fewer than 200 members, "embedded in wider networks of more or less sympathetic neighbors among a total population of almost 700,000 within a twenty-five-mile radius of the reactors" (124). And exactly this phenomenon is to be explained. To be sure, even in large groups free riding varies. But even if 50 percent of a large population participate in demonstrations against a government the question is why the other 50 percent do not participate. It is strange – to say the least – if in view of such greatly varying participation rates there are scholars who regard "free riding" as an irrelevant problem. It is therefore important to look at possibilities to solve this problem.

McAdam (2004) takes issue with the free rider problem as well. In his opinion, the traditional formulation of the problem is one "in which outsiders must be induced to join a movement" (228). This situation never occurs in reality. "Instead, insiders are threatened with the loss of member benefits for failure to take part" (228). This is again a misunderstanding: a "free rider" is, by definition, somebody who benefits from a public good without having contributed to its provision. These "free riders" may be "outsiders," i.e. non-members of a social movement who consume a public good such as nuclear power. Assuming that at least part of these outsiders are against nuclear power, we find that only a tiny percentage engages in some action against nuclear power. One question then is how the free rider problem is or can be solved for those "outsiders." The free rider problem does not imply at all that these "outsiders" and non-participants must be "induced to join a movement." There may be other forms of actions for the provision of a public good that are not related to a movement. Examples are the protests against the communist regimes in 1989–1990. Is it not worthwhile to explain those protests and to explain why many citizens did not join? The formulation of the free rider problem (see before) does not at all preclude that somebody is a member of a movement. In this case, McAdam is right: the movement often provides selective incentives for participation. But not all movement members participate. Why not? A question McAdam does not answer. Thus, the free rider problem also obtains for members of social movements.

It is odd why the free rider problem raises so much concern among social movement scholars. The issue is so simple: many of those who have shared goals do not participate to attain those goals. They let others do the work and enjoy the results of their efforts. The question is why some participate and others do not. This is all. It is difficult to understand what the problem is with this simple question.

We will return to the free rider problem in later chapters. We will there discuss other objections against its relevance and formulation, viewed from the perspective of specific social movement theories.

Critical mass, political entrepreneurs, and the distribution of incentives

It often "takes some minimum number of people or some minimum accumulation of seed money to draw in the participation and contributions of others" (Marwell and Oliver 1993: 1). This minimum number is the *critical mass*. This "minimum number" may be ordinary citizens, political entrepreneurs or leaders.[26] An example are the citizens who were the first to participate in the Monday demonstrations against the communist regime in Leipzig in the fall of 1989. These citizens' protests contributed to the rise of numbers in future Monday demonstrations. Examples are further activists or leaders of social movements or other groups like unions who organize a demonstration or other collective events. In such cases, a group of individuals are the first who become active to achieve some goal, and then others follow suit. Two questions arise: (1) Why are some individuals the first to contribute? (2) What could the incentives be that the key group provides to others so that their participation increases?

In regard to the first question, collective action theory suggests that there are special incentives that lead to the participation of the members of a key group. In terms of the micro model specified before, we would assume that those who first participate in a demonstration will be those whose discontent and perceived influence is particularly high and who are exposed to other incentives such as encouragement of friends and acquaintances to a high degree. Depending on the kind of organizing activities, the resources which the entrepreneurs dispose of and the resources they are willing to invest are important. If time and other resources are precious and very productive in other uses – a self-employed lawyer may lose a fortune when he or she becomes an activist in a social movement – this means that the costs of contributing to the public good are high.

The kinds of incentives for participation of a key group may be different. For example, some group members may wish to gain a reputation in their group or expect to become a candidate for a party position or a functionary of a union.[27] These may be people for whom the public good is irrelevant. In Olson's theory, such motivations are typical for those who are active in large groups. Here public goods preferences are irrelevant because the individual's contribution is negligible. In contrast, we have argued before that also in large groups public goods preferences matter because perceived influence varies. Further, the interdependence of incentives is relevant for participation.

If the key group is a critical mass, i.e. raises the participation of others, incentives must be provided that increase their participation. One such incentive is that the key group reduces the costs of participation for others. For example, when the key group organizes a demonstration in order to change a government decision and spreads information about the venue of the demonstration, the costs of political action decrease for all others: they just need to go to the venue of the demonstration and save the costs of organization or of engaging in other activities. The activities of the key group will further bring about positive incentives for others. When others get to know that a key group bears the costs of initiating collective action, it is likely that this gives rise to positive incentives for participating among group members. The micro model specified before suggests that a norm of participation will be activated – it is unfair to let others do the work; friends and acquaintances will encourage participation. Thus, the participation of the key group raises the net utility of participation for others.

However, the increase of this net utility may not be high enough. In other words, the key group may have influenced the costs and benefits of many others, but it is still more beneficial to stay home than to contribute. The key group will only be a critical mass if the *discrepancy* between the overall utilities of participation vs. non-participation is not too high. More precisely, the net utilities of others for contributing and not contributing must be distributed in a certain way.[28] Thus, if the activities of the key group raise benefits or lower costs of participation to an extent that the net utilities for participation of others becomes higher than the net utility of non-participation, then the key group becomes a critical mass. If the discrepancies are relatively low, the key group will be more successful because the incentives for participation need not rise much.

To illustrate the role of discrepancies of net utilities for participation and non-participation let us look at Figure 3.6. Let there be six groups. The vertical axis represents net utilities, the horizontal axis depicts the six groups. Assume that the net utilities of a contribution to a public good are the same for each group (see line N_1), but the net utilities for non-participation (see line N_2) differ: they are lowest for group 1 and highest for group 6. In this scenario, group 1 and 2 will be active because only for these groups is the net utility of participating higher than the net utility for non-participation. For group 3, the net utility of non-participation is only a little higher than for participation. The discrepancy is thus very low – in contrast to group 6 where this discrepancy is high. Therefore, in order to get group 6 to participate a key group must provide strong incentives. In real situations, it is to be expected that those groups with high discrepancies cannot be "converted."

Now assume that the net utilities of participation rise from N_1 to $N_{1'}$. This might be due to incentives provided by a key group. In this situation, a new group becomes active, namely groups 3. Group 4 is just a little below the borderline. If the participating groups succeed in increasing the incentives to participate only a little,

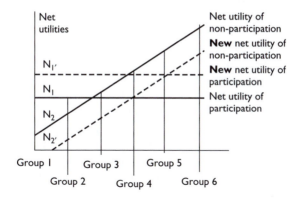

Figure 3.6 Groups with different net utilities of participation and non-participation

then group 4 becomes active. Next assume that the net utility of non-participation decreases from N_2 to $N_{2'}$. Now groups 1 to 5 become active. Group 6 is still not reached.

The figure illustrates how important the distribution of net utilities and, thus, costs and benefits for participation and non-participation is. It can easily be seen that there will be situations where a key group will not be able to provide incentives to get other individuals to cooperate. Another extreme situation is that the discrepancies of all groups are so low that only little effort of a key group is needed in order to achieve an overwhelming mobilization.

The process of sequential and cumulative participation that is elicited by a key group can be depicted by a flowchart (Figure 3.7). The process begins with the

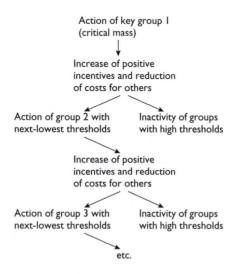

Figure 3.7 The dynamics of collective action with a critical mass and continuous thresholds

contributions of a key group. Thus, it is assumed that there is a group with relatively high incentives to participate. The activities of this group raise incentives for others. If the thresholds (i.e. the size of the net utilities for non-participation) for other groups are not too high, other groups participate etc. An unfavorable distribution of thresholds may leave the initial group isolated. At the other extreme is a favorable distribution that leads to a cascade of participation until the whole group contributes. This process will stop at some point when the increase of incentives is not big enough to instigate other groups to participate.

Three points are worth noting. (1) One is that hypotheses about the effects of a critical mass are propositions that refer to the micro and macro level: these activities are a variable on the macro level which affect variables on the micro level, namely the incentives of individual actors that are not members of the critical mass. It is also possible to formulate these hypotheses on the macro level: collective action of a key group affects collective action of other groups. But implicitly there are clear macro-to-micro links: it is assumed that collective action of a key group affects individual incentives that then translate into collective action.

(2) Even if a critical mass operates, there may be other sources of incentives. For example, repressive actions of governments may thwart activities of key groups so that the incentives they provide do not suffice to get other groups to participate. In other words, their thresholds increase. Thus, in order to explain processes of collective action, it is important to specify all actors that are involved in providing incentives.

(3) Although the work on critical mass and political entrepreneurs is clearly a progress, compared to Olson's original work, this work still needs to be further developed. In particular, more theory and research is needed to specify hypotheses addressing the question: when is a key group more or less successful in spawning incentives for others to participate? What exactly are the incentives that are provided?

Spontaneous coordination

The previous section addresses the process of collective action that is initiated by a critical mass. There are two different processes involved. The typical process in democratic societies is that an organization or a social movement – the political entrepreneurs – organize collective action. The group coordinates action and suggests what is to be done, how and where. The group thus bears part of the costs of participation and provides some positive selective incentives to cooperate and removes incentives for non-participation. If the group is lucky, i.e. if the distribution of incentives in the population is "right," collective action is triggered to an extent that additional amounts of the public good are provided. This is the *organization model* of collective action.

The previous section alluded to another model which may be called the *spontaneous cooperation model* of collective action. In contrast to the organization model, collective action may occur without any organization. The spontaneous demonstrations that contributed to the collapse of the former communist regimes in

Eastern Europe illustrate this model. One example are the demonstrations in Leipzig (East Germany) in the fall of 1989. On October 9, 1989, more than 70,000 citizens convened at a central square (the Karl Marx Square) in the center of Leipzig. This demonstration was not organized. How can this spontaneous demonstration be explained?[29] In 1989, when the liberalization of communist countries adjacent to East Germany took shape, citizens became increasingly dissatisfied that the communist regime of East Germany did not even allude to providing more freedom such as the possibility of free travel to western countries. Furthermore, data indicate that at that time perceived personal influence was high: many citizens thought that if they would protest now the regime could no longer refuse to provide more liberties. Although discontent and perceived influence were widespread, the data show that their intensity varied across the population. Even if it can be assumed that many citizens of Leipzig were ready to express their discontent through some action, the question for the single citizen was how he or she could do this. There was no social movement or organization that was able to organize any anti-regime action. Nonetheless, on October 9 more than 70,000 citizens demonstrated on the Karl Marx Square in the center of Leipzig. How can this be explained? October 9 was a Monday, and there were smaller demonstrations on previous Mondays. Why on Mondays and why on the Karl Marx Square? Close to the Square, peace prayers have taken place since 1982 in the Nikolai Church, always on Mondays, in the late afternoon. These events turned to venues for those who wanted to leave the GDR (i.e. East Germany) and for those who wanted to stay and change regime politics. After the peace prayers, people went from the Nikolai Church to the adjacent Karl Marx Square. These gatherings were regarded as protests by the regime, and they were violently terminated by police forces with many citizens being arrested before October 9. There was no indication that the police force would behave differently on this day. Nonetheless, the largest demonstration took place since the worker uprising in 1953.

These events can be phrased in terms of the theory of collective action: there were intensive public goods preferences (more freedom) and relatively high perceived influence which varied across the population, along with other incentives (see the references in note 29). For part of the population, there were thus strong incentives to participate in some anti-government action. On the other hand, it is likely that participants expected high costs due to police repression.

Assume now that citizens want to show the regime their discontent. Citizens knew about the peace prayers and that they could expect to find other dissatisfied citizens at the Karl Marx Square after the peace prayers. They further knew that a relatively large number of participants at the Karl Marx Square would be noticed by the regime as a signal for widespread discontent. This cognitive expectation was one of the incentives for the choice of the venue where one could reveal his or her discontent to the regime.

Why didn't the threats of repression deter people from going to the Karl Marx Square? Potential participants probably reasoned that just going to the center of Leipzig could not per se be regarded as an act of protest by security forces; being arrested one could have argued that one was about to visit friends or to do some shopping. Thus, perceived costs were low – despite the likelihood of state repression. Indeed, although the threat to severe repression was clearly announced by the government and communicated by the media and by word of mouth by the regime before October 9, our data indicate that many citizens did not believe that there would be bloodshed or severe repression.

The data further show that not only strong discontent and high perceived personal influence, but also social incentives contributed to attending the demonstrations (Opp and Gern 1993): participation in the demonstration on October 9 was particularly high when persons had friends who were critical of the regime or had already protested. Social networks thus played a role where people encouraged each other to participate. Another indicator of this is that many participants attended the demonstration together with others.

In contrast to demonstrations before October 9, 1989, this demonstration was not crushed and there was no violence on the side of the demonstrators either. This apparently set the stage for the next Monday demonstration on October 16 with a much larger number of participants. For these demonstrations, the participants of the demonstration of October 9 were the critical mass: it is plausible that this demonstration brought about encouragement by friends and acquaintances to participate in the next demonstration; a norm to participate was probably activated as well not to let the others do the work. Furthermore, the absence of repression on October 9 led to the expectation that repression would not occur on October 16 either. The next "layer" of participants were then those with the lowest discrepancy of net utilities of participation and non-participation. These discrepancies were apparently small and distributed in a way that subsequent demonstrations became always larger. Thus, the critical mass was an important factor.[30] Imagine if there had been a bloodshed on October 9 and hundreds of demonstrators had been shot. The key group would probably not have attracted any new participants, and the participants of the first demonstrations would probably not have returned.

The incentives to participate in the next demonstration did not only come from the participants of the previous demonstrations. External events like the decisions of the GDR government changed incentives as well (see, for details, the literature mentioned before).

The interesting features of this example are, first, that the critical mass was no group, social movement or group of leaders who bore the costs of organization. The key group consisted of ordinary citizens. Furthermore, the micro model outlined before can be applied to explain the participation. Finally, the joint action had consequences that none of the participants had foreseen: the protests contributed to the collapse of the communist regime and finally to the unification of East and West Germany. Such successes of citizen protests are rare. However, nobody expected this outcome, although participants believed in some success in regard to more freedom (see the previous references).

This example is certainly special, but there are many other instances of spontaneous cooperation. The day before the Iraq war began in March 2003, many citizens gathered at US embassies. There was no organization. In general, important events of various kind are an occasion where people gather at central squares in a city or other places to express their discontent. This is illustrated by the regular gatherings at the grave of the Czechoslovakian student Jan Palach who died on January 16, 1969, after self-immolation as a protest against the communist regime. Already the funeral became a venue for a mass demonstration. One condition for gatherings at certain places is that people expect to meet others there. Only then those gatherings are regarded as expressions of discontent by the targets.

A quite different example for spontaneous cooperation concerns the individual sanctioning of undesirable behaviors such as smoking. Scientific research on the dangers of second-hand smoking increased the amount of sanctioning of smokers in interaction situations where a smoker and a non-smoker meet. The more frequently smokers are sanctioned, the more likely it is that a generally accepted anti-smoking norm emerges. Such a norm is a public good (or, for smokers, a public evil). Sanctioning smokers is thus a contribution to a public good. Who is the critical mass? It is likely that there are always groups of non-smokers for whom being exposed to smoke was particularly costly. This is the key group. Their sanctioning is often visible to others. When these others observe that the sanctioned smokers refrained from smoking at least temporarily and that smokers do not react aggressively, this may suggest to them that sanctioning smokers is not costly and successful. Thus, sanctioning of a key group raises the sanctioning benefits for others.

Very often smokers are sanctioned not in order to contribute to a general norm but just to prevent being exposed to smoke. Thus, there are contributions to a public good which are not intended to bring about the public good – its provision is a by-product of the sanctioning – and which are not organized. Many individuals have the same interest and perform similar behaviors independently of each other whose side effect is the provision of a public good. Nonetheless, the first sanctioners were a critical mass. This critical mass is not as easily observable as in the case of the Monday demonstrations. Therefore, the incentives for further sanctioning they provide is probably low. The smoking example illustrates that the process of sanctioning is not only set in motion by a critical mass. Lawmakers set incentives as well by prohibiting smoking at various places. This is a signal of a prestigious group that a certain behavior is illegitimate. It is plausible that this lowers the costs of sanctioning those who perform this behavior as well.

Sanctioning systems, norms, and social networks

If contributions to the provision of a public good are at issue in everyday life, sanctioning of non-contributors is ubiquitous: people encourage each other to contribute, they punish non-cooperators and they appeal to norms that cooperation is fair or a duty.[31] It thus seems, that "collective action can be organized through a sanctioning system consisting of norms requiring cooperation" (Heckathorn 1989: 80). However, as Heckathorn notes and as has been said before in this chapter, contributing to setting up or sustaining a sanctioning system is a contribution to a public good as well: it is a second-order public good which is instrumental to bring about the first-order good. To be sure, there is a regulatory interest (Heckathorn) for a sanctioning system. That is to say, it is in every member's interest that contributors are rewarded and non-contributors punished with the consequence that everybody contributes to the provision of a public good. But the members of a group are faced with the same problems that originate when the first-order public good is to be provided. To illustrate, assume there is a large group and the free rider problem is salient because personal influence is considered negligible and because there are no other incentives. Thus, direct contributions to the provision of the public good such as curbing pollution or joining a social movement are absent. What could be the incentives in this situation to punish friends and neighbors if they do not contribute? It was already described how odd it is to punish others for non-contributions or reward them for contributing: assume that you – the reader – do not contribute and a friend expresses his or her disapproval and even threatens to break up with you if you do not contribute. Apparently, your friend would expect you to do an absolutely futile thing: to perform an action that is like asking the president of the United State to give you a million dollars. You would probably break up with your friend due to his or her rather insolent request. The puzzle is that we observe that in those kinds of situations *imposing sanctions on non-contributors* is widespread. Why do people sanction behavior that is apparently futile?

"Futile" means that a person has no immediate advantage of sanctioning. This situation is also given in third party punishment which can be observed in everyday life and in experimental settings (see, e.g., Fehr and Fischbacher 2004). This is a situation where individuals sanction others although they themselves are not affected by the others' behavior. For example, a person may sanction B because B insulted C. Again, sanctioning seems nonsensical – unless one assumes the existence of norms such as norms of fairness or cooperation.

The second puzzle is that we do not only observe that there is sanctioning of useless behavior, but that there is also a *sanctioning norm* (see, e.g., Axelrod 1986; Horne 2007 with further references), i.e. there is a metanorm of sanctioning: it is regarded as a duty to sanction non-cooperators. How can a norm emerge to sanction a useless behavior?

A third puzzle is that there is a general *norm of cooperation*. To be sure, this norm is conditional, and one condition for the norm to hold is that the respective action is successful. But another condition is that there is an obligation to participate if discontent is high (see Jasso and Opp 1997). This implies that even if participation is futile one has to contribute when there are strong grievances. Thus, there is a norm to do useless things. The puzzle is how such a norm can originate.

One possible answer is that persons learn in their socialization process to reward contributors and punish non-contributors, that it is a duty to sanction and to contribute to the provision of the first-order public good. Since socialization processes are different for different people, we can expect that sanctioning and norms obtain in different intensities in a population. So there is some variation in sanctioning, in the sanctioning norm and the norm to cooperate.

This explanation does not solve the puzzles mentioned before, it moves the explanatory question one step back. It is certainly correct that children learn to sanction, etc. from their parents. The question that remains is why parents and other socialization agents teach their children behavior and norms that in many situations do not make sense.

Another solution has been suggested: integration in social networks promotes cooperation and sanctioning (see Coleman 1990: chapter 10 and 11). The idea is that it is less costly and more rewarding to sanction when individuals are connected by social bonds. For example, it is easier for individuals who know each other to pool their sanctions against a non-cooperator than for unconnected individuals. All this may be true. But even if sanctioning is relatively "cheap" in social networks, why should individuals sanction in situations where the public good can apparently not be provided by the individual's direct or indirect contribution?

A related argument has been that punishing those who do not punish is a low cost activity, at least lower than contributing directly to the provision of a first-order public good. For example, punishing a person who does not go to a demonstration is less costly than participating in the demonstration. But this argument is not convincing. First of all, sanctioning non-contributors need not be a low cost activity at all, one may reckon with aggressive reactions to a negative sanction. But even if we grant that sanctioning is a low cost activity, the problem is that there are many low cost activities that are not performed. The benefits must be higher than the costs in order be performed. So why is sanctioning chosen? What are the benefits? Thus, the low-cost argument does not solve the second-order free rider problem.

The only convincing solution is, in my opinion, that the inclination to sanction and the capacity to internalize norms of cooperation or of fairness are part of our evolutionary heredity. It seems that the evidence is in favor of a gene-culture coevolution of human altruism.[32] The basic idea is that in earlier times groups were small. In this situation, sanctioning and sanctioning norms were likely to increase "fitness" or, in modern terms, were likely to contribute to the provision of the desired public goods for the group. Such a sanctioning trait has become part of our genes and is transmitted to present day *Homo sapiens*.

It is not possible and not necessary either to go into the details of evolutionary explanations. For explanations of collective action in real life situations it is only important to look at some of the consequences of the numerous empirical studies and theoretical arguments of the literature alluded to in the previous notes.

1. Explanations of collective actions in real life situations must take into account the variations in regard to the positive or negative sanctioning of cooperators or defectors across individuals, and in regard to norms of cooperation, sanctioning, and fairness.[33] These are the initial conditions in explanations. Thus, when we want to explain collective action we have to determine empirically what the distribution of these variables is in a certain setting.

2. The internalized norms often require behavior that is costly and does not have any material or immediate advantages. One of these norms that is relevant for explaining cooperation is the norm to sanction non-cooperators even in situations where individual cooperation will not have visible effects for the individual.

3. At first sight, it seems that some of the previous statements contradict the theory of collective action. But this is not the case. If those who sanction non-cooperators have followed a norm, they get internal positive sanctions such as a

good conscience; if they do not adhere to the norm, they experience internal negative sanctions such as shame and a bad conscience. These costs and benefits depend on the extent to which a norm is internalized. Furthermore, sanctioning or following a norm gives rise to external costs and benefits. For example, expecting a severe counter reaction from a punished person will lower the likelihood of future sanctioning.

The problem of not having an elegant solution to the second-order free rider problem does not diminish in any way the utmost importance of sanctioning behavior, norms of cooperation and sanctioning norms for explaining collective action. In the extreme case, punishing of non-cooperators may lead to universal cooperation, when purely instrumental behavior would not work (see, e.g., Fehr, Fischbacher and Gächter 2002).

The previous points, based on the research on sanctioning and sanctioning norms, are familiar to sociologists and social psychologists. Economists have rediscovered them. In contrast to sociologists, economists have conducted experiments, and their hypotheses are based on a general theory of action. For sociologists, it is good to see that some of their basic ideas are confirmed. Nonetheless, it seemed useful to present these ideas to emphasize their relevance for explaining collective action.

An important consequence of the previous discussion for the theory of collective action is that it clearly confirms the importance of selective incentives: sanctioning and fairness norms are selective incentives. The research further suggests that there is a difference between the second- and first-order free rider problem: norms of fairness and of cooperation that are incentives for rewarding contributors and punishing non-contributors help to solve the second-order free rider problem. It is important that these norms are at least to some extent independent of the effectiveness of the contributions.

4. Summary and conclusions

This chapter has focused on one of the most controversial theories in the social sciences, namely the theory of collective action. This is the only theory addressed in this book that is not directly concerned with protest or social movement participation. But because protest and social movement participation are forms of collective action, the theory can be and has been applied to explain protest behavior. In order to be able to assess the strengths and weaknesses of the theory and, accordingly, of its application to the field of protest and social movements we have devoted a separate chapter to it. However, this chapter is not intended to be a comprehensive treatment of the theory. We selected those propositions and findings that seem particularly relevant for explaining social movement phenomena.

The question Olson tries to answer is when individual actors with a common goal act in order to achieve their goal. If this goal is achieved, then, by definition, a public good is produced. This is a good (i.e. everything that provides utility) which, if it exists, can be consumed by every member of a group. Olson's question thus is: when do members of a group contribute to provide the public good?

Olson's procedure to answer this question is different from all other theories addressed in this book: Olson explicitly applies a general theory of action, i.e. a micro theory, to explain contributions to the provision of the public good. This procedure is discussed in detail in chapter 1 of this book.

The basic proposition – the group size proposition – stipulates: the larger the group, the less likely is it that a public good is provided. If a collective good is provided by a large group, then this can only be due to selective incentives. These are, by definition, benefits occurring when one contributes and costs obtaining when one defects. In contrast, the benefits of the public good can be enjoyed by every member of a group, regardless of his or her contribution. One major reason why large groups are usually not capable of providing a collective good is that the individual contribution has only "negligible" (Olson's term) effects.

The first contribution of this chapter, that is important for later chapters, is the reconstruction of Olson's theoretical argument as a micro-macro model. The theory of collective action consists of three parts, and each part has its own strengths and weaknesses. (1) The first part is a *micro model*. It explains the individual's contribution to the public good and involves individual incentives such as the interest in the public good, the efficacy of a contribution to the public good, the costs of the contribution, and selective incentives. (2) The second part is the *macro proposition* about the effect of group size on public goods provision. This is the most controversial part of Olson's theory. (3) The third part are *bridge assumptions,* i.e. hypotheses connecting the micro and the macro level. Olson's implicit argument is that group size as a macro variable affects the individual incentives (micro variables) that, in turn, affect contributions to the public good which, in turn, aggregate to collective action. This micro-macro model is spelled out in detail in this chapter.

In the discussion of the major weaknesses of the theory that are relevant for explaining protest and movement phenomena, we first extend the micro model. We specify in detail the incentives relevant for contributions to the public good. An important point is that the incentives are interdependent. This model is further discussed in the next chapter.

Another major problem is Olson's micro-macro model. The validity of the group size proposition hinges on the validity of the assumed effects of group size on the incentives. These relationships are discussed in detail and found very problematic.

We then present and discuss important extensions of the theory of collective action. One is the introduction of production functions. They specify relationship between the number or proportion of contributors on the one hand and the amount of the public good produced on the other. This extension of the theory shows that the relationship between group size and public goods production can be manifold. We discuss the possibility to explain production functions. An important distinction is made between production and mobilization functions. The latter specify the relationship between the number of contributors and the effect on the number of new contributors. Mobilization functions are important in the field of social movements because protesters do not provide the good themselves, their major aim is to mobilize adherents in order to put pressure on third parties like governments. The final part of this chapter discusses various mechanisms (i.e. processes) of public goods production.

The major task now is to apply the theory to social movement phenomena. The next chapter is devoted to this task. At the end of the next chapter we will outline to what extent the theory can be a backdrop for the discussion of the other theories discussed in the book.

4 Protest and social movements as collective action

This chapter focuses on the application of the theory of collective action, outlined and discussed in the previous chapter, to explain protest and social movements. It is clear that the theory can be applied: political protest is a contribution to public goods, and the major goal of social movements is to provide public goods. There is meanwhile a burgeoning literature where the theory is applied. Two early examples are Oberschall's (1980) detailed explanation of the events around the Davis Cup matches at Vanderbilt University in Nashville, Tennessee, on March 17–19, 1978 (see also Oberschall 1979), and Hechter, Friedman, and Appelbaum's explanation of collective ethnic action (1982). More recent applications are the explanation of the rise and decline of the civil rights movement (Chong 1991), the explanation of mobilization in a mining village in Spain (Linares 2004) (this study will be discussed in detail below), the explanation of the protests and revolutionary events in Eastern Europe and East Germany (Goldstone 1994; Karklins and Petersen 1993; Kuran 1995; Lohmann 1993, 1994; Olson 1990; Opp, Voss, and Gern 1995; Pfaff 2006), and the explanation of insurgent collective action during the civil war in El Salvador (Wood 2000, 2003). General critical reviews are rare (see Marwell and Oliver 1984; Moore 1995 who focuses on rebellion, i.e. violent collective action). Further, there are applications of the theory to explain rebellion (Leites and Wolf 1970; Muller 1979; Opp 1989),[1] revolutions (Salert 1976: chapter 2; see also Taylor 1988, and Goldstone 2001, 2002 for a review of the literature)[2] and many other phenomena (see, e.g., the work of Oberschall such as 1979, 1980 and 1994).

The present chapter begins by spelling out some differences between protest and other forms of collective action. The best way to show how collective action theory can be applied to explain protest and other social movement phenomena is to present a case study where the theory has actually been applied: we will describe and discuss Linares's qualitative study about mobilization in a mining village in Spain (Linares 2004).

The most devastating critique of the theory of collective action is Fireman and Gamson's claim that collective action theory is not suitable for explaining social movement phenomena. We have not found any refutation or detailed discussion of this critique in the literature. This may mean that the critique is generally accepted or that it is so obviously wrong that a discussion is not necessary. But because the critique is, if it is correct, a very severe challenge to collective action theory, it is important to discuss the critique at this point.

We saw in the previous chapter that one ingredient of the theory of collective action is a micro model that explains protest behavior. This micro model is further extended to be more useful for the explanation of protest behavior.

The next sections then address in general the question of how to apply collective action theory to explain social movements phenomena: we outline a two-step procedure for applying the theory of collective action. We conclude with some suggestions on what social movement research can learn from the theory of collective action.

1. Protest and collective action

As we have alluded to already in the previous chapter, protest is a form of collective action. Protesters have a wide variety of common goals such as closing down nuclear power plants, preventing or ending wars or effecting less pollution. These are public goods: if the goals are achieved every member of a group enjoys them (or suffers from them, depending on the point of view). "Social movements" are groups of individuals with at least some key goals in common (see chapter 2). Protests and social movement activities are thus contributions to the provision of public goods. Thus, the theory of collective action can be applied to explain political protest.

There are nonetheless some differences between protest and other forms of collective action. These differences might require different explanatory hypotheses. Three differences seem most important. (1) Protesters do not provide the public good themselves. Instead, only third parties like governments are capable of providing the public good. Protesters try to influence the decisions of the government to yield to their demands. This is different for other types of collective action where the actors themselves provide the public good.

In terms of a micro-macro model this means that the relationship from individual contributions to a public good is empirical (see chapter 3: subsection "Micro-to-macro relationships: Is the public good an empirical or analytical function of individual contributions?").

The consequence for explaining the provision of public goods is that not only contributions have to be explained but the behavior of third parties as well. The reason is that the third parties provide the good. In explaining public goods provision there are thus two phenomena to be explained: protest and the decisions of the third parties, i.e. the provision of the public good.

Due to this difference between protest and other types of collective action two types of functions must be distinguished, as we saw in chapter 3 (see Figure 3.5): one is a mobilization function describing the extent to which collective action instigates non-mobilized actors to participate; the other is a production function which describes the extent to which the contributions by protesters affect the extent to which the public good is provided by third parties.

(2) The kinds of public goods protesters are seeking to produce are often vague. Goals such as to ban war or terminate hunger in the third world are not

as clear as building a bridge across a certain river. Furthermore, activists often pursue goals that are not stated explicitly. For example, students sometimes protest for a goal that they know they will not achieve such as increasing the university budget in order to hire more teaching personnel. The real reason for their protest may be different: they may actually pursue some subsidiary or secondary goals such as informing others about the political situation, "raising consciousness," or gain support by other students. In studies about social movements care must be taken to ascertain the real goals of protesters or social movement activists.

Those two distinguishing features of protest behavior do not pose principal difficulties of applying the theory of collective action. It complicates social movement research because in explaining public goods provision one has to consider the reactions of third parties and one has to look carefully at the actual goals groups or actors want to achieve.

2. How to apply collective action theory: a case study about the mobilization of a mining village in Spain

In this section we present Francisco Linares's case study about the mobilization and protests of the inhabitants of a Spanish mining village where a new open mining pit was to be built (Linares 2004). The question Linares addresses is "how it was possible for the inhabitants of this village to remain mobilized for three and a half years" (438 – all page numbers in this section refer to this article). Finally, the mine was closed, but the explanation of the outcome of the mobilization process is not subject of the study. Linares leaves it open whether this outcome was brought about by the activities of the residents or by other events.

There are numerous case studies in the social movement literature. The first reason for choosing the Linares study is that the description of the case is not too voluminous so that the reader of this chapter is not distracted with too many details. The second reason is that it is a qualitative study, based on documents and informal interviews. This should counteract the widely held view that collective action (and rational choice) theory is heavily quantitative. Obviously, this is not the case. The third reason is that Linares applies the whole "toolkit" of new developments of collective action theory, particularly game theory, critical mass theory, and production functions. Finally, there are some open questions so that this section is not only a recount of the article.

The situation in Llano del Beal

Mining in the mountains of Cartagena-La Unión (in the south-east of Spain) can be dated back to Roman times. In the second half of the nineteenth century 56 percent of Spain's lead ore was produced there. Several factors then led to the decline of mining. From 1953 onwards, the mining company Peñarroya invested in a new development of mining activities. The plan was to substitute underground mining for surface mining. In 1986, the company employed 484 people. However, the quality of the ore had declined. At the beginning of 1987 the continuation of mining depended on a new open pit called Los Blancos III. This had to be authorized by the Ministry of Industry and the local government.

This new pit was to be built close to the village Llano del Beal (LdB) which had (together with two other villages in the community) 2,138 inhabitants in 1991. Between half and two-thirds live in LdB. This village has a doctor's practice, a school, and a pharmacy. There was also a Residents' Association. In the 1970s and 1980s, some public investments were made such as road surfacing and street lighting. Some of these services came about as a result of the residents' persistent demand to the distant Cartagena City Council. It is also important that the majority of the working population was forced to look for work outside the community.

In general, due to the mining crisis LdB was "one of the most underprivileged districts in the run-down municipality of Cartagena" (441). Furthermore, the population suffered from the production in two open pits that began in 1972 (Los Blancos I and II): there were the daily explosions and the traffic of lorries and machineries. These pits had been closed in 1985. The population of LdB suffered even more after the start of Los Blancos III in 1984 (before the permission of the ministry) which was located 800 m from the village.

This pit was to be developed in several steps. The procedure was to fill in the pit of each phase of the construction process with the waste extracted in successive phases. The last phase consisted of mining on the south side of the village. The end of the "local environmental destruction" would be the restoration of the part of the pit close to the village.

In a meeting of the Peñarroya company and the Residents' Association on June 4, 1987, the company showed a scale model. The residents realized that in fact "half of the village was taken away," as one interviewee noted (443). After this meeting the Residents' Association representatives informed the other residents in an assembly that took place on August 31, 1987. "This gathering could be described as the opening shot of a marathon of resistance which lasted for three and a half years, until mining finally came to an end in May 1991" (444). The situation in LdB is summarized very succinctly in a letter by a retired miner to the government Ombudsman in September 1987:

> The Mining and Metallurgic Company of Peñarroya-Spain Ltd. is preparing to develop an open pit in the village in order to extract underground minerals, a plan which involves demolishing 25 houses, resulting in the deterioration of the remaining houses and the village becoming a living hell of 24 hours a day, causes being: noise, vibration from the borers and the constant dust which we will all have to breathe.
>
> May I bring to your attention the fact that there are 3500 people living here and 60% of us either are silicosis sufferers or retired, without a means of leaving the village. We will have to fight to the death, all we can do is defend ourselves and shed whatever blood is necessary so that the conflict brought on by Peñarroya becomes a national scandal. (444)

Although this letter is written by a single person we may surmise that it is a joint product of a group of residents and captures the grievances of the residents, along with their determination to oppose the planned pit.

The repertoire of resistance and the features of the residents' movement

The residents engaged in various activities. (1) They negotiated with the authorities by organizing numerous meetings with representatives of the local and regional governments and the company. (2) The residents engaged in various initiatives in order to put pressure on the government. For example, petitions against the company's plans were presented at the Cartagena Town Hall. (3) Legal actions were carried out by the Residents' Association such as demonstrations, sit-ins, and camp-outs. This included judicial action. (4) Illegal actions were taken as well such as "blocking the path of the lorries and machinery and interrupting the mining work" (445).

The center of the resistance was a hut "set up at the highest point of the village ... From there, the residents could easily maintain a constant monitoring of the work of the machines" (445).

The Residents' Association was the driving force of the activities of the residents. Their committee consisted of 30 members who regularly met. Members were some highly regarded residents of the village such as the doctor and the school principal. They were the major representatives of the residents and the interlocutors of the institutions involved in the conflict. Linares notes that in regard to the various activities there were no status differences in the sense that the views of the "leaders" were respected and not discussed. At the meetings "... there was no 'you are the doctor' and 'you're this', I mean there we were arguing, and we were equals ..." (447), as one interviewee put it.

Decisions the committee made had to be approved in assemblies of the residents. These assemblies had a high attendance, sometimes of 1000 or 2000 people. These assemblies were held in the village square or in the church. This size suggests that almost every inhabitant participated.[3]

Linares points out that achieving the goal of the residents to prevent the pit implies supporting the abolition of jobs at the mine. Linares explains that this "contradiction" disappears because the residents felt that they "were nothing more than an instrument used immorally by the company" (448). This seems to mean that the residents thought the company worked together with the government without any consideration of the needs of the residents. Anyway, it seems that the consequence of fewer jobs if the goals of the residents were met was not important for the citizens in this case.

Initial mobilization: suddenly imposed grievances and incentives to collective action

The reader may pause for a moment and think about answering the following questions: (1) How can the initial mobilization be explained? (2) How can the long duration of the mobilization be explained? The following sections provide an answer to these questions.

The start of the mobilization process was the meeting on June 4, 1987, when it became clear to the residents what the consequences of the planned pit for their houses and the quality of life had been. This event is an example of what is called in the social movement literature a "suddenly imposed grievance" or a "critical event." This event changed the major incentives for collective action of most of the residents. The event is a factor at the macro level, whereas the incentives are variables at the micro level. Linares does not provide an explicit micro model, but he mentions various kinds of costs and benefits which are ingredients of the micro model that has been discussed in the previous chapter and will be extended later in this chapter. In order to explain the mobilization in detail the question then is: which incentives did the critical event change?

First of all, the expected *grievances* increased, i.e. the residents expected a drastic decline of a whole bunch of public goods – where the term "good" is hardly appropriate, one should rather speak of a public "bad." Linares notes, as has been said before, that there might have been conflicting goals: a success in preventing the new pit would have the consequence that no new workplaces were created. But Linares argued that this did not play a role because the residents were concerned about the apparent cooperation of the company and the government which did not consider the needs of the citizens. It seems that the resentment about this cooperation was so strong that it made up for the loss of workplaces. Another explanation of why the loss of workplaces was not regarded as important might have been that the expected consequences of the planned pit were much more concrete and thus more threatening than the future loss of workplaces. In other words, the shadow of the future was small.

Another incentive for collective action is a *norm to cooperate*, i.e. a felt obligation to contribute to the public good. Norms are conditional. The norm to contribute holds in particular, if grievances are high (see our discussion of the micro model below). Furthermore, if grievances are regarded as illegitimate, a norm of cooperation also becomes activated. Both conditions obtained in this situation. It is thus plausible that the expected further deterioration of the living conditions triggered off moral indignation.[4]

The increased grievances and activation of a norm to cooperate further gave rise to strong *social incentives*: if intense grievances are regarded as unjust and if a norm to cooperate is activated, friends and acquaintances will be encouraged to participate, and defectors will probably be sanctioned negatively. It is likely that the social incentives were relatively strong because there were dense social networks with frequent interactions. One reason for these extensive interactions were low status differences. The few inhabitants with a higher status such as the doctor, the pharmacist, the school principal, and the priest were apparently quite well integrated in the group.

The *costs of participation* were mostly the time forgone that could have been used for other purposes. Since there were many unemployed and retired residents there was a substantial number of people for whom enough time was available at low cost. The situation was different for employed persons, especially for the leaders in the Residents' Association. They were busy in their job and participation in the various activities of the residents might have been very time consuming and, thus, costly. Linares does not provide information whether this caused any problems.

Linares notes (see above) that some infrastructure in the community came about as a result of the residents' persistent demands on the distant Cartagena City Council. There was thus some experience of protest in the past. It seems plausible that protests became less costly when there has been some previous participation. More importantly, the past group success might have been another incentive for participation (see the micro model exhibited in Figure 3.3 in the previous chapter).

The critical event explains why mobilization did not occur earlier. As we have seen before, the LdB residents were suffering from the ore production already before the meeting. The goal to live without noise and pollution existed before the decisive assembly. It seems plausible that the presentation of the plan for the new pit came as a shock which raised the incentives to a level that set off the mobilization activities.

Explaining different forms of resistance and "exit"

As we saw above, the residents chose a whole array of activities to reach their goals, including violent actions. How can it be explained that these and no other actions were chosen? Linares does not discuss this question. When we apply the micro model outlined in the previous chapter, the answer is as follows. First of all, the behavioral alternatives which the residents chose are well known as normal possibilities to influence governmental decisions. All these actions are thus among the perceived behavioral alternatives of all citizens. But there are certainly more alternatives than those that have been chosen. For example, terrorist activities or murders were not performed by the residents of LdB. Why, then did the residents choose the actions described above? The micro model would suggests that three factors are relevant: the expected success (and, thus, personal influence) of the actions, their normative acceptability, and their low costs. We can only speculate that the residents thought that the mix of actions they chose promoted their goals best.

A problem is the choice of violent actions. There were relatively few people who engaged in these activities, and there were apparently negative sanctions (460). Violence was thus costly. Since relatively few residents engaged in these actions it is plausible that many considered them not efficacious or regarded them as morally not acceptable. But incentives are different. So it may be that those who engaged in violent acts saw their efficacy differently and perhaps accepted some of the common justifications for engaging in violent actions. One is that the intense grievances imposed by the company justify violence. These are speculations because Linares does not present data that can be used to test these hypotheses about the choice of violence.

An open question that is not addressed by Linares is why the residents did not choose the exit option, i.e. move to another place. Linares does not provide information whether in the negotiations of the Residents' Association with the company and the government one of the options had been a move of the whole village to another location. The exit option from the point of view of a resident is only addressed in the letter of a retired miner, quoted above, which is here repeated: "May I bring to your attention the fact that there are 3500 people living here and 60% of us either are silicosis sufferers or retired, without a means of leaving the village. We will have to fight to the death, all we can do is defend ourselves and shed whatever blood is necessary so that the conflict brought on by Peñarroya becomes a national scandal" (444). Thus, the costs of moving were in general probably high for a single resident. The quotation also suggests that the company and the state did not provide the money for a perhaps very expensive resettling. These are again speculations. Linares does not present hypotheses and data that explain why the exit option was not viable.

The coordination of collective action

Even if the planned pit had triggered strong incentives for collective action the question arises how coordination was achieved. There were various forms of *joint* action and not just isolated individual actions such as writing a letter to the government, attacking representatives of the company, or running around with a banner demanding "we don't want the pit." If there is joint action two questions must be answered. The first is why it is in the interest of the actors to initiate some joint action – a demonstration or as an initial step establishing an organization. In most cases and in LdB the answer is that from the perspective of the actors involved joint action is probably considered much more successful than isolated action.

The second question is to explain the *forms* of coordination the actors have chosen. In chapter 3 we discussed various mechanisms describing how coordination can come about. The main mechanism in LdB was *leadership*: there existed a group, the Residents' Association, which has acted already in the past in the interest of the residents. One could almost say that it was "natural" that this group took the lead of organizing joint action. A committee with 30 members from the Association met regularly and discussed problems and possible solutions. That the Association or members thereof took the leadership was also to be expected because some members with a high status in the village were active in the association (see above).

Although the Association was the "backbone" of the various activities, as Linares put it (446), just about 30 residents in the committee were probably not enough to achieve the common goal. When we imagine that they were the only residents who actively opposed to the planned pit, the authorities would probably not have even considered to change their plans. For example, assume a demonstration is announced and only the members of the committee show up. The government and the company would certainly not have been impressed. We can further expect that the members of the Association would terminate their activities if the turnout would be so low. However, as we have seen before, a great deal of the residents cooperated.

Why did so many others follow suit? Put otherwise, why was the Association a "critical mass" that set off a process that involved many other residents in the various forms of collective action mentioned above? A first important consequence of the activities of the Association was that it *lowered the costs of collective action* for the other residents. For example, if there is somebody who takes the time to organize a demonstration or a meeting with the authorities, participants not involved in the organization save time. But this is certainly not enough for widespread collective action in LdB. Several features of the village, of the residents and their social networks mattered as well.

As was noted above, the *high intensity of the incentives across the population* was an important condition for the widespread participation. But was the intensity high enough? This is likely if there is *inequality* in regard to the intensity of the incentives. In particular, if there are residents with a very strong interest in the public good who believe that they can make a difference (high efficacy) they will be among the first who follow suit. If these persons further dispose of resources (such as knowledge about the legal situation, skills to bargain), hold strong obligations to participate and are exposed to strong social incentives, the likelihood that they participate is particularly high. It is important to note that the *same individuals* must be exposed to these incentives. If, for example, some individuals have a strong interest in the public good, but others think they are influential (but are not interested at all in the public good), and still others accept a strong participation norm (and are not interested and do not feel their participation makes a difference), participation is less likely.

If there is inequality the incentives may still not be strong enough to set off a general mobilization process. Another condition is that there is a pre-existing *favorable distribution of incentives* (see the previous chapter). This means the following. Assume there are a few persons with very high incentives to participate. The activities of the leaders then lower the costs to an extent that these persons participate as well. This may lead to lowering the costs and increasing the positive incentives to a next layer of the population to an extent that they now will participate. Thus, there must be a pre-existing distribution of incentives such that if one group becomes active the next follows suit. Such a spiral of protest will stop if the difference between the various net utilities of participation is too big or if everybody participates. In terms of thresholds, there must be a certain distribution of the size of net utilities of protest so that participation of one group raises the incentives of another group to an extent that for this other group the net utility of protest becomes higher than that of inactivity and so on.

It is a common assumption that the participation of individuals raises the positive incentives to participate for yet inactive individuals. Why? One possibility is that a *fairness norm* is activated: if others participate I should not let them do the work. This will probably raise *social incentives* among the population: if there is an obligation to participate friends and acquaintances will be encouraged to participate as well. Linares describes in detail processes of positive sanctioning (457–458). These sanctions increase if an increasing number of individuals participate.

It is to be expected that dense networks will lead to strong social incentives. These include "hypocritical" sanctioning (see Heckathorn 1996), i.e. residents do not participate themselves but reward others for participating. Strong positive social sanctioning took place in LdB: there were "close ties," i.e. "there was frequent face-to-face interaction, but also a highly centralized and closed social network within the community" (455).

This dense network was brought about by the structure of the village: the small size and the remote location forced people to interact, but also "that the community had only one school, one doctor's surgery and one pharmacy and that they have to use the same stores (bakeries, grocer's, etc.) and the same recreating areas" (455).

There is another type of incentives which may be called *situational incentives*: when people convene there is a sense of community, a great deal of fraternity, a sense of harmony and strong emotion (460). These are certainly not incentives that individuals expect to obtain when they participate for the first time. But when they have participated, they will expect these situational incentives next time.

The mobilization process

The mobilization process took time (see the description of the events above) and occurred in several phases. The process resembles, according to Linares, an S-shaped production function (see Figure 3.4 in the previous chapter). It is important to note that this function is actually a *mobilization function* (see chapter 3, section 3 and Figure 3.5): the vertical axis does not represent the amount of a public good provided, because no public good was provided during the mobilization process. As Linares notes, his case study is about mobilization or, in terms of the theory of collective action, contributions to the public good and not about its production. The provision of the public good, i.e. withdrawal of the plan to build the pit, occurred after the mobilization and is only addressed in passing (438). It is even left open whether the contributions of the citizens played any role for the decision of the authorities and the company.

Thus, what Linares describes is the mobilization function and not the function that relates number or proportion of contributors to the amount of the public good produced. In the S-shaped function the first accelerating part means that there are a few people who act first. In LdB this is the Residents' Association or its committee. Their activities attracted an increasing number of residents over time who became active as well. Thus, the curve gets to the point where it increases linearly. Linares notes that the majority of the residents participated but there was also a number of non-participants. For example, "for families of the employees of the mining company and for those individuals who remained loyal supporters of the socialist party (groups which bore a higher cost)" the value of the public good was lower and perhaps the costs of participation higher. This held also for those whose houses were located at the side of the village that was not affected by the mining activities. It thus seems, that to a small extent *material selective incentives* were important: to those who were likely to be affected most by the mining activities, the loss of their houses was likely. Although they were promised to be compensated, the threat of losing a house is certainly an incentive to do something about it. But all this did not apply to those whose houses were in some distance to the location of the pit to be built. So there began the decelerating phase where the curve flattens. This means that after a substantial number of the population has become active additional supporters could not be recruited.

The structure of the theoretical argument

The case study consists of two parts. The first one consists of the description of the setting where the mobilization took place. Linares then gives an account of the major actor on the side of the citizens (namely the Residents' Association, i.e. pre-existing leadership), the company and the government, the close-knit networks in the village and the distribution of the incentives. These are, in terms of the theory of collective action, the initial conditions. It is important to note that they are specific to the situation and that they must be determined empirically (see chapter 1). The importance of these factors is that they determine whether collective action origi-nates if something happens in this setting.

This "something" is the critical event, i.e. the information that part of the village is supposed to be destroyed. This event triggered the mobilization process by rais-ing the incentives to various forms of collective action. This is a macro-to-micro (top-to-bottom) relationship: it is assumed that a macro event changes the values of various micro variables. The respective actors are the residents who are in part members of the Residents' Associations, the latter being a collective actor. The other two collective actors – the company and the government – which in fact seem to act jointly do not take action, they reveal their plan to build the new pit and stick to it, at least in the period Linares is concerned with.

The mobilization process consists of actions of the committee or of the Residents' Association respectively, and of joint action of subgroups of the resi-dents. These are forms of collective action and, thus, a dependent macro variable. These episodes of collective action, in turn, change incentives on the individual level. The process is thus a chain of events running back and forth between the macro and micro level. Figure 4.1 illustrates this process.

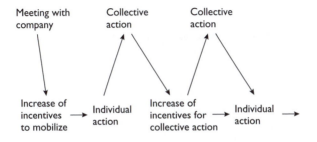

Figure 4.1 The process of mobilization: the example of Llano del Beal

The role of production functions, game theory, and micro-macro modeling in explaining mobilization

Linares suggests a particular production function, but in fact this is a mobilization function (as we have seen before, see chapter 3, section 3). He further applies game theory. To what extent does this improve the incentives-driven explanation outlined before?

In regard to the explanatory value of the mobilization function we saw in chapter 3 (section 3), that mobilization (or production) functions do not explain collective action but are the outcome of mobilization processes. This can be demonstrated for LdB. If the mobilization curve is S-shaped, then at the beginning relatively many people must be active in order to mobilize others. The number of people mobilizing and being mobilized depends on the incentive structure and the activities of the collective actors. The respective production or mobilization function can thus be derived or predicted. The curve then succinctly informs us about the course of the mobilization process, but it does not explain it.[5]

What role does game theory play in the explanation of the mobilization process in LdB? Linares's starting point is the work of Heckathorn (1996). One of his ideas is that the game structure may change in the course of the mobilization process, and different games may apply to different groups. Linares argues that "it is evident that at the beginning of the mobilization the incentive structure for, at least, some subset of the population must have been analogous to that of the privileged game in which the dominant strategy is to 'cooperate'" (452). This means that it is best for an actor to cooperate (i.e. participate in the mobilization activities in LdB) if others cooperate; but if others do not cooperate, it is best to cooperate as well, although the benefit of cooperation is lower than in the former case (451). The quotation implies that the game is – as the mobilization or production function – an outcome of the incentive structure. For example, if the incentives are very strong for a group of residents then they will participate whatever the others do. This means that "cooperation" is a dominant strategy.[6] The important point in this context is that not only the production function, but the structure of a game is a result of the incentive structure. The game then succinctly shows the payoffs (which are a function of the totality of incentives at work) of a group of actors, depending on the actions of the other actors. Thus, the burden of the explanation is the specification of the detailed incentive structures that generates collective action.

A thought experiment: Under what conditions would mobilization have been different?

A limitation of a case study is that we do not know exactly how strong the influence of each factor is that set in motion and sustained the mobilization process. But it is nevertheless tempting to speculate on what could have happened if certain features of LdB would not be present. To avoid *ad hoc* answers to this question a theory must be applied like the theory of collective action.

Imagine there is a village of the same size as LdB with the following features:

there is no "critical mass." Assume, for example, there is no pharmacist, no priest, etc. and no citizen organization like the Residents' Association. Assume further that there are no close-knit ties between residents so that the facilitating incentives for collective action mentioned above (such as meeting at the same stores) do not exist. Another condition could be that there were various requests to the government to provide some services in the past but no request was successful. This suggests that perceived personal influence is very low. Would a mobilization process have originated after the critical event? The least we could say is that in this scenario collective action would have been much less likely than in LdB. The reason is that most of the factors promoting collective action in LdB were not present or were present to a lower degree in the imagined community.

An interesting question is how group size is related to the mobilization process in LdB. Linares classifies LdB as a small group. Is a village with about 2,000 or even 1,000 inhabitants a "small" group? If we assume this for a moment, it seems that the features that Olson links to a small group size (see chapter 3, Figure 3.2) are largely present in LdB. We can imagine that in a village with a population of say 20,000 or 50,000 inhabitants, many features of LdB would not be present. Networks would be less dense – not everybody would meet at the same stores – and inequality would be higher. But if in such a village a Residents' Association existed, a process of mobilization would probably also have been set in motion. But the number of people mobilized would probably be lower, and the mobilization curve would probably be S-shaped.

Such speculations are useful to see how the theory of collective action can be applied to specific situations and what possible problems are. The theory directs our attention to certain kinds of factors, namely incentives. We further dispose of a more specific "tool kit" (Linares's term), i.e. ideas such as critical mass, political entrepreneurs, and an inventory of possible incentives. We can then determine in new situations what the conditions were that triggered collective action or that prevented it. We can also see the limits of certain study designs. For example, if we had several case studies beside LdB where mobilizations were more or less successful, we could construct a data base that would allow quantitative analyses and thus explore the weights of various factors.

What about resources, political opportunity, identity, and framing?

The reader who is informed about the major theoretical perspectives in the field of social movements and political protest will wonder that so far nothing has been said about resources, political opportunities, identity, and framing. Several questions arise. (1) How could variables of these approaches be integrated into to the previous explanation? (2) If those perspectives are theories, one would like to know whether they imply a different explanation or would only suggest new questions to be asked. Thus, the question is whether and, if so, in what respects Linares's explanation could be improved or extended when those perspectives are applied. We will take up these questions in chapter 12 when we have discussed these perspectives in detail and have seen what their strengths and weaknesses are. We can then build on these analyses in order to judge whether they can modify or extend the explanation of the mobilization process in LdB presented so far.

Open questions

The reader will have noticed that not every step in the explanation could be supported by data. For example, the answers to the questions of why the exit option was not chosen or why coordination took place and not only isolated individual action were speculative. Such answers should not be understood as circular arguments where on the basis of the dependent variable the independent variables are "inferred." The theoretical speculations are hypotheses that need to be tested.

It might be argued that the research presented is an example of collective action but does not have anything to do with social movements and political protest. The Residents' Association comes at least close to a "social movement": it is a group, i.e. a collectivity of actors who want to achieve their shared goal or goals by influencing decisions of a target. This is the definition proposed in chapter 2 (section 3) for "protest group" which is the subject of this book and which includes social movements. Furthermore, the whole village is a "protest group" in this sense – with the exception of those who have not been mobilized. But even if this is not accepted, there can be no question that the activities of the residents are examples of protest – in whatever sense this term is used (see, again, our definition in chapter 2, section 3).

Each explanation considers certain phenomena, namely initial conditions, as given. In the present example, it is not explained how the Residents' Association came into being. It is further not explained why the government and the company acted as they did. Although these are interesting questions, they have not been answered in this investigation. A given explanation cannot address all interesting questions.

What are the special characteristics of the previous explanation, i.e. how does this explanation differ from other explanations that do not apply the theory of collective action? Social movement scholars might argue that many of the factors in the explanation are widely used in explanations of mobilization and political protest that are not based on the theory of collective action. This holds in particular for social networks, grievances, duty to participate, and efficacy (i.e. perceived personal influence). The basic difference to other explanations is that explanations based on the theory of collective action are an *incentive-driven approach*: changing incentives explain the mobilization process. These incentives change due to macro events (the critical event at the beginning of the process and then various collective action events). This is the second basic feature: *micro-macro modeling*. We will later return to the procedure to explain macro events and macro processes.

3. Is collective action theory not appropriate for social movement explanations? A note on Fireman and Gamson and other critics

This question seems odd at this point because the previous sections have shown that collective action theory can be applied to explain protest or social movement phenomena. But perhaps the previous theoretical arguments and all studies, based on collective action theory, are seriously flawed? This must be the case, otherwise it could not be claimed that "Olson's utilitarian logic does not fit social movements, or for that matter, collective action in general" (Fireman and Gamson 1979: 9 – all page numbers in this section refer to this article). But the authors go one step further: they suggest an alternative theory. Let us first look at Fireman and Gamson's critique and then at their alternative theory.

The tautology charge again

In the following discussion we take it for granted that it is necessary to apply the *wide version* of the theory of rational action to explain social movement phenomena (for details see chapter 1, section 1). This version admits various non-economic incentives such as informal rewards and internalized norms as possible incentives to protest. We are aware of the fact that Fireman and Gamson do not accept this version of the theory of rational action. Their attack is directed at the narrow version. They argue that a wide version is tautological (20). Thus, the wide array of incentives that may give rise to protest action is, in their opinion, to be excluded from the theory. We have discussed the tautology charge in detail in chapter 1, section 1. The conclusion from this discussion is very clear: Fireman and Gamson's tautology charge is not tenable. Chapter 1, section 1, shows in detail why the authors' critique is mistaken. Even if this analysis would not be accepted the tautology charge would be very implausible because the authors themselves invoke various non-material incentives (as we will be shown below) as explanatory factors for social movement phenomena, but without any theoretical basis. Thus, explanations with norms and similar factors are tautological if these explanations are based on the theory of collective action, but they are not tautological when the factors are employed without applying (at least explicitly) any theory. A statement is either tautological or not tautological. But to argue that given hypotheses are tautological if they are based on a general theory of action and are not tautological if they are asserted *ad hoc* (i.e. without explicitly subsumed under a theory) is so weird that it does not need any comment.

Why is collective action theory supposed to fail?

Fireman and Gamson's critique denies the validity of Olson's micro model. Their critique can be summarized in two points. (1) The authors reject Olson's basic hypotheses that, for example, "group interest" (the authors mean the preference for public goods) is irrelevant in large groups and that selective incentives matter. (2) It is further argued that selective incentives are not necessary to mobilize individuals. To what extent is this critique acceptable?

(1) The authors draw some conclusions from Olson's theory that at first sight indeed seem counter-intuitive. For example, Olson's theory would imply that it is a waste of time "for organizers to demonstrate to potential constituents that their goals are worthwhile and their strategy is viable" (11–12). The organizers "need

only be concerned with who may be most interested in the selective incentives they can offer" (12). This is "hard to believe" (12).

The problem with this argument is that it is not based on an alternative general theory of action. Instead, the authors simply find Olson's argument implausible, but they do not cite any empirical evidence for their claim.

Could the authors nonetheless be right? When we apply an extended micro model presented in the previous section admitting beliefs such as perceived (and not actual) personal influence and non-economic incentives, we may specify conditions for the correctness of the authors' hypothesis. For example, when we assume that individuals do not think that their participation matters (i.e. perceptions of efficacy are completely lacking) and when we further assume that there are no indirect effects of the collective interest (i.e. the grievances) on the other incentives (see chapter 3, section 2, and the heading "The micro model revisited," where the interdependence of incentives is discussed) the authors draw the correct conclusion. Indeed, group interest is not an incentive to protest. But if these restrictive conditions do not hold – e.g. people think that their contributions make a difference – then the interest in the public good matters. We discussed this in detail in the previous chapter. We see here the weakness of Fireman and Gamson's critique: they just tell us that they find a certain implication of a theory implausible. They do not apply any theory, and they do not bother to specify conditions when their claim may hold and when not. In particular, the theory of collective action, based on a wide version of rational choice theory, does not in general imply that the organizers "need only be concerned with who may be most interested in the selective incentives they can offer" (12).

(2) The authors argue that "resourceful actors often facilitate mobilization without promising or providing selective incentives. Particularly in the early stages of mobilization, organizers try to convince ordinary constituents *not* that joining in collective action will bring about benefits only for those who join, but rather that collective action will bring about a collective good" (18). In other words, organizers raise *expected group success*. We saw in chapter 3 (section 2, heading "The micro model revisited", where "The role of expected group success" is discussed) that group success does not have a direct effect on collective action, but an indirect effect under certain conditions. As was said before, further research is needed to test this hypothesis and the model of the previous chapter.

The authors further hypothesize that organizers

1   help constituents to understand their common stake in a collective good,
2   alert constituents to threats and opportunities,
3   propose a course of action,
4   gather and communicate commitments,
5   organize decision making,
6   coordinate decision making, and
7   coordinate action (19).

"... if these tasks are done well, then in some situations many ordinary actors mobilize without selective incentives" (19, the numbering is not in the original text).

A detailed analysis of the organizer's activities reveals that the organizers are in fact creating incentives, if their help or activities are accepted or effective. Let us look at the activities listed above and "translate" them.

1   ... = the organizers try to raise the perception of collective efficacy or try to establish the perception of some public good (i.e. an awareness that there is a common concern or, equivalently, shared goal);
2   ... = the organizers raise the subjective probability that there will be threats (and thus increasing expected costs) or they raise individual efficacy;
3   ... = the organizers suggest new behavioral alternatives that have so far not been taken into account;
4   ... = the organizers activate a norm to participate;
5   ... = the organizers diminish costs of participation by bearing the costs of organizing collective action;
6   ... = same as (5);
7   ... = same as (5).

To be sure, the authors' description of the activities of organizations may be interpreted in different ways, but our interpretation suggests that the *activities mentioned are in fact an attempt to either increase public goods incentives (discontent or influence) or selective incentives*. The conclusion thus is, that the authors' argument does not support their hypothesis that organizers succeed in mobilization without providing selective incentives. The authors show exactly the opposite. Perhaps "selective incentives" are understood only as economic or material incentives. If this is meant, then indeed organizers do not provide selective incentives. But this understanding is clearly not in line even with Olson's theory (see our discussion in the previous chapter about the selective incentives in Olson's theory).

But when we apply the micro model suggested in chapter 3 there might indeed be cases where political action comes about in situations where organizers need not provide selective incentives. For example, if grievances and perceived individual influence are very high organizers may just provide some coordinating activities that reduce the costs of participation in order to trigger joint action.

Fireman and Gamson's alternative theory

The alternative to Olson's theory consists of a list of factors that are allegedly contradictory to what Olson claims. The authors provide a long list and we will mention only a few of the factors: ideology, class consciousness (all on p. 16), commitments to contribute, norms against free riding, expectations about whether others will contribute (all on p. 17), solidarity (16, 21–23, see also Gamson 1992: 55), urgency (27–28), necessity (28–29), opportunity (30–31), loyalty and responsibility (31–32).

The first point to be noted is that this is not a theory at all: a simple enumeration of factors is not yet a theory. What is left open is how exactly these factors are related to which dependent variables. For example, what form of protest is to be expected, if "ideology" becomes stronger? Second, no empirical evidence is provided for the impact of these factors on protest action. Third, one would like to know what the relationships between these factors on the one hand and other micro theories of protest are.

Conclusion

From the perspective of a wide version of the theory of rational (and, thus, collective) action, some of Fireman and Gamson's critique can very well be integrated into the theory of collective action. Some of the factors the authors mention refer to public goods preferences (such as urgency) or selective incentives (such as a norm against free riding). But there are factors the authors mention where this is not clear. Further theory and research is necessary to further clarify the meaning of these factors and then analyze their relationship to existing theory.

It would be interesting to see how the authors would explain the mobilization of Llano del Beal. When we look at the authors' list of factors that are allegedly not part of the theory of collective action one wonders that at least some of these factors are part of the above explanation. This supports our conclusion that – from the perspective of contemporary theory of collective action – Fireman and Gamson's critique and alternative can largely be integrated in the theory of collective action.

4. A micro model of protest behavior

One conclusion of our discussions in the previous chapter and in chapter 1 is that an explanation of protest events or of relationships between protest and other macro variables requires a micro model of protest behavior. The previous chapter provides a detailed discussion of a micro model explaining the participation in collective action in general. In this section we will extend and apply this model to explain protest behavior.

The basic model

Olson's micro model consists of the following major types of incentives: (1) preferences for public goods, and (2) "noticeability" of one's behavior (i.e. perceived personal influence); both may be called *public goods incentives* or *public goods motivation*; (3) the *costs* of providing the public good (in particular time and other resources, i.e. opportunity costs); and (4) *selective incentives*. When this micro model is to be applied to explain protest behavior or other activities related to social movements, it is useful to specify the kind of incentives in more detail. This is the goal of this section.

Public goods preferences

Protesters and social movements have quite diverse goals. Grievances or discontent means that certain goals are not achieved. The amount of discontent is a function of the intensity of the preference for the respective public goods and the extent to which the good is not provided. For example, if somebody has a very intense preference for peace and if a cruel war is looming, discontent is high.

The kinds of discontent or grievances depend on the specific case. In general, it is useful to distinguish two kinds of discontent: one is discontent with decisions of some authorities (such as a government), the other discontent with the political system in general. The latter is often called political alienation.

There is a long-standing discussion on whether discontent (or grievances) has an effect on protest behavior. We will not go into this discussion at this point.[7] It seems that most scholars will now agree that most of the time a simple additive effect of grievances – especially if grievances of a large population are at issue – does not obtain. But this does not imply that grievances are irrelevant. A plausible hypothesis is that grievances instigate protest behavior if the actors think that their protest makes a difference. Thus, there is an *interaction effect* of grievances and perceived influence on protest behavior which will be discussed in the next section. In other words, the effect of grievances depends on the amount of perceived influence and vice versa. This implies that very intense grievances will not affect protest behavior when people think that their participation does not matter.

As was discussed already in the previous chapter (section 2, subsection "The causal interdependence of incentives"), grievances have indirect effects on protest, i.e. increasing grievances will raise other incentives to protest such as social sanctioning.

Perceived personal influence and group efficacy

We mentioned in the previous chapter that not the actual but the perceived influence is relevant. Olson has assumed that individuals' beliefs match reality. Thus, in a large group personal influence is negligible. Numerous empirical studies show very clearly that even in large groups perceived influence is not negligible and there is variation in influence.[8] People thus overestimate their influence.

As we argued in chapter 3 (section 2), the perception of group success is not supposed to have a direct effect on protest behavior but an indirect one: it has a positive direct impact on perceived influence and on other incentives. We specified in detail the complex relationships between perceived influence, group success, and other variables in the previous chapter that are summarized as a causal diagram in Figure 3.3.

Moral incentives

Many activists feel that they have an obligation to protest, i.e. they have internalized a protest norm.[9] It is important to note that a protest norm – as most norms – is conditional. This is to say, it holds only under certain conditions (Jasso and Opp 1997; Opp, Voss, and Gern 1995). For example, people feel obliged to protest if discontent is high or if there is some chance of success. People may think it is justified not to protest if severe repression is likely.

If these conditions are present then the respective protest norm is activated. Thus, the norm does not emerge, it is activated or applied.

Social incentives and protest promoting network integration

One of the most widely accepted hypotheses with ample empirical support is that integration into social networks encouraging protest is an important cause for engaging in protest behavior.[10] "Encouragement" of protest means that social rewards for protest behavior is provided to a large extent. An indicator for such social incentives is membership in certain kinds of social networks. These are groups (such as citizen initiatives or social movements) but also personal networks such as friends, family, or acquaintances.

It is important to note that not every network promotes protest. For example, membership in a golf club will hardly influence protest behavior – unless there is a government decision to close down the club. Only those networks matter where protest behavior is valued positively or positively sanctioned.

Identity

Most social movement scholars argue that "identity" does not fit into a micro model that is based on the theory of rational action. However, an analysis of the various definitions of "identity" shows that at least some definitions of this term refer to selective incentives. This holds for "identification" with a group: if somebody is strongly attached to a group this means that she or he is interested in the welfare of the group. That is to say, for those identifying with a group it is rewarding when he or she acts in the interest of the group, and it is costly if he or she does not. We will further discuss identity as a determinant of protest behavior in chapter 7.

Situational incentives

It may happen that incentives emerge during a protest event like a demonstration. For example, during the Monday demonstrations in Leipzig in October 1989 participants prevented other demonstrators from taking violent action against the security forces. These are, thus, negative sanctions of certain behaviors during a protest event. We further saw when we described Linares's case study that social incentives originated during the meetings of the residents.

Such situational incentives help to explain the form and development of protests. For example, depending on the composition of the group at an event, violence may emerge or a demonstration may remain peaceful. But the incentives may also be relevant as a motivation to participate in the next event: people may expect that the next demonstration is a "social event" as well. It may be doubted, however, that many participants are just interested in the social event. It seems more plausible that situational incentives are secondary incentives that just occur as a by-product of a protest event, but that they are not the major conditions for participating.

Costs: time and resources

The costs Olson refers to are time and resources required to produce a public good. These are opportunity costs, i.e. utility forgone. It is plausible that these variables play a role in explaining social movement activities as well. It is often hypothesized that for self-employed persons and for parents with many children, the costs of participating in protest activities are relatively high. However, it is not always the case that self-employed persons and parents protest less frequently. It seems, thus, that opportunity costs are often not the decisive incentives. It is unfortunate that opportunity costs are usually not measured directly. One could ask respondents in a survey, for example, what activities they would give up if they decided to participate in a demonstration during the coming week. The next question then could be how valuable these activities are. The prediction would be that those with the most valuable alternatives protest least frequently. Another possibility is to present the respondents with items like "I don't have time to protest" or "I am so busy that I had problems in finding the time to demonstrate." We have included such items in some of our own studies (available only in German) but have not found any effects. A possible explanation is that the protest activities are most of the time not very time consuming so that opportunity costs are largely irrelevant.

It is not implausible that costs matter only when they exceed a certain threshold. For example, for a student who expects that he or she might not pass an oral exam next day when he or she participates in a demonstration instead of learning for the exam, the costs will be so high that he or she will defect. But a single mother with three children might take the children to the demonstration, or a self-employed person might participate in protest action when he or she takes a break anyway.

The interdependence of incentives

In most micro models about protest in the literature the incentives are considered independent of each other. This seems to be a questionable assumption. As chapter 3, section 2, and in particular Figure 3.3, suggest, there are causal interdependencies between various incentives. Although there is some empirical evidence for this claim, research has been rare that tests hypotheses about causal interrelationships between incentives.

Other incentives

Depending on the situation and, thus, on the form of protest that is to be explained other incentives may be relevant. It seems that material incentives are in general not important if protest behavior is to be explained. But there are exceptions: in the case study presented above, those who are employed at the mining company would lose their jobs if the protesters had been successful. In general, this may be an incentive not to participate in protest behavior (although, as we saw above, it has probably not been important in Llano del Beal). Further, some of the "solidary incentives" mentioned by Clark and Wilson (1961: 134–135) may sometimes determine protest. Examples are "status resulting from membership, fun and conviviality, the maintenance of social distinctions." We believe, however, that the kinds of incentives mentioned above are the most important ones that affect protest behavior.

Indirect indicators for incentives

Researchers often do not measure incentives directly but use proxies. Demographic variables are popular indirect measures. For example, Schussman and Soule (2005) measure "biographical availability" by "the respondent's age, education, marital status, presence of children, family income, student status and employment status" (1088; similarly Beyerlein and Hipp 2006). A problem with such indicators is that they measure a vast number of different phenomena. Take the example mentioned above: a plausible assumption is that the opportunity costs are high for single mothers with, say, three children. But they might decide to take the children to the demonstration. So there might be no or very low opportunity costs. Thus, "marital status" is not or often not related to costs of participation. The problem of using indirect indicators becomes also apparent if one does not find the expected relationship between the respective indicator and the dependent variable. For example, assume we do not find that marital status which is used as an indicator for costs has any effect on protest participation. Does this imply that the respective proposition to be tested (opportunity costs have a negative effect on protest behavior) is falsified? It would be very bold to draw this conclusion because the indicator may be invalid. Most researchers are inclined to argue that perhaps the indicator was not good enough. Indeed, this is plausible. But if this is granted the question arises as to why one uses such indicators at all. It sometimes seems that one simply tries them out: if the indicator works, the respective proposition is regarded as confirmed. If the indicator does not have the expected effect, one blames the indicator. However, if one does not like the proposition to be tested, one considers it falsified.

To conclude, it seems very problematic to use demographic variables as proxies. They are useful as control variables: relationships between theoretical variables (like the incentives) should remain stable if demographic variables are included as control variables. It may be of further interest to explain relationships between demographic variables and protest. For example, when we find that social class correlates positively with protest our micro model should allow for an explanation of this finding.

Similar micro models

There are micro models in the literature which use a different terminology, but a closer look at the meaning of the variables indicates that in fact they are similar to or even identical with the variables of the micro model suggested in the previous section. But there are also alleged determinants of protest that differ from the variables of the micro model suggested before. In this and the following section, we will look at some alternative micro models suggested in the literature and compare them with the micro model of this and the previous chapter.

Cost, risk, biographical, and structural availability

McAdam (1986; see also Wiltfang and McAdam 1991) addresses the question "why does one individual get involved while another remains inactive?" (64 – this and all subsequent numbers in this section refer to this article). He distinguishes between low-risk/low-cost activism on the one hand and high-risk/high-cost activism on the other (67). "Cost" refers to "the expenditures of time, money, and energy that are required of a person engaged in any particular form of activism" (67). These are opportunity costs, as defined above. The term "risk" is defined as "the anticipated dangers – whether legal, social, physical, financial and so forth – engaging in a particular type of activity" (67). In terms of the micro model specified above, "risk" refers to all kinds of behavioral consequences that an individual expects to some extent and that he or she values negatively (i.e. have a negative utility). "Risk" thus includes state repression and negative informal sanctions. So far, McAdam's model squares with the previous micro model.

Then McAdam introduces "attitudes" prior to activism that "virtually preclude a segment of the population from participating in even the safest forms of activism" (68). It seems that "attitudinal availability" refers to the acceptance of the goals of a movement (or other groups) which organizes protest events (68). McAdam thus seems to refer to the preferences for the public good. In other words, when individuals do not share these preferences, they are not available for a movement. Our "translation" would again make McAdam's model consistent with the previous micro model. In terms of this model, the question would be whether other incentives could not offset a lack of interest in the public good. This question is not addressed by McAdam.

But he mentions one finding from several studies that "prior contact with a recruiting agent" (68) is important for movement participation. Does this only hold when there is some "attitudinal availability"? If the answer is yes, there would be an interaction effect. Another question is how the variable "prior contact with a recruiting agent" fits in our previous micro model. McAdam answers this question by arguing: "The explanatory power of this factor derives, I suspect, from the significant social costs of non-participation that such contact introduces into the calculations of potential recruits" (68). The explanatory variable thus is "expected negative sanctions" which is part of "social incentives" of the previous micro model.

It is further in line with our previous micro model when McAdam assumes that individuals weigh the costs and benefits before they participate: "the potential recruit is likely to weigh the risk of disappointing or losing the respect of his friends against the personal risk of participation" (68). To be sure, the wide version of rational choice theory which is applied in this book does not require that persons calculate. It only requires that individual behavior is governed by costs and benefits. Whether people calculate can be explained by the theory because "calculation" is a kind of behavior. In general, individuals will calculate when much is at stake if a wrong decision is made. But McAdam may be interpreted as claiming that in general the costs and benefits are relevant for movement participation.

So far, McAdam addresses low-cost and low-risk activity. His assumption is that this kind of activism is the route to high-cost and high-risk activism. But not all who engage in the first will proceed to the second. One condition for getting through the first stage is "biographical availability" (70; see also Schussman and Soule 2005; Beyerlein and Hipp 2006). This factor is defined as "the absence of personal constraints that may increase the costs and risks of movement participation such as full-time employment, marriage, and family responsibilities" (70). It seems that this is identical with the costs (or opportunity costs) mentioned before. But mentioning "family responsibilities" suggests that more is implied. This could be negative sanctions coming from family members when one participates in high-cost and high-risk activities; and perhaps it refers to internalized norms to bear the "responsibilities" as a member of a family. Thus, "biographical availability" is consistent with the previous micro model, but it is not entirely clear what exactly the costs and benefits are that are at stake and that this concept refers to.

Another variable used is "structural availability" (see again McAdam 1986: 65; see also Schussman and Soule 2005: 1086) referring to the "presence of interpersonal networks which facilitate recruitment to activism" (Schussman and Soule 2005: 1086). Obviously, these are rewards or costs of participation obtained from members of certain groups. This variable is included in the above model as "social incentives."

This discussion of McAdam's model shows that the author uses terms that at first sight seem to refer to variables not consistent with a wide rational choice model. On closer analysis, however, it is clear that McAdam implicitly applies a wide version of rational choice theory. It remains an open question why this theory is not applied explicitly (there is no reference to the literature on rational choice and collective action). It is further not clear, why McAdam does not systematically discuss the whole array of possible costs and benefits that could explain high-risk and high-cost activism. In this context, the important point is that McAdam actually proposes a micro model of protest behavior that is clearly based on a wide rational choice approach and that is perfectly compatible with our own micro model. In contrast to the previous model, however, McAdam uses broad classes of incentives, and it is not clear what exactly these incentives are. Thus, instead of using variables like "biographical availability" it is preferable to decompose these factors into specific incentives. This would also solve the problematic measurements which use demographic variables like Schussman and Sole (2005) or Beyerlein and Hipp (2006).

Value expectancy models

Value expectancy theory has been introduced to the sociology of social movements by Klandermans's attempt to provide a "Social Psychological Expansions of Resource Mobilization Theory" – which is the subtitle of his article (1984).[11] In this section, we will discuss the author's application of the theory. We will address his claim to "expand resource mobilization theory" in the next chapter.

It is first important to note that value expectancy theory (VET) is a version of rational choice theory (see chapter 1, section 1), as Klandermans also correctly notes: "value expectancy theory is a rational-choice theory" (584 – page numbers in this section refer to Klandermans's article). When we compare his application with our previous micro model, the different terminology suggests that it is not consistent with our model. However, when we analyze the meaning of the variables of Klandermans's and our own model, we find that both models are largely equivalent, but there are also differences. Let us look at the details of Klandermans's model.

The dependent variable in Klandermans's model is *"willingness to participate"* referring to whether individuals think they will participate in political action in the future (590). It is not explained why the dependent variable is not actual behavior. An argument for this choice might be that individuals often make correct predictions about their future behavior so that "willingness" is a proxy for actual behavior. If this is the assumption it would be desirable to test it, i.e. to measure actual behavior as well.

As independent variables Klandermans distinguishes between a collective motive, a social motive, and a reward motive. These variables are very similar to some of the variables of our micro model. The *collective motive* describes the value of the public good to an individual. This is, in terms of the above model, public goods preference or discontent. It is also consistent with the previous model, that this variable has no additive, but a multiplicative effect: whether the public goods motive affects participation depends on the extent to which an individual expects his or her participation to make a difference. Klandermans distinguishes three expectations: (a) the expectation that the individual's participation is successful; (b) the expectation that joint action is successful; and (c) the expected number of participants.

These variables differ from those in the previous model in the following respects. Variable (a) is identical with our variable "perceived personal political influence." In our model only this variable has a direct effect on protest behavior. Variable (b) is our variable "group success." We argued that this variable has only an indirect effect on the dependent variable – via perceived personal influence (see chapter 3, section 2, subsection "The micro model revisited"). Variable (c) – the expected number of participants – has no direct effect on protest in our previous model either (see again our discussion in chapter 3, section 2).

Klandermans's model further includes *social motives* which refer to social incentives in the previous model. *Reward motives* are, in terms of the previous model, material incentives.

Thus, the model of Klandermans and our own model only differ in regard to the expectation components. As was said earlier, further research is needed to test these alternative propositions.

The micro model in previous research

It is important to note that the variables of the previous micro model have been widely used by scholars who are not committed to the theory of collective action. Various forms of public goods preferences (i.e. discontent) are included in most explanations of political protest, although it is still debated under what conditions discontent matters. "Perceived influence" or "efficacy" have been a standard variable in political action research since the famous study of Campbell, Gurin, and Miller (1954). Moral incentives are included in various studies as well. For example, Verba, Schlozman, and Brady (1995: 117–120) examine the effects of "civic gratifications" on political action. This variable refers to moral incentives. The importance of integration into social networks (i.e. social incentives) has already been a central variable in explaining mass movements in the work of William Kornhauser (1959; for a critique, see, e.g., Oberschall 1973: 102–145). In this work, the variables have been used as *ad hoc* hypotheses, i.e. not integrated in a theory.

Alternative micro models

Many other factors are used in the literature to explain protest behavior.[12] How are these factors related to the factors of the previous micro model? There are several possibilities. One is that the factors actually are the same as in our micro model, but that different terms are used by the respective authors. Thus, an analysis of the meaning of the factors would indicate that they refer to incentives. For example, we will see later (chapter 8) that frames in the sense of "schemata of interpretation" (Snow *et al*. 1986: 464) refer to beliefs. Lofland (1996: 250) notes that "perceived influence" is such a belief. Thus, at least some frames refer to incentive variables. We will see later that "collective identity" is an incentive as well (see chapter 7): the concept mostly refers to social relationships such as group membership and group identification (Gould 1995: 13–23). The latter can be expressed by an "individual announcement of affiliation," such as "I am a member of Solidarity" (Friedman and McAdam 1992: 157). In this sense, "collective identity" is close to "social incentives." Friedman and McAdam even argue that "collective identities function as selective incentives motivating participation" (1992: 157). Thus, it seems that many factors are at first sight different from the incentives; but a closer analysis of their meaning reveals that they are incentives. Another example is "post materialist value orientations" that is supposed to affect political participation (Barnes *et al*. 1979; Inglehart 1979). This variable refers to public goods preferences (Opp 1990).

But there are factors that are not incentives. This holds for "prior contact with a member of a movement" which was already mentioned before (McAdam 1986; Snow, Zurcher, and Ekland-Olson 1980). McAdam describes how this variable is related to incentives: "The explanatory power of this factor derives, I suspect, from the significant social costs of non-participation that such contact introduces into the calculations of potential recruits" (McAdam 1986: 68). The relevant variable is thus costs of non-participation (or rewards for participation). McAdam argues that contact with a member of a movement increases these costs. Thus, factors may not be part of our micro model but may be *empirically related to incentives*. Statistically this means that if these factors and the respective incentive variables are included in a regression (or, in general, in a multivariate) analysis, only the incentives should have effects.

But it may also hold that a factor that is not an incentive has a separate causal effect. This means that the incentive model is falsified. That is, not only incentives but other factors as well have an impact on protest behavior. If that is the case, the theory that underlies the previous micro model is falsified and has to be modified or replaced by a superior theory.

What is to be explained? The "repertoire of contention"

The dependent variable of the theory of collective action is "collective action." The form of action depends on the kinds of incentives. For example, if persons believe that legal political action is more efficacious than violent action, if individuals expect strong negative sanctions if they engage in violence, and if they have internalized strong norms that forbid participating in violent action, it is likely that legal forms of action are chosen.

Often incentives are not that specific that they refer to exactly one form of behavior such as participating in a demonstration and nothing else. Often incentives refer to classes of political action. For example, important others may reward some form of political action like demonstrating, working in a protest group or signing a petition. There will be neither rewards nor even negative sanctioning for violent forms of action. Then there will be specific incentives that determine which specific action is chosen. For example, if there is a protest group in the neighborhood, a person may discuss this with his or her friends and incentives emerge in the interaction situation. The outcome of the discussion may be that the local protest group consists of "extreme" political activists and should not be joined. There are thus negative incentives to join the group or participate in activities organized by the local protest group. Instead, the group agrees that they will join a demonstration that is announced but is not organized by the local protest group.

The latter example suggests that one condition for the choice of an action is what behavioral alternatives are perceived. This is a major condition value expectancy theory states (see chapter 1): only those actions are performed that are included in the perceived behavioral alternatives of an individual. If we do not simply want to regard these behavioral alternatives as given, several interesting questions arise.

One is what the actual behavioral alternatives are in a given society and in a given period that are typically perceived by individuals if they are politically dissatisfied and want to effect social change. This is a descriptive question. If it is clear from what behavioral alternatives people can choose, the next step is to specify the incentives for the choice.

Another interesting descriptive question is whether the repertoires of contention are rather constant or subject to change over time. For example, did the activists of the civil rights movement dispose of the same repertoire of contention as the peace activists in the twentieth century? It is clear that there are differences. Sit-ins, boycotts, occupation of buildings, street blockades, silent protest marches, or hunger strikes were not available at all times. What repertoires of contention are given in which historical periods?

There are two explanatory questions. First, how can this changing stock of a repertoires of contention in a society at a given period be explained? Second, which of the actual available behaviors are perceived by a group in a given situation?

It is not possible to explore these questions in detail in this book. This would require another chapter. The important question at this point is to what extent changing repertoires of contention and the perception of these repertoires can be explained by rational choice theory or the theory of collective action. Little work has been done to answer this question. A repository of historical data and explanatory hypotheses is the work of Tilly (see in particular 1978: chapter 5; 1979). It would be interesting to discuss and extend Tilly's hypotheses from the perspective of a general theory of action.

Are protesters "rational"? The meaning of "rationality"

So far the term "rationality" has neither been used nor defined. The reason is that it is not needed. The theories that have been presented include all what is necessary to explain protest-related phenomena. The term "rationality" is not only not needed, it is harmful because it is the trigger of numerous misunderstandings and uninformed objections to the theory of rational action. It is one of those concepts that have dozens of different meanings. In criticizing versions of the theory of rational action the critic selects some meaning of this term and then criticizes the theory because people are not "rational" in this sense, whereas the theory claims that human beings act "rational." In general, the critic is often right with the assertion that people are not "rationally" in a certain sense. But the problem is that this does not in any way falsify the theory of rational action. For example, Jasper (1997: 23) asserts that for M. Olson "rationality ... consisted of calculation" and then assumes that this is how "rationality" is used in the theory of rational action. However, as was said already in chapter 3, this is plainly wrong. Proponents of the theory only assume that individual behavior is governed by costs and benefits. "Calculation" is a behavioral choice that depends on costs and benefits. For example, if much is at stake people calculate but when they buy a yoghurt, calculation does not occur. Thus, in this sense rational choice theory does not assume "rationality." Again, the theory only assumes that behavior depends on costs and benefits. This could be called "rational" behavior. In this sense, then, the theory actually claims that individuals act "rationally," but only in this sense. As long as the theory is correct, every human being acts "rationally" in this sense. This holds for protesters as well as for non-protesters.

The suggestion for critics of rational choice theory is to look at its substantive propositions. If the critic maintains that people don't act "rationally" and, accordingly, the theory is wrong, the question should always be how the term "rational" is used by the critic. Only then it can be judged whether "rational" behavior is implied by the theory of rational action or not.

5. Guidelines for explaining macro events and macro relationships: the two-step procedure

Applying the theory of collective action to explain protest behavior implies adopting a micro-macro perspective. This has been discussed in chapter 1 (see the illustration in Figure 1.1) and in chapter 3 where Olson's implicit micro-macro model has been reconstructed. In this section, we will provide some more specific suggestions about how to proceed when a macro event, i.e. collective protest, or a macro relationship is to be explained.

The basic explanatory component for explaining protests is always the change of incentives. In order to predict or explain protest episodes or their absence it is of utmost importance to analyze the incentive structure in the social situation where protest takes place. Are there groups that provide different incentives such as social movements or other organizations? What about the distribution of incentives in the population? What exactly were the incentives that led to protests? Maybe there are comparable situations – such as nuclear power plants in France and Germany – but only in one situation are there extensive protests. What are the different incentives in these situations? Assume, protests increase and then decline. The explanation should look at the change of incentives because they – and not the macro events – are the proximate causes of any collective action. Thus, explaining changing protests requires looking at changing incentives.

But this is not satisfactory. Assume that we know that in the period of May to October 1989 in East Germany various incentives that are included in our micro model increased so that protests were expected to increase as well. Assume that this explanation is correct. Nonetheless, we will not be satisfied with it. We want to know *why* the incentives have changed. This is the second step in the explanation of collective political action, namely explaining the change of incentives. In general, the explanatory burden of the explanation of incentives is on macro events. For example, the changing incentives in Leipzig in the fall of 1989 were brought about by various decisions of the government.

Many – perhaps most – protest episodes begin with a clearly identifiable event that changes individual incentives to protest. Examples abound: it may be a catastrophe like a nuclear accident, a planned war like the Iraq war, a new law like a change in the abortion or immigration law, a decision or action of a government or organization such as the plan to build a new highway. Such critical events have also influenced the origins of the East European protests that have been often used as illustrations in this book, and the case study of Llano del Beal that was presented above. Critical events may also be the protest of a group which is a "critical mass" and causes a "positive feedback" (see Biggs 2003 with further references).

But there are more subtle social changes that bring about protest events. A type of situation that is well documented in the literature is increasing relative deprivation (see, e.g., Davies 1969). The well-being of a group may grow slowly over time, but then the development suddenly stops. Expectations that the standard of living further rises become disappointed and discontent increases. If other incentives are strong enough this slowly emerging deprivation may be the catalyst for collective protest. Another example: scientific evidence accumulates showing that certain human behaviors like smoking and CO_2 emission are hazardous to health. Again, discontent increases and, as a consequence, a demand for change originates that may be a trigger for various protest events.

Furthermore, general changes of preferences, values, or norms may contribute to protests. For example, an increasing preference for equality may trigger protests by women for equal rights. Changes of general preferences, values or norms may be adopted by powerful actors and serve as justifications for various forms of collective action. For example, if the public view is no longer in favor of nuclear power stations, this view will be increasingly spread among the members of social movements, unions and other organizations. The expectations of political entrepreneurs such as movement activists to mobilize a sizable part of the population may increase and lead to mobilization attempts and, finally, to large-scale protests.

Whether the critical events are spectacular incidences or slowly emergent social changes, they are macro phenomena. But they are only one component of the whole process of emerging collective action. Their effects depend on how these changes impinge on individual incentives to collective political action. Even if such events are triggers of protest, this is only possible if other incentives are relatively strong. As we saw before, just an increase of deprivation is not enough to bring about collective action. As we will see, for example in the chapter on political opportunities (chapter 6), the argument that political opportunity structures bring about protest is at least incomplete: only if changing opportunities and other conditions, namely a favorable incentive structure, are present collective action will ensue.

Often there is not one protest event but there are successive protest episodes. Examples are the Monday demonstrations in Leipzig and other East European cities or a whole series of demonstrations against the Iraq war. Our case study of Llano del Beal also illustrates that protests are often not isolated incidences. The basic procedure in explaining series of protests actually is a *sequential application of the basic model*. Let us illustrate this with the upper part A of Figure 4.2 which shows the most elementary model. The first step is always to look at the changing incentives. The second step then is to identify the macro events that have changed the incentives. Now assume that such a macro event triggered a protest action – via a change of incentives. Will this be only a single protest? Assume that the event is a new immigration law that led to large-scale protests shortly after the law has passed. If this critical event does not change, it is likely that the incentives do not change either and continue to trigger protest action. Actually, however, protests will not continue forever in such a situation, even if the critical event remains. One reason might be that the declared willingness of the government not to change the law – which is again an event – diminishes incentives such as perceived influence. There might not be a declaration, but if the government does not cave in, this may be interpreted as a signal that a change of the law and, thus, group success is unlikely. The objective event such as an existing law thus does not change, but accompanying events such as reactions or non-action of a collective actor may have different effects over time.

These examples as well as the upper part A of Figure 4.2 illustrate that an explanation of a protest series requires a repeated application of the same procedure. Repeated protests depend on existing incentives which, in turn, are influenced by macro events. This is then the procedure of explaining dynamic trajectories of protest events or protest cycles (see in particular Tarrow 1998: part III). What the trajectory is depends on the macro changes and the changes of incentives. It is unlikely that there are laws about certain stages (or cycles) of protests (see also chapter 10). These would be macro laws. The reason is that the specific situation (i.e. the incentive structure) and the macro changes are so variable that the effects of given macro changes will be very different. This explains why so far macro laws about "cycles" or trajectories of protest or collective action have not yet been discovered.

However, real protests are more complicated. Part B of Figure 4.2 takes this complexity of protest processes into account. The upper part A of the figure assumed that there are events and that there are protests. In other words, protests cannot be events. However, as the case study and theoretical contributions to critical mass phenomena suggest, events can also be collective protests that change individual incentives which, in turn, may further instigate protests. This is indicated in part B by a line from "protest" to "event." The line symbolizes an analytical relationship, that is individual protests make up collective protest events, i.e. critical events.

So far it was assumed that protest does not have any feedback effects. In other words, protest does not change the incentives on the micro level. As was said in chapter 4, section 2, there are no clear and confirmed hypotheses in the literature. To remedy this situation changes of incentives after individuals have protested were looked at, i.e. without determining whether they were brought about by the respective individual's protest behavior. Nonetheless, arrows from "protest" to "incentives" on the individual level were inserted as a reminder for further research to provide the respective hypotheses.

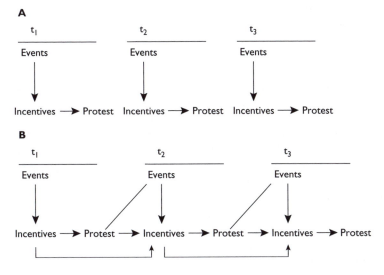

Figure 4.2 Explaining the development of protest over time

Another assumption in model A was that there are no relationships between incentives. This is a simplification because incentives are interdependent. In the course of protest events various conditions will change, which, for example, influence protest norms or sanctioning behavior which will change incentives.

Part B of the figure suggests heuristic guidelines for explaining specific series of protest events. It involves a *two-step procedure*: the starting point and first step of explaining protests and protest processes is always determining changes of incentives. They are the proximate causes of protest behavior. What the incentives are if specific protest events are to be explained must be determined empirically. This first step also involves looking at the dynamics of the incentives due to their interdependence.

This step explains protest, but another step is needed: one will usually not be satisfied with stating that incentives have changed that brought about a certain behavior. One would like to know *why* the incentives changed. This is the second step. The causes for the change of incentives are macro events. They change over time and affect incentives. Explaining a series of protests therefore involves a successive determination of what has changed on the macro level.

So far we have looked at changes in protests over time that were influenced by macro events. Another issue is often to explain *relationships between macro events* where one macro event is collective protest. For example, it might be observed that increased state repression sometimes leads to more and sometimes to less collective protest. There is thus sometimes a positive and sometimes a negative correlation between two macro events. Furthermore, we find an inverted u-curve (with repression as the x-axis and protest as the y-axis). Another example for a relationship to be explained is that between social class and movement participation: mostly educated people are movement participants. Social scientists are not content with just reporting such relationships, they want to explain it. The argument in chapter 1, section 4, was that only a micro-macro explanation is satisfactory. This corresponds to the two-step procedure outlined in this section: one has first to specify the individual incentives that are the proximate conditions for protest behavior; the next step then is to explore in detail under what conditions macro events such as increasing repression or different kinds of repression affect those individual incentives. In this instance, both steps are closely interwoven: when the incentives are specified one will look for those incentives that might be changed by the macro events. Nonetheless, it is important to note that both steps are involved. This is different when changes of protests over time are to be explained. One could first look at the change of incentives and then in a next step at the macro changes that could have caused the change. In this instance, thus, the steps can be nicely separated. Nonetheless, the two steps are always involved.

The two-step procedure emphasizes a particular part of a micro-macro explanation. As we saw in chapter 1, the incentives are a component of a micro model that has to be applied. This is implied in the first step: it is obvious that the incentives whose change is to be ascertained are part of a micro model. The macro-to-micro relationship – from individual to collective protest – is also implied in the two-step procedure since the focus is on collective action. The two-step procedure thus highlights – under a different perspective – micro-macro modeling.

So far we have distinguished two levels of analysis: the micro and macro level. It may be argued that this distinction is too rough. There are many different levels. For example, Gerhards and Rucht (1992: 558) introduce the concept of "mesomobilization actors" which they define as "those groups and organizations that coordinate and integrate micromobilization groups" and not individuals. This is, it might be argued, again a simplification. For example, levels may be: citizen groups, movement organizations, local government, or federal government. The question arises, which levels should be distinguished if a micro-macro analysis is undertaken? Assume that the behavior of individual actors is to be explained. They may be faced with incentives from various collectivities such as social movements, unions, police and state government. Which groups play a role depends on the explanatory problem. Assume that activities of groups are to be explained such as the attempts of a social movement to mobilize union chapters. From the perspective of the theory of collective action, the behavior of members of the union chapters is to be explained. They are faced with incentives of the mobilizing activities of the movement. Thus, actually the micro and macro level is involved. In this case, further organizations may be of interest. For example, an employer organization may try to neutralize the effects of the activities of the movement. From the perspective of the actors whose behavior is to be explained, the employers are another group. The theoretical analysis would treat the employer organization as another group, i.e. macro factor.

Both examples suggest that a priori classifications of levels does not seem useful. Distinctions should be theoretically motivated and depend on the research question. To answer explanatory questions by applying the theory of collective action, the identification of the actors that could drive the process of collective action is important. These actors may belong to different levels which can then be distinguished. But ultimately, the procedure of a micro-macro explanation suggests that a micro level is always the focus of an explanation – see the basic micro-macro scheme in Figure 1.2 of chapter 1; the explanatory burden is then located "above" this level – which consist of several levels.

6. What can we learn from the theory of collective action for the explanation of social movement phenomena?

This and the previous chapter – and to some extent also chapter 1 – have shown that the theory of collective action is not without problems. However, some of its features are worth being taken account of in explanations of social movement phenomena. We will summarize those features in this section. They are all well illustrated by the previous case study.

(1) The most important point is that it is useful to apply a general theory of action. This is at present a wide version of the theory of rational action (including, in particular, value expectancy theory). This theory has sharply to be distinguished

from a narrow version mostly used in neo-classical economics and often in game theory. It is high time that social movement scholars stop mixing up both versions and indulge in the common misunderstandings (see in particular the discussion in chapter 1).

(2) In applying the wide version of the theory of rational action it is important to note the following points: (a) Non-material incentives seem most important to explain protest behavior, but depending on the situation, material incentives may matter as well; (b) incentives have to be empirically ascertained because they vary across situations. It should be obvious that the concrete kinds of incentives that operate in specific situations can never be part of a theory.

(3) A basic feature of the theory of collective action is that it is made up, among other things, of an explicitly stated micro model. This has to be adapted to the specific kinds of collective action (like protest). For example, the general model includes a norm of cooperation. This is a norm to protest or an accepted justification for violence when protest behavior or violent political action is to be explained.

(4) The micro model that is a component of the theory of collective action is based on the general theory of action that is applied in this book.

(5) Another basic feature of the theory of collective action is that it is made up of a systematic and explicit micro-macro explanation. This distinguishes it from all other approaches, and this is, as will also be seen in later chapters, the basic strength of the theory.

(6) Micro-macro explanations involve a two-step procedure. One step of explaining protest is to look at the change of incentives, the other is to explain those changes of incentives. They are triggered by macro events.

(7) Social movement scholars often seem to think that the theory of collective action requires quantitative analyses and the application of mathematics. This belief is simply wrong. The case study discussed at length in this chapter is a qualitative study. Although the author applies game theory, the basic study uses informal reasoning. This openness to quite different methods does by no means imply that the widespread ambiguity in regard to concept and theory formation in the social movement literature is accepted. Most proponents of the theory of collective action prefer rigorous theorizing.

As a conclusion, the previous points indicate that an explanation that applies the theory of collective action is much more detailed than explanations by other approaches: it looks at the individuals and at structures and dissects the interplay between these different levels.

7. Summary and conclusions

Whereas chapter 3 provided an outline and discussion of the theory of collective action, the present chapter applies this theory to collective *political* action, i.e. to the explanation of protest behavior. This requires a detailed discussion because protest differs from collective action in general: a major difference is that the protesters usually do not provide the public good by themselves. Instead, they put pressure on third parties to provide the good. Thus, in order to explain public goods provision, the behavior of third parties has to be explained.

The best way to learn how the theory of collective action can be applied to explain protest is to analyze a specific case: we looked at the mobilization and various activities (including protests) of the inhabitants of a Spanish mining village where a new open mining pit was planned (Linares 2004). The case study illustrates how existing incentive structures (i.e. a distribution of incentives) and certain macro events are a fertile ground for a very successful mobilization process of almost the whole population: there is an organization, namely the Residents' Association, and a relatively dense network of the inhabitants. This makes communication, mutual encouragement, and sanctioning easy. Incentives further include a high level of dissatisfaction and strong social incentives. The event that precipitates almost complete mobilization of the residents was an assembly where it became known that the plan to build the pit would lead to strong grievances such as the demolishing of houses, noise and constant dust, i.e. "a living hell of 24 hours a day," as one of the residents put it. This event has changed various incentives that brought about legal as well as illegal action of different sorts by the residents for three and a half years. It is shown how different aspects of this process can be explained by the theory of collective action. One specific feature of the explanation is that it is an incentive-driven approach that explores in detail how macro changes bring about micro changes and how these, in turn, change macro events.

The theory of collective action is controversial in the social movements literature. After the case study we discussed some arguments that purport to show that the theory is not useful to explain protest behavior: we refer to Fireman and Gamson's (1979) attack. We tried to show that their arguments are mistaken.

A major feature of the theory of collective action is its micro-macro orientation. This implies that a micro model, i.e. a theory about the conditions of individual protest participation, plays a major role. Such a theory was outlined in the previous chapter and is extended for protest behavior in this chapter. We further discuss similar and alternative micro models suggested in the literature. This discussion indicates that there are more common features between the different models than might be expected.

The case study shows that the explanation moves back and forth between the micro and macro level. Based on this study and on other previous discussions we provide some guidelines suggesting how to proceed in micro-macro explanations. The basic procedure in explaining successive protest events is first to look at the change of the incentives of the actors. The next step then consists of looking at the macro events that changed the incentives. These macro events may also be collective protests. This procedure is repeatedly applied when series of protests are explained.

Finally, it is discussed what can be learnt in general from the theory of collective action when protest is to be explained. One of the conclusions is that an explanation that applies the theory of collective action is much more detailed than explanations of other approaches: it looks at the individuals and at structures and dissects the interplay between these different levels.

There is one explanatory problem that has largely been neglected so far in this book and that will not be addressed in detail in the following chapters: the formation of groups, including social movements. We will return to this issue in the final chapter 12 (see the section "What is to be explained?").

5   The resource mobilization perspective

The oldest genuine sociological approach to social movements and political protest that is still widely applied is the resource mobilization perspective – sometimes called "solidarity theory" or "resource management approach." We prefer the term "resource mobilization perspective" (RMP). The basic article is "Resource Mobilization and Social Movements" by John D. McCarthy and Mayer N. Zald from 1977. We will first present their theoretical perspective and show the implicit causal structure of their propositions. We further propose a causal model, based on the authors' orienting statements. Other topics of this chapter are a suggestion for a definition of "resources" and "mobilization," a detailed critical analysis of the approach, and some theoretical suggestions on the conditions when resources are mobilized and when resources affect political action.[1]

1. Resources, grievances, and strategic actors: J. D. McCarthy and M. N. Zald's theory

The main target of the authors is the deprivation and relative deprivation approach advanced by authors such as Gurr (1970), Turner and Killian (1972), and Smelser (1963). One of the major assumptions of this work is that variables like discontent, generalized beliefs, or ideological justifications give rise to protest behavior. Another assumption is that structural conditions influence discontent. McCarthy and Zald list several studies that cast doubt on the validity of these assumptions. The authors suggest a new approach in which movements are regarded as political actors who have goals which they try to achieve by using unconventional means.

The authors call their approach a *"partial theory"* (1213, 1237 – numbers in parenthesis refer to pages of McCarthy and Zald's article). This means that certain conditions are regarded as given. For example, the theory is based upon the American case and uses case material of the left, and, thus, ignores organizations of the right. It is not explored in detail what exactly this means for the validity of the propositions. Do the propositions not hold true for organizations of the right or are organizations of the left only illustrative cases for the theory, so that using case material of the left does not affect the validity of the theory? Furthermore, in the formulation of their specific hypotheses (1224–1236) the authors repeatedly point out that other conditions are relevant (see, e.g., their comments on hypothesis 1 on

p. 1225). But what exactly the effects of these additional variables are is not clear. Does it mean, for example, that the propositions are wrong if other conditions obtain? Or does it mean that the other conditions are additive variables that explain a greater variance?

In a review of their approach, the authors state that the theory holds under certain *scope conditions* (Zald and McCarthy 2002: 150–151). In short, the setting where the hypotheses are supposed to hold is a free society where voluntary associations can be founded, where freedom of speech is accepted, where mass media may report protests and grievances, and where small groups cannot gain legislative office. Perhaps this is what "partial theory" means: the theory is "partial" in the sense that it holds only under certain conditions. We will discuss these scope conditions later in this chapter.

The subject of the theory

The focus of the authors' article is "the dynamics and tactics of social movement growth, decline, and change" (1213). In addition, the authors are concerned with the "success" of a movement (1213, 1216). The units of analysis are thus social movements and other collective actors and not individual actors.[2]

Taken literally, explaining the "growth" of a movement means that a movement already exists. But when one looks at existing research and reviews of the approach, the *emergence* of movements is clearly supposed to be the subject of the perspective as well. This is also the subject of the specific propositions to be discussed below. Perhaps "growth" of a movement also implies that a movement comes into existence, i.e. "grows" from non-existence to existence.

It is important to note that neither *protest behavior* nor the *mobilization of resources* is mentioned as the subject of the theory. Initiating protests and mobilizing resources would count as tactics of a social movement.

The orienting propositions

Before the authors suggest a detailed causal model they list some variables that they think are important to explain social movement phenomena. What exactly these variables explain is not clear. The authors' propositions are thus orienting statements and not full-fledged theoretical propositions. The perspective "emphasizes" (1213) the relevance of the following factors (1213, 1216, 1222, 1236):

1 social support and constraint of social movement phenomena (1213);
2 existing variety of resources that must be mobilized (1213);
3 linkages of social movements to other groups (1213);
4 external support as a condition for the success of a movement (1213);
5 tactics used by authorities to control or incorporate movements (1213);
6 the aggregation of resources such a money, labor and facilities "is crucial to an understanding of social movement activity" (1216);
7 some minimal form of organization (1216);

8   involvement of individuals and organizations from outside is of "crucial importance" for "a movement's successes and failures" (1216);
9   infrastructure such as communication media and expense, levels of affluence, degree of access to institutional centers, pre-existing networks, and occupational structure and growth (1217, 1225);
10   exercise of social control or repression of authorities (1222, 1225);
11   entrepreneurial attempts to meet preference demand (1236);
12   political freedom (1225).

What are the dependent variables? It is not clear what exactly the effects of the variables listed above are. For example, what is the impact of "social support and constraint of social movement phenomena" (no. 1 in the list)? Will we expect that high social support in a population and small constraints have a positive effect on the *growth* or the *success* or the *stability* of a movement or on all three? No. 6 states that the aggregation of resources such as money, labor and facilities "is crucial to an understanding of social movement activity." The variable to be explained here is not growth, success, or stability of a movement but what the movement or its activists do; but the kind of activity is left open. This is a clear orienting statement: it is only said that a variable has some effect on movement actions, but the reader is not told what exactly the effect is.

Can these factors explain the *emergence* of a new movement? Some of the variables presuppose that a movement exists already. This holds, for example, for no. 4 in the list: "external support as a condition for the success of a movement" implies that there is already a movement. Factors 9 to 11 could refer to a situation where movements do not yet exist and where the emergence of a movement is likely.

The authors further describe the "strategic tasks" of social movements: these are "mobilizing supporters, neutralizing and/or transforming mass and elite publics into sympathizers, achieving change in targets" (1217). This seems to suggest that if these tasks are fulfilled movements will grow and succeed. Again, these are orienting hypotheses which are – at least in part – included in the previous list.

The authors refer several times to costs and rewards that are important for individual behavior. They also mention Olson's theory. But they never show how exactly a cost-benefit approach fits into their macro propositions. We will return to this question later on when we discuss the RMP.

The role of grievances

The authors argue that there is "ambiguous evidence" (1215) for the assumption that deprivation (i.e. grievances) and relative deprivation are key variables for the explanation of protest behavior and social movements. The conclusion from this research is not, as one would suspect, that deprivation is no longer considered to be an explanatory variable. Instead, the authors "want to move from a strong assumption about the centrality of deprivation and grievances to a weak one, which makes them a component, indeed, sometimes a secondary component in the generation of social movements" (1215).

What exactly could it mean to "lessen the prevailing emphasis on grievances" (1215)? Assume that the "old" theory asserts that deprivations are a cause for protest and that the size of their effect is b_1:

$$Old\ theory\ T_1\!: Protest_1 = a_1 + b_1\ Deprivation + b_2\ OtherFactors$$

Thus, if deprivation increases by one unit then protest rises by b_1 units – if other factors remain constant. If it is claimed that a new theory "emphasizes" the effects of a factor less than older theories, this could mean that b_1 in the older theory is larger than the respective coefficient in the new theory. If this coefficient is b'_1, the new theory would state:

$$New\ theory\ T_2\!: Protest_1' = a'_1 + b'_1\ Deprivation + b'_2\ OtherFactors$$
$$b_1 > b'_1.$$

Since it is left open what exactly the value of b_1 in the "old" theory is, it is also not clear whether any coefficient we estimate is larger or smaller than that in the "old" theory. Or perhaps it is meant that the (standardized) coefficients of other variables are larger than the coefficient of deprivation?

The authors' proposition about the role of grievances can be interpreted differently. In an earlier paper the authors argue that the RMP "does not necessarily deny the existence of grievances. It stresses the structural conditions that facilitate the expression of grievances" (McCarthy and Zald 1973: 1). Similarly, in an article where the authors review their approach they assert that "groups with few resources are less able to act on grievances or perceived injustices" (Zald and McCarthy 2002: 149). This means that grievances don't have additive but *interaction effects*. In other words, the effects of grievances depend on the values of other factors. These factors could be facilitating structural conditions or resources groups dispose of. Which "structural factors" are interacting with grievances is not specified.

The authors further argue that grievances are not given. Instead, "grievances and discontent may be defined, created and manipulated by issue entrepreneurs and organizations" (1215). This argument does not speak against the importance of grievances as an explanatory variable for social movement activities. The argument is an empirical proposition about the causes of grievances, but it does not imply anything about grievances as a cause of protest. Even if political entrepreneurs define or create grievances, they may nonetheless be important factors that instigate protest behavior. Figure 5.1 symbolizes this causal structure: the authors argue that the activities of political entrepreneurs generate grievances; these grievances may, in turn, have a positive effect on protest. Thus, there are two causal

Activities of
political ———→ Grievances ———→ Protest
entrepreneurs

Figure 5.1 The influence of political entrepreneurs on creating grievances

processes: the first is the effect of "activities of entrepreneurs" on "grievances," the second of "grievances" on "protest." Thus, the assumption that political entrepreneurs create grievances is irrelevant for the effect of grievances on protest.

A further argument against using deprivation as a variable is that it is *ubiquitous*. This is a plausible assumption: if a factor is a constant it cannot be used to explain the great variation in protest behavior. But the argument implicitly assumes that the grievance variable is a *dichotomy*: grievances are present or absent. But grievances can be conceived as a *quantitative* variable: they can be more or less intense. Even if grievances are ubiquitous they may differ in intensity. If this is granted, grievances may in principle explain variations in protest behavior, even if *some* grievance is ubiquitous.

The grievance proposition is controversial. Especially in the work of Edward J. Walsh and associates (see, e.g., Walsh 1988) grievances are regarded as important determinants of protest behavior.

It is striking that the authors do not refer to the theory of collective action (see chapters 3 and 4 in this book): grievances are public goods preferences. As such, they interact with perceived influence and have various indirect effects on other incentives. Thus, the role of grievances in this theory is clearly defined.

Conceptual foundations

In the next part the authors introduce several new concepts. Some of them are now widely used. We will briefly report their definitions. A *social movement (SM)* is defined as "a set of opinions and beliefs in a population which represents preferences for changing some elements of the social structure and/or reward distribution of a society" (1217–1218). The authors mean not just any preferences but "mobilized or activated (effective) demand (preferences) for change in society" (Zald and McCarthy 2002: 148). A *"counter movement* is a set of opinions and beliefs in a population opposed to a social movement" (1218).

What is normally called a "social movement" is denoted as a *"social movement organization" (SMO)*. This is "a complex, or formal, organization which identifies its goals with the preferences of a social movement or counter movement and attempts to implement these goals" (1218). A *"social movement industry" (SMI)* consists of all SMOs "that have as their goal the attainment of the broadest preferences of a social movement" (1219). A still more comprehensive group is the *"social movement sector" (SMS)* which "consists of all SMIs in a society no matter to which SM they are attached" (1220).

Next the authors distinguish between types of individuals or groups based on their relationship to SMs or SMOs. *"Adherents"* are individuals or groups who accept the goals of a movement, whereas *"constituents"* are those individuals or groups who provide resources for the SMO. *"Bystander publics"* are "non-adherents who are not opponents of the SM and its SMOs but who merely witness social movement activity" (1221). The term *"opponents"* is not explicitly defined, but apparently refers to individuals or groups who do not accept the goals of a SMO and probably do not contribute resources either.

Three other concepts are defined: *"potential beneficiaries"* are those "who would benefit directly from SMO goal accomplishment" (1221); *"conscience adherents* are individuals and groups who are part of the respective appropriate SM but do not stand to benefit directly from SMO goal accomplishment" (1222). *"Conscience constituents* are direct supporters of a SMO who do not stand to benefit directly from its success in goal accomplishment" (1222).

The "illustrative hypotheses" as a causal model

The next part of the paper consists of eleven explicitly stated hypotheses, i.e. it is clearly stated what the dependent and independent variables are. The authors discuss each hypothesis in detail, but they do not address the relationships between the hypotheses. One question is whether the hypotheses have dependent or independent variables in common. If this is the case, the hypotheses form a complex causal model. Thus, it is not clear what exactly the structure of the variables of the hypotheses is. We clarify this structure by depicting the hypotheses as a causal diagram (see Figure 5.2). The reader may for the time being ignore the two boxes and the dashed arrows.

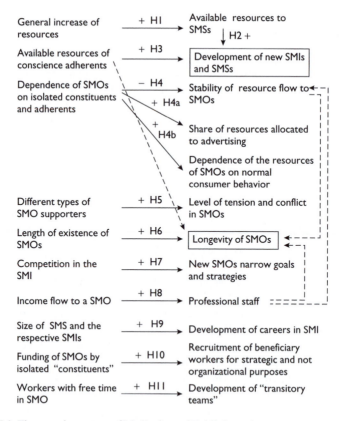

Figure 5.2 The causal structure of McCarthy and Zald's hypotheses

Hypothesis 1 posits that a general increase of discretionary resources, i.e. time and money, in a society will lead to an increase of the resources that are available to the SMS.[3] As for most of their hypotheses, the authors mention other factors that are relevant for the validity of this proposition. For example, the priority of the goals of the population is important: if the priority is to spend the additional resources for the satisfaction of basic needs few resources will go to the SMS.

The next two hypotheses have the same dependent variable: the development of new SMOs and SMIs. *Hypothesis 2* reads: The more resources are available to the SMS, the more new SMIs and SMOs will develop that compete for these resources. *Hypothesis 3* addresses the resources of "conscience adherents": the greater the amount of resources available to them, "the more likely is the development of SMOs and SMIs that respond to preferences for change" (1225). This hypothesis holds regardless of the resources available to those who directly profit if the SMOs reach their goals.

Let us look at the relationships between the variables of hypotheses 1 to 3 in Figure 5.2. We see that the general increase of available resources in a society has only an indirect effect on the development of new SMOs – via "available resources to SMSs." Thus, two variables affect the "development of new SMIs and SMSs." Among the major phenomena to be explained according to the goal of the article – namely the growth, decline, change, and success of social movements – only the growth (or the emergence) of movements is addressed by the eleven propositions. Further, only two variables are specified that directly affect SMO emergence. The box around "development of new SMIs and SMSs" symbolizes that this is one of the central variables the RMP tries to explain.

In their comment on hypothesis 3 the authors mention again Mancur Olson. From the perspective of the theory of collective action, the question arises as to why individuals contribute resources to support a social movement organization. It seems that the conscience adherents' contribution is only attributed to their interest in the public good. Because they are members of a large group the question arises why they contribute and not free ride. Hypothesis 3, thus, "turns Olson on his head" (1226): contrary to Olson, grievances (i.e. public goods preferences) trigger contributions to the public good in large groups. There is no discussion on why Olson should not be left on his feet, i.e. what the evidence or theoretical rationale for McCarthy and Zald's alternative hypothesis is.

The next hypothesis addresses the consequences that occur when different kinds of constituents or adherents contribute resources. Those who contribute can be isolated individual adherents or constituents, but also groups (1229–1230). *Hypothesis 4* reads that the flow of resources will be less stable, if a SMO largely consists of isolated constituents. These are less closely related to the movement, whereas there are closer contacts with non-isolated groups. The consequence is that there is strong competition for the isolated adherents. One will thus expect what *hypothesis 4a* claims: "The more dependent a SMO is upon isolated constituents the greater the share of its resources which will be allocated to advertising" (1230). Furthermore, if a SMO is dependent on isolated adherents, resource flow will resemble normal consumer behavior, i.e. it will change according to tastes, mood, time of the year, etc. (*hypothesis 4b*).

A strategy of SMOs to bind constituents is to set up local chapters. But, as *hypothesis 5* asserts, this leads to high tensions if conscience as well as beneficiary constituents are members. The reason is that conscience constituents are often members of several SMOs and have conflicting loyalties and are fickle (1232) because they have wide-ranging concerns.

Hypothesis 6 addresses the consequences of a larger or smaller resource flow: "Older, established SMOs are more likely than newer SMOs to persist throughout the cycle of SMI growth and decline" (1233). Put differently, the longer a SMO has persisted, the longer will be its expected existence. The authors argue that longevity is positively related to legitimacy. In addition: "Older organizations have available higher degrees of professional sophistication, existing ties to constituents, and experience in fund-raising procedures" (1233). We framed "longevity" in Figure 5.2 because this is a central variable in the explanatory aims of the RMP.

The idea of *hypothesis 7* is that companies differentiate their products if competition gets harder. The same holds for SMOs: "The more competitive a SMI ..., the more likely it is that new SMOs will offer narrow goals and strategies" (1234).

The subject of hypotheses 8 to 11 is the internal organization of SMOs. If the income flow to a SMO is large, the cadre and staff will become professional and these groups will become relatively large. The reason is that organizational problems amount and that these are solved more likely by full time personnel (*hypothesis 8*). *Hypothesis 9* states: The larger the SMSs and SMIs become, the more likely it is that careers will become possible within SMOs. What are the consequences if a SMO is supported by isolated constituents? *Hypothesis 10* asserts that such SMOs recruit beneficiary constituent workers "for strategic purposes rather than for organizational work" (1235). "Beneficiary constituent workers" are persons who provide resources and profit if the movement accomplishes its goals. The hypothesis maintains that these persons are used to wield influence outside the organization. The reason is probably that for those SMOs soliciting outside resources is more important than internal organizational work.

In order for a SMO to thrive it is not only important to recruit supporters with money but also with discretionary time. According to *hypothesis 11*, if SMOs consist of many workers with discretionary time at their disposal, it is likely that transitory teams develop. That is to say, many supporters can be sent to demonstrations and other events, which may recruit new supporters.

Macro and micro versions of the resource mobilization perspective

Perrow (1979; see also Zald and McCarthy 2002) distinguishes Resource Mobilization (RM) I and RM II. It is not clear what exactly the different propositions of the two versions are. One difference is that the early articles of McCarthy and Zald from 1973 and 1977 suggest an "entrepreneurial theory of movement formation in which the major factor is the availability of resources, especially cadres and organizing facilities" (Jenkins 1983: 530). Zald and McCarthy (2002: 158) speak of the "organizational entrepreneurial variant." The other is the "political process or political opportunity" variant. The latter focuses on "political structures, opportunities, and constraints" (Zald and McCarthy 2002: 158–159).

The latter variables are the key explanatory variables of the political opportunity structure perspective that will be presented and discussed in the next chapter 6. It is therefore useful to continue with the RMP as it is presented in the basic paper of the authors and in other work and take up RM II, i.e. the political opportunity structure perspective, in the next chapter.

RM I and RM II are macro versions of the perspective. McCarthy and Zald's article clearly shows this. However, there is a micro version of the RMP as well. Anthony Oberschall, one of the founders of the perspective, suggests: "Participants in popular disturbances and activists in opposition organizations will be recruited primarily from previously active and relatively well-integrated individuals within the collectivity, whereas socially isolated, atomized, and uprooted individuals will be underrepresented, at least until the movement has become substantial" (Oberschall 1973: 135). McAdam, McCarthy, and Zald (1988: 703) succinctly summarize this proposition by stating: "The greater the density of social organization, the more likely that social movement activity will develop." In general, the integration of individuals into social networks promotes their protest participation. Piven and Cloward (1991: 442) regard this proposition as "one of the RM school's most fundamental causal propositions." Indeed, from the perspective of the RMP this is not implausible: a person who is member of a social network – which may consist of friendship relationships or relationships to group members – may dispose of resources in the sense that one may recruit others in the network to participate in protest action at relatively low costs. Thus, individuals in networks are easily available as targets of mobilization and can easily address others as targets of mobilization.

The most elaborate micro model of political participation in which resources play a central role is Verba, Schlozman, and Brady's (1995; see also Brady, Verba, and Schlozman 1995) "Civic Voluntarism Model" (CVM). The most important resources are free time, money, and various civic skills such as the ability to communicate effectively or organizational skills.[4] It is important to note that the CVM includes resources only as one of several variables – we will return to the CVM later (see section 10).

This work indicates that individual resources are manifold. Integration in social networks is only one resource. "Civic skills" is a whole complex of other individual resources.

2. The causal structure of McCarthy and Zald's approach: a critique and extension

Although the "illustrative hypotheses" seem to be clear and straightforward, there are several problems which will be addressed in this section. In contrast to the "illustrative hypotheses," the orienting propositions seem to address the basic dependent and independent variables of the approach. It seems therefore worthwhile to try to use them to construct a causal model that connects these variables. Such a model will be suggested in the final part of this section.

Explicit propositions and implicit modifications: missing variables and causal relationships

One problem with the 11 explicit propositions is that the authors' comments suggest various other factors and caveats that often render the explicit propositions invalid. For example, hypothesis 1 is valid "ceteris paribus," i.e. only under certain conditions (1224–1225). One is that if wants are not satiated (to what extent?) additional resources are devoted to satisfy these personal wants and not to support SMOs. Thus, contrary to hypothesis 1, additional resources in a society will not be transferred to SMOs in this situation. We thus conclude that the model is incomplete because relevant variables which the authors mention in the text are not included in the propositions.

The causal diagram in Figure 5.2 shows that most of the propositions consist of one independent and one dependent variable. It is extremely implausible that any phenomenon in the social sciences is caused by only one independent variable. To be sure, the comments of the authors include other variables. The question is why they are not included in the hypotheses. One might speculate that the hypotheses include only those variables the authors deem most important. Anyway, the model should perhaps not be regarded as a full-fledged theory but as a collection of theoretical ideas that need further elaboration.

Assume the model depicted in Figure 5.2 includes the relevant variables and is thus not misspecified in regard to the kind of variables included. The question arises whether there are not other relationships between the variables that the authors did not address. A few of these relations are symbolized by the dotted lines in the figure. For example, the longevity of a movement will depend, among other things, on the available resources provided by conscience adherents. They are devoted to the goals of a movement and may thus have an interest in supporting it. Another example: if there is a professional staff this will probably increase stability of resource flow because the staff has established and continues to establish connections to various groups who support the SMO.

What is the difference between preferences and grievances?

The authors define "social movement" as "a set of opinions and beliefs in a population which represents preferences for changing some elements of the social structure" (1217). These "preferences" are a condition for the emergence of social movements. What is the difference between having "preferences for change" and "suffer from grievances in regard to the status quo"? For example, social movements with the goal of preventing a war have a "preference" for preventing the war; this means the same as being dissatisfied with the prospect of a possible war. In terms of the theory of collective action, this means "preferences for a public good."

If a "preference" for some situation and "dissatisfaction" with this situation are the same, there is some contradiction in the theory. In the first part of the paper grievances are played down. In the second part they are reintroduced with another name: they are now called "preferences." Thus, it seems, grievances play a major role for movement related phenomena.

The orienting propositions: a reformulation as a causal model

The orienting hypotheses the authors provide at the beginning of their article address the major independent as well as dependent variables of the approach – see our previous list. It is odd that the authors do not use this list to construct an informative theoretical model. We propose such a theoretical model that is depicted as a causal diagram in Figure 5.3. The model does not include general conditions such as infrastructure or the constitution of a society which are mentioned by the authors. These are scope conditions: only if they are given does the model hold true.

There are three dependent variables the RMP focuses on, namely emergence, growth (or decline), and success of SMOs. We assume that there is one causal relationship between these key variables: "growth of a SMO" has a positive effect on "success of a SMO."

Our model includes five variables which have direct effects on each of the three explanatory variables. One refers to the general preferences of a society for social change. It is assumed that this leads to societal support for the goals of a social movement – see the variable at the upper left of the figure. This is in fact the authors' definition of "social movement." The effect of this variable on each of the three key variables takes account of the authors' hypothesis that general preferences (or demand for change) are often taken up by social movements or political entrepreneurs and are important for the emergence, growth and success of a

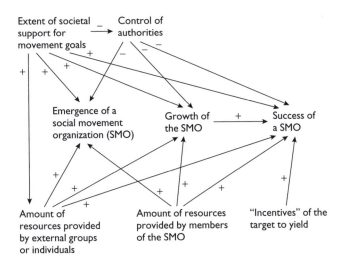

Figure 5.3 The orienting propositions: a suggestion for a causal model

movement. Two variables refer to resources: the resources provided by external groups – i.e. external support – and the resources provided by members of a SMO. "Control of authorities" is the only variable that has negative effects.

It was emphasized already several times that the success of a SMO is not only determined by features of the movement but by incentives of the targets to meet the SMO's demands. For example, we know from public choice theory that voter support is important. If a government has a strong majority that guarantees its re-election, movements may be large but nonetheless not successful. This is the variable "'incentives' of the target to yield" to the goals of a movement.

The exogenous variables have some further relationships with each other. For example, if there is large societal support for a cause, then large organizations have an incentive to provide support for movements which pursue this cause.

This causal model is just a beginning. Empirical tests and perhaps an elaboration of the model are necessary. We believe that it captures better the major ideas of the approach than the "illustrative hypotheses."

In further developing the model the following questions need to be answered. How do the orienting propositions and in particular the model of Figure 5.3 fit into the authors' "illustrative hypotheses"? The answer to this question is that there are only lose connections. "Growth" and "success of a SMO" which are major explanatory variables in the orienting propositions are not part of the "illustrative hypotheses." Only resources are part of both sets of hypotheses. We do not know why this is so. What is missing in the model of Figure 5.3 are the activities of the movement. It goes without saying that tactics and strategies are a condition for success and for the mobilization of resources. The implicit assumption seems to be that the resources available are used in a strategic way that is most likely to yield success. Maybe a separate model is necessary to explain SMOs' strategies and tactics. We will take up this issue in section 10.

3. Conceptual problems: the meaning of "resources" and "mobilization"

Although McCarthy and Zald call their theoretical perspective "resource mobilization approach" (1213), they do not define the basic terms "resources" and "mobilization" explicitly. In his introduction to a collection of Zald and McCarthy's essays Gamson (1987: 1) states that the concept of resources is a "mushy concept" and that it has not been clearly defined by McCarthy and Zald themselves or by other scholars. Instead, McCarthy and Zald (1977) and other authors list various kinds of resources such as money, facilities and labor (1216), and legitimacy (1220). They further introduce the term "*discretionary resources*" which refers to time and money (1224). This is a hint at the meaning of "resources": maybe they have something to do with the actors' control over goods.

In a review of their approach in 2002 the authors write: "Our version of RM [resource mobilization – KDO] locates many of the resources in the larger society. These include all levels of government, foundations, religious institutions, and conscience constituencies, groups that support the movement's goals, even though its members are not eligible to receive the direct output of the policy/political changes that the movements advocate" (Zald and McCarthy 2002: 150). This suggests that "resources" do not only include tangible goods such as money and facilities but features of institutions and groups. What exactly these features are is not clear from this quotation.

When we look at the literature the concept of resources comprises available financial means, access to media, support by sympathizers, loyalty of groups or members or third parties, availability of rooms (for meetings or office work), rights, knowledge and abilities or skills actors dispose of (see, e.g., Freeman 1983: 195ff.; Gamson 1968: 94; Gamson, Fireman, and Rytina 1982: 23; Jenkins 1983: 533; Oberschall 1973: 28; Tilly 1978: 7; Walsh 1988: 8; see also the review by Jenkins and Form 2005: 337).

What could be a general definition that comprises all these phenomena? It seems that resources refer to *goods*. This is, by definition, everything that has utility. But not all goods are resources. For example, the money of Bill Gates is a good, but certainly not a resource of a social movement. The previous examples suggest that only those goods are resources that actors can use to achieve their goals. Such a definition seems useful because "resources" is a variable that should help to explain social movement or protest activities. These become more likely if actors have some control over goods. This is the case for the time and money of a deprived actor but not for the time and money of Bill Gates (although this could become useful for achieving social movement goals).

The goods mentioned may be used by individual as well as by collective actors. Although the RMP is a macro perspective it often refers to individual actors, as will be seen later (see section 6). We therefore suggest to define resources for individual as well as collective actors and arrive at the following definition:

Definition of "resources": Resources are goods (i.e. everything that has utility) which individual or collective actors can control.

The definition by Gamson, Fireman, and Rytina (1982: 23) is very similar: "By resources, we mean those objects which can be used by the group to achieve its collective goals, and the control of which can be transferred from one person to another. Money, weapons, printing presses, and the like are examples." Resources are thus properties of groups (in contrast to our definition that includes individuals as well); but only those objects are resources that can be transferred from one person (and not group) to another. "Intelligence" or "skills" would thus not be a resource. We do not find any reason why this definition is chosen. Thus, our definition is broader.

What does "mobilization" mean? The definition by Jenkins (1983) captures what McCarthy and Zald seem to have in mind: "Mobilization is the process by which a group secures collective control over the resources needed for collective action" (Jenkins 1983: 532). We suggest to expand this definition to include also individuals – as in the definition of "resources": "mobilization" may therefore also mean *individual* efforts to gain control over goods.

Jenkins's definition uses control as a dichotomy: a group "secures collective control" or does not secure collective control. Instead, it seems more useful to conceptualize "control" as a quantitative variable. Thus, if a group wishes to gain *more* control – for example more money or support – this is a mobilization process as well. We thus arrive at the following definition:

> *Definition of "mobilization"*: "Mobilization" refers to activities of a movement organization or of an individual actor to gain more control over goods that contribute to achieve the goals of the movement organization or the individual actor.

An illustration of these definitions of "resources" and "mobilization" is McCarthy and Wolfson's (1996) study of groups against drunk driving. Although the authors do not provide an explicit definition of resources and mobilization in this article, they measure various activities or strategies of the movement in order to achieve its goals, and the outcomes of these strategies. They are attempts to mobilize resources. The mobilization activities include public education (bringing problems and consequences of drunk driving to the attention of wide audiences) and legislative action (attempts to "change laws, authorities, and/or regimes" (1072)).

It is very awkward that the basic concepts of the RMP are still not clearly defined. In their own review of their approach, McCarthy and Zald do not provide a clear definition either. Their only comment is that "critics noted the unexamined use of these categories, calling for a more refined specification of resources" (2002: 154–155). The primary problem is not to provide some new classification of resources which includes, among other things, "symbolic resources" (155). The problem is to specify in detail what the concept of resources means and which of the possible definitions is more or less theoretically useful.

4. What kind of resources bring about what kind of movements and strategies? Problems of the explanatory power of the perspective

Piven and Cloward (1991: 436–439) criticize that McCarthy and Zald do not distinguish between "normative and non-normative" forms of protest. The latter refer to violent and illegal forms of collective action such as riots, insurrections and invasions of official buildings (437). It is not clear why such a distinction should be made. But the critique points to the following problems of RMP. First of all, it cannot explain the specific forms of protest behavior and of social movements. When do riots occur? When do the movements choose to stage a peaceful and not a violent demonstration?

Second, it cannot be explained what kinds of SMOs, SMSs or SMIs originate under what conditions. Hypothesis 2 illustrates this: it is claimed that increasing available resources to the SMS raises the likelihood "that new SMIs and SMOs will develop" (1225). It is left open of what kind these movements are. Any kind of SMI or SMO is possible, ranging from a terrorist organization to a religious movement.

There are several scope conditions, as we saw before. For example, the perspective refers to a democratic society where a free flow of resources is institutionally allowed. This amounts to a lack of empirical content: we do not know how social movements or social movements related phenomena come about if these conditions are *not* given. For example, how to explain protests in authoritarian societies where the transfer of resources is severely restricted? To be sure, it is perfectly legitimate to state scope conditions. But a good theory is capable of deriving implications about what happens if certain scope conditions do not prevail.

5. The implicit background theory

The RMP – and McCarthy and Zald in particular – assumes, among other things, that political actors and, thus, SMOs have goals. In order to achieve their goals one strategy is to mobilize resources. This implies that SMOs act in order to get something that is valuable to them, i.e. they act according to their preferences. It further means that SMOs have certain beliefs. Such beliefs include the assumption that the mobilization of resources is instrumental to achieve their goals. Thus, political actors do not choose *any* strategy but the strategy that they think is best suited to achieve their goals. Finally, it is assumed that SMOs do not always succeed in mobilizing resources. In other words, there are constraints.

McCarthy and Zald also explicitly reveal their background theory when they write that an explanation of collective behavior "requires detailed attention to the selection of incentives, cost-reducing mechanisms or structures, and career benefits that lead to collective action" (1216). One paragraph later the authors continue that there is "a sensitivity to the importance of costs and rewards in explaining individual and organizational involvement in social movement activity."

These assumptions are a description of the theory of rational action. In a nutshell, this theory holds that preferences and constraints are the major determinants for a behavior and that actors choose what they think is best for them (see chapter 1, section 1). Several quotations in the previous presentation of the theory make it abundantly clear that the implicit theory applied is the rational choice approach. This is also noted by various critiques, accounts or reviews of the approach (see, e.g., Jenkins 1983). Zald, one of the founders of the RMP, himself states that the RMP's "underlying psychological decision model has been a utilitarian model of cost/ benefits" (1992: 335).

Why, then, is this theory not applied systematically and explicitly? Most of the propositions of the RMP are *ad hoc*, i.e. it is not clear what their relationship to the implicit general theory is. It is also not clear why the theory is not applied explicitly.

Had this been done, the authors would have come across the following problem. The units of analysis of McCarthy and Zald's theory are collective actors such as social movement organizations and not individual actors. The problem then is how to assign preferences and constraints to collective actors. It seems that the procedure of economists is adopted: they assume that the collective actors are in fact representing the goals of a collectivity of individuals. This is plausible for social movement organizations as well: "the" goal of a SMO is in fact the common goal of the members. A problem exists when the goals of a movement are not homogeneous. We will discuss this problem in chapter 8, section 2. At this point we assume that the aggregation problem (i.e. defining the goals of a group as a function of the goals of the group members) is solved. Nonetheless, it is important to point out that this does not imply that only the macro level is important. Social movements are concerned with recruiting or mobilizing individual actors. Thus, the micro level is always involved.

Applying the underlying theory explicitly might have also given guidelines to define the basic concept of "resources" in a theoretically meaningful way. The definition we suggested above is based on the rational choice approach. It seems to be theoretically fruitful because the availability of resources is a factor – but not the only factor! – that contributes to action.

6. The structure of the perspective: the implied and missing micro-macro model

The RMP is a macro perspective: the units of analysis are SMOs and other collective actors. However, McCarthy and Zald refer to the micro level numerous times in their basic article. As was shown in the previous section, the implicit general theory applied is rational choice theory. This is a micro theory. How are the individual costs and benefits related to macro factors such as societal resources? The answer is clear: "Costs and rewards are centrally affected by the structure of society and the activities of authorities" (1216). This means that there are effects running from variables of the macro level (such as "the structure of society and the activities of authorities") to the micro level ("costs and rewards" for participation). But which macro factors have which effects on which micro variables? The previous quotation is only an orienting hypothesis, not an informative theoretical proposition that exactly specifies which variable has which effect on which other variable. The orienting proposition is a bridge assumption, in this case a macro-to-micro hypothesis. It is thus part of a micro-macro explanation, but only a part.

The authors further note that the *infrastructure* of a society affects the dynamics of social movements (see the list above). This includes communication media, levels of affluence and access to institutional centers and networks, occupational structure (1217), transportation, political freedom, the extent of repression, and the available technologies for resource mobilization such as mass mailing techniques (1225). These factors "may affect the cost for any individual or organization allocating resources to the SMS, serve as constraints on or facilitators of the use of resources for social movement purposes" (1225). This includes again a macro-to-micro proposition. It is, however, again left open which costs or benefits exactly are affected in what way by these macro-factors.

Let us illustrate a micro-macro model of the resource mobilization approach with Figure 5.4. Take the new communication technology such as the internet as a kind of macro resource. Which effects could this have on incentives at the micro level? First of all, the internet will lower the costs of organizing protests: less time

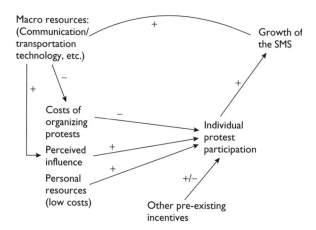

Figure 5.4 Example of a micro-macro model with "resources" as a macro and a micro variable

and money are required to reach others and to spread information about venues for rallies.[5] These lower costs increase the likelihood of individual protest. It is further plausible that in general resources on the macro level increase personal perceived influence. People might think that the possibility to send many messages and appeals to different potential participants greatly enhances the chances of mobilizing others and, thus, personal influence as well.

The micro level includes two variables or sets of variables that are not influenced by the macro variables of the model: individual resources such as available time and other pre-existing incentives. This may include an unconditional norm of cooperation or fairness.

In regard to personal resources, other macro variables not included in the model may influence personal resources. For example, laws about working hours increase free time. These personal resources have a positive effect on protest behavior. Thus, there may be incentives that are not affected by the macro variables of a given macro model, but by other macro factors.

The micro-to-macro transition is from individual protest to "growth of the SMS." This could be an empirical relationship: the more individuals participate in various protest actions the more they are willing to work in social movements. However, the relationship may also be analytical: the size of the social movement sector may be defined as the amount of individuals in a society who engage in protest activities.

This causal model should only be an illustration of how micro-macro models with resources as variables can be constructed. It should further illustrate that the theoretical arguments of the authors implies such a model.

One limitation of this model is that there is only one macro variable. A second problem is that the micro model is incomplete – see the discussion in chapter 4, section 4. As a matter of fact, the RMP does not dispose of a micro model. McCarthy and Zald note in a recent review of their approach that one "of the major problematic of the broader RM program ... has been the explanation of individual decisions to participate in movement activities" (Zald and McCarthy 2002: 156). This insight is not new: already Jenkins (1983: 549) complained about 20 years before that it is an important task of RMP to develop "a more sophisticated social psychology of collective action."

This task has not yet been seriously tackled so far, as is illustrated by a recent review of the RMP. Here the authors hypothesize that social movement participation "emerges out of biographical circumstances, social supports, and immediate life situations" (Zald and McCarthy 2002: 150). This is hardly an informative model. For a more informative model the authors seem to rely on other work when they state that "a social psychological theory of micro mobilization has been developed that utilizes subjective-utility theory" (Zald and McCarthy 2002: 157).[6] They refer, among other things, to Klandermans' book (Klandermans 1997). Does this mean that this is "the" micro model of the RMP? In their review of the RMP Zald and McCarthy (2002: 160) regard "frame and script analysis" as tools "that serve as powerful complements to the original branches of RM that had largely ignored how beliefs, frames, and ideologies operated." Does this mean that a micro model should be based on the framing approach? What does such a micro model look like?

All these questions are not answered. It is striking and very difficult to explain that on the one hand there is a clear micro-macro orientation with the rational choice approach as the implicit underlying theory, but that on the other hand neither micro-to-macro nor macro-to-micro relations nor an explicit micro model are modeled in any detail.

7. How is the free rider problem solved?

In their first hypothesis the authors assume that a general increase of resources in a society will increase the amount of resources available to the SMS. This presupposes that those whose resources increase are willing to transfer some of their resources to SMOs. Why should they do this? The members of a society are a large group. Why should they support a social movement? This question is not answered. In their hypothesis 3 it is assumed that the "conscience adherents" – these are individuals who do not directly profit when the SMOs reach their goals – are willing to transfer part of their resources to SMOs. This, so the authors, "turns Olson on his head" (1226). In other words, Olson is wrong. But the authors beg the question of what the incentives for the support of the conscience adherents are. Why do they participate? Perhaps one should leave Olson on his feet.

The authors note that "transitory teams" often work for a SMO. These teams consist of "workers assembled for a specific task, short in duration" (1227). They "can be expected to receive solidary incentives from such involvement – selective benefits of a nonmaterial sort" (1227). Do the authors refer to social rewards or rewards from conforming to an internalized protest norm? Do the other types of contributors to a SMO also receive those incentives? Are those incentives sufficient to solve the free rider problem?

SMOs compete for resources, i.e. they mobilize resources, sometimes directly from adherents (1227). How do they manage it to convince others to transfer resources? What kinds of strategies do they choose? Is the choice of certain strategies sufficient to solve the free rider problem?

McCarthy and Zald treat SMOs as firms (see, e.g., 1227). However, firms sell private goods, whereas SMOs try to provide public goods. They thus resemble interest organizations and not so much firms. Olson argued that an interest organization in a society has only a small impact on providing public goods for its constituency so that selective incentives are necessary. What are the selective incentives for SMOs? Do they also receive private goods and, if so, which ones from whom?

To conclude, an important question that is not answered is what motivates individuals or organizations to invest time and other resources in order to provide the public good. It is stunning that the authors mention this problem but do not provide a clear and systematic answer to this question.

To be sure, the authors time and again refer to Olson, but how the theory of collective action is related to the RMP is not clear. This ambiguity is borne out when the authors write that the RMP is "shaped, but not bound, by the problem of collective action as described by Mancur Olson (1965)." What does this mean? Is Olson a sort of heuristic and, if so, how exactly does the theory of collective action "shape" the RMP? Why is Olson or a modification of his theory not used as a general theory to derive new hypotheses?

In their article of 1977 the authors seem less critical of Olson than later (Zald and McCarthy 2002: 156–157): there they cite various objections to Olson's theory. This may imply that they consider Olson's solution to the free rider problem problematic. This may be true (see chapter 3). But this critique does not at all imply that the very question of how the free rider problem is solved is obsolete or irrelevant. At least we do not find any argument in favor of such a claim. Instead, the authors simply seem to ignore the problem. After citing various objections to Olson they characterize their own approach: "Our approach focused upon organizational needs and the organizational provision of opportunities for participation and mobilization, what has subsequently been called a supply side explanation of individual participation. Subsequent research has shown that one of the best predictors of whether a social movement adherent participates is whether or not she is asked to do so, consistent with our supply side account of the process" (Zald and McCarthy 2002: 157). It is hardly plausible that being asked is the only selective incentive for participating in protests or for becoming a member of a SMO. Furthermore, many people protest or become members without having been asked.

We conclude that the authors seem to recognize that the free rider problem is a serious issue but that they do not solve it, they simply ignore it. They do not provide any reason for this.

8. Are there falsifications of the resource mobilization perspective?

To what extent is the RMP empirically confirmed? It seems that there is overwhelming evidence indicating that resources are important for all kinds of movement related phenomena. For example, McCarthy *et al.* (1988: 75) found in their study about groups against drinking and driving: "The more plentiful both material and human resources are in a community, the more likely is the development of most organizational forms." This is a confirmation of hypotheses 1 to 3 of the causal model of the 1977 paper (see Figure 5.2 before). Are there clear falsifications of the RMP or at least disconfirmations of some of its propositions? I have not found any rigorous research that provides clear negative evidence for propositions of the perspective. However, it seems that there are some conditions or types of situations where basic propositions of the perspective are wrong or, more cautiously, problematic. Some of these situations and conditions are outlined in this section.

When do resources trigger protest?

It was argued in chapters 1 and 3 that the validity of macro propositions depends, among other things, on the effects of the independent macro variables on the incentives of the micro model. Our detailed discussion of Olson's theory clearly demonstrates this: group size – a macro variable – only prevents collective action if group size has certain effects on the micro level. More specifically, the effects of group size on collective action depend on how group size affects the individual incentives to contributions to the public good.

The same holds for the macro variables of the RMP. Resources on the macro level will lead to collective protest events only if resources change the individual incentives in the "right" way. In short, if there are resources, but if micro mobilization does not obtain there will be no individual protest and, accordingly, no collective protest either.

Can we imagine situations where there are resources but where protest does not obtain because resources do not set in motion micro mobilization? Let us again look at Figure 5.4. It seems plausible that in general the availability of resources like the internet lower the costs of mobilization attempts. But how many users of the internet or of cordless phones actually try to mobilize others? Thus, existing technology that lowers the costs of communication is not sufficient to increase protest. Other, additional incentives must obtain.

The model claims that a cheap communication technology raises perceived political influence (see Figure 5.4). But this may not hold for those "free riders" who believe that their influence in a large group is negligible. For others the rise of influence by new developments of the internet may be so low that it does not suffice as an incentive to protest.

Let us take another resource that is part of McCarthy and Zald's (1977) hypotheses 1 and 2 (see Figure 5.2). The authors indicate in their comments that an increase of free time and income will only facilitate SMO emergence if other needs are not salient. In terms of the incentives to protest, an increase of free time will only raise collective protest or lead to the foundation of new movements if these factors increase perceived influence, activate a norm to protest, etc. Even if perceived influence is high due to some macro resources, people may be rather satisfied with their standard of living and the political situation so that any increase of general resources will not instigate any protest behavior.

The importance of the relationship between resources on the macro level and individual incentives on the micro level is also addressed by the comments of McCarthy *et al.* on the macro proposition mentioned before (see 1988: 75), when they discuss how resources in a community may affect the founding and growth of local citizens' groups, namely via individual actors who use the resources: "The more resources available to potential activists, the more likely such groups are to form and grow" (75). The resources the authors consider are, among other things, income and education. These are "discretionary" resources (McCarthy and Zald 1977: 1224). The hypothesis thus reads: "More affluent and better-educated individuals are, in general, more likely to form groups." Thus, in order to form groups resources must be available to those individuals who are willing to engage in activities against drunk driving. In other words, *only if* the *same* individuals who have a strong interest in doing something against drunk driving also dispose of "discretionary" resources, then groups are formed. One condition for the effects of resources and collective protest on the macro level is that there is no separation of interest and resources across individuals. If those individuals dispose of resources who are not interested in social movement activities, then a high concentration of resources in a community will not be associated with the founding of social movement related groups.

The general conclusion thus is that changing macro resources are only conducive to collective protest or to the emergence of new SMOs if they change incentives on the micro level, i.e. if they instigate micro mobilization processes. But this need not be the case.

Protests without resources?

According to Piven and Cloward (1991: 447–453) the RMP implies that "collective protest episodes are always sponsored by organizations" (449). There are many examples where protests come about without organizations. Many of the East European protests in 1989–1990 (which Piven and Cloward mention) were spontaneous and thus not organized. Incidentally, such spontaneous protests are rarely addressed in the social movement literature and by the RMP in particular (an exception is Rosenthal and Schwartz 1989).

Is this critique justified? When we look at the orienting propositions and the illustrative hypotheses, or at McCarthy and Zald, it is difficult to see how the RMP can explain such spontaneous collective protest events. The "illustrative hypotheses" (see Figure 5.2) address the emergence of SMOs, but spontaneous protests are, by definition, not organized or engaged in by SMOs. Our reconstruction of the orienting hypotheses (see Figure 5.3) also explain SMOs and can thus not be applied to explain spontaneous protest action. The conclusion thus is that the RMP is wrong: there is protest even if the major independent macro variables such as societal support for movements are absent. Put briefly, there are protests without resources on the macro level.

These facts do not falsify the RMP if it only claims that resources are a sufficient condition for protest events. In other words:

> If there are resources (RES), then there is collective protest and there are SMOs (PrSMOs). It is not true: if PrSOMs, then RES.

This means that the RMP can predict correctly that given organization and resources trigger protest events. But if there is no organization and if no general resources for a movement are available, protest events may occur as well. The RMP would not be false in this case. This is what it means that RES are a sufficient condition for PrSMOs. RES are thus not a sufficient *and necessary* condition. In other words, the following proposition is *wrong*: "If there are RES, there are PrSMOs; if there are PrSMOs, there are RES." Only the first part of the proposition is correct.

Table 5.1 (which is a truth table as it is common in formal logic) clarifies these different types of statements. Assume that "resources" and "protest and social movement organizations" are dichotomous variables. Each can thus be true (i.e. there are resources or not, and there are protest and SMOs or not). Columns 2 and 3 list the four possibilities. For example, RES and PrSMOs may both be true (line 1) or false (line 4) or one may be true and the other false (lines 2 and 3). Column 5 shows for which combinations of T and F the statement "if RES, then PrSMOs" is true or false. It is only false if the RES is true and PrSMOs false. In all other cases the statement is correct. The table further shows when the hypothesis that RES are a necessary condition for PrSMOs is correct, and for which truth values it is correct that RES are a necessary *and* sufficient condition for PrSMOs. For example, if RES are a necessary and sufficient condition for PrSMOs, then it must hold that if we find PrSMOs, then RES must be given and vice versa. Thus, if Piven and Cloward's critique is correct, the RMP could be saved when we reformulate it as claiming that variables like organization and societal resources are sufficient conditions for collective protest and SMOs.

It is not clear whether proponents of the RMP conceive resources as only

Table 5.1 Resources (RES) as sufficient conditions for collective protest and social movement organizations (PrSMOs).

No. of line	Protest or Social Movement Organizations (PrSMOs)	Resources (RES)	RES is a necessary condition for PrSMOs	RES is a sufficient condition for PrSMOs	RES is a sufficient and necessary condition for PR
			if PrSMOs, then RES	if RES, then PrSMOs	if RES, then PrSMOs and vice versa
1	2	3	4	5	6
1	T	T	T	T	T
2	T	F	F	T	F
3	F	T	T	F	F
4	F	F	T	T	T

sufficient or as necessary or as both, necessary and sufficient, conditions. The argument in this section suggests that resources are only sufficient conditions. This means that the RMP has a relatively low explanatory power: when there is protest we do not know whether it came about by resources or organization or whether it was spontaneous. But this statement must be qualified, as the argument in the previous section suggests: it happens that there are resources but that these resources do not bring about protest or SMOs.

Taken together with the argument of the previous chapter – that often resources do not trigger the relevant incentives to protest – we may conclude that resources on the macro level are *at best* (or at most) sufficient conditions.

Organizational integration and protest: the micro version of the resource mobilization perspective

To what extent is the micro version of the RMP asserting a positive impact of social integration and protest participation? Piven and Cloward (1991: 442–447) argue that the integration of actors into groups has different effects on protest behavior: sometimes such integration makes protest more likely, sometimes less likely. The authors further show that there are different propositions in the literature. For example, high "biographical availability" means that there are few social ties. This, it is argued, makes protest participation more likely (see also chapter 4, section 4). On the other hand, membership in groups is regarded as impeding mobilization. The finding that "integration" sometimes increases and sometimes lowers protest does thus falsify the RMP.

The hypothesis that group integration triggers protest is based on the assumption that group integration is related to resources available to the group members, as was said before.

To be sure, there is evidence for the hypothesis that social integration, i.e. membership in social networks, matters for protest (see also chapters 3 and 4). But there is also disconfirming evidence. For example, Biggs (2006) found that students who lived in dormitories (an indicator for social integration) did not participate significantly more frequently in sit-ins. In my own research I found clear evidence that not only integration in a social network mattered but only integration in networks that provide rewards for protest (see Opp 1988, 1989; see also Opp 1989: chapter 5). Thus, integration into social networks only matters under certain conditions, depending on the incentives that are provided in networks. If, therefore, resources in the form of network involvement matter, they are not the only variable: rewards related to networks matter.

But why should a special kind of resource, namely integration into networks, matter if it is held that in general resources play a role for protest? Does the micro version imply that every resource a person disposes of matters for protest? Or might it be the case that, for example, integration into social networks is irrelevant, but that "civic skills" are important? The problem is that the micro version of the RMP does not specify what kind of resources affect what kind of behavior. We will take up this problem in section 10.

9. Recent developments

There is a burgeoning literature that is based at least to some extent on the RMP or on theoretical ideas of this approach. We conclude from our reading of this literature that in regard to major deficiencies outlined before there is only very limited progress.

Conceptual problems

We saw that the basic concepts of the RMP are not clearly defined. There are no attempts to provide a clear definition of the basic concepts, namely "resources" and "mobilization," and compare the theoretical fruitfulness of alternative definitions. What is also missing is a look at the definitions of "resources" in other disciplines like economics. This is surprising because McCarthy and Zald borrow some ideas from economics by comparing social movements with firms. But the theory of the firm in economics is not systematically applied.

Macro theory

McCarthy and Zald's basic article mentions various macro variables but does not connect them to a causal model, comparable to the model suggested in Figure 5.3. The situation has not changed: there is still no full-fledged macro theory that includes resources and other macro variables, which specifies their complex inter-relationships in order to explain what form of movement or collective action emerges. There is no theory with the explanatory power of the theory of collective action. However, there are several explicit macro propositions addressing specific questions. Examples are the hypotheses proposed in an article by Zald and Ash (1966) that was published ten years before the founding paper by McCarthy and Zald (1977)! This article addresses in general the "Growth, Decline, and Change" of social movements. There are two other articles, one by Zald and McCarthy (1980) addressing cooperation and competition among movement organizations, another by Zald and Berger (1978) that is concerned with social movement phenomena within organizations. There is much other interesting work (e.g. Khawaja 1994, with many further references). However, all these contributions are not a general theory that can be applied to a wide range of different phenomena to yield specific predictions. And the propositions are not theoretically derived from a more general macro theory.

The microfoundation of the perspective

As we saw before, McCarthy and Zald do not provide a clear micro model of polit-ical participation. So far, there is only B. Klandermans's article that is explicitly aimed at providing "social psychological extensions of resource mobilization the-ory" – this is the subtitle of the article (Klandermans 1984). We have discussed Klandermans's model and other micro theories in chapter 4, section 3. One may conclude that there is by now a satisfactory microfoundation of the RMP. However, it is not systematically used to build micro-macro explanations – see the next section.

The missing micro-macro models

It was shown that McCarthy and Zald (1977) implicitly apply a micro-macro model. But so far systematic micro-macro modeling is largely missing. A fruitful beginning seemed to be Klandermans's (1984) article which suggests a micro model of participation which was designed to be an expansion of the RMP. But Klandermans does not answer explicitly the question of how exactly this micro model can be used to "expand" the RMP. He provides micro-macro links only implicitly. This becomes particularly clear when he discusses why the union failed to accomplish its goal. There were "external events" (595) such as the adamant employers and the loss of a strike of the West German unions. One of the effects was that on the micro level the "collective motive to participate vanished" (595).

Klandermans suggests another macro-to-micro proposition. When he addresses the different extent of the willingness to strike in different plants, he provides some evidence about the strength of the unions in the plants. His hypothesis is: "The stronger the position of the union, the greater is the chance that colleagues will motivate people to participate ..." (596). In other words, "strength" of a union (macro level) has effects on the change of certain incentives (micro level).

A careful reading of Klandermans's article suggests that he advances the model depicted in Figure 5.5. To be sure, there are clear relationships between the macro and micro level. But the kind of relationships – whether they are causal or analytical – is never spelled out. It is also important to note that the causal propositions from the macro to the micro level are at least in part orienting statements. "Union action" has not always an effect on the change of incentives, as Klandermans's case study illustrates. It is further not clear, what kinds of external events in general have

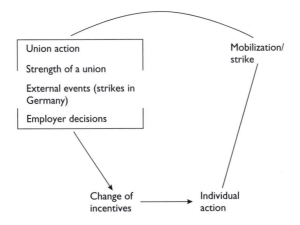

Figure 5.5 The implicit micro-macro model in Klandermans 1984

which effects on which incentives. Furthermore, micro-to-macro relationships are not based on theoretical arguments. It is difficult to understand why Klandermans never formulates a micro-macro model explicitly. One may conclude that Klandermans's "expansion" of the RMP is very limited: it is an explicit formulation of a micro model, everything else is not spelled out in detail.

The proliferation of orienting propositions

The RMP has brought about a vast number of empirical studies. But in regard to theory development, mostly new orienting propositions are provided. It is consistent with this judgment that in Zald and McCarthy's review of their approach (2002) the headline of the section presenting their major propositions is "orienting propositions" (151). For example, they point out that – apart from resources – various other factors might be relevant for explanations of social movement phenomena. They mention as examples culture, framing, and emotions. But what exactly the effects – compared to resources – are and how the causal interrelationships of these variables are, is left open.

There are further many simple hypotheses with one independent and one dependent variable. Here are a few examples. Zald and McCarthy (2002: 149) note that there are many demands for change in a society such as preferences for a cleaner environment. These preferences for change are "more or less tightly linked" to "the organizational growth, decline, or adaptation of SMO." The hypothesis seems to be: The more intense and common preferences for change are, the more likely is the growth of SMOs. Another hypothesis is that "groups with few resources are less able to act on grievances or perceived injustices" (149). McCarthy and Wolfson (1996: 1072) suggest: "the more effort activists expend, the more resources will be mobilized, all other things being equal." It is hardly plausible in these examples, that the independent variable is the only one that has an impact on the dependent variable. Incidentally, the ceteris paribus clause ("all other things being equal") should be ignored because it makes a proposition unfalsifiable unless the factors that are to be held constant are known.

Most of the studies of the RMP are case studies which explain mobilization attempts, protests or the rise, stability or decline of specific social movements or similar groups. The focus of these studies are resources. McCarthy and Wolfson's research (1996) mentioned in the previous paragraph is an example (see also a related article by McCarthy et al. 1988). This study focuses on mobilization activities of groups and members of groups and organizations against drinking and driving. The article raises interesting questions such as: When do mobilization activities have which effects? Variables are outlined that describe properties of the groups engaging against drunk driving. Examples for these properties are group age and the organizational structure of the groups (1072–1073). Although these are important variables, features of the target are missing. Further, micro-macro relationships are not spelled out but only adumbrated. For example, the authors argue that different organizational structures are less successful than others in recruiting and motivating local activists "because the incentives that motivate activism at the two levels, differ" (1073). What exactly are the effects of which organizational structures (macro level) on which incentives (micro level)?

Another important question is: What are the mobilization activities of the different groups? To be sure, a description of the different activities is a necessary first step for their explanation. But a detailed theoretical analysis of why different individuals or groups choose different mobilization activities is missing. The theoretical analyses provided by proponents of the theory of collective action about political entrepreneurs could be integrated in the "thick" descriptions of McCarthy and Wolfson's study.

The study of organizational processes: a research agenda

If, as in McCarthy and Zald's original work, social movement "organizations" are the subject of their approach, it is a next plausible step to apply existing approaches that directly address organizations and firms in general. This could be economic analyses of firms, but also approaches in sociology or political science that address organizational processes. Topics are, for example, the emergence and change of organizations and the supply and demand of labor. The latter is relevant for SMOs because they demand labor – often unpaid – to achieve their goal. Another topic is organizational decision making.

The application of these approaches is so far a research program. Debra Minkoff and John McCarthy (2005) provide a detailed review and discussion of the pertinent perspectives. It remains to be seen whether this research program yields informative proposition for explaining social movement phenomena.

Conclusion

Compared to the original article by McCarthy and Zald (1977) discussed in this chapter, there are no pathbreaking new theoretical developments. There is, however, a vast number of very interesting empirical studies that use theoretical ideas from the RMP. But the major theoretical problems are still unsolved.

10. Theoretical suggestions

In this section three theoretical questions will be addressed that are basic to the RMP and to the explanation of social movement related phenomena in general. There are so far no detailed answers to these questions. One question focuses on the behavioral options or, equivalently, on the possible strategies that individuals or groups face. For example, individuals or groups may attack a target directly or try – as a first step – to mobilize supporters or money and other material resources. When will which strategy be chosen? A second theoretical question is when actors decide to assign more or less resources to a group. Finally, we will take up the question of what role resources play in decisions to become politically active. This section does not offer full-fledged theoretical models but rather explanation sketches. The major point to be made is that the previous theoretical tool-kit, i.e. the micro model and the two-step procedure, can be used to answer all three questions. Detailed theoretical models must be left for further research.

Direct action, mobilizing resources, or investing in organization as behavioral alternatives

In explaining protest behavior social movement scholars usually do not take into account what exactly the behavioral alternatives, i.e. strategies, are that individuals or groups face. Social movements or protest groups usually choose various kinds of activities to reach their goals and not just direct protest action such as staging demonstrations. The case study described in chapter 4, section 2, illustrates this.[7] In this section, we will suggest some theoretical ideas about conditions for the choice of strategies that need further theoretical elaboration and empirical test. The major thrust of the argument is that the micro model suggested in chapter 2 is capable of answering questions about the choice of strategies.

Assume there is a group of individuals who know each other. They have a common goal and are dissatisfied, and they are willing to do something in order to change the situation. They may consider three behavioral alternatives. One is *direct action* such as organizing demonstrations, suing or negotiating with the goal of putting direct pressure on the target to meet their demands. A second option is to first *mobilize resources* such as recruiting others who are willing to support them in different ways. Such support may consist in giving legal advice, commitment to participate in future direct action, or to invest time in organizing action. Finally, the group members might think about setting up first some *organization* such as developing some explicit rules about the division of labor and about leadership functions. Which of these alternatives are chosen in what sequence? Or is there sometimes only one "best" strategy so that alternatives are not taken into account?

To answer this question the micro model specified in the previous chapter and the underlying general theory (in particular value expectancy theory) can be applied. The basic theoretical idea is that the group members will discuss the advantages and disadvantages of each strategy and then make joint decisions, where each member has weighed the pros and cons. If differences in (cognitive and normative) beliefs of the group members are small, a unanimous opinion about strategies to be chosen may emerge quickly.

These perceived advantages or, put differently, costs and benefits need not be instrumental. That is to say, actors need not calculate what the most efficient strategies are, in their view. Culture in the sense of ideological beliefs may be important. Normative views of participatory democracy that require unanimity may be important (see, e.g., Polletta 2005 for an interesting case study). If such views are strong, actors may dispense with efficiency. Thus, which organizational form will be adopted very much depends on the beliefs and values of the group members.

To illustrate these ideas we will look at two possible sequences. One sequence is the following:

Sequence 1: Mobilization, organization, direct action.

When will this sequence be chosen? Assume that the group is relatively small. The members might reason that it is too small to be successful. That is to say, their *expectation of success of joint action* and, as a consequence, their *perceived personal influence* will be higher when they mobilize others and, in addition, put some effort into organizing their activities. But the necessary condition for expected group success and personal influence is that there is an *expectation of successful mobilization.* If the members would expect that they will not be able to recruit more resources the sequence will not even begin. Another important variable is the *costs of mobilization.* Maybe the group members think that they could mobilize further resources, but that this will take too much time.

But assume the group decides to mobilize resources and recruits a great number of supporters. The group members may reason that some organization is necessary to optimally assign the resources and organize direct action. For example, rules may be suggested to set up some division of labor – such as taking the different steps to organize direct action. As a final step direct action is taken.

These factors may also help to explain another sequence:

Sequence 2: Direct action, mobilization, organization.

Assume the members think that an announcement (per email to friends and acquaintances) to convene at some place and express their grievances will be likely to recruit a great number of participants so that one will be heard. That is to say, the expectation of the success of joint direct action (and, thus perceived individual influence by direct action) is relatively high, and the incentives to undertake this action are high as well. This direct action may generate the expected attention in the press; this leads to the expectation that direct action with a larger group would be necessary to achieve the group's goals. Successful mobilization activities start. Next, organizational activities follow as a preparation for further action.

These examples suggest that we can specify various conditions for the termination of a sequence at a certain point. For example, in sequence 2 direct action may not get the expected attention so that the group decides not to take any further action in the future.

The sequences were explained by looking at changes or certain values of micro variables that triggered the sequences. In addition, the two-step procedure described in chapter 5, section 5 could be applied: macro events such as government decisions may influence the individual incentives that set in motion a certain sequence.

When do individuals decide to transfer resources to a social movement organization?

The previous section assumed that individuals face three options: engaging in mobilization of resources, direct action or investing in organizing collective action. In this section, we will address the other side of the coin: we do not focus on activities to mobilize resources but on the decision to provide resources. The option many individuals face is whether to support a movement by transferring some resources like money and free time. A basic assumption of the RMP is that organizations or groups mobilize and use resources in order to achieve their goals. But the availability of resources depends on the extent to which *individuals* assign resources to SMOs (see hypotheses 1 to 3 of Figure 5.2). These individuals may also be representatives of organizations. The first step in explaining the successful *mobilization* of resources of SMOs thus is to answer the question under which conditions individual actors decide to *transfer* their resources to support a movement. To answer this question, let us start with a simple example: assume some person P had a salary increase of $200. When will P spend the money to support a given movement – say, the anti-nuclear movement?

The answer to this question follows from our micro model. The reason is that the provision of resources to a SMO is a kind of contribution to a public good. One kind of contribution is direct action like protest behavior. Another contribution is indirect: one provides resources that the movement can use to contribute to the public good. In fact, providing resources is a second-order public good (see chapter 3). It seems plausible that the following conditions are relevant for a transfer of resources to a movement or group.

1   A first condition is that *the resources an individual disposes of can actually be used by a movement*. For example, if P wins a monthly subscription of a newspaper it would be difficult to transfer this resource to use for a movement. However, there are many resources such as money, free time, and knowledge that can be used and transferred to a movement.

2   Another variable is the *cost of transferring a resource to a movement*. For example, assume a lawyer has the knowledge that would be highly relevant to a SMO and would probably increase its chances of success. Nonetheless, the time and money forgone when advising the movement might be too costly for the lawyer.

3   The next factors refer to public goods preferences, alternative conflicting goals, and perceived influence.

   a   P may share the goal of a movement, but the *intensity of conflicting goals* may be still higher. For example, P may urgently need some new books for his or her study which increase the likelihood of a good grade – which may be his primary goal. Therefore, the resources will be put to personal use.

   b   P's decision to transfer the money or at least part of it would further depend on the *extent to which he or he shares the goals of the movement*. In other words, the intensity of the preference for the public good is relevant.

   c   P will consider the *efficacy* of the resource transfer for the provision of the public good. P may think that the resources he might be willing to transfer would not make the provision of the good more likely. It would be an interesting question for further research whether efficacy of resource transfer and efficacy of direct action differ.

4   There may be *moral incentives* that prevent or promote the assignment of resources to the movement. For example, P may feel obliged to first pay his

debts to a friend or his or her parents before giving money to a movement. Or P may feel obliged to support a movement even if his or her support might not be efficacious.

5   *Social incentives* are relevant as well: positive or negative rewards from important others to support (or not support) a movement are an incentive for transferring resources.

To conclude, the previous argument suggests that the micro model can be applied to explain when individuals transfer resources or engage in direct action. Which decision is made depends on the extent to which the incentives of the micro model are stronger for one than for the other alternative.

Individual resources as a condition for protest

The RMP comes in different versions. One is a micro version (see above, section 1) claiming that individual resources trigger political action. We discussed already one hypotheses of this version stating that social integration – which is an individual resource – matters for protest. We saw that this hypothesis is not valid.

We further discussed McCarthy and Zald's (1977) hypotheses 1 and 2 (see Figure 5.2) that a general increase in resources in a society leads to a greater availability of resources to SMSs and to the development of new SMIs and SMSs. This suggests that on the micro level individuals whose resources increase decide to transfer resources to SMOs or invest to found new SMOs. However, individuals transfer resources only under certain conditions (as McCarthy and Zald themselves emphasize). Some hypotheses about these conditions have been discussed in the previous section.

In general, the previous two sections indicate that the availability of individual resources is only one condition that leads to either direct action or indirect contributions to collective action. To be sure, available resources lower the costs of contributing to public goods. But other costs and benefits that are included in our micro model are important as well. In the extreme case, resources may be completely irrelevant. For example, a politically satisfied person who is not interested in politics at all may dispose of plentiful resources which will not at all be conducive to protest. On the other hand, incentives to political action may be high, and a little increase in resources (such as free time) may then trigger protest.

This argument is in line with Verba, Schlozman, and Brady's "Civic Voluntarism Model" (1995) which also includes, apart from resources, other factors. As the authors put it: "Resources appear to matter for political participation. Resources are, however, only one of the components of our Civic Voluntarism Model" (343). Some of these factors such as political efficacy are part of the micro model specified in the previous chapters. Other factors such as political interest are different. Those factors, we would argue, are only relevant if they are associated with incentives. We do not agree with the authors in regard to their critique of explanations of political participation, based on a rational choice approach (see, e.g., 1995: 383–387). It seems that they are attacking a narrow version that is not the one advanced in this book (see chapter 1). What can be learned from their book is the detailed measurement of resources by survey research.

The work of Edward J. Walsh and associates about mobilization in the wake of the nuclear accident at Three Mile Island in 1979 further illustrates the role of individual resources.[8] One of the basic hypotheses is that "both grievances and structural situations of aggrieved groups should be treated as variables in the RM [resource mobilization] perspective" (Walsh 1981: 1). More specifically, Walsh argues that "suddenly imposed or abruptly realized and continuing major grievances" make mobilization likely when there is some "threshold level of resources able to be activated when perceived grievances increase dramatically" (Walsh 1981: 18). Why will grievances operate if there exists a certain level of *individual* resources? To be sure, resources reduce the costs of mobilization and activism. But only changing costs may not be sufficient. Assume that all the other incentives of our micro model are very low. Plenty of resources would not be sufficient. It seems plausible that the accident raised perceived influence in the population that protests against nuclear energy could now – after the accident – be successful because the danger of nuclear energy may have become evident to everybody. It is further plausible that the accident triggered various other incentives: a protest norm (moral indignation) may have been activated which further led to mutual rewards for participation (social incentives). The grievances due to the accident may further have influenced other incentives (see our discussion of the interdependence of incentives). Although all these hypotheses are not tested in the research by Walsh and associates, the detailed account of the mobilization process after the nuclear accident in Three Mile Island suggests that these speculations seem plausible. At least the research suggests that individual resources alone are not enough. They are only important when they are embedded as a component in a whole set of incentives.

11. Resource mobilization and collective action theory

How are both theoretical perspectives related? When we compare their theoretical structure, both consist of macro variables. But whereas the major macro variable in the theory of collective action is group size, the RMP consists of a whole array of other macro variables. As we saw before, a clear microfoundation of the RMP is missing. This is another major difference to the theory of collective action.

The dependent variables of the RMP are manifold and not clear. But the RMP as well as the theory of collective action focus on collective political action. Thus, both approaches are comparable.

As far as the micro version of the RMP is concerned, it is compatible with the micro model suggested in the previous two chapters. "Resources" are part of this model: they refer to costs of collective action, i.e. they are behavioral constraints or opportunities in terms of the theory of collective action. But resources are only one class of incentives relevant for political action.

We saw that the RMP lacks explanatory power inasmuch as the kinds of movements or political action are not explained. It was shown in chapter 3 that this is possible with the theory of collective action – via incentives of the micro level.

To conclude, the RMP and the theory of collective action are not contradictory theoretical approaches. The rich macro structure of the RMP can be supplemented by the micro model and by micro-macro hypotheses, i.e. by bridge assumptions.

12. What can we learn from the resource mobilization perspective for the explanation of social movement phenomena?

There is no doubt that the RMP consists of many important macro factors that often have some effect on collective political action. These macro factors are the "infrastructural options and supports" (Zald and McCarthy 1987: 45). Bringing these factors to the fore is a major achievement, compared to the state of the sociology of social movements before the new perspective has emerged. However, as our presentation and critique of the RMP indicates, the approach is incomplete in several respects. Future theory and research should concentrate on macro-micro explanations and elaborate in detail what exactly the effects of the various macro variables on the incentives of the micro model are under various conditions.

As long as this microfoundation is absent, the existing inventory of macro factors could be used as heuristics: when it turns out that the change of macro resources is accompanied by changes of protest events one could try to find independent evidence about the kind of incentives that have been influenced by the change of resources. If direct measurement is not available, there might be proxies such as the extent to which an "alternative sector" exists in a region or to what extent voters of a certain party like the Green Party in Germany who are close to social movements live in certain areas in a region. These indicators suggest strong individual incentives to protest behavior.

13. Summary and conclusions

We began by reconstructing the propositions in McCarthy and Zald's article from 1977 which is regarded as the founding work of the resource mobilization perspective (RMP). The authors' "illustrative propositions" as well as their orienting statements were reformulated as two causal models. It is important that the RMP comes as a macro and as a micro version, the former being the mainstream perspective which the discussion in this chapter focuses on. The major conceptual problem of the perspective is the concept of resources which we tried to clarify. Important for the major argument of this book is that the background theory of the approach is the theory of rational action and that implicitly a micro-macro model is used which is not spelled out in detail. Deficits further exist in regard to the explanatory power of the approach. For example, it cannot explain the form of social movements and political action.

We further discussed the validity of the perspective: it was argued that the micro model specified in previous chapters can be used to derive situations where available resources – the major variable of the perspective – do not bring about social movement related phenomena. The RMP has further difficulties in explaining spontaneous protests. The conclusion then is that resources are at best only sufficient conditions for protest. In other words, if there are resources, protest ensues; but if there are no resources protest may obtain too. Thus, one cannot conclude that if there is protest there must have been resources.

The chapter further discusses some theoretical hypotheses about when actors decide to mobilize resources, to take direct action and to invest in organizing a group. Further, it is discussed when actors decide to transfer resources to a movement or a group.

Is the RMP compatible with the theory of collective action that was discussed in chapter 3? A major difference consists in the substantive content of the macro variables, and in the lack of a microfoundation of the RMP. The major contribution of the RMP for the explanation of political action is the rich array of macro factors that often lead to political action by changing the incentives on the individual level. But these factors often do not bring about political action when the "right" incentives do not change. Thus, the RMP badly needs a microfoundation. Furthermore, hypotheses and research on macro-to-micro and micro-to-macro links are needed.

The argument that available resources often do not lead to protest because the incentives do not change to an extent that triggers political action is not based on existing empirical research. As was said above, there is so far no disconfirming evidence of basic propositions of the RMP based on rigorous research. This may have different reasons. One is that the RMP is difficult to falsify. This is certainly due to the broad concept of resources *and* due to the fact that it is not specified what kinds of resources are relevant for what kind of movement related phenomena. Thus, if *some* kind of resource is found to bring about *some* protest or group formation, this is a confirmation. The reason for all the confirmations may be that it is not difficult to find always some existing resources if there is protest. To illustrate, let us look again at a hypothesis mentioned already by McCarthy *et al.* (1988: 75): "The more plentiful both material and human resources are in a community, the more likely is the development of most organizational forms." Are any resources relevant? Which resources are conditions for which kind of organizational forms? To be sure, in their research the authors define resources clearly and provide some quantitative analysis by comparing various groups. But in the analysis of single cases one might select a case where there has been protest. One will certainly find some resources. Because it is not specified what kind of resources lead to what kind of political action, one can claim that the hypothesis is confirmed. It is thus difficult to find falsifications of the RMP

For a rigorous test of hypotheses of the RMP, it would be important to find cases where there are resources but no protest. This is the kind of situation that would be a falsifying instance for the RMP.

It would be a worthwhile undertaking to look in detail at the existing research that is relevant for testing or applying hypotheses of the RMP. Such a meta-analysis should develop criteria for test rigor. For example, have at least two cases been compared so that a falsification was possible? Is there any information in the paper or research about why certain samples or cases have been selected?

6 Political opportunity structures, protest, and social movements

It seems that the political opportunity structure (POS) perspective – also called the "political process model" – has edged out the resource mobilization perspective which was dominant in the 1970s. To be sure, Eisinger's seminal paper of 1973 laid the foundation of the POS perspective and was thus published earlier than McCarthy and Zald's founding paper of the resource mobilization perspective in 1977. But the POS perspective could establish itself as a distinctive approach only in the beginning of the 1980s.[1] In this chapter we begin with a detailed restatement and discussion of P. Eisinger's theory. We then address major conceptual problems of the perspective. One issue is whether POSs should be seen as objective or subjective "chances of success." POSs are defined as changes in the political environment that influence the "chances of success." The definition thus contains a causal statement. Is this really useful? We further compare the concepts of POS and resources. As in the previous chapters, we look at the explanatory power of the POS perspective, we ask whether there is an implicit micro-macro model, and analyze how the free rider problem is solved. We further review the empirical evidence for the perspective. Among other things, we present several types of situations where the perspective does not work. In the section on recent developments we analyze the models by D. McAdam and S. Tarrow. In regard to the general objective of the book, the section on the synthesis of the POS perspective and the theory of collective action seems particularly important.

1. The political environment and the chances of success: P. Eisinger's theory

We will first discuss the basic concept that gave the perspective its name: political opportunity structure. We will then deal with Eisinger's basic propositions.

The concept of political opportunities

Eisinger (1973) concentrates on the effects of the "political environment" (11 – all subsequent numbers in parentheses refer to pages in this article) which is the "context within which politics takes place" (11). This context is called the "structure of political opportunities" (11):

That is to say, such factors as the nature of the chief executive, the mode of aldermanic election, the distribution of social skills and status, and the degree of social disintegration, taken individually or collectively, serve in various ways to obstruct or facilitate citizen activity in pursuit of political goals. Other environmental factors, such as the climate of governmental responsiveness and the level of community resources, help to establish the chances of success of citizen political activity. In short, elements in the environment impose certain constraints on political activity or open avenues for it. The manner in which individuals and groups in the political system behave, then, is not simply a function of the resources they command but of the openings, weak spots, barriers, and resources of the political system itself. There is, in this sense, interaction, or linkage, between the environment, understood in terms of the notion of a structure of political opportunities, and political behavior. (11–12)

This extensive quotation provides a definition of POSs as well as the basic proposition.[2] In regard to the definition, Eisinger lists some macro factors – called political opportunity structures – such as "governmental responsiveness" which more or less promote the *attainment of individual goals*, i.e. increase "the chances of success of citizen political activity." Three features of this definition are important. (1) Variables of the political environment are only called "POS" if they are related to the goals of individuals. Thus, in order to know whether a factor is a POS we have to ascertain the goals of the actors. What these goals are is not specified. They must be ascertained empirically. Only then it can be decided whether a POS exists. (2) The "chances of success" are objectively defined, i.e. from the viewpoint of an observer. They are thus *objective probabilities*. Accordingly, the "analyst" determines (12) how likely it is whether or to what extent some factor from the political environment leads to a group's goal attainment (i.e. "chances of success"). The perception of citizens or groups is not part of the definition. (3) It is of utmost importance to note that in order to determine whether a certain factor of the political environment is a POS or not, one has to establish a *causal relationship*, i.e. the question must be answered to what extent a factor changes the probability that goals are achieved.

Let us illustrate the concept of POS by some examples from Eisinger's article. He argues that mayor-council governments are "more accountable, and hence more available, to citizens than manager-council governments" (17). The reason is that the "mayor must please a constituency; the manager is a professional, hired by the city council, who maintains his office at their sufferance" (17). In this example, the openness of the political environment is determined by looking at the incentives of an incumbent government to please citizen groups. The existence of such incentives will make it more likely that the "chances of success" of certain groups are relatively high if they engage in some political activity. Thus, the objective probability is determined indirectly via incentives to please citizens.

Another indicator for an open POS is whether a city has received "Model Cities planning funds" (21). When a city has received such funds "this may serve as an indication of responsiveness to what is often the most frequently named problem facing the cities – the lack of decent housing" (21). Thus, the government took certain action, namely applying for "Model Cities planning funds." This suggests that the government is motivated to satisfy certain citizen demands. Again, the "chances of success" are not directly measured. Instead, indirect indicators are used which may provide some hint at incentives or motivations to satisfy citizen goals, if there is some political behavior.

The theory

As the previous quotation indicates, POSs have an impact on "political behavior." Eisinger emphasizes that protest is "in part" (14) a function of political opportunities. What exactly is this function? Two conflicting hypotheses are discussed. One is the *linear model*, i.e. there is a negative linear relationship between POSs as the independent and protest as the dependent variable (see Figure 6.1): if POSs are very low protest is high; increasing opportunities reduce protest behavior. The *curvilinear model* which Eisinger advances and which he finds supported by his data resembles an inverted u-curve (see Figure 6.1): if opportunities are very low protest is absent; increasing opportunities raise protest. When political opportunities exceed a certain value protest declines. In other words, mixed systems, i.e. systems where opportunities are in part open and in part closed trigger the highest extent of protest.

The relationship between POSs and protest is a macro proposition. Most scholars who advance such propositions are not satisfied with them. They provide a micro-macro model to explain the macro relationship. Eisinger is no exception. The question is why there may be a linear or a curvilinear relationship. The linear model holds if protest is a "frustrated response" (14): groups which are "unable to gain access to decision-making councils by conventional means" (14) express their frustration by protesting. Low POSs thus lead to high protest. If the system opens up frustration and, thus, protest decrease. This resembles a frustration-aggression mechanism.

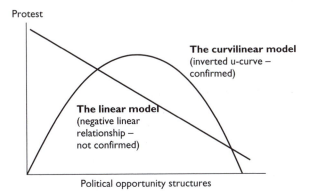

Figure 6.1 Two hypotheses about the relationship between political opportunity structures and protest

The curvilinear relationship assumes, contrary to the linear model, that protest first increases and then declines if POSs increase. Why? Eisinger seems to assume that there are rising expectations that political authorities will yield to the demands of the groups. In a mixed system (which is in part open and in part closed) "the pace of change does not keep up with expectations" (15), i.e. expectations change faster than the change of the political opportunities (or the decisions of the authorities). Protest is an expression of "impatience" (15). This could mean that the rising expectations generate discontent. If the system is largely open the citizens' demands are increasingly met so that protest declines.

Eisinger distinguishes between protest behavior and violence, and discusses various differences between them. The previous propositions refer to protest which is the focus of Eisinger's article. We will therefore not discuss his propositions about violence.

As was said before, protest is only "in part" a function of opportunities. When Eisinger discusses the results of his test of the POS proposition, he concludes that opportunities are only "mildly related" (25) to protest or that opportunities play only a "small part" (28) for the explanation of protest. The question then arises as to what the other factors are. One hypothesis is that protest "is a product ... of a cost-benefit calculation ..." (13). In contrast to the POS proposition, this is a hypothesis on the individual level. What is the relationship between both propositions? As we saw before, Eisinger explains protests by certain effects of the changing opportunities: if they are closed, frustration is high; if they open up, frustration decreases (the linear model). In the curvilinear model, opportunity structures generate expectations and, if they are not fulfilled, discontent originates. These expectations are beliefs about the likelihood that certain public goods are provided. "Frustration" is discontent with the provision of public goods. The explanation Eisinger suggests is a micro-macro explanation and thus insinuates a micro-macro model.

Eisinger mentions other factors that influence protest (25–26). Deprivation is one factor. This seems to be a property of individual actors. Another factor is "organizational needs" of elites who employ protest in order to enlarge their organization. A third factor refers to certain demands that are not part of routine politics. An example is the demand of student power in the university. These causes "are in some degree shaped by the nature of the political system" (26). "Deprivation" is certainly a micro variable. The other two factors are macro variables referring to "needs" or "demands" of groups. When we assume that these are ultimately needs or demands of the members of the groups then – again – a macro-to-micro relationship is implied. This time this is an analytical relation: the macro-needs are needs of individuals that have certain effects on political behavior.

The micro-macro model suggested by Eisinger can be depicted as a causal model that is depicted in Figure 6.2. On the macro level, a curvilinear relationship between opportunity structures and collective political action is assumed (arc 1). The question that Eisinger does not answer is whether this is a *causal* relationship or only a *correlation*. We assume that the relationship is not causal because it is explained by the effects that opportunity structures have on individual incentives to participate. As we saw before, opportunities affect incentives (arrow 2) which, in turn, lead to

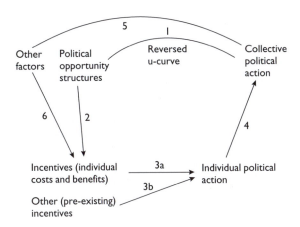

Figure 6.2 Eisinger's theory of political opportunity structures

individual participation (arrow 3a) that aggregate to collective political action. Opportunity structures thus have an *in*direct and not a direct effect on collective political action. We further include "other factors" in the diagram which correlate with political action (arc 5). It is plausible that these other factors have also effects on the micro level incentives (arrow 6). One may speculate that not all micro factors are changed by changing opportunities. For example, the goals of the groups exist before the opportunities change and are not influenced by changing opportunities. Only the likelihood of goal attainment is changed. There are thus pre-existing incentives – see the figure (arrow 3b).

Let us now look at the theory again, but this time together with the definition of POS. Figure 6.3 highlights that the definition of POSs includes a causal statement. Thus, only if it has been determined empirically that a certain factor has a causal effect on goal attainment then POSs are given. The theory asserts that protest obtains if the factors of the environment *and* their effect on goal attainment are given. For example, if a new coalition has been formed *and* if it has been established that this coalition increases the likelihood of goal attainment, then the theory predicts that protest increases. The figure further includes what we have seen before, namely that POSs affect the incentives to protest.

Eisinger's test of his theory

Eisinger analyzes the incidence of protest, based on articles in local newspapers, from 43 American cities. These data include indicators of protest as well as various other indicators that measure, according to Eisinger, POSs. The problem with the data is that POSs are not measured directly. That is, Eisinger applies many untested propositions linking his indicators to POSs. Two examples were mentioned above when we illustrated the POS concept. One was that the mayor-council governments

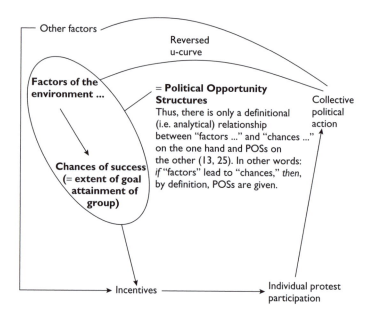

Figure 6.3 The definition of POSs and POS theory

provide more opportunities than manager-council governments. The reason is that the "mayor must please a constituency; the manager is a professional, hired by the city council, who maintains his office at their sufferance" (17). It is not tested empirically whether mayor-council governments increase the objective probability of goal attainment of politically active groups to a higher extent than manager-council governments. This problem exists for all the measures Eisinger employs. Sometimes the assumptions are more, and sometimes less plausible, but Eisinger never provides empirical evidence that the indicators he uses are linked to the probability of goal attainment of certain groups.

It is important to note that other factors are not measured either. Eisinger is only concerned with indicators for POSs and their relationships to protest. This procedure implies the assumption that POSs are always related to protest – whatever the values of the other variables are. There is thus an additive effect of POSs which can be expressed as an equation:

$$PROTEST = a_1 + b_1\ POS + b_2\ FACTOR1 + b_3\ FACTOR2 + \ldots +$$

For example, assume collective deprivation is one of the other factors. Now assume that the form of government in a number of cities changes from manager-council to mayor-council government, i.e. there is an increase of POSs. At the same time, the collective deprivation strongly decreases. When we control for this factor we would nonetheless find a positive coefficient and thus a positive effect for POS.

When we assume that Eisinger's data provide a test of his theory then the curvilinear proposition is confirmed, but it is certainly a very weak confirmation. The graph of the function (27) shows many outliers, and a rigorous regression analysis with an additive and quadratic term is not provided. Nonetheless, a visual inspection of his graph seems to be compatible with an inverted u-curve. So we conclude that Eisinger's test can only be regarded as a very first and preliminary examination of his proposition.

2. Conceptual problems: What are political opportunity structures?

The basic concept of the perspective is burdened with several problems. One is whether POS should be defined objectively or subjectively. Another is what the difference is between political and other – non-political – opportunities. A third question is whether a priori classifications of dimensions of POSs are meaningful. Finally, the question arises as to what the difference between resources and opportunities is. These problems are discussed in this section.

Objective or perceived opportunities?

There are two definitions of POS in the literature. According to the *objectivist definition* POSs are defined as environmental changes that change the objective likelihood of goal attainment. Thus, an omniscient observer determines whether there has been a change in the likelihood of goal attainment. It is irrelevant whether the actors are aware of these changes or not. The second *subjectivist definition* posits that POSs are only given if there are perceived changes in the environment, i.e. if (subjective) expectations of success change. POS theory would thus claim that only changes in perceived goal attainment matter. These perceptions need not be based on any objective change. What are the advantages and disadvantages of an objectivist and a subjectivist definition?

The objectivist definition

As an illustration of the problems of this definition let us return to Eisinger's concept. As was noted above, he defines opportunity structures as environmental variables that increase or lessen the probability of goal attainment of individuals ("chances of success") if groups are politically active. He thus refers to *objective probabilities*, i.e. probabilities that are not distorted by the actor's perceptions but which are objectively given, from the viewpoint of third parties such as social scientists. When Tarrow (1994) and Kriesi *et al.* (1992), two of the major proponents of POS theory, mention as a type of opportunity the availability of influential allies they refer to objective phenomena (Tarrow 1994: 86–89). The same holds for the definition by McAdam (1995: 224): "By expanding political opportunities I mean changes in either the institutional features or informal political alignments of a given political system that significantly reduce the power disparity between a given challenging group and the state." The "objective" feature of the definition is that there needs to be a reduction of the power disparity – from the perspective of an observer. In their review of the field McAdam, McCarthy, and Zald (1988: 699) define "political opportunity structure" as "the receptivity or vulnerability of the political system to organized protest by a given challenging group." Goldstone and Tilly (2001: 182) provide an objectivist definition as well: they define "opportunity" as "the probability that social protest actions will lead to success in achieving a desired outcome" (see also 183, where the definition is explained).[3]

One problem with the objectivist definition is the measurement of the objective probability of goal attainment in case of political action. Assume, for example, the outcome of an election led to the formation of a grand coalition of the conservative and socialist party. What is the objective probability that the environmental movement can accomplish its goals? It is difficult to imagine that anybody can answer this question. So far the proponents of POS theory have not suggested any rigorous measurement devices. In empirical studies it is usually decided *ad hoc* whether there has been a change of opportunity or not. Our discussion of Eisinger's study has illustrated this.

Lacking a rigorous measurement procedure, there is a second best device to get some indication for existing POSs: it is to look at *incentives to authorities or politicians to meet certain demands of groups*. This is the procedure that was applied in Eisinger's seminal paper and that was discussed before. This procedure is only a second best solution because there are usually no data about the incentives of authorities to take into account the goals of certain groups, but we can make plausible guesses. For example, it is plausible that in a democracy the incentives of governments to consider the goals of groups are higher than in a dictatorship. Or assume that the Green Party which is to a great extent based on the social movement sector joins a government. This will certainly increase incentives of the government to meet demands of the alternative sector. In this particular case, it may be argued that the party program includes certain goals and that therefore representatives of the party will try to realize these goals, and these goals benefit certain groups. A related argument is provided by Meyer and Minkoff (2004: 1468–1469) who take the difference between Democrats and Republicans in congress as an indicator of "general political opportunity structure."

Another problem of ascertaining POSs arises if there are different groups with different and conflicting goals. There may be a pro-abortion and an anti-abortion movement, a pro- and anti-nuclear movement, etc. Thus, what "provokes mobilization for one movement or constituency may depress mobilization of another and be completely irrelevant to a third" (Meyer and Minkoff 2004: 1461). If opportunities are defined as the extent to which changes in the political environment change "the" chances of success it is meant to what extent the goals of all groups are accomplished. How does one proceed to arrive at an overall measure of the extent to which in the whole polity the chances of success change? We need some device for setting off the increasing chances of some and the decreasing chances of other groups.

The previous discussion refers to problems of defining the concept and of applying it to empirical cases. Another problem is the theoretical fruitfulness of an objectivist definition. As a variable of POS theory this definition implies that perceptions are irrelevant. That is to say, if by some operational definition scholars detect that the objective probability of goal attainment for a certain group increases, the prediction is that this affects protest behavior. Misperceptions are irrelevant. This is hardly plausible, and there is empirical evidence that perceived changes of the political environment matter, as will be seen below.

Why do proponents of POS theory adopt an objectivist definition? It seems that the assumption is made that in general changes of opportunities are correctly perceived (see, e.g., Tilly 1978: 133). However, this is often a problematic assumption. For example, Kurzman (1996; see also Kenny 2001) describes a mismatch between "structural opportunities" and perceived opportunities in the Iranian revolutionary movement from 1977 to 1979. A mismatch may also occur because the opportunities that are described in the literature are often rather complicated so that an ordinary citizen will hardly perceive them correctly. For example, opportunities may change in the form of a changing "political alignment of groups within the larger political environment" (McAdam 1982: 40). It may be difficult for an ordinary citizen to perceive the sometimes subtle changes in power structures *and* to assess the change of the objective probability to attain political goals if groups are active. "Political opportunity structures are comprised of specific configurations of resources, institutional arrangements and historical precedents for social mobilization, which facilitate the development of protest movements in some instances and constrain them in others" (Kitschelt 1986: 58). One can imagine how difficult it is even for social movements or interest groups to assess whether a change of a "specific configuration of resources, institutional arrangements and historical precedents for social mobilization" increases or decreases the probability of goal attainment (or of mobilization or political action).

These difficulties in ascertaining objective opportunity structures are anything but a minor problem. The theory becomes amenable to *ad hoc* explanations (see, e.g., Gamson and Meyer 1996: 276) and to strategies that immunize the theory against falsification. For example, one might observe certain changes of political action over time. One might then look for macro factors that have changed as well, and it is very likely that one will always find such factors. These factors are then identified as the "political opportunities" that have brought about the protests. This is a circular argument, and we suspect that this is sometimes used in empirical case studies: it cannot be ruled out that authors select cases where protest and certain changes of the political environment occurred together so that POS theory is confirmed. As long as there are no clear measurement procedures it is easy to classify or not to classify changes of the political environment as changes of opportunity structures.

The subjectivist definition

According to this definition, POSs are given if changes in the political environment give rise to changes in the (subjective) expectation of success (i.e. perceived goal attainment). Such a *subjectivist definition* is provided by Tarrow who defines "political opportunity structures" as "... dimensions of the political environment that provide incentives for people to undertake collective action by affecting their expectations for success or failure" (1994: 85; see also Tarrow 1996: 54; for similar definitions see Kriesi 1995: XIII; Klandermans 1997: 168 – both refer to Tarrow).[4] In other words, features of the political environment are, *by definition*, only "opportunity structures" if they change "expectations for success or failure." If the (objective) "chances of success" in Figure 4.3 are replaced by "expectations of success," the figure captures the subjectivist definition. In this definition, it is irrelevant whether the chances of success are perceived correctly. The environmental factors, as they are perceived, affect political action.

There are fewer problems with this definition than with the objectivist definition. (1) The measurement is less problematic because we don't need to ascertain objective probabilities but only the individual's perceptions. These can be and often have been measured by surveys.

Another possibility to get some hint about perception is to look at the *incentives* for activists or other persons to scrutinize the political scene for finding weak spots that allow to improve the group's situation. Activists thus may continuously analyze the political situation and try to explore whether there are any signs for increasing chances of success. Although incentives to screen political events in regard to the chances of goal attainment may be high, it may be difficult to guess to what extent a given political change affects the chances of success. For example, if a new government is elected it may be more difficult to predict chances of success than after some time when the government has set up a working program. Thus, it is important to what extent there are *visible signals* for groups that protest or other forms of collective action will be successful (see Meyer and Minkoff 2004: 1470–1471). These signals may be party programs or various statements of politicians about their political views.

(2) How an overall assessment of the expected chances of success can be arrived at is not clear in either definition. Perhaps the following procedure might be appropriate: when we dispose of a subjective measure of the perceived chances of success for each group we may form simply an additive scale, where subjective probabilities are subtracted when groups believe that their chances of success are reduced and added when groups think their chances of success increase.

(3) When we subscribe to the assumption that human behavior depends on perceptions then the subjectivist definition is theoretically preferable to the objectivist one. Whereas POS theory that includes the objectivist proposition yields wrong predictions if environmental factors are not correctly perceived, POS theory that includes the subjectivist definition solves exactly this problem. We fully agree with McAdam, Tarrow, and Tilly (2001: 43): "No opportunity, however objectively open, will invite mobilization unless it is a) visible to potential challengers and b) perceived as an opportunity."

(4) It may be argued that the previous point is correct but that we would nonetheless like to know what the actual probabilities are, i.e. under what objective conditions individuals form which beliefs about reality. This is certainly an interesting question. But, as was said before, the objective probabilities are most often difficult

to obtain. In such situations hypotheses about conditions for misperception cannot be tested. But in general it would be a very interesting extension of the POS perspective to explain how political changes are perceived and under what conditions. But this is an additional question and it does not speak against the fruitfulness of using a subjectivist definition.

To conclude, a subjectivist definition seems superior to an objectivist one. In other words, it is preferable to define "political opportunities" as changes of the political environment that change the expectations of success.

The previous discussion implicitly assumed that it is useful to include a causal statement in the definition of POS. We think that this is not useful. This question is discussed below (see the section "Do we need a 'causal definition' of political opportunities?").

Why focus on "chances of success"?

Eisinger's definition of POS includes a causal relationship between changes of the political environment and the "chances of success." The "chances of success" are only one incentive that may affect protest behavior. As our micro model in chapters 3 and 4 suggests, there are many other incentives, and the "chances of success," i.e. (actual or perceived) group success, is not even the incentive with the strongest effect. The question arises of why the definition includes just this incentive? Why not define a POS as an environmental change that changes some incentive? Thus, if one wishes to include incentives in the definition of POS it is an open question why just one incentive is included and, if it must be one incentive, why the "chances of success"?

Political, cultural, and other opportunities

Eisinger (1973) refers to "political" opportunities. The question that he does not answer is what distinguishes political from non-political opportunities. There is no clear answer either in the subsequent literature.

After Eisinger's article various classifications of opportunities are suggested. For example, Koopmans and Statham (1999: 228) introduce "discursive opportunity structure" (see also, e.g., Ferree 2003: 309; McCammon *et al.* 2007: 731), Kurzman (1998) deals with "organizational opportunities," and McAdam (1994: 39; 1996: 25) addresses "cultural opportunities." There is ample opportunity to introduce numerous other kinds of opportunities. For example, why not distinguish "economic opportunities," "cognitive opportunities," and "emotional opportunities"? Such classifications raise several questions.

(1) What exactly is the meaning of these new kinds of opportunities – compared to "political" opportunities? There are no clear demarcations of all these types of opportunities. Are these different concepts or can all be subsumed under an overarching concept "opportunity"? For example, what exactly is the difference between POS as defined above (i.e. a change in the political environment that changes the – subjective or objective – chances of success of groups) and "discursive political

opportunity structure"? This "may be seen as determining which ideas are considered 'sensible,' which constructions of reality are seen as 'realistic,' and which claims are held as 'legitimate' within a certain polity at a specific time" (Koopmans and Statham 1999: 228). It seems that the meaning of this term does not have anything to do with the chances of success of a group; it refers to the extent to which ideas are classified ("realistic," etc.) by a group. But since the authors refer to "opportunity" it is suggested that the term is similar to "political" opportunity structure. The problem of such new classifications of opportunities is that it is not clear what exactly they mean, and what their relation to the original meaning, suggested by Eisinger and many other scholars, is.

(2) What are these classifications good for? It is a weakness and not a strength of a "theory" when classifications instead of informative propositions abound. If the concept of opportunities is defined precisely, classifications are not needed. If a clear definition exists it is clear what phenomena – whether cultural, discursive, or economic – are opportunities. When we explain some protest event we could simply explore the situation and find the kinds of opportunity (i.e. the initial conditions) that matter. A good theory does not need classifications.

Is it theoretically fruitful to formulate POS theory only for "political" opportunities? Whatever "political" means, they are not sufficient to explain protest behavior. To illustrate, the increase of gasoline and oil prices would certainly not be termed a "political" opportunity. But they might have effects on protest behavior. One consequence of rising oil prices is that heating and driving becomes more costly. Many people might compensate these costs by working more. This increases opportunity costs, also for protesting. Driving to a demonstration site becomes more expensive as well. Another example: a decrease in postage or a decrease in the costs of using the internet lowers the costs of mobilization, but can hardly be called a "political" opportunity. Thus, POS theory should not include only "political" opportunities but opportunities in general.

The "dimensions" of political opportunities

It is common in the literature to distinguish different dimensions of POSs. For example, Tarrow (1998: chapter 5) lists five "key dimensions": "(1) the opening of access to participation; (2) the evidence of political realignment within the polity; (3) the appearance of influential allies; (4) emerging splits within the elite; and (5) a decline in the state's capacity or will to repress dissent" (76). McAdam (1996) provides a comparative discussion of dimensions suggested by several authors. Jasper and Goodwin (1999: 32–33) enumerate still other dimensions mentioned in the literature. In understanding what such dimensions refer to it is important to note that dimensions are not definitions of POS. Those who suggest dimensions assume that it is clear what the meaning of POS is. Further, dimensions are not classifications of POSs. Thus, Tarrow's dimensions refer to one and only one kind of opportunity structure and are not different kinds of POSs. Dimensions involve empirical propositions: it is claimed that the dimensions *affect* POSs. For example, according to Kitschelt "four factors [i.e. dimensions of POS – KDO] *determine* the openness of political regimes to new demands on the input side" (Kitschelt 1986: 63, italics added).

The question arises as to whether it is meaningful to classify certain dimensions (i.e. variables) of the political environment once and for all as political opportunities. For example, Kriesi *et al.* (1995: XIII) hold that "the POS is made up of four components: national cleavage structures, institutional structures, prevailing strategies, and alliance structures." Thus, a cleavage or, to mention another example, a "political realignment within the polity" are always political opportunities. This means – according to the definition of POS – that in all these situations the likelihood is high that in general the goal achievement of groups increases. If a subjectivist definition is adopted then the presence of the dimensions should increase the subjective probability of goal attainment. For example, according to Tarrow's dimension (4) it should hold true:

> If splits within the elite emerge, then the probability increases, that the goals of political groups are achieved (objectivist definition).

Apparently, the authors who suggest dimensions of POS implicitly assume that such a relationships exist. But what is the evidence for the existence of these relationships? For example, is it always and without exception the case that a split of an elite in general increases the likelihood that groups can accomplish their goals? There might be situations where groups exist with certain goals, but where none of the elite group accepts these goals and, thus, is not willing to support them. The same holds for political realignment.[5]

How problematic it is to specify dimensions that are assumed to have fixed relationships to probabilities of goal attainment is indicated by disagreements between authors about what the relevant dimensions are. McAdam (1996) notes that the dimension of state repressiveness is not consensual among the authors he discusses (28).[6] But McAdam thinks that this factor should be in the list of POSs. He further pleads to omit two dimensions that other authors include. What are the reasons? In regard to repression, the argument of McAdam is that there is "considerable empirical evidence attesting to the significance of this factor in shaping the level and nature of movement activity" (28). Let us look more closely at this argument. According to the definition of POS, repression (or repressiveness of a regime) is a POS *if* it increases the likelihood of goal achievement. If this is the case, then this increases protest. More formally, the argument reads:

$$(Decreasing\ repression \rightarrow Increasing\ probability\ of\ success) \rightarrow Protest$$

McAdam argues for including repressiveness in the list of POSs because it "shapes the level of social movement activity" – see the previous quotation. Thus, the dependent variable – movement activity – is seen as an indicator for the relevance of the independent variable. This is clearly a *circular argument*. That is to say, the incidence of the dependent variable is seen as a proof for the incidence of the independent variable. It seems that other authors provide similar types of argument.

Our conclusion from this discussion is that it is highly questionable to provide a priori lists of dimensions and claim that these are related to an increase or decrease of POSs. Dimensions involve empirical propositions, and it must therefore be tested empirically whether they affect the actual or perceived goal attainment of groups. In regard to repression, for example, it is well known that it may have quite different effects under different conditions: sometimes it has a deterrent and sometimes a radicalizing effect, and sometimes it has no effect at all. It is thus not recommendable to include repression in any list of "dimensions" of POSs with fixed effects on chances of success.

In general, thus, using a dimension to measure POSs without providing evidence for its effect on (objective or subjective) goal attainment is completely *ad hoc* and unacceptable. However, this is common practice (see also Meyer and Minkoff 2004: 1458–1461).

A possibility to "save" the dimensions is to regard them as possible indicators or heuristic rules of thumb that may help to find out whether changes in the political environment change the actual or perceived chances of success. A list of possible dimensions so far used in the literature is thus useful. But applying them needs a further step: providing data to examine the extent to which they change goal attainment of groups.

Do we need a "causal definition" of political opportunities?

The concept of POS is defined as a change in the political environment that raises the (actual or perceived) chances of success, i.e. the chances that actors' goals are realized if they engage in political action. The causal statement in this definition is:

changes in the environment → goal attainment in case of protest.

Why do we need to include this causal statement in the definition of the POS concept? I have not found any discussion of this point in the literature. An argument against a "causal definition" is this: various case studies refer to phenomena that proponents of the POS perspective call "political opportunities," but in these studies we do not find any definition that includes a causal statement and, in addition, the term "POS" is not even used. We will first illustrate this kind of study with an example and then draw some conclusions.

In analyzing the collapse of the communist regime in East Germany in 1989–1990 various changes in the economic and political environment occurred. These changes began with Gorbachev's glasnost and perestroika in 1985. This included, among other things, granting the Russian people more freedom and making the military backing of the East German regime less likely. Another event was the crackdown on the Chinese student movement in June 1989. The institution of the Monday prayers in Leipzig since 1982, the decision of Hungary to open its border to Austria and the decision of border officials on November 9, 1989, to open the border to West Berlin are events that contributed to the origin of the East German protests in 1989 and the collapse of the communist regime. These and other factors are included in detailed studies that try to explain the East German revolution (see, e.g., Opp, Voss, and Gern 1995; Pfaff 2006).

One of the questions raised in the literature is why these factors have instigated the protests. This is an important question. The reason is that it is hardly plausible that a Leipzig citizen goes to a demonstration because Gorbachev changed politics. The answer to this question is that these macro factors are relevant because they changed various incentives on the micro level. For example, the study by Opp, Gern, and Voss (1995) uses survey data that indicate that some of the events mentioned before increased people's belief that their protest could make a difference. In other words, the macro events are systematically connected to the micro model.

The case study of the protests in the Spanish mining town Llano del Beal that was described at length in chapter 4, section 2, proceeded in the same way. There were macro changes and these were related to the incentives of individual actors.

There are further many studies where the concept of POS is used but where the question arises of whether one could do without this concept. An example is the study on coalition formation in the pro-choice movement in the US by Staggenborg (1986). She argues that coalition work is influenced by "two different sorts of environmental conditions. First, coalitions were formed to take advantage of environmental *opportunity* in the period after 1970, the year in which repeal victories were won in four states including New York. These victories created a climate in which nationwide victory seemed possible, if only a big push could be made. Thus, environmental opportunities made coalition work and the organization of coalitions by 'entrepreneurs' like the SWP [Socialist Workers Party – KDO] attractive prior to the 1973 victory" (380, italics in the original). Couldn't one do without the concept of opportunity? A strict use of the concept would require that the author provides some evidence that the victories increased the chances of success. As is normal in the literature, such evidence is not provided. Now assume that the concept was not used, i.e. imagine the expression "to take advantage of environmental *opportunity*" would be deleted. The hypothesis then would be that repeal victories "created a climate in which nationwide victory seemed possible if only a big push could be made." The hypothesis is that the victories had some effect on "a climate in which nationwide victory seemed possible." In other words, the victories (macro level) affected expected group success (or, put differently, the "chances of success"). This is an empirical hypothesis. There is no need and no advantage either to include it in a definition. The issue is what effects the victories had. Perhaps there were effects on other incentives such as increased positive sanctioning of participation. Thus, the concept of POS is simply superfluous.

The important point in this context is that in the studies cited and in much other work *there is no definitional (i.e. analytical) relationship between certain changes of political environment and incentives, and in particular the "chances of success," involved.* The researchers did not even use the term POS, or, if it is used, it is superfluous.

When we forgo the concept of POS, the question arises: how does the researcher select the macro events that may be conducive to protest – via a change of incentives and the chances of success in particular? The answer is that the researcher *consults previous empirical studies, applies his or her everyday understanding of the situation, gathers information from all kinds of sources such as participants in the collective action events, journalists or colleagues, diaries or newspaper reports.* Not least, the researcher *applies existing theory.* Then hypotheses are suggested about what features of the political environment changed which incentives – and not only the "chances of success" which is just one incentive of the micro model discussed in previous chapters. Finally, these hypotheses are tested.

This is exactly what is done when the concept of POS is used. In applying this concept in a rigorous way one must provide evidence for the effect of environmental changes on incentives (and, in particular, on the chances of success). But, as said before, there is no need and no advantage either to include this empirical knowledge in a definition.

To illustrate this procedure I will briefly describe how I proceeded in explaining the emergence of the protests in Leipzig in 1989 (Opp, Voss, and Gern 1995). My major reason for beginning this project was that the protests in 1989, in a situation where strong repression was to be expected, were a puzzle and may falsify existing sociological theory, in particular the theory of collective action. Based on this theory, the theoretical approach that emerged during the events at the end of 1989 was that the focus of the explanation should primarily be on the individuals who participated in the activities. Their behavior had to be explained. How? Based on existing research on social movements and protest, the initial assumption was that the major incentives that had been shown to be important in western settings might also explain the protests of the GDR citizens. But this answer was not very satisfactory. The question was how the macro events mentioned before, that are meanwhile adopted as common sense explanations of the East German revolution, were related to the incentives. The idea was that these events have changed the incentives. These are thus macro-to-micro relationships. The next major question was: which events affected which incentives? The major work to be done was then to specify these bridge assumptions.

In order to formulate the hypotheses all available sources were consulted. For example, we conducted qualitative interviews, read newspapers, looked at interviews published in media, read protocols of meetings of the Politbureau and so on. We came up with various hypotheses about what events could have changed which incentives. These hypotheses were then tested in a first survey of the Leipzig population, conducted in the fall of 1990.

Two features of this work are important in this context. Although the term "political opportunity structure" is not used at least some of these factors refer to phenomena that could be called POSs. For example, Gorbachev's new political orientation would count as an opening POS. The second feature is that no definitional relationship was involved between some variables of the political environment and incentives.

What would be the advantage of applying the concept of POS in this research? For each macro factor, we had to examine whether it changed the "chances of success." For example, did Gorbachev's policy change affect the chances of success of the GDR citizens? What about the crackdown on the Chinese students? What about the initial protests in September 1989: were they a POS for the other Leipzig citizens who did not yet protest? Thus, we would mainly be concerned with solving some definitional issues such as: is change X a POS, is change Y a POS and so on? Even if we had answered these questions, we would not yet have achieved an explanation. The question then would be what role the other factors played that were not POSs.

In contrast to the POS approach, the *procedure* illustrated by the previous example is to *look at environmental changes and formulate hypotheses about which incentives for which individuals (or groups of individuals) for which behavior have changed due to the environmental changes*. Again, these "elements" of the environment may be political, cultural, or "discursive." The point is that the researcher formulates propositions about what effects these elements may have on collective action and is not involved in any definitional issues.

This procedure is not new at all. It describes exactly how proponents of the theory of collective action (and rational choice theory) proceed. They focus on the effects of various features of the environment in which individuals and groups act. For example, explanations of the effects of property rights, of health insurance, of increases of gasoline prices, tax increases, bans on smoking, and of legal punishment are addressed.

Nonetheless, the POS perspective could help us to find the relevant factors. The existing literature could be used as a heuristic device. This is elaborated in section 11.

What is the difference between resources and opportunities?

An unsolved issue is how resources and opportunities are to be demarcated. Are there differences at all and, if so, how are both concepts be distinguished? It is not surprising due to the lack of clarity of both concepts that there are different views about their relation and, therefore, also about the differences between the RMP and POS theory. For example, Tarrow (1991b: 14) regards POS theory as an alternative to RMP. But when Tarrow writes that POSs "emphasize resources *external* to the group" (Tarrow 1994: 18) POS theory and RMP are no longer contradictory, they complement each other: there are different types of resources that instigate social movement activities: resources that groups possess (or control) and those they do not possess (or do not control). The consequence would be that POSs "are a necessary complement of resource mobilization theory" (Rucht 1994: 301, translation by KDO). Kitschelt (1986: 59) regards both perspectives as "loosely linked," without saying what this means. Similarly, for Zald (1992: 333) POS theory is a "variant" of the resource mobilization perspective (and the theory of collective action) without explaining what a "variant" is. In the same vein, McAdam, McCarthy, and Zald (1988: 697) claim that the approaches are "not incompatible," but differences consist in "emphasis and empirical focus." Resource mobilization, the authors argue, "tends to emphasize the constancy of discontent and the variability of resources in accounting for the emergence and development of insurgency ...", whereas POS "emphasizes (a) the importance of indigenous organization, and (b) a favorable 'structure of political opportunities' (Eisinger 1973)." When we look at the factors that proponents of the RMP and POS theory actually advance in their writings, it seems that the former are more concerned with "discretionary" goods, i.e. goods that an individual has control of (see our definition in chapter 5, section 3). In the POS perspective, the larger political environment is addressed such as political freedom, new political alignments, elite splits or population growth (for the latter see Goldstone 1991). Thus, a possible distinction could be that *resources* refer to discretionary goods whose use actors can control. In contrast, *opportunities* are elements of the environment that objectively or subjectively are relevant for goal attainment but cannot be controlled by actors.

This distinction seems to make sense if one looks at the writings of authors of the RMP and POS perspective. But common usage does not imply theoretical fruitfulness. A first problem might be how precise the distinction is. It is based on a dichotomy: control and no-control of goods. But "control" is a quantitative variable, i.e. one may have more or less control of a good. Or perhaps POSs are elements of the environment actors *cannot* control? The cutting point is then no control and some degree of positive control. Take the constitution of a society that is changed to allow more freedom of assembly. Actors can normally not control the constitution, but they can take advantage of it, i.e. the constitution is relevant for goal realization. The same holds for the internet: actors can normally not control it, they can only use it for their purposes.

Another question is whether such a distinction is theoretically needed. This question is discussed below. But for the time being, we may conclude that a relatively clear and probably most generally accepted distinction is the one mentioned in the previous paragraph.

3. What form of political action can be explained?

Eisinger distinguishes between protest and violence. He argues that both types of action are determined by different factors: protest (which seems to be legal mass action) is dependent on calculation, whereas violence is a frustrated response. Whatever one may think about this explanation – we will not discuss it but refer to the micro model discussed in chapter 4 – Eisinger does not address the question of what kinds of POSs trigger what kinds of political action.

There are discussions in the literature about the form of protest that different POSs might give rise to (see, e.g., McAdam 1996: 29–31; Kitschelt 1986: 66–67), but POS theory does not include propositions that are specific enough to allow predictions about what kind of POS generates what kind of protest or collective action.

However, Marks and McAdam (1999: 102) suggest the following theoretical argument: "Organizers are also very likely to tailor their efforts to the specific kinds of changes they see taking place in the political systems they seek to challenge. In particular, *where* and *how* they seek to press their claims will reflect their view of where the system is newly vulnerable or receptive to their efforts." This suggests an extension of POS theory that is not formulated in a general way. The idea seems to be that actors choose the action that is, in their view, most instrumental to reach their goals. Thus, the incentives prevalent in the specific situation are relevant for the form of action that is chosen. This is the application of a micro model of political action that closely resembles the model suggested in chapter 4 of this book.

It is further not clear whether the phenomena to be explained are protest or social movements. In Eisinger's theory "protest" is the dependent variable, Tarrow (see, e.g., 1998: 77) posits that expanding opportunities lead to the emergence of movements.

Whatever exactly the dependent variable is, POS theory does not consist of propositions that are capable to explain, for example, when demonstrations, riots, mobilization activities, blocking streets, etc. are to be expected. However, an application of the micro model and additional hypotheses about effects of "POSs" on the incentives yields propositions explaining the form of protest.

4. The missing micro-macro model and the implicit background theory

The previous discussion of the POS perspective indicates that two questions are not answered. (1) What exactly are the micro variables that prompt individuals to participate? Although the major authors address the micro level, no clear micro model is specified. (2) It is further not clear what opportunity structures affect which micro-variables (i.e. incentives). In other words, the top-down relationships from the macro to the micro level are not spelled out. These problems are succinctly diagnosed by Koopmans (1995: 15): "A basic shortcoming of all existing studies using the POS concept is that they lack a clearly stated motivational theory that would explain how these structural phenomena enter the strategic choice situations of individuals and organizations" (see also McAdam 1982: 48). In a similar vein, McAdam, McCarthy, and Zald (1996: 5) argue: "Mediating between opportunity, organization, and action are the shared meanings and definitions that people bring to their situation. At a minimum people need to feel both aggrieved about some aspect of their lives and optimistic that, acting collectively, they can redress the problem. Lacking either one or both of these perceptions, it is highly unlikely that people will mobilize even when afforded the opportunity to do so."

Despite these programmatic statements, none of these authors provides a clear and empirically-tested micro model that explains individual actions nor a clear set of propositions about the effects of macro-structures on individual-level variables. When we look at the various micro-level factors that are mentioned by advocates of POS theory at least some of them are very close to those of our own model suggested in chapter 4 (see, e.g., McAdam 1982: chapter 3; Tarrow 1991b: 15; Tilly 1978: 99).

It is striking that the leading authors of the POS perspective apply a version of the theory of rational action. The basic hypothesis that costs and benefits affect behavior was clearly stated by Eisinger (see the previous discussion). Tilly applies this theory as well. His "central assumptions" are: "1. Collective action *costs* something. 2. All contenders count costs. 3. Collective action brings benefits, in the form of collective goods. 4. Contenders continuously weigh expected costs against expected benefits ..." (1978: 99). Kriesi *et al.* refer to the "costs and benefits of a movement's mobilization" (1995: xv). Tarrow (1996) holds that the "incentives to confrontation and violence" are great when the state is strong (46), and McAdam (1982) refers to the "myriad of interpersonal rewards that provide the motive force for participation" (45).

Do proponents of POS theory also subscribe to the proposition of utility maximization? To be sure, we have never found a statement that uses the expression "utility maximization," but there can be no doubt that this assumption is made. It is held that actors choose the strategies and tactics that are instrumental – from the perspective of the actors – to best realize their goals, given the opportunities the actors are faced with. This amounts to the proposition that political actors maximize (or optimize) their utility. Thus, proponents of POS theory *implicitly* assume that actors maximize utility.

5. Other factors: the incomplete macro model

We mentioned already Eisinger's claim that protest has many causes and that POSs are of minor importance. It seems that the latter assumption is not shared by most contemporary proponents of POS theory. They ascribe opportunity structures a major role as causes of political action (see, e.g., McAdam, McCarthy, and Zald 1996: 3; Tarrow 1991, 1998), otherwise it would be difficult to explain the vast literature on POSs.

Nonetheless, all proponents of POS theory seem to agree that other factors – beside opportunity structures – are important determinants of protest. What these factors are, however, is not clear. Various authors mention different factors.[7]

The question arises as to how these factors are selected. For example, why do McAdam, McCarthy, and Zald (1996: 8) think that "sufficient organization" is necessary for POSs to trigger protest? Or why is "indigineous organizational strength" (McAdam 1982: 51; see also section 8 in this chapter, where McAdam's model is discussed) regarded as an independent variable beside POSs? The answer could (and should) be that a theory has been applied. But none of the authors derives hypotheses about other factors from a theory. The introduction of other factors is *ad hoc*.

Another question is whether the other factors do have an additive or multiplicative effects. The following hypothesis (Tarrow 1998: 71–72) suggests interaction effects: "When combined with high levels of perceived costs for inaction, opportunities produce episodes of contentious politics" (1998: 71). In other words, the impact of POSs depends on the costs for inaction. This is, by definition, an interaction effect: the impact of one variable (namely POSs) depends on the value of other variables (costs for inaction).

Thus, an important agenda for future research is to specify additional factors. But this should not happen *ad hoc*. Instead, the factors should be derived theoretically. Furthermore, attention should be paid to the kind of relationships of the additional factors *and* POSs on protest.

6. How is the free rider problem solved?

It is rare that proponents of POS theory discuss in detail the free rider problem. A reason may be that the approach does not provide a solution. Assume that some changes on the macro level increase the likelihood that groups can achieve their goals. This means that the probability of goal attainment of *collective* action increases. This alone is not a sufficient incentive for an individual actor to partici-pate in or organize collective action. This is in line with the theory of collective action: increasing opportunities mean that the likelihood that the public good is provided increases. But increasing expected group success is not enough for col-lective action to ensue (see our micro model in chapter 4).

Increasing POSs may not only increase expected *group* success but also *individ-ual* influence. But, again, this alone is not sufficient to trigger protest action either. Only if it is assumed that increasing POSs generate other incentives such as moral or social incentives that are strong enough to bring about protest, then POSs solve the free rider problem.

But this is a strong assumption. Various cases to be discussed below indicate that there are POSs or changes in POSs that are not conducive to protest. The reason is that sufficient selective incentives are not generated. Thus, the POS perspective does not solve the free rider problem.

It is ironic that one of the major proponents of the POS perspective, whose "political process model" will be discussed below in section 8, grants this implic-itly. He argues that the free rider problem is solved below the level where opportu-nity structures are located: according to McAdam (1982), the "established structure of solidary incentives" (45) is important, i.e. "indigenous organizational strength" (see McAdam's model; see also McAdam 1988: 136). These established incentives solve the free rider problem (45). This is exactly Olson's solution! Thus, POSs do in general not contribute to the solution of the free rider problem. Only in the extreme case, when POSs lead to dramatic changes of (selective) incentives is the free rider problem is solved.

7. When is the theory wrong?

A major problem of assessing the confirmation or falsification of the theory is that POSs are always measured indirectly, i.e. by using proxies. There is no test for whether these proxies really measure POSs, i.e. the chances of success. It is there-fore typical to use indicators for POSs in a largely arbitrary way. The previous dis-cussion of Eisinger's test of his theory is an illustration of this problem. The consequence is that confirming evidence may be due to choosing the "right" indi-cators, i.e. indicators that in fact did affect the chances of success.[8] In discussing the evidence for and against POS theory we will assume that the measurements are sound – which is admittedly a bold assumption. For example, we assume that POSs are more open in a democracy than in an authoritarian regime. Although the (objec-tive or subjective) likelihood of goal attainment is never tested in a rigorous way the cases are relatively simple so that is is plausible that POSs change in the way indicated below. If that is denied the critic must claim that the theory is not testable at all and, thus, has not been tested. Even if these problems let the reader conclude that there are no rigorous tests, the existing studies and cases give some preliminary evidence about the extent to which the POS perspective is empirically valid.

Confirmations

There are many studies which confirm the POS perspective. An example of a quantitative multivariate macro study is Jenkins, Jacobs, and Agnone's analysis of African-American Protest in the United States from 1948 to 1997. However, the study also illustrates the problems of the perspective. Instructive is the discussion of the dimensions of POS whose effects are tested. The authors look at various possibilities of how these dimensions could influence protest. Then they formulate specific hypotheses about their effects. These hypotheses are based on various untested plausibility assumptions. In particular, it is not tested whether the POS dimensions the authors select really do influence the expected or real chances of success. One result that is worth noting is that it is not opportunities alone but other factors as well that affect protest.

We will not discuss this and other research that confirms the POS perspective. The reason is that the problems of a theory become only apparent when we look at cases where the perspective is wrong or at least problematic. The focus of this section is therefore on disconfirming evidence.

Falsifications

Whether a certain study falsifies or confirms POS theory depends on what version of the theory is considered. In what follows we assume a positive linear relationship, i.e. the theory we adopt reads that increasing POSs cause increasing protest. Our reading of the literature suggests that most scholars in the field subscribe to this hypothesis. This is equivalent with the first increasing part of the inverted u-curve of Figure 6.1.

As was seen before, there is a subjectivist and an objectivist version of POS theory. All cases to be discussed falsify the subjective as well as the objective version – with the exception of case 6 (see below).

When is the POS proposition falsified? If POSs change and if there is no parallel change of protest the hypothesis is falsified. "Parallel change" means that if POSs rise, remain stable, or decrease, protest must also rise, remain stable, or decrease. Table 6.1 lists these cases.

There are several empirical cases where the expected parallel changes do not take place. Figure 6.4 summarizes these cases that we will now discuss.

(1) Eisinger argues that sometimes opportunities increase but that powerful actors will not wield their power. This may happen, for example, when an increase of opportunities does not increase the perceived "chances of success of citizen political activity" (Eisinger 1973: 11–12) to a sufficiently high extent so that it is not worthwhile to incur the costs of mobilization. In other words, the effects of

Table 6.1 Possible combinations of changing opportunities and protest where the political opportunity proposition (increasing opportunities lead to increasing protest) is falsified

Change of opportunities	Change of protest
Increasing	Stable
	Decreasing
Stable	Increasing
	Decreasing
Decreasing	Increasing
	Stable

political opportunities on the incentives to participate may be so low that individuals do not find it worthwhile to use the opening opportunities. There is thus an increase in opportunities, but no increase in protest.

(2) One of the major goals of the protesters in East Germany and in Eastern Europe in 1989 and 1990 was to *create* opportunities. The success of the large-scale protests and thus increasing opportunities *de*creased political discontent and thus diminished the incentives to protest. The goals of the actors to create new opportunity structures have been fulfilled. Furthermore, in the process of the provision of the new opportunities other goals of the actors have been attained as well. In this

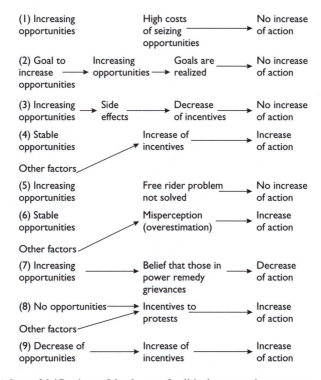

Figure 6.4 Some falsifications of the theory of political opportunity structure

situation, no further political action will ensue. Once again, this is a case where opportunities increased but protest did not.

(3) Expanding political opportunities may have negative side effects: they may *de*crease the major incentives to participate. In East Germany, for example, many people felt that in the new democratic order, i.e. after considerably expanding opportunities, there are so many "voices" that it takes a much higher effort than in the former communist Germany for a group to be heard. In everyday language, East Germans say that one could not demonstrate under communist rule; afterwards, one can demonstrate but it does not have any effect. Thus, increasing POSs may generate increasing political competition which, in turn, decreases perceived personal influence and perhaps other incentives. Increasing opportunity structures may thus be a *dis*incentive to political action and reduce protest.

(4) Individual incentives to participate may change although opportunities are stable. McAdam (1995) mentions "spin-off movements" "for whom the opportunities argument is clearly untenable" (226). These are movements which "draw their impetus and inspiration from the original initiator movements" (219). For example, the German student movement owes much to the American New Left (226). Thus, not expanding opportunities but previous movements (the initiator movements) are relevant. A further illustration are police raids that change individual incentives to participate in or organize joint protests (see as an example 224–225). Another example is the explanation of the Iranian revolution by Kurzman (1996). He provides data for his hypothesis that during the revolutionary period between 1977 and 1979 the state was not vulnerable, i.e. opportunities for a revolution did not change, but that opportunities were misperceived which increased protests. Thus, there were stable opportunities but increasing protest.

(5) Assume that opportunities increase in a society and that the citizens regard joint action as successful. The expected success of *joint* action does not mean that the *individual* incentives to participate are high (see, e.g., Finkel, Muller, and Opp 1989). In this situation, the free rider problem becomes particularly salient. The individual actor could believe that many others will participate, that their protest will provide the public good, and that his own participation is therefore not necessary. Thus, increasing opportunities are only effective if there is an increase of perceived personal influence or other incentives to protest. In other words, increasing opportunity structures need not provide the incentives to overcome the free rider problem.

(6) One of the assumptions made by many proponents of POS theory is that opportunity structures are perceived correctly, as was seen before. Misperception of opportunity structures might have the effect that an actual change of opportunity structures does not lead to behavioral changes that POS theory would predict. Kurzman (1996) shows that an overestimation of actually stable opportunity structures led to an increase of protest. This case falsifies the objectivist version of the theory only.

(7) Assume that there is a political party like the Green Party in Germany whose goals are to a great extent identical with the goals of various social movements. If this party is elected the representatives of the social movements may reason that the

party will realize their goals so that protest is no longer necessary. That is to say, although opportunities increase protest does not increase.

(8) POS theory treats changing opportunities as exogenous factors which trigger protest. In recent work, opportunity structures are also treated as dependent variables (Gamson and Meyer 1996; Tarrow 1996). That is to say, it is hypothesized that protesters sometimes create opportunities. If opportunities are supposed to increase protest, then it is a falsification of the perspective if there are no opportunities and people nonetheless protest because other factors trigger protest. But if there are already opportunities to some extent and people want to extend their opportunities by protesting, the perspective is not falsified.

A case where opportunities did not exist – however this term is defined – but where nonetheless collective action could be observed was the uprising in the Warsaw Ghetto in 1943. Einwohner (2003) argues "that collective action in the Warsaw Ghetto emerged not in response to opportunity but to a lack thereof; in fact, it was only once the ghetto fighters became aware of the hopelessness of their situation that they began to plan for resistance" (652). The explanation is that resistance was due to honor and dignity. These concepts refer mainly to normative phenomena and certain objectives such as "regaining the respect that had been denied them during Nazi occupation" (667). This is thus a situation where opportunities neither existed nor increased, but where collective action originated.

(9) Increasing state repression or repressiveness has been regarded as a decreasing POS (see, e.g., McAdam 1996: 27–28; see also Eisinger 1973). Repression should thus lower protest. However, repression has not only a deterrent effect but sometimes a radicalizing effect. The explanation is that an increasing repression that is regarded as illegitimate triggers moral indignation and social incentives which, in turn, increase protest (see, e.g., Opp and Roehl 1990). Thus, increasing repression does not always have the effect it is supposed to have, if the POS proposition is valid.

This enumeration of situations is not exhaustive. The point is that there are situations where it is highly implausible that POS theory is valid. The question then becomes: What are the conditions when changing opportunities generate changing protest? We will return to this question later in this chapter.

Is there any possibility to reject these cases as falsifying instances of the POS perspective? One strategy is to invoke other factors that explain why POSs don't have the expected effect. However, such arguments are *ad hoc* and in fact make the theory unfalsifiable, i.e. it would immunize the theory against critique. Another strategy is to assume a curvilinear relationship and argue that in case of non-parallel changes the value of the POS is at the peak of the curve or at the declining part of the curve. However, this would again immunize the theory against critique. So the conclusion is that the cases described are situations where the POS perspective is incorrect.

A partial confirmation

There are few rigorous quantitative and multivariate tests of POS theory. Among the best tests of POS hypotheses available is Meyer and Minkoff's study (2004).

They use data referring to the civil rights movement. Their dependent variables are civil rights protest mobilization, organizational formation, and policy outcomes between 1955 and 1985. The authors specify two models: a structural model which refers to "formal changes in rules and policies affecting political access, as well as the changed practices that follow them," and a signals model that "includes issue-specific and general opportunity variables that savvy activist entrepreneurs could read as invitation to mobilize" (1470). An example for an indicator of the structural model is the time when the protest took place: "years after 1965" is a dummy variable with value 1 "for those years following the passage of such critical legislation as the Civil Rights Act of 1964 and the Voting Rights Act of 1965, both of which marked a significantly more open political and legal environment for civil rights activism. This legislation legitimated black activism as well as grassroots mobilization by diverse marginalized groups" (1468).

Indicators of the signals model are, among others, Democratic advantage in Congress and the incumbency of a Democratic President. These indicators "may represent both an actual increase in elite support and a signal that opportunities for activism are favorable" (1470).

The results are not very impressive. For example, in a partial ("issue-specific") model of the structural model the post-1965 variable has a negative effect with a $p<10$ on civil rights protest (Table 5). That is to say, that increasing opportunities did not raise but depressed protest. In the full structure model the variable is no longer statistically significant (Table 5). The variable does not have a significant effect on civil rights SMO formation (Table 6) either. The effect is positive and in the full structure model significant for the third dependent variable (civil rights budget – Table 7). "Democratic advantage in Congress" is only significant in the full signal model with civil rights protest as a dependent variable. "Democratic President" has no significant effect on civil rights protest, but statistically significant effects on civil rights SMO formation. There is also a significant effect in the structure model of the third dependent variable (civil rights budget), but not in the signal model with this dependent variable.

Similar results obtain for the numerous other indicators. A glance at Tables 5 to 7 shows that most of the indicators are statistically not significant. In general, thus, the findings provide – at best – only a partial confirmation of the POS hypotheses.

The indicators the authors use may be flawed. Although the authors' arguments for choosing these indicators are plausible, there are no data that provide a test of the assumption that the indicators affect the perceived or actual chances of success. But since the authors regard their indicators as valid measures of POSs, it would amount to an immunization of the theory against empirical critique if one would doubt the validity of the indicators after they have not shown the expected effects.

However, several indicators have the expected effects, and the authors focus on these indicators when they assess the extent to which their hypotheses are confirmed. Their general conclusion is that "insurgents responded to structural changes in the polity and signals from particular institutional actors to mount protest campaigns in the 1950s" (1484). Indeed, some indicators and findings point in this direction, but only some indicators, many others do not.

Another problem of the research is that the causal order of POSs and social movement phenomena is hardly unidirectional, i.e. from POSs to protest. At least some aspects of the POS addressed in the article are influenced by protest activities such as media attention or perhaps the civil rights budget. If this is correct then protests or SMO emergence originated when only few or perhaps even no POSs existed. The causes of protest were then not POSs but other factors.

In assessing the authors' findings, it is important to note that only indicators of POSs are part of the models. Other factors are not considered. We thus don't know to what extent POSs really explain social movement phenomena. If Eisinger is right other factors are more important. Even in recent models of proponents of POS theory (see below, where we discuss models of McAdam and Tarrow) other explanatory factors are included. It cannot be ruled out that the other factors have a much higher explanatory power than POSs. Another possibility is that including other factors renders POS indicators insignificant due to intercorrelations of the factors.

Sometimes effects of POSs and other factors are multiplicative. For example, POSs may only work if sufficient pre-existing incentives for protest or SMO are given. In McAdam's terms (1982), "indigenous organizational strength" where the free rider problem is solved is important. The research does not show to what extent the hypotheses are only valid under certain conditions.

These limitations are not meant as a critique. The authors are well aware that their study is not the final word in testing POS theory (see in particular 1484–1485). Further research is needed to build on this study and improve the design as suggested. If the approach advanced in this book is applied, future studies should include hypotheses and data about the specific effects of POSs on micro processes.

Macro variables as proxis for incentive structures

When McAdam discusses "indigenous organizational strength" he refers, among other things, to "established structures of solidary incentives" (45) – see the quotation above. A similar variable is used by other authors as well. For example, Jenkins, Jacobs, and Agnone (2003) include the variable "indigenous group organization" in their research which "provides leadership and organizers, collective solidarity, and social networks" (278). This means that the authors implicitly apply a micro model claiming that incentives affect protest action. However, the incentives are not specified in detail. The authors use a macro variable and posit that this is related to a certain incentive structure. This is an empirical proposition. For example, Jenkins, Jacobs, and Agnone measure indigenous group organization by membership in certain groups such as the annual membership of the National Association for the Advancement of Colored People (NAACP, see 289). The study is concerned with macro events: the dependent variable is counts of the number of African-American protests between 1948 and 1997, based on newspaper data. The implicit assumption is that individuals who are members of the NAACP are faced with protest promoting incentives. But what the incentives are is not spelled out. In this particular case, this is a plausible hypothesis, based on knowledge of the values and goals of the groups and the activities of the civil rights movement. Thus, a macro variable is used as a proxy for a distribution of incentives on the micro level.

A similar proxy is used in research with individual data: it is common to employ membership in protest encouraging networks as a proxy for social incentives (see, e.g., my own work such as Opp and Gern 1993). Again, this is an empirical assumption and based on knowledge about the groups.

The important point is that a pure macro model may include macro variables that are disguised micro variables: a macro variable actually measures incentives on the micro level. This is typically the case for macro variables that refer to indigenous organization of the population.

When we interpret McAdam's model in this way, the causal diagram must be changed: "indigenous organizational strength" must be dropped because it is already included in the micro variables (see Figure 6.6, where McAdam's "political process model" is discussed in detail).

When does the curvilinear relationship hold? Implications from the theory of collective action

The previous discussion of the validity of POS theory suggests that POSs affect protest only under certain conditions. What are these conditions? One possibility to answer this question is to apply a more general theory such as the theory of collective action or rational choice theory. In this section, we will examine what the predictions of these theories are in regard to the kind of relationship between POSs and protest: when will we expect a linear and when a non-linear relationship?

Let us first look at Eisinger's own explanation of the linear and curvilinear relationship. The negative linear relationship – see Figure 6.5A – comes about if frustration is transformed to an aggressive response. When opportunities are closed, frustration is high and turns into protest. If opportunities open up, frustration is reduced and protest thus decreases. Eisinger's data do not support the negative relationship. But the relationship might hold in other situations and originate from another mechanism. Assume that there are low opportunities and a critical mass begins successfully to mobilize. These political entrepreneurs may create strong expectations that protest will open up opportunities, and, thus, the perceived influence will increase. There may further be strong pre-existing protest supporting networks. Initially, thus, protest is high. Then individuals may largely get what they want. The incentives to protest decrease.

The curvilinear relationship – Figure 6.5B – is also explained by the change of incentives in the course of protest: if opportunities are largely absent this means, among other things, that repression is strong and, thus, the costs of launching political action are high. If opportunities open up, there are rising expectations. If opportunities exceed a certain point, expectations and satisfaction increase. Tilly (1978: 135–137), Muller (1985), and Muller and Weede (1990) provide similar theoretical arguments.

When will there be a positive linear relationship between POSs and protest– see Figure 6.5C? As was said before, most scholars seem to believe that POSs and

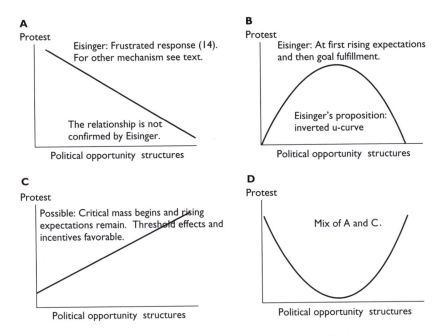

Figure 6.5 Some possible relationships between political opportunities and protest

protest are related in this way (see, e.g., Goldstone 2004: 349). How can this relationship be explained? Initially, there could be a critical mass which is successful in mobilizing others. Expectations rise continuously when opportunities open up. Other pre-existing incentives remain strong as well or increase. There is thus rising protest until the goals of the groups are largely accomplished. Graph C does not tell the whole story because protest will never remain at the highest level forever, as the graph suggests. There is thus some mechanism that reduces protest. Thus, the line in graph C must be prolonged by a declining curve.

We can further imagine a relationship that resembles a u-curve (Figure 6.5.D).[9] The first part up to the inflection point may be caused by the mechanism for the negative relationship in graph A: a critical mass instigates protest and the protesters' goals are largely achieved. But then new groups may arise who argue that the protesters could achieve more than was granted: aspirations, expectations, and other incentives increase. But protest would not remain high over time, as graph D implies. After protest has reached high levels it will decline again by a mechanism that was described before when we discussed the declining part of the graph B. The curve of C should thus be prolonged by a declining part so that it resembles a S-curve.

The previous explanation of diverse relationships between POSs and protest illustrates arguments suggested in chapter 1. Just looking at the relationship between macro variables like POSs and collective protests is only a first step. Determining whether the relationship is linear or not is not sufficient either. The next step is to explain under what conditions a relationship has what form. The previous theoretical argument further illustrates that macro propositions are no lawful statements: there is no law about the relationship between POSs and protest. Relationships vary under different conditions. The discussion of the empirical evidence shows this very clearly. The task then is to apply general theoretical hypotheses and explain under what conditions which relationship holds. It goes without saying, that this amounts to micro-macro modeling, as the explanation of the four curves illustrates. A detailed analysis of concrete trajectories of protest and changing opportunities could and should make use of the "tool kit" of collective action theory described in chapter 3.

8. Recent developments and lingering problems: an illustration with two versions of the theory

We will now discuss two versions of POS theory that are based on the original model by Eisinger, but modify it. These versions of the POS perspective are widely cited and proposed by two influential proponents of the perspective: Doug McAdam and Sidney Tarrow. Their models are thus indicators for the state of the arts.

D. McAdam's political process model

A relatively clearly specified version of POS theory is McAdam's widely cited "political process model" (1982: chapter 3). McAdam summarizes the model that explains movement emergence as a causal diagram (51). The upper diagram of Figure 6.6 is identical with McAdam's graph, except that we draw straight instead of curved arrows. The political process model asserts that the emergence of social movements is determined by expanding opportunities, indigenous organizational strength of the population, and cognitive liberation. In addition, "expanding political opportunities" and "indigenous organizational strength" have a positive effect on "cognitive liberation" and are influenced by "broad socio-economic processes." The hypothesis about the effects of "broad socio-economic processes" is only an orienting statement because it is not clear which "broad economic processes" exactly affect opportunities or indigenous organizational strength. We will therefore not further discuss this hypothesis.

To what extent does McAdam's model go beyond our reconstruction of Eisinger's theory (see Figure 6.2)? Both models accord that POSs are not the only relevant explanatory variable. In contrast to Eisinger who claims that several other factors are to be included in explaining political action, McAdam's model suggests only one other factor. However, in his discussion of the model McAdam mentions other factors as well. For example, it is not only the level of organization of the population ("indigenous organizational strength"), but the level of organization of the "aggrieved population" (40). Thus, "grievances" of the population are another factor. We thus conclude that Eisinger as well as McAdam believe that beside POSs several other variables affect political action.

McAdam's Causal Diagram

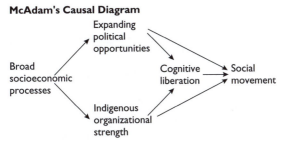

The Diagram as a Micro–Macro Model and Its Problems

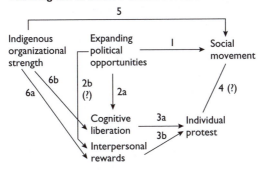

Figure 6.6 D. McAdam's (1982) political process model about movement emergence: two
graphic representations

Another common feature of both models is that the additional factors are not
derived from a theory, they are introduced *ad hoc*.

The relationship between POSs and political action in Eisinger's model is curvilinear. It is not clear what the relationship is in McAdam's model. It seems that
McAdam assumes a positive linear relationship: increasing POSs raise political
action.

In our reconstruction of Eisinger's model the relationship between POSs and
political action is not causal, it is a correlation. In contrast, McAdam's model postulates a causal relationship. This is implausible, as was argued before, because the
macro relationship is explained by processes on the micro level.

This is done in McAdam's model as well. "Cognitive liberation" seems to be a
property of individual actors. It is defined as "the collective assessment of the
prospects for successful insurgency" (40). This sounds like the variable "perceived
group success" in our micro model. But it may also mean "perceived individual
influence" – again a micro variable. This interpretation is suggested by a quotation
from Piven and Cloward 1979: McAdam points out that "cognitions" are important
for a successful insurgency. One of these cognitions is "a sense of efficacy; people
who ordinarily consider themselves helpless come to believe that they have some
capacity to alter their lot" (50, the quotation is from Piven and Cloward 1979: 3–4).
This is exactly the variable "perceived personal influence" from our micro model.

But "cognitive liberation" could also be interpreted as a macro variable: "collective assessment of successful insurgency" in the previous quotation could mean that the members of a group share a perception of joint success. If this is meant then this macro property is an aggregation of individual cognitions. These are then an independent variable of the micro model. Thus, "cognitive liberation" seems to refer to a micro variable, either to personal influence or to perceived group success, that affects individual protest participation.

How is this micro variable related to the macro variables in the model? This question can be answered easily when we move the macro variables to the upper and micro variable to the lower level in the figure. The result is the lower graph of Figure 6.6. The numbers at the arrows correspond to the relationships of Figure 6.2, i.e. to Eisinger's model, so that the two models can be compared. Let us look at McAdam's model in more detail.

McAdam's model in the lower panel of the figure consists of only one micro variable, namely cognitive liberation. However, when we look at his comments on "indigenous organizational strength" he argues that, among other things, the "established structure of solidary incentives" is important, i.e. "the myriad interpersonal rewards that provide the motive force for participation in these groups. It is the salience of these rewards that helps explain why recruitment through established organizations is generally so efficient. In effect these established 'incentive structures' solve the so-called 'free rider problem'" (45). This quotation clearly refers to the micro level: interpersonal rewards trigger individual protest participation (arrow 3b).

Are cognitive liberation and interpersonal rewards the only micro variables? This is hardly plausible. As was said before, grievances of the population is mentioned in McAdam's text, along with indigenous organization. "Grievances" are probably a micro variable as well which is a component of the micro model. The question then arises whether the effect of influence ("cognitive liberation") and grievances is multiplicative or additive. McAdam further mentions the costs authorities incur in repressing insurgent groups as a determinant of repression (43). If costs are relevant for authorities they are certainly relevant for insurgents as well. But this variable is not included in the micro model.

Thus, a careful reading of the text clearly indicates that McAdam applies a micro model. But what the variables of this model are, is not clearly spelled out. His reference to beliefs about efficacy, interpersonal rewards, and costs further suggests that he utilizes a general background theory. This seems to be a version of the theory of rational action. Again, this is not clearly stated, but the text suggests it.

What about bridge assumptions, i.e. the bottom-up and top-down relationships between the macro and micro level? McAdam claims that "indigenous organizational strength" has a positive effect on "cognitive liberation" and "interpersonal rewards" (see arrows 6a and 6b). "Expanding political opportunities" affect "cognitive liberation" (arrow 2a). We do not learn whether expanding POSs further affect interpersonal rewards (arrow 2b). However, this seems plausible: if people recognize that changing political circumstances make their goal achievement more likely, they will reward each other for participating in joint action.

The bottom-up relationship between individual "protest" and "social movement emergence" is not addressed. It is thus not clear whether it is an analytical relationship (see arrow 4) or an empirical one.

To conclude, McAdam's "political process model" is very similar to Eisinger's theory: it is a micro-macro theory, but neither the micro theory nor the bridge assumptions are spelled out.

These problems are not solved in McAdam's second model either (52) that purports to explain movement *development and decline*, whereas the model discussed before explains movement emergence. In regard to this second model, it is not clear why it is needed at all. If a model explains the *emergence* of a movement, then changes of the values of the independent variables of the model lead to *growth or decline* of a movement. For example, if a movement exists and if opportunities shrink, the model of Figure 6.6 implies that there will be fewer movements. A second model that explains the development and decline of a movement is thus not needed.

A problem of McAdam's second model is that there are contradictions to the first one. For example, a new variable "level of social control" is added to the model: it affects the growth and decline (new model) but not the emergence of a movement (old model) which is not very plausible. "Cognitive liberation" is not retained in the new model but replaced by "collective attribution." It seems, however, that both terms have the same meaning (see 53). Let us assume that this is the case. In the new model, this variable is now no longer a *cause* of protest or, as McAdam now puts it, of the "level of insurgency"; instead, "level of insurgency" *affects* "collective attribution." The latter variable thus does not contribute anything to explaining "insurgency" or protest. A consequence is that there are no longer any micro-macro relationships. "Level of insurgency" is only explained by macro factors. Another problem of this new model is that it postulates feedback effects between most of the variables. Such models are mathematically not identifiable and, thus, not testable. But we can interpret these feedback effects as orienting statements that have to be further developed.

It would perhaps be best to integrate both models. One possibility is to include the "level of social control" as an additional macro variable in the first model. Next macro-to-micro relationships must be added. We leave the specification of such a model to further research.

It is further striking that neither Eisinger nor McAdam explicitly apply a general theory to specify the macro factors. They invoke just plausibility but no theoretical underpinning.

There is one other difference between Eisinger's and McAdam's model: whereas Eisinger claims that POSs have only a small effect, McAdam's model is silent about the strength of the impact of POSs.

An open question is whether the effects of the independent variables are really additive. One plausible hypothesis is that there is an *interaction effect* of POSs and indigenous organizational strength on political action. This would be the case if, for example, POSs do not affect protest if there is no indigenous organization.

We conclude that the structure of the original Eisinger model and the model of McAdam is identical: both are micro-macro models and they are incomplete.

However, substantively there are differences between the models. A progress is that McAdam explicitly adds "indigenous organizational strength" as a factor beside POSs and that at least some micro variables and bridge assumptions are explicitly stated. In general, most of the problems of Eisinger's model are still unsolved.

S. Tarrow's model

In this section we will analyze hypotheses by Sidney Tarrow suggested in his book on the POS perspective (Tarrow 1998, first edition 1994 – page numbers refer to the 1998 edition). In contrast to McAdam, Tarrow does not provide a causal diagram, and he does not formulate his hypotheses explicitly so that the reader can recognize what exactly the dependent and independent variables are and how they are related. Accordingly, we have to reconstruct Tarrow's propositions and will display them as a causal diagram (Figure 6.7). The numbers next to the arrows correspond to those of the figures of the causal models of Eisinger and McAdam (Figures 6.2 and 6.6). We begin with a quotation that summarizes some of Tarrow's hypotheses (Tarrow 1998: 71):

> Contention increases when people gain the external resources to escape their compliance and find opportunities in which to use them. It also increases when they are threatened with costs they cannot bear or which outrage their sense of justice. When institutional access opens, rifts appear within elites, allies become available, and state capacity for repression declines, challengers find opportunities to advance their claims. When combined with high levels of perceived costs for inaction, opportunities produce episodes of contentious politics.

"Contention" refers to action of individuals: "Contentious forms of collective action ... bring ordinary people into confrontation with opponents, elites, or author-ities" (4). Nonetheless, the proposition seems to refer to the macro level, i.e. to joint action. We assume that this is an aggregation of individual action – see Figure 6.7, arrow 4.

"External resources" and "opportunities" are two macro variables which lead to contention. Tarrow further mentions threats which individuals are exposed to. As later parts of the text suggest, this means repressive acts of governments. Thus, so far the macro theory posits that external resources, opportunities, and threats affect collective contentious political action.

Tarrow also addresses the micro level by mentioning costs that individuals can-not bear. The costs refer to costs of inaction that are mentioned later in the quota-tion. Another variable on the micro level is the individual's sense of injustice that is "outraged." This variable refers to strong grievances.

Next Tarrow briefly summarizes his dimensions of POSs (see the sentence beginning with "When institutional access ..." and ending with "advance their claims"), which have already been discussed before.

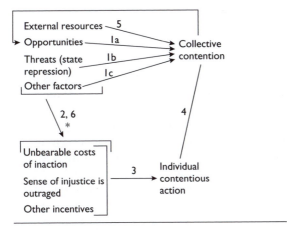

* Note: It is not clear whether *all* macro factors affect micro factors
or whether some micro factors are given (pre-existing incentives,
see Figure 6.2). It is further not clear whether some macro factors
are analytically related to the micro level.

Figure 6.7 S. Tarrow's (1998) model about political opportunities and contention

The last sentence claims that opportunities "produce episodes of contentious politics" when they are "combined with high levels of perceived costs for inaction." Thus, POSs alone are not sufficient. They lead to contention only if costs for inaction are high.

The latter is a micro variable. It is not clear how POSs are related to this micro variable. One possibility is that POSs affect the costs of inaction. Given existing grievances, a closed opportunity structure may further increase the costs of remaining inactive. An example may be the situation described by Eisinger in which a closed opportunity structure increases grievances that actors will no longer tolerate. But high costs of inaction may also be due to a natural disaster or another critical event such as a nuclear accident.

In view of Tarrow's general assumption that POSs affect incentives we assume that the previous passage describes a macro-to-micro proposition (i.e. a bridge assumption – see arrows 2 and 6): contention originates when macro variables affect individual incentives which lead – via individual contentious behavior – to collective action.

This list of macro factors, beside opportunities, is by far not complete. Tarrow lists a great number of other factors. We illustrate this by quoting a passage after the previous quotation:

Of course, changing opportunities must be seen alongside more stable structural elements – like the strength or weakness of the state and the forms of repression it habitually employs .... Moreover, external opportunities do not necessarily produce sustained social movements. The process requires challengers to employ known repertoires of contention, to frame their messages dynamically, and to access or construct unifying mobilizing structures. (71–72)

We will not list all the other factors Tarrow mentions in his book. The figure just includes "other factors" as a reminder that the causal diagram is incomplete. Whatever these other factors are, Tarrow's theory is problematic in several respects.

(1) It is not clear why the other factors are introduced. There is no explicit theory that is applied. The other factors are based on plausibility considerations.

(2) If several other factors are relevant, the question arises as to how important POSs are. Tarrow does not answer this question.

(3) It is not clear whether the independent variables have additive or interaction effects. For example, Tarrow claims in the first quotation that contention increases "when people gain the external resources to escape their compliance and find opportunities in which to use them." This seems to mean that the effect of opportunities depends on the extent to which external resources exist and vice versa. This is an interaction effect which means that the effect of a variable depends on the values of another variable. In the second quotation, Tarrow argues that effective opportunities require challengers who employ know repertoires, etc. This seems to be an interaction effect as well.

(4) Let us turn to the micro model. We have included as incentives in Figure 6.7 only costs of inaction and grievances. But Tarrow time and again refers to "incentives" without specifying exactly which incentives these are. Thus, Tarrow uses a micro model but does not specify the variables it consists of.

The frequent use of the term incentives suggests that Tarrow uses an implicit general theory of action that resembles a wide version of the theory of rational action. But the application of this theory remains implicit. We therefore include in the figure "other incentives" as a reminder that the micro model is incomplete.

(5) This holds for the macro-to-micro relationships as well: they are not clearly specified. It is not even clear which of Tarrow's assumptions refer to the micro or to the macro model. The reader may examine this by looking at the previous quotations.

(6) How is the free rider problem solved in Tarrow's model? Although Tarrow mentions incentives time and again he does not discuss where these incentives come from and whether or when they are sufficient to solve the free rider problem.

The reader may recognize that these are the same problems we found in the models of Eisinger and McAdam. However, there is one hypothesis that is not included in the models before: it is the feedback effect of contention on POSs. It is important to note that this hypothesis is only a problem if contention occurs when no POSs exist. This would not be in line with the theory if its claim is that POSs generate protest. This would imply that no protest is to be expected if no POSs exist.

Another difference between Tarrow's model and the other two models by Eisinger and McAdam is that Tarrow tries to incorporate the framing perspective – see the last sentence of the second quotation. But so far this is more an orienting statement claiming that framing is relevant: it is not yet specified in detail how movement activities or opportunities influence framing. We will address these issues in chapter 8.

Has there really been made progress between the first version of the theory in 1973 and the version in Tarrow's book from 1998? On the one hand, some new orienting statements are included. Many new factors, beside POSs, are addressed. But the major problems that were discussed before are still unsolved.

Conclusion: unresolved issues and extensions of the perspective

The two models discussed represent very well the state of the arts. Our reading of the extensive literature suggests that all proponents of POS theory subscribe to the model exposed in Figure 6.2 – with the exception of relationship 1: most authors favor a linear relationship. However, no author advances this theoretical model explicitly. One has to work hard to find the often vague adumbrations which suggest this model.

But there are also disagreements which can be identified by using the Figure. (1) Although the basic independent macro-variable is always "political opportunity structure," there are different definitions of this variable. (2) As was said already, there is no agreement in regard to the kind of relationship between POS and protest behavior. Whereas Eisinger suggests a curvilinear function (relationship 1 in Figure 6.2), other authors are skeptical (e.g. Kitschelt 1986: 62), others do not address the relationship explicitly. It seems that most social movement scholars assume a *positive* linear relationship: the more open POSs are the more frequently people protest. (3) Authors further differ in regard to the anchoring of POSs on the micro-level (see arrow 2 of the Figure). These differences concern (a) whether authors mention specific micro variables at all, (b) the kinds of micro variables authors suggest (see arrow 3 of the Figure), and (c) the effects of opportunity structures on micro variables (arrow 2 of the Figure) which are rarely addressed in detail. (4) In regard to micro-to-macro relationships (arrow 4 in the figure) authors seem to assume a simple aggregation of the sort that collective protest is a function of the number of protest acts of individuals. (5) Authors differ in regard to the "other factors" that are claimed to be important beside opportunity structures. (6) In specifying the "other factors" authors do not apply a theory. (6) It seems that proponents of POS theory also differ in regard to the form of political action that is explained.

There is vast number of writings that use the POS variable and other factors to explain specific movement related phenomena, and the hypotheses are formulated for the specific single cases. In particular, among the other factors are framing activities of SMOs. Some of these studies are discussed in the next chapter. It is difficult to see whether there are any new *general* propositions about the effects of POSs.

One important new development is that no longer are only the effects of POSs on mobilization or collective action addressed. A growing number of studies focus on the success of social movements. Especially prominent is political mediation theory with the important contributions of E. Amenta and collaborators (see, e.g., Amenta, Bernstein, and Dunleavy 1994; Amenta, Neal, and Olasky 2005). Since the theme of this book is mobilization and collective action, we will not discuss this type of work.

9. Political opportunities and collective action: a synthesis

Although POS theory refers to the macro level, its basic idea is that POSs affect protests via changing incentives on the micro level. These incentives, in turn, lead to individual protest participation which translates into collective political action. This theoretical structure implies a micro model: incentives lead to individual political action. Such a micro model is available in the theory of collective action (chapters 3 and 4). This theory further relates macro variables – in particular group size – to the micro level. It thus seems plausible that POS theory and the theory of collective action can be integrated. This section addresses the question of how such an integration looks.

Let us assume that some change of a macro variable leads to increased chances of success for some groups. By definition, thus, POSs increase. We use here the subjectivist definition of POS which means that a change of POSs affects the perceived chances of success. Let us look at this proposition – perceived POS triggers collective protest – from the perspective of the theory of collective action. Is the variable "perceived chances of success" a component of this theory? POS theory assumes that groups have *goals* they want to accomplish. This is equivalent, in terms of the theory of collective action, to *public goods preferences* that are not realized. Thus, POS and collective action theory include the goals of groups as a theoretically relevant variable. "Chances of success" is a component of the theory of collective action as well: it refers to *expected group success* (see chapter 3 and the model summarized in Figure 3.3).

Although both theories include group goals and expected group success as independent variables, the theories differ in regard to the assumed effects. According to POS theory, "chances of success" is a major variable that affects political action. This is in stark contrast to the theory of collective action: in the collective action model summarized in Figure 3.3, "expected group efficacy" (which is equivalent to expected "chances of success") does not have a direct effect on political action, it affects this variable only indirectly. This is plausible, as was argued in chapter 3: perceived group success compounds the free rider problem: why should an individual participate if the others' action provide the public good? If the others do not act, then the individual's participation is superfluous. However, as our previous argument indicates, perceived group success may affect other incentive variables and may thus indirectly affect protest action.

But even if we assume that perceived group success has a direct effect on political action, this is only one of several incentive variables. There is no evidence so far for a particularly strong effect of this variable. Other incentives are perceived *personal* influence and the intensity of the group goal, i.e. of the intensity of the preference for the public good. Both variables have an interaction effect. Furthermore, social and moral incentives are important. Finally, there are interdependencies of the incentives. Proponents of POS theory do not consider these theoretical relationships.

Thus, the first step of integrating POS theory and the theory of collective action is to supplement POS theory with the micro model of the theory of collective action. Some variables from POS theory are included in this micro model, but, in general, the micro model implicitly applied by proponents of the POS perspective is an incomplete or, more precisely, incorrect version of the micro model of the theory of collective action.

The next step must then be to formulate propositions about the effects of changes of the political, economic, etc. context on the incentives of the extended micro model. Proponents of POS theory often mention incentives in general that are affected by changes in the political structure. What is needed are more specific hypotheses about the effects of the political environment on the incentives of an extended micro model.

There is another common feature of POS theory and the theory of collective action. POS theory claims that beside POS "other factors" determine collective political action. The theory of collective action does not restrict the relevant macro factors in any a priori way so that "other factors" may be included as relevant macro variables as well. Thus, any factors POS theory takes into account may, but need not, be macro variables that affect incentives.

Although the theory of collective action is compatible with the assumption that various macro factors affect incentives to protest, there is no definition with a built-in causal statement like the definition of POS. As we saw before, this causal part of the definition is superfluous. When we eliminate the causal statement in the POS definition we may dovetail "POS" and "other factors" to one complex factor that refers to "changes in the social context" or "societal changes." We have then to examine to what extent these factors affect incentives, as was argued before.

There is another assumption of POS theory that was included in the models of McAdam and Tarrow and that is compatible with the theory of collective action: there may be *pre-existing incentives* that are not influenced by macro changes. McAdam calls these "indigenous organizational strength." These are "pre-existing incentives" which refer to the distribution of incentives in the population, i.e. protest promoting incentives on the micro level actors are faced with.

We saw that the relationships between macro factors and incentives may be analytical or empirical. Adherents of the POS perspective never discuss this kind of relationship between the macro and micro level. Applying the theory of collective action would thus force adherents of the POS to specify the bridge assumptions.

The previous theoretical argument leads to the following conclusions. (1) Both theories, i.e. POS and collective action theory, can very easily be integrated. The idea is to treat the political, social or economic environment, or anything that has been termed "POS" as possible macro factors and explore their relations to the independent variables of an explicit micro model, taken from the theory of collective action. The "other factors" of POS theory are included in this set of possible macro factors.

(2) This integration implies that the critique of POS theory is correct: it becomes abundantly clear that POSs are only one factor that affects protest. Increasing POSs need by no means raise protests. It depends on many conditions whether a change of POSs has any effects. Applying the integrated POS-collective-action theory implies that various scenarios can be generated, where a changing POS may generate more or less political action of a certain form. Figure 6.5 depicts some of these scenarios. This is also in line with Eisinger's original formulation. These scenarios are based on the integrated theory which provides theoretical reasons why changing POSs sometimes have an effect on protest and sometimes don't, and why the trajectories of the rise and fall of protest are different.

(3) Applying the micro model of the theory of collective action can also help to explain the forms of collective action that actors choose. Relevant are, e.g. efficacy considerations or moral reasons (see in detail chapter 3).

(4) The argument in this section further suggests that the causal statement in the definition of POS is not helpful, to say the least. As a matter of fact, exploring the effects of a change in the social context – be it political, economical, social, or whatever – requires proposing and testing hypotheses about the effects of certain macro factors on incentives, as was shown in detail before. Definitional relations between factors and incentives are unnecessary. Whether these macro factors are the dimensions listed in POS theory or other factors is irrelevant.

A proponent of POS theory could nevertheless try not to give up distinguishing between POS factors and other factors. For example, the distinction could be: POSs are factors that change the "chances of success," whereas other factors don't. Thus, "other factors" will change only other incentives and not the chances of success; if a factor changes the chances of success it is a POS. Although this distinction, as any distinction, may be made, the question is what it is good for. The alternative is, as described before, to explore which factors of the societal context have which effects. This must be done, regardless of this distinction.

10. What can we learn from the political opportunity structure perspective for the explanation of social movement phenomena?

The vast number of studies which use POS as a variable confirm the general idea, which is a common place by now: the political environment may trigger protest behavior. The term "political" must be understood in a very wide sense. These studies provide specific information about what the relevant dimensions of the political environment *might* be. This work can be used as an inventory of *possible* macro variables. If a study is to be undertaken to explain some protest event the work on POS can be used as a heuristic device to generate hypotheses about which changes in the political environment might have changed incentives. But whether incentives have changed must be determined empirically.

It is important to note that the dimensions need not change incentives, as was shown before. Changes of incentives have to be determined empirically. This is typical for a general theory. The kinds of POSs that generate collective action in specific situations are the initial conditions in the explanation (see chapter 1) and must therefore be determined empirically. Such initial conditions cannot be parts of a theory. This is similar to the theory of rational action which does not provide any information about what is rewarding or costly for a group. Again, the kind of costs and benefits are the initial conditions of the theory that must be ascertained empirically.

11. Summary and conclusions

This chapter began with an exposition and critical analysis of Peter Eisinger's founding paper of the political opportunity structure (POS) perspective. Its major hypothesis is that POSs are related to collective political action. Eisinger's data support a curvilinear relationship, namely a reversed u-curve: if POSs are low and increase, protest rises up to a certain point. If POSs further increase, protest declines. The basic concept, POS, is defined as some feature of the political environment that has a positive effect on the "chances of success of citizen political activity." In order to ascertain in a specific situation whether there is a POS one has thus to test a causal statement: is there an effect of a change in the political environment on the objective probability that a group attains its goals? If so, a POS is, by definition, given.

Eisinger's theory is a macro proposition, but in explaining the curvilinear relationship he refers to the micro level and offers bridge assumptions linking the micro and macro level. One of these assumptions is that an opening opportunity structure leads to rising expectations of the individual actors that the authorities yield to the demands of a group. Eisinger further hypothesizes that the costs and benefits of political action are important determinants of political action. But he does not apply this proposition systematically to derive testable propositions about the effects of POSs on political action. Thus, Eisinger – along with other major contemporary proponents of the POS perspective, as is shown in detail when the theories of McAdam and Tarrow are discussed – puts forward a micro-macro explanation, but does not explicitly formulate micro-macro models, they are only hinted at. The free rider problem is not even addressed, let alone solved.

Eisinger further claims that POS and political action are only "mildly related" and that other factors such as deprivation are relevant. There are no general hypotheses about what these other factors are. Furthermore, Eisinger does not apply a theory to generate hypotheses about these other factors. This holds true for contemporary proponents of the POS perspective as well.

One problem of Eisinger's POS concept is that it refers to objective probabilities which are difficult to measure. Furthermore, it seems theoretically more plausible to replace objective by subjective (i.e. by the actors' perceived) probabilities. One of the advantages of a subjectivist POS concept is that perceived probabilities are easier to measure. The major argument for using subjective POSs is the following: it is well known that only changes of stimuli that actors perceive are relevant for their behavior, whatever the objective change may be. Another problem of the POS concept is that the difference between political and non-political opportunities is not clear. Finally, the literature does not provide an answer to the question of what the advantage is to include a causal statement in the definition of the POS concept.

Although there is a burgeoning literature on the POS perspective, the major problems of Eisinger's version of POS theory are not solved. For instance, it is still not clear why or under which conditions POSs trigger protest, i.e. there are no clearly specified and tested micro-macro models. This is illustrated with the theories of two major proponents of the perspectives that are analyzed in detail in this chapter, namely D. McAdam's political process model and S. Tarrow's theory.

One major problem is still what a clear and theoretically fruitful definition of the POS concept is. To be sure, there are various distinctions between kinds of POSs, but their clarity leaves much to be desired. For example, what exactly is a cultural opportunity? There are also many suggestions about "dimensions" of POS. For example, a split of government is seen as a dimension of a changing POS. However, according to the definition of POS, it is necessary to test for each "dimension" whether it leads to changes of the (actual or perceived) "chances of success" of a group of actors. This is typically not done in applications of the POS perspective. Instead, it is simply claimed on plausibility grounds that some change of the political environment is a POS. Another unsolved conceptual problem is the difference between resources and opportunities.

If, as proponents of the POS perspective themselves argue, the effects of POSs depend on the extent to which they change incentives on the micro level, we would expect that POS theory is often invalid: we can imagine many situations where a change of the POS does not affect the incentives to an extent that protest is brought about. But it is also to be expected that researchers are often lucky when they find situations where POSs affect political action by changing incentives or because pre-existing incentives were strong enough so that a little change of POS was sufficient to bring about political action. Accordingly, it is not surprising that there are falsifications, confirmations as well as mixed evidence, as this chapter shows.

We will not repeat our discussion of all the problems of the POS perspective at this point. We will only summarize some of our theoretical suggestions. One is that it does not make sense to include a causal statement in the definition of the POS concept. The strategy should be to formulate hypotheses about effects of changes in the general social context (including political, economic, or any other features of the macro environment) on incentives to political action and then test these propositions. The reader is referred to the detailed discussion of this procedure before. For this purpose, a detailed micro model of political action, that is available in the literature and discussed in detail in chapters 3 and 4 in this book, should be used. If this is not regarded as fruitful, proponents of the POS perspective should suggest a superior model.

Another suggestion, discussed in this chapter, is to integrate POS theory and the theory of collective action. This is easy because there are strong similarities between both theories that are disguised by a different terminology. For example, if there are increasing "chances of success" this implies that there are group goals or, in terms of the theory of collective action, preferences for public goods. The "chances of success" refer to the efficacy of collective action for the provision of a public good. These variables are components of the theory of collective action. The next step then could be to take advantage of the huge amount of scholarly research in the tradition of the POS perspective where we find numerous hypotheses about the effects of specific features of the political, economic, and social context that could be used as an orienting hypotheses or as a heuristic device to develop informative propositions about effects of macro variables on incentives.

The message of this chapter is that the many problems of the POS perspective can be solved by a synthesis of this theory and the theory of collective action along the line sketched above. This suggestion of a synthesis will be elaborated in the next chapters: it will be argued that identity and framing extend the micro model of political action in specific ways. Chapter 11 will then describe the synthesis in more detail.

7 Collective identity and social movement activity

This and the next chapter focus on two perspectives that are distinct from the perspectives addressed so far. One basic thrust of the new perspectives is a critique of the collective action, resource mobilization and political opportunity structure perspectives. It is not claimed that their substantive propositions are wrong but that something is missing: the actor is ignored. This means that the actors' definition, understanding, and interpretation of the situation and their construction of meaning must be considered in a full explanation of social movement phenomena. The identity and framing perspectives thus build on qualitative traditions, based on the work of authors like George Herbert Mead and Herbert Blumer. This implies a specific theoretical as well as methodological approach. In regard to the first, proponents of the perspective reject "rationalistic" theories or assumptions advanced by the collective action, resource mobilization, and political opportunity structure perspectives. In regard to methodology, a constructivist approach is accepted (see the brief discussion in chapter 12).

Despite these differences we believe that our procedure of analyzing the theoretical perspectives related to social movement phenomena will be acceptable to all social movement scholars. "Rationalistic" as well as "qualitative" social scientists want to formulate clear and informative propositions, and they want to find out whether they are valid. Therefore, it is legitimate to apply the kind of analysis advanced in this book to the identity and framing approaches as well.

The earliest work that is devoted to the identity perspective for the field of social movements and political protest is Melucci's article from 1988.[1] We will therefore analyze this article first. In doing so we suggest a causal model of "identity processes" based on Melucci's theoretical argument. We then turn to the recent literature on collective identity and discuss particularly the meaning of the concept of collective identity and problems of identity theory. After reviewing empirical research we suggest how to synthesize identity theory and the theory of collective action. This new version of identity theory is then discussed in detail.[2] Chapter 9 suggests some new hypotheses about identity that are derived from the theory of cognitive balance.

1. Constructing collective identity and protest: A. Melucci's theory

Like most other work that proposes a perspective that is new to the field, Melucci attacks traditional views. These are previous substantive propositions such as imitation or irrationality as explanations of social movement phenomena. He further criticizes previous methodological assumptions such as treating collective phenomena as a "unitary empirical datum" (330 – numbers in parenthesis refer to Melucci 1988). Instead, Melucci argues, it is useful to "consider the collective phenomena as the result of multiple processes" (331). No social scientist will probably disagree with this. The question is what exactly these "multiple processes" are. So what is Melucci's theory?

The subject of the theory

Melucci is concerned with "collective action." Because his subject is social movements it seems that he refers to all kinds of social movement related actions, which include protest behavior. His question is when individuals act together. In other words, he is interested in "processes in which the actors produce meanings, communicate, negotiate, and make decisions" (331). The focus is thus on individuals. The outcome of joint individual action may be a demonstration or a social movement.

The procedure reminds of the theory of collective action. Here the question is when individuals with a common goal act in order to achieve their goal. Melucci is concerned with a very similar or perhaps with the same question. His starting point is also a collectivity of actors. The question that is not answered is how this collectivity is defined. It is not implausible that the minimal defining characteristic is a common goal. If this is correct the questions of Melucci's theory and the theory of collective action are identical: When do people with a common goal act to achieve their goal?

The propositions: a reconstruction as a causal model

Melucci defines "collective identity" only at the end of his article, i.e. after the presentation of his theory. We will proceed in the same way. Melucci suggests numerous factors that are related to collective action. The problem is that it is not clear what exactly the independent and dependent variables are and how they are related. In order to make sense of Melucci's theoretical considerations we will begin with a quotation that captures his main ideas. We will then make some suggestions about how the factors he mentions could be related. The model that in our opinion is the closest match to Melucci's text is depicted in Figure 7.1.[3]

> In the view I am proposing here collective action is thus considered as the result of purposes, resources, and limits, as a purposive orientation constructed by means of social relationships within a system of opportunities and constraints (332). The actors "produce" the collective action because they are able to define themselves and to define their relationship with the environment

(other actors, available resources, opportunities and obstacles). The definition that the actors construct is not linear but produced by interaction, negotiation, and the opposition of different orientations. Individuals contribute to the formation of a "we" (more or less stable and integrated according to the type of action) by rendering common and laboriously adjusting at least three orders of orientation: those relating to the *ends* of the actions (i.e. the sense the action has for the actor); those relating to the *means* (i.e. the possibilities and the limits of the action); and finally those relating to relationships with the *environment* (i.e. the field in which the action takes place. (332–333)

The reader may recognize most of the variables mentioned from the previous discussion of the collective action, resource mobilization, and political opportunity structure perspectives. New is the emphasis on negotiation and interaction, the formation of a "we" and the definition of the situation. Thus, Melucci does not argue that other approaches are principally flawed. The argument is that they are incomplete. The question then becomes how exactly these additional elements are related to the variables of the previous approaches. The text does not say this, but we think that the following theoretical reconstruction is compatible with the text and makes sense.

Opportunities and constraints are here conceptualized as macro variables. They define the limits of collective action. Furthermore, the properties of the actors that matter for collective action are "purposes, resources, and limits." "Limits" are included in opportunities and constraints. Melucci further mentions "social relationships." They affect the micro variables, as Melucci writes: "purposive

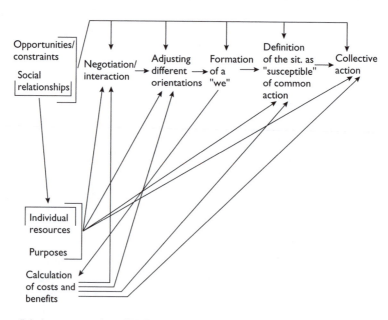

Figure 7.1 A reconstruction of Melucci's implicit model (Melucci 1988)

orientation" is "constructed by means of social relationships within a system of opportunities and constraints." The micro model thus consists of "individual resources" and "purposes." The third variable – cost-benefit calculation – will be discussed below.

The "definition" of the situation is important for collective action: collective action is "produced" or, as he also says, "constructed" (332), "because" the actors are able to define that situation as one that is "susceptible" (332) to collective action. The term "because" signifies a causal relationship: the "definition" of the situation has a direct effect on collective action. It seems plausible that this "definition" is relevant immediately before collective action comes about. It is the recognition that collective action will be worthwhile. "Definition" is a cognition: actors "define in cognitive terms the field of possibilities and limits which they perceive" (332). Melucci could mean that this is an overall cognitive assessment of the features of the situation where the actor compares the situation he or she perceives with the beliefs he or she has stored in his memory (i.e. in his or her mental system).

This "definition" is "produced by" negotiation and interaction. These are thus variables that have a causal impact on "definition." Melucci further mentions that the "definition" is influenced by the "opposition of different orientations." But later he writes that "tensions" between ends, means and the environment are adjusted. It seems plausible to assume that negotiations and interaction between the actors bring about such adjustment. This adjustment leads to the formation of a "we."

How does the theory of collective action fit into this model? Melucci mentions this theory (339), but then cites the critique of Fireman and Gamson (1979, see our discussion in chapter 4, section 3). He accepts this critique and, accordingly, ignores the theory in the remainder of his article. Nonetheless, he does not deny that "cost-benefit calculation" is involved in collective action. However:

> ... collective action is never based solely on cost-benefit calculation ... Some elements of participation in collective action are endowed with meaning but cannot be reduced to instrumental rationality (they are not ir-rational but neither are they based on calculation logic). (343)

We will discuss this argument below. At this point, we will only ask how "cost-benefit calculation" can be integrated into the model. To be sure, there is cost-benefit calculation, according to Melucci. It is not clear, however, at which points in the model people consider costs and benefits. A bold assumption would be that costs and benefits are taken into account not only for actions – this is the common assumption in the theory of rational action – but for acquiring beliefs and attitudes as well. If this assumption is made, then there should be effects of "calculation" on all dependent variables of the model – with one exception: Melucci assumes that identity influences calculation (342). If we assume that a we-feeling is an important part of an identity, then there should be an arrow from "formation of a 'we'" to "calculation." These assumptions are included in Figure 7.1. A more modest assumption is that "cost-benefit calculation" is only involved if behaviors (and not beliefs or attitudes) are at issue. Then arrows should only point from "calculation" to "negotiation and interaction" and to "collective action."

So far the theoretical argument was reconstructed as a normal causal model, i.e. as a set of general propositions. But the argument could also be interpreted as a possible process of successful collective action: there are opportunities so that collective action is in principle possible. There are sufficient resources and strong social relationships. Interaction processes and negotiations lead to the formation of a "we," etc. There are other processes. For example, a group may be so homogeneous that negotiation is not necessary. The situation is immediately "defined" as susceptible to collective action. This second interpretation means that "there is" a process depicted in the figure, and "there is" another process, etc. The open question then is under what conditions which process is to be expected. A more theoretically fruitful interpretation is the first one: it is a theory and not just a set of "there is" (i.e. existential) propositions.

To summarize, let us look at Figure 7.1. The macro variables are opportunities, constraints, and social relationships on the one hand and the variables describing the process from negotiation to collective action on the other (see the upper level of the figure). In contrast to previous models, the macro variables are interrelated: opportunities/constraints facilitate or impede the process that leads to collective action. Furthermore, there is a causal chain connecting the other variables on the macro level.

There are three micro variables in Melucci's model (see the lower level of the figure) that are only influenced by opportunities/constraints and social relationships. The micro variables affect the variables included in the causal chain (from "negotiation" to "collective action") – with one exception: "calculation of costs and benefits" does not affect the formation of a we; instead, the latter affects the calculation of costs and benefits.

Readers who compare Melucci's text with our reconstruction will probably arrive at other causal models (see also note 3). This is not surprising when a text is so ambiguous. We have also tried out various possible models and selected those that in our opinion come closest to the text and, if the text was not clear, which seemed most plausible.

The concept of collective identity

So far the term "collective identity" has not been mentioned, we encountered only the expression "we-feeling" as a component of this variable. Our reconstruction of Melucci's theoretical argument shows that this is one of several variables of his theory. It is therefore a bit surprising that this variable gives the approach its name and that it is in the title of Melucci's article. If "collective identity" is such an important term, it is further surprising that Melucci defines it only at the end of his article. Here is his definition:

> Collective identity is an interactive and shared definition produced by several individuals and concerned with the orientations of action and the field of

opportunities and constraints in which the action takes place: by "interactive and shared" I mean a definition that must be conceived as a process, because it is constructed and negotiated through a repeated activation of the relationships that link individuals (342). Collective identity as a process involves at least three fundamental dimensions ... : (1) formulating cognitive frameworks concerning the ends, means, and field of action, (2) activating relationships between the actors, who interact, communicate, influence each other, negotiate, and make decisions, (3) making emotional investments, which enable individuals to recognize themselves. Collective identity is thus a process in which the actors produce the common cognitive frameworks that enable them to assess the environment and to calculate the costs and benefits of the action; the definitions that they formulate are in part the results of negotiated interactions and of influence relationships; and in part the fruit of emotional recognition. (343)

This text does not provide a clear definition in the sense that the author stipulates how to use a term or an expression. The quotation includes a mix of definitional criteria and empirical hypotheses. So let us disentangle the text. First of all, "collective identity" is a "shared definition"; according to the second part of the quotation this "shared definition" refers to *common cognitive frameworks*. Then the kind of these frameworks is specified: they are about means and ends and are "concerned with the orientations of action and the field of opportunities and constraints in which action takes place" (first part of the quotation). It seems that Melucci refers to certain shared *beliefs* (or perceptions) about "the field of opportunities and constraints in which action takes place." The beliefs could refer to cognitive expectations about the reactions of authorities in case of protest, to expectations about the success of joint action and about the success of mobilization attempts. This interpretation of Melucci's text is confirmed by the second quotation where Melucci writes that the frameworks enable the actors "to assess the environment and to calculate the costs and benefits of the action."

Mentioning "goals" as part of cognitive frameworks means that individuals know their goals. If the frameworks are common, this implies that "collective identity" also implies *common goals*. The reference to means may imply that "collective identity" may also refer to *common values and norms* in regard to the means that are employed to achieve the goals.

The second feature mentioned is "activating relationships between actors." This means that relationships may be taken advantage of if mobilization is at issue. A "collective identity" thus also refers to the *social network* actors are part of.

Further, "emotional investments" are part of the definition. It is not clear what these investments are. Do they refer to *emotional bonds* to other actors in the social network or "in the same boat," i.e. to those who have the same goals? We do not know.

So far we referred only to a part of the previous text. We commented on those sentences that seemed to be concerned with a definition of "collective identity." But the text also includes empirical hypotheses. For example, Melucci emphasizes that collective identity must be conceived "as a process, because it is constructed and negotiated through repeated activation of the relationships that link individuals." Similarly, later in the text Melucci states that "the definitions are in part the result of negotiated interactions ... and in part the fruit of emotional recognition." These are apparently empirical statements that assert, for example, that the beliefs, etc. change all the time and are brought about by negotiation. It doesn't make sense to include these empirical statements in the definition because this would imply that there is no theory any more.

The definition refers to *common* beliefs, goals, etc. It is not clear what the groups are whose beliefs are relevant. As was suggested before, the respective "group" could be any collectivity of actors with a common goal. Thus, we arrive at the following reconstruction of Melucci's definition:

> A *collective identity* exists, by definition, if there is a group (i.e. individuals with at least one common goal) with common beliefs, with common normative convictions, that is connected by social relationships (i.e. there is a social network) and by emotional bonds.

This definition implies that a "collective identity" is a property of groups (i.e. a macro property). Further, it is a qualitative variable. In other words, groups have or do not have a collective identity. It is not possible that there is more or less collective identity.

The definition leaves it open as to which kinds of beliefs must be shared, and to what extent they must be shared so that we can speak of a collective identity. Which goals and normative convictions must be common and to what extent must they be shared? What properties must the social network have in order for a collective identity to exist? For example, is the density relevant? If emotional bonds are relevant: to what extent must the group members be tied? As long as these questions are not answered, it is not possible to determine *whether* a group has or does not have a collective identity. Neither is it possible to ascertain the *extent* to which groups have a collective identity.

The same problems exist when collective identity is a property of individual actors. For example, assume that a person has, by definition, a collective identity when he or she shares beliefs with other members of a group, shares goals with these members, etc. In other words, it is not clear when an individual has or does not have a collective identity or when there is a collective identity to a more or less high degree.

A critique of Melucci's theory

Some problems of Melucci's model are problems of the identity approach in general. But some concern Melucci's model in particular. We will discuss the latter first.

Where is collective identity in the model?

It is surprising that Melucci's hypotheses do not mention the concept of "collective identity." It is only defined at the end of Melucci's article. Why, then, does he define the concept of collective identity at all if it is not needed in his propositions?

If we look at the propositions on the one hand and the definition of collective identity on the other, we find that some of the definitional properties of the definition are included in the model. This holds, for example, for social networks and for goals. The "we" in the model may refer, among other things, to emotional bonds: if persons develop a we-feeling this means that they feel attached to certain groups or individuals. Thus, it seems, that "collective identity" captures various features that are included as variables and relationships between variables in the model. Again: why do we need a new concept that designates several components of a theoretical model and is not included in the model as a theoretical concept?

Can different forms of collective action be explained?

Melucci does not discuss how different forms of collective action can be explained. For example, when do people use violent strategies and when to they choose conventional forms of political action such as organizing or participating in demonstrations? Such questions are not addressed. It is also difficult to see how such hypotheses can be derived from our reconstruction of Melucci's model.

The prevalence of orienting hypotheses

Most of Melucci's theoretical ideas are orienting hypotheses: he mentions numerous factors that in his opinion have some relevance. But it is not clear what effects these factors have on what other factors. Thus, informative propositions are rare in Melucci's article. To illustrate, here is a typical sentence from Melucci's article: "The collective phenomenon is in fact the product of differentiated social processes, of elements of structure and motivation, that can combine in a variable manner" (331). What exactly are the "social processes" that produce the "collective phenomenon"? What "elements of structure" and what "motivation" lead to what kind of "collective phenomena"? How do these variables "combine" into what processes or other phenomena? The sentence says that the collective phenomenon *can* combine in a variable manner. "Can" implies that it is also possible that the collective phenomenon *does not* combine. This sentence in fact does not give any information: it leaves everything open.

Orienting statements are typical for the vast literature on collective identity. As a further illustration, the reader may look at the review of Polletta and Jasper (2001) and try to find informative propositions.

Problems with micro-macro modeling and with the micro model

The micro-macro model in Figure 7.1 is incomplete. To be sure, there is a macro level, there is a micro level, and there are macro-to-micro relationships. There are several micro-to-macro relationships. The three micro variables have direct effects on the macro level variables. This is highly implausible. For example, collective action on the macro level comes about through individual behaviors, which consist of contributions to collective action. Thus, the three micro variables should have an effect on other micro variables which, in turn, affect variables on the macro level.

What could be the effects of the independent micro variables on variables of the micro level? Let us start with an example. When groups of individuals negotiate and interact this presupposes that *single* individuals decide to enter a negotiation or to interact with others. Thus, the independent micro variables should affect the individual decision to negotiate and interact. This variable then has an analytical relationship to the macro level variable "negotiation/interaction." In other words, when several individuals decide to enter a negotiation, this adds up on the macro level to "negotiation/interaction" of groups or several individuals.

This argument holds for the other macro variables in the causal chain as well: each has an equivalent on the micro level. Before "adjusting different orientations" on the macro level originates, individual actors have to adjust their orientation. The antecedent of the "formation of a we" in a group is that individuals form such a "we." The same holds for "definition of the situation as 'susceptible' of common action": before this becomes a shared belief of a group, individuals must have developed such definitions. Finally, collective action on the macro level is based on

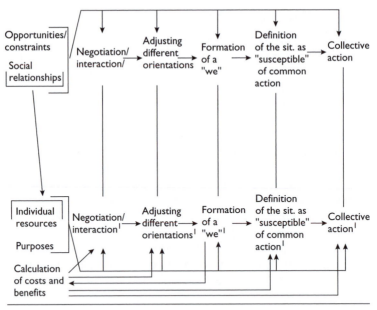

I These variables refer to individual decisions in regard to negotiations and to adjusting different orientations; they refer to individual formations of a "we," to individual definitions of the situation as "susceptible" of common action, and to individual contributions to collective action.

Figure 7.2 A modification of Melucci's implicit model as a micro-macro model (Melucci 1988)

individual contributions to collective action. All these micro variables have analytical relationships to the macro level.

There are causal relationships between the variables on the macro level. These relationships should obtain between the respective variables on the micro level as well.

Figure 7.2 displays this modified model. It includes all variables and relationship of the model in Figure 7.1, but extends the micro level and adds micro-to-macro relationships.

Part of the micro model in Melucci's theoretical argument suggests relationships between incentives (individual resources, purposes) and contributions to collective action. This model does not square with the findings of empirical research (see chapter 4, section 4). "Purposes" are preferences for the collective good. Thus, variables like perceived influence, moral and social incentives are missing. "Calculation of costs and benefits" should not be included as a separate variable. It is a mental process where individual resources, purposes and other factors are considered to reach a decision. We can thus conclude that this part of the micro model is incomplete.

The three micro variables have not only an effect on collective action but on other variables as well. There is so far no empirical evidence that tests this extended micro model. One can thus only speculate whether this model is plausible. Let us look at some of Melucci's hypotheses in this extended model.

One hypothesis is that strong incentives (individual resources, purposes) for collective action set in motion negotiation and interaction. Strong incentives to collective action are present in small and homogeneous groups with intense grievances, high perceived influence and a felt moral obligation to protest. An implication from Melucci's model is that in such a group negotiation would originate among the members. But what is to be negotiated in such a homogeneous environment? The topics of negotiation among the members could be the goals to be realized, the efficacy and legitimacy of means that might be employed to reach the goal. Thus, high homogeneity in groups where the incentives to collective action are strong will not have any issue to negotiate. If heterogeneity is very high negotiations will not occur either: it might not be seen as promising to invest effort to reach agreement (see the discussion in chapter 3, section 1, subsection "Missing macro-to-micro relationships").

It is further plausible that negotiation and interaction will not always lead to "adjusting different orientations." If the group is too heterogeneous negotiations will not be successful.

Does a we-feeling emerge when different orientations become homogenized? A we-feeling in the sense of a positive attachment to a group probably needs more than just reaching some agreement or adaptation of orientations. But if a we-feeling affects collective action it should be included in the micro model at the first stage, along with individual resources and purposes. It should then also have a direct effect on collective action.

The definition of the situation as susceptible to collective action should not only be influenced by a "we-feeling," but by the incentives of the first stage (individual resources, purposes) as well. This definition is a general assessment of the situation, and for this the incentives are relevant as well.

Another problem is to what extent costs and benefits are not relevant when identity in the sense of a we-feeling plays a role. If this factor is a cognition such as "I am a member of the anti-nuclear movement," it may not have any effect at all. If the members of an anti-nuclear group have developed a we-feeling this means that one feels attached to or identifies with the movement or is proud of being a member. If this is a motivation to engage in collective action, why should this exclude any consideration of costs and benefits? For example, a group of students with a strong "affiliation" to the anti-nuclear movement may calculate whether it is useful to them to participate in a demonstration on the next day when this may jeopardize a good grade in the written exam that takes place one day after the event. We will discuss this problem of calculation later in detail.

This discussion indicates that the causal chain on the micro and macro level will occur only under certain conditions. Further research is needed to explore what these conditions are.

What is the implicit background theory?

If a factor like collective identity is supposed to affect a behavior the question is from what theory this proposition can be derived. Why should we expect that collective identity triggers protest behavior or affects any other phenomenon? Melucci does not provide any general theoretical basis for all the causal relationships he proposes in his model.

The only general theory he mentions in his article is rational choice theory. However, Melucci argues that this theory cannot be applied for a complete explanation of the effects of identity. Nonetheless, his implicit background theory is the theory of rational action. Melucci argues that individuals have purposes. He thus assumes that individuals' behavior is goal directed. This assumption implies that individuals do what they think is best to realize their goals. Goal attainment is impeded by constraints. This includes, among other things, individual resources. This is a variable in Melucci's micro model. The general micro theory that Melucci implicitly applies is thus a version of the theory of rational action. To be sure, Melucci emphasizes the limitation of this theory – this is almost a must of a proponent of identity and framing theory – but he does not provide any detailed discussion of this claim.

How is the free rider problem solved?

To be sure, Melucci mentions the free rider problem (339). But then he criticizes Olson's theory and does not further address it. Even if his critique of Olson's theory is correct, this is not yet a good reason to do away with the free rider problem. This is actually a general problem, not tied to any specific approach: it refers to the question of why so many individuals with a common goal do not act in their interest. A theoretical perspective that does not provide a solution to this problem is flawed. In regard to Melucci's theory it is not clear what a solution to the free rider problem looks like.

Conclusion: What can we learn from Melucci's model?

Despite the many problems of Melucci's theory his theoretical argument actually adumbrates an integration of the perspectives discussed before. His model includes general opportunities, individual resources, and incentives. The chain of effects, ranging from negotiation to collective action, is an interesting extension of the models discussed so far. Although the causal process depends on various conditions, it is one possible mechanism to explain collective action. What we further can learn from Melucci's argument is that variables from different sociological schools can be integrated into a unified theoretical structure – see our causal model summarized in Figure 7.2. "Negotiation" or a "we-feeling" are variables from symbolic interactionism. However, Melucci's argument is mostly on the level of orienting propositions. Further theoretical efforts are needed to elaborate Melucci's ideas so that they become informative and testable propositions.

2. Conceptual problems: What is a "collective identity"?

There are numerous definitions of identity or collective or social identity in the literature. Almost all the definitions have one feature in common with Melucci's definition: they are surprisingly vague. This has been noted by several authors. Gamson, for example, holds that the concept of collective identity "sometimes seems excessively vague and difficult to operationalize" in the social movements literature (Gamson 1992: 60; see also Snow and Oliver 1995: 588). Nonetheless, there are several dimensions that most definitions have in common, which are summarized in Table 7.1.[4] "Collective identity" is often defined as a property of individual actors. The first panel of Table 7.1 lists the dimensions that are most often used in the literature to define "individual" identity. The first three characteristics refer to various properties of individual actors (which are also perceived) which are not attitudes or other psychic features. For example, a person may have the collective identity of a woman (membership in a category), of a teacher (a role or status), or of a member of the peace movement (membership of a group). Sometimes these features are not denoted by "collective identity" but simply by "identity." For example, Gould (1995) characterizes union membership as an "identity" (and not as a collective identity) and explains that individuals may give priority "to the identity of parent, child, tenant, debtor, member of an ethnic group, U.S. citizen or any other social role; and these may in some circumstances directly compete with occupational identity" (Gould 1995: 14). This definition thus combines characteristics 2 and 3 of the table. The last category in the table refers to emotional attachments or attitudes. This includes "identification" with a group that is often used if "collective identity" is discussed (see, e.g., Klandermans and de Weerd 2000; Biggs 2006). Laitin (1998: 11) notes that "people's identities change with the level of aggregation: within their community, they may identify themselves on the basis of

Table 7.1 Dimensions of the concept of "collective identity"

I.   Collective identity as a property of *individual* actors
1. (a) Being member of a category (woman, American) or (b) having a position on a dimension (e.g. the dimension may be "income," and the position may be "a yearly income of $60,000")
2. Having a status or role (teacher, father)
3. Being member of a group (peace movement, citizen initiative)
4. Having positive feelings toward (being attached to, identifying with) a category or group or status or role
II. Collective identity as a property of *collective* actors
1. Shared views of members on social environment
2. Shared views of members on goals
3. Shared views of members on limits and success of collective action

socioeconomic background ..." Thus, "identity" and "identification" are used inter-changeably. Later, Laitin explicitly defines "identity": "Identities are therefore categeories of membership that are based on all sorts of typologies – gender, race, class, personality, caste" (21).

Collective identity is further regarded as a property of collective actors or of groups – see part II of the table. Many authors agree that a collective identity is some-thing that the members of a group of individuals share. This leaves the following questions unanswered: (1) What or how many views must be shared in order to assign a collective identity to a group? (2) To what extent must a view or the views be shared? (3) Is "collective identity" a qualitative concept with two values (a group has it or does not have it) or is it a quantitative concept (a group may have it in different degrees)? (4) If "collective identity" is a qualitative concept, to what extent must which views be shared so that one can say a group has a collective identity? If "col-lective identity" is a quantitative concept, how is it constructed from the views of the group? For example, let there be two beliefs that all members share, ten beliefs that 40 percent of the members share, and fifteen beliefs that 5 percent share. Is there a collective identity or to what extent does the group have a collective identity?

To illustrate these problems, let us look at the discussion of the concept by Klandermans (1992: 81). A collective identity is given, among other things, if the members of a group "develop shared views of the social environment, shared goals, and shared opinions about the possibilities and limits of collective action. Groups can be more or less successful in developing a collective identity." In regard to question 1, what views of the social environment must be shared? Is it only views that are regarded as important? In regard to question 2, to what extent must views be shared – do all members have to share the views, 80 percent, 55 percent? The last sentence suggests that collective identity is a qualitative concept (question 3). In regard to question 4, Klandermans does not discuss how a "collective identity" is constructed from these different criteria.

Whatever the answers to these questions are, it is interesting that a collective iden-tity of a group is, by definition, a function of the views of the members of the group. Thus, in order to arrive at a definition that can be applied a measurement instrument must be constructed that relies on the distribution of properties of members.

A consequence of the ambiguity of "collective identity" as a property of groups is that it is at present hardly possible to provide a rigorous test of propositions with this concept. The reason is that it cannot be decided whether a group has a collective identity or not.

There are numerous definitions in the literature. How do some definitions that are not explicitly mentioned in the table fit into the definitions summarized in the table? "Collective identity" is often defined as a we-feeling with a certain group – see the definition by Melucci discussed above. This can be interpreted as an identification or emotional attachment to a group (Table 7.1, dimension I.4). Another definition refers to a collective identity as a statement claiming "we are ..." For example, assume that people "define their identity in religious terms – that is, if they say to themselves, 'We are primarily Jewish, Christian, or Muslim, and not German, French or Iranian'" (Kopstein and Lichbach 2005: 24). This means that people regard themselves as members of categories (Table 7.1, dimension I.1) – they consider themselves as Jewish, etc. What does it mean if somebody feels "primarily" German, etc.? Perhaps not only a cognitive judgment is referred to but in addition some feeling of attachment. One may consider himself or herself primarily, say, Christian and not German means not only a cognition that one is Christian but an emotional attachment: I feel "closer" to Christians than to Germans.

Which definition of collective identity is theoretically most fruitful? It is striking that we have not found any author who gives some detailed justification of why he or she defines the concept in a certain way. The question of which definition has theoretical import can only be answered if theoretical propositions are formulated that include the concept. It can then be examined for which concept the theory is correct. For example, a basic proposition is, as we will see, that collective identity is a determinant of protest. In a first step we could conduct a thought experiment and ask: is the proposition plausible if we define "identity" as being a member of a category (see Table 7.1, dimension 1a), or a member of a group, or if "collective identity" is a positive attitude toward a group? Such different hypotheses must then be tested to find out which definition has the highest theoretical import. Such research has so far not been conducted.

3. Identity theory: recent developments

In this section we will focus on the two major propositions of the identity approach: one is that identity is a determinant of protest, the other claims that protest affects identity. We close with a brief conclusion on the present state of identity theory in the social movement literature.

Identity as a determinant of political protest

The basic proposition in the literature on social movements reads that identity has a positive effect on collective action and particularly on protest behavior.[5] I call this the *identity-proposition*. As we saw before, identity may be an individual or a collective property. There are thus two versions of the identity-proposition, one for individuals and another for groups:

> *Identity-proposition 1*: The stronger the collective identity of individuals, the more likely they engage in protest behavior.

> *Identity-proposition 2*: The stronger the collective identity of a group, the more likely the group engages in collective protest.

Proponents of the identity perspective agree that identity is not the only factor that affects protest, but that it is a very important factor. For example, Klandermans (1992: 81) asserts that groups can be more or less successful in developing a collective identity. "If a group fails in this, it cannot accomplish any collective action." If this is true, identity is indeed a very important variable: the quotation maintains that other variables are irrelevant if there is no collective identity. Perhaps other authors are less convinced of the importance of the variable. According to Polletta and Jasper (2001: 284), for example, "... the forms of protest they [individuals] choose are *also* influenced by collective identities" (italics not in the original). Thus, identity is only one of several factors.

The question arises which other factors are determinants of protest behavior. We will not list here the factors that are proposed to have an effect, in addition to identity. Some of the factors will be mentioned when we discuss empirical studies where hypotheses about collective identity are tested. At this point, it is important to note that there is no theory that the authors apply in order to generate propositions about what these other factors are.

Due to the different definitions of the identity concept the question is which definition is theoretically fruitful, i.e. yields a true identity proposition. Let us first look at the first identity proposition and the different definitions listed in Table 7.1.

Definitions (1a) and (1b): It seems to be irrelevant for protest behavior whether a person falls in a certain category. For example, the mere fact that somebody is male or has a certain income is not related to protest behavior. Being in a certain category will only be relevant if this is connected with certain incentives to protest. For example, if being poor (such as having an income of less than $600 per month in the USA) is related to integration in protest promoting networks and other incentives, we will find a correlation of being in a category or having a certain property on the one hand and protest behavior on the other. Thus, the relevant factors are not mere category membership but the additional factors related to category membership.

Definition (2): The same holds for having a certain role or status: being a father or a school teacher is in itself irrelevant. Protest participation will only be likely if, for example, school teachers have a strong internalized protest norm, are organized in networks for collective action, etc. Again, the major factors of the explanation are the incentives related to the respective status or role.

Definition (3): Being a member of a network per se is also irrelevant. Mere membership does not matter but the kind of the network. For example, being member of a golf club will normally not predispose a person to participate in any protests. Again, the major factor are the incentives prevalent in a group.

Definition (4): Identification with any group will not affect protest, but only identification with certain kinds of groups. For example, identifying with a golf club or with a university will not necessarily lead to protest. But identifying with the peace movement will make protest more likely. The question then is what the conditions are when identification with a group generates protest. This question will be discussed later in this chapter.

Let us turn to the identity proposition referring to groups. As was said before, the problem of this proposition is that it is not specified what exactly has to be shared that is important for protest behavior. The general idea of the proposition is that *homogeneity* of a group is positively related to collective action. As our discussion in chapter 3 indicates, relevant common features are, for example, goals or beliefs about the efficacy of tactics. Such homogeneity lowers the costs of joint action. It is further important that some inequality of resources exists – see the discussion of critical mass and threshold effects. Thus, "collective identity" as a property of groups is relevant for protest, but not any homogeneity, only homogeneity of certain factors. What these factors are is discussed in various theoretical approaches in the social movements literature. The identity-proposition 2 can thus be seen as an orienting statement and not as an informative proposition.

Political action as a determinant of collective identity

So far the causal effect runs from identity to political action. Another hypothesis is that protest changes identification with a group (see, e.g., Calhoun 1991: 59; Klandermans 1992: 82). Teske claims that activists "develop certain identities for themselves. This is the identity-construction approach to political activism" (Teske 1997: 121). The claim is that activism leads to fundamental changes in the beliefs, values, norms, and attitudes of the activists (see Teske 1997: chapter 4). What exactly these consequences are "varies widely from activist to activist" (123). However, three consequences stand out: one is the development of intense relationships with other activists (122–123). This suggests: the more individuals protest, the more intense is their involvement in political groups. Second, new emotional attachments to other individuals and groups – i.e. group identifications – originate. The author further emphasizes the "moral meaning" of activism.

It is plausible that not every political action changes group identification. The question thus is what the conditions are when social movement participation affects group identification. This question is largely left unanswered in the literature. So there is so far no clear answer to the question of when political action generates a collective identity.

Other determinants of identity

Various other theoretical ideas are proposed in the literature addressing factors that influence the formation of identities. For example, institutions and culture may affect identity (Polletta and Jasper 2001: 288). But which institutions generate identification with which groups? Which aspects of culture determine which kind of group identification? The existing literature does not provide answers to these questions.

Conclusion

When we look at the present state of the identity approach in the social movement literature and compare this with Melucci's theoretical contribution, we may conclude that his theoretical ideas are not further developed. We do neither know what exactly the effects of identity – in whatever sense – are on protest or collective action. We do not know either what the conditions for the formation of identities are. Authors do not even bother to provide a clear definition of "identity" or "collective identity" if they engage in developing theory or reviewing the state of the arts (like Polletta and Jasper 2001).

4. Empirical evidence

Although it is widely accepted that identity is a pivotal variable in social movements research, it is astounding that there are few empirical studies that provide a rigorous test of a micro-model of protest behavior that includes identity as well as other variables. It could be argued that the number of studies is irrelevant. It is more important whether existing studies provide supporting evidence. And this seems to be the case: empirical studies "overwhelmingly support" the identity-proposition, i.e. the assumption that "a strong identification with a group makes participation in collective political action on behalf of that group more likely" (Klandermans 2004: 364). Is the evidence really so overwhelming? The existing studies that test this proposition show several deficiencies, and there are falsifications of the identity-proposition.[6]

(1) Some of the studies explain the *intention* or the *willingness to participate* (see, e.g., Kelly and Kelly 1994; Kelly and Breinlinger 1996; Stürmer *et al.* 2003). Since the identity-proposition refers to behavior, a test should include behavior as a dependent variable and not only intention.

(2) Identification or identity is *measured differently*. For example, Kelly and Breinlinger (1996) measure identity as self-perception as an activist; de Weerd and Klandermans (1999) distinguish four components of identification where one is "attachment to the group or category." Simon and associates use still other measurements (see, e.g., Stürmer and Simon 2004). Thus, it seems that different versions of the identity-proposition are tested – unless it is shown that the different measurements are indicators of the same latent variable. But so far this has not been shown.

(3) There is sometimes *deficient measurement*. For example, Kelly and Breinlinger (1996; see also Kelly and Kelly 1994) measure identity with the item "I identify strongly with the union" (Kelly and Kelly 1994: 59; similarly de Weerd and Klandermans 1999; Simon *et al.* 1998; Stürmer and Simon 2004). It is highly problematic to use terms like "identification" in a questionnaire that even scholars use in different and ambiguous ways. In one of their studies, Kelly and Breinlinger

(1996) measured "identification as an activist" (Kelly and Kelly 1994: 65) by asking respondents to what extent they would describe themselves as "someone who is actively involved in promoting women's issues." It is hardly surprising that an independent variable that consists of a measure referring to a self-description as someone who performs protest behavior (an "activist") correlates strongly with actual protest behavior. This procedure does not provide an independent measurement of the dependent and independent variable.

(4) To be sure, there is empirical support for the identity-proposition, but it is certainly not "overwhelming." For example, for the dependent variable "intention to protest" the identity-proposition is confirmed (for confirmations see Kelly and Breinlinger 1996; Simon *et al.* 1998; Stürmer and Simon 2004; Stürmer *et al.* 2003).[7] But there are also *falsifications*. For example, Kelly and Breinlinger (1996) find that gender identity (in the sense of "feeling close to women") does not have an effect on actual protest participation in a multivariate analysis. De Weerd and Klandermans (1999) do not find effects of "identification" in several analyses. The research by Mühler and Opp (2004: chapter 8.1) provides a falsification of the identity-proposition as well: only if the salience of identifying with certain groups was very strong, identification had the expected positive effect on protest behavior. For lower values of salience, the effect of identification was negative. Biggs (2006) finds that identity in the sense of identification with a respondent's race was insignificant for explaining protest participation.

(5) Research designs to test the identity proposition are relatively *simple*: interaction effects as well as feedback effects are rarely tested, and there are few panel studies.

In general, thus, there is some support for the identity-proposition, but there are also falsifications. Furthermore, the measurement of identity is often different and problematic. This state of empirical research suggests that further research is urgently needed. There are no studies that provide a rigorous test of hypotheses on the effects of protest and other factors on identity.

5. Synthesizing collective identity theory and the theory of collective action

In this section a synthesis of the identity perspective and the theory of collective action is suggested. The theory of collective action is based on rational choice theory. The synthesis that will be proposed suggests that collective identity is a kind of a selective incentive. This presupposes that having an identity and acting according to this identity is related to costs and benefit. Both claims are discussed in this section. We will finally take up a thesis by Melucci that identities influence cost-benefit calculations.

The two paradigms: collective identity and cost-benefit calculation

It is widely held that the identity perspective contradicts rational choice theory. Melucci, for example, argues that "collective action is never based solely on cost-benefit calculation ... Some elements of collective action are endowed with meaning but cannot be reduced to instrumental rationality (they are not ir-rational but neither are they based on calculation logic)" (Melucci 1988: 343). Klandermans's (2004: 364) position is similar: "there is much more in being a movement partici-pant than perceived costs and benefits," and this "much more" is social identity. Polletta and Jasper (2001) also claim: "Collective identity does not imply the rational calculus of evaluating choices that 'interest' does" (285, but see also 298).[8]

Thus, there seem to be *two paradigms* of explaining social movement phenom-ena, one is based on identity, the other on interests. Simon *et al.* (1998; similarly Klandermans 2002 and 2004: 364; Stürmer *et al.* 2003) argue: "There seem to exist two independent pathways to social movement participation or at least to willing-ness to participate. One pathway appears to be *calculation* of the costs and benefits of participation (including normative considerations). ... The second pathway seems to be *identification* with the movement or, in other words, adoption of a dis-tinct activist identity. Here, calculation processes should be of less importance than identification or self-definition processes ..." (656).[9] It is first important to note that the definition of identity used here is identification with a group (see Table 7.1, def-inition I.4). This is in line with our previous argument that this concept seems to be theoretically the most fruitful definition of "collective identity."

The assumption of the two paradigms can be tested. For example, one could investigate the decision processes of subjects with and without an identity and examine to what extent calculation (i.e. conscious weighing of advantages and dis-advantages of a behavior and then choosing the behavior that seems best) occurs. However, this is not done so far. So we can only speculate whether it is plausible that in general calculation does not take place or is rare if there is a strong identifi-cation with a group.

Consider the following scenario. A demonstration against an authoritarian regime is planned by a social movement, and demonstrators expect violent police action. Assume that demonstrators think that the demonstration will probably change the regime's behavior and that individual contribution matters, but that it is highly likely that demonstrators will be injured and arrested. It is implausible that in such a situation participants will not deliberate whether it is worthwhile to par-ticipate, even if they strongly identify with the movement. People will reflect on the consequences of their participation by considering possible imprisonment, injury, and other personal disadvantages on the one hand, and the benefits of the public goods to be provided on the other.

Another scenario is a planned demonstration of a social movement in a demo-cratic society. It is plausible that often those who strongly identify with the move-ment will spontaneously participate. There is thus no calculation. But this need not be the case. Assume there is a demonstration and a student's examination takes place the next day. The student is afraid that he might get a worse grade if he or she participates. Will the student really spontaneously decide to demonstrate and not consider the possible cost?

Thus, it is plausible that there are situations where people identify with a move-ment and where they decide to participate without considering consciously the costs and benefits. There are other situations where there is strong identification but nevertheless still a concern about the "advantages" and "disadvantages" of partici- pating in movement activities.

But let us look at situations where no calculation takes place. Does this imply that costs and benefits do not play any role for the decision to participate? Many spon- taneous activities are carried out because the benefits are, compared to the costs, so high that people do not think about costs and benefits, but that does not mean that costs and benefits are irrelevant. Even murders out of passion are governed by costs and benefits.

If this is denied, that is, if it is assumed that costs and benefits are irrelevant in sit- uations in which identification with a group is high, the question arises: How do proponents of the identity perspective explain the behavior of identifiers? Do people choose their action by chance? When we would ask individuals who strongly identify with a movement and spontaneously participated in a demonstra- tion why they acted for the group, the answer would probably be that it was a pleas- ure for them to support the group or that the group deserved their support or that they felt an obligation to act on behalf of the group. Those who identify with a group would probably feel uneasy or would have a bad conscience when they did not act in the interest of the group. This indicates that costs and benefits are involved, even if people don't calculate and strongly identify with a group.

The situations outlined before can be classified in the following way. Two dimensions were at issue: one is calculation. That is to say, there may be situations where people calculate and situations where people do not. Secondly, costs and benefits may be considered or may not be considered. Combining these two dimen- sions results in four scenarios which are summarized in Table 7.2. Let us look at each of those scenarios in more detail.

The argument advanced so far claims that there are situations where people cal- culate and there are situations where people don't. But in both cases costs and ben- efits may enter the decision to participate. There are thus four different situations, depicted in the four entries of Table 7.2. Which of these situations are allowed or are consistent with which theoretical position?

Table 7.2 Differences between rational choice and identity theory

Calculation	Consideration of costs and benefits	
	Yes	*No*
Yes	(1) Consistent with rational choice theory Inconsistent with identity theory in case of identification	(2) Inconsistent with rational choice theory Not explicitly addressed by identity theory
No	(3) Consistent with rational choice theory Inconsistent with identity theory in case of identification	(4) Inconsistent with rational choice theory Identity theory in case of identification

Entry 1 in the table refers to a situation where there is calculation and where costs and benefits are taken into account when a decision is made. This is a situation where rational choice theory can be applied. What about identity theory if individuals identify with a group? As the previous arguments of proponents of the identity approach indicate, there is no calculation: in a situation where individuals identify with a group there will be spontaneous protest in the interest of the group. Thus, identity theory implies that in a situation where individuals identify with a group there is neither calculation nor action that is governed by costs and benefits.

Entry 3 of the table is incompatible with identity theory. First of all, if individuals identify with a group there is no calculation but spontaneous action. The previous citations indicate that in a situation where people identify with a group, costs and benefits are not considered either.

Is the situation in entry 3 possible according to rational choice theory? In other words, is it possible that people do not calculate but that nonetheless behavior is governed by costs and benefits? The answer is clearly "yes." It is a typical misunderstanding that rational choice theory assumes calculation, as was emphasized several times in this book (see, e.g., chapter 1). This misunderstanding is also widespread among social movement scholars, as the literature quoted above shows. They believe that the theory of collective action and rational choice theory presuppose that individuals calculate. To be sure, this was and is an assumption made by some neoclassical economists and game theoreticians, but it is not part of a relatively wide version of a rational actor model that is increasingly applied in the social sciences and in this book as well (for details see Opp 1999 – see also chapter 1, section 1 of this book). In this version of rational choice theory, the assumption is that individual behavior is governed by costs and benefits and not that these costs and benefits are always calculated. Such an assumption of universal calculation would indeed contradict all we know about human behavior (for a summary see Wilson 2002). Leading economists also subscribe to this wide version of the theory of rational actions. For example, Gary Becker (1976: 7) emphasizes: "... the economic approach does not assume that decisions units are necessarily conscious of their efforts to maximize or can verbalize or otherwise describe in an informative way reasons for the systematic patterns in their behavior" – Becker mentions Milton Friedman (1953) who makes the same point. Although Herbert Simon would not regard his idea of "bounded rationality" as part of the rational choice tradition, it is in fact in line with a wide version of this theory: "Rationality is bounded when it falls short of omniscience. And the failures of omniscience are largely failures of knowing all the alternatives, uncertainty about relevant exogenous events, and inability to calculate consequences" (Simon 1979: 502). We find similar arguments in textbooks on game theory (see, e.g., Morrow 1994: 20). Thus, the theory of rational action does not assume that individuals calculate but only that costs and benefits govern their behavior.

Rational action theory as well as social psychological theories go one step further: they explain under what conditions individuals calculate. For example, if choosing the "wrong" alternative is very costly, it "pays" to calculate.[10] Fazio

(1986, 1990) delineates in detail conditions that lead to more or less spontaneous action or calculation. In short, if the risks of a decision are high, there are strong incentives to calculate. To be sure, identification with a group makes it in principal beneficial to act on behalf of the group. If this benefit is relatively high, compared to the costs, there is no incentive to calculate the costs and benefits. But this holds for any situations where strong positive incentive for a behavior obtain. For example, in case of very strong internalized norms and weak other incentives, calculation is unlikely. So there may be situations where a strong identification prevents calculation of the costs and benefits of a behavior that is in the interest of a group, but if much is at stake, even strong identification will not automatically lead to act on behalf of a group. In such a situation, identification is just one of the benefits or costs of a behavior, and the actors will face a decision situation with several options.

This implies that it may be that those who identify with a group do not calculate costs and benefits in certain situations. But this does not imply that we need two *theories* to explain protest participation, one that includes costs and benefits and the other identity and not costs and benefits as independent variables. Thus, whether people calculate or do not calculate can be explained by applying rational choice theory.

To summarize the argument so far, it is implausible that in general those who identify with a group do not calculate or calculate less than those who do not identify with a group. But even if there are situations where group identification keeps individuals from calculating, the identifiers' behavior will depend on its costs and benefits. The extent to which people calculate is a question of the costs and benefits of calculation. The general implication of this argument is that it may be granted that there are different "pathways" or processes that lead to protest participation, one that involves mainly calculation and one that is more spontaneous and identity-driven, but, again, we do not need two *theories* to explain political action.

The implication is that rational choice theory is not restricted to situations in which individuals calculate, it can be also applied when people don't calculate. In this situation, costs and benefits are involved as well.

Entry 2 of Table 7.2 is clearly a situation that will not exist according to rational choice theory: it denies that there are situations where behavior is not guided by costs and benefits. This situation is neither mentioned in the identity literature. Therefore, we will not further discuss entry 2.

Entry 4 is the situation identity theory focuses on, as the previous quotations suggest: people who identify with a group do not calculate and their behavior is not based on considering costs and benefits. However, as was said before, the proponents of this approach do not answer the question of how people make decisions in such situations. Further, entry 4 is a situation that should not occur if rational choice theory is valid.

To conclude, the position advanced in this book is that there are situations where calculation obtains and other situations where people do not calculate. In all situations, individuals consider costs and benefits. This holds regardless of identification with a group.

Collective identity as a selective incentive

When we assume that individuals who identify with a group decide on the basis of costs and benefits, the next question is how identity is related to the theory of collective action: Is identification a variable of the theory of collective action? The variables of this theory are costs and benefits. "Identification" can thus only be a variable in the theory if individuals who identify with a group incur costs or obtain benefits if they participate or defect.

This question is not identical with the argument discussed in the previous section. The question there was whether in situations where individuals identify with a group calculation obtains and whether in these situations costs and benefits govern behavior. This does not yet presuppose that identification per se is a cost or benefit.

This is the assumption advanced in Hirschman's theory (1970) that explains how people react if the quality of a product declines. The variable of Hirschman's theory that is of interest here is "loyalty" to an organization. "Loyalty" is defined as "attachment to an organization" (Hirschman 1970: 77–78) or as "affection for an organization" (78). This definition is identical with the definition of identification mentioned before. One of Hirschman's hypotheses reads that "loyalty" to a firm makes "exit" (buying a product from another firm) less likely and that "loyal" customers are motivated to do something to improve the quality of the product ("voice"). Hirschman's background theory is the theory of rational action. So the question arises what the relation is between loyalty on the one hand and costs and benefits on the other. Hirschman argues that loyalists will be "unhappy" (88) if they switch to another organization. That is to say, loyalty is a "penalty for exit," which is "internalized" (98). This suggests that *loyalty to a group means an interest in the well-being of the group*. In other words, the stronger the identification with a group, the more rewarding is the well-being of a group. If there is such an interest in the welfare of a group then action (in Hirschman's terms: voice) that is expected to improve the well-being of a group is beneficial as well. Thus, if individuals strongly identify with a group they get high (internal) benefits if they act in order to improve the situation of the group, and they incur costs if they are inactive.[11]

Dissonance and balance theory (Festinger 1957; Harmon-Jones and Mills 1999; Heider 1958) also suggest that identification with an organization incurs costs if the organization is deteriorating and if the individual remains inactive. In other words, if an individual likes (or identifies with) a group and at the same time realizes that protest (or "voice") would make the organization better off, dissonance, i.e. a psychic costs, would obtain if the individual would not protest.[12]

If identification with a group refers to behavioral costs and benefits the question arises whether these incentives are public goods incentives or selective incentives. The previous argument implies that acting on behalf of the group confers benefits, whereas defection is costly for those who identify with a group. The costs and benefits are thus linked to contributing or defecting. Therefore, identification with a group is a selective incentive and not a public good incentive.[13] The theory of collective action and the previous argument thus provide some theoretical support of the identity-proposition.

Based on the previous argument, the identity-proposition, referring to individual actors, can now be formulated more accurately in the following way:

Revised identity-proposition 1: The stronger individuals identify with a group, the more rewarding is action in support of the group and the more likely is participation in the interest of the group.

According to the theory of collective action, identification should thus contribute to participating in action to the benefit of the group.

Do identities influence "cost-benefit calculation"?

Proponents of the identity approach argue that collective identities provide "the base for ... calculating costs and benefits of action" (Melucci 1988: 342; see also Gamson 1992: 57). Those who advance this claim seem to believe that this falsifies a rational choice approach: cost-benefit calculation – the assumption seems to be – is something that is independent of identity, i.e. it should not be influenced by identity. Similarly, it could be argued that the acceptance of moral norms and of cognitive beliefs about, for example, the efficacy of one's behavior affects calculation.

First of all, the claim that identity (as well as all kinds of beliefs or preferences) affect cost-benefit calculation is correct. It is obvious that one's cost-benefit calculation is different if one identifies with a group (i.e. if one has the goal of supporting a group) or if one does not care about the well-being of a group. In a similar vein, the cost-benefit calculation of somebody with a strong moral belief that one must participate in collective action against nuclear power is different than the calculation of somebody who does not hold this belief. In other words, identification and other beliefs change the costs and benefits of an individual and thus change the calculation.

Second, the claim that identity (and other incentives) influences cost-benefit calculation is by no means contradictory to rational choice theory and, accordingly, not inconsistent with the theory of collective action. To show this let us assume that public goods preferences in a large group do not lead to contributions to the public good. Thus, the result of cost-benefit calculation is that individuals decide to abstain. But now assume there are selective incentives such as an identification with a social movement or moral beliefs. That leads to a change of the cost-benefit calculation, because now other costs and benefits come into play: the existence of selective incentives will now ensue in contributions to the public good, if the selective incentives are strong enough. Thus, it would contradict collective action theory if identity (and other beliefs) would *not* alter "calculation."

We can thus conclude that indeed a collective identity influences the costs and benefits for and, thus, affects cost-benefit calculation of collective action in various ways. Having said that one wonders why this is so often emphasized by proponents of the identity approach. And one wonders why those who emphasize the obvious, further believe that this is an argument against the theory of collective action. We leave it to the reader to seek an explanation for this strange belief.

The extended theory of collective action thus includes as an additional selective incentive identification with a group. This means that both approaches – the identity approach and the theory of collective action – are no longer contradictory; they can be integrated.

6. Problems of the extended theory of collective identity

We will now examine to what extent the revised identity proposition meets the criteria that we have applied to the theories discussed in previous chapters. We will focus on collective identity in the sense of identification with a group.

Can the forms of political action be explained?

The revised identity proposition asserts that identification with a group provides a motivation to act *in support of the group*. This implies that individuals will consider to choose those actions that support the group. Thus, the identity proposition explains the form of action that those who identify with a group will choose.

But there may be conflicting incentives. For example, assume that a person who strongly identifies with a group is convinced that only violent action will contribute to achieve the goals of a group. If the person feels a strong obligation to engage in peaceful collective action, there is a conflict of motivation. The question now is what the stronger motivation is. In general, however, a relatively strong identification with the group and the belief that only violent action could help the group makes it more likely that violent action will be chosen. Thus, the revised identity proposition is capable of contributing to an explanation of the form of collective political action.

The generation of micro-macro models

Although the theoretical synthesis of the identity proposition and the theory of collective action does not provide a micro-macro model, we can include collective identity as one of the incentives of the micro model and then generate explicit propositions about the effects of the macro factors discussed in earlier chapters on collective identity. The question is whether group size, the various kinds of resources, and opportunity structures affect collective identity. It is not implausible that such effects exist. For example, if a group has a high reputation and is regarded as successful, this will increase identification with the group. This hypothesis is compatible with the attitude theory by M. Fishbein and I. Ajzen (see chapter 1, section 1). This theory explains in general the attitudes toward an attitude object. An identification with a group is a positive attitude toward a specific attitude object. The basic idea is that identity with a group originates if the group has many positive features that are valued very positively and are ascribed to the group with a high subjective probability. Thus, it is likely that identification with a group increases if people believe that it has many features they value positively. So far a micro-macro model with hypotheses about the effects of the political, economic or societal environment on identification as a micro variable is missing.

What are the other factors?

Our theoretical argument that collective identity is a selective incentive has an important implication: there is now a general theory that can be applied to generate hypotheses about the other factors that might influence collective action: they are the incentives of the micro model specified before. It is thus no longer necessary to specify these other factors *ad hoc*.

How can identity theory solve the free rider problem?

As was said before, Melucci does not address this problem. But perhaps the free rider problem is not a problem at all? Accordingly, Polletta and Jasper (2001: 284) claim that "those who do participate usually do so in the absence of selective incentives or coercion, Olson's (1965) solution to the free-rider dilemma. Collective identity seemed to capture better the pleasures and obligations that actually persuaded people to mobilize. Identity was appealing, then, as an alternative to material incentives." In other words, people participate if there is a collective identity. There is thus no free rider problem.

This argument has several implications. First, when the authors claim that selective incentives are not necessary for collective action to originate, they refer to material incentives – see the end of the quotation. However, as we saw before, a wide version of the theory of collective action and rational choice includes also non-material incentives. Then the argument that the free rider problem is solved without selective incentives if there is identity is incorrect because collective identity is such an incentive.

Second, collective identity is related to "pleasures and obligations that actually persuaded people to mobilize" (see the quotation). In other words, an existing identity is connected with strong benefits ("pleasures and obligations") which "persuaded people to mobilize." There are thus no longer two paths to collective action: one via identity, the other via incentives. Identity *is* a set of incentives. Thus, the authors' argument supports our previous analysis that collective identity is a (obviously, a non-material) selective incentive.

Third, the claim of the authors seems to be that a collective identity is sufficient to instigate collective action. However, the authors add later that protest is "*also* influenced by collective identities" (284, italics not in the original text). There will thus be situations where people have developed a collective identity but that this will not be sufficient to instigate participation. Existing research and the micro model developed earlier indicate that collective identity is just one of many possible selective incentive. There is no evidence so far that it is a particular important incentive, but there is evidence, as we have seen, that it is no important incentive at all.

Can there be collective action without collective identity?

Some scholars would probably emphatically deny that there may be collective action without a collective identity. As Klandermans puts it (1992: 81): if a group cannot develop a collective identity "it cannot accomplish any collective action." However, Polletta and Jasper (2001: 291) argue that "mobilization does not always require preexisting collective identities." They refer to the work of James Jasper (Jasper 1997; Jasper and Poulsen 1995). For example, catastrophes such as Three Mile Island may mobilize people without any existing collective identity. Another example are the protests in 1989 and 1990 in former communist countries. Participation in these situations apparently did not require identification with a group.

Thus, if there is protest there need not be a collective identity. But if there is a collective identity there is some likelihood that it influences protest – depending on its strength and other incentives. This is quite consistent with the theory of collective action. As has been said before, it has to be determined empirically what the selective incentives in the specific situation are (see chapter I).

Explaining collective identity

As we saw before, the literature does not provide clear and informative hypotheses about the origins of collective identity. Social movement scholars will probably agree that it is an interesting question how identities come about. A possibility to explain identity in the sense of "identification with a group" is to apply a general theory. The best candidate is the theory by M. Fishbein and I. Ajzen. Identification is an attitude toward a group. The Fishbein/Ajzen theory in general explains attitudes. It would be an interesting task for future research to apply this theory to generate propositions about the conditions for a change of identities.

The assumption of continuous negotiations

A basic assumption of proponents of the identity approach that can be found in almost every writing is that actors continuously negotiate. As Melucci (1988: 333) puts it: collective actors "continually negotiate and renegotiate all these aspects of their action." This thesis raises several questions.

(1) Why is this hypothesis needed for the explanation of protest or social movements? If negotiation is ubiquitous, it cannot explain the changing incentives and protests.

(2) It could be argued that some negotiation may be ubiquitous, but that the extent or intensity of negotiation varies. In other words, negotiation is a variable. The question then is what the effects on protest are if negotiation is more or less intense. This question is not answered in the literature.

It seems plausible that very intense negotiation prevents any decision-making. The implication then would be that movements and protests would never originate. This is obviously an empirically false hypothesis.

(3) There can be no question that members of many groups negotiate various issues. These include the goals to be achieved, moral issues about acceptable strategies and beliefs about the efficacy of direct action or mobilization. The following questions are of interest: Under which conditions will negotiation occur to what extent? What are the outcomes of these negotiations under what conditions? For example, if there is a certain initial distribution of beliefs in a group and if negotiation begins, who will change his or her mind, i.e. what beliefs will prevail? To what extent does the intensity of negotiation and the outcome depend on the leadership structure or on status differentials?

These questions refer to the decision-making processes of groups. They are rarely discussed in detail in the social movement literature (but see, e.g., Downey 1986). It would be important to formulate propositions that explain these processes and their outcomes. The identity approach directs our attention to the existence of these processes but there is no contribution to provide detailed answers to these questions.

7. What can we learn from the identity approach for the explanation of social movement phenomena?

An important contribution of the identity approach is that it directs the attention to subjective phenomena. This is a welcome extension of the resource mobilization and political opportunity perspectives. To be sure, the theory of collective action disposes of a micro model that includes subjective phenomena, but this micro model so far did not include "identity." The identity approach suggests a new variable that can be integrated in existing micro theories of political action.

The literature on identity abounds with orienting hypotheses. They include, for example, many ideas on what factors might change identities. There are other ideas about phenomena that have not yet been the subject of social movement research. We refer the reader to Figure 7.2. Among other things, negotiation and the emergence of a we-feeling might be new dependent or independent variables that might be integrated into a micro-macro model explaining various social movement phenomena. These ideas could be used as a starting point to formulate testable and informative propositions. For example, Melucci's ideas outlined earlier are still waiting for a theoretical effort to transform them into a full-fledged, informative, and testable theory.

8. Summary and conclusions

This chapter began with a detailed analysis of Melucci's basic article (1988) of the identity perspective in the field of social movements and political protest. We tried hard to extract a causal model from Melucci's text which is not very clear. It is interesting that Melucci's model includes basic variables of previous approaches and adds new variables. Thus, the identity perspective is not an incompatible alternative to previous approaches. In regard to the variable that gives the approach its name, namely "collective identity," it is surprising that this term does not show up in the presentation of his theory. The variable that is often included in or identical with the definition of "collective identity" in the literature is a we-feeling. Only after the presentation of his theory Melucci discusses "collective identity." He does not provide a clear definition. It seems that "collective identity" exists if there is a collectivity of individuals with common beliefs, common normative convictions, with social ties (i.e. there is a social network) and with emotional bonds. Some of these phenomena are components of Melucci's theory. It thus seems that "collective identity" comprises several variables included in his propositions.

Melucci's theory is a micro-macro model. What is new is that the micro model is much more complex than the micro models discussed in the literature (see Figure 7.2). However, its empirical validity is questionable. It would nonetheless be an interesting task to try to use Melucci's variables to expand existing micro models. Although Melucci holds that the effects of identity on collective action cannot be explained completely by a version of the theory of rational action, he actually applies it. He assumes that human behavior is goal-oriented and that resources are relevant. This implies that people try to realize their goals by taking account of the available resources or constraints – a basic assumption of the theory of rational action. Melucci further mentions explicitly that cost-benefit calculations take place. In general, it seems that Melucci's implicit background theory is actually a version of the theory of rational action. The free rider problem is not solved in Melucci's theoretical argument.

Turning to the development of the literature after Melucci's article, several definitions of the identity concept are discussed (for a summary see Table 7.1). It seems that "identity" is most often used in the sense of identification with a group. We employ this definition as well in the remainder of the chapter. In regard to the theoretical development, the basic proposition is still that collective identity has an effect on protest behavior – we call this the "identity-proposition." Although researchers agree that other factors are relevant as well, there is no agreement in regard to what factors these are. There is no theory either that is applied to generate hypotheses about these factors. And there is no theory that implies that collective identity will affect protest behavior.

Our review of empirical research that tests the identity-proposition shows that the empirical evidence is mixed. There are confirmations, but also falsifications.

The most important part of this chapter is, in our opinion, the synthesis of the identity proposition and the theory of collective action. The argument is that identifying with a group means that a person has an intrinsic interest in the well-being of a group. If individuals have developed such an intrinsic interest, then acting in the interest of a group is beneficial, whereas not acting to improve a group's well-being is costly. In terms of the theory of collective action, identification with a group is thus a selective incentive. Taking this into account allows it to integrate the identity-proposition and the theory of collective action: identification with a group is thus one of various possible selective incentives. This integration is important because it is now possible to apply a theory to generate hypotheses about the other factors that are relevant, apart from collective identity. We discuss various implications of this synthesis that will not be summarized here.

As a general conclusion, the identity approach has added a new variable to the micro model of political protest, and it has again emphasized the importance of subjective factors. However, it is unfortunate that the approach so far consists mostly of orienting statements. Many variables are mentioned, but informative hypotheses are rare. It would be an important task for further research to utilize the rich reservoir of theoretical orienting ideas in the identity literature to build rigorous theoretical micro-macro models and then test them.

8   How framing influences mobilization and protest

The framing perspective that is presented and discussed in this chapter is the most recent attempt to break new theoretical ground. The major question is when the arguments that social movements articulate are accepted by unmobilized individuals (or other third parties). The empirical hypothesis is that acceptance of these arguments makes collective action more likely. Formulated in terms of the framing perspective, the issue is when social movements succeed in aligning their frames to the frames of non-mobilized individuals or groups. It is claimed that such "frame alignment" increases the likelihood of social movement participation.

In presenting and discussing the basic concepts and propositions of the framing approach we proceed as usual: we begin with the basic theoretical article of the framing perspective (Snow *et al.* 1986), discuss its problems, and look at recent developments.

In regard to methodology, most adherents of the framing perspective advance a constructivist approach. The basic methodological orientation is thus identical to that of the identity approach (see the brief discussion of the constructivist approach in chapter 12). We repeat here what has been said at the beginning of the previous chapter: we believe that our procedure of analyzing the theoretical perspectives related to social movement phenomena will be acceptable to all social movement scholars, including proponents of the framing perspective. All social scientists want to formulate clear and informative propositions, and they want to find out whether they are valid. Therefore, it is legitimate to apply the kind of analysis advanced in this book to the framing perspective as well.

The major points made in this chapter are that the framing perspective has much in common with the perspectives discussed before: rudimentary micro-macro modeling and a background theory that resembles a wide version of the theory of rational action are applied. Basic concepts need clarification. We review some empirical evidence that shows no falsification, but hardly provides severe tests of framing propositions. How the framing perspective can be synthesized with the other perspectives is discussed in chapter 11. In the next chapter we will apply the theory of cognitive balance to derive some new propositions about framing.

1. Frame alignment processes: D. Snow, B. Rochford, St. Burke, and R. Benford's contribution

The basic article which laid the foundation of the framing perspective is the work of David Snow and his associates (Snow *et al.* 1986).[1] The authors address the "support for and participation in social movement organizations (SMOs) and their activities and campaigns" (464).[2] In other words, the dependent variable is individual protest behavior. It is thus not the emergence of SMOs that is to be explained. In order to provide valid explanations of protest behavior, the authors argue, it is useful to look at social psychological as well structural and organizational factors. The authors' aim is to contribute to linking these two types of factors, i.e. micro factors ("social psychological" factors) and macro factors ("structural and organizational" factors). In doing so they elaborate "frame alignment processes" (464). These are processes by which SMOs link or align their "interpretive orientations" (464) to those of non-mobilized individuals. As examples for such interpretive orientations the authors mention "some set of individual interests, values and beliefs and SMO activities, goals, and ideology" (464). Thus, frame alignment processes refer to processes that lead to more congruence or homogeneity of the frames of SMOs and non-mobilized persons. In this section, we will first look at the authors' definition of "frames." We then describe their classification of frame alignment processes and finally present their hypotheses.

The framing concept

The authors' concept of frame is based on Erving Goffman's book *Frame Analysis* (1974). The following quotation is from this book. The authors define frames as

> "schemata of interpretation" that enable individuals "to locate, perceive, identify and label" occurrences within their life space and the world at large. By rendering events or occurrences meaningful, frames function to organize experience and guide action, whether individual or collective. (464)

In order to understand the theoretical argument of the authors it is necessary to clarify this definition. First of all, what does "interpretation" mean? According to Goffman (1974), frames refer to the "organization of experience" (11) or to a "belief system" (27). Contemporary social psychologists would also speak of a mental model, a cognitive structure or a cognitive framework. We will use these terms interchangeably. These expressions refer to everything that an individual has stored in his or her memory. This "everything" can be broken down into single cognitive elements (or, equivalently, cognitions) or sets of cognitive elements. Thus, a "frame" is a *mental model which consists of cognitive elements*.

What are the cognitive elements of a mental model or frame? The authors mention the following elements. A mental model first comprises *concepts* such as "traffic light" or "restaurant." These expressions refer to real phenomena. For example, a person having stored the concept "traffic light" in his or her memory has also stored the referents of the concepts, that is, the person may point to (i.e. identify) phenomena in the real world that are "traffic lights." Furthermore, mental models consist of *cognitive beliefs* such as the hypothesis that reducing man-hours of workers leads to a decrease in the unemployment rate. A belief about one's personal influence is a cognitive belief as well. A frame also includes *norms, values, attitudes*, and *goals*. These are *non-cognitive beliefs*. Thus, one may have stored the (normative) belief that one must not kill or that the Grand Canyon is a great destination (a positive attitude toward an attitude object). *Discontents, normative justifications* (e.g. violence against a target is justified if the target has used violence in the past) and *attributions of causality* (certain measures of the government lead to lower unemployment) are among the cognitive elements of a mental model as well.

It is important to note that *some of these cognitive elements are incentives, i.e. costs and benefits to participate*. For example, the micro model of the theory of collective action discussed in chapters 3 and 4 includes discontent, perceived influence, and norms. These are also cognitive elements of frames. This partial equivalence of incentives and cognitive elements of frames is the key to integrate the framing approach with the other theoretical perspectives, as will be shown in detail in chapter 11. To illustrate, if incentives are a subset of the cognitive elements of frames, then the framing approach can be linked to the micro model of political action developed in previous chapters.

It is further important to note that not the real external constraints or behavioral opportunities such as actual repression of security forces are cognitive elements, but their mental representation. This implies that the mental representation may be at odds with reality.

What does it mean when Goffman writes that a framework "allows its user to locate, perceive, identify and label a seemingly infinite number of concrete occurrences defined in its [the framework's – KDO] term" (Goffman 1974: 21)?[3] Let us look at an example. Assume a person wants to cross a street and sees a traffic light at the other side of the street. An element of the person's mental model is the category or concept "traffic light." This element allows him to *locate* the traffic light in the sense that the person has stored beliefs about the type of locations where traffic lights are found. If expressions like "traffic light" are available in memory, they direct attention to the respective real phenomena – the referents of the concept. In other words, the person *perceives* a traffic light. The person is further able to *identify* something in reality as a "traffic light." If somebody points to an object that is a traffic light and asks somebody else "What is this?" the person will *label* it "traffic light."

Subsets of a person's cognitive elements are often denoted by names. For example, Snow *et al.* mention *injustice frames* and characterize them in the following way. Individuals do no longer see certain features of their lives as misfortune and as immutable but as (1) unjust, (2) mutable, and (3) individuals regard noncompliance to rules as legitimized. When the authors write that certain features of reality are "interpreted" as unjust, etc. this means that certain cognitive elements of a person's frames (i.e. a person's mental models) are activated and applied: individuals perceive certain features of reality, and they have beliefs about what is just and unjust, what is mutable or immutable and when it is legitimate to break rules. The perception of reality thus activates certain cognitive elements that are related to reality.

Let us illustrate with an example how persons arrive at the view that a specific event in reality is "unjust," etc. Assume an individual has stored the following cognitive elements – call this an "injustice frame":

1   A government must not take measures that exacerbate the living conditions of citizens.
2   Such measures are unjust.
3   If a government takes unjust measures then citizens are allowed to engage in illegal action directed against the government.

These cognitive elements direct the attention of citizens to certain aspects of reality. For example, if a government takes certain measures, a citizen will collect information about the consequences for the citizens. Assume that citizens read in a newspaper:

4   Government G has taken measures to build a highway.
5   These measures aggravate the living conditions of the citizens.

The citizens now compare this empirical information with their mental models. The cognitive elements (4) and (5) are compared with the mental model consisting, among other things, of elements (1) to (3). Accordingly, the citizen classifies the situation as "unjust" (cognitive element (2)) and infers element (3). One could say that in this process certain aspects of reality are perceived and aligned with the existing cognitive elements stored in memory. This may lead to an "activation" (or "inference") of norms or readiness to act. Snow *et al.* would probably say: the situation is "interpreted" as unjust, mutable, and illegitimate action is regarded as justified.

The process described before consists of the following steps:

a   there are the frames (mental models) of individuals, i.e. the mental models that individuals have stored in their memory;
b   there is observation of reality that results in new cognitive elements (e.g. the perception of certain government measures);
c   there is a match (or alignment) of the cognitive elements of the pre-existing mental model and the new cognitive elements; and
d   there are inferences and, among other things, the activation of norms and action preparedness.

One may call step (c) an "interpretation" of reality, i.e. establishing a link between cognitive elements of a given frame and new cognitive elements formed by observing reality. Perhaps "interpretation" could include step (c) as well. It is not clear what Snow *et al.* mean by "interpretation."

The authors also use the concept of *framing*. This concept refers to two different phenomena: (1) the process of communication in which actors articulate their frames,[4] and (2) a cognitive process such as applying, adopting or changing frames (see, for further references, Steinberg 1998: 845–846).

Types of frame alignment processes

"Frame alignment" means, as was mentioned before, "the linkage of individual and SMO interpretive orientations" (464). In other words, the mental models of SMOs on the one hand and unmobilized individuals are linked. The authors distinguish four types of frame alignment processes.[5]

(1) *Frame bridging.* This is "the linkage of two or more ideologically congruent but structurally unconnected frames regarding a particular issue or problem" (467); it is "the linkage of a SMO with what McCarthy (1986) has referred to as unmobilized sentiment pools or public opinion preference clusters" (467). There is thus no change of the frames of the unmobilized individuals, there is only an increasing awareness of the unmobilized persons that their frames and those of SMOs coincide. It is important to note that the bridging is "effected primarily" by activities of SMOs, interpersonal networks or mass media (468). "Primarily" implies that not only activities of SMOs, etc. "effect" bridging.

Frame bridging is, according to the authors, the most typical kind of frame alignment. The authors provide many examples, based on detailed case studies, indicating that frame bridging often occurs. They use this material for illustrating the other forms of frame alignment as well. We will not describe this rich material in detail but refer to it only occasionally. We will focus instead on the kinds of frame alignment processes the authors outline.

(2) *Frame amplification.* This type of frame alignment is given if there is some "... clarification and invigoration of an interpretive frame that bears on a particular issue, problem or set of events" (469). This type of frame alignment is further broken down into two types. One is "value amplification" (469). This is given if SMOs refer to values that seem to be important to prospective supporters but that have not yet been important for collective action. The second type of frame amplification is "belief amplification." Examples are beliefs such as "capitalists are exploiters" or "black is beautiful" (469). Whereas values refer to the goals of movements, beliefs are cognitive elements that "support or impede action in pursuit of desired values" (470).

The authors further distinguish between five kinds of beliefs referring to the seriousness of the problem, to the attribution of causality or blame, to "stereotypic" properties of antagonists, to the efficacy or probability of change of collective action, and to the necessity of "standing up." As an illustration the authors describe protest against the relocation of a Salvation Army shelter. Beliefs that the shelter "destroys the neighborhood," that the homeless are criminal or alcoholic or mentally deranged are examples for the beliefs that the activists wanted to transmit.

As noted before, some of these cognitive elements are incentives of the micro model laid out before (chapters 3 and 4): examples are discontent, efficacy, and protest norms.

(3) *Frame extension*. It happens that the goals of SMOs "may not be rooted in existing sentiment or adherent pools, or may appear to have little if any bearing on the life situations and interests of potential adherents" (472). In order to connect the different frames of the SMO and the unmobilized persons a SMO will have to show that its frame is congruent with the life situation and with the interests of the non-mobilized individuals. In doing so SMOs "elaborate goals and activities so as to encompass auxiliary interests not obviously associated with the movement" (472). The examples of the Nichiren Shoshu and Hare Krishna movements illustrate this alignment process. These movements first tried to find out what the interests of the prospective members were and then told them that these interests could be realized by the movement. The authors cite from an interview with somebody who was recruited: the member of the movement told the person that there were many pretty girls at the meeting. This motivated the person to go to the meeting. But the motivation to join was the "happiness and friendliness of the members and the fact that I kind of liked the chanting." This is a classic example of a group that tries to find *selective incentives* to recruit members. However, the authors note, those recruited by using selective incentives later adopted the basic goals of the movements.

(4) *Frame transformation*. It happens that "programs, causes, and values that some SMOs promote ... may not resonate with, and on occasion may even appear antithetical to, conventional lifestyles or rituals and extant interpretive frames" (473). In this case only a frame transformation of the non-mobilized individuals can lead to a frame alignment. Furthermore, the authors introduce another classification. They distinguish between the transformation of domain-specific and global interpretive frames (474–475). The difference is that the scope of the changes required is larger in the latter case.

The theory

Two questions have not yet been answered. (1) Which effect does a successful frame alignment have on collective political action? Assume a movement succeeds in aligning its frames to those of non-mobilized prospective members. Is this sufficient to become involved in political action? (2) When are social movements successful in linking their frames to the frames of unmobilized individuals? Both questions will be addressed in this section.

Does frame alignment lead to political action?

The authors are very clear in this respect: "... frame alignment is a necessary condition for movement participation, whatever its nature or intensity" (464; see also 467, 471, 476). Applying formal logic, a condition C is necessary for something to be explained (E – for "explanandum") if the following condition is met: if E is present, C exists as well; but if C is given, E may, but need not occur. Thus:

> *Frame-alignment proposition:* If individuals participate in movement activities, frame alignment has always taken place (i.e. frame alignment is a necessary condition for social movement activity to occur).

The implication is: if frame alignment has been taken place this is not sufficient for protest participation. Thus, when we find that sometimes frame alignment occurs but not protest the authors' proposition is not falsified, because frame alignment is not sufficient for participating protest action. This is consistent with the authors' statement that "participation in SMO activities is contingent *in part* on alignment of individual and SMO interpretive frames" (476, italics not in the original). The authors thus do not answer the question of what the sufficient conditions for protest participation are. We will return to this question later on.

When does social movement activity generate frame alignment?

The authors propose two hypotheses. The first can be put in the following way – it may be called the frame-resonance proposition:

> *Frame-resonance proposition:* "the higher the degree of frame resonance, the greater the probability that the framing effort will be relatively successful, all else being equal." (477)

"Success" means that the transmission of the frame is achieved. "Resonance" is high if the movement frame suggests "answers and solutions to troublesome situations and dilemmas that resonate with the way in which they are experienced" and if these answers are "believable and compelling" (477).

The second proposition refers to framing "hazards" or "vulnerabilities" (477) that may accompany each frame alignment process. The authors may have in mind the following proposition:

> *Frame-vulnerability proposition:* the more frame alignment attempts by SMOs are fraught with hazards and vulnerabilities, the less likely framing efforts will be successful.

The authors do not define in a general way what they mean by "hazards" or "vulnerabilities." Instead, they illustrate these concepts for each frame alignment process with examples. If *frame bridging* is used by competing SMOs it often happens that individuals are "inundated by a barrage of similar impersonal appeals" (477). This has the effect that frame bridging is likely to be unsuccessful. A "vulnerability" in *frame amplification* obtains "when a movement fails to consistently protect or uphold those core values or beliefs being highlighted" (477). It may also happen that a value becomes "discredited" and thus "may drag associated frames along with it" (477). This will be the case, one might suspect, if the "discredited" value is very important in the mental model, i.e. if it is firmly linked to the other cognitive elements. Movements choosing *frame extension* may fail to deliver the promised benefits. The previous example of the "pretty girls" may illustrate this: if there are no pretty girls and no other benefits such as friendly people there is a "hazard" or "vulnerability." Such failures may undermine the credibility of a SMO. This further holds when a frame is extended by including goals and issues that are only loosely connected to the original goals and issues. The authors mention as an example when proponents of nuclear freeze link their goals with a defense of social welfare programs (478). Again, these "hazards" jeopardize the success of frame extension. A risk of *frame transformation* is, for example, that there is sometimes a great enthusiasm that refers to elements that are external to the frame of a movement. This may undermine the integrity of a movement (478) and, thus lets frame transformations fail.

The basic framing model

Let us summarize the theoretical propositions discussed so far in a causal diagram. The factor that initiates a process of mobilization and collective action is the attempt of SMOs to link their frames to the frames of unmobilized third parties. These efforts are a causal factor that influences frame alignment. The other factor that makes frame alignment more likely is high frame resonance. If, however, hazards and vulnerabilities are high, frame alignment becomes less likely. The more the frames of SMOs and unmobilized individuals are aligned, the more likely is mobilization and/or collective action of the unmobilized individuals.

2. Conceptual problems

In reading the previous presentation of the framing approach by Snow *et al.* the reader might have noticed that some of the concepts are difficult to understand or, more precisely, in need of clarification. In this section we will look at some of the ambiguities. We will first briefly comment on the frame concept. We then turn to the concepts "hazards" and "vulnerabilities," to the demarcation of types of frames and to the classification of frame alignment processes.

The meaning of "frame"

There can be no question that the initial definition based on Goffman's work is far from clear, as the previous discussion shows. But when we apply hypotheses and findings of social psychology and define a frame as a mental model or a cognitive structure, i.e. everything that a person has stored in his or her mind, it is relatively

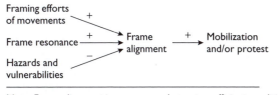

Note: Frame alignment is a necessary, but not a sufficient condition for mobilization and/or protest (see text).

Figure 8.1 The basic framing model

clear what a "frame" is. Snow *et al.* further list the elements frames may comprise. Important for the field of social movements are goals, norms, beliefs such as perceived influence or expected sanctions, attribution of causality for a grievance and normative justifications.

It may be difficult to ascertain empirically what the cognitive elements of a frame of specific individuals are. For example, assume that a researcher is interested in the cognitive elements that are linked to the discontent of a person with a decision of a government to restrict immigration. To what extent does an individual regard this decision as "unjust"? Which norms does the decision violate? To what extent does an individual believe that he or she can change this decision by participating in protest behavior? Problems in measuring the elements of a frame may be that individuals have not yet thought about these matters or that they may give social desirable answers in interviews. But these are matters of empirical research and not of the vagueness of the framing concept.

"Frame" is a very broad concept like "reinforcement" in learning theory, "benefits" in rational choice theory or "behavioral consequence" in value expectancy theory. Such concepts encompass a wide variety of phenomena, but they are nonetheless clear. As we saw in chapter 1, it is a common misunderstanding that broad concepts are vague. The concept of "man" is very broad, but clear, whereas the concept of "hero" is narrow but vague. However, there may be one important difference between "frame" on the one hand and "reinforcement," for example, on the other: the latter is part of a well confirmed and informative theory. Is that also the case with "frame"? We will return to this question later.

Frame analysts, it is argued, "tend to depict frames as relatively stable meaning systems, akin to modular texts or maps, which can endure for long periods of time" (Steinberg 1999: 741). All variables of a theory can be more or less stable. It is a matter of empirical research to determine (and explain) the stability of frames. We do not yet know how long a given frame remains stable. But it is plausible that the stability of a frame is so high that it can be measured. This suffices to make predictions or test propositions with the frame concept.

Frames of individuals and frames of social movements: the aggregation problem

Frames are features of individual actors. "Social movements do not frame issues; their activists or other participants do the framing" (Benford 1997: 418). Although the definition of Snow *et al.* (1986: 465) also clearly refers to individuals, as we have seen before, their aim is to elaborate "frame alignment processes," referring "to the linkage of individual and SMO interpretive frames" (464). Thus, the authors address *individual* (the frames of unmobilized individuals) and *collective frames* (the frames of social movements). This is also typical for the social movement literature: social movements and not (only) individuals are the subject of the analysis.

The question then is: how can collective frames (i.e. frames of a social movement or, in general, of a group) be defined? If this question is not answered a theory of frame alignment that addresses collective frames cannot be applied because it is not clear how a movement frame can be ascertained. This question is not addressed in the article by Snow *et al.*, and I have not found any other discussion of this issue either.

Collective frames can be defined in different ways. (1) If "frames" are properties of individual actors, a collective frame of a group is a function of the individual frames. What could that function be? The theory of collective action (chapter 3) suggests one possible answer. The theory applies to individuals with common goals. Accordingly, the frame of a social movement could be defined as the *shared frames of the members* of the movement.

(2) Whereas the theory of collective action focuses on the question when individuals with common goals act collectively to realize their goals, the social movement literature is concerned with groups where homogeneous frames of all members need not exist. It is probably normal that SMOs consists of various fractions with different frames. For example, in the anti-nuclear movement there are fractions that wish to shut down all nuclear power plants immediately, whereas others demand closure within a certain period of time. Further, some fractions approve of violence, while others advocate legal action only. What is "the" frame of a movement if it consists of subgroups whose frames differ? If the question is when SMOs are successful in transmitting their frames the question is what frames are *externalized*, i.e. are presented to unnmobilized individuals. It is plausible that movement activists often present those frames that movement groups or their majority agree upon when they try to mobilize individuals. Then "the" frame of a movement is the externalized frame, i.e. the frame that is articulated by movement activists.

If different groups of a movement externalize different frames, the question then is to what extent these different frames are transmitted. It may happen that different groups of activists succeed in transmitting different frames to different groups of unmobilized individuals, or that some groups are more successful in transmitting "their" frames. An implication is that a movement may have different frames, which are the frames of different subgroups.

Frames can be defined in this way also when SMOs are organizations like firms. There is a hierarchical structure and collective decisions are made. Their outcomes are the frames, i.e. goals, strategies, norms, and beliefs, etc. Movements are thus treated as unitary collective actors. Similarly, economists deal with firms which have preferences such as profit maximization and are subjected to the constraints of the market and to state regulations. Again, in this situations "the" frame is the frame that is presented by the leaders of the firm or the SMO to the public.

It would be an interesting task to examine how the spate of work about framing of SMOs solves the aggregation problem, i.e. how the researchers argue when they refer to collective frames. The general procedure is simply to claim that movements have certain frames without addressing the aggregation issue explicitly. In empirical studies – see the research discussed below – data about movements or groups are used. Here the aggregation problem is solved, but how it has been solved remains in the dark.

What is meant by "resonance" and "hazards" of frames?

It is claimed that a strong *resonance* of the frames of a SMO on the one hand and unmobilized individuals on the other will make frame alignment attempts successful (see 477 and above). But when are frames more or less "resonant"? The authors' definition reads, as we saw before: resonance is high if the movement frame suggests "answers and solutions to troublesome situations and dilemmas that resonate with the way in which they are experienced" and if these answers are "believable and compelling" (477). This definition is problematic for two reasons. First, it is a common requirement for proper definitions that the term to be defined must not occur in the definition. In this case, "resonance" is given, by definition, if frames "resonate" – which is not very informative, to say the least, if one wants to know what "resonance" means. Second, it is not clear how it can be determined whether certain arguments ("answers and solutions" to problems) are "believable and compelling." This can only mean that the unmobilized individuals accept the frame of the movement. That is to say, frames are aligned. But then "resonance" can no longer *explain* alignment because it *means* alignment!

What could a measure of resonance of frames of a SMO and unmobilized individuals look like? Frames consists of cognitive elements such as goals, values, norms or cognitive beliefs. This means that each single cognitive element may be more or less resonant. The *total* resonance of a given frame is then a function of the resonances of the cognitive elements. The difficulties of determining the overall resonance of a frame is illustrated by an example depicted in Figure 8.2.

The first problem in determining frame resonance is to specify the elements of a frame. That is to say, it must be clear what exactly the elements of the respective frames are. Only then is it possible to look at the relationships between the frame

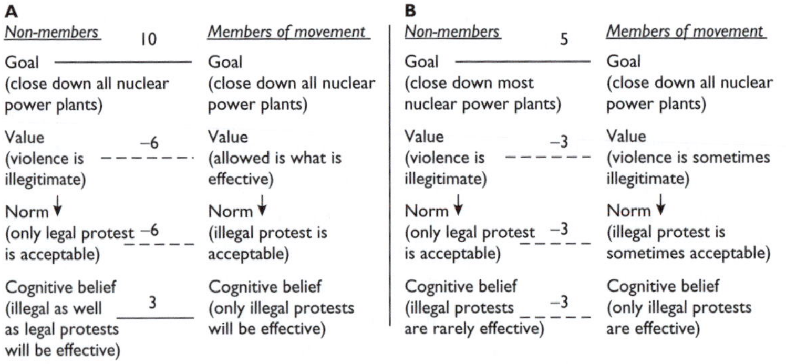

A

Non-members	10	Members of movement
Goal ————————		Goal
(close down all nuclear power plants)		(close down all nuclear power plants)
Value	−6	Value
(violence is illegitimate)	− − − − − −	(allowed is what is effective)
Norm ↓		Norm ↓
(only legal protest is acceptable)	−6	(illegal protest is acceptable)
Cognitive belief	3	Cognitive belief
(illegal as well as legal protests will be effective)		(only illegal protests will be effective)

B

Non-members	5	Members of movement
Goal ————————		Goal
(close down most nuclear power plants)		(close down all nuclear power plants)
Value	−3	Value
(violence is illegitimate)	− − − − −	(violence is sometimes illegitimate)
Norm ↓		Norm ↓
(only legal protest is acceptable)	−3	(illegal protest is sometimes acceptable)
Cognitive belief	−3	Cognitive belief
(illegal protests are rarely effective)		(only illegal protests are effective)

Legend: *Solid line*: agreement or indifference; *broken line*: disagreement; *numbers*: degree of agreement (1 to 10) or disagreement (−10 to −1); 0 is indifference; *arrow*: justification.

Questions: (1) How resonant are the two frames in the left panel, and how resonant are the two frames in the right panel? (2) Are the two frames in the left panel more resonant than, less resonant than or as resonant as the frames in the right panel?

Figure 8.2 Measuring the "resonance" of frames

elements. Let us assume that the cognitive elements of a given frame are known – see the figure.

How could "resonance" be measured? The underlying idea of the authors' definition seems to be that resonance is high if the similarity of the frames is high. The frame-resonance proposition would then assert that high similarity of frames will make frame alignment likely. This is at least a plausible hypothesis, and we will therefore assume that resonance can be interpreted as similarity. If the authors do not agree the question arises as to what their definition is and how it can be transformed into a measurement procedure.

In panel A it is assumed that there is a group of non-members (i.e. unmobilized individuals) and a group of members of a social movement (i.e. the activists). The cognitive elements of the frame of each group are listed in the two columns. These elements are goals, certain values, a norm, and a cognitive belief – see the figure. The degree of similarity or, equivalently, "resonance" of the elements of the two different frames is symbolized by lines. A solid line means agreement or indifference, and a broken line means disagreement. The value range is from maximal similarity $(+10)$ to indifference (0) to maximal dissimilarity (-10). Panel A in the figure shows that the unmobilized individuals and the SMO fully agree on the goals, namely to close down all nuclear power plants. Thus, similarity of the cognitive elements gets the maximum value 10. But there is strong disagreement on the norm to engage in legal or illegal protest (-6). This norm is justified by a value (i.e. a general norm) referring to violence in general.[6] There is further some agreement in regard to the perceived efficacy of legal and illegal protest (3), but the agreement is relatively low when we compare it with the maximum value 10. Panel B shows another scenario in which in general disagreement is not very high (there are three values with -3), but agreement is not high either (there is one value of $+5$).

How could the resonance of the whole frame in panel A be determined? Let us look at two possibilities. (1) If agreement is perfect each line would have value 10. Thus, the higher the sum of the single resonances the higher is the total resonance. This sum could be divided by the maximum possible resonance of the entire frame. Degrees of resonance may thus range from 1 (highest resonance) to -1 (lowest resonance). The maximum sum of each of the panels A and B is 40. The actual sums are 1 in A and -4 in B. So resonance would be $1/40 = .025$ in panel A and 1 in panel B. Resonance is thus higher in panel A than in B.

(2) Another possibility is to add for each cognitive element the absolute value of the difference to the maximum values. The intuitive idea is that resonance is large if the distance between the actual value for a given cognitive element and the maximum value 10 is large. Assume the value for a given cognitive element is 3. The distance to the maximum value is $3-10 = -7$, so the absolute value is 7. If the actual value is -4 the distance is $-4-10 = -14$, the absolute value is thus 14. The sum of the absolute values for a given frame like panel A captures the distances. A high value means low resonance. The respective sum in panel A is: $(10-10) + (-6-10) + (-6-10) + (3-10) = 0 + 16 + 16 + 16 + 7 = 55$; for panel B the respective sum is: $(5-10) + (-3-10) + (-3-10) + (-3-10) = 5 + 13 + 13 + 13 = 44$. Thus, the "distances" of the cognitive elements to the maximum value 10 are larger in graph A than in B.

Resonance is thus smaller in graph A than in graph B. This is the opposite of the previous measure 1.

It is certainly possible to suggest other measures. The selection criterion for a definition in this context is whether it is theoretically fruitful. In other words, is the frame resonance proposition plausible if we use the first or the second definition? Or are other definitions theoretically more fruitful?

The example illustrates how important it is to specify the cognitive elements of a frame. This is typically not done in existing research: frames are assigned labels (such as "injustice frame"), but it is far from clear what the elements of the frames are. We will return to this point in the next section.

The authors further use the term *hazards* or vulnerabilities of frame alignment processes. It seems that this concept refers to factors that impede or compromise the alignment of frames. To clarify what "hazards" are is thus not a simple definitional issue but a theoretical question. In other words, the task is to propose hypotheses that make alignment processes more or less successful. As our presentation of the theory shows the authors do not provide general propositions but just examples.

The demarcation of types of frames

The literature abounds with classifications of frames. Noonan (1995), for example, explores the development of a maternal frame, a feminist frame and a "working-class radicalism" frame. She further speaks of a "master frame" – a term that is also frequently used in the literature. Benford (1997: 414–415) briefly discusses "a rather long laundry list of types of frames." Another list of frames referring to the proponents of women in juries is provided by McCammon *et al.* (2007: 728). These classifications are burdened with two problems.

One is that it is rarely spelled out in detail what exactly the cognitive elements of the respective frame are and how they are related.[7] For example, sometimes elements are "inferred" from other elements, sometimes elements justify other elements. To be sure, the name of the frame refers to at least one element. For example, an "injustice" frame has something to do with an actor's feeling that something is unjust. But what exactly is the structure of the frame? What are the actors' goals? What are the norms the actor applies that lead to labeling some decisions or events as unjust? What exactly are the beliefs involved in the frame? An application of a norm to a specific event – such as "the decision to construct a highway in area A is unjust" – implies certain beliefs about the consequences of the decision or about the motives of the decision maker. Authors who address an "injustice frame" or a "maternal frame" (Noonan 1995) never specify in detail the cognitive elements and their relations the respective frames consist of. In regard to "master frames" it is only clear that the respective frames are in some sense more general than other frames. But what the relationships between the elements of this general frame to the more specific frames are remains in the dark.

Beside the vagueness of the various classifications, a second problem is their theoretical utility. Benford does not "call into question the analytical utility [of the frames] for the specific study to which it was applied" (1997: 415). "Analytical utility" can have three different meanings. (1) One is that the frame points to descriptively interesting phenomena. For example, a researcher might wish to describe how a "maternal frame" changed over time. (2) "Analytical utility" may further mean that it is interesting to explain a frame (or a change of a frame). However, there is so far no theory that can explain the origin of frames, as the previous discussion has shown already. (3) A third meaning of "analytical utility" could be that a frame is an interesting independent variable. The question could be, for example, what kind of frame leads to which kind of political action. Perhaps Benford has this type of "analytical utility" in mind. A theory that posits that frames of type A lead to political action of type B requires that in a specific situation where political action of type B is to be explained, frames must be empirically ascertained. The frames would be initial conditions in the explanation. However, all the classifications of frames are not components of a theory that allow us to predict the kind of political action that the frame brings about. Thus, the "analytic utility" in the sense of theoretical import of the existing classifications of frames has so far not been shown.

The classification of frame alignment processes: their clarity and analytical fruitfulness

The authors distinguish four types of frame alignment processes, as we saw before. One problem is that it is not clear what exactly the differences between these processes are. For example, when does frame bridging end and when does frame amplification begin? Actually, there is an underlying continuum. At one end, there is a situation where a frame of a movement and an unmobilized individual are identical; at the other end, there is a situation where no element of the frame of the movement and the individual is equal and where a frame transformation of the unmobilized individuals takes place. It is always difficult to impose a classification on an underlying quantitative variable because the choice of the cutting points is largely arbitrary. This is particularly difficult if the underlying quantitative variable is not clear, as is the case for the alignment processes.

But even if a classification is possible the question is why it is needed. Why not use the quantitative variable? It is not clear at all why the classification is needed: it is not part of a theory. Why did the authors not first propose a theory and then decide whether a classification is needed? The literature is full of classifications that never became part of a fruitful theory and finally were forgotten. The authors might argue that their classification is a first step to a theory. In general, successful theories in the social sciences did not begin with vague classifications. Anyway, so far the authors have not shown that their classification is theoretically fruitful: it is neither an independent nor a dependent variable of a theory.

3. The structure of the theory: the implicit micro-macro model

The framing perspective consists of a multi-level theoretical system. This becomes clear already at the beginning of the authors' article when they argue that there is

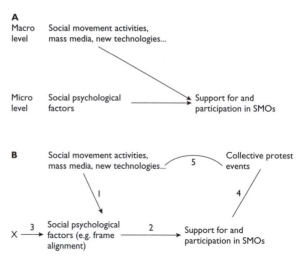

Figure 8.3 Kinds of micro-macro models in Snow *et al.* (1986)

growing recognition that a thoroughgoing understanding of support for and partic-ipation in SMOs "requires consideration of both social psychological and struc-tural/organizational factors" (464). The social psychological factors are, among others things, frame alignment processes which are affected "primarily by organi-zational outreach and information diffusion through interpersonal or intergroup networks, mass media, the telephone and direct mail" (468). The first variable men-tioned is "support for and participation in SMOs" which is the dependent variable on the micro level. The first quotation suggests that "structural/organizational fac-tors," i.e. variables on the macro level, as well as social psychological factors, i.e. variables on the micro level, affect individual protest behavior. Graph A of Figure 8.3 depicts this model.

In the second quotation, it is spelled out in more detail what these macro factors are. Furthermore, frame alignment processes are introduced as the independent micro variable. This variable is affected by the macro factors, especially by social movements' efforts to effect frame alignment (see arrow 1 in graph B of Figure 8.3). "Frames" of the unmobilized as well as mobilized individuals are among the micro factors that trigger support for and participation in SMOs (arrow 2).

Not only macro factors affect frame bridging. The authors mention that frame bridging may also occur between movements (467). This means that mobilized individuals interact. This is captured in the figure by arrow 3: we denote the inde-pendent variable as "X" because the authors only provide an orienting statement. We further assume that not only individual protest activities but protest events such as demonstrations are to be explained. These are macro events, and they are a func-tion of individual protest behaviors. This aggregation is analytical which is sym-bolized by a line (arrow 4). For example, if the theoretical argument predicts that many individuals will convene at a certain location at a certain time carrying posters with political messages then this means that there will be a "demonstration."

The final part of graph B is the relationship between the macro events (see line 5). Assume we find that the developments of new technologies as well as certain strategies of SMOs are related to an increase of collective events such as rallies or demonstrations. In other words, there is a positive relationship between, for example, activities of SMOs and protest events. This relationship is usually formulated as a causal effect, i.e. the assumption is that social movement activities *bring about* protest events. If our reconstruction of the theoretical argument of the authors in graph B is correct, the relationship between the macro variables should not be a direct but an indirect causal effect, i.e. the relationship should be correlational: social movements activities lead to changes of individual factors which bring about collective protest. This is in line with the micro-macro models discussed in previous chapters.

How can the model summarized in Figure 8.1 be integrated into the model of Figure 8.3B? The model in Figure 8.1 claims that framing efforts of SMOs, frame resonance, and hazards and vulnerabilities affect frame alignment. The first variable is included in the macro variable "Social movement activities ..." in Figure 8.3B. This is plausible for the other two variables as well: "resonance of frames" are a property of frames of SMOs, and "hazards and vulnerabilities" are processes at the macro level.

The important point in this section is that the framing perspective – along with all the other perspectives discussed so far – includes actually a micro-macro model. It is further worth noting that this model is not spelled out in detail.

4. Why do people change and use frames? The implicit background theory

Assume an unmobilized person P is approached by a member of a SMO. At the beginning of the conversation it turns out that P shares the movement's goals, but is skeptical about the movement's belief that illegal protest is efficacious. Furthermore, P does not agree at all with the movement's normative claim that illegal protest is a legitimate strategy. Assume the frames of the SMO and of P are the same as in panel A of Figure 8.2. After a long conversation, P changes his or her mind: he or she accepts the normative claim that violence in this particular case is acceptable and efficacious. Why does a person alter cognitive elements of a frame when he or she interacts with an activist of a SMO (or with somebody else)? Cognitive dissonance theory and balance theory (see chapter 1.1 and the next chapter) provide an answer to this question. Assume that P finds O (the SMO member) very likeable and learns in the conversation that O accepts a cognitive belief B that P does not accept. This situation where I realize that my friend O has an opinion (B) that I reject is a dissonant or an unbalanced situation. This means that this situation causes psychic strain. One possibility for P to reduce this strain is to change his or her opinion in regard to B, i.e. to accept the belief of O. The general theoretical idea that underlies these theories is that individuals try to avoid unpleasant (or costly) situations and have an incentive to change the situation. Psychic strain is such a cost that individuals want to avoid.

Many adherents of the framing perspective strongly reject this idea which is the basic idea of rational choice theory. Not so the authors. They do not principally reject the perspective, they explicitly state that they "do not quibble" (470) with value-expectancy theory which is a version of rational choice theory. The authors even mention the possibility that "costs or risks of participation" (467) may be involved in shifts of interpretive frames. But the authors criticize that "little attention is given to the actual process by which certain lines of action come to be defined as more or less risky, morally imperative in spite of associated risks, or instrumentally pointless" (466; see also 470–471). This may be correct, but the question that is not addressed is to what extent value-expectancy theory *could* give more attention to these processes.

Although it is plausible that changes in frames can be explained by applying a general theory, such as the theory of cognitive dissonance, and although the authors grant this possibility they do not apply such a theory explicitly. We don't learn the reason or reasons for this neglect, although there are convincing general arguments in favor of applying general theory (see chapter 1, section 3). In regard to framing, the application of general theoretical hypotheses might yield predictions about changes of specific cognitive elements under various conditions, as we will see below (see chapter 9).

Many authors in the framing literature plead for applying social psychology. But they don't look at well confirmed social psychological theories such as value-expectancy theory, the theory of cognitive dissonance, balance theory or the attitude theory of M. Fishbein and I. Ajzen. This latter theory explains, among other things, attitudes. This is one factor that is changed during frame alignment processes. So this theory could be applied. Again, the authors don't let us know why this well-known and in social psychology prominent theory is ignored and why other theories are not utilized either.

Assume there exist frames in the sense of widely accepted general arguments from the cultural context. An example is the norm that men and women should be treated as equals. In pursuing their cause groups decide which frame they use in their struggle to persuade opponents. The frames they select for this purpose are called "strategic frames" (Benford and Snow 2000: 624). Apparently, activists calculate which frames may be best suited to achieve their goals. For example, in the struggle of women in the first half of the twentieth century to convince lawmakers to give women an opportunity to sit on juries the activists consciously selected those frames that they thought would help them to be represented in juries (McCammon *et al.* 2007). This is a clear rational choice argument. When reading the description of the processes that lead to using frames one often thinks the respective paper is from the public choice literature. Thus, in explaining the use or application of frames or, put simpler, the provision of certain arguments, it is obvious that a rational choice perspective helps and is actually employed. Implicitly, this perspective is also applied when changes of frames are explained.

Babb (1996) addresses the question of what happens when a widely accepted ideology contradicts empirical reality. In her conclusion she refers to the theory of cognitive dissonance (Festinger 1957) and to the study by Festinger, Riecken, and

Schachter (1956) about the effects of a failed prophecy and explores some of the implication of the study and the theory for the question at issue. The theory claims that changes in cognitions depend on the amount of cognitive dissonance, which is an unpleasant psychic state, i.e. a cognitive cost. Thus, changes in "frames" have something to do with costs and benefits. The short discussion by Babb (1996: 1050) shows that cognitive dissonance theory can be applied to social movements phenomena and in particular to explain frame changes. Chapter 9 of this book will explore the application of balance theory which is similar to the theory of cognitive dissonance to explain identity and framing processes.

Many other authors emphasize that the creation and use of frames are decisions, often by political entrepreneurs, where several options exist. There is thus a "strategic" or "rational quality of social movement framing activities" (Noakes and Johnston 2005: 24 and 2). This does not imply that one person can control the creation or spread of frames. Instead, the decisions of many actors and their interactions are involved (Noakes and Johnston 2005: 24). To mention another example: McVeigh, Myers, and Sikkink (2004: 655) describing the process of framing of movements emphasize that "movement leaders and members continuously revise and modify frames, attempting to find new ways to connect with potential supporters and to reach new audiences. As a movement attempts to extend its influence across many communities, intimate knowledge of the values and concerns held by potential supporters in those communities can be extraordinarily valuable. Local concerns can be incorporated into the movement's framing, providing additional incentives for individuals to join the organization." A clearer description of decision processes that are involved in frame adoption and that show that costs and benefits play a major role in these decisions is hardly possible. But the question remains as to what exactly the costs and benefits for adopting or changing frames are. This can only be ascertained if the underlying version of rational choice theory is applied explicitly and systematically.[8]

5. Is frame alignment a necessary condition for social movement participation?

The authors hypothesize, as was said before, that frame alignment is a necessary condition for protest participation. What this means can most clearly be explained with a so-called truth table in formal logic (see Table 8.1). The compound sentence "frame alignment is a necessary condition for protest" consists of two constituent sentences: "there is frame alignment" (abbreviated as FA) and "there is protest" (abbreviated as PR). Each of these sentences may be true (T) or false (F). There are thus four possibilities – see columns 2 and 3 of the truth table: either both sentences FA and PR are true (line 1) or false (line 4) or one of the sentences is true and the other false (lines 2 and 3). A "necessary condition" means that if there is protest (i.e. if PR is true) than there is always FA (i.e. FA is true) – see line 1 and column 4. In this case, thus, the compound sentence "FA is a necessary condition for PR" is true (see column 4). But if we find that there is protest (PR is true) and no frame alignment (FA) then the compound sentence is false (line 2, column 4).

Table 8.1 Frame alignment (FA) as a necessary or sufficient condition for protest participation (PR)

No. of line	Protest (PR)	Frame alignment (FA)	FA is a necessary condition for	FA is a sufficient condition for PR	FA is a sufficient and necessary condition for PR
			if PR, then FA	if FA, then PR	if FA, then PR and vice versa
1	2	3	4	5	6
1	T	T	T	T	T
2	T	F	F	T	F
3	F	T	T	F	F
4	F	F	T	T	T

T means *true* and *F* means *false*.

What about the other combinations of truth values in lines 3 and 4? Assume FA is true and PR false, i.e. we find that there is frame alignment but people do not protest (line 3). This is compatible with the assumption that FA is a necessary condition for PR because this does not exclude that if there is not PR there is nonetheless FA – "necessary condition" means that if there is protest there must be FA. Thus, if the constellation of truth values in line 3 holds, then the proposition that FA is a necessary condition for PR is true. The same holds for line 4, i.e. if there is neither FA nor PR. If FA is a necessary condition for PR then this does not preclude that there are cases where there is neither FA nor PR.

Two questions are of interest. (1) Assume it is true that FA always exists if there is PR (line 1), but that there maybe FA that is not associated with protest (line 3). Is this a satisfactory hypothesis in regard to its explanatory value? (2) Is the hypothesis correct that FA is a necessary condition for PR? This question will be discussed in section 9 when we look at empirical evidence for the framing perspective.

Let us first look at the explanatory value of the hypothesis that FA is a necessary condition for PR. Assume there is frame alignment (FA is true), but protest does not occur (PR is false) – see line 3. This does not render the proposition that FA is a necessary condition for PR false. Nonetheless, we are left with the question: if there is frame alignment why doesn't it lead to protest? In other words, we want to know under what conditions frame alignment brings about protest.

The hypothesis that FA is a necessary condition for PR is unsatisfactory for another reason. FA and PR are employed as dichotomous variables. However, protest is used as a quantitative variable in theory and research. If protest is quantitative and FA dichotomous: what does it mean that FA is a necessary condition for protest? Does it mean that if we find the slightest amount of protest that there will be FA? Further, as we saw before, FA is actually a quantitative variable as well: there are different degrees of frame alignment. If, thus, frame alignment as well as protest are quantitative: what is the relationship between the two variables, i.e. in what sense is FA a "necessary condition" for PR? Do the authors mean that for every amount of protest there should be some minimal amount of frame alignment? Assume frame alignment and protest can vary between 0 and 10. Perhaps the authors then mean:

If protest > 0, then there is frame alignment > 0.

Even if that is meant it is unsatisfactory that the proposition does not say anything about the effects of different degrees of frame alignment on different degrees of protest or to what extent we will expect what amount of frame alignment if there are different amounts of protest.

So far it was assumed that the authors are aware of the exact meaning of "necessary condition." Since sociologists are normally not familiar with formal logic this assumption may be false. This is suggested by the following quotation: "... participation in SMO [social movement organization – KDO] activities is contingent *in part* on alignment of individual and SMO interpretive frames" (476, emphasis not in the original). What exactly the other factors are is not clear. Leaving this aside, this statement may mean: if there is FA then there is PR, but protest may also be brought about by other factors. But then FA would be a sufficient condition for protest – see column 5. In other words, the hypothesis that the authors probably have in mind reads:

If there is frame alignment, there is protest.

This hypothesis is only false if there is frame alignment but no protest. FA is thus a sufficient condition for protest (see column 5 of the table). The problem of this proposition is, again, that FA and PR are actually quantitative variables, and it is a loss of information to dichotomize quantitative variables.

There is still another possible interpretation of the authors claim that FA is a necessary condition for PR. In his assessment of the framing perspective Benford (1997: 415) argues in regard to injustice frames: "Before collective action is likely to occur, a critical mass of people must socially construct a sense of injustice." In other words, this frame must be present before collective action obtains. This means that the frame is a cause of protest: it triggers protest and there is an injustice frame if protest occurs. This seems to mean that frame alignment is a *necessary and sufficient condition* – see column 6 of the table:

If there is frame alignment, then there is protest; if there is protest, then there is frame alignment (or, equivalently: if, and only if there is frame alignment, there is protest).

This proposition is false if there is PR and no FA or if there is no PR but FA (see column 6 of the table). Again, the problem is why quantitative variables are dichotomized.

If the latter interpretation of the authors is correct this suggests that an increase of FA leads to an increase of PR and vice versa. We may thus formulate a quantitative hypothesis – which may then be regarded as another interpretation of the authors:

> The more frames of SMOs and unmobilized individuals are aligned, the more likely the unmobilized individuals will engage in protest behavior.

This hypothesis asserts a positive linear relationship, where the x-axis symbolizes the amount of FA and the y-axis the amount of PR. The points in the scatter diagram are individuals with different degrees of protest and frame alignment. A problem of this hypothesis is that there is so far no measure of the degree of FA so that it is not testable for the time being.

To conclude, it is not clear whether the authors really mean that FA is a necessary condition in the strict sense. Other interpretations are plausible as well. All these interpretations are burdened with problems. The basic question is: Which of the different propositions is valid? We will defer this question until we discuss the empirical evidence for the framing perspective.

6. How is the free rider problem solved?

The authors do not explicitly address the free rider problem. The question that is to be answered reads why individuals are supposed to participate if their frames are aligned to those of social movements? For example, assume individuals acquire an injustice frame that exactly matches the frame of a movement. Is this sufficient for participation in movement action? The single individual is still a member of a large group. From the perspective of the theory of collective action, an injustice frame is very similar to the preference for a public good: in this case, the individual wants to combat injustice. Having an "injustice frame" means high discontent, the normative belief that certain government decisions are regarded as unjust and perhaps that certain targets are held responsible for the grievances. Why should an individual protest if just some cognitive elements change? We do not learn why the authors did not address this question.

It is rare that the free rider problem is mentioned in the framing literature, let alone discussed. An exception is Polletta (1998: 139) who argues: "Concepts like 'frame' and 'framing' have proved useful" in solving the free rider problem. She then reviews some ideas of the framing literature without showing how this literature can solve the free rider problem. Actually, Polletta mentions various incentives that are components of the micro model of chapters 3 and 4 such as injustice (i.e. public goods preferences), identity (a selective incentives – see the discussion in chapter 7), and sense of collective efficacy. These are not all the incentives that could instigate protest behavior. However, Polletta's argument can be interpreted in the following way: frames or framing involves or leads to collective goods and selective incentives. *If* this is correct, then the framing perspective can indeed solve the free rider problem. However, it remains to be shown that frames or framing alone is really linked to public goods or selective incentives that may bring about protest. Chapter 11 will show in detail that this is correct only under certain conditions.

7. Framing and the form of political action: an unanswered question

Assume frame alignment is successful: unmobilized individuals have adopted the frames of a movement, and this instigates political participation. What form of participation will individuals choose? Will they blindly follow the activities organized by the movement? When we apply the micro model discussed in chapters 3 and 4 incentives such as perceived personal influence and moral beliefs would be relevant. For example, an individual might choose those behaviors that he or she thinks are most efficacious, if they are morally acceptable. If the "efficacy frame" would be identical with the movement frame then indeed the individual would follow the movement's lead. But "frame alignment" may not be perfect so that individuals follow the movement's lead only to some extent. It is a weakness of the framing literature that there is no detailed discussion of the implications of the approach for the form of action that individuals choose.

8. When does frame alignment succeed?

A major question of the framing approach is under what conditions efforts of social movements change the frames of unmobilized individuals. The authors' hypotheses are that "frame resonance" increases the likelihood of successful frame transmission and that "hazards" and "vulnerabilities" lower those chances.

The assumption is that frame alignment is effected by movement activities. The standard scenario is that a movement or activists of a movement come into contact with unmobilized individuals. The likelihood that these contacts lead to frame alignment is high if the frames are already highly similar (i.e. if there is high "resonance") and if there are little hazards or vulnerabilities. However, there is also frame transformation. In this case, there are no similar frames and nonetheless the movement succeeds. The question is not addressed what the activities of a movement are that will bring about such effects.

It seems that often the assumption is that movement activists simply talk to third parties and are then successful. The "importance of being asked" (Varese and Yaish 2000; Brady, Schlozman, and Verba 1999) for recruitment to various kinds of action suggests this. However, just addressing others is not enough: some tactics are more successful than others. Snow *et al.* (1986) mention a promise of movement activists to unmobilized individuals that there will be nice girls in a meeting. This suggests that movement activities are more likely to align frames if selective incentives are promised. Is this always the case? The question that is not answered is what kinds of movement activities are under what conditions more or less successful in bringing about alignment.

In regard to the effects of social movement activities on frame alignment, another question is not answered. In the standard scenario it is assumed that the movement changes frames of unmobilized individuals. If there are interaction processes, it is not very likely that only one of the partners influences the other one. Often there are mutual influence processes. In regard to social movements, activists might realize in encounters with third parties that some of their arguments are not convincing. There will then be discussions with fellow activists which may lead to a change of frames of the movement. An important question thus should also be what exactly the conditions are for changes of frames of social movements when they try to influence unmobilized individuals.

9. Recent developments

After the Snow *et al.* paper of 1986 a spate of studies has been published that applies the framing perspective to social movement phenomena. It is typical that the focus is not exclusively on framing, but that other factors are considered as well. To what extent have the major problems of the approach sketched before been solved? In particular, are there conceptual clarifications? Is there progress in regard to theory? These are the questions that are addressed in this section.

"Frame" and other concepts and their usefulness

There has not been any detailed effort to clarify the framing concept. Most of the time, the original unclear definition of Snow *et al.* (1986, see above), based on E. Goffman's definition, is quoted. Snow and Benford (1988: 198) vary their original definition: framing means to "assign meaning to and interpret relevant events and conditions in ways that are intended to mobilize potential adherents and constituents, to garner bystander support, and to demobilize antagonists." In a footnote, then, they refer to their original definition (Snow *et al.* 1986). Another variant of the frame definition that was mentioned already (Snow and Benford 1992: 137) reads that a frame "refers to an interpretive schemata that simplifies and condenses the 'world out there' by selectively punctuating and encoding objects, situations, events, experience, and sequences of actions within one's present or past environment." These definition are not clearer than the original one: they include unclear concepts such as "meaning" and "interpretation," and we do not know what it means to "simplify" or "condense" the world. It is further not clear whether the three definitions have the same meaning. This does not seem to be the case. For example, the original definition did not refer to intentions to mobilize or demobilize others. If the definitions are different, one would like to know what exactly the differences are, why they were changed and which definition is theoretically fruitful.

The literature further abounds with new concepts and new classifications. For example, Snow and Benford (1988) distinguish between diagnostic framing, prognostic framing, and motivational framing. It is further typical that various ideologies, norms, etc. are labeled with new concepts. For example, Noonan (1995) distinguishes a feminist frame, a master frame of the left and a working-class radicalism frame. What exactly the cognitive elements of these frames are is not clear.

The introduction of the framing concept is a success story in the sense that there is hardly an article on social movements or political protest that does not use this term. It almost seems to be a sign of scientific reputation to designate simple arguments, beliefs or norms as frames. Is this inflationary use of the framing concept justified? One justification could be that the phenomena subsumed under the frame concept and, thus, the concept of frame is part of a theory with high explanatory power. Examples for such concepts are cognitive dissonance or reinforcement. However, it can hardly be said that the framing concept is a component of an informative theory, as was seen before.

The frame concept may further be useful because it denotes new phenomena which social movement scholars have not been concerned with before the introduction of this concept. But this is not the case. In the old days one would have spoken about a movement's agenda, ideology, program, claims, beliefs, ideas, themes, or goals. These terms are still employed in work on framing. It is not clear what exactly their difference to the frame concept is and why the old-fashioned concepts are not used.[9] To illustrate, McVeigh, Myers, and Sikkink (2004) address, among other things, the "frames" of the Ku Klux Klan and their effects on mobilization. One of their findings is:

> "The progressive economic themes included in the Klan's *framing* should have *resonated* strongly in underindustrialized counties and in counties dependent on corn production" (661, italics not in the original) and should thus make mobilization in these counties likely.

The same idea could have been expressed without the concepts "framing" and "resonance," and without any change of meaning. The sentence would then read:

> "The progressive economic themes included in the Klan's *agenda (ORIGINAL: framing)* should have *been widely accepted (ORIGINAL: resonated)* ... in underindustrialized counties and in counties dependent on corn production" (661, italics not in the original) and should thus make mobilization in these counties likely.

In replacing "resonate" with "accept" is probably a clarification because it is not clear what exactly "resonate" means.

It is perhaps more convincing when the same author formulates the question she addresses in plain English and then in the framing terminology:

> The theoretical question is "what happens when a social movement's ideology does not fit the perceptions of its constituents." This lack of fit means a gap between ideology and experiences (Babb 1996: 1033).

> "What happens when a frame that resonates with extant traditions and beliefs also contradicts experience?" (Babb 1996: 1034).

Even if the framing terminology seems often (or, more cautiously) sometimes superfluous because other terms are clearer, it may nonetheless have two advantages. One is that it denotes a very wide class of phenomena for which there was no or no clear equivalent concept in the social movement literature before the introduction of "frame." That does not seem to be the case. A second advantage may be that the frequent use of the concept may instigate scholars to improve framing theory. But maybe this expectation is too optimistic. Many scholars seem very satisfied with using and extending the frame terminology without any further development of theory.

The article by McVeigh and colleagues mentioned also illustrates that the framing terminology often pretends to ask questions or formulates hypotheses that can be couched in terms of existing approaches. The previous quotation (and the text of the article) suggests that the authors are concerned with the public goods the Klan decided to offer to its potential constituency. Thus, the Klan and the constituency have common goals. There is thus a collective action problem and the theory of collective action (see chapter 3) could be applied to solve the problem. Using the framing terminology disguises that an old problem is addressed and that solutions already exist. The framing terminology conceals this.

Theory

Social movement scholars by now agree that frames alone are not sufficient to bring about mobilization or other effects. Other factors must be considered as well. Thus, in recent theory and research framing is only one variable in multi-factor models. This development raises two questions: What exactly are the framing variables? Which other factors are to be included? In this section these questions are addressed. We further provide a critical analysis of other theoretical developments.

Diagnostic, prognostic, and motivational framing

Several studies take up a distinction introduced by Snow and Benford (1988: 200–204). In short, they distinguish between three kinds of frames: diagnostic frames which involve "identification of a problem and the attribution of blame or causality"; prognostic frames which do not only "suggest solutions to the problem but also ... identify strategies, tactics, and targets"; and motivational frames which refer to "the elaboration of a call to arms or *rationale for action* that goes beyond the diagnosis and prognosis" (italics in the original).

The authors' hypothesis is that these are the three "core framing tasks" (199). In other words, "variation in the success of participant mobilization, both within and across movements, depends upon the degree to which these three tasks are attended to. The more the three tasks are robust or richly developed and interconnected, the more successful the mobilization effort, *ceteris paribus*" (199, italics in the original). This hypothesis is then illustrated with the peace movement.

The first part of the sentence is a clear general hypothesis: social movements who engage in diagnostic, prognostic, and motivational framing are more successful in mobilizing adherents than movements who do not engage in these framing activities. The second part qualifies this proposition: the question arises of what it means that the three tasks are "robust," "richly developed" and "interconnected." Another problem is the ceteris paribus clause. Unless the factors that must be constant are specified, such a statement is untestable, as is well know from the philosophy of science: the ceteris paribus clause claims that the framing tasks only work when no other factors change. If these factors are not specified, any falsification can be "explained" by arguing that some other factor prevented mobilization. So it would be of utmost importance to specify the other factors.

In a later article Cress and Snow (2000) hold that those frames must be "coherent" and "well-articulated" (1072). They further suggest that "how SMOs attend to the tasks of diagnostic and prognostic framing" is important (1072). However, as long as it is not precisely specified when frames are "coherent" or "well-articulated" and what kind of activities SMOs must perform in order to be successful, the proposition is not informative and not testable either.

Leaving that aside, it is plausible that the substantive content of the three frames is important for their success. In their work on the Ku Klux Klan, McVeigh, Myers, and Sikkink (2004: 655) note: "A movement may construct a collective action frame that does well in attracting members in one structural context, but fails to mobilize in another. That same frame can also align or alienate the general public and its representatives, depending upon the patterns of structural differentiation in the broader arena of conflict." This suggests that the content of the frame matters. But whether it matters or not depends on the context. It is thus not useful to delineate the content of these frames in a general way, but in relation to the kinds of groups the movement intends to mobilize or to convince. But what should such a general group-specific characterization look like? This question is not yet answered. Intuitively, "resonance" may be important, i.e. the relationship of the movement frames to the frames of the targets. But this refers us back to the question of how this factor is to be defined. Thus, somehow diagnostic, prognostic, and motivational framing matters, but how is not known.

Frame resonance, frame alignment, and mobilization

A basic idea of the framing perspective is that high "frame resonance" makes framing efforts and thus alignment more likely; this, in turn, increases the chances of mobilization. Benford and Snow (2000: 619–622) provide some new hypotheses about the causes of frame resonance by extending their argument from an earlier article (Snow and Benford 1988). They argue that two "sets of interacting factors account for variation in degree of frame resonance: credibility of the proffered frame and its relative salience" (619). In other words, if a frame is credible and salient to targets of mobilization, movements that try to align their frames to those of non-mobilized individuals will be likely to bring about resonance and, as a consequence, mobilization, and collective action.

It is striking that in their original article (Snow *et al.* 1986: 477 – see the quotation above) the authors seem to *define* resonance as the degree to which the movement frame suggests "answers and solutions to troublesome situations and dilemmas that resonate with the way in which they are experienced," and the degree to which these answers are "believable and compelling" (477). Now they (Snow and Benford 1988) address "credibility" and the "salience" of a frame as *causal*

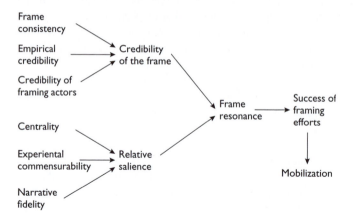

Figure 8.4 Frame resonance and mobilization: Benford and Snow's model (2000)

factors for resonance. This is difficult to reconcile. Let us assume that "resonance" of two frames is to be defined as their similarity, as was suggested above, and that "credibility" and "salience" are causal factors of resonance.

These two factors – credibility and salience – are, in turn, each affected by other factors. Credibility of a frame "is a function of three factors: frame consistency, empirical credibility, and credibility of the frame articulators or claimsmakers" (619). Salience to targets of mobilization is influenced by three factors as well: centrality, experiential commensurability, and narrative fidelity. The authors thus specify a causal model that is displayed in Figure 8.4. This model has several shortcomings.

One is that the concept of frame resonance is, as was shown above, extremely vague. Before such a model is testable it is thus necessary to clarify one of its basic variables. However, the authors' reasoning might be understood in a different way. In structural equation modeling (with statistical programs such as Amos, EQS or Lisrel) latent variables are used that are then measured by empirical indicators. For example, the latent variable "discontent" could be measured by interview questions referring to the extent to which the respondents are dissatisfied with various decisions of the government. As far as the previous framing model is concerned, "resonance" could be measured by the two factors in the model that immediately affect "resonance"; each of these factors then could be measured by the factors that affect these variables. But then the causal arrows should run from resonance to the next level of the model ("credibility" and "salience") and from there to the lowest level ("frame consistency," etc.). If the framing model is understood as a measurement model, a vague characterization of the latent variables is often regarded as satisfactory, the emphasis is then laid upon the empirical indicators assigned to the latent variables.

Benford and Snow nowhere refer to their dimensions as latent variables: they use a causal language claiming that, for example, credibility and salience *affect* frame resonance. Thus, the interpretation of the "resonance model" as a measurement model is not supported by the text. But one could modify the model so that the resonance model becomes a measurement model. The problem then is that the lowest level is missing: a measurement model consists at the lowest level of indicators such as interview questions that measure the latent variables. The authors could argue that the specification of a measurement model is a task for further research.

But this task would be extremely difficult because not only the meaning of "resonance" but the meaning of the other variables is extremely ambiguous as well. This is the case despite the authors' comments on these variables. Even in a measurement model the latent variables must be so clear that they can give suggestions for measurement procedures, because the latent variables are a guideline to the selection of the indicators. Otherwise, any indicator could be assigned to a latent variable.

This vagueness is also a problem when we interpret the previous hypotheses as a causal model. Although the authors comment on each concept they do not provide clear meanings. Let us illustrate this with "frame consistency":

> A frame's consistency refers to the congruency between an SMO's articulated beliefs, claims, and actions. Thus, inconsistency can manifest itself in two ways: in terms of apparent contradictions among beliefs or claims; and in terms of perceived contradictions among framings and tactical actions (as between what the SMO says and what it does). Hypothetically, the greater and more transparent the apparent contradictions in either realm, the less resonant the proffered framing(s) and the more problematic the mobilization. (620)

"Consistency," "congruency," and "contradictions" are apparently used interchangeably. The term "contradiction" has a clear meaning in formal logic: it refers to a certain relationship between sentences. The authors distinguish between two such contradictions: between beliefs, and between framings and tactical actions on the other. Thus, "frame inconsistency" would exist if a movement simultaneously claims that one should shut down nuclear power plants and that one should not shut down nuclear power plants. These are two contradictory normative beliefs. But how can "framings" and "tactical actions" contradict each other? The authors add in parenthesis as an example a "contradiction" between what the SMO says and what it does. But this is not a contradiction in the logical sense. For example, it is not contradictory when a movement says "we will demonstrate tomorrow" and then decides not to demonstrate. Thus, "contradiction" is apparently not used in the common logical sense. But what the meaning of the term is is not clear.[10]

Another question is whether consistency (whatever this means) does in fact capture the meaning of resonance of the early article. In Snow *et al.* 1986 it seems that "resonance" refers to a relationship between frames of movements and non-mobilized individuals and not only to relationships of cognitive elements among the frames of a SMO.

Other work does not provide clearer definitions. This holds in particular for the definition of resonance because this seems to be a key variable in explaining mobilization. An extensive discussion of this and other concepts of the framing per-spective is provided by Noakes and Johnston (2005: 11–16) which builds on an arti-cle by Benford and Snow (2005). Although Noakes and Johnston extend and modify the conceptual distinctions by Benford and Snow, the basic concepts are retained. But Noakes and Johnston seem to be more aware of the problems of the concepts than Snow and Benford. Noakes and Johnston note that resonance "cap-tures an important aspect of framing processes, but the question remains whether frame resonance, per se, can be operationalized and measured in ways that impart confidence – and some degree of precision – about its effects on mobilization processes" (Noakes and Johnston 2005: 16). The reason why operationalization is so difficult may be that scholars so far did not provide a clear definition of the con-cept.[11] Perhaps we do not need a general concept of resonance? Perhaps it is only necessary to look at subsets of cognitive elements that are at issue (or are addressed) in encounters of movements and unmobilized individuals? The configuration of those elements in terms of balance or imbalance then leads to certain changes in the cognitive structure. This procedure will be discussed in the next chapter.

Extending the range of application

The original article on framing by Snow and collaborators (1986) is concerned with the effects of framing on collective political action. The standard scenario is that a movement tries to align its frames to unmobilized individuals who are then mobi-lized and engage in movement participation. Recent work has extended this sce-nario: the targets are no longer only unmobilized individuals but lawmakers, governments or other third parties. For example, Cress and Snow (2000) explain the attainment of the goals ("outcomes") of 15 homeless social movement organi-zations. Two of these outcomes are "representation," which refers to "formal par-ticipation of SMO members on the boards and committees of organizations that are the targets of influence" (1066); and "resources" which are "material concessions received by the homeless SMOs from the targets of their collective action" (1067). McCammon *et al.* (2001) explain why suffragists gained voting rights in 29 states in the USA. All this work uses as one independent variable ideas from the framing approach. The question is to what extent frames of the claimsmakers change the frames of the targets, and the targets are no longer unmobilized individuals. They may be lawmakers or organizations as well.

   There is in principle no objection to extend the range of application of the fram-ing approach. It implies that more phenomena can be explained than before. However, such an extension of the universe of discourse is theoretically only use-ful if there is a theory that can explain frame alignment or, in general, framing processes of this extended set of targets. But such a single theory does not yet exist, as the previous discussion attests.

Multi-factor models

It is plausible that mobilizing supporters or convincing adversaries cannot only be explained by framing activities and existing frames of collective actors. Other factors are relevant as well. But what are these factors? Authors do not systematically apply a general theory in order to generate the relevant factors. This will be illustrated by the empirical studies discussed below. The typical procedure in selecting those additional factors is to apply orienting propositions. For example, in explaining the success of the women's suffrage movement McCammon *et al.* (2001) start from the idea that resource mobilization, political opportunities and cultural framing may be relevant factors. They then construct a causal model that is inspired by these ideas. It is important to note that this is not a precise theory-driven derivation of hypotheses (see our discussion in chapter 1, section 5). The procedure is to use theoretical ideas that serve as a heuristic foundation for the formulation of specific testable propositions. It is typical that a great number of quite diverse factors that seem relevant are then labeled *ad hoc* as opportunities or resources. For example, it is rarely specified how the concept of opportunity is used. It sometimes seems that the standard definition of a political opportunity as a change in the political environment that enhances the chances of success is used. But then it is not shown in detail whether the chances of success really changed, it is just assumed. As was shown in chapter 1, all this is a factor-driven and not a theory-driven procedure.

To illustrate, in the theoretical argument by McCammon *et al.* (2001) one major variable is changing gender relations, i.e. the rise of the "new woman" including receiving extensive education, working outside the home and entering professional careers. It is assumed that this factor altered the attitudes of political decision makers about the role and ability of women. The authors now call this a "political opportunity for suffrage" (51): "shifts in political circumstances altered the political calculus on which decision-makers based their actions, providing a *political opportunity* for suffrage." What is the meaning of "political opportunity" in this context? Did the changing gender relations raise the chances of success? How does one proceed to rule out the opposite effect: a possibility would be that the decision makers tried harder to keep women from gaining voting rights. Thus, the term "political opportunity" is not applied in a rigorous way. The question arises why it is used at all. What would have been lost if the last part of the sentence "providing a political opportunity for suffrage" is deleted? What then remains is a rational choice argument that certain changes of the position of women in the society were recognized by politicians. Their cognitive beliefs about the abilities of women were then changed. The next step would be to specify in detail the pressures political decision makers have been exposed to in order to vote for women's suffrage. Actually, this is what the authors do.[12]

Due to this lack of application of an informative theory it is not surprising that the additional factors selected are different. This can be seen, for example, by comparing of the articles by Cress and Snow (2000), McCammon *et al.* (2001), and McVeigh, Myers, and Sikkink (2004). For each research, the question arises as to what the relevant factors – beside frames or framing activities – are. The perspectives applied in most of the work do not provide informative propositions for specific research questions.

Although the recent work committed to the framing perspective does not explicitly apply general theoretical propositions, it is surprising how often theoretical arguments address the costs and benefits of the collective actors involved in the specific case. These cost-benefit arguments also concern the use and change of frames. However, there is never a systematic application of this approach to generate the theoretical model. It would be an interesting exercise (perhaps of a paper in a seminar) to reconstruct the arguments of these (and many other) articles by applying systematically the theory of collective action and rational choice theory.

Orienting hypotheses

As was suggested already before, a great deal of recent work in the framing tradition does not propose informative theoretical propositions but orienting statements. Here are some examples provided by Noakes and Johnston (2005) which they have found in the literature:

1   "framing can be purposive action" (7) ;
2   "the role of social movement entrepreneurs in the construction of collective action frames is crucial" (7);
3   "frames can also be communicated through nonverbal devices" (8);
4   "symbols of the dominant group are sometimes used as tools for constructing collective action frames" (11).

There are many other orienting hypotheses in the literature. Here is another example:

5   "Collective action frames are constructed in interpersonal interaction" (Klandermans, de Weerd, Sabucedo, and Costa 1999: 137).

These are orienting statements insofar as they do not specify in detail what kinds of phenomena are to be explained and what exactly their conditions are. Statement (1) points out that framing activities are determined by goals of the actors. But we are not told what goals lead to which framing attempts and not to other activities, and which other conditions, beside "purposes," are relevant. If it is said that framing "can" be purposive action, then this implies that there are situations where it "may not" be purposive action – hardly a very informative statement. Hypothesis (2) refers to the actors who are involved in framing activities. It is emphasized that one actor is particularly important, but we do not learn what the other actors are, why social movements are important, when they are successful, etc. Statement (3) informs us that frames are not only communicated verbally. But the statement does not tell when frames are communicated in one or the other way and what the differential effects are. Statement (4) leaves open when symbols of the dominant group are used and when not, it is just said that "sometimes" symbols are used. In regard to statement (5), one wishes to know under what conditions which frames emerge (or, to use a more impressive term, are "constructed").

   These are a only a few examples. The question arises of why the framing literature still abounds with such kinds of statements. Orienting statements are perhaps important as a first step in the development of theoretical propositions. But it is worrying if a major part of the theoretical production 20 years after the basic theoretical article of Snow *et al.* (1986) still consists of orienting propositions.

Other open questions

A major shortcoming in the development of the framing approach is that there is still no theory that explains in detail what effects certain frames or successful frame alignments have on the *form of collective action* that is performed. As was seen before, this question was not answered in the founding paper either.

Another question is how the *form of frame* can be explained that is adopted by collective actors or individuals. One of the few scholars who addresses this question is Diani (1996). He asks what kind of political opportunity structures create which types of frames (see Figure 1 on p. 1056). However, the hypotheses consist only of dichotomous terms. Further, one would like to know *how* and *why* different types of opportunity structures lead to certain types of frames. For example, why should a situation where there are high "opportunities for autonomous action within the polity" and high "opportunities created by the crisis of dominant cleavages" lead to "realignment frames"? Another deficiency of Diani's hypotheses is that only very broad phenomena are explained such as "realignment frames" or "inclusion frames." When we assume that it is clear what cognitive elements these frames consist of, the theory only predicts that exactly one set of frames such as an inclusion frame originates. It would be interesting to know what elements of frames are brought about by which macro factors.

There is also no progress in *micro-macro modeling*. Time and again studies include macro as well as micro variables. The article by Diani (1996) mentioned in the previous paragraph is an example: he argues that opportunities affect frames. But more complex macro models with an explicit micro theory are not provided.

The questions of proponents of the framing approach focus on the effects of framing efforts of the mobilizing agents on the mobilization and the frames of their targets. A typical question is, as was seen before, when social movements succeed in aligning the frames of unmobilized individuals. It is rarely asked when those who engage in mobilizing or framing efforts change their own frames. This question is addressed, for example, by Cornfield and Fletcher (1998; see also Esacove 2004; Evans 1997): they investigate why the American Federation of Labor (AFL) has changed its legislative agenda or, in the jargon of the framing perspective, has extended its frames. To answer this question the authors develop a "market model" and a "political model." This is an interesting set of hypotheses that could be formulated in a more general way so that it can be applied to other cases as well.

10. The validity of the framing approach

To what extent are propositions of the framing approach confirmed or falsified in empirical research? We will first take up the question of whether frame alignment is a necessary condition for collective action, suggested in the founding paper of Snow *et al.* (1986). We will then look at some empirical studies to explore which propositions of the framing approach have been tested and what the outcome of these tests were.

Is frame alignment a necessary condition for collective action?

One of the propositions in the founding paper by Snow *et al.* (1986) is that frame alignment (FA) is a necessary condition for protest (PR – see the previous discussion). The following two scenarios suggest that this proposition is not valid.

Scenario 1: There are protests without any involvement of a movement. This holds for some of the east European revolutions. For example, the demonstration in Leipzig on October 9, 1989 was not organized by any movement. People convened spontaneously on the Karl Marx Square in Leipzig. There are many other similar cases. For example, if nations are involved in events such as wars, protesters often convene at the respective embassies in order to express their discontent. These gatherings occur spontaneously, and no movements are involved. There are thus protests, but no frame alignment of unmobilized protesters and social movements has taken place.

Scenario 2: Assume there is large number of groups and organizations who joined to organize a large demonstration against unemployment. The name of this group is "coalition against unemployment." The local press publishes a note that a coalition of very heterogeneous groups is worried about increasing unemployment and asks all those who share this concern to convene at a certain place at a certain time. Assume that potential participants know only the goal of the demonstration and the place and time where it takes place. Has there been some frame alignment? One could assume that "frame bridging" has taken place (see before), i.e. "the linkage of two or more ideologically congruent but structurally unconnected frames regarding a particular issue or problem" (467); it is "the linkage of a SMO with what McCarthy (1986) has referred to as unmobilized sentiment pools or public opinion preference clusters" (467). To be sure, there is a coincidence of the goal of the organizers on the one hand and of many non-mobilized individuals on the other. But an alignment as defined by the authors has not taken place. There is thus PR without FA.

Is FA a sufficient condition for PR? This means: if there is FA, then there is also PR; if there is no FA, PR may or may not obtain. It is only excluded that there is FA but no PR. Collective action theory implies that just an alignment of some cognitive elements of a frame is not enough to generate PR. For example, assume that movement activities have the effect that unmobilized individuals accept justifications for violent behavior and some of the movement's beliefs in regard to who is guilty of the grievances. These are not sufficient incentives to bring about protest. Thus, we will often find FA but no PR. FA is thus not a sufficient condition for PR.

Is there empirical confirmation of the framing perspective?
A selective discussion of empirical studies

There is a vast number of empirical studies that include some hypotheses on framing. We will select two recent studies that in our opinion are pieces of good empirical research and that are among the most rigorous investigations that test or apply propositions of the framing perspective.

Cress and Snow 2000

We begin with an article by Cress and Snow (2000). It is particularly interesting how an empirical test of framing hypotheses where one of the founders of the perspective is involved solves problems of operationalization mentioned before. The authors explain the extent to which 15 active homeless social movement organizations (SMOs) have attained their goals. They specify four types of outcomes sought by the homeless such as office space for the movements and securing accommodative facilities for beneficiaries of the movement.

The framing hypothesis applied in the research reads that SMOs that attend to the three "core framing tasks" (diagnostic, prognostic, motivational framing – see above) are "likely to be more successful in securing their proximate goals" (1071). The authors add that attainment of the movement goals should be "partly contingent on the development of coherent and well-articulated accounts of the problems and who and what is to be blamed (diagnostic framing) and what needs to be done in order to remedy it (prognostic framing)" (1072). It was said before, that it is hardly clear what "consistent" and "well-articulated" frames are. One is thus curious whether the measurement adds some clarity to these concepts.

Applying ideas from the founding paper by Snow *et al.* (1986), the research problem refers to frame alignment of the homeless SMOs and their targets. One major condition for the success of SMO activities to align their frames and the frames of their targets is the resonance of the frames. Furthermore, possible "hazards" and "vulnerabilities" (see before) could jeopardize success and are thus important for the success of the framing activities of the SMOs as well. It is very disappointing that these basic ideas are not subjected to the test. This research would have been an opportunity to examine to what extent elusive concepts like "resonance" could be utilized in empirical research. Instead, the authors focus only on SMO activities that are supposed to explain frame alignment.

The authors further specify several other factors such as viability of the SMO organization (measured, among other things, by the frequency of meetings), the use of disruptive tactics, existence of sympathetic allies and the presence of city support.

The central question in this context is how the authors measure the provision of "consistent" and "well-articulated" frames by the movement. Unfortunately, the coding of the material the authors use is badly documented and not clear: the authors illustrate their operationalization in only one paragraph (1079). They construct two dichotomous frame variables: using prognostic frames and using diagnostic frames. Those concepts refer to certain statements of movements. If they use more extensive arguments related to the diagnosis of the problem, this is classified as articulate framing and, thus, as diagnostic framing; otherwise diagnostic framing is not present. "Prognostic framing" – a dichotomy as well – is measured similarly. It is striking that motivational framing is not part of the study. It is further striking that "consistency" is not addressed and a "well-articulated" frame becomes simply an "articulated" frame. There is thus a gap between the operationalizations and the theoretical propositions.

Based on the operationalization, the framing hypothesis the authors actually test reads:

> If a social movement articulates statements referring to (a) what is problematic, in need of amelioration and who is to be blamed (diagnostic framing), and to (b) what needs to be done (prognostic framing), goal attainment is likely.

Every social movement scholar would probably agree that this proposition is plainly wrong. There is a huge number of social movements and other groups that provide extremely extensive arguments but are not successful at all. For example, Gamson (1990) has shown that more than half of the organizations he analyzed did not succeed, and it can be assumed that they provided extensive arguments for their goals. In one of the few studies that addresses the failure of a movement Voss (1996) shows that the Knights of Labor's various framing activities could not prevent their collapse and were thus not successful. But, of course, sometimes articulating goals suffices for attaining them. The question thus should be under what conditions movements are successful. Although the authors mention this burgeoning literature on movement success they do not formulate conditions about the success or failure of framing activities.

What were the results of the study? The authors carry out a "qualitative comparative analysis" (QCA, 1079). They discuss the relevance of the independent factors for each of the four outcomes separately. "Taken together, our findings identify the importance of organizational viability and framing activities for obtaining targeted outcomes by homeless SMOs" (1101). Thus, there is confirming evidence for the propositions tested – given the authors operationalizations.

The authors criticize quantitative approaches because "they have additive and linear assumptions about the influence of variables" (1079). This is incorrect: modern multivariate analyses can handle non-additive and non-linear effects, as every advanced textbook in statistics testifies. Furthermore, the hypotheses of the authors are linear and additive – see the previous hypothesis that the authors tested. It is thus strange that the authors did not try a quantitative analysis as a supplement to the QCA. The 15 cases with 6 independent variables can easily be subjected to a logit or OLS regression analysis. Since the data are available (Table 3) we constructed a data file. First, the bivariate correlations of the two framing variables (diagnostic and prognostic framing) with each of the four outcome variables (representation, resources, rights, and relief) ranged – with one exception – from .22 to .87. Only "prognostic frame" and "resources" showed no correlation ($r = .02$).

To simplify the analysis we constructed a scale by adding the four outcome variables. This was legitimate because they loaded on one factor. Next we performed a regression analysis with the 6 independent variables (prognostic frame, diagnostic frame, SMO viability, disruptive tactics, sympathetic allies, city support) and the dependent outcome scale. Due to multicollinearity, the variable "diagnostic frame" was dropped from the analysis. This suggested to construct a scale by adding the two frame variables. The next regression analysis consisted of this scale and the four other independent variables, and the dependent outcome scale. Due to high multicollinearity we carried out a stepwise regression. The variables left were the frame variable (Beta = .62, p = .001) and the variable "sympathetic allies" (Beta = .40, p = .028), with an adjusted R^2 of .81. This is a clear confirmation of the importance of the framing variables in this research.

This confirmation is very surprising. The question now arises why such a simple and incorrect hypothesis that clearly contradicts all we know about social movement activities and movement success is confirmed. To answer this question requires us to look in detail at the research setting which cannot be done at this point because this requires some intimate knowledge of the research site. A speculation is that the measured variables highly correlated with other non-measured variables that refer to "resonance" in the sense of similarity of various frames. The conclusion from the research is that the framing proposition tested is clearly not falsified but confirmed. However, it can certainly not be claimed that this is a serious test of basic propositions of the framing approach.

McCammon et al. 2007

McCammon *et al.* (2007) "explore movements' capacity to produce political change through framing" (726). Their example is the U.S. women's jury movement whose aim is to attain the right to sit on juries. The basic idea is that the success of frames "in persuading lawmakers to redefine the law one must consider not only the content of the frames but also the broader circumstances in which framing takes place" (726). In other words, "movement actors must incorporate or respond to critical discursive elements in the broader cultural environment" by tapping into a "hegemonic discourse" (726). The authors discovered numerous frames – each is denoted by a different name (see the summary in Table 2). For example, the "similarity master frame" emphasizes "the similarities between women and men and the need to treat men and women equally" (728). This over-arching frame includes various subframes such as the rights frame claiming that men and women have the same rights. The "difference master frame" includes, among other things, the peers frame claiming "that the courts were harmed by women's absence ..." (729).

The authors suggest several hypotheses about when frames are effective. One hypothesis they come up with after a long theoretical argument is that some frames such as the rights, duty, and peers frames "should be effective in inducing lawmakers to expand jury laws to include women because these frames align with a hegemonic legal discourse" (733).[13] Furthermore, some additional factors are specified. It is innovative that the authors suggest and test interaction effects.

The data are annual state-level measures of 15 states in the USA. In this context, the measurement of frames is of interest: their operationalization is based on a content analysis of historical sources. The authors "recorded the content of the frame and then tallied the number of times annually that activists in a state used each type of frame (e.g. the duty or peers argument)" (738). The empirical analysis thus only includes the type of frame used (see Tables 3 to 5). Thus, the proposition that is actually tested reads:

> If a social movement uses a frame claiming a change of behavior of third parties, they will meet the demands of the movement.

This is similar to the hypothesis of the study discussed before (Cress and Snow 2000) that frame articulation generates frame acceptance and goal attainment.

The findings show that the use of some frames matter, namley the rights, duty, and "war shortage or quality frame" (Table 3). In other words, using these frames is related to the passage of state women jurors laws between 1913 to 1966. The authors hold that the background theory they use to generate the specific hypotheses about the women's jury movement is confirmed as well: "There is substantial evidence in the findings that the context in which movement framing takes place moderates the political effectiveness of discursive tactics." They then qualify this statement by adding that: "Not all contexts, however, are shown to influence the effects of movement framing" (740).

Are these findings really a confirmation of the grand theory that is applied? All the hypotheses about resonance, counterframing or discursive opportunity structure discussed in the authors' article are not tested. This implies that the frames of lawmakers and their "resonance" with the frames of the women were not measured. In order to test the relevance of frames taken from the cultural context one should include situations where the arguments (i.e. frames) are *not* taken from "hegemonic discourse." But this is not done. It can thus not be ruled out that new arguments that are not rooted in widely held views are much more effective or perhaps only effective under certain conditions. Resonance may not be effective as well. For example, if the frames of the jury movement on the one hand and politicians on the other are very different and if the politicians think that adaptation of their frames to those of the movement will yield the support they need to remain in power, they will change their views. All this is not tested.

In their statistical analysis the authors test several models. Each model consists of all the other factors, but only one type of frame is included. For example, model 1 in Table 4 is made up only of the other factors, it is the base-line model; model 2 includes these other factors and, in addition, the variable "duty frame." The third model includes again all other factors, but this time only the competence frame. It is not clear why the authors did not test a model that includes all frame variables simultaneously. This would be important in order to see whether the effects of the frames are perhaps canceled out.

The authors could argue that they have tested predictions from a theory and that this is a legitimate procedure. However, this argument presupposes that there is a clear theory from which predictions are logically derived and then tested. But the authors' background theory consists only of orienting hypotheses that are used to generate and not to derive the predictions to be tested in a rigorous way. There is neither a clear formulation of the theory nor of the logical derivation.

In sum, the article showed that among the list of frames that were hypothesized to affect the behavior of the lawmakers some proved to be effective for the behavior of the law makers. The conclusion is that there is no falsification of frame hypotheses, but there is no serious test of basic propositions of the framing perspective either.

Conclusion

The two studies discussed are good empirical investigations, that include hypotheses about framing. We thus assumed that they would provide rigorous tests of basic framing propositions. We saw that both articles apply a complex background theory, but test only very simple propositions: as a matter of fact, they examine whether the use of certain frames (or, in plain English, arguments) has effects on the behavior of third parties such as city governments or lawmakers. The hypothesis actually tested reads, when we renounce the framing jargon:

If movements use arguments, they are heard.

To be sure, the authors of the articles do not formulate the hypotheses which they test in this way. Their theory is about resonance, hegemonic discourse, etc. but what is actually tested is the simple hypothesis mentioned before. In a nutshell, there is grand theory, and only very little of this theory is tested. Further, all we know suggests that the simple propositions that are tested are wrong. Nonetheless, the propositions are not falsified. But it often happens in the social sciences that wrong hypotheses are confirmed. The interesting question is why this was the case in the two studies. We will not go into this question. For the purposes of this section it is only important that there is no falsification of the hypothesis tested.

The bulk of empirical investigations in the framing perspective are qualitative case studies. They are burdened with even more problems than the studies discussed before. An example is the research by Noonan (1995) who provides rich historical material about the history of Chile and the women's movement. The author summarizes her argument in the following way (104–105). The question is how the traditional responsibilities of women "translated into political power, especially in protests against Pinochet in the 1980s" (104). The explanation "lies in collective action frames." Due to changing state forms women's pre-existing maternal frame was mobilized "to identify the culpable parties, guide their action, and justify their 'nontraditional' behavior" (104). Women thus had, in contrast to men, a "mobilizational opportunity" (104).

The problems of this and other investigations are that it is not clear whether the postulated causal effects do really exist. The evidence is that certain phenomena are present, but the claim that they are causally related is not substantiated. This lack of providing conclusive empirical evidence for the validity of hypotheses from the framing approach holds for the numerous other case studies using framing concepts as well.

To conclude, the judgment by one of the major proponents of the framing perspective from 1997 is still valid today:

> While the case study approach has yielded scores of rich investigations of social movement dynamics, we have failed to demonstrate that one of our central theoretical constructs – collective action frames – affects mobilization. (Benford 1997: 412)

In general, thus, one must conclude that more than 20 years after the basic article by Snow *et al.* (1986) has been published there is no rigorous test of the basic propositions of the framing approach. We speculate that the major reason is the vagueness of basic concepts and hypotheses.

It is further worth noting that interaction effects are rarely tested and that panel or time series studies with individual data (and not protest events) are rare. This is a cautious formulation – actually, I have not found any. The absence of rigorous dynamic studies with individual data implies that the causal order of the variables has not yet been tested so far. Another feature of the existing research is that in specifying the other factors no theory is applied. The authors simply use variables from previous research such as various kinds of opportunities, but without examining whether their defining characteristics are present in the research situation. This holds, for example, for "political opportunities." Their existence is not determined empirically, i.e. there is no evidence that an event that is termed "political opportunity" actually has changed the chances of success of groups.

11. Synthesizing the framing approach and other perspectives

So far each chapter in this book includes a section where it was shown how the approach under discussion could be synthesized with the perspectives discussed before. This chapter departs from this procedure for two reasons. One is that the integration of the framing perspective is more complicated than the integration of the previous approaches so that it is useful to devote a separate chapter to it. The second and major reason is that the synthesis of the framing perspective with the other approaches is the major goal of the book, and this definitely deserves a separate chapter. Chapter 11 suggests this synthesis.

12. What can we learn from the framing perspective for the explanation of social movement phenomena?

The major achievement of the framing perspective is that cognitive structures are considered in the social movement field in much more detail than before. It is not quite correct if the turn is described as "bringing ideas back in" (Oliver and Johnston 2005: 185). Ideas in the sense of ideologies were part of social movement research long ago. However, looking at whole cognitive structures of interacting individuals and their changes in the course of interaction was new. More specifically, the new questions are how movements act to change the cognitive structure of targets and under what conditions movements are successful in changing "frames" of targets.

The drawback is that framing theory is heavily underdeveloped after more than 20 years of its inception, as the discussion of this chapter indicates. Nonetheless, there are many ideas that wait to be formulated in a more precise manner and tested rigorously. These ideas could be further developed by applying general social psychological theories (see chapters 1 and 9). Although there is much talk in the literature that social psychology is relevant, social psychological theories are rarely addressed in the framing literature (one of the few exceptions is Babb 1996). For example, there is a vast social psychological literature on interpersonal influence. Just to mention an example, many hypotheses discussed in the book by Cialdini (1984) could be applied to social movement phenomena. The vast literature on religious conversion could be consulted by social movement scholars as well.

Many empirical studies that address framing formulate new explanatory hypotheses for the specific case they investigate. Often these hypotheses are based on orienting statements. For example, McCammon *et al.* (2007: 731) "theorize that specific discursive elements and structural circumstances in the broader cultural and political context will moderate the capacity of a collective action frame to win the support of lawmakers." Then specific hypotheses are formulated where the kinds of discursive elements and structural circumstances as well as the decisions of lawmakers to be explained are specified. It would be an interesting question to explore to what extent these hypotheses can be formulated in a more general way so that they can be applied to other explanatory problems. That would be one possibility to generate new hypotheses about framing.

13. Summary and conclusions

The chapter began with the discussion of the founding article of the framing perspective by Snow *et al.* (1986). The basic idea is that an alignment of the frames of a social movement and unmobilized individuals makes collective action more likely. What are frames? Modern social psychologists would speak of mental models (i.e. everything that is stored in the memory of an individual). These mental models (or, equivalently, cognitive structures) consist of cognitive elements. These are cognitive beliefs (such as the perception of personal influence) as well as non-cognitive beliefs (such as norms). It is important to note that frames comprise, among other things, incentives: a norm to participate is an incentive to collective action and at the same time a cognitive element in a frame.

The authors' theoretical propositions are, in short, that frame alignment is a necessary condition for movement participation, that strong "resonance" of frames of a movement and of non-mobilized individuals makes framing efforts successful and increases the likelihood of collective action. However, various "hazards" and "vulnerabilities" impede the success of framing efforts.

The major part of the present chapter is concerned with various problems of the founding paper and of the subsequent development of the framing approach. One problem is that individual actors do the framing, but that frames are ascribed to social movements. We discuss several solutions of this "aggregation problem." Another issue is the demarcation of frames: what are, for example, the cognitive elements a feminist frame or an injustice frame consist of? It is further very difficult to tell what "resonance" of frames means and how it can be measured. This holds for "hazards" or "vulnerabilities" as well.

An important result of our reconstruction of the founding paper is that an implicit micro-macro model is used. Another result is that a version of the theory of rational action is implicitly applied as a background theory to explain the change and use of frames and their effects on collective action. For example, assume that unmobilized individuals and activists with different mental models (or frames) meet. A change of frames of the unmobilized individuals will occur when in their interaction with the movement they realize that certain cognitive elements do not fit in with those of the movement; this causes cognitive dissonance or imbalance which is an incentive for the change of the cognitive structure. Imbalance or dissonance are unpleasant or costly for individuals. Thus, the change of frames is a function of costs and benefits. This holds for using frames in order to mobilize others as well.

It is claimed that frame alignment is a necessary condition for social movement participation. It is argued (see also the section on the validity of the framing perspective) that this is a questionable assumption.

In regard to recent developments, several propositions are discussed that are found problematic. We further review some empirical studies. It is interesting that these studies test very simple propositions such as: the articulation of frames of movements leads to their acceptance. It is unexpected that such hypotheses are not falsified, although they contradict everything we know: movements' goal attainment depends on many factors and not just on articulating their goals. It is not clear why there is no falsification.

The points made in this chapter suggest that the framing perspective has many shortcomings. Nonetheless, it was and is a welcome extension of existing approaches. The most important innovation is that cognitive structures are introduced into the social movements field. There are many ideas in the literature, mostly orienting propositions, that could be used as a heuristic foundation for suggesting more precise and informative propositions. The next chapter suggests some new propositions by applying a general social psychological theory. Chapter 11 will then show how the framing approach can be synthesized with the other perspectives discussed before.

9 Identity, framing, and cognitive balance

Toward a new theory of identity and framing

The previous two chapters have shown that there is a dearth of clear and informative hypotheses about the origin and effects of collective identities and framing processes. One possibility to generate such hypotheses is to apply a general theory (see chapter 1). This is the strategy employed in this chapter. We apply balance theory (BT) in order to suggest some propositions about collective identity and framing. The goal of this chapter is to show that BT can be fruitfully applied to generate new hypotheses about social movement phenomena. In particular, BT can be applied to address questions that are asked but not answered in an adequate way in the framing and identity perspectives. The chapter is not intended to provide a full exploration of the possibilities to apply BT to the social movement field. We will confine ourselves to a few topics hoping that other scholars continue our efforts.

Balance theory seems ideal to deal with phenomena that are addressed in the framing approach: it focuses on mental systems, or cognitive structures that consist of cognitive elements, and it assumes various relations between these elements. For example, proponents of the framing approach have sketched processes of frame alignment. These can be addressed by BT: its subject are cognitive elements and their relationships, and it specifies the conditions under which a cognitive structure changes. Collective identity in the sense of identification is a cognitive element that may be at odds with other cognitive elements. Thus, BT seems suitable to generate hypotheses about collective identity as well.

We will first introduce the reader to the basic ideas of BT. For those who are not familiar with this theory reading the chapter requires perhaps some more effort than reading previous chapters. Impatient readers may look only at the propositions which are easily identifiable in the text. After the introduction to BT we address identification with SMOs (social movement organizations) and suggest propositions about conditions for a change of identification and its effects on framing and social networks. We further deal with frame alignment and frame resonance and discuss the relevance of cultural resources (or "discursive opportunities"). Another theme is the explanation of collective action by applying BT. After sketching several mechanisms for cognitive reorganization (i.e. for the change of frames) we ask what movement scholars can learn from BT.

1. A very short introduction to Fritz Heider's balance theory

There are several versions of BT. This chapter is based on Fritz Heider's theory (Heider 1946, 1958) and in particular on its formalization by Cartwright and Harary (1956).[1] We will outline the theory step by step and illustrate it with social movement phenomena.

Simple cognitive structures and the basic theoretical idea

The building blocks of the theory are entities and relationships between these entities. The *entities* are p (a person), x (some impersonal object such as an event, an idea or a thing) and o (some other person or group). A cognitive structure (this concept is explained below) may consist of any number and kind of entities and their relations.

There two kinds of *relations* between the entities: L is a liking or, in general, an affectual relationship; its opposite is ~L (disliking). Examples for L are: like, love, esteem, has a positive attitude toward, value, identify with. Such relationships are symbolized as pLo which means p likes, loves, etc. o and p~Lo.

U is a unit relationship; its opposite is ~U. Examples are: similarity, proximity, causality, membership, possession or belonging (U) and their opposite (~U). pUx means p owns x, p is familiar with x, etc.

It is important that the theory always assumes the perspective of the person p. Thus, oLx (i.e. the other person o likes x) means that o likes an object x from the perspective of p, i.e. p perceives that o likes x. An assumption that is often made is that the situation is perceived similarly by all actors a cognitive structure is made up of and that the situation is perceived correctly. oLx then means that p as well as o (and perhaps others as well) perceive a positive attitude of o toward x and that such an attitude actually exists. Let us call expressions such as pUx or pLo a *cognitive structure*. This term thus refers to any set of entities and the relations between them. The simplest cognitive structure consists of two cognitive elements and a relationship such as pLo.

Heider defines *balance* and *imbalance* of a cognitive structure in the following way. (a) If there are two entities balance exists if the relationship between the entities is positive (negative) in regard to all meanings of L and U. For example, balance is given if p likes, admires o and regularly meets o. An imbalanced state exists, e.g. if p dislikes o, but regularly meets with him.

(b) Now assume that there are three entities, for example pLo, pLx and oLx; this cognitive structure may mean: p and o are friends (p likes o); both p and o have a positive attitude toward the SMO x. Balance exists if all three relationships are positive in all respects or if two are negative and one positive. In the example, there is a balanced state: p and o are friends and they both like the SMO. Imbalance exists, for example, if p and o like the SMO (x), but if p does not like o.

So far we have only introduced concepts but not yet theoretical propositions. A basic proposition reads that imbalance is a psychological unpleasant or uncomfortable state. In other words, if there is imbalance there is tension or strain. This is plausible, as one of the previous examples illustrates: if p likes o, but if both have different opinions about an issue x such as nuclear power, i.e. p likes x and o dislikes x, then there is imbalance, and this is unpleasant. In other words, *imbalance is costly*.

Another of Heider's assumptions is that *if no balance exists, it is likely that balance will be established.* Balance may be brought about through action or cognitive reorganization. For example, in the unbalanced situation where p and o like each other, but where both have different opinions about an issue x, one (p or o) may change his or her opinion about x. This is an example of cognitive reorganization. An example for action in order to restore balance would consist of breaking up the relationship with o.

Thus, BT is an application of the wide version of the theory of rational action. A particular situation – imbalance – is assumed to be costly. Rational action theory then would predict that individuals have an incentive to change the situation. Various options will be considered and the option is chosen that is best for the individual. BT adds special assumptions about these options and their costs and benefits.

The basic theoretical idea of BT can be summarized by a causal diagram (Opp 1984: 31) – see Figure 9.1. The initial situation is imbalance. This leads to an unpleasant or costly state, whereas balance is, in Heider's term, "comfortable." This is a causal hypothesis: Heider argues that imbalance generates "forces" that lead to action or cognitive reorganization in order to restore balance. This is again a causal assumption. Balance, then, has the effect of diminishing or eliminating tension.

The causal diagram also indicates where the theory might be problematic. First of all, "balance" is a dichotomous variable, but there may be more or less balance. How can this quantitative variable be defined? An answer will be given below. If this problem is solved then the proposition is: the higher imbalance, the more costly is the situation and, thus, the higher is the likelihood that balance is restored.

Another possible weakness of the theory is that the diagram does not yet specify what kind of action or cognitive reorganization is brought about when imbalance obtains. If this is left open the theory is not very informative. The idea of explaining the specific consequences of balance (for details see below) is that those changes are effected that are least costly or most beneficial to an individual.

We will finally introduce two concepts that we need later. A *path* is a sequence of at least two different points connected by lines. A *cycle* is a path that begins and ends with the same points. Now assume that a positive line is assigned +1 and a negative line –1. A *sign of a path* is the product of the values (–1 or +1) of its lines.

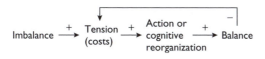

Figure 9.1 The basic theoretical idea of balance theory and other versions of cognitive theories

Similarly, the *sign of a cycle* (we also speak of the value of a cycle) is the product of its lines. Thus, the balanced cycles have a positive sign, the unbalanced cycles a negative sign.

Illustrations

We will now illustrate the previous conceptual apparatus and the theoretical propositions with some graphs (Figure 9.2) referring to social movement phenomena. The convention in the graphs is that lines symbolize U- or L-relationships. Positive relations are symbolized by solid lines, negative relations by dashed lines. Let us assume that the symbols p, o, and x have the following meaning:

x = a public good (such as less pollution, no war, rejection/acceptance of a certain immigration bill)
o = a social movement organization
p = a person

There are eight possible configurations of a system consisting of p, o and x – we speak of pox systems – which are shown in the figure. Graphs A to D are balanced.

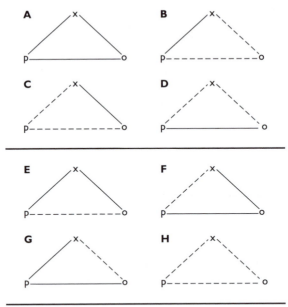

Example: x = public good (less pollution, acceptance or rejection of an immigration bill, less nuclear power), o = social movement organization; p = person.
Note: Solid lines = positive relations; dashed lines = negative relations.

Figure 9.2 Some examples for balanced and imbalanced cognitive structures

This means, according to the previous definition, that in each balanced graph either all three relationships are positive in all respects or that two relations are negative and one positive. Graphs E to H are unbalanced.

Let the L-relationship between p (an individual) and a SMO (o) be *identification*, i.e. p identifies with the SMO. The relationship px and ox refer to L-relationships such as attitudes. For example, p may perceive that the SMO is in favor of an immigration bill (ox is positive), whereas p is against the bill (px is negative). Graphs A to D show several configurations of identification and attitudes toward an issue. Graph B means, for example, that p does not identify with the SMO o and that both, p and o, have different opinions about the immigration bill. This is a balanced state which is plausible: if I don't like somebody I have no problems when we disagree on certain issues. But if I identify with a movement (po is positive) I am concerned when I realize that some views of the movement differ from my own views (see graph F or G). Such a situation is imbalanced.

As was said above, the hypothesis is that imbalanced states are likely to be transformed into balanced ones. This means that each of the four imbalanced states E to H will become one of the balanced states A to D, but it is left open which of these balanced states will originate. For example, state E may become A, i.e. p develops a movement identity. In order to establish balance, p could change his or her opinion in regard to the immigration bill. Thus, so far it is left open which imbalanced state is transformed to which balanced state. The theory only states: if there is an imbalanced state E to H, then state A or B or C or D will emerge. It will be discussed later how this hypotheses can be reformulated so that predictions become more specific.

Let us look at a more complex example. Assume there is a SMO aiming at the representation of women in juries in the first half of the twentieth century in the US (see McCammon *et al.* 2007). Figure 9.3 shows the two major actors: the SMO and the federal government (FG). Assume further there is disagreement about two issues: the FG claims that women and men have not the same abilities and that women should not be members of juries (lines 5 and 6). The SMO disagrees (lines 1 and 2). There is further a unit relation between the SMO and the FG (line 3) meaning that FG is the target of the SMO. The SMO and the FG hold that if women have the same abilities as men then women should also be represented in juries (line 4).[2]

The procedure to determine balance of a graph is as follows.[3] First assign +1 to positive and −1 to negative lines. Multiply for each possible cycle the values of the lines. If the sign of each cycle of a graph (i.e. a cognitive structure) is positive (i.e. +1) balance exists; otherwise there is imbalance. The *degree of balance* could be computed by dividing the number of balanced cycles (i.e. cycles with positive values) by the number of all possible cycles.

In determining balance of the graph in Figure 9.3 we first draw all the possible cycles of the graph. The four graphs A to D are the cycles consisting of three cognitive elements (and, thus, three lines). There are further three cycles with four elements and four lines each – see graphs E to G. The solid and dotted lines correspond to the lines of the upper graph. The numbers −1 or +1 within the graphs signify imbalance (−1) or balance (+1). In total, there are 3 balanced and 4 unbalanced graphs. The degree of balance is thus 3/7 or .43.

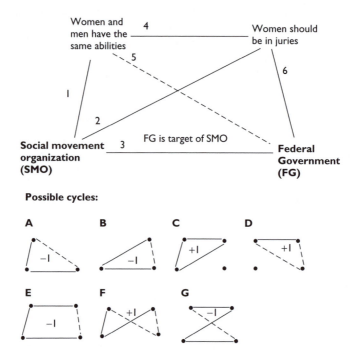

Figure 9.3 Opposite opinions of actors in a conflict situation

How could balance increase? One possibility is that the negative lines become positive. This means that the government accepts the beliefs that women and men have the same abilities and that women should be represented in juries. Another possibility is that the movement adopts the views of the government, i.e. lines 1 and 2 become negative. Another possibility is that line 6 becomes positive and lines 2, 3, and 4 become negative. In this case, thus, only lines 1 and 6 are positive, all others are negative. This change of four lines is rather implausible: it seems plausible that the actors try to restore balance by changing as few lines as possible.

What would happen if the opponents agree that equal abilities is no justification for admitting women to juries because this is a naturalistic fallacy (see the previous endnote)? This implies that line 4 becomes negative. Then C and D become negative, and E and G become positive. Thus, imbalance does not change. This sort of cognitive reorganization is thus implausible.

The question arises which of these possible changes is most likely. We will turn to this question in the following section.

Balance in complex structures: additional propositions

The previous propositions have several shortcomings. (1) It is not specified which changes of all possible changes occur if imbalance obtains. If cognitive systems consist of four or more cognitive elements, the number of possible balanced states is still larger and, thus, predictions about what happens in an unbalanced situation are still less specific. Thus, so far the theory has little explanatory power.

(2) The theory does not distinguish between *degrees* of L and U. But the intensity of a relationship is relevant for the psychic tension and, thus, for the likelihood of a change. For example, if in graph F in Figure 9.2 px is the weakest and po the strongest relation, it is likely that px and not po or ox change. In other words, changing the relations po or ox would be more costly than changing one's view about pollution.

We will now introduce some hypotheses that address these problems. These hypotheses are based on a wide version of the theory of rational action.[4] The following hypotheses are thus not only plausible but backed by a general theory. They are also found in the literature on balance theory. The initial assumption for applying this theory is the implicit hypothesis in all versions of cognitive consistency theories, namely that imbalance or dissonance or cognitive inconsistency is costly. In other words, imbalance is an unpleasant psychological state. The theory of rational action as well as BT would thus predict that individuals want to avoid or change imbalance. In other words, individuals wishing to maximize their utility will try to reduce psychic costs or effect changes that incur lower costs. Thus, when cognitive structures are imbalanced, i.e. costly, those changes are preferred that are least costly. The question now arises how this proposition can be applied to make predictions about changes of unbalanced states more specific.

A first idea is that it is in general less costly to change one relationship than two or more. For example, assume a person p likes another person o (or identifies with a SMO o) and learns that they differ in regard to their opinion about x: o likes x, whereas p dislikes x. This is graph F in Figure 9.2. One possibility to achieve balance is to change p~Lx to pLx. Another possibility to restore balance is to alter more than one line. For example, assume p discusses the utilization of nuclear energy (x) with friends and finally agrees that nuclear energy is acceptable. At the same time p begins to infer from some previous discussion with o that o only pretends to be in favor of x because his friends have this opinion so that in fact o rejects x. Thus, oLx becomes o~Lx. This prompts p to break up his relationship with o so that pLo becomes p~Lo. This is the situation of graph B in Figure 9.2. Such a change would be unlikely because, as said, changing only one line is less costly than changing two or more lines. Our first proposition thus reads:

(1) The higher the number of lines is whose change leads to balance, the higher are the costs of restoring balance. Thus, in restoring balance the lowest possible number of lines is changed.

When we assume that the intensity of a line is important for its change, hypothesis 1 is only valid if the lines do not differ in intensity. This implies that there could be situations where a change of two lines is less costly than changing one intense relation.

The idea that the intensity of a relation matters can be formulated as a hypothesis in the following way:

(2)   The more intense a L- or U-relationship is, the higher the costs of changing it and, thus, the less likely the relationship is changed.

It is plausible that it is more pleasant to transform a negative into a positive relationship than to change a positive to a negative one. For example, balance in graph E (Figure 9.2) can be restored by changing pLx to p~Lx or by changing p~Lo to pLo, assuming that oLx is given. Given equal intensity of the relationships it is less costly to develop a liking relation to o than a negative attitude toward x. Thus:

(3)   It is more costly to change a positive line to a negative one than a negative one to a positive one. Thus, it is more likely that balance is restored by changing negative to positive than positive to negative lines.

So far we dealt with complete graphs, i.e. with graphs in which all possible lines between the entities are drawn. But this is not always the case. Assume that p likes o and that p has a positive attitude toward x. But p does not know what o thinks about x. This means that the line between o and x is missing. If p likes o he or she would certainly be interested in knowing how o thinks about x. Thus, not knowing what o thinks about x is costly to p. It is therefore plausible that there is a tendency toward completeness. In other words:

(4)   If graphs are incomplete (i.e. if lines between points are missing), it is likely that relationships are added so that balance increases.

A graph describes the situation as it is perceived by the reference actor p. The common assumption is that p is not idiosyncratic so that the perceived structure matches the actual one. In the situations that are addressed in this chapter, o is often a group or SMO, as the previous examples indicate. It is a plausible assumption that from the perspective of p relationships in which o and not p is involved are difficult to change. For example, an individual will usually not assume that he or she is able to change an SMO's ideology (or "frames"), i.e. an oUx relationship. A plausible assumption thus is:

(5)   If o is an organization or a large group, changes of relationships in which only o and not p is involved are more costly and, thus, less likely than relationships in which p is part of.

Since this chapter provides the first application of BT to the field of social movements and protest, we will not apply BT in all its complexity but make some simplifying assumptions. One is that relationships are symmetric. This means: if there is a relation R between p and o (pRo), this relationship holds also for o and p (oRp).

Thus: if pRo, then oRp. An example is interaction: if p interacts with o (pIo) then o interacts with p (oIp). Assuming symmetric relationships implies that if there is a relationship pLo, then there is also a relationship oLp. Although this is often not the case the assumption is in general plausible because BT predicts that asymmetric relationships (p loves o but o hates p) do not last long, they tend toward balance. The reason is that an asymmetric relationship is imbalanced[5] and, thus, costly, and it is therefore likely that it changes. We further assume that there is no misperception. In a next step, these assumptions should be dropped. But this is not done in this chapter but must be deferred to further research.

2. When movement identification changes frames

We will first deal with situations where a person p and a SMO o are the actors. There is further an issue x such as a government decision. x is thus an attitude object. From the perspective of an individual, x may be a belief (such as knowing that the government has made a certain decision) or a value or a whole set of cognitive elements such as a frame or an ideology. Thus, x can be conceived of as a homogeneous mental system. Cognitive systems as units of analysis are also addressed by social movement scholars when whole frames are at issue. What x refers to depends on the perception of the reference actor p. For the sake of simplicity, we assume that x is a goal such as advancing a liberalized immigration bill. There may be different relationships between p, o, and x. We start with the cognitive system of the first graph of panel A in Figure 9.4. Assume that p has developed a strong identification with an SMO, symbolized by the bold line between p and o. There is thus an intense L relationship between a person p and the SMO. Furthermore, p is approached by social movement activists and realizes that they pursue goal x. The graph is incomplete. Because, as we saw, there is a tendency toward completeness the prediction is that a positive attitude of p toward x will develop – see the second graph of the panel A. The circles highlight the relations that have changed, compared to the previous graph. To summarize:

> *Hypothesis 1*: If individuals strongly identify with a social movement organization and have not yet developed attitudes toward some of the movement's ideas or toward a whole movement ideology (or, equivalently, toward a frame), it is likely that a positive attitude toward these ideas or toward the ideology will emerge.

Put in the jargon of the social movement literature: If there is a strong collective identity and if adherents are not yet informed about some components of the SMO's frames, mobilization attempts will be successful: they are easy because just providing some information about the movement's stance is sufficient to align the SMO's frame with the frame of the unmobilized individual.

Let us look at another situation – see panel B of Figure 9.4. Assume again that p strongly identifies with a SMO. But this time p has a strong stance toward x: p rejects the immigration bill. However, assume that px is less intense than po

(1) When does identification of a person p with a SMO o influence attitudes or beliefs x, e.g. a public good such as advancing a liberalized immigration bill? The relationship po means that p strongly identifies with the SMO. **Circles** indicate that there is a change of the line(s).

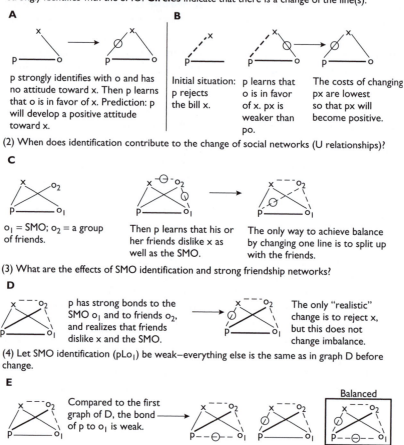

A

p strongly identifies with o and has no attitude toward x. Then p learns that o is in favor of x. Prediction: p will develop a positive attitude toward x.

B

Initial situation: p learns that p rejects o is in favor the bill x. of x. px is weaker than po.

The costs of changing px are lowest so that px will become positive.

(2) When does identification contribute to the change of social networks (U relationships)?

C

o_1 = SMO; o_2 = a group of friends.

Then p learns that his or her friends dislike x as well as the SMO.

The only way to achieve balance by changing one line is to split up with the friends.

(3) What are the effects of SMO identification and strong friendship networks?

D

p has strong bonds to the SMO o_1 and to friends o_2, and realizes that friends dislike x and the SMO.

The only "realistic" change is to reject x, but this does not change imbalance.

(4) Let SMO identification (pLo_1) be weak—everything else is the same as in graph D before change.

E

Compared to the first graph of D, the bond of p to o_1 is weak.

Balanced

Figure 9.4 Frame resonance and mobilization: Benford and Snow's model (2000)

(so the px line is a little thinner than the po line). Thus, p is strongly committed to the SMO, but his or her view about the immigration bill is not that determined. Now p learns that o is in favor of the bill (see the second graph in panel B). It is unlikely that the strong bond of p to o changes. It is further unlikely that p believes he or she can change the position of the SMO toward the bill. The prediction thus is that p will change his or her attitude toward the immigration bill. In other words:

> *Hypothesis 2*: If individuals strongly identify with a SMO and learn that they do not accord with certain attitudes or beliefs of the movement the individuals will adapt their attitudes to those of the SMO.

This holds, as was said before, only if the px relation is relatively weak, compared to the po relationship. In reality, it is unlikely that px and po have exactly the same intensity. But assume this is the case. Assume further that it is abundantly clear that the SMO is in favor of the bill. This means that the individual will hardly misperceive the SMO's stance on the bill. In this case, p might not be able to transform the imbalanced situation to a balanced one. We will discuss a similar situation later. But, as said, such situations are rare so that actually the weakest relation will be changed.

3. Movement identification and the change of social networks

We will now explore how identification with a social movement changes social networks – see panel C of Figure 9.4. The initial situation consists of four units: a person p, an issue x, a social movement organization o_1 and a group of friends o_2. Again we assume that p strongly identifies with the SMO o_1. p concurs with the SMO that the new immigration bill x is to be valued positively (i.e. pLx and o_1Lx obtain). We further assume that p is member of a personal network of close friends o_2, there is thus a liking relation pLo$_2$. This is a private network, and political matters are rarely discussed. The new immigration bill changes this situation and p learns that his friends have strong reservations against the bill and also dislike the movement – see the middle graph in panel C of the figure. This is an unbalanced situation: p identifies with the SMO and shares its opinion, but p realizes that his or her friends don't like the movement and don't share its opinion about x. Several cycles are imbalanced – the reader may check this by examining which of the seven cycles (see Figure 9.3) are balanced or imbalanced.

What happens in this situation? Since there is a strong relationship between p and the SMO it is unlikely that this bond changes. It is further implausible that p changes his or her perceptions that his or her friends don't like the movement. Neither will p change perceptions about the attitudes of o_1 and o_2 to x. We will assume that the facts are so clear that only a neurotic person will misperceive the situation, and we further assume that our actors are not neurotic. Is there a possibility that a change of one line restores balance, and that this line will not be the strong identification with the movement? Indeed, balance would be restored by splitting up with the friends (see the graph right of the arrow). This is likely because the relationship to the friends, compared to that to the movement, was more of a superficial nature. This may be the case if, as we assume, the friends are a sports group.

It was assumed so far that there is only one strong relationship, namely that between p and the SMO. But now assume that x is very important to p. This would then make it still more likely that p breaks up with his friends. Thus:

Hypothesis 3: If individuals have strong ties to a SMO and less strong ties to friends, and if it turns out that the friends and the SMO have conflicting views, integration into personal networks will decrease or will be terminated. This is the more likely, the more important the movement's stance is to p.

It might be argued that an individual who strongly identifies with a movement and supports its ideological position will hardly have friends whose members dislike the movement and reject its position on a certain issue or its ideology in total. However, friendship groups often form on the basis of common interests, irrespective of political issues. Nonetheless, critical events may obtain which elicit heated discussions. It may then turn out that there are basic political disagreements that were unknown. An event such as the terrorist attack on September 11, 2001, may instigate discussions in non-political friendship groups and it may suddenly become apparent that some friends approve of the attacks and, in general, justify terrorism against the USA.

Balance could also be established by changing the xo_2 and o_2o_1 lines in the second graph of panel C. Then all lines would be positive. But this is implausible. Breaking up with friends (see the last graph in panel C on the right) is less costly than trying to convince friends to change their opinion about x and at the same time convert friends to movement adherents.

4. Conflicting frames and strong ties to movement and friends: a case where imbalance remains

Let us now alter the situation described in the second graph of panel C in the following way. Assume that there are strong friendship ties, i.e. an intense L-relationship between p and his or her friends – see the first graph in panel D of Figure 9.4. Everything else remains as in the second graph in panel C: p identifies strongly with the SMO (o_1), and there is disagreement on an issue x between p's friends (o_2) one the one hand and p and the SMO on the other. In terms of the framing perspective, the frames of p and the SMO on the one hand and the friends on the other differ. In addition, p's friends don't like the SMO. What will happen in this situation?

This is a tough situation for p. The bonds to friends and the SMO are so strong that a change would be very costly. Changing the xo_1 and xo_2 relationships is costly or even impossible from p's perspective (p is not neurotic and misperceives clear facts). The same holds for the relationship of friends and the SMO: p will probably not know how to get his or her friends to like the SMO. The only possibility from the perspective of p is to change his or her mind in regard to x (see the right figure in the panel D). But this does not change imbalance. The number of positive cycles divided by the number of all possible cycles is in both graphs 3/7. Since change of a structure is more costly than no change the prediction is that p will stay with an imbalanced structure. Thus:

> *Hypothesis 4*: If individuals have strong ties to an SMO, strong ties to friends, and if it turns out that the friends and the movement have conflicting views, imbalance will not be restored.

5. Friendship networks, conflicting frames, and movement identification

In the situation depicted in panel C of Figure 9.4 there was strong identification with a SMO, whereas panel D assumed, in addition, strong friendship ties of p. We now explore the situation in which the only strong relationship is between p and his or her friends. The assumption that there is disagreement will not be changed. This situation is depicted in the first graph of panel E of Figure 9.4. What will happen in this unbalanced situation?

As in the previous situations, it is plausible that the following changes are unlikely because they are very costly: p does not change the intense friendship ties to o_2; p will further feel that he or she cannot change the relationships between friends and the SMO, between friends and the attitude object x, and between the SMO and x. Thus, from the perspective of p there are two options left: Either po_1 becomes negative, or px becomes negative, or both become negative. Let us look at each of these cases.

In case 1 (first graph after the arrow in panel E) po_1 has turned negative. When we compute balance by dividing the number of positive by the number of all cycles, balance is 3/7. The next graph in panel E where px becomes negative is also imbalanced with $B = 3/7$. The third graph in the panel, however, where po_1 as well as px become negative is balanced: all possible circles are positive. It is thus to be expected that p will change his or her opinion, and will break up with the SMO. To summarize:

> *Hypothesis 5*: If individuals have weak ties to a SMO, strong ties to friends, and if it turns out that the friends and the movement have conflicting views (i.e. frames or cognitive elements), the individuals will adopt the views of the friends and identification with the movement will cease.

This hypothesis assumes that restoring balance is a primary goal of individuals. Although changing several relations at the same time and changing positive to negative relations lines is costly, the change to a balanced state in this situation seems to be less costly than staying in imbalance.

The initial situation in the framing approach (Snow *et al.* 1986, see chapter 8 of this book) is that there are unmobilized individuals and a SMO that tries to mobilize these individuals by aligning their frames to those of the SMO. There is thus not yet an identification with or membership in the movement. Assume now that there have been interactions between movement activists and unmobilized individuals. The result of such encounters is depicted in graph A of Figure 9.5. To begin with, let there be a U-relation between the unmobilized individual p and the SMO (bottom line in graph A), i.e. p knows the movement, but there has not yet developed a movement identification, i.e. a liking relation between p and the SMO. Person p now learns that the SMO has the goal G, i.e. to stop the utilization of nuclear energy. (It may also be assumed that not only this goal but a complete "frame" or ideology of a SMO is at issue. But in order not to complicate the argument, it is assumed that only the goal mentioned is involved.) Furthermore, assume that p has learned that the SMO believes that violent action helps to achieve this goal, that the SMO approves of using violent tactics and also plans violent actions. To be sure, p accepts the SMO's goal to stop nuclear energy, but p rejects violence on moral grounds. Nonetheless, p shares the movement's belief that violence (and not other tactics) will lead to abolishing nuclear power plants. This is an unbalanced situation: B = 3/7. Intuitively, it is plausible that this situation is unpleasant (i.e. imbalanced): on the one hand, p knows that the SMO accepts violence, and, on the other, p rejects this; but p accepts the movement's goal and belief that violence leads to goal achievement. Will there be frame alignment, i.e. a change of p's cognitive structure so that it matches the cognitive structure of the SMO?

It is easy to see that balance is achieved if p changes his or her attitude toward violence and thus accepts the use of violence (see graph B). Note that this prediction holds under the conditions comprised in graph A. One of these major conditions is that no line is particularly intense. For example, the situation would be different if p's rejection of violence would be a very strongly held moral principle. Thus:

> *Hypothesis 6*: If mobilization attempts of an SMO reach unmobilized individuals p, if p and the SMO share a relatively large number of beliefs or attitudes, it is likely that the movement will succeed in aligning the discrepant cognitive elements, i.e. p will adopt the movement's frame (or cognitive elements). This is the more likely, the lower the strength of p's attitudes and beliefs is.

Now assume that the encounter of SMO activists with the unmobilized individuals p brings about antipathy to the SMO – see panel C in Figure 9.5. That is to say, there develops a disliking relationship between p and SMO (see the negative line from p to SMO). To be sure, there is a positive U-relationship (p knows the movement) which is not included in the graph but the disliking relationship is stronger so that the overall relation between p and the SMO is negative. Again, this is an

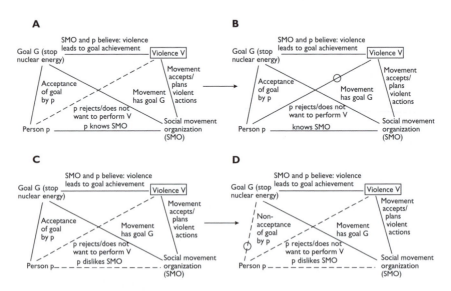

Figure 9.5 Applying balance theory to explain "frame alignment"

imbalanced situation: $B = 3/7$. The simplest way to restore balance by changing only one line is to reject the goal to stop nuclear energy – see graph D. Thus, although there is already partial agreement between p and the SMO there is no alignment. On the contrary, p changes his or her previous acceptance of the SMO's goal. Thus:

> *Hypothesis 7*: If mobilization attempts of an SMO reach unmobilized individuals p, if p share a relatively large number of beliefs or attitudes of the SMO, and if a disliking relationship between the p and the movement develops, it is likely that the movement will not succeed in aligning the discrepant cognitive elements. On the contrary, there will be disalignment (i.e. the distance between the frame of p and the SMO will increase). This is the more likely, the lower the strength of p's attitudes and beliefs is.

6. Block alignment of frames, frame completion, and frame resonance

So far we looked at single cognitive elements of a SMO and individuals p. Next we will address whole frames, i.e. certain sets of cognitive elements. We assume that the frame elements of a frame are clearly identified. The first graph of panel A of Figure 9.6 shows a situation of an unmobilized individual with a frame (or, in terms of BT, a cognitive structure) consisting of elements 1 to 4. There is so far no contact between p and a SMO. The SMO's frame consists of elements 1, 2, ~3, 5 and 6. Equal numbers in the frames of p and the SMO symbolize identical elements. Element ~3 (such as a negative attitude toward violence) is the opposite of 3. Thus, actually there is, in terms of the framing approach, some "resonance" between the two frames, i.e. some cognitive elements are identical, namely elements 1 and 2. The SMO and p differ in regard to element 3. Element 4 is in the frame of p but not in the frame of the SMO. Elements 5 and 6 are components of the SMO's frame, but not of p's frame. The first graph A on the left is an account of the situation from the perspective of an observer, i.e. before interactions between p and the SMO occur. This is the reason why the first graph departs from the graphs common in BT.

At this point we do not yet address relations between the cognitive elements. In reality, however, such relations may exist. For example, a cognitive element that is a value may justify another cognitive element, namely a norm. We will later drop this assumption that cognitive elements are unconnected.

Now let an activist try to mobilize p – see the second graph B of Figure 9.6. This leads to an U-relation between p and the SMO (that is henceforth called "o" for "other") signifying that p now knows o and interacts with its activists. Furthermore, p recognizes that there is some "resonance" or, in plain English, similarity between the frames of p and o: p and o agree on elements 1 and 2. There is thus a U-relation between p on the one hand and elements 1 and 2 on the other, and between o on the one hand and elements 1 and 2 on the other. But p and o differ in regard to element 3 so that there is a negative relation between o and element 3. There are no connections between p and the elements 5 and 6. Furthermore, o is not related to element 4 because this is only in the frame of p.

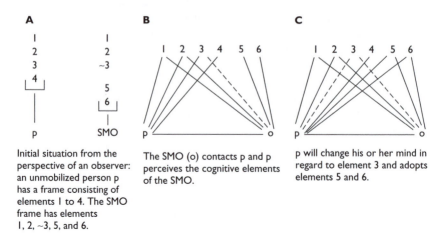

Initial situation from the perspective of an observer: an unmobilized person p has a frame consisting of elements 1 to 4. The SMO frame has elements 1, 2, ~3, 5, and 6.

The SMO (o) contacts p and p perceives the cognitive elements of the SMO.

p will change his or her mind in regard to element 3 and adopts elements 5 and 6.

Figure 9.6 Block alignment of frames and frame completion

What happens after the encounter of p and o? Let us look at the cycle p3op which has a negative value. There is thus imbalance. What change is most beneficial or least costly to p? It is assumed, as before, that a change of the relationship between o and element 3 is not possible because p will not consider it successful to change the SMO's stance toward element 3. Another possibility is to dissociate with the SMO, i.e. to change the positive line between p and o to a negative line. To be sure, this would remove imbalance from the p3op system, but two cycles would become imbalanced, namely p1op and p2op. Thus, the best option from the perspective of p is to change the attitude toward element 3 – see graph C. This argument suggests the following hypothesis:

> *Hypothesis 8*: If there is a relatively large "resonance" between the cognitive elements of the frames of unmobilized individuals and a SMO (i.e. if there is a relatively great similarity of attitudes and beliefs of p and the SMO), it is likely that the unmobilized individuals will change their beliefs and attitudes that are not resonant (i.e. dissimilar) by taking over the views of the SMO.

In other words, there is a sort of *block alignment* of cognitive elements of a frame: the more cognitive elements of p and an SMO are equal or "resonant," the more likely it is that discrepant views become homogeneous because p will change his or her views by adopting the views of the SMO.

In the initial graph A p's frame does not include elements 5 and 6. The proposition that claims that the missing lines of incomplete graphs will originate suggests that relations between p and the two elements 5 and 6 will emerge. There is thus *frame completion*.

> *Hypothesis 9*: If there is a relatively large "resonance" between the cognitive elements of the frames of unmobilized individuals and a SMO (i.e. if there is

great similarity between the attitudes and beliefs of p and the SMO), it is likely that the unmobilized individuals will take over cognitive elements of the SMO that are not yet included in their frame.

What about element 4 that is included in p's frame but not in the frame of the SMO? The tendency to completion might lead to the opinion of p that in fact the movement will not be against element 4 which may be a belief about dangers of nuclear energy. Perhaps p thinks that element 4 "fits" into the movement's ideology or frame because the SMO holds many beliefs about dangers of nuclear energy. If p believes that the movement disapproves of element 4 then p will take over this opinion.

The tendency toward completion applies to dyadic relationships (i.e. relationships between two elements) as well. For example, it was assumed that there is only a U-relation between p and o. Balance would increase if, in addition, a L-relationship between p and o would emerge. This means that there will originate positive identification with the SMO. Another type of U-relation would be membership in the SMO. But there might be other cognitive elements that prevent the development of such additional relationships. For example, membership may be costly or inconsistent with expectations of friends and would thus compromise leisure activities that p engages in or friendships.

Does the situation change when we assume that there are connections between the cognitive elements of a given frame? Actors normally believe that the cognitive elements of their frames are not inconsistent. Otherwise, imbalance would exist and there would be incentives to change the frame. This means that either cognitive elements are unconnected or there are positive relations between them. For example, actors may think that certain elements logically imply others or justify others. This would imply that in our example in Figure 9.6 some of the elements 1 to 6 are positively related. This then means that new cycles must be added. For example, if elements 1 and 2 are positively related, there would exist the new cycle p12p.

But there might be complications: unmobilized individuals could believe that the frame of a movement is inconsistent. For example, some beliefs of a SMO might be inconsistent with general values, or empirical statements of the movement may be inconsistent with empirical findings. This will then add negative cycles to the cognitive structure. For example, assume that p thinks that 4 and 5 are inconsistent. There would thus be a negative line between elements 4 and 5. The cycle p45p and the cycle p45op would thus be negative and imbalanced. What exactly happens when such additional conditions obtain must be further explored which will not be undertaken in this chapter but will be left for future theory development. In this chapter it is assumed that there will be no or only positive relations between cognitive elements.

It is important to remember that the hypotheses in this section – as in the previous sections – hold only under certain conditions. These are specified in the graphs. For example, if the relationship between p and element 3 is very strong, compared to the other relations between p and the cognitive elements, p might be better off to break up the relationship with the SMO. This will be particularly likely if the bonds to the movement are weak and if the other relations to beliefs and attitudes are weak as well. This suggests that many other hypotheses could be derived by changing the conditions included in the graph.

7. Cultural resources and framing

Various authors emphasize the "importance of a frame's consistency with the available cultural resources" (Hewitt and McCammon 2005: 37 with further references). In terms of BT, this idea suggests that cognitive elements that are generally accepted in the population and are referred to in mobilization attempts make frame alignment or mobilization more likely. Is this consistent with or does this follow from BT? Or does this hold only under specific conditions?

Let us return to the example displayed in Figure 9.4 which we slightly modify. This time, there is an unmobilized individual p and a SMO o. The latter has contacted p and p perceives a discrepancy in attitudes in regard to the right of women to be represented in juries r). There is thus imbalance – see Figure 9.7, graph A.

Now assume the movement uses "discursive opportunities" by invoking an argument for its claim that is generally accepted: women should be allowed to be members of juries "because" men and women have the same abilities. The argument thus consists of a cognitive belief b (women and men have the same abilities), a norm r (women have the right to be in juries), and a relationship between b and r (b justifies r): the argument is that r holds "because" b is the case. In terms of BT, there is a U relation between b and r. p further perceives that the movement accepts belief b. Finally, p believes that women and men have the same abilities. The new lines in graph B are encircled.

Does the inclusion of the "cultural resources," i.e. the claim that b is a good reason for accepting r, change anything in the balance of the original graph A? The introduction of the new argument, i.e. of the new entity b and the new relations, has not resulted in balance: there is still one negative line and thus imbalance. However, it seems plausible that the costs of rejecting r become higher: whereas p first had just disagreed with the view that women have a right to be in juries (graph A) and realized that this is not in line with the SMO's view, there is now an argument that suggests that p's view is wrong. Holding this view becomes more costly: there are now several unbalanced circles. It is further important, that p accepts this argument. Before the mobilization activities of the movement, p was not aware of the connection between some generally held beliefs and the particular norm r. The best option to reach balance seems to be to change the relation pr. To summarize:

Hypothesis 10: If mobilization attempts expand the cognitive structure of individuals by adding cognitive elements and, in addition, relations between the elements of the structure that are taken from the general culture, if these new cognitive elements and relationships raise imbalance and the costs of holding the original relations between elements, it is likely that the cognitive elements of the SMO are adopted.

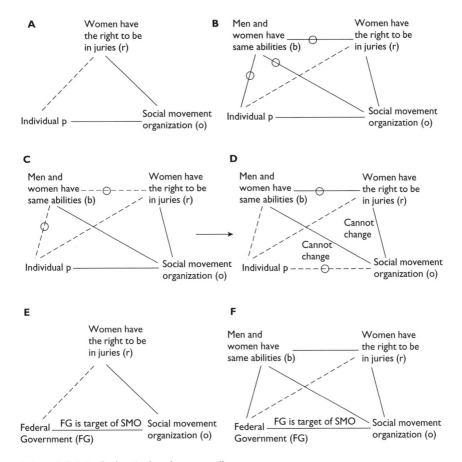

Figure 9.7 Introducing "cultural resources"

The important conditions thus are that there is some imbalance, that adding new cultural items raises imbalance and that changing the original beliefs restores balance. This is a special situation, and we can imagine that reference to cultural items will not always restore balance.

It was assumed that the new elements are shared cultural items. However, the situation is the same if the new cognitive elements are not taken from the culture but are invented by the individual or are results of new scientific studies. New findings about smoking may support beliefs about the dangers of second-hand smoking.

Under certain conditions the SMO's framing attempts may backfire. In the previous example it was assumed that p accepts the argument of the SMO (see the pb relation in graph B of the figure). But there is no guarantee that this is always the case. It seems plausible that in the example many men do not believe that men and women have the same abilities. Further, the argument is, as was noted before, a typical naturalistic fallacy: a norm (women should be members of juries) can never be logically derived from an empirical statement (men and women have equal abilities). For such a derivation another normative statement must be added such as: if individuals have the same abilities, they should have the same rights. So let us assume that those who are targets of mobilization attempts do not accept the SMO's argument – see graph C of Figure 9.7. Thus, pb and br are negative (see the encircled lines of graph C which indicate changes, compared to the previous graph B). What will happen in this situation? We assume that p cannot change the SMO's relationships to r and b. There is thus one way to achieve balance by changing only two lines: the individual accepts the argument, but breaks up with the movement. Thus, p believes that if b then r, but he or she holds that neither b nor r can be maintained. This is graph D.

It may be argued that the previous prediction is implausible because an argument rooted in the general culture is accepted by individuals that are targets of mobilization. This allegation presupposes that there is actually a "general culture" that is accepted by every member of a society. However, societies are made up of many groups that differ in regard to many cognitive beliefs, norms, values, and attitudes that are held. There are thus beliefs etc. that are not accepted by everybody. It is therefore possible that movements provide arguments that are perhaps widely accepted but not by certain groups that the SMO wants to mobilize. Mobilization attempts might thus fail and even eliminate initial sympathies. Thus:

> *Hypothesis 11*: If mobilization attempts confront individuals p with arguments from the general culture (i.e. the SMO tries to make use of "cultural opportunities" or "cultural resources" – whatever these expressions mean) that p does not accept, it is likely that relationships to a movement become more negative than before the mobilization attempt and that frame alignment fails.

So far we dealt with the situation in which an unmobilized individual and a SMO interact. The example in Figure 9.3 refers to lawmaking: the issue is whether the federal government accepts arguments from the larger culture and then promotes a law to allow women to be represented in juries. The previous argument can be applied to this situation as well. In contrast to the previous figure, graph E in Figure 9.7 takes the Federal Government (FG) as a reference actor. The question then is how the FG reacts to the efforts of the SMO to bring a new argument to its attention. The structure of graph F is identical with that of graph B. So the previous argument holds for this situation as well. The conclusion is that BT can be applied to many situations where quite diverse actors are confronted with new arguments and where some actors want to align their frames to those of other actors.

8. Collective action and balance theory

When will a person engage in collective action? If the micro model proposed in chapters 3 and 4 holds it should be possible to represent this model as a cognitive structure. Assume there are three actors: person, person's friends and a SMO. Relevant cognitive non-personal objects are goals, norms, and collective action.

Let us look at two situations. The left graph A of Figure 9.8 shows a completely balanced situation: person has positive relationships with friends and a SMO, and friends have positive relationships to the movement as well. All accept the same goals and norms and engage in some form of collective action. Furthermore, all think that the goals can be achieved by collective action (see the solid line between "goals" and "collective action"). Thus, this is a clear case where the actors involved will engage in collective action. Even if there is not yet a relation between person, friends, and the SMO on the one hand and collective action on the other, it is to be expected due to the tendency to completion that these missing lines will originate.

Now look at a completely different situation depicted in the second graph B: now only person and his or her friends have ties. Person does not know which goals and norms his or her friends accept (the respective lines from graph A are deleted). Furthermore, neither person's friends nor person participate in collective action. Person and friends are, intuitively speaking, very far away in their "ideology" from the SMO. This situation depicted by graph B is imbalanced. For example, the circle "person-collective action-goals-person" is negative. This holds for the circle "person-goals-collective action-friends-person" as well. How could balance be restored or increased? We will not explore all the possible balanced states but only note that engaging in collective action would not restore balance. This is an example of a situation in which mobilization attempts by a SMO will at least not immediately bring about collective action. If mobilization attempts are to be successful, the SMO has to change a lot of things. One could be to establish positive liking relations to person and friends. If these L-relations become very intense then perhaps person and friends adapt their goals and norms to those of the movement. But to establish liking relations to persons whose beliefs and attitudes are very different from the SMO is very difficult. Perhaps SMOs will not even attempt mobilization if they recognize the heterogeneous frames.

The examples suggest that BT can be applied to explain collective action. An interesting question is whether BT is consistent with the micro model developed previously. We leave it to further research to explore whether this is the case and whether new and interesting hypotheses can be derived that explain which

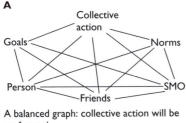

A balanced graph: collective action will be
performed.

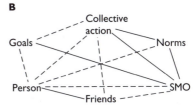

An imbalanced graph: collective action
is not performed by person and friends.
Their performane of collective action
would not lead to balance.

Figure 9.8 Explaining collective action

balanced states would imply performing collective action. Another question that has been hinted at is when SMOs decide to attempt mobilization. Since they dispose of limited resources they will not approach every group but consider for which groups mobilization will be most successful.

9. Mechanisms of cognitive reorganization

It is a common assumption that individuals "interpret" reality. The various kinds of cognitive reorganization outlined in BT and in particular in the theory of cognitive dissonance can be used to specify in what sense individuals "interpret" reality. In this section, some of these kinds of cognitive reorganization will be described, focusing on the social movement field. The literature on BT is rather silent on these mechanisms. In contrast, the literature on dissonance theory describes these mechanisms in much more detail (see, e.g., Festinger 1957), but they can be easily integrated into BT, as this section indicates.

Cognitive adaptation

Ideologies are typically ambiguous: it is not clear what exactly the goals are that should be realized, what means are supposed to be efficacious, and what moral values are accepted. For example, if the goal is "environmental protection" it is at least unclear to what extent pollution or other environmental problems are to be coped with. Will even the slightest CO_2 emission be condemned? If a SMO is against the utilization of nuclear energy it is not clear, for example, whether all nuclear power plants should be closed down immediately or whether they should all (or in part) be closed down within a certain period of time.

What are the consequences of such unclear movement agendas for mobilization? Assume that a SMO tries to mobilize individual p, and p comes across a movement agenda that is to some extent unclear. For illustrative purposes, assume that the SMO claims to be in favor of liberalizing immigration laws – let this be cognitive element i (for "immigration"). How will p react? Assume that p has developed some identification with the SMO. Given that cognitive balance is a pleasant psychic state p will "interpret" the cognitive element i so that it does not cause imbalance. "Interpretation" could mean the following. (a) If the individual's cognitive system disposes of a similar element e (such as: each year 100,000 more immigrants should be let into the country) p will assume that i is identical with e. (b) Assume p has so far no opinion about i. He or she will simply include i in his or her cognitive system. (c) Assume p does not have any opinion about i but has various beliefs about empirical effects of the number of foreigners in a country. For example, one belief may be that foreigners raise cultural diversity which is valued positively. In this case element i fits very well in p's cognitive system. But assume p believes that an excessive number of foreigners raise the crime rate which is regarded as negative. The individual might then think that the SMO will certainly not be in favor to let an "excessive" number of foreigners into the country.

Person p will not always succeed in adapting an element of a movement frame so that cognitive balance is preserved. Assume p believes that each additional foreigner increases crime and that a SMO is clearly in favor of more immigration. This would clearly contradict p's views and would thus increase or generate imbalance.

The idea that individuals strive for balance and that cognitive adaptation is one way to achieve this pleasant state indicates that frame alignment will be the more successful the more an SMO "frames" its agenda in a way that is so vague that it does not blatantly contradict the views of a large number of potential supporters. Alignment will be the more successful the higher the identification of p and the SMO is. Strong identifiers will "interpret" the unclear movement frame so that it becomes consistent with their own frame. Thus:

> *Hypothesis 12:* If the cognitive elements of a SMO frame are relatively vague, unmobilized individuals p will assume that the movement elements are "resonant" with their own cognitive elements. This is most likely if p strongly identifies with the SMO.

The search for new cognitive elements

Let us take up the example of Figure 9.7, graph A: p is against a bill that gives women the right to be in juries, whereas the SMO propagates this goal, and p is aware of this. The example assumes that the SMO provides the argument that men and women have equal abilities and that this speaks in favor of women's representation in juries. This is graph B of Figure 9.7. Now p could choose not to change one of the lines of the graph but thinks about searching for new arguments. An additional argument, i.e. an additional cognitive element, could be that men and women have equal rights and that this speaks in favor of women's jury representation. This would make it even more likely that p changes the negative line pr into a positive one.

If p searches for new cognitive elements it may also happen that p finds elements that increase *im*balance. To avoid such costs p will primarily search for cognitive elements that increase or at least do not lower balance. The example from cognitive dissonance theory to illustrate this is that individuals who have bought something will not look for negative information about the product (post-decisional dissonance). However, there are situations where imbalance cannot be avoided. An example is the evidence for health hazards of smoking that can hardly be denied, not even by heavy smokers. In general, thus, the search for cognitive elements does not guarantee an increase in balance. We can even imagine situations where individuals find cognitive elements that are completely dissonant with their cognitive system and generate large-scale changes.

It would be interesting to explore what the conditions are when individuals choose the option to search for new cognitive elements if they are the object of mobilization attempts by SMOs. Perhaps this is a rather costly procedure because the new element must be integrated into the cognitive structure, i.e. new relations between elements must be generated. This is rather costly. So it seems that searching for new cognitive elements is only chosen if changing existing relations between elements does not yield balance.

The differentiation of cognitive elements

Assume individual p reads that a SMO, he or she identifies with, is in favor of violence. In contrast, p is only in favor of violence against objects, but not against persons. The individual might reason that a SMO in a democratic society "can't" advocate a principle that in fact takes into account to hurt or even kill opponents. In p's opinion, the movement "must" mean only violence against objects. The element "violence" is thus partitioned into "violence against persons" and "violence against objects." This partitioning prevents imbalance and thus preserves the positive relationship between p and the movement.

Changing the strength of a cognitive relationship

Another mechanism for maintaining balance is to diminish the importance of a relationship. Assume again that p learns that the SMO he or she identifies with is in favor of violence, whereas p rejects violence of any kind. p may think that this is not really the opinion of most of the members and that violence is only advanced for tactical purposes, i.e. in order to intimidate the targets of the movement. It is important to note, that diminishing the strength of a relation does not really avoid imbalance but only diminishes it.

When is which mechanism chosen?

So far we have not yet provided a general answer to the question under what conditions which mechanism will be chosen. A first hypothesis is that the kind of mechanism depends on its availability. This refers first to the cognitive repertoire of a person p. For example, p may not know that balance can be achieved by differentiating cognitive elements. Even if a mechanism is part of the person's cognitive repertory he or she may not see any possibility to apply the mechanism. For example, p may not find a possibility to differentiate cognitive elements or may not be able to discover new arguments. Or a SMO's agenda may be so clear that there is no room for "interpretation."

Even if all the mechanisms are in p's cognitive repertoire the costs of using them may be too high or the person may not be able to use them. For example, just deciding to lower the intensity of a liking relationship will not work: I cannot decide that I will now change my identification with a SMO. Or assume that p is shocked about finding clear evidence that the leading activists of a SMO are willing to commit violent acts; p will hardly be able to change or misperceive this fact and adopt the belief that the SMO is against violence – even if this might restore balance.

Balance theory does not dispose of clear hypotheses that state the conditions when which of these mechanisms will be used. To derive such propositions is an important task for future research.

10. A change of perspective: the movement as reference actor

So far the standard scenario was most of the time an unmobilized person p and a SMO that tried to mobilize p – for an exception see Figure 9.3. One of the major questions then is when the SMO will align its frame to that of p. Unmobilized individuals are thus mostly the reference persons of the previous applications of BT. Subsequent research has expanded this scenario by addressing other reference actors such as lawmakers and SMOs (see also Figure 9.7, graph E). However, so far the SMO is rarely taken as a reference actor. But this is a fruitful line of inquiry because, as has been noted in the literature, SMOs may also change their frames when they note that such changes would increase their mobilization chances. However, the common assumption is that SMOs impose their frames on unmobilized individuals.

An interesting application of BT would be to formulate models that treat p and SMOs simultaneously as reference actors. For example, the situations displayed in Figure 9.7, graphs A to D, could be modeled for p and then for the SMO. If the situation is seen from the perspective of the SMO the lines from SMO to r and from SMO to b need no longer be considered given. However, in this particular case it is hardly plausible that the SMO will give up its major goal to get women into juries. It will be more likely that the SMO invests more resources in convincing potential supporters to accept its views. For example, the SMO will try to expand the cognitive structures of the individuals by new cognitive elements. In other situations when ideas are at issue that are not that central the movement may eliminate cognitive elements. For example, when activists realize that certain arguments are vigorously rejected by others the SMO might eliminate them from their cognitive repertoire and, thus, from their agenda.

This suggests that many new hypotheses can be derived by considering the perspectives of different actors. Depending on the choice of the reference actor, there are different relations that are easier or more difficult to change. For example, an unmobilized person will not consider changing the cognitive elements of a SMO, but activists of a SMO may consider and effect such changes. The reference actors to be chosen may not only include SMOs, but other actors like governments or organizations, and unions or churches as well.

11. What can we learn from balance theory for the explanation of social movement phenomena?

The previous theoretical arguments undergird one major critique of the framing perspective: new categories for frames such as the maternal frame are invented, but it is rarely spelled out what exactly the cognitive elements are these frames consist of. Furthermore, it is not spelled out in detail either which elements change in a framing process. The application of BT shows that fruitful hypotheses about frames and their change can only be derived if the cognitive elements of frames and their relations to each other are specified. BT forces the researcher to look in much more detail at the frames than has been done before. In particular, an analysis of relations between cognitive elements is of utmost importance to explore changes that are to be expected. This is rarely done in the social movement literature. Exceptions are Gerhards and Rucht 1992 and, based on this article, Johnston 2005. Social movement scholars should also look at the analysis of "cognitive maps" in political science such as Axelrod 1976 and Gallhofer and Saris 1996. This literature may give suggestions for the reconstruction of the frames of actors such as SMOs, unmobilized individuals and other organizations.

BT further suggests that in each situation only a specific section of the cognitive structure is relevant. In other words, there is a salient situational set of cognitive elements that is relevant for the explanation of changes of cognitive elements. But due to interaction processes between actors this set will be expanded. As is argued in the literature, items from the larger culture may be brought into play or SMOs may invent new elements and relate them to existing cognitive elements. Thus, again, it is important to ascertain the relevant elements of a cognitive structure in a situation where framing processes are to be explained.

This chapter further shows that concepts and hypotheses from the framing perspective can be reformulated in a clearer way. It seems fruitful to apply the conceptual apparatus of BT to concepts and hypotheses of the framing literature. A beginning has been made in this chapter. The result is not just a reformulation but a restatement. This means that existing ideas in the movement literature are used to propose clearer and more informative hypotheses by applying BT.

The previous considerations show an important feature of applying BT: it is of extreme importance to specify the situation that is the starting point of an explanation. That is, the initial task is to outline exactly the points and the lines of a cognitive (or social) structure. For example, will we deal with a situation where attitudes toward an issue such as a law or a government decision are very intense? How strong are the bonds between a person and a SMO? Thus, pre-existing relationships between cognitive elements (including cognitive representations of friends, acquaintances and so on) are of extreme importance if the effects of certain critical events are to be assessed. An important lesson from BT especially for the framing approach is to specify in much more detail the initial situation than is common in the literature.

What can BT *not* teach us? One argument could be that BT is a psychological theory and thus "reductionistic." For example, Benford (1997) rejects "to psychologize what is sociological" (420). The argument is that "we must keep in mind that frames are modes of interpretation that are socially/culturally constructed" (420). Would the application of BT contradict this claim? Obviously, no. It was shown that framing involves some mode of "interpretation" in the sense that the perception of reality depends on the existing cognitive elements – see the previous discussion of mechanisms of cognitive reorganization. Further, BT is perfectly compatible with the notion that frames are "socially/culturally constructed": frames are acquired during social interactions, and their change depends on the situation and, in particular, on social interactions. Instead of just pointing out *that* cognitive structures emerge and change when individuals interact – which nobody denies – BT explains *how* the "construction" of frames happens.

In contrast to Benford's argument, the previous discussion shows how cognitions and social structure can be related. The cognitive structures that are subject of the theory consist, among other things, of cognitive elements that represent macro properties such as mobilization activities of SMOs. But in addition, detailed cognitive processes are subject of BT. This is exactly what proponents of the framing perspective aim at.

There is no question that the application of BT – as the application of any theory in the social sciences – is not without problems. One is the complexity if a cognitive system consists of a great number of cognitive elements. This may make the theory unmanageable. However, modern computers and algorithms suggested in the literature (see note 1) allow the handling of a large number of cognitive elements and cognitive structures. As we saw in this chapter, a theoretical strategy is to treat certain sets of cognitive elements as a unit (see the discussion of block transmission of frames). A possible "reduction of complexity" also seems empirically plausible: when we assume that human cognitive abilities are very limited it is implausible that very complex structures will ever exist empirically.

Although there is supporting empirical evidence for BT, there are also falsifications. But this is typical for every theory in the social sciences. What counts as an asset is that the theory has yielded numerous interesting predictions (see, e.g., Davis 1963 and the references in note 1). Even if this does not convince a reader the least one could say is that BT can be used as a heuristic device to generate hypotheses that then must be tested. We hope that this chapter has shown that BT can fruitfully be applied at least as a heuristic device to generate new hypotheses and to clarify and modify theoretical ideas of the framing approach and the social movement literature.

12. Summary and conclusions

It is rare that general theories such as value expectancy or balance theory (BT) are systematically applied by social movement scholars to generate propositions. To utilize such a possibility seems particularly fruitful in a field that is in need of clear and informative propositions. In this chapter we applied the social psychological BT in order to suggest some propositions referring in particular to collective identity in the sense of group identification and to framing.

A first section introduces the reader to the basic ideas of BT. We then suggest 12 propositions referring to collective identity, framing, social networks, and other phenomena. We further discuss how to explain collective action by applying BT and what kinds of cognitive mechanisms might be applied when frames are imbalanced. In this summary, only some of these propositions and ideas will be sketched. We began by exploring a situation in which a strong identification with a social movement organization (SMO) obtains. It is assumed that unmobilized individuals p have not yet developed a certain opinion toward an issue. If there are contacts between p and the SMO, then p will adopt the SMO's opinion. In this situation it is thus easy for a SMO to align its frame to that of p. Another situation is that p realizes discrepancies between the SMO's and his or her own frame. If there is a strong identification with the movement and if the beliefs of p are not strong, there is again no problem for the SMO to impose its frames on p.

Another situation is that there are strong bonds of p to a SMO and relatively weak relationships of p with friends. Now assume there is a critical event like a nuclear accident and p notes that his or her opinion differs from those of his or her friends; furthermore, the friends don't like the SMO. The prediction is that the least costly reaction of p is to break up relationships with friends. A more difficult situation obtains when p has intense relationships with friends as well as with the SMO. The prediction is that p will change his or her opinion in regard to the issues x. This is plausible because it is rather costly to change the friends' or the SMO's views on certain issues.

The success of mobilization attempts of a SMO hinges on several conditions. Assume that the unmobilized individuals p realize that they and the SMO share a relatively large number of beliefs or attitudes. It is then likely that the SMO will succeed in aligning the discrepant cognitive elements, i.e. p will adopt the movement's frame. This is the more likely, the lower the strength of p's attitudes and beliefs is.

However, the situation changes if there develops some antipathy between p and the SMO. In this situation, alignment of the SMO frame and that of p does not take place. Balance is achieved if p rejects the SMO frame altogether. This is the more likely, the lower the strength of p's attitudes and beliefs is.

Other situations addressed in this chapter refer to conditions that lead to the alignment of entire frames. One condition is frame resonance, that gets a clearer meaning if BT is applied. If relations between cognitive elements in the frames of p are missing, frame completion originates. We further deal with the question whether an SMO's reference to "cultural resources," i.e. to cultural items that are widely shared, will always be successful. This is not the case: we describe a situation where reference to the general culture even eliminates sympathies with SMOs.

Proponents of the framing approach emphasize that individuals "interpret" reality. Applying BT clarifies what this could mean: we specify various mechanisms of cognitive reorganization. An example is cognitive differentiation: a person may perceive a movement's positive attitude toward some issue such as violence which the person rejects. But then the person may further explore the movement's ideology and finds out that the movement is only in favor of violence against objects and not against persons (a distinction made by the German student movement). This, then, comes close to the person's conviction and thus diverts imbalance.

We further discuss what can be learned from BT for the explanation of social movement phenomena. One important lesson is that the detailed specification of the cognitive elements of frames is necessary for the explanation of framing processes. Another lesson is that the initial situation is important for the kind of changes in frames. It is thus important to specify the initial situation. For example, changes of frames depend on the strength of the relationship between p and the

SMO or on the intensity of an attitude toward an attitude object. The previous chapter about framing shows that basic concepts and hypotheses of the framing approach are ambiguous. BT can be used as a toolkit to provide clearer concepts and hypotheses. Application of BT further modifies existing propositions of the existing framing literature.

This chapter is only a beginning of exploring the implications of BT for the explanation of social movement phenomena. The analyses in this chapter indicate that many other interesting and new propositions can be derived. A next important step would then be to devise research designs to test these propositions.

We anticipate that proponents of the framing approach will be skeptical about the fruitfulness of BT, for whatever reasons. If that is the case we would like to ask the major proponents of the approach to derive the previous propositions or, perhaps, improved alternatives, from their approach. As long as this is not possible BT is clearly a good way to start a framing approach that begins to propose informative hypotheses, based on a general theory, that can be tested.

10 The dynamics of contention approach – retreat to history?

The approach presented in this chapter is the outcome of a long-term project that began in the early 1990s. It consisted of various meetings that resulted in several books.[1] This chapter is primarily based on McAdam, Tarrow, and Tilly's book (2001) in which their new approach is described and discussed in great detail. In order to save space we use the acronym DCA for "dynamics of contention approach." We will first present this approach and then discuss its major strengths and weaknesses.

1. The dynamics of contentious politics: D. McAdam, S. Tarrow, and Ch. Tilly's new agenda

The first innovation of the DCA is an expansion of the field of study. It follows a detailed critique of the existing theoretical approaches aimed at explaining social movements and protest. Then the authors present their own approach and provide many detailed applications. We will focus on the authors' approach and discuss applications only for illustrative purposes later.

The new field of study: contentious politics

Many scholars in sociology and political science are specialized in studying particular kinds of contentious action where groups struggle to achieve their goals. Examples of such struggles are (9)[2] revolutions, protests, strikes, wars, ethnic mobilization, democratization, and nationalism (see also Tarrow 2001: 7). The authors suggest looking at common features of these phenomena. For this purpose, they coin a new term, namely "contentious politics" which they define in the following way:

> Contentious politics refers to "episodic, public, collective interaction among makers of claims and their objects when (a) at least one government is a claimant, an object of claims, or a party to the claims and (b) the claims would, if realized, affect the interests of at least one of the claimants" (5).

There are two implications of this definition. One is that "regularly scheduled events ... such as parliamentary elections" are excluded. They are not "episodic."

The other implication is that non-public episodes in which, for example, organizations such as churches, firms, or unions are involved are not "contentious politics."

Why is this broad definition chosen? The major argument is that the different forms of contention "result from similar mechanisms and processes" (4) that are subject of the book. Put differently, the broad definition is regarded as theoretically fruitful: similar causal processes generate the phenomena subsumed under the term "contention" or "contentious politics." Accordingly, the authors wish to find "parallels, connections, and variation" between contentious episodes (10) or "recurrent causal mechanisms" (10).

However, the authors "do not claim that these episodes ... conform to a single general model" (6). In other words, the authors reject the application of general theories, including general theories of action. This claim is based on a critique of the theoretical perspectives advanced in the social movement literature (14–16), of the covering law model (13–14), and of "rationalist analyses" (21). We will return to the role of theories in the DCA later in this chapter.

Problems of the social movement literature

A new approach becomes more convincing when it can be shown that the existing theoretical perspectives are heavily flawed. Indeed, this is what the authors claim. In their critique they refer to the resource mobilization, political opportunity, and framing approach which are the dominant explanatory schemes in the literature.

What are the basic shortcomings of these approaches that disqualify them from explaining contentious politics? There are "four major defects" of these classic social movement perspectives (42). (1) There is a focus on static and not dynamic relationships; (2) the classic perspectives do not work well for broader episodes of contention; (3) the classic perspectives are formulated for the American political system of the 1960s and do not sufficiently emphasize threats and organizational deficits; (4) the classic perspectives do not focus sufficiently on the later phases of contention; and (5) later they add (51) that the classic movement perspectives mostly address one actor such as a social movement organization, whereas the DCA focuses on multiple actors.

The authors construct a causal diagram (17) that summarizes the major independent variables of the "classic approach," namely mobilizing structures, opportunity and threat, framing processes, and repertoires of contention.[3] The dependent variable is "contentious interaction." They then raise several other questions this theoretical scheme cannot answer. The general thrust of the criticism is that the approaches are not capable of explaining relatively specific phenomena such as the forms of contentious politics. In other words, the classic approach "provides relatively weak guides to explanation of action, identities, trajectories, or outcomes" (37). "Relatively weak" suggests that the approaches are not entirely inadequate. It is thus not inconsistent when the approaches are not completely dismissed but used as a "source of ideas." In the last chapter of their book the authors conclude: "we have insisted on the uselessness of choosing among culturalist, rationalist, and structuralist approaches to contentious politics but adopted insights from all three where we found them helpful" (305). It seems thus that the authors' position toward the classic approaches is ambivalent: on the one hand, they outline basic weaknesses, on the other they do not want to eliminate them entirely. The authors' approach is eclectic. But which ideas are useful for what explanations is not said.

Although the previous quotation indicates that the authors apply ideas from the three different orientations ("culturalist, rationalist, and structuralist") they make clear that collective action and rational choice theory are not seen as a viable theoretical approach. We will discuss this allegation below.

The new approach: dynamic, recurrent mechanisms instead of theories

We insinuated already that the authors wish to discover recurrent, dynamic causal mechanisms or processes. The authors define "mechanism" and "process" in the following way:

> *Mechanisms* are a delimited class of events that alter relations among specified sets of elements in identical or closely similar ways over a variety of situations. (24, italics not in the original)

> Social *processes*, in our view, consist of sequences and combinations of causal *mechanisms*. To explain contentious politics is to identify its recurrent causal mechanisms, the ways they combine, in what sequences they recur, and why different combinations and sequences, starting from different initial conditions, produce varying effects on the large scale. (12–13, italics in the original)

A "mechanism" is thus a causal relationship: it is a class of *events* that "alter" or, equivalently, have a causal effect on certain *relations* among *elements*. But not any change of relations among elements is a mechanism; a mechanism is given only if events change relations "in identical or closely similar ways over a variety of situations." It is not specified (as, for example, in balance theory) what the elements and relations are that may be part of a mechanism. It is not said either what is meant by "identical or closely similar ways."

Let us try to clarify these terms. Assume there is a nuclear accidents like Three Mile Island in 1979. This event has altered relations among elements. *Elements* may be groups, organizations, societies or individuals, but also objects such as nuclear power plants. "Elements" that were involved in the nuclear accident were individual actors, all kinds of groups such as protest groups and the government, but also the nuclear power plant.

What could be new *relations* between these elements that were spawned after the accident?[4] Existing protest groups recruited new members, i.e. new interactions emerged. Thus, an "event" altered a certain kind of relationship between actors. What other relationships could be involved? One is perception – "person A perceives a phenomenon B" is a relation. Thus, if individuals after the accident have changed perceptions about the danger of nuclear power plants or beliefs about authorities, these changes could be part of a mechanism. Attitude changes such as a more negative evaluation of nuclear power would be a relation between elements as well: "person A values B" is a relation.

Is there anything that could be altered which is not a relation? For example, "protest" could be formulated as a property of an individual actor, i.e. "actor a protests" (symbolically: Pa). But it can also be expressed as a relationship such as "actor a protests against government decision b." The problem is that everyday natural language is flexible so that often different symbolizations of attributes are possible. The authors do not provide any rule specifying which attributes are relations and which are not.

Mechanisms exist only, according to the definition, if the changes occur "in identical or closely similar ways over a variety of situations." Assume that various changes after the Three Mile Island accident were observed and compared to changes after other nuclear accidents. Assume further that in all those cases new groups emerged, protests were staged, and attitudes toward the government became more negative. Thus, "a delimited class of events" (nuclear accidents) "that alter relations among specified sets of elements in identical or closely similar ways over a variety of situations" (emergence of new groups, etc. in different nuclear accidents) is given and, thus, a mechanism.

As will be seen later, the authors specify numerous mechanisms that often consist, among other things, of single causal statements. In the previous example, thus, various mechanisms could be distinguished. One could be "the emergence of groups," another the "valuation of objects" which has changed after the nuclear accident (an "event" in the terminology of the authors). We will later discuss some of the mechanisms the authors suggest in more detail.

The authors aim at specifying *dynamic* mechanisms, i.e. social processes. These are sequences of mechanisms (see the quotation above), in other words: "Processes are regular sequences of such mechanisms that produce similar (generally more complex and contingent) transformations of those elements" (24). The simplest mechanism is a one-step causal sequence. That is to say, a class of events has several effects that conform to the above definition. An illustration is:

Nuclear accident → formation of new protest groups.

A process would be:

Nuclear accident → formation of new protest groups → repressive action by government → new protests → decision of government to shut down nuclear power plants.

This sequence only counts as a process if it is regular and brings about "similar (generally more complex and contingent) transformations" of the elements. "Regular" might mean "at least twice."[5] Our illustration would conform to this definition if such processes can be observed not only once but are "regular" and bring about similar transformations. For example, the same process might be observed at the Chernobyl disaster in 1986.

There is still another requirement mechanisms must fulfill. "Contention" refers to "episodic" events or processes, as was seen above.

Another emphasis in the authors' approach is that explanations of contention must take into account several actors and their relations. In this respect, the authors want to go beyond the extant social movement agenda that, in their opinion, focuses just on one actor.

The authors further delineate the procedure of their "explanatory agenda" (28–29): the first step is to identify contentious episodes with some problematic feature; then processes within these episodes are located that bring about that problematic feature; then the "crucial" causal mechanisms are searched. In a final step the goal is to find similar episodes in different historical periods. The authors illustrate the procedure with a set of episodes "in which people respond to increased repression by striking back at their enemies instead of fleeing or subsiding into passivity" (29). Then processes such as mobilization or polarization are discovered. "Within those processes we will find such mechanisms as collective attribution of threat and reinforcement of commitment producing crucial effects" (29). This, then, is a "causal account of resistance to massive threat" (29). The next step is to search "similarities and differences with conflict streams that have occurred elsewhere or in the same system in different historical moments" (29). When this step is taken the "entire stream of confrontations" is taken as a single episode (29).

A final example might further clarify what the authors aim at. The cases they discuss at the beginning of the book and which are taken as examples throughout the book are the French Revolution, the American civil rights movement and Italian contention in the sixties. In these different cases, the authors find "a number of common mechanisms that moved the conflicts along and transformed them: creation of new actors and identities through the very process of contention; brokerage by activists who connected previously insulated local clumps of aggrieved people, competition among contenders that led to factional divisions and re-alignments, and much more. These mechanisms concatenated into more complex processes such as radicalization and polarization of conflict; formation of new balances of power; and re-alignments of the polity along new lines" (33).

The authors also make clear what they reject: they do not want to identify "necessary and sufficient conditions for mobilization, action, or certain trajectories" (13). First of all, this is a very strange statement, because in their research program they wish to identify mechanisms and "the ways they combine, in what sequences they recur, and why different combinations and sequences, starting from different *initial conditions*, produce varying effects on the large scale" (12–13, italics not in the original). Thus, the authors explicitly state that they wish to discover *conditions*. Isn't it then of utmost importance to learn whether these conditions are necessary or sufficient?

Furthermore, the authors do not want to apply general theories, i.e. they do not intend "to pour all forms of contention into the same great mold, subjecting them to universal laws of contention and flattening them into a single two-dimensional caricature" (13), or, put differently, "stamping of the same general laws onto all the world's contention" (314) is rejected. Two points are noteworthy. One is the disparaging language that indicates a rather emotional rejection of the application of theories or general laws in the field of contentious politics. Instead, arguments would be preferable which are missing. We will return to this point later. A second noteworthy point is that the authors only refer to "universal laws of contention." Later they point out that their aim "is not to construct general models of revolution, democratization, or social movements" (37). In general, it seems that the authors are against theories of the middle range referring to phenomena that can be subsumed under "contention." This position does not imply that the application of general theories is inappropriate as well. However, general theories are rejected as well. We will return to this claim later.[6]

Collective action theory is not included in the "classic approach," although M. Olson's book was published already in 1965 and, thus, earlier than the basic writings of the other approaches. However, in looking beyond the "classic social movement agenda" to "intellectual resources" that could be applied to the field, the authors mention "rationalist analyses" (21). But this approach is entirely dismissed. We will return to this point later when we discuss the problems of the DCA.

The authors themselves summarize their agenda in a succinct way: they seek "explanation of contentious politics by identifying crucial mechanisms and processes within and across episodes" of contention (84).

2. Critique of the approach

The DCA raises various questions. One is whether the alternative approaches are so deficient that it is useful to dismiss them. A second set of issues concerns the research program of the DCA. These are the questions that are addressed in this section.

How bad is social movement theory?

To what extent is the authors' critique of social movement theory sound? Some points the authors raise are not well taken. One is that the classic social movement perspectives are static. The authors themselves show in their arguments that a theory that does not include time as a parameter can be applied in explaining a process of collective action sequentially (see also chapter 4 in this book). For example, assume the amount of mobilized resources is relevant for the growth or decline of the social movement sector; a trajectory of growth and decline of social movements can then be explained by a growth and decline of resources the movements were able to mobilize. It is a misunderstanding that a theory must explicitly refer to time in order to be applied to explain social processes.

It is also not correct that the classic agenda only provides "accounts of single actors rather than relations among actors" (72). For example, our reconstruction of the resource mobilization perspective (chapter 5) shows that a complex network of actors is the subject of the theory. In the political opportunity structure and framing perspective at least two actors are involved. Even if several actors and their interaction is not explicitly modeled, it may nonetheless be possible to apply the basic propositions of the approaches to derive propositions about behavior of several actors. This question is not discussed by the authors.

A problem of the authors' critique of the classic social movement perspectives is that it is not based on a clear reconstruction of the approaches. Chapters 5 to 8 of this book show how ambiguous the structure of their propositions is. So the question is what the hypotheses are that the authors refer to in their critique. It seems that they just look at the core variables: resources, opportunities, frames, and identities (see Figure 1.2, 17). But there is much more than just these core variables, as we have seen in previous chapters.

There are many shortcomings of social movement theory that the authors do not address. Major critical points raised in the previous chapters of this book are not discussed. For example, conceptual problems of the basic variables such as "resources" or "political opportunities" are not mentioned. Problems of the framing approach are still more severe, as chapter 8 indicates. Thus, the state of social movement theory is more problematic than the authors' critique suggests.

The rejection of "rationalist analyses"

As was said before, the application of collective action theory, rational choice theory or any other theory is not regarded as fruitful. What are the reasons? The devastating critique (22–24, 57) is a caricature of the theory of collective action and the rational choice approach. It is typical that no literature is cited for which the critique holds. For example, who regards "individual minds as the basic, or even the unique, sites of social reality and action" (23)? One wonders how insane proponents of "rationalist analyses" are supposed to be.

When the authors discuss their own approach they refer to Hedström and Swedberg's book (1998) that advances a mechanism-based approach. The authors make clear that they do not accept "methodological individualism" because Hedström and Swedberg "focus only on mechanisms that operate at the individual level" (25). This is a clear misunderstanding. The thrust of methodological individualism as it is pursued by modern rational choice theory is a micro-macro orientation (see, e.g., chapter 3 of this book).

Another misunderstanding is that "general models like rational choice ... purport to summarize whole categories of contention and move toward the analysis of smaller-scale causal mechanisms ..." (24). Since rational choice theory is capable of explaining very specific phenomena there is no necessity to refer to "whole categories of contention." The categories chosen may be more or less specific, depending on the research question. Further, there is no necessity to move "toward the analysis of smaller-scale causal mechanisms." Existing work analyzes, among other things, large-scale historical processes, as the work of Douglass North and others attests (see, e.g., North and Thomas 1973; North 1981).

A dynamic analysis is by no means outside the agenda of "rationalist analyses." It concurs, for example, nicely with the application of balance theory (chapter 9). As Doreian (2002: 117) notes: "... studying event sequences seems the most useful way of discerning the operation of balance theoretic processes. With that knowledge gained, generalized mechanisms and their operation can be elaborated." Applying rational choice theory to explain social processes is straightforward: the basic idea is that changes in the independent variables of the theory, i.e. changes of incentives, determine changes of behavior which then results in macro phenomena (see, for details, chapter 1). In regard to the explanation of mechanisms – also in the sense of social processes – the collection of essays in the book by Hedström and Swedberg (1998) show how rational actor theory can be applied.

There are other grave misunderstandings. In their first programmatic statement of the DOC approach McAdam, Tarrow, and Tilly (1996) concede that proponents of the rational choice perspective are correct "to stress the importance of incentives to the study of individual activism" (25). The critique then is that they fall short "in their extremely narrow – and generally materialist – conception of incentives." Another charge is the "traditional rational choice imagery of isolated individuals" (26). Tilly (1997) in responding to Lichbach (1997) writes that Lichbach fails to recognize the "radical limitations" of rational choice theory: the theory accounts only for "conscious decisions" (108), it explains "only one kind of decision: whether to participate in an action or not" (109). All this – and much more in Tilly's article – is plainly wrong, as our discussion of the theory of rational action and micro-macro modeling in chapter 1 clearly shows. The only interesting point in such blatant misrepresentations of a theory is how it can be explained that renowned scholars do not bother to read the rational choice literature more carefully. This is a personal remark and, maybe, it should be kept private. But for a proponent of the rational choice approach it is of utmost frustration to see that a serious discussion is not possible because it is not even known what its basic propositions are.

There is another point why the rejection of "rationalist analyses" is difficult to understand: it contradicts the author's own agenda. As we will see, the authors apply the resource mobilization and political opportunity structure perspectives throughout their book. We have shown in chapters 5 and 6, that these approaches are based on rational choice theory. Thus, the question arises how one could accept and apply – at least to some extent – certain propositions (namely the resource mobilization and opportunity structure perspectives), but not the underlying theory.

The general claim that "rationalist ... approaches do not provide sufficient means for the task at hand" (73) is thus unwarranted. The existing work in the tradition of the theory of collective action shows the opposite. Apart from our discussion in previous chapters, the following example illustrates this. The protest cycle model, developed by S. Tarrow, posits increasing conflict and diffusion of collective action before activities decline (for a summary see 65–66). The authors then state that the weakness of this model is that the process does not need to follow the neat parabolic trajectory. Many things may happen that generate other trajectories. This would also follow from collective action theory. The process of collective action will not take a lawful course but depends on the existing conditions. Collective action theory even helps to explain under what conditions which trajectory is to be expected. In a former chapter (chapter 6, Figure 6.5) such conditions were specified for different trajectories of protest. This example and the existing work of the theory of collective action casts serious doubt on the authors' contention that a "rationalist" framework is doomed to failure.

Should a bad theory be applied?

To be sure, there are many flaws of social movement theory, but is this a justification for not further applying it? One will dismiss a theory only if no better one is available. This seems to be the authors' position as well: they state that the classic approach "provides *relatively* weak guides to explanation of action, identities, trajectories, or outcomes" (37, italics not in the original), and they recommend the use of perspectives as a "source of ideas." They even "call upon the major concepts developed out of the study of social movements in western democracies since the 1960s to make a start" (33). Actually, these concepts are applied throughout the book. This becomes clear in their theoretical framework in Figure 2.1 (45): it comprises "attribution of threat/opportunity" (this is the major variable of the political opportunity structure approach), "organizational appropriation" (i.e. appropriation of resources, the major variable of the resource mobilization approach). "Framing" is not explicitly included in this scheme, but used as a key factor throughout the book (see, e.g., 48).[7] The same holds for "identity" (see, e.g., 56–56). Thus, the authors actually apply the traditional approaches: throughout their book resources, opportunities, identities and frames carry the explanation of contention in their case studies.

The problems of the social movement perspectives imply that many explanations the authors suggest are highly problematic. For example, assume one finds that after the occurrence of a class of events certain episodes of collective action obtain such as the formation of terrorist groups and new political parties. The traditional social movement approaches are not capable of explaining that exactly these outcomes were to be expected. They predict only, at best, that some form of political action will occur. Thus, the theory does not imply that those specific events originate. The dubious explanatory strategy is: changes in resources, opportunities, frames, or identities are identified; then these changes are regarded as the causes of specific forms of contentious politics that have been observed. This causal attribution is *ad hoc*, it does not follow from the theory. In other words, the theory applied does not imply that the specific phenomena originate.

Another problem of the authors' application of social movement theory is that unclear concepts such as opportunities are applied *ad hoc*. That is, certain phenomena that preceded changes in contention are simply called "opportunities" without providing empirical evidence whether the (actual or perceived) chances of success have changed.

Thus, it is legitimate to apply social movement theory if the authors think there is no better alternative. However, one should then be aware of the major problems and describe them, including an outline of the possible flaws in the explanation.

Broadening the field of study

The authors anticipate one critique of their claim to broaden the field of study: the definition of "contentious politics" is too broad (5). Our discussion in chapter 1 showed that a wide working definition of a concept is theoretically fruitful. Thus, instead of concentrating on specific phenomena like revolutions or strikes it seems useful to switch to a broad explanandum that encompasses these and other phenomena.

Could the definition of "contentious politics" not be even broader? For example, why must a government be a claimant? A strike in which opponents are unions and firms or employer organizations would not fall under "contentious politics." Furthermore, the criterion "public" excludes, for example, protests of an association of tenants against owners of a housing unit who raise rents. Why are such restrictions theoretically fruitful?

Whether a broad working definition is theoretically fruitful must be tested if a theory has been formulated. It can then be examined whether the theory can explain the different phenomena designated by the broad concept. But if no theory is applied, which is a claim of the authors of the DCA, the theoretical fruitfulness of the broad concept cannot be tested. Nonetheless, those who do not subscribe to the authors' rejection of theories could test whether "contentious politics" is a theoretically fruitful concept. That would be an interesting question as an explanandum of the theory of collective action.

The authors' criterion for the fruitfulness of the broad definition is whether for all the different phenomena subsumed under "contentious politics" at least some identical mechanisms can be found. The detailed case studies suggest that at least for many kinds of contention identical mechanisms exist. But it is not clear whether a wider definition is not even more useful. Are there common mechanisms for those kinds of "contention" that do not fall under the umbrella of "contentious politics"? For example, why not study *conflict* in the sense of "interaction among makers of claims and their objects"? Although this definition comprises more cases than one would probably like to study, one may simply concentrate on the cases of interest. This would be a similar procedure as suggested in chapter 2 when we defined "protest."

The focus on dynamics

The claim to intensify the study of dynamics is like carrying coal to Newcastle: numerous scholars try to explain the development of protest or, in terms of the DCA, of contention over time. Examples are explanations of revolutions such as the East European revolutions beginning in 1989. So the focus on dynamics is not new and generally accepted.

However, the authors are right that often just the emergence of a movement or certain protest events are explained. But this is interesting and important work as well. First, data on dynamics are often not available, and a "static" explanation is better than no explanation. Second, explanation of a single event may be the first step in a dynamic explanation. Nonetheless, no scholar will probably disagree that in principle dynamic analyses are an important research agenda in the social sciences in general and that more effort should be invested in explaining processes of contention over time.

From single to multiple actor explanations

The authors are right when they assert that social movement studies often concentrate on one actor although, as was said already, this is not generally true. Many accounts in the social movement literature include several actors. Are these accounts principally flawed? If that would be the case it would no longer be legitimate to focus on the development of specific movements like the civil rights movement in the USA or the anti-nuclear movement in Germany. Furthermore, it would no longer be legitimate to look at the development of protest in a single country like Switzerland.

In this work scholars focus on one actor. But this does not imply that other actors are completely ignored. It is obvious that in explaining the development of the civil rights movement other actors like the church are taken into account. However, the focus on a given movement means that the behavior of the other actors is not explained. Instead, their action or reaction is taken as given and its effect on the development of a movement is explained.

Is such work problematic? First of all, explanations focusing on one actor are not wrong, if they take into account reactions of other actors which are taken as given. However, such explanations are incomplete: the explanation of the reactions of the other actors is missing. Is this a flaw? Every explanation takes certain facts as given. If that is rejected, an *infinite regress* would be the consequence: if one has explained a certain phenomenon with, say, factor x as a cause, the explanation is regarded as flawed because x is not explained. If then x is explained by, say, factor z, it is criticized that z is not explained. This critique could continue infinitely. To avoid such an infinite regress one should accept every correct explanation and at the same time suggest that it would be interesting to explain the causal factors. For example, in explaining the development of a movement that is influenced by the church, a next interesting research question would be to explain why the church supported the movement.

Focusing on one actor is often a first step of a more complete explanation. For example, a researcher may begin by explaining the development of a social movement. It turns out that the support of important societal actors changed over time. A next step could then be to explain why the support of these actors changed.

This strategy of avoiding an infinite regress is also implicitly followed by the authors. They too take many phenomena as given. For example, the mechanisms the authors proposed are not explained. For example, it is not explained why the "itinerant workers" (i.e. the "brokers") diffuse information or, in general, why people or institutions take the role of brokers. Furthermore, the authors time and again emphasize that they provide "partial explanations" (see, e.g., 306). Thus, incomplete or partial explanations are the rule in the social sciences, and one should not condemn them. It is preferable to try to improve our knowledge by engaging in new research to close the gaps.

To conclude, focusing on one actor is a legitimate research goal. Depending on the explanatory problem, the action or reaction of other actors must be taken into account as given. If their behavior is not explained, this does not invalidate the explanation, it is incomplete. A next fruitful question would then be to explain the behavior of other actors as well.

The comparative agenda and the search for empirical regularities

A major goal of the DCA is to compare mechanisms in different situations. The finding is that "similar mechanisms and processes play significant parts in quite different episodes, but produce varying overall outcomes depending on their sequence, combination, and context" (306).

One ingredient of this agenda is comparative research. This is hardly a contended research program in the social sciences. "Comparative politics" or "comparative sociology" are special fields of study. There are even journals devoted to comparative research.

What are the results of the comparisons? For example, the authors identify "three crucial processes that recur in roughly the same form in a wide variety of episodes of contention" (314). One is the "constitution of new political actors and identities within contentious episodes" (314, for other examples see below). These mechanisms are thus "empirical generalizations" or "empirical regularities." The authors even speak of "partial theories" about "robust causal similarities" (33). This means that the hypotheses refer to specific times and places and are thus no theories or lawful statements.

However, the research agenda comes very close to formulating theories in the strict sense when the authors recommend to "establish scope conditions with regard to time, space, and social setting under which such partial theories hold and those in which they do not" (33). Why could the specification of scope conditions not result in general propositions? Why is that principally excluded? This is the major problem of the approach which will be discussed in detail in the next section. As long as the "mechanisms" specified do only refer to special cases our general knowledge about social processes is not enhanced. The mechanisms provide existential statements such as:

> There are episodes of contention in which new actors are constituted.
> There are episodes of contention in which brokers diffuse information among actors.

Such "there-are"-statements are not very informative. We do not learn under what conditions which mechanisms obtain. When we wish to analyze new episodes of contention we always must investigate whether a mechanism is present. Is such a procedure really an explanation? We doubt it. The following sections will further pursue this question.

Do mechanism-based explanations require theories?

As was shown before, the authors reject any theory at all and, thus, do not intend to propose new theoretical propositions either. This implies that the covering law model of explanation is rejected as well. There is no detailed discussion of this position. Nonetheless, it is important to discuss the arguments for such an important claim.

The authors' aim is explanation. For example, they claim that "mechanisms and processes" are the "workhorses of explanation" (30). Thus, mechanism-based explanations include causal statements and, thus, causal explanation. This is also in line with the authors' claim to "offer new answers to old questions" (36), because the old questions refer to causal relations such as (38): "Under what conditions will normally apathetic, frightened, or disorganized people explode into the streets, put down their tools, or mount the barricades?"

The basic point that mechanisms and processes are sequences of causal statements is also undergirded when we look at the definition of "mechanisms": they are defined, as was seen above, as a "limited class of events that alter relations among specified sets of elements in identical or closely similar ways over a variety of situations." The expression "a limited class of *events*" is equivalent to "a limited class of *conditions*." For example, a nuclear accident is an event and a condition for spawning social processes such as group formation and protest.

The major problem of simply denoting some events x as causes and other events y as effects is that this is completely *ad hoc*, i.e. arbitrary. The reason is that any argument is missing that provides evidence for the claim that x causes y. How do the authors know, for example, that in a certain episode "social appropriation" has caused "innovative action" (316)? Is it the authors' intuition that speaks in favor of this statement? That would be hardly a satisfactory answer. Is it prior research that is in line with the causal statement? If this is the case, how do the authors know that the results of prior research hold in the new setting as well? The only adequate answer is that a general statement is invoked, i.e. a law or theory, that states (or implies) that social appropriation in general leads to innovative action. It seems that the authors advance this proposition, as their causal diagram (317) suggests. However, the authors never provide an explicit answer to the question of how they validate their causal claims.

The previous paragraph is a short summary of the detailed discussion of the role of laws or theories in explanations that was given in chapter 1. To reiterate, theories such as those presented in chapter 1 state that in general certain conditions have certain effects. In specific situations then the theories allow the researcher to identify the specific conditions that have brought about a phenomenon. To reiterate, doing away with theories leaves the question unanswered how the researcher can identify causes.[8] The authors of the DCA do not provide an answer to this question either.

Perhaps the most convincing argument for the covering law model in the present context is that the authors violate their own methodology of not applying theory permanently. Although the "classic" movement perspectives are criticized, the authors apply them in their substantive analyses of mechanisms throughout their book.

The authors' "dynamic, interactive framework for analyzing mobilization in contentious politics" which is depicted as a causal diagram (45) is a system of general propositions, i.e. a theory. One of the statements is that "attribution of threat/opportunity" has a causal effect on "social appropriation." As this lawful statement illustrates, the explanatory value of the authors' propositions in the causal diagram is relatively low. The laws can best be characterized as orienting statements. For example, it is not explained what kind of "social appropriation" the actors choose. The causal diagram includes "innovative collective action" as a dependent variable, and it is claimed that "organizational appropriation" has an effect on "innovative collective action" (45). Again, this is a law. But it lacks information: the form this action takes is left open. Thus, again, the causal diagram depicts a system of lawful statements.[9]

It is important to note that at least four of the variables in this diagram are mechanisms, as the authors state later on when they discuss mechanisms operating in the course of the French revolution (61). There are thus causal relations between the mechanisms. These are lawful statements as well. To illustrate, the authors assume that there is a causal feedback effect between the mechanisms "identity shift" and "category formation" (317).

The effects of specific mechanisms the authors suggest are often formulated in a general way. For example "brokerage" means that previously insulated individuals or groups will be connected (a more precise definition is given below). It is then assumed that this mechanism has an effect on mobilization or contentious politics. This is a general statement in which it is claimed that a mechanism has some effect. Furthermore, for some of the mechanisms it is claimed that they can be found in all processes of mobilization. This is a lawful statement as well. For example, when the authors discuss the mechanisms "collective attribution of opportunity and threat," "social appropriation," and "brokerage," they speculate that these mechanisms "will turn out to be robust components of any process of mobilization and demobilization" (123). To be sure, "this speculation needs to be refined, replicated, and tested" (123); but there can be no question that the authors propose a law.

The book is full of all sorts of other lawful statements. For example: "... shared prior knowledge, connections among key individuals, and the on-the-spot direction guide the flow of collective action" (49). This hypothesis does not refer to any time and place and is thus a lawful statement. But, again, it is only an orienting statement: it is not specified what kind of prior knowledge, what kind of connections between what kind of individuals affect what form of collective action. The authors' hypotheses about identities are clearly general, i.e. lawful statements as well (56). To provide a final illustration, the authors claim that a mobilization process "consists of a combination of attribution of opportunities and threats, social appropriation, construction of frames, situations, identities and innovative collective action" (70). This is a proposition, not confined to any time and place and, thus, by definition a law or lawful statement. These examples could be multiplied.

Sometimes the authors apply pure rational choice theory. For example, when they analyze the strategic situation of contentious actors, they look at the behavioral alternatives of a single actor and the distribution of possible outcomes. This could be a textbook example for an application of the theory of rational action.

To summarize, there can be no doubt that the authors apply laws or theories – whatever their explanatory power might be. If laws or theories are applied, why not in an explicit and rigorous way? The answer seems to be that the authors are not aware that they actually apply laws or theories. They claim: "No general law has been proposed here for the study of contentious politics, nor will it be in our book" (70). As has been shown before, this is plainly wrong.

In regard to the kind of theories that can be applied an important distinction is to be made: application of theories is not equivalent with "general models of revolution, democratization, or social movements" (37). These kinds of theories must be distinguished from general theories of action. The authors reject the application of theories in general. However, one might take the position that valid macro theories about protest, democratization, etc. do not exist and will probably not be discovered. This is plausible from the perspective of general theories that show that macro propositions hold only under certain conditions, as was seen in previous chapters. However, general social psychological theories exist that are well confirmed and that can be applied to explain contentious politics (see chapter 1 in this book). But, as was shown before, the authors reject any kind of theory.

To conclude, the authors (1) do not provide detailed arguments why they do not want to apply theories. (2) The major argument in favor of applying theories is that they are the only way to avoid *ad hoc* causal statements: theories provide information about which conditions lead to which effects. (3) The authors violate their own methodological rules by applying not only the key propositions of the existing social movement perspectives, they further suggest several causal models, each depicted as a causal diagram, which are clearly theories. Furthermore, the models assume that there are lawful relations between mechanisms. (4) In addition, the book is full of other lawful statements, including explicit applications of rational choice theory.

The perspective applied: To what extent do the proposed mechanisms explain episodes of contention?

The major part of the authors' book consists of detailed analyses of 15 episodes of contention (see Table 3.1 on p. 76 where the cases are listed). In addition, the authors specify numerous mechanisms (I counted 22)[10] that are introduced in different sections of the book and are applied to several episodes of contention. In order to judge the merits of the approach it is not only important to look at the proposed research program, but also at the empirical analyses in which the program is applied. The reason is that the research program and its application may be inconsistent. One such inconsistency was already discussed: we saw that the claim was to refrain from applying theories, but actually theories have been applied. This section looks at the logical structure of the mechanisms the authors propose: are they really singular causal statements or are they general propositions? It is not possible and not necessary either to analyze each of the mechanisms. We will concentrate on a few and leave it open whether the results of our analyses hold for the other mechanisms as well. We think, that they hold, but because it is not shown, we confine our judgment to the mechanisms analyzed.

Collective attribution of threat and opportunity

This mechanism "involves (a) invention or importation and (b) diffusion of a shared definition concerning alterations in the likely consequences of possible actions (or, for that matter, failures to act) undertaken by some political actor" (95). Thus, this mechanism is given if there is a diffusion of a group of actors' shared belief that the consequences of their behavior change. This mechanism is applied, for example, to contribute to the explanation of the Mau Mau revolt in Kenya in the early to mid-1950s (92–93). The parties involved in this insurrection "interpreted major social changes as significant threats and opportunities" (95–96). One of these major social changes was "the postwar trend toward decolonization and the wave of nationalist movements" (96). For the white settlers and the colonial government this trend was a threat. They probably suspected that their power would be compromised. The Kenyan nationalists, however, "viewed these events as evidence that an unprecedented opportunity for independence lay at hand." The authors posit that the result of this situation was "increased mobilization in Kenya and elsewhere in Africa" (96). Thus, major social changes affected the consequences of behavior for certain groups. In particular for the nationalists the consequences of political action changed: the likelihood that their collective action contributed to political independence of their country increased.

What exactly is meant by the "mechanism" of collective attribution of threat and opportunity?[11] The definition refers to "alterations in the likely consequences of possible actions" without specifying what the actions and the consequences are. If it comes to the explanation of specific episodes of contention, the respective actions and the consequences must be determined empirically. Thus, the "mechanism" is a change of a set of variables: the likelihood of various consequences for given actions may more or less change. It is important to note that the definition of the mechanism does not say anything about the *effects* of these variables. It only says that perceived consequences change. If that is the case the mechanism is given. But that does not mean that these consequences affect behavior. At least this is not part of the definition of the mechanism.[12]

Social appropriation

This mechanism denotes the "active appropriation of sites for mobilization" (44). It is introduced when the authors describe mobilization in the civil rights movement (47–48) and refers to capacity of challengers "to appropriate sufficient organization and numbers to provide a social/organizational base – and not that organization itself – which makes mobilization possible. Would-be activists (members no less than challengers and subjects) must either create an organizational vehicle or utilize an existing one and transform it into an instrument of contention" (47). This "process of social appropriation" applies, the authors note, to all groups involved in a contentious episode.

The mechanism refers to the process of mobilizing resources. There may be numerous forms of resources, as was seen in chapter 5. They range from the "appropriation of sites" to the activities that make organizations to allies. The mechanism thus signifies mobilization activities. This is a variable: mobilization activities may be more or less frequent or more or less intense. But it is also plausible that the mechanism denotes a successful mobilization. The mechanism then describes a causal relationship between activities and outcomes: "social appropriation" is given *if* actors gain control of resources (i.e. are successful in mobilizing resources).

Assume that the latter is the correct interpretation. What is explained by the mechanism? It is *not* explained what the conditions are when actors succeed in appropriating resources. Second, it is left open what the effect of the "appropriation" is on collective action or contentious politics. Third, we do not find clear hypotheses about possible indirect effects of "appropriation" on collective action or contention. For example, appropriation may increase perceived influence which, in turn, makes collective action of contention more likely.

It is important to note that the definition described in the previous paragraph includes a causal statement.[13] The problem is that a causal effect must be established before we know whether a mechanism is given.

Brokerage

This mechanism is defined as "the linking of two or more previously unconnected social sites by a unit that mediates their relations with one another and/or with yet other sites" (26). It is a mechanism that relates groups and individuals that were previously unconnected. For example, there may be two tribes in different villages that have no connection. A broker who may be a single person may initiate contacts and speak on the behalf of the groups to, say, a district police commissioner (142). Brokerage "also operates with cliques, organization, places and, at the limit, programs" (142).

In the literature on collective action and social movements the "broker" is often a leader or a political entrepreneur. But the concept of broker is wider: it may also include groups and individuals that are not directly involved in a struggle. For example, in the account of the Mau Mau revolt the authors mention "itinerant traders" who did not establish new connections between villages or groups but functioned as agents of diffusion of certain information. They performed this function already long before the conflict. In general, brokers include "local elites, arbitrators, biculturals, interpreters, interlocutors, political entrepreneurs, nobles, priests and chiefs" (142).

In what sense is "brokerage" a "mechanism"? It denotes a causal effect: *if* individuals link certain sites, then, by definition, these individuals are brokers and the process is, by definition, "brokerage." Note, that this definition includes a causal statement: whether "brokerage" obtains can only be determined if there are individuals or groups and if their activities establish some relation.

What aspects of an episode of contentious politics does this mechanism explain? First, it is not explained under what conditions individuals are successful brokers. For example, the "itinerant traders" may not be trustworthy and their messages would not diffuse. Second, it is not explained either what the effects of successful brokerage are. For example, assume the itinerant traders' activities actually contributed to the diffusion of information. They are thus successful brokers. It is left open what the effect of the diffusion of certain messages on mobilization or political action are. Third, brokerage could have indirect effects on mobilization or collective action. For example, the messages diffused by brokers might increase political discontent which, in turn, spawns new protests. All these questions are not answered. The mechanism thus explains very little, if it explains anything at all.

Certification and decertification

Certification refers to the "validation of actors, their performances, and their claims by external authorities" (121). Accordingly, decertification is "the withdrawal of such validation by certifying agents" (123). This mechanism is illustrated with the trial and imprisonment of Jomo Kenyatta and other Kenyan nationalist leaders in the Mau Mau revolt. This was an "effective" decertification of Kenyatta, the other leaders, and even the Mau Mau rebellion (122).

This mechanism is a variable: actors may more or less certify or decertify other actors. Certification may be more or less successful. That is to say, if there are certifying or decertifying efforts by the government or by insurgents others need not accept them. The extent to which certification efforts are successful has thus to be explained. If such efforts are successful, the next question is what their impact is on mobilization and contentious action or on factors that, in turn, influence mobilization or contentious politics. These questions are not answered by the mechanism.

Category formation

A "category" denotes "a set of sites that share a boundary distinguishing all of them from and relating all of them to at least one set of sites visibly excluded by the boundary" (143). For example, a new category is formed "when Bosnian Serb leaders decree who in Bosnia is a Serb and who not" (143).

This mechanism is a variable. It seems to be a dichotomous variable: a category may be applied or not applied. The authors discuss various effects of category formation. Their proposition is that "category formation powerfully affects the identities in the name of which participants in contention interact" (144). But these effects are not identical with the mechanism. Separate analyses are necessary to discover the effects of category formation. Again, the mechanism does not explain anything, it is just a variable.

Conclusion

The question of this section has been to what extent the specific mechanisms the authors propose explain aspects of contention. The mechanisms discussed in this section show that there are two types of mechanisms. One consists simply of variables. An example is category formation which refers to applying or not applying some category to a class of objects. These mechanisms do not per se have any explanatory power, they are concepts or variables. In order to explain anything the variables must be related to other variables. This is what the authors actually do: they suggest various hypotheses that include these concepts. But it is important to note that these mechanisms themselves do not explain anything.

The second type of mechanisms are causal statements. For example, "brokerage" means that some relations between objects are established. More precisely, "brokerage" is given *if* objects are connected. Thus, the definition includes a causal statement. The problem is that we know only whether a definition is given if the causal effect has been determined in a particular situation. What exactly do such mechanisms explain? The answer is: very little. First of all, it is not explained when the effect the mechanism refers to obtains. For example, when is brokerage successful? Second, it is not explained what the effect on contention is. Third, it is not explained whether there is any indirect effect on contention via other variables. For example, if brokerage is successful, it may increase discontent which, in turn, affects contention.

These conclusions are based on the mechanisms analyzed before. We do not want to carry out the same analyses as before for all the 22 mechanisms that we have counted in the book. Our judgment is, however, that the other mechanisms are not different.

However, the authors include the mechanisms as components of many new hypotheses in their book. For example, we pointed already out that causal hypotheses are suggested that link the mechanisms to other variables. This is the major thrust of their book. But this means that the explanation is carried by those additional hypotheses. A problem of these additional hypotheses is that the explanations are not based on the explicit application of theory.

3. The free rider problem and the missing micro-macro modeling

The DCA is a macro perspective. It can thus not be expected that it includes explicit micro-macro modeling. As is typical for macro approaches, the micro level is often invoked but explicit micro-to-macro or macro-to-micro hypotheses are not proposed. This holds for the DCA as well. The question of how macro changes will motivate individual actors to participate in contentious action is not regarded as a problem. Thus, there is no detailed discussion of the free rider problem.

In a companion volume to the *Dynamics of Contention* book (Aminzade *et al.* 2001) McAdam (2001: 223–224) emphasizes the importance of micro-macro links. However, we do not find systematic micro-macro modeling in the sense that a micro theory is applied and that then the bridge assumptions are specified. In a similar vein the free rider problem is addressed in this volume. Aminzade and McAdam (2001: 17) critize the "formulation" of the free rider problem as the claim that selective incentives matter. It is argued that "this formulation ignores the power of emotions to shape both the assessment of potential gains and costs involved in any line of action the individual might take and perhaps to motivate action directly quite apart form any instrumental calculus of risks ad rewards. Intense fear can motivate action, even in the face of extreme risks and seemingly no hope for payoff" (17). It is no problem for the underlying theory of rational action if emotions have a causal impact on costs and benefits. For example, if fear of severe repression increases the costs of participating, then a negative selective incentive obtains; if positive sanctions come from friends if one participates, then a positive selective incentive obtains. The authors argue that emotions may not only affect incentives but may also supplant them. However, if fear (or other emotions) are costs or benefits, then, by definition, they *are* selective incentives. The mentioning of an "instrumental calculus" underlying the theory of collective action suggests that the authors refer to a narrow "economistic" rational actor model. Apparently, they think that selective incentives are material or "tangible" costs and benefits. As has been shown in chapter 1, a wide version of the theory of collective or rational action does not assume calculation or any "instrumentality" and includes all kinds of incentives. Therefore, the argument of the authors need not concern us here since we do not subscribe to the narrow version of "rationalist" analysis they criticize. Again, we find here the common misunderstandings of what rational choice theory actually claims.

4. What is a "mechanism"?

The term "mechanism" is defined in the following way, as was seen above: "Mechanisms are a delimited class of events that alter relations among specified sets of elements in identical or closely similar ways over a variety of situations" (24). When we presented this definition before we mentioned already some ambiguities. Leaving these aside, the question arises as to why this and no other definition is chosen. In answering this question it must be considered that the authors want to address similar processes that can be found in different settings. This is their dynamic and comparative focus. But why is it then necessary to restrict this agenda to events that alter "relations" among elements, and why must these alterations happen in "identical or closely similar ways over a variety of situations"?

An alternative specification of a process that does not change the authors' thrust is the following. Explaining complex processes means that one wishes to avoid simple explanations that consist of an independent and a dependent variable. An example is the statement "increased opportunities have brought about the revolutions in Eastern Europe." Explaining processes means to explain what happened between the class of events (namely, the increased opportunities) and the outcomes (namely, the revolutions). One could also say that the previous statement is a black box explanation: it does not address what happened between the opportunity changes and the revolutions. In other words, the aim is to extend such simple

Figure 10.1 An alternative definition of "mechanism"

explanations by specifying intervening variables or processes. The "mechanisms" could then be defined as the intervening variables or processes. Figure 10.1 (which is taken from Hedström and Swedberg 1998: 9) illustrates the structure of a mechanism. The "class of events" is the "input" in the figure, the effects of the events – whatever they may be – are the output. The intervening variables or processes are the mechanism. This is a clear and straightforward definition.

If this is too broad one could add some rules about the kinds of mechanisms that one wants to discover. For example, one rule could be to find common mechanisms in different settings. Another rule could be to find mechanisms that change relations between groups. In this case the relations should be specified. But why should such a restrictions be imposed?

It goes without saying that theories can and must be applied to establish what kind of input leads to which intervening processes and which intervening processes lead to what outcomes. Furthermore, as was emphasized, the definition of a mechanism is not only applicably to micro-macro relationships. To be sure, the micro-macro model (see, e.g., chapter 1) includes a mechanism. But the intervening processes may be located at the macro level.

The definition of mechanism proposed here avoids ambiguities, and captures the thrust of the research program of the authors of the DCA.

5. What can we learn from the dynamics of contention approach for the explanation of social movement phenomena?

One important innovation is the broadening of the field of inquiry. However, it has to be examined whether the specific definition of "contentious politics" is fruitful. Perhaps some restrictions of the definition could be dropped.

Some of the DCA's methodological postulates are important for further theory and research in social movements, protest and related phenomena. This holds, first of all, for the focus on dynamics, i.e. the explanation of processes of contention. A second fruitful postulate is to analyze in more detail the relationships between all major actors of an episode of contention. A third welcome part of the DCA agenda is to shift attention or at least to devote more attention from contentious episodes in the West to contentious politics "within and across world regions" (305). Fourth, more emphasis on comparative analysis seems acceptable as well.

To be sure, these claims are not new in the social sciences. But in the social movement literature and in political sociology in general there is no agenda that advances these claims simultaneously. For detailed explanations of the processes of protest, collective action or contention it seems important that more scholars try to pay attention to these postulates.

There is a lot that can *not* be learned from the DCA. Perhaps the most important deficit is the abomination of theory. The best argument against the rejection of any theory is that the authors themselves implicitly apply theories of various kinds throughout their book. Nonetheless, there is still too little theory. For example, most of the causal allegations are *ad hoc*: simply asserting that x is a cause of y without invoking any general theoretical foundation means that arguments are missing that could give good reasons for the causal statement.

We are also skeptical in regard to the explanatory value of the mechanisms the authors suggest. As the analysis of the examples in particular indicates, the mechanisms are either variables which per se do not explain anything, or they are defined as causal relations. Even if these statements are given (e.g. if there is a broker) they explain little.

6. Summary and conclusions

The most recent perspective focusing on social movement related phenomena is the "Dynamics of Contention" approach (DCA), advanced by D. McAdam, S. Tarrow, and Ch. Tilly (2001). The claims of this research program can be summarized as follows: (1) The field of study should be extended to "contentious politics" which is much wider than social movements and protest. It includes, for example, phenomena like strikes, ethnic conflicts, and democratization. (2) In contrast to the traditional social movement literature, the DCA focuses on social processes that consist of sequences and combinations of social mechanisms. These are given if a class of events alters relations between actors or other "elements in identical or closely similar ways over a variety of situations" (24). (3) A major difference to other approaches is that the DCA rejects any application of theory. In particular, the authors criticize "rational analysis" (i.e. the theory of collective action and rational choice theory) as inadequate.

The DCA has strengths and weaknesses. On the positive side is the critique of the "classic" social movement perspectives (resource mobilization, opportunities, framing), although several flaws that were discussed in previous chapters in this book are not mentioned. The extension of the field of study is welcome: it may yield more interesting information about differences and commonalities of various phenomena. Further strengths of the DCA is the focus on dynamics, the suggestion to consider in more detail all actors involved in contentious episodes, and the emphasis on comparative analysis.

The weaknesses of the DCA clearly predominate. A problem with the authors' critique of the extant social movement perspectives is that a theory is usually not eliminated unless there is a better one. The authors do not suggest any theoretical alternative at all. Despite the weaknesses of the "classic" social movement perspectives the authors apply them as a "source of ideas." Taking into account all the problems of these perspectives discussed in the previous chapters, the authors' explanatory accounts in their book are burdened with the respective problems. One and perhaps the major problem of the DCA is the outright damnation of theory. This includes in particular the rejection of "rationalist analyses," i.e. the theory of collective action and rational choice theory. This position is not supported by any detailed arguments. The most convincing counter-argument against the rejection of theory is the authors' implicit application of various theories, including hypotheses from the rational choice approach, throughout their book. A further problem of the DCA is that mechanisms that include causal statements are *ad hoc* if no theory is applied. In other words, only a theory can support the claim that a certain variable x has a causal effect on y. A detailed analysis of some of the great number of specific mechanisms the authors propose indicates that the explanatory power of the mechanisms to explain processes of contentious politics is rather limited.

The DCA focuses on macro propositions: it is a structural approach, as it is often called. It is therefore not surprising that micro-macro relations are not considered explicitly and systematically, and that the free rider problem is not addressed adequately. Another problem is why the authors define "mechanisms" in a certain way, given the thrust of their research program. In order to avoid the ambiguities and restrictions of their definition of a "mechanism" we suggest to denote intervening processes that occur between an event (or input) and its effect (or output) as mechanisms. Additional methodological rules can then be formulated to focus on the discovery of similar processes across types of contention or settings or on mechanisms where relationships between actors are altered due to critical events.

In general, thus, the DCA is no alternative to the existing perspectives that explain social movement phenomena. However, important questions are raised that are neglected in the existing literature. This does not imply that the specific analyses of various episodes of contention throughout their book are worthless. But they need a theoretical underpinning. Thus, the dynamics of contention approach is certainly an interesting addendum to the literature, but there are no sufficient arguments to give up the "classic" social movement agenda and in particular "rationalist analysis," i.e. the theory of collective action and general theories of action.

11 The structural-cognitive model

A synthesis of collective action, resource mobilization, political opportunity, identity, and framing perspectives

This chapter builds on the analyses of the previous chapters and is actually a synopsis of the major critique and extension of the existing theoretical perspectives. It is shown more explicitly than previously how the critical analyses and extensions yield a synthesis that is called the structural-cognitive model. This model is presented in the first part of this chapter. The second part provides several illustrations that suggest ideas of how the model could be applied.

1. The idea of a synthesis: the structural-cognitive model

The basic idea of the synthesis is a theoretical model that links the macro and the micro level. Such a model is exhibited in the upper graph of Figure 11.1. Let us first look at the macro level (arrow 4 of graph A). Some perspectives focus on propositions referring to this level. This holds in particular for the political opportunity and resource mobilization perspectives. An example is the hypothesis that increasing political opportunities lead to collective political action. A first important point in this context is that this hypothesis is actually not a causal but a correlational statement (for details see chapter 1). The reason is that the relationship between the macro variables is explained by reference to the micro level. Proponents of the political opportunity structure (POS) perspective argue that POSs influence incentives for political action. This implies that POSs affect collective political action via individual incentives. The relationship between POS and collective action is thus not a direct but an indirect causal effect – via the micro level. This holds for other macro propositions as well.

Other theoretical perspectives focus on the micro level. This holds for the identity and framing perspectives. In other words, the goal is to specify conditions for the change of individual behavior, attitudes or beliefs (arrow 2 of graph A). Thus, these perspectives are mainly concerned with a micro model. Especially in chapters 1, 3, and 4 we discussed in great detail existing hypotheses about individual protest action and suggested some extensions of extant models. It is claimed that the model specified there can fruitfully be applied to explain protest behavior on the micro level. Furthermore, it was suggested to apply general social psychological theories (see also below).

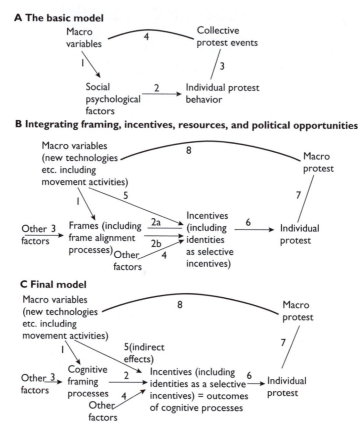

Figure 11.1 The structural-cognitive model: a synthesis of the major theoretical perspectives about social movements and political protest

There is one perspective that addresses both levels: the theory of collective action. For example, it is argued that discontent with the provision of public goods, the extent to which individual contributions matter, and selective incentives determine individual contributions to the provision of the public good. One of the macro propositions reads that in large groups the provision of public goods is unlikely. As we saw in chapter 3, this macro proposition is explained by relating its independent variable, namely group size, in specific ways to the independent variables of the micro model. However, it took a lot of effort to find out what exactly the micro-macro model was.

When we ignore the theory of collective action for a moment, the question arises whether micro and macro approaches are just two different schools that deal with different phenomena or whether there is some connection between micro and macro propositions. Actually, social movement scholars link both levels in their work. In each chapter of this book we analyzed in detail to what extent the major proponents of all approaches address the micro and the macro level. Our analyses clearly revealed that scholars from all perspectives use micro-macro explanations. For example, we find micro-macro explanations in the contributions by – in alphabetical order – B. Klandermans, D. McAdam, J. D. McCarthy, A. Melucci, and D. Snow and associates. This is a clear and unexpected result of the theoretical analyses provided in this book. But these micro-macro explanations were rarely proposed in an explicit and clear way. One has to read the texts very carefully to reconstruct the theoretical arguments of the authors.

How do the authors connect both levels? The procedure is to *explain macro relationships by invoking processes on the micro level*. Take as an example the proposition that increasing political opportunities raise collective action. The question arises, how such a relationship can be explained. For example, why should a person participate in a demonstration if on the macro level some political opportunity structure changes? The answer is that political opportunities affect collective action *because* opportunities change individual incentives (arrow 1 in graph A). This is a macro-to-micro relationship, i.e. a *bridge assumption*. It specifies how macro variables affect the micro level and thus "bridge" micro and macro level. This is thus a top-down relationship. More precisely, the macro-to-micro relationship indicates how macro variables affect factors on the micro level that lead to individual political action.

What about the relationship between individual protest behavior (micro level) and collective action (macro level)? The idea is that if a macro change has an impact on the individual determinants for protest then this change of individual motivations affects many individuals. This then leads in the aggregate to collective action (line 3 of graph A). Of course, a collective protest event is not just a summary of individual protests. The factors on the micro level must be specific enough to explain what form of individual protest participation is most likely. If this is the case then a collective action event like a demonstration indeed "consists of" the actions of many individuals. There is thus a micro-to-macro relationship which is also a *bridge assumption* – in this case a bottom-up relationship. But in contrast to the macro-to-micro bridge assumption this one is not an empirical but an analytical relationship: it is just an aggregation (such as the crime rate is an aggregation of individual criminal behavior).

To summarize, an explanation of a macro proposition such as "rising political opportunities increase collective action" reads that opportunities have an impact on individual determinants of protest behavior which, in turn, lead to the rise of individual action, which translate into collective action.

The fact that this kind of explanation is pursued – more or less explicitly – in the social movement literature suggests that micro-macro explanations are regarded as important. Why are they important? They answer the question of why a certain relationship originated and thus add *depth* to an explanation. One will not be satisfied just by noting that, for example, a repressive act of a government increased (and did not deter) political action (a macro proposition) but one wishes to know why that unexpected effect occurred. This question is answered when we know why *individuals* involved in the event reacted in a certain way when they were exposed to repression. The conclusion thus is that micro-macro explanations are in principal fruitful. Pure macro explanations do not answer important questions.

If this is accepted one wonders why such explanations are only adumbrated in the social movement literature. A full-fledged micro-macro explanation requires a clear micro model (arrow 2 in the figure). However, when micro-macro explanations are suggested the full micro model is rarely specified. It is typical that the authors just mention "incentives" as effects of macro changes or at best a single variable such as "cognitive liberation." Bridge assumptions are not spelled out either. For example, what exactly are the effects of a change of given macro factors? How exactly does individual action translate into collective action? These questions are largely not answered in the social movement literature.

Providing answers to these questions is the basic idea of a synthesis of the different approaches suggested in this book. The vast literature on social movements and political protest disposes of a great inventory of macro propositions. They can be a starting point for micro-macro explanations.[1] On the individual level, there are many propositions referring to the conditions that lead to individual protest behavior; other general propositions can be applied to generate such conditions. We are referring to propositions from the framing perspective, from identity theory, and from social psychological theories such as value expectancy theory or attitude theory (see, e.g., the theory by M. Fishbein and I. Ajzen). In chapters 3 and 4 a micro model is suggested that could be used – for the time being – in micro-macro explanations. Depending on the problem other theories such as balance theory (chapter 9) can be applied as well. An important task for future research is to improve these models.

Another ingredient of micro-macro explanations are macro-to-micro propositions (top-down hypotheses). This part of micro-macro explanations is perhaps the least developed in the social movement literature.

Finally, micro-to-macro propositions (i.e. bottom-up bridge assumptions) are at issue. As far as protest is concerned, these seem to be simple aggregations from individual to collective action. Thus, if incentives for many individuals to participate in a demonstration are strong, individuals will convene at a certain place at a certain time. This then is, by definition, a demonstration.

To summarize, the synthesis of the existing approaches aims at focusing on developing and testing micro-macro explanations. This approach is called the *structural-cognitive model* (SCM). This expression should emphasize the basic feature of the synthesis: it connects the macro level with the micro level. The term "cognitive" suggests that one major variable on the micro level is that individuals perceive (or recognize) the macro changes. In other words, the "definition" of the situation is important for individual action. Thus, structures (in a wide sense) *and* their perception are relevant. But "cognitions" also refer to other beliefs and, in general, to all kinds of elements in the mind of individuals, i.e. in the individual's cognitive system, that are relevant for protest behavior. In order to avoid the misunderstanding that a micro theory is limited to isolated individuals we repeat that beliefs also refer to the perception of social relationships. To be more specific, if we apply a theory such as value expectancy theory, the independent variables of this theory are the "cognitive" side of the SCM. All macro or social variables that have an impact on these variables are the "structural" side of the SCM. In a nutshell, the SCM is a micro-macro model.

To be sure, the proposed synthesis pursues the implicit research program of the existing theoretical perspectives. But it also corrects existing theorizing on the macro level. It was shown in previous chapters time and again that the application of general social psychological theories (including value expectancy theory, balance theory, cognitive dissonance theory, and attitude theory – for a detailed discussion see chapter 1) corrects macro propositions: it shows under which conditions they are valid. This implies that the SCM can also be applied when "other factors" are invoked. For example, scholars agree that identity alone or framing processes alone are not sufficient as determinants of collective action. Other factors are relevant. But what are these other factors? They are typically introduced *ad hoc*, i.e. not by applying a theory. The SCM claims that the explanatory power of the existing social psychological theories should also be explored in generating propositions about the "other factors."

2. The missing link: framing and the structural-cognitive model

The micro model which was suggested in chapters 3 and 4 is an application and extension of value expectancy theory that was first introduced to the field of social movement research by Bert Klandermans. It includes the major micro variables based on the theory of collective action. It was further discussed when we looked at macro factors such as societal resources or opportunities and their effects on individual incentives (chapters 5 and 6).

One problem in regard to a synthesis of existing micro theories was put forward by proponents of the identity approach: it is argued that two different micro theories are needed: one that addresses the effects of incentives, the other that addresses the impact of identity as conditions for protest. However, identity can be integrated into the micro model as a specific kind of incentive (chapter 7).

Another major problem that has not yet been addressed – neither in this book nor in the literature – is what a synthesis of the framing perspective and the micro model based on value expectancy theory could look like. A suggestion to answer this question is the aim of this section. Graph B in Figure 11.1 depicts the argument in graphical form.

The basic proposition of the framing perspective (see Snow *et al.* 1986 and chapter 8 of this book) is that social movement activities, i.e. certain factors at the macro level, lead to frame alignment processes on the micro level (see relationship 1 in graph B of Figure 11.1). The authors restrict their analysis to the alignment of frames of social movements and unmobilized individuals. In a more general theory of protest and social movement activities, framing processes in general should be the focus of attention. This is also the recent development in the social movement literature. For example, young people may change their views on violence when they watch the atrocities of war on TV. Thus, social movement activities are not necessary to change frames. Therefore, the macro factors are no longer only movement activities but, in addition, other properties of the larger social structure (some of which Snow *et al.* mention) such as wars, natural disasters, or splits in a government. This is taken into account in relationship 1 that addresses not only movement activities but macro factors in general.

Another assumption of the framing perspective is that frame alignment has a direct effect on protest behavior ("support for and participation in SMOs," as Snow *et al.* claim) – see arrow 2 in graph A of the figure. The reason why this relationship is not included in graph B will be discussed below.

Value expectancy theory claims that perceived behavioral consequences, their valuation and subjective probabilities are the major determinants of protest behavior. How can these variables – which we will call for ease of reference "incentives" – be integrated into the framing model? One possibility is to extend the framing model by including incentives as an additional set of variables. The hypothesis thus would be that frame alignment, along with public goods preferences and other incentives determine protest (see arrow 6 in graph B). This would be a strategy that many movement scholars pursued, as we saw in chapter 1: if you want to explain protest activity (or any other social movement phenomena) simply add all the variables that are ingredients of the current theoretical perspectives. Such a strategy is unsatisfactory in this context for the following reason. The micro model is based on a theory which states that incentives are determinants of protest behavior. If we simply add "frame alignment" as another variable the question arises whether this is a type of incentive, i.e. part of the theory. If it turns out that "frame alignment" has nothing to do with incentives then the framing perspective would be an alternative theory to the incentive theory and would thus falsify it. Thus, simply adding frames and incentives as two separate types of factors without any detailed theoretical analysis is not meaningful.

The question then is how frame alignment is related to the incentive variables of the micro model of the theory of collective action. Frames are, as we saw before (chapter 9), mental models (or, equivalently, cognitive structures or belief systems), composed of cognitive elements. These cognitive elements are manifold and include the mental representation of incentives. To illustrate, when the authors discuss "frame amplification" (Snow *et al.* 1986: 469) they deal with "value amplification" and "belief amplification." In other words, values and beliefs are among the cognitive elements of frames. Certain values such as a protest norm are part of the micro model of protest. The same holds for discontent or grievances which are also a component of frames. "Perceived personal influence" is a belief and thus part of the mental model as well. "Group membership" or "membership in protest encouraging networks" refer, first of all, to real phenomena, but they become effective as conditions for protest only if they are perceived, i.e. if they are part of a mental model. Since the (perceived) incentives are a subset of the cognitive elements of frames there is an *analytical relationship* between "frames" and "incentives" which is symbolized by the line 2a in graph B. In other words, the elements of frames that are conducive to protest do not have an effect on incentives, they are incentives themselves. This means that there is not an empirical but an analytical relationship.

It is important to note that frames include not only incentives to protest but many other cognitive elements as well. But in order to explain protest only the incentives of the micro model are relevant.

Does this mean that in order to explain protest only the tiny part of a frame that refers to the incentives, is relevant? The answer is clearly "no." The reason is that the cognitive elements are related to each other. For example, several cognitive elements may be balanced or unbalanced (see chapter 9). Assume that an unmobilized individual A has a close friend B, and both usually don't talk politics. But then members of a terrorist group in the town where they live are arrested. Now A learns that B justifies terrorist acts whereas A thinks that violence in general is immoral and cannot be justified. This is an unbalanced situation: if I have a friend and learn that the friend has a different opinion on important matters, this causes psychic tension. Balance and dissonance theory predict that there is some likelihood that there will be a change in the cognitive elements: maybe A and B will no longer interact, or one of them changes his or her mind in regard to the moral evaluation of violence, including a norm to protest. Thus, the relationships between the cognitive elements of a frame may lead to changes of some incentives, such as the perceived justification of using violence. This means that framing processes also have an *empirical impact* on incentives. This is symbolized by relationship 2b in the figure.

Not only frames and framing processes explain incentives. For example, assume a movement member provides certain information about features of the movement – see the example of the "pretty girls" in chapter 8. This means that a belief about selective incentives is acquired due to information from a third party. Thus, other factors on the individual level may directly affect incentives – see arrow 4 in graph B.

In regard to relationship 3 in graph B, framing processes may originate on the micro level due to interaction between individual actors. This is what symbolic interactionists and proponents of the identity approach emphasize. Determinants of frames are thus not only variables on the macro level.

Another factor that is relevant for the framing processes that occur due to external events (such as social movement activities) is the given cognitive structure of a person. If in the previous example person A only weakly rejects violence and friendship with B is important to A, then A will change his or her moral views on violence due to interaction with B. The given cognitive structure of the interacting parties is thus among the factors which affect frame alignment and is subsumed under relationship 3.

The framing perspective holds that frame alignment has a direct effect on protest behavior – see relationship 2 in graph A. This is not plausible. If frame alignment is relevant because it is equivalent to incentives or has an impact on incentives, then it is likely that frame alignment influences protest via incentives. Thus, we assume that frame alignment has only an indirect causal effect on protest behavior. In graph B there is thus no arrow from "frames" to "individual protest."

Relationship 7 in graph B (and relationship 3 in graph A of Figure 11.1) refers to the relationship between protest on the individual and collective level, i.e. to how individual protests "translate" into collective protest. This relationship is not explicitly addressed in the framing perspective. This neglect is common among all perspectives in the social movement field (see, e.g., chapter 3).

Snow *et al.* (1986) assume that macro factors affect frame alignment processes (arrow 1 in graphs A and B). Previous chapters show that macro factors are also addressed in the theory of collective action, in the resource mobilization perspective and in the political opportunity structure perspective. These macro factors directly affect incentives (see relationship 5 in graph B).

A problem with the model in graph B is the relationship between frames and incentives: on the one hand, frames *include* incentives – this is the *analytical* relationship 2a. On the other hand, framing processes, i.e. cognitive processes such as changes of beliefs or attitudes, have an *empirical effect* on incentives – see the empirical relationship 2b. This implies that given macro factors (arrows 1 and 5) such as political opportunities affect frames as well as incentives which are part of frames (see relationship 2a). Thus, macro factors impinge on the same incentives twice. Similarly, the micro factors that influence frames and incentives may be the same (see arrows 3 and 4) – again because frames and incentives are partly identical (i.e. they are analytically and not empirically related).

To avoid these problems it is useful to separate cognitive *processes* (or, equivalently, framing processes) from the *outcomes* of these processes. Thus, cognitive *processes* would be perceiving repression or changing a belief – see the previous examples about a change of an attitude toward violence. The *results* or outcomes of these processes are then beliefs or attitudes such as a negative attitude toward violence. There is thus an empirical relationship between the *process* and its *outcome*.

When we make this distinction we can simplify the model in graph B and transform it into the model in graph C. This latter model does no longer include incentives twice. Thus, arrows 2a and 2b in graph B become arrow 2 in graph C. The frames now include only framing processes whose outcomes are, in part, incentives such as beliefs about influence. These processes may – indirectly – also lead to action, but only if they lead to a change of incentives. *This is in fact the synthesis of all the approaches discussed so far.* The exception is the dynamics of contention perspective which jettisons theory entirely. This has been discussed in chapter 10.

It will often be difficult to provide data about cognitive processes set in motion by macro changes. The SCM suggests looking at pre-existing cognitive structures and then examining how a new event such as repressive action by police forces changes the cognitive structure and, as an effect, influences incentives. If such data about cognitive processes are more difficult to come by than data about changing incentives, it seems plausible to focus on incentives. For example, it might be easier to ascertain whether expected repression changes discontent, activates norms and increases social incentives than to get information about individuals' existing cognitive structures and their changes. Thus, a simplified application of the SCM would be to provide macro-to-micro relations by looking at the *indirect* effects of macro changes, i.e. on the effects on incentives (see arrow 5 in graph B of Figure 11.1).

3. How existing social movement theory fits into the structural-cognitive model

It is important to note that the SCM is in one respect not contradictory to existing perspectives in the social movement literature. It pursues explanatory strategies in an explicit way that remain largely implicit and undiscussed in the existing literature. This close relationship between these perspectives and the SCM is depicted in Figure 11.2. The contents of the figure are actually a summary of results of the chapters that address the reconstruction of the different approaches. We showed there for each perspective how and to what extent micro-macro explanations were used.

The *framing perspective* deals with macro-to-micro relationships (effects of social movement activities on frame alignment) and – in our extended model – with the relationships of framing and incentives. As we saw before, we dropped the direct effect of framing on protest. The *resource mobilization and political opportunity structure perspectives* focus on the macro model and – implicitly – adumbrate macro-to-micro relationships. The *theory of collective action* is the only one that explicitly addresses micro and macro relationships, but the theory does not mention framing. The *identity approach* is mainly a micro model, although there are hints of effects of macro structures on identity formation. The micro-to-macro relationship from individual to collective protest is not addressed by any perspective (we discussed it in chapter 3). For details the reader is referred to the chapter where the respective theoretical approach is discussed.

4. The structural-cognitive model applied: some illustrations

Does the SCM explain protest events better than existing theories? The best answer to this question is to apply the model to specific kinds of protest events. Such

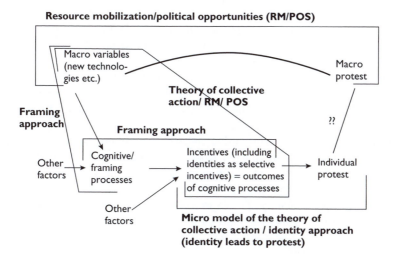

Figure 11.2 Questions addressed by the social movement perspectives

applications require detailed data that refer to the variables of the model. For example, we need information about framing processes and incentives on the micro level, and we need to know which macro changes have altered these processes and incentives. To apply the model requires new research projects or the analysis of existing data sets. This cannot be provided in this book. The book is about theory and not about the analysis of specific protest events or social movements. What can be done, however, is to look at some protest events and social movements and provide explanation sketches or, more precisely, show what questions are to be asked, what the answers might be from the perspective of the SCM, and to what extent questions and possible answers differ from those of other approaches.

This is the subject of the remainder of this section: we present and discuss four cases that are rather different so that one can see how the SCM can be applied in quite diverse circumstances. We begin with a worldwide movement, the anti-globalization movement. We then turn to a movement of Latin America: the Landless Rural Workers' Movement of Brazil. The next case is the American Civil Rights Movement. Finally, we will discuss a case where protest originated without a movement and without organization: the East German revolution. Here we will focus on the protests in Leipzig (East Germany) in October 1989 that contributed to the demise of the communist regime.

How can we proceed to apply the SCM to these – and other – cases? Since the SCM provides a micro-macro explanation and is based on the theory of collective action, we draw on the procedure outlined in chapter 4, section 4. In explaining protest the first natural step is to describe the protest events. Since the SCM can provide very detailed explanations of behavior, the researcher has to decide how specific the explananda should be that are addressed. For example, is the aim to account for the development of protests over time or is the form of protest to be explained? Or is the issue where the protests took place?

Since the SCM implies micro-macro explanations, one may begin with the micro level. A useful starting point is the situation that instigated the protests and the agenda of the protesters, i.e. their grievances or, equivalently, the extent to which they want the provision of certain public goods. The next step is too look at the other incentives which are suggested by our micro model (chapter 4).

Figure 11.1 suggests further to look at cognitive processes. They precede incentives. A full explanation thus should specify which cognitive structures exist and how they influenced incentives.

Explaining protest events means looking at changes of protests – at least from a situation without protest to a situation where people took action. The SCM explains these changes by looking at changes of incentives and cognitive processes. However, this does not yet provide a satisfactory explanation. Even if we know which incentives or cognitive processes have changed over time, the question is why this happened. This then leads us to the macro level. The question to be answered reads: what changes of macro events have affected which incentives and cognitions in what way?

If protest on the macro level – such as a demonstration – is to be explained, a final step is to provide hypotheses or assumptions that transform individual action to collective action. This is the micro-to-macro transition.

As was said before, it is not possible to answer these questions for the cases selected. What we can and will do is to briefly describe the cases and then make suggestions of how the SCM could be applied. We hope that other scholars use these suggestions, extend them and engage in research that tests the SCM. We further hope that this book will be used in classes and that the cases – or perhaps other cases – are discussed more extensively by applying the SCM. Perhaps students will conduct small projects in writing seminar papers or theses to answer some of the questions outlined below.

The anti-globalization movement

The movement, that is sometimes also called the "Global Justice Movement," has engaged in numerous large-scale protests.[2] One of the first took place on June 18, 1999, in several cities and was called the "Carnival Against Capitalism." Perhaps the most well-known protest is "The Battle of Seattle" on November 30, 1999, with more than 50,000 participants. The occasion of the protests was a conference of the World Trade Organization (WTO) that aimed at a new round of market liberalization.[3] Numerous similar protests have happened. Examples are protests in Davos, Switzerland, on occasion of the World Economic Forum on January 2000, and at the occasion of the 27th G8 summit in Genoa, Italy, in July 2001. The movement further has set up its own annual meeting, the World Social Forum (WSF) to coordinate and develop strategies and to discuss globalization issues (see for a short overview Reitan 2007: 10–13).

What is the agenda of the anti-globalization movement? The major issue is "globalization" in the economic sphere referring to the growing interconnection of national economies in regard to the expansion of international free trade, the flow of capital, the transfer of technology, and the migration of labor.[4] Although this process can be traced back at least to the middle ages, it accelerated in the nineteenth century and in particular after the collapse of communism in 1989/1990. There are different assessments of the consequences of this process and the possibility to stop or reverse it. The members of the anti-globalization movement see mostly negative consequences. They criticize in particular the unfettered activities and power of transnational corporations. Their targets are further trade agreements and international organizations (such as the World Bank or the International Monetary Fund) that promote globalization. Although the unifying agenda of the various movements is a rejection of globalization or, as advocates of the movement like to say, of neoliberal globalization, their specific agendas differ.[5] Furthermore, the belief is that globalization is not irreversible and can be shaped, stopped or reversed.

The anti-globalization protests are organized by a great number of different groups and organizations that form a large network. The agenda of these groups is most of the time not specifically targeted to fight globalization, this is just one of the issues in their agendas. The globalization issue fits in the general goals of the organizations that can be located at the left political spectrum: the organizations favor socialism, environmentalism, human rights or labor rights. An organization that focuses in particular on globalization issues is ATTAC.

This very short description may make it plausible that a detailed explanation of the protests and the movement would take at least another book. Instead we will sketch the questions that are of interest and some possible answers, taking the perspective of the SCM.

What is to be explained? One interesting phenomenon is the form of the protests, i.e. the specific tactics used (including more or less violent behaviors). Another is the size: there were around 50,000 participants in Seattle. For the G8 summit in Genoa 200,000 participants were estimated. For a worldwide organizational effort even 200,000 participants is not overwhelming. Why? The composition of the protesters was international. Which countries had most participants and why? An important issue is the location of the protests. Why were certain locations chosen?

Beginning with the micro level and the incentives to participate the question arises what the motivations for participation might have been and might be. The public evils that existed from the perspective of the participants could only be changed by an international cooperation of many governments. This is the goal of the movement. To what extent do or did the participants believe that their protests will really change the world? It seems that perceived personal and collective efficacy matter because it is emphasized time and again that globalization can be changed. Or is this only propaganda to mobilize others? Perhaps the major participants want to achieve only little changes such as preventing a trade agreement at a certain international meeting. A detailed analysis of the efficacy beliefs (individual and collective) would be interesting. But perhaps the anti-globalization protests are mainly driven by moral incentives? If so, what exactly are these moral views (i.e. what is the conditionality of the norms)? It is further of interest to explain why the protests are organized and, thus, not spontaneous. This suggests strong social incentives distributed by groups and organizations.

The major protests that were organized so far required sophisticated logistics that can only be provided by long-term activists with organizational skills who are integrated in organizations. How strong are these social incentives? An indicator could be the length of stay in an organization. Perhaps there is bridge burning (i.e. contacts exist mostly with other activists) which is an indicator for strong social incentives and strong negative sanctions if one wants to leave an organization. Another question could be what the mental models of devoted activists look like.

Let us turn to the macro-level. How do the organizations mobilize individuals and other groups? Or are the participants in the protests mainly members of the organizations? Are expenses for participating in protests paid for? Are there other "selective incentives"? Do different organizations use different mobilization strategies? Since anti-globalization activists are probably strongly rooted in an anti-capitalist ideology it would be particularly interesting how effective they can change the mental models of which kind of non-mobilized individuals. Successful mobilization of a large number of new activists seems rather limited, from the millions of people all over the world who are against globalization or feel they are the losers of globalization there are only few who participate. Thus, the free rider problem is particularly salient and should be addressed.

Which macro events were relevant for the change or generation of incentives to participate? One question is why the protests did not take place earlier. As was said before, globalization exists for a long time. One major macro variable for the growth of the anti-globalization movement might be modern communication technology and the decreasing costs of transport. These are important because the movement is transnational. What role do such technological innovations play for the development of the movement? International summits were the major critical events or occasions for the protests. Did the events change incentives? For example, did they further increase discontent with globalization and raised other incentives? It seems that the outcomes of the big meetings were not affected by the protests. Did this decrease perceived influence or perhaps increase "moral indignation"?

Some of the protests were not only violent on the side of the protesters, but on the side of the security forces as well. Which role did repression play for further protests? Did it raise expected repression and, if so, did that have a deterrence or a radicalization effect on participation?

The SCM posits that framing processes affect incentives. It is striking that the views about globalization are so different. Typically, those who are ideologically more on the left, denounce globalization, whereas those more on the right defend it. It seems plausible that globalization more or less fits into pre-existing mental models of a certain type. What exactly are the cognitive elements of those mental models that are more or less consistent with particular beliefs about consequences of globalization? Another interesting theme would be the extent to which specific decisions of international organizations or agreements at international meetings lead or have led to a cognitive reorganization of those mental models.

How do explanations of the SCM differ from existing explanations of the anti-globalization movement? The SCM provides a full-fledged explanation by looking at the individual participants, their social context and at the macro level. Further, it concatenates these levels. The macro level encompasses the immediate context of personal networks and membership groups as well as the decisions of national and international organizations and governments. The difference but also the similarity to a more traditional approach can be seen by comparing the previous explanation sketch and the explanation provided by della Porta *et al.* (2006: 21–23). The authors' explanatory model is just a conglomerate of the by now common variables, each taken from one of the existing approaches (see in particular the graph on p. 22). The authors thus employ not a theoretical but a factor explanation (see chapter 1). But there are also agreements such as a micro-macro approach (23). However, in the approach favored by della Porta *et al.* there is no systematic application of a micro-model and there is no explicit micro-macro modeling. Nonetheless, it would be interesting to examine the extent to which the empirical material in this book and in other work on the anti-globalization movement could be used to answer questions from the perspective of the SCM. The rich material in the book by Reitan (2007) could also be used for this purpose.

The movement of landless rural workers (MST) in Brazil

This movement[6] is not only of interest because it "is unquestionably the most dynamic and influential political movement in Brazil today" (Hammond 1999: 1), it "is Latin America's premier grassroots movement and one of the world's most remarkable peasant organizations" (Carter 2005: 4; see also Veltmeyer and Petras 2002).[7]

The kind of activities the movement engages in are illustrated by a report of the BBC news from May 2, 2000:

> Members of the landless movement clashed with police and invaded public buildings and farms in a wave of protests in Brazil. In the worst clash, at least 200 people were arrested and several were injured in the southern state of Parana. A convoy of 30 buses carrying more than 1,000 peasants were stopped on the main road to the state capital, Curitiba, by riot police who fired teargas and stun grenades. The Landless Rural Workers Movement (MST) and other groups are demanding land distribution and more credits for poor rural workers.[8]

This quotation first illustrates that the actions of the movement are organized occupations of unused or unproductive land of large landowners and of public buildings. If land is occupied settlements are established with schools, healthcare, etc. This goes along with organizing security teams to avoid evictions by the police. Among the activities of the MST are further marches, pickets, group meetings, sit-ins at government buildings, building takeovers, rallies, hunger strikes, road blockades, protest camps, and participation in election campaigns. The movement further continuously bargains and collaborates with numerous state agencies. Another kind of activity is to set up cooperatives and food processing plants. Among the activities are further the organization of national congresses. For example, in June 2007 the fifth national congress took place in Brasilia with 17,500 delegates from 25 states across the country and 200 international guests.[9]

The movement was founded in January 1984 in the city of Cascavel in the southwest of Paraná. It began with a three-day meeting of about 100 landless workers, held at the diocesan center. The MST quickly expanded to other regions.

What are the grievances? One feature of Brazil is the extreme concentration of land. According to data from 1996, 1 percent of the landholders are in control of 45 percent of the farmland; 37 percent of the population holds 1 percent of the land. This has historical origins: before independence of Brazil, the Portuguese crown gave large property to privileged colonial families. This inequality did not change after independence from Portugal in 1822 (see Carter 2005 with further references). In addition, due to modernization in the agrarian sector many small farmers lost their livelihood. This also led to a decreasing demand of farm labor. Furthermore, industrial developments such as the construction of large dams displaced many small farmers. There was thus a great number of landless peasants, and a great deal of the arable land owned by relatively few families is unused.

The primary goal of the movement is agrarian reform claiming that land of the large landowners is to be distributed to the landless. But the target is also neoliberal policies. In a final letter to Brazilian society at the 2007 congress the MST declared that it will continue to "struggle so that all of the large landholdings are expropriated, with the properties of foreign capital and the banks being prioritized" (quoted from the article by Kenfield in the previous note).

The activities of the movement provoked harsh counter reactions such as armed resistence by the land owners by hiring gun men. It also happened that the police executed members of a landless organization and that the members faced other repercussions.

The movement and its development raises many interesting questions that could be addressed by applying the SCM. The MST is an organization of poor people. How is it possible that they can set up such a successful movement? Answering this question means first of all to specify the individual incentives, based on the micro model of protest outlined in chapter 4. The history of the movement is well documented and may provide information about major incentives. Perhaps the emergence of the movement is the result of political entrepreneurs, i.e. of the activities of a few poor people who actually disposed of personal resources such as rhetoric and organizational skills.

If our micro model is correct efficacy beliefs are a major incentive. To what extent did the founders believe in the efficacy of their organization and that their participation could make a difference? To what extent were these beliefs influenced by past events such as the first occupation of land in 1979 in Rio Grande del Sur under a military dictatorship?

The grievances existed for a long time. Why was the movement only founded in 1984 and not earlier? How did the incentives on the micro level develop over time? How can the great variety of movement activities be explained, including violent and illegal actions? Which role did perceived normative obligations or efficacy considerations play? It is plausible that various justifications for violence are accepted. The existing mental models could be analyzed in regard to the "fit" of such justifications into pre-existing cognitive elements. How can the drift to anti-neoliberalism be explained, i.e. why did neoliberalism not fit into the cognitive model of the MST agenda?

Apparently, the movement is very successful in mobilizing others. What are the (selective) incentives that are provided by the movement and why are they effective? What selective incentives are provided by groups that support the MST (like the church)?

This book has not addressed the extent to which social movements are successful in realizing their goals. The reason for this omission is space limitations. Nonetheless, movement success is an important question. In particular in regard to the MST, the achievements are numerous. Examples are land reform settlements for 350,000 families and 1,800 schools (Carter 2005). How could the movement be so successful? The SCM could be extended to tackle this question: it has to be determined what the incentives are for the government and other authorities to yield to demands of the MST? But in regard to a general land reform the MST is not (yet?)

successful. Why? "Success" means that targets of the movement make certain decisions, based on incentives. Thus, the SCM could be applied to explain the decisions of targets as well.

A basic claim of the SCM is to provide micro-macro explanations. That means that not only the change of incentives over time is to be ascertained, but it is to be explained which macro events changed these incentives. One question would be why incentives remained high or even increased despite severe repression. Accordingly, one wishes to know what effects government reactions and repressive acts from landowners had on incentives to participation. What were the effects of President Luiz Inácio Lula da Silva's new government that was first elected in 2002 and then re-elected in 2007? The activities of the MST generated extensive media coverage. How did this change which incentives for whom?

The fruitfulness of a theoretical model is best judged by comparing it with other theories. In regard to the MST we have not found a clearly specified theoretical explanation so that the contribution of the SCM to the explanation of the MST cannot be assessed.

The American civil rights movement

It is difficult to tell what the exact date of the origin of the movement is. According to Aldon Morris (1984: ix), it was June 1953 when "the first major battle of the modern civil rights movement took place in Baton Rouge, Louisiana."[10] At that time blacks boycotted the city's segregated bus system. Immediately afterwards similar confrontations took place at other locations. The most well known event is probably the bus boycott in Montgomery, Alabama, in December 1955. Rosa Parks was arrested for refusing to give up her seat near the front of a bus to a white man. Fifty leaders of the black community (including Dr Martin Luther King Jr) organized the boycott. Other major events were a sit-in campaign in 1960: four students repeatedly went to a Woolworth's lunch counter in Greensboro, North Carolina, and were refused service. An article in the New York Times inspired similar actions across the south.

In 1961 students took bus rides – called Freedom Rides – through the South. Their aim was to test to what extent new laws against segregation in interstate travel facilities, including bus and railway stations, were heeded. In 1962, in the Mississippi Riot, a riot broke out after a black student wanted to be enrolled at the University of Mississippi. Two students were killed. In August 1963, the famous March on Washington took place, organized by civil rights activists, where Martin Luther King Jr gave his "I Have a Dream" speech. This brief list of activities of the movement illustrates that the action repertoire was manifold, peaceful as well as violent. Protests were mostly organized by quite diverse groups and organizations across the US, but first primarily in the South.[11]

Among the activities of the movement were also more conventional tactics such as trying to change public opinion through press releases, speeches, and lobbying. Another tactic was legal action which became the main tactic of the NAACP – see below.

The movement's goals are related to the situation of blacks, especially in the South of the USA. Morris (1984: 1–4) describes this situation as a "tripartite system of domination" that Southern whites had created by the 1950s. This system consisted of economic, political and personal discrimination. In regard to economic domination, blacks had the lowest-paying and dirtiest jobs, and blacks were controlled by whites. Political discrimination means that in the South blacks were not part of the political process: there were no black officials in governments, there were only white policemen, and the courts consisted of white judges and juries which decided in favor of whites. Personal discrimination refers to the system of segregation that labeled blacks as an inferior race. Blacks had to go to different schools, had to use different toilets, waiting rooms, there was segregation in transportation facilities, cemeteries, theaters, and restaurants. The general goal of the movement was to change this situation, i.e. to fight racial discrimination of African-Americans.

The movement consisted of various organizations. The most important pre-existing organization or institution that supported the battle for civil rights in various ways was the Church. "Churches provided the movement with an organized mass base; a leadership of clergymen largely economically independent of the larger white society and skilled in the art of managing people and resources; an institutionalized financial base through which protest was financed; and meeting places where the masses planned tactics and strategies and collectively committed themselves to the struggle" (Morris 1984: 4).

The NACCP (National Association for the Advancement of Colored People) was founded in 1909 and 1910 by a group of black and white intellectuals to fight for civil rights. The organization was based in the North. The NAACP "became the dominant black protest organization for the first half of the twentieth century" (Morris 1984: 15).

Over time many other organizations have formed. Examples are the Marcus Garvey movement proclaiming a black nationalist "Back to Africa" message in the 1920s, and A. Philip Randolph's March on Washington Movement (MOWM), organized in 1941. The Congress of Racial Equality (CORE) was founded in 1942. The Student Nonviolent Coordinating Committee (or SNCC, pronounced "snick") was one of the important organizations of the civil rights movement in the 1960s. It played a major role in the sit-ins and Freedom Rides, and in the 1963 March on Washington. Another organization is The Southern Christian Leadership Conference (SCLC). It was closely associated with its first president, Martin Luther King Jr.

The activities of the movement were accompanied by severe repression: there were beatings, heavy court fines, arrests, imprisonments, killings, and assassinations. Examples are the assassination of Martin Luther King Jr on April 4, 1968, the bombing of the Sixteenth Street Baptist Church by the Ku Klux Klan in September 1963 in Birmingham where four little girls were killed. In the 1961 freedom rides there was violence at many stops along the way.

The movement had many successes. Often authorities had to give in to the demands of those who resisted segregation. Court decisions were in favor of civil rights. For example, in 1956 a federal court ordered that buses in Montgomery had to be desegregated.

What can the SCM contribute to explain the dynamics of the civil rights movement? A good starting point is to look at those who were suffering from white domination. One striking phenomenon is that the great majority of blacks were silent, only relatively few took action. Thus, the free rider problem is clearly salient. A question then is what the individual motivation was to become active. This implies looking also at those who remained inactive. Was it mainly moral indignation that instigated participation? Or did activists, in contrast to the silent majority, think their action could make a difference? A clue for explaining many activities might be that they targeted local issues such as the bus boycotts. Here perceived influence could be much more salient than if the issue were a national one. Perhaps also important were social incentives because protest was strongly anchored in groups or organizations.

In looking at the incentives the question arises as to what the cognitive processes have been that changed incentives to become active. Perhaps there were preexisting cognitive structures that predisposed certain groups of individuals to become more involved in civil rights action than others. These are questions that refer to the micro level.

The explanatory strategy of the SCM is to explain changes of micro variables by macro events. For the civil rights movement numerous critical macro events took place. They included spectacular activities such as civil disobedience by ignoring certain rules such as segregation. Court decisions, killings, and repressive acts such as brutal police actions were critical events as well. How did these events affect individual incentives? A particularly interesting question is why the high costs of engaging in the movement did not have a deterrent effect for the activists. To what extent were those who refrained from supporting the movement afraid of repression? Answering this question requires a detailed analysis of the incentive structure of activists and non-activists. Thus, an explanation of the development of the movement would consist, among other things, of looking in detail at the continuous macro-to-micro effects of critical events on incentives and framing processes. In which situations (or for what groups of individuals) were the effects strong enough to engage in further action? These actions, then, become new critical events such as demonstrations or riots. These are micro-to-macro relations. The ensuing macro events again change incentive structures.

Important macro factors include organizations or, in general, groups that played a major role in the civil rights movement. As was mentioned, the church was a particularly important collective actor. How did the church act to change which incentives for which groups? A further step in the explanation of the civil rights movement could be to explain why various groups supported the civil rights movement in various ways. It would also be interesting to look at the processes that led to the formation of new groups. Again, micro-macro modeling would be the explanatory strategy.

What would be gained by applying the SCM? It would be an interesting task to compare the explanations of the movement by the SCM with two widely cited and important explanations of the development of the civil rights movement, namely Aldon D. Morris's *The Origin of the Civil Rights Movement* (1984) and Doug McAdam's *Political Process and the Development of Black Insurgency, 1930–1970* (1982). Morris mainly uses the resource mobilization approach (chapter 11), but complements it with other theoretical hypotheses. For example, he uses Max Weber's theory of charismatic leadership and movements, and he applies ideas of the collective behavior tradition to explain aspects of the movement. McAdam focuses on the political opportunity structure approach (i.e. the political process model that he developed in the book) that was discussed in chapter 6. Although Morris's explanation is closer to the SCM than McAdam's, both lack systematic micro-macro modeling.

Perhaps closest to the SCM comes the study by Chong (1991). His explanatory arguments are based on the theory of collective action. Nonetheless, systematic and detailed micro-macro modeling as would be suggested by the SCM is missing as well.

Applications of the SCM would not provide a completely new explanation that is incompatible with those accounts. However, the detailed specification of incentives and the effects of macro changes on those incentives, the transition from micro-processes to macro events (such as anti-segregation protests), and, in turn, their effect on further incentive changes would certainly add important new insights in explaining the trajectory of the movement.

The East German revolution

Our last case differs from the previous cases in many respects. One major difference is that in the decisive first phase of the revolution in the communist German Democratic Republic (GDR) in the fall of 1989 social movements were not involved. Various political groups that would normally not be called a social movement entered the scene only later. This case is interesting because existing social movement theory has problems in explaining the East German revolution and spontaneous protests in general. Does the SCM fare better?[12]

Let us first describe the emerging protests in the GDR, especially in 1989. Since the foundation of the GDR on October 7, 1949, protests of various kinds have occurred, albeit mostly on a relatively small scale. The protests mainly consisted of demonstrations. Large-scale demonstrations took place in June 1953 when workers demonstrated against increasing work quota. But the demands then became broader and included resignation of the East German government. The protests were crushed with the help of Soviet troops. Since that time protests were rare. This changed when on May 7, 1989, a local election took place the results of which were obviously tampered with. Several demonstrations followed immediately after this became known. From the end of September 1989, after the summer break, there was a dramatic upsurge in the number of demonstrations and participants. This holds in particular for the number of participants of the Monday demonstrations on the Karl Marx Square and adjacent streets in Leipzig. These demonstrations took place after the prayers for peace that had been held in the Nikolai Church since

1982. The demonstrations in Leipzig were a major trigger of the revolution in the GDR, and as such are of particular interest. Approximately 800 to 1,200 people took part in the Monday demonstration on the 4th of September. The numbers increased until about 70,000 on October 9, 1989.

All the demonstrations before October 9 were immediately dissolved by the security forces. The demonstration on October 9, 1989, was the largest demonstration in the GDR since June 17, 1953, and the first demonstration that was not violently terminated. On October 9 demonstrations were also held in other locations in the GDR, but with far fewer participants. Both the demonstrations in Leipzig and in almost all the other locations were non-violent. All demonstrations were illegal, as they had been neither registered nor permitted.

Other activities against the communist regime were the foundation and the call for the foundation of oppositional groups. For example, on August 13, 1989, about 400 members of various opposition groups met in the community hall of the Confessional Church in Berlin-Treptow. The Social Democratic Party (SPD) was founded in East Germany on October 7, 1989. The call to found the New Forum was issued on September 10, 1989. All these initiatives were directed against the communist regime that tried to prevent the foundation of the new groups.

There were, in addition, many small individual groups such as artists, church groups or workers' groups, who wrote and distributed declarations, wrote open letters or petitions demanding reform.

All these forms of protest increased during 1989. On November 9, 1989, when the Berlin Wall opened, the protests decreased. Actually, the communist regime has lost its power. On March 18, 1990, the first free election to the national East German parliament (Volkskammer) took place. On October 3, 1990, East and West Germany were reunited.

What was the situation in which the protests took place? East Germany was a communist authoritarian regime, with one reigning party, a strong repressive apparatus (the STASI, i.e. state security). After the Berlin Wall was built on August 13, 1961, traveling to western countries was severely restrained. All opposition to the regime was suffocated. Apart from widely spread political dissatisfaction there were economic problems. For example, people suffered from scarcity of everyday commodities, and had to wait for years to get a car. The look and quality of the East German car "Trabant" (called "Trabi") can serve as a symbol for the short supply of goods that were often of low quality. The dissatisfaction was particularly high because the comparison group was West Germany with a clearly higher living standard and a democratic market order.

What can the SCM contribute to the explanation of the East German revolution? We have already briefly provided an answer to this question in chapter 1, section 2, and in chapter 6, section 2 (subsection "Do we need a 'causal definition' of political opportunities?"). We will take up these considerations here and extend them. A starting point in explaining the revolution is – as before – the micro level: what were the incentives that were conducive to the large-scale protests? Figure 1.1 shows, among other things, the micro model that captures the major incentives whose relevance was tested in our research (see the previous note). This research provides evidence that those incentives have changed dramatically in the year 1989. What were the events that suddenly led thousands of people to protest against the communist regime, after decades of quiescence? First of all, there were various internal events, i.e. certain decisions of political bodies in the GDR, in 1989 and before. They include, among other things, the outcome of the communal elections held on May 7, 1989, that, as was said, were obviously having been tampered with. This event increased the population's dissatisfaction with the regime. This was also the effect of the celebrations of the 40th anniversary of the GDR on October 7, 1989. The regime praised the achievements of socialism in the GDR although the discrepancy between the regime's claims and reality were becoming more and more obvious. Second, external events, i.e. the decisions of third countries, changed incentives. These include the continuation of liberalization processes in other countries of the Eastern bloc. For example on May 2, 1989, Hungarian border police started to remove border fortifications at the Austrian border. This led to increasing (relative) dissatisfaction because there was no sign of liberalization in the GDR. It increased perceived personal and collective influence: the citizens believed that the GDR authorities could no longer resist reforms if, in addition to the external events, protests in the country would increase. These are examples that illustrate how macro-to-micro relations can be modeled.

An interesting question was how the protests could emerge without any organization. Let us assume that an average citizen is highly motivated to express his or her dissatisfaction. This citizen is aware that for the regime even a mere collection of persons may be perceived as an act of protest and will be sanctioned. If dissatisfied individuals want to convene with other dissatisfied individuals to signal political discontent, the question arises of where and when he or she can find such individuals. Thus, there must be some expectation that one will find others at a certain place at a certain time. If this is the case then a tacit coordination of individuals occurs without any necessity for organization or mobilization.

Assume such an expectation exists. Will individuals not be deterred in going to the meeting point because of possible repression? If one expects to meet only a few persons, there is a relatively low risk of governmental sanctions because one's presence will not be regarded as an act of protest. There may be many reasons for being at a certain place at a certain time. The larger the number of individuals, the greater the likelihood that the security forces assume a protest and intervene. However, the large number makes it relatively unlikely that a single person gets arrested or hurt. If a person is arrested he or she can always claim that he or she was just taking a stroll through the streets. Thus, in this situation expected repression is probably not that strong that it will suffocate any protest.

But, again, how could an expectation develop to meet others at a certain venue at a certain time? If one wants to meet others in a town with a clearly defined urban center, one will go to one of its large squares. For the citizens of Leipzig the Karl Marx Square was such a meeting place. But at what time should one go to the Karl Marx Square? Leipzig citizens were well aware that since 1982 prayers for peace have been held in the Nikolai Church every Monday from 5 to 6 pm. The Nikolai Church is nearby the Karl Marx Square. It was further common knowledge that the peace prayers were increasingly attended in 1989 by discontented citizens who wanted to leave the country and wanted to express this wish, and that many who left the church after the peace prayers crossed the adjacent streets and went to the Karl Marx Square. Thus, it was known that one had to go to the Karl Marx Square on Mondays in the evening to meet dissatisfied people.

This brief explanation sketch illustrates how an incentive-based approach can explain protests that are not organized. The basic idea is that there is some structure of incentives that instigates a group of people to decide independently to convene at a certain venue at a certain time.

Explaining the East German revolution further means explaining the reactions of the regime. For example why did the government not terminate the protests violently as in all the years before? For limitations of space, we must the reader refer to Opp, Voss, and Gern 1995.

We collected several data sets to test our propositions. One major data set was a representative survey of Leipzig citizens in the fall of 1990 referring to the situation in the fall of 1989. These data support the micro model as well as many of the macro-to-micro propositions. The explanation of the decisions of the regime received support by documents such as the minutes of sessions of the Polit Bureau or reports by the Stasi (state security).

Existing explanations are not completely inconsistent with the explanation outlined before. They propose also the internal and external events as causes. However, they do not provide macro-to-micro explanations. That is, the black box from the events to the behavior is not filled: it is unknown why the events changed the protests. The SCM provides the missing macro-to-micro links. Furthermore, existing explanations do not explicitly apply a theory. It is further difficult to see how the existing approaches, in particular the macro approaches, can explain how the spontaneous protests could emerge.

Discussion

There are differences and similarities between the cases discussed in this section. Social scientists are more interested in finding common features of events that can be subsumed under a single category such as "episodes of contention" – a term borrowed from the dynamics of contention approach (see chapter 10) – than looking at differences. One goal of the latter approach is to discover mechanisms. We doubted that this contributes much to explaining the dynamics of contention. However, this does not imply that it is not of interest to find some general features of protests. What could be possible interesting generalizations inspired by the SCM? Perhaps one could look at the kinds of individual actors that initiate collective political action, the political entrepreneurs. To be sure, this would not be new: critical mass theory in particular and the theory of collective action have emphasized their importance. But what the specific kinds and perhaps strength of the incentives are has not been investigated. Another central question would be to specify the incentives that are most likely to change if macro changes affect protest events. For example, what is the role of perceived influence? Is this the major factor that instigates collective action if critical events occur? Addressing this question may remind the reader of the lists of "dimensions" of political opportunity structures which we criticized (chapter 6). The problem with these dimensions is that their effects on incentives is never spelled out, let alone tested. From the perspective of the SCM such a list would serve as a heuristic device that can be used to ease finding macro-to-micro relationship in tackling specific research questions.

The protests dealt with in this chapter took place relatively recently so that data about many features of these protests are available. This is different for protests that took place in the distant past such as the Russian or French revolution. In particular, it is difficult to obtain subjective data for these cases. Although this is possible if the main actors of an event are still alive, it is often expensive, and major actors will not be ready to be interviewed or the information one receives is biased. In this situation the only possibility is provide *informed speculations* about what incentives might have motivated actors to behave in a certain way. The basis of such speculation may be various documents such as minutes of meetings, recorded speeches, diaries, and novels of the time that document everyday behavior and customs. Historians can teach us how we can use various documents to get information on certain attitudes, beliefs, and preferences. Even if personal data are available those documents could be used as additional evidence. Thus, just doing away with the SCM by pointing out how difficult it is to get subjective data is not convincing. There are many sources that give at least some evidence for hypotheses on the relevant incentives.

The micro part of the SCM does not only consist of the theory of rational action, but of social psychological theories that can explain features of protest events that are of interest to social movement scholars. The suggestions in the previous sections to apply the SCM were mostly based on the theory of rational action. But in regard to looking at changing cognitive structures balance theory could be applied, as chapter 9 has shown. In explaining changing attitudes toward a regime or its policies the Fishbein-Ajzen theory could be applied. Thus, it is important to keep in mind that rational choice theory is not the only theory that is capable of forming the micro basis of the SCM.

5. Summary and conclusions

This chapter has argued that a major lacuna in social movement theory and research is the lack of micro-macro explanations. Although all theoretical perspectives propose such explanations, their theorizing remains most of the time implicit. This is the basic idea of synthesizing the approaches. They emphasize the micro and macro level to a different degree. Macro propositions lack explanatory power: they do not tell us why they hold. For example why does repression sometimes deter and sometimes instigate protest? Micro propositions do not tell us which changes on the macro level affect the individual motivations to protest. The SCM claims that a full-fledged explanation requires us to consider the micro and macro level and connect them by so-called bridge assumptions. In applying the SCM it is suggested that we utilize to a much higher extent certain social psychological theories (see chapter 1) that have so far been applied only rarely in social movement theory and research.

Why is this synthesis useful? It shows that the perspectives no longer contradict each other. This is an important result and takes issue with much of what has been written in the social movement literature. The basic contention of many social movement scholars seems to be that framing and identity approaches on the one hand and rational choice, resource mobilization and political opportunity perspectives on the other are incompatible. Sometimes the dividing line is seen between rational choice approaches on the one hand and everything else on the other. Our synthesis and the discussion in previous chapters show that these allegations are highly problematic, to say the least. Rigorous research addressing the identity and framing approach confirm this (see, e.g., Klandermans and associates' work about testing identity propositions): clear theoretical hypotheses are formulated and tested by the common methods of empirical research. However, there are also movement scholars who think that the various approaches are not contradictory but complement each other. But none of these scholars analyzes in detail how the approaches are related or could be integrated. It seems that they have a simple additive model in mind that just combines factors (see our discussion in chapter 1). In contrast, we provide an integrated theoretical model and not just add various variables in an *ad hoc* fashion.

We have not addressed in detail the dynamics of contention perspective in this chapter. How is it related to the SCM? As our discussion in chapter 10 showed, this approach has not added new theory to the field. However, new questions have been asked. A synthesis with the SCM would consist of answering these new questions with the theoretical toolkit of this model.

12 General discussion, conclusion, and an agenda for future research

This chapter begins with a summary of the most important strengths and weaknesses of the theoretical perspectives explaining social movement phenomena. Then the proposed alternative, the structural-cognitive model, is outlined. Next we take up the case study from chapter 3 as another illustration (in addition to the case studies discussed in the previous chapter) of the theoretical approach proposed in this book. In particular, it will also be discussed to what extent existing social movement theory can improve the explanation outlined in chapter 3. The final section before the usual "Summary and conclusions" then proposes an agenda for the development of future theory and research.

1. The major strengths and weaknesses of extant theories of social movements and political protest

The previous chapters have discussed the major problems of the theoretical perspectives as well as their achievements in great detail. In this section, we highlight only those shortcomings and strengths that seem most important. Let's start with the problems.

(1) The first major obstacle to find out what the problems of the theories are is that it is not clear what exactly their propositions are. It took a lot of effort to reconstruct them, i.e. to suggest what exactly the dependent and independent variables are and what the concepts could mean. This is the first problem. And it is not only the problem of the founding work but of subsequent developments as well. Assuming that the reconstructions suggested actually represent the propositions the authors had in mind, the following flaws stand out.

(2) The approaches – with the exception of the theory of collective action – have little explanatory power. This means in particular that they cannot explain the specific forms of social movement phenomena. Typical is the proliferation of a vast number of orienting statements. That is to say, classes of variables are mentioned that are supposed to have some influence on some vaguely described classes of dependent variables.

(3) It is not clear what the relationships are between the social movement theories. For example, does the political opportunity structure perspective contradict the resource mobilization perspective? If not, what exactly is the relationship?

Is one implied by the other? The recent trend is to pull all the key variables together in peaceful co-existence. In explaining specific social movement phenomena it is then examined to what extent certain values of the independent variables exist. So it may turn out that some events that are called political opportunities exist or are increased. These are then *ad hoc* attributed as causal factors to "explain" certain phenomena. This is not theoretical integration, as was shown in chapter 1, it is an eclectic *ad hoc* procedure. We called it factor explanations, in contrast to theoretical explanations that consist of applying theories.

(4) Most of the approaches – with the exception of the theory of collective action – have no explicit theoretical foundation. That is there is no explicit theory that is applied to derive specific propositions. This implies, for example, that it is not clear why social movement scholars are convinced that identity or resources matter. What is the underlying theory that supports such claims? There are allusions, as our analyses indicate, but there is a lack of explicit and systematic applications of theories.

(5) The macro (or structural) approaches neglect the micro level. For example, if it is claimed that a change of political opportunities alters collective political action it is ignored why individual actors should change their political behavior if somewhere in the society some political opportunities change. In other words, the explanations are superficial in the sense that it is not really explained why political action changes: the process or mechanism on the individual level that instigates protest is not considered explicitly. However, it seems that macro theorists are uneasy with pure macro hypotheses: they typically invoke processes on the micro level to explain the macro outcomes. But this occurs mostly implicitly. That is to say, no explicit micro-macro explanation is provided.

(6) The approaches that are primarily micro-oriented do in general not engage in relating the micro variables to the macro level. For example, if identity or framing matter one would like to know what changes on the macro level (such as a nuclear accident or a change of government) have exactly what effects on the values of these variables. Again, there is in general no micro-macro explanation.

(7) Our analyses in the previous chapters have shown that all perspectives implicitly apply a micro model. But no perspective specifies this model in detail. The micro models suggested explicitly in the literature are rarely used.

(8) The empirical validity of most of the approaches is questionable. If there is research that can be regarded as a test we often find falsifications. In this situation one would expect serious attempts to modify the underlying theories or conceive new ones. However, this is not a central agenda in the social movement field. The "solution" to problems of the approaches is factor explanations, as was said before.

There are many problems that are specific to each approach, as the discussion in the book shows. We will not repeat the results of these detailed analyses here. The major deficiencies mentioned in this section already suggest that an improvement of the state of theory is necessary.

Each of the previous chapters that address one of the approaches includes a section about what can be learned for the explanation of movement related phenomena. The most important point is that the factors the perspectives emphasize can be integrated into a theoretical framework that was the subject of the previous chapter and will be shortly outlined in the next section.

2. The alternative: the structural-cognitive model as a theory-based micro-macro explanation

The alternative suggested to the extant social movement perspectives is the structural-cognitive model (SCM) proposed in chapter 11. The two most important ingredients of this model are the following.

(1) A basic claim of the SCM is that micro-macro explanations are desirable. This means that the macro approaches – the resource mobilization and opportunity structure perspectives – are no longer self-contained theoretical paradigms. Instead, they are propositions to be explained. For example, assume that protests increase after a new coalition in the parliament has formed. Proponents of the political opportunity structure perspective would probably be satisfied by stating that this is consistent with their theory that changing opportunities raise protests and that the new coalition was such a changing opportunity.

This would be unsatisfactory from the perspective of the structural-cognitive model. First of all, it is not at all clear that the new coalition was a political opportunity. That has to be determined empirically by examining whether the (actual or perceived) chances of success have changed. Even if this has been determined empirically and even if it has turned out that the new coalition has changed the "chances of success," the explanation would not yet be satisfactory: it has to be explained why the new coalition has brought about protest. The question is what effects the new coalition has had on the incentives of various actors to engage in some form of collective action. The perceived "chances of success," i.e. the likelihood that joint action would raise goal attainment, is only one variable. The micro model specified in chapter 4 includes many other variables that are more important than the expected success of a group.

Looking at the effects of macro changes on the incentives for various groups implies that the process of collective action is explained. Perhaps there was a particularly strong change of incentives for a particular group that initiated a protest. Then other groups with a low threshold of participation followed suit. This, in turn, changes incentives of other actors, etc. Such an explanatory strategy yields a full-fledged explanation that proceeds from a change of a macro variable and ends in a macro change of collective action.

(2) Another important feature of the SCM is that it provides a synthesis of the different approaches in the following way.[1] The macro variables such as societal resources and political opportunities are used as factors that may but need not affect incentives on the micro level. Empirical research and theory must determine what the effects of such macro changes are.

These and many other macro variables affect micro variables. We assume that all relevant macro changes first enter the cognitive system of individuals and set in motion cognitive processes (i.e. framing processes). These effects on the cognitive system may create incentives to protest (see, for details, the previous chapter and

Figure 11.1). This happens if macro changes meet with a mental model with a "favorable" cognitive structure. Chapter 9 suggests what that means. These incentives then have a direct impact on protest.

Incentives include material as well as non-material costs and benefits. Among the non-material incentives is identity or identification with a group. Thus, existing approaches such as the framing or identity perspectives are parts of a micro theory that is a component of the SCM.

To conclude, the SCM provides micro-macro explanations and thus avoids the explanatory incompleteness of pure macro and pure micro approaches. The model further accomplishes an integration or synthesis of the approaches.

3. An illustration: Is something missing in the explanation of collective mobilization in Llano del Beal?

Chapter 4, section 2, applied the theory of collective action which was the theme of chapter 3 to the field of social movements and political protest. The application was illustrated with a case study: a long-term protest in a small Spanish mining village – Llano del Beal (LdB) – against the construction of a new pit. The question we will now address reads: to what extent do the existing social movement perspectives improve the explanation of the mobilization and protests in LdB? F. Linares (2004), the author of the study, does not discuss alternative explanations. Nonetheless, it is interesting to explore whether the approaches discussed after chapter 4 will complement or perhaps invalidate Linares's explanation. Finally, it will be shown how the SCM fits into the explanation outlined in chapter 4, section 2.

To be sure, Linares does not refer to the resource mobilization perspective, but the term "resources" is used several times in the article and refers to personal investments for the production of the public good. The author further addresses resources of groups. It is not spelled out what this means, but it seems to refer to the size of the group and the resourcefulness of the members. "External help" (472, note 16) is also mentioned as a resource of the protesters. This reference to resources in an explanation that applies the theory of collective action confirms what has been said in chapter 5: resources are a component of the theory of collective action and of rational choice theory in general.

What about political opportunities: are there events in LdB that have changed the actual or perceived chances of success of the protesters? Linares does not mention the term. What proponents of the political opportunity structure (POS) approach would probably do in this situation is to classify *ad hoc* various events that occurred at LdB as a POS. For example, an encounter of the company that intended to develop the pit on the one hand and representatives of the residents on the other could be called a "political opportunity." The residents were informed about the meeting in a well attended assembly. "This gathering could be described as the opening shot of a marathon of resistance which lasted for three and a half years, until the mining finally came to an end in May 1991" (Linares 2004: 444). Linares describes the ensuing activities in detail. We can thus assume that the encounter has changed various incentives. But Linares does not present data that could provide information about what incentives changed for which groups of residents. That would be important to know, because this would explain mobilization and protest.

Is the meeting or the encounter a POS? We don't know this because Linares does not present data that show whether the meeting has changed the (actual or perceived) "chances of success" of the residents – the defining characteristic of a POS. What is important to know is which events have changed which incentives. "Chances of success" (or, in other words, perceived group success) is only one of those incentives and, as has been argued before, not a very important one. Whatever the importance of this incentive is, it is a component of the theory of collective action. We thus don't need the POS concept. What we need is detailed propositions about the effects of macro changes on incentives. These propositions are not offered by the POS perspective.

Linares's account does not mention "identity" either. As was shown in chapter 7, "identity" in the sense of "identification" can be integrated into the theory of collective action as a possible incentive. Could the identification with the village have had any impact on the mobilization and protests in LdB? We do not know. Most residents have lived in the village for a long time, and some identification may have developed. But it is implausible that identification would have had a strong effect on the emergence of protest. The issue was the quality of life in the village and thus a severe grievance. It is plausible that social incentives and an acceptance of a norm of protest drove participation. From Linares's account it seems further plausible that perceived personal influence mattered, i.e. residents believed they could influence the government to stop the construction of the pit, and in this case grievances would be a strong incentives. Based on our micro model (chapter 4), grievances might also have indirect effects on protest – via changes of the norm to protest and social incentives. But it cannot be excluded that those who were strongly attached to the village had an additional incentive to protest. Thus, including identity in the model could have improved the explanation but would not have invalidated it.

"Framing" is not addressed in Linares's article either. As was shown in chapter 11 (see Figure 11.1), framing processes shape incentives. If framing processes are not included in an explanation, the incentives explanation is still valid, but something is missing. That is the case in Linares's study. How the individuals' beliefs, values, attitudes, and norms have changed in the course of the mobilization is not known, but would be an additional interesting aspect of the explanation.

Could the dynamics of contention approach (DCA) add something to the explanation of the protests in LdB? First of all, these protests are an example of "contentious politics" (see the definition cited in chapter 10) so that the DCA can be applied. But since the events in LdB are only a single episode and since the DCA is concerned with at least two cases, "mechanisms" or "processes" are not at issue and not discussed by Linares. Nonetheless, it could be examined to what extent the mechanisms or processes identified by McAdam, Tarrow, and Tilly (2001) exist in LdB. For example, is there "collective attribution of threat and opportunity", "social appropriation," "brokerage," etc. (see chapter 10, section 2)? We can safely assume that these (and perhaps most of the other) mechanisms suggested by the authors can be found in LdB. For example, a "broker" was the residents' association that negotiated with the company and the government on behalf of the residents. What does it contribute to the explanation of the processes in LdB when we know that the residents' association was a "broker"? Substantively, that is what was described in the case study, but there was no new term for this process. Now we have a new term and can call this process "brokerage." But this term does not add anything to the explanation. Assuming that the other "mechanisms" existed in LdB as well we could nicely apply all the new concepts to denote phenomena that have been described by Linares with a new vocabulary. However, this would not improve the explanation at all.

Those who advance the DCA might argue that it is interesting to know that "attribution of threat and opportunity," etc. are present in LdB as well as in many other episodes. This may be granted. But the question is what this information does add to explaining processes of contention in all these cases. Our answer is: very little.

To what extent does the SCM go beyond the explanation outlined in chapter 4, section 2? Compared to the graphic representation of the SCM in the previous chapter 11, Figure 11.1C, the explanation in chapter 4 has all the ingredients of the SCM – the micro model and bridge assumptions linking the micro and macro level – with one exception: cognitive processes are missing. Thus, the explanation could be improved by knowing what the mental models of the residents and of different groups of the residents were and how the situation changed which cognitive elements.

When we compare such a full fledged explanation with the explanation that could be provided by the existing theoretical perspectives – see the first part of this section – it is evident that the SCM provides a much more satisfactory explanation.

4. An agenda for future theory and research

The SCM suggests an agenda for future theory and research. Compared to existing social movement theory, new questions are to be explored and additional analytical steps in explaining social movement phenomena must be taken. Furthermore, research designs are recommendable that include subjective data.

Exploring the microfoundation of contentious politics

The first major component of the agenda is to *apply and further develop general social psychological theories*. Imagine that the recommendation to apply micro theories would be followed by the authors of all the case studies of protest and social movements, including the proponents of the dynamics of contention approach. This would lead, as was argued in chapter 1, to deeper and more valid explanations. We would learn why, i.e. under what conditions, macro relations hold and why they hold.

This first component of the agenda does not imply that the existing general micro theories are perfect. On the contrary, there are different social psychological theories (see chapter 1), and we need to integrate them. Further comparative tests are important. This means, among other things, that we need some overarching general micro theory that includes the specific existing theories as special cases.

A first step of integrating and improving general micro theories should be that social movement scholars delve more deeply into the work about these theories. This would avoid the numerous misunderstandings and misrepresentations of these theories. This holds especially for the theory of rational action. We have mentioned in almost every chapter caricatures of this theory that were attacked by movement scholars. The discussion thus suffers from various typical misunderstandings.

It is further necessary that the micro theories referring to protest or contention (see chapters 3 and 4) are refined. This could be done by applying, among other things, the *general* micro theories (such as the attitude theory by Fishbein and Ajzen): it could be examined to what extent they are consistent with the *specific* micro hypotheses about protest. And it could be explored whether the application of the general micro theories in different fields could yield suggestions for factors that might operate in the field of protest and social movements as well.

Micro-macro analyses

Arriving at deeper explanations means to learn how the macro (or structural) factors influenced the motivation of the actors involved in the protest and how this change of the incentives brought about the behavior to be explained. This means that micro-macro analyses are important in explaining collective political action. Thus, if specific episodes of contention are to be explained, one should no longer only look at structural factors. The goal should be to examine explicitly how structural factors have changed individual incentives of different groups of actors. That is the second component of the agenda: engage more than before in micro-macro explanations.

Theoretical integration

The third component of the agenda takes up the integrative thrust of the SCM: an important topic should be to further explore the relations of the existing social movement approaches to the structural-cognitive model. This implies several tasks.

One is to elaborate relationships between the macro factors spelled out in the resource mobilization and political opportunity perspective on the one hand and individual incentives on the other. These are top-down or macro-to-micro relationships. For example, if opportunities or – in general, elements of the political environment – change: what are the most common effects on the independent variables of the micro model of protest outlined in chapter 3? The common hypothesis that macro changes are only related to the "probability of success" is inadequate:[2] if this variable has any direct effect on behavior at all, it is certainly not the most important variable, as has been argued in chapter 4. This part of the agenda would yield an inventory of empirical generalizations about effects of macro factors on the theoretically relevant micro variables that could be used in further research.

Another possibility of integration concerns the micro approaches. We have discussed the identity approach and have argued that "identification" is one of the possible incentives to collective action. As was seen before, the concept of identity has many different meanings. It would be important to reconstruct other meanings in a precise way and examine to what extent these identity-concepts can be linked to the structural-cognitive model. Can they also, like identification, be integrated as incentives into the theory of collective action?

How are emotions and culture related to the structural-cognitive model? A detailed answer would require another chapter. A few comments must suffice. A common misunderstanding is that rational actor theory cannot deal with culture. Culture consists of a vast number of phenomena. For example, most of the constraints and preferences – variables of the theory of rational action – are part of the culture of a society. Thus, variables of this theory *denote* cultural elements. Furthermore, cultural items may *influence* preferences and constraints. In the socialization process, preferences and beliefs are learned. On the macro level, cultural items may *affect* the micro variables of the applied micro theory. Thus, even a superficial analysis indicates that "culture" can easily be integrated into the SCM. More thorough theoretical analyses are necessary to examine whether this claim is correct. In passing, it may be of interest that the explanatory relevance of culture has not gone unnoticed by proponents of rational choice theory (see, e.g., Bednar and Page 2007).

Emotions are very popular in the social movement literature and are a major issue in rational choice theory as well. One important point for integrating emotions and the SCM is that some emotions are *equivalent with* variables of the theory of rational action. For example, "anger" about a political decision is an intense discontent or preference for the provision of a public good. Furthermore, emotions may *affect* incentives. Examples are "hate" or "jealousy": in crimes of passion these emotions will lead to misperception of the consequences of a crime. In both cases there is no contradiction between rational choice theory and emotions. Does this hold for other kinds of emotions as well? An important question in regard to explaining social movement phenomena would be to what extent emotions are related to the independent variables of the micro model that explains social movement participation.

A topic that is rarely addressed by social movement scholars is the influence of personality characteristics. In one of the few discussions and reviews of personality characteristics and protest Snow and Oliver (1995: 577–579) conclude that research on the effects of personality characteristics suggests that they have some merit in explaining protest behavior. It would be interesting to analyze to what extent personality characteristics are compatible with rational choice theory or with other social psychological theories that may be used as a microfoundation for explaining social movement phenomena.

Numerous other substantive questions could be tackled from the perspective of the SCM. One question could be when social networks matter. Research shows that social networks have quite different effects, depending on the situation (for a short review of the state of the arts see Vala and O'Brien 2007: 79–81). There is a whole list of effects. But what the conditions are for these effects is still an open question. Applying the micro model or the theory of collective action could specify under what conditions which network structures have which effect on protest or other activities – via the incentives.

Proponents of the dynamics of contention approach emphasize dynamics. To what extent is the SCM capable of explaining processes of contention? Interesting existing work on the dynamics and cycles of protest is found in the work of Biggs (2003, 2005), Minkoff (1997) and, of course, Tarrow (see, e.g., 1998: chapter 9); for a review and discussion see Koopmans 2004. Work on the emergence of revolutions is pertinent here as well.

These are only few of the questions that need further inquiry. Again, the major thrust of the agenda is to provide full-fledged explanations which include, among other things, a micro-macro perspective. Another ingredient is a general theory of action as the theoretical foundation. This is in particular a broad rational choice theory that includes various other micro approaches such as identity and framing, as has been shown before.

The agenda pursued in this book is inconsistent with each of the single existing theoretical paradigms of social movement research. As a matter of fact, it modifies these approaches by integrating them into a single theoretical model. For example, it is argued that the macro approaches such as the POS perspective are not valid: POSs affect protest only if the impact on the incentives is strong enough. In a micro-macro model that is equivalent with the structural-cognitive model POSs are related to incentives. Only after integration of the approaches into the SCM it becomes apparent that they are no longer inconsistent: they become ingredients of the SCM.

There is another difference between this model and a theoretical strategy discussed in chapter 1 which simply lumps together the key variables of the different approaches – we called this "factor explanation." Instead, we favor explanation by applying theories. In other words, in this book we engage in "paradigm warfare" (Tarrow 2004). Wars and warfare are really bad things. Thus, "attacking" paradigms is warfare and, because wars are horrible, this must be stopped. In contrast, factor explanations – the alternative strategy to theoretical explanations – are peaceful. The idea is: everything social movement scholars have written is good and true, only different aspects of reality are emphasized. We strongly disagree with this view. First of all, the term "warfare" is a very inappropriate expression that has no place in a scientific discourse. If scientists discuss theories this has nothing to do with a war: no person is killed or injured. In science scholars try to test and falsify theories in order to find better explanations. The latter is the explicit goal of the theoretical sciences, and trying to discover theoretical problems is the ideal strategy to achieve this goal. This is accomplished by comparative theory testing which philosophers of science consider the best strategy of achieving scientific progress. In contrast to the "everything-is-good" strategy, the structural-cognitive model does not provide factor explanations but suggests theoretical integration and, thus, applies theory. To use the term "warfare" is, to say the least, an awkward description of the scientific enterprise of comparative theory discussion.

Extending existing research designs

Most empirical research on social movements and political protest uses macro data such as protest event data or documents referring to activities, goals, or ideologies of groups such as social movements. The SCM requires subjective data: explanations that address the effects of macro events on incentives need to ascertain characteristics of individuals. This means that research that takes the SCM seriously must find ways to look at the cognitive processes, incentives and actions of individuals.

What is to be explained?

The dynamics of contention approach has extended the universe of discourse to be studied by social movement scholars. There is one set of explanatory questions that has been neglected so far in this approach and in the vast literature on social movement phenomena: it is the origin of groups and social movements in particular. The focus of the literature is on explaining mobilization and protest. But how do social movements originate in the first place? This is not identical with the question of the growth and decline of movements. This question presupposes that movements exist already. Macro hypotheses claiming that under certain conditions new social movement organization originate (see the hypotheses discussed in chapter 5) do not address the process of emergence in any detail. The question is to explain the first steps of the origin of a movement or of groups akin to movements.

It seems plausible that the theory of collective action can be applied. If there is no group and if there are individuals with common goals one option is to form a group. But what are the incentives that lead to the formation of groups? If there are incentives to form a group, what is the kind of group that is set up? An important agenda for future research is a focus on group emergence.

There is some recent work on coalition formation (see, e.g., Staggenborg 1986; van Dyke 2003) that could be used to generate hypotheses on group formation. Forming a coalition means that groups emerge that consist of groups. Perhaps the decision processes of collective actors can be used to model similar decisions of individual actors.

"Natural science" or "constructivist" framework in the explanation of contention?

There is one difference in the writings of the theory of collective action, the resource mobilization perspective, and the political opportunity structure approach on the one hand and the identity and framing approach on the other which has not yet been addressed in detail in this book. Proponents of the latter perspectives pursue another methodological orientation: for the framing perspective, "ethnomethodological and phenomenological approaches have seemed appropriate" or a "constructionist standpoint" (Benford 1997: 412; see also, e.g., Adair 1996; Johnston 2002; Morris and McClurg Mueller 1992). Proponents of the identity approach will subscribe to this methodological orientation as well. This holds, for example, for Melucci who is a major proponent of the identity perspective (see chapter 7). He advances a "constructionist" view (1989: part I) as well.

It is not possible to discuss these different orientations in detail. This would require another chapter, and this book is already too long. We will only make two comments. One is that it is so far not clear what exactly a "constructivist" perspective means that is held by social movement scholars. There are many different conceptions of "constructivism" (see, e.g., Hacking 1999; Kukla 2000). Before it is not known what version of "constructivism" social movement scholars advance, it is not possible to discuss the strengths and weaknesses of their orientation.

In looking in detail at the texts in the social movement literature that use a constructivist terminology it seems that it is just another language for familiar phenomena. Two examples illustrate this. (1) Melucci (1988: 331) addresses the following question: "By means of what processes do the actors construct a common action?" Apparently, this statement can be translated as: "By means of what processes do the actors *perform* a common action?" (2) The same author argues (340): "The expectation is a construction of social reality that enables an actor to relate to the external world." This seems to mean that expectations are *influenced* by social reality and that these expectations then enable "an actor to relate to the external world."

It seems that differences between orientations are diminished or perhaps even disappear if concrete research projects are undertaken. The research cited in chapters 7 and 8 is qualitative as well as quantitative, and the propositions tested are formulated as normal causal or correlational statements.

These comments suggest that we should not take the alleged different philosophical orientations in the study of protest and social movements too seriously. It seems that the common methodological orientation of all social movement scholars is to formulate testable propositions and to test them in a way that falsification is possible.

5. Summary and conclusions

This chapter first summarizes the most important strengths and weaknesses of the existing theoretical perspectives in the field of social movements and political protest. We then provide a short overview of the alternative theoretical framework suggested in this book, namely the structural-cognitive model.

We presented a case study about the development of protest in a Spanish mining village in chapter 4 that should illustrate the application of the theory of collective action. Nothing has been said there about the relevance of the resource mobilization, political opportunity structure, identity, and framing approach for the explanation of the protests. In the present chapter, it is discussed to what extent these approaches could improve the explanation of protests. The answer is that improvements will probably be minor. It is further argued that the application of the theory of collective action in chapter 4 is largely consistent with the structural-cognitive model: only cognitive processes are missing.

Based on these considerations we outline an agenda for future research. One component is a further exploration of the microfoundation of explaining contentious politics. In other words, further research is needed to refine the micro theories applied in micro-macro explanations. A general demand of the agenda is to focus on micro-macro analyses because only they provide full-fledged explanations.

More effort needs to be invested in the further development of the intended theoretical integration which is a major goal of the structural-cognitive model. For example, it has to be explored how emotions, culture, and personality characteristics can be integrated into the model. A final point addressed is the different philosophical orientations in the field: we find a "natural science" orientation on the one hand and a "constructivist" stance on the other. Our brief discussion suggests that one should not take these different orientations too seriously: if it comes to specific research it seems that the differences are minor or even non existent.

The list of theoretical perspectives addressed in this book is not complete. There are other research programs, but they are just suggestions in an initial phase, i.e. there is not yet a voluminous body of work that pursues these research programs. Examples are Koopmans's suggestion for an evolutionary perspective (Koopmans 2005) or Zald's reconceptualization of social movements (Zald 2000a, 2000b). We will not discuss such perspectives. This should not be understood as any judgment about their fruitfulness. The reason for omitting them is simply that this book is already long enough, so that it did not seem useful to include other additional material.

Notes

1. What kind of theory do we need and what is a good theory?

1 In this book the concepts "theory," "perspective," and "approach" are used interchangeably. This is done in the social movement literature as well. Actually, none of the "approaches" this book focuses on is a theory in the strict sense, namely a set of general propositions that are used to derive other more special propositions. The "approaches" are a rather loose collection of hypotheses and concepts. They got their name due to the major factors they focus on, such as resources, political opportunities, identities, and framing. Only in the present chapter are we concerned with theories in the strict sense.

2 The expressions "micro-macro" and "macro-micro" relationship or model have the same meaning throughout the book.

3 In what follows we do not distinguish between different macro levels. Sometimes reference is made to the meso level. For example, the society may be the macro level and social movements the meso level. We will leave it open how many macro levels can and should be distinguished. This depends on the explanatory questions. If it turns out to be useful to distinguish several macro levels then the following argument on the micro foundation of macro propositions holds for each macro level.

4 This chapter will thus not provide an introduction to or treatise of the philosophy of the social sciences. This is the topic of numerous textbooks. One of my favorite books about philosophy of science in general is Chalmers 1982. Two books which focus on theory construction and explanation and are thus particularly relevant for this context are Little 1991 and Reynolds 2007 (first 1971).

5 See Merton (1957: 5–10); 1967: chapter 2. For a discussion and further references see Opp 1970.

6 There is an extensive literature that describes and discusses RCT. See in particular Becker (1976: chapter 1); Frey 1999; Heap *et al.* 1999; Sandler 2001. For the application in sociology see the reviews by Hechter and Kanazawa 1997; Voss and Abraham 2000. See also the references in Note 9.

7 Authors not only fail to distinguish different versions of RCT, they misrepresent its contents in other ways. For example, relative deprivation theory is not to be included in rational choice approaches (Snow and Oliver 1995: 583), and it is further not a "core feature" that there are "conscious intentional decisions" (Snow and Oliver 1995: 584). The theory posits that costs and benefits govern human behavior. This does not imply that there needs to be calculation. This is a behavioral alternative, and it can thus be explained when people calculate.

8 This assumption is discussed in chapter 7, section 4.

9 For details about this wide version see, e.g., Boudon 1996; Frey 1999; Goldthorpe 1998; Hedström 2006; Hirshleifer 1985; Opp 1999; Simon 1983. A detailed discussion of the narrow and wide version is provided in Opp 1999. For an account and a discussion related to protest and social movements see Oberschall (1993: 32–38).

10 See the findings in Henrich *et al.* 2004.

11 For a detailed analysis of the tautology charge and other objections against a wide version of RCT see Opp 1999.

12 Another example is the statement "if persons are members of a social system, they interact with each other." It is analytically true because "social system" is defined as a set of individuals who interact with each other. Thus, the sentence is equivalent to "if individuals interact with each other, they interact with each other" which is true.

13 The reader who wants to consult a treatise on formal logic may look at textbooks such as Suppes 1957 (new paperback edition 1999), McKay 1989 or Priest 2000.

14 For detailed expositions and discussions of the theory see, e.g., Feather 1982; Eagly and Chaiken (1993: 231–241). One of the first scholars who applied the theory to explain social movements activities is Klandermans 1984. Although this article is very frequently cited with approval (see, e.g., Snow *et al* 1986: 470) VET is very rarely applied in the social movements literature. This holds for the other theories discussed in this section as well.

15 Substantively, this means that the effect of a goal (or utility), such as a cleaner environment on, e.g., demonstrating, depends on the likelihood with which the achievement of the goal is expected (this is perceived influence). There is thus an interaction effect of "utility" and "probability" on behavior.

16 First see Fishbein and Ajzen 1975. See in particular Ajzen 1991 and further Ajzen 1988, 1996. For recent reviews see Ajzen and Fishbein 2005; Armitage and Conner 2001; Ajzen and Manstead 2007.

17 The basic reference of dissonance theory is Festinger 1957; more recently see Harmon-Jones and Mills 1999. The initial paper of balance theory is Heider 1946. See further Heider 1958; Cartwright and Harary 1956. Both theories are described in Eagly and Chaiken 1993.

18 For exceptions see de Weerd and Klandermans 1999; Klandermans and de Weerd 2000; Reicher 1984, 1996.

19 There is an extensive literature on SIT. See in particular Abrams and Hogg 1990, 1999; Ellemers, Spears, and Doosje 1999; Ellemers 1993; Mäs 2005; Mummendey *et al.* 1999.

20 The quotation illustrates the way some scholars criticize a theory: they use swearwords ("obscurantism") instead of providing detailed critical analyses. This kind of "criticism" will be ignored in this book.

21 The following model is based on extensive empirical and theoretical work on the East German revolution. See particularly Opp and Gern 1993; Opp 1994; Opp, Voss, and Gern 1995. See also Pfaff 2006 with a similar theoretical approach.

22 For the sake of simplicity, we neglect at this point another important proposition (see chapter 4): the incentives are *interdependent*. For example, the felt obligation to participate in protests (moral incentives) holds under certain conditions, and these conditions changed during 1989. For example, many respondents in our interviews believed that there is a duty to participate if one feels that protesting makes a difference. Thus, an increase in perceived influence further increases moral incentives.

23 Basic references are Hempel and Oppenheim 1948; Hempel 1965. For a discussion see, e.g., Little 1991.

24 They even state: "That there must be a link between the two [micro and macro level – KDO] should be obvious" (709).

25 This holds also for scholars who are not suspicious of being in favor of a rational choice perspective where micro-macro modeling is typical. See, e.g., Noakes and Johnston (2005: 1–2 and 20–22); Benford 1997: 416. See also McAdam 1988 who already discusses some macro-to-micro relationships in more detail than most other authors in the social movement literature. One of the few articles that addresses micro-macro models in detail is Gerhards and Rucht 1992.

26 See, e.g., Zald and McCarthy (2002: 161–162) who advance this procedure and who mention various empirical studies that examine the importance of the different factors.

Goodwin and Jasper (1999: 52–53) and McAdam (1999, see the new introduction) also advance factor explanations.

27 In regard to the causal diagram by McAdam, Tarrow and Tilly (2001: 17) mentioned before it is left open which kinds of mobilizing structures, etc. influence which types of "repertoires of contention."

28 This is based on Karl R. Popper's idea of empirical content. See, e.g., Popper 1959: chapter 6 and passim.

29 For a basic reference on concept formation see Hempel 1952. I do not know any better treatise on concept formation.

2 Protest, social movements, and collective action: conceptual clarifications and the subject of the book

1 Many other definitions are listed in Diani (1992) who also discusses common dimensions of the definitions.

2 See, e.g., the detailed case study by Downey (2006), based on the work of Lofland (1989, 1993): Downey describes in detail the strategies of certain movements during World War II.

3 Group size, selective incentives, and collective action

1 All subsequent numbers in parentheses refer to pages in this book.

2 For reviews of the theory, its critique, and its further development see in particular Hardin 1982; Heckathorn 1989, 1996, 2002; Lichbach 1995, 1996; Macy 1990, 1991; Marwell and Oliver 1993; Oliver 1993; Sandler 1992; Udéhn 1993.

3 See 1–3, 16–22 and 57–60. Olson mentions also sociological functionalism which is consistent with the general assumption he criticizes.

4 Marwell and Oliver (1993: 4) argue that collective action is any activity "aimed at" the provision of the public good. This implies that an activity that unintentionally leads to the provision of a public good – such as the unintended consequences of the demonstrations in communist countries in 1989 where the actors achieved much more than they dreamt of – is not an instance of collective action. Since we do not see any reason to exclude such events from the theory, it is preferable not to include the aim of the actors in the definition of collective action.

5 As was said before, the theory of collective action is about individual actors, whereas this example addresses firms. However, each firm can be treated as a single individual actor. It is assumed that the decision-makers in the firm have identical preferences and react in the same way to constraints.

6 Olson further assumes that the elasticity of demand is low: if the price decreases at a certain percentage, the demand increases at a lower percentage.

7 It is a misunderstanding that the market-example is used as an "analogy" for other groups (Fireman and Gamson 1979: 15). Olson only *illustrates* his theory with a group of firms in a competitive market. This does not at all imply that other groups are substantively similar to market groups. The theory is so general that it can be applied to very heterogeneous groups.

8 Olson introduces several classifications of groups such as privileged (i.e. small) groups, intermediate and latent (i.e. large) groups, but he also uses the quantitative formulation several times in the text.

9 We will not present Olson's formalization of his theory. This has been criticized convincingly by Kimura 1989; Marwell and Oliver (1993: 39–42); Sandler (1992: chapter 2). We will also not deal with the part of the theory about optimality. We are interested only in the extent to which a public good is provided, be it suboptimal or optimal.

10   As was said in chapter 1, the terms "micro-macro" or "macro-micro" model are used interchangeably.

11   For this distinction see chapter 1, section 1.

12   The updating of wrong beliefs is a complicated process which we will not address in this book. See, e.g., Breen 1999; Matsueda 2006. The simple assumption that in general beliefs adapt to reality is certainly not correct.

13   For a similar modeling see Finkel, Muller and Opp 1989: 887.

14   Empirical research on the conditionality of a norm to protest showed that perceived personal influence is a condition when participating in protest is regarded as a duty. See Jasso and Opp 1997; Opp 2001; Opp, Voss, and Gern (1995: 81–90).

15   See, e.g., Klandermans 1984, see also chapter 4, section 4, of the present book where Klandermans's model is discussed. See in particular Biggs (2003; see also 2005) for a good review of the literature and a discussion of "positive feedback," i.e. effects of recent participation of groups or individuals on the participation of others. In this section, we focus on the *expected* number of participants, whereas Biggs deals with the question of how actual recent participation affects later participation. This may have an effect on expected participation which, we assume, is the more important variable for explaining collective action. Nonetheless, some of Biggs's propositions (2003: 224–228) hold for the effects of the expected number of participants as well.

16   For a detailed discussion of the measurement argument against the wide version of the theory of rational action see Opp 1999.

17   For some empirical evidence for the following hypotheses see Jasso and Opp 1997; Opp, Voss, and Gern (1995: chapter 12).

18   For empirical evidence see Opp and Roehl 1990; Opp 1994. For a recent discussion of the effects of repression in general see Boykoff 2006; Davenport, Johnston, and Mueller 2005; Goldstone and Tilly 2001. See also a special issue of the journal "Mobilization": vol. 11, no. 2, June 2006.

19   Some of the following critique of the group size proposition has already been noted in the literature. There are also many other theoretical discussions and arguments specifying conditions for the validity of the group size propositions. See in particular Oberschall 1979; Oliver and Marwell 1988; Marwell and Oliver (1993: chapter 3); Hardin 1982; Sandler 1992. See further Bonacich *et al.* 1976; Chamberlain 1974; Frohlich and Oppenheimer 1970.

20   This book includes the ideas and sometimes the text of previous articles. In regard to the critical mass and production functions see, e.g., Oliver, Marwell, and Teixeira 1985.

21   The following argument applies to mobilization functions as well. For the sake of simplicity, we will focus on production functions.

22   This is actually the implicit argument in work that addresses production functions. See, e.g., Oberschall (1994: 80–84) where he explains several forms of production functions. The incentives that make up a production function may also depend on the characteristics of the public good. If, for example, a bridge is to be built there will be a step function because a bridge can only be used if it is finished.

23   It is now common to use the ambiguous term "mechanism" which sounds very scientific. In this book "mechanism" means "process." We thus use both terms interchangeably.

24   A goldmine of solutions to the free rider problem are the two voluminous books by Lichbach (1995, 1996).

25   Ferree further argues that there are many instances where selective incentives are not necessary (see 1992: 38–39). First of all, this is quite consistent with the version of the wide rational actor model used in this book: if perceived influence and discontent are high this may suffice to bring about collective action. Secondly, Ferree has a very narrow definition of selective incentives that seems to exclude non-material incentives. This is, as we saw, one of the typical misunderstandings of the theory of rational action that ignores the wide version.

26   See Frohlich, Oppenheimer, and Young 1971. See further Chong (1991: 125–133);

Marwell and Oliver 1993; Oberschall 1980; Popkin 1988; White 1988. See also the discussion of charisma as a particular ability of leaders to mobilize people, i.e. as a particular ability to change costs and benefits of others' behavior (Andreas 2007: 437). For the importance of "leadership capital" see Nepstad and Bob 2006. The basic idea that the behavior of certain groups of individuals influences the costs and benefits and, thus, the behaviors of others is much older. It is spelled out in detail particularly in Schelling 1978. For a discussion of leadership referring to social movement phenomena see Aminzade, Goldstone, and Perry 2001.

27 See also the literature referred to in the previous note. Frohlich, Oppenheimer, and Young (1971) in particular describe the incentives of political entrepreneurs.

28 This argument is referring to *thresholds*. Basic references are Granovetter 1978; Macy 1990, 1991; Braun 1995. See also Biggs (2003; 2005) who addresses the question of "positive feedback," i.e. the extent to which people engage in collective action when others do.

29 For the following argument which is supported by survey data see Opp, Voss, and Gern 1995. See further Pfaff 2006.

30 See the analyses of this process by Braun 1995; Lohmann 1994; Prosch and Abraham 1991.

31 There is meanwhile a vast number of experimental and other studies showing that in general there is a strong tendency to punish defectors or "suckers." See, e.g., the work of Ernst Fehr and co-authors, such as Fehr and Gächter 2000, 2002; Fehr, Fischbacher, and Gächter 2002; Fehr and Fischbacher 2003. See further Boyd *et al.* 2003; Horne 2007.

32 This is only a very rough characterization. For detailed discussions of evolutionary explanations, with further references, see, e.g., Fehr, Fischbacher, and Gächter 2002; Fehr and Fischbacher 2003; Henrich and Boyd 2001; Henrich *et al.* 2006; Price, Cosmides, and Tooby 2002.

33 This assumption is also made in the literature mentioned before. It discusses what happens *if* there are defectors, cooperators, and sanctioners in different quantities in a group setting. For example, what are the consequences of cooperation if there are many or few "strong reciprocators," i.e. persons who are willing "(I) to sacrifice resources to be kind to those who are being kind ... and (II) to sacrifice resources to punish those who are being unkind" (Fehr, Fischbacher, and Gächter 2002: 3).

4 Protest and social movements as collective action

1 Leites and Wolf's (1970) work seems to be the first application of a rational choice approach, that underlies the theory of collective action, to protest related behavior.

2 There is an article by Olson whose title suggests that he explains social movement phenomena (Olson 1986), but in fact it is an excerpt from his book of 1982.

3 A similar case where complete mobilization was achieved is Ermershausen in Bavaria (Holtmann and Killisch 1989). The issue was a government decision that aimed at integrating the largely autonomous village Ermershausen into a larger administrative unit and thus stripping it from its autonomy. The citizens fiercely opposed it and finally had success (personal communication from Everhard Holtmann, April 5, 2007).

4 Linares claims that norms *emerged* during the mobilization process. But his explanation of norm emergence is not convincing. It is more plausible that a cooperation norm existed and was *activated* during the process. In what follows I will therefore not discuss Linares's theoretical account of norm emergence.

5 Linares assumes that there is an S-shaped function. According to his description of the mobilization process, it seems more plausible to assume a decelerating function (see chapter 3, Figure 3.4, curve 5). That is to say, after the initial assembly the Residents' Association became active and, it seems, was able to mobilize a relatively large number of citizens. Thus, a few active people mobilize many others so that the curve is steep at the beginning and then flattens out.

6 Similarly, Goldstone (1994: 134) argues that an assurance game obtains if there are strong norms of cooperation. This means that there are general incentives to participate if others participate, but if others do not participate, it is best not to participate. See also Chong (1991: chapter 6).

7 See, e.g., the reviews by Finkel and Rule 1986; Gurney and Tierney 1982. See further, e.g., Law and Walsh 1983; Opp 1988, 2000; Useem 1980; Muller 1979, 1980; Muller and Jukam 1983. See further the discussion in the resource mobilization perspective on the role of deprivation, first in McCarthy and Zald 1977.

8 See, e.g., Finkel and Muller 1998; Finkel, Muller, and Opp 1989; Gibson 1991; Moe 1980; Muller and Opp 1986; Opp 1988, 1989; Opp, Voss, and Gern 1995.

9 See, e.g., Chong (1991: 93–100); Fleishman 1980; Jasso and Opp 1997; Marwell and Ames 1979; Muller 1979; Opp 1986; 1989; Opp, Voss and Gern 1995.

10 A basic article is Snow, Zurcher, and Ekland-Olson 1980. See further the chapters in Diani and McAdam 2003, in particular Passy, Oliver and Myers, Gould and McAdam; see further Gould 1991, 1993; Klandermans 1984; Marwell, Oliver, and Prahl 1988; McAdam 1986; 1988; McAdam and Paulsen 1993; Nepstad and Smith 1999; Oegema and Klandermans 1994; Opp and Gern 1993; Opp 1988, 1989, 1989b; Schussman and Soule 2005; Verba, Schlozman, and Brady 1995; Walsh 1978; for reviews and discussion see Kitts 2000; Passy 2001; Snow and Oliver (1995: 573–577).

11 The theory has been applied to protest behavior much earlier. See, e.g., Muller 1979. More recent work includes Finkel, Muller, and Opp 1989; Finkel and Muller 1998; Muller and Opp 1986; Opp 1986.

12 See, e.g., the lists of factors in Lofland 1996; Milbrath and Goel 1977. Wiltfang and McAdam 1991: note 1 also provides a list of various factors that have been used to explain activism. For reviews of the literature see Leighley 1995; Moore 1995; Whitely 1995.

5   The resource mobilization perspective

1 An early review of the approach is Jenkins 1983. McCarthy and Zald review their approach themselves several times: see Zald 1992; McCarthy and Zald 2002; Zald and McCarthy 2002. A collection of their articles is published in Zald and McCarthy 1987. The edited book by Zald and McCarthy (1979) comprises interesting articles related to the resource mobilization perspective. Other basic references are Gamson 1968, 1975; Oberschall 1973; Tilly 1978; Zald and Ash 1966. For critical analyses of the perspective see Buechler 1993; Kerbo 1982; Kitschelt 1991 and the response by Zald 1991; Perrow 1979; Pichardo 1988; Piven and Cloward 1991 (this is identical to Piven and Cloward 1992); Snyder and Kelly 1979; Turner 1981. It is interesting that McCarthy and Zald's article from 1977 is regarded as the major founding paper of the perspective. Many ideas of this paper are already included in Zald and Ash 1966 (which in my opinion should be regarded as the basic article of the approach). For a short but informative overview of the great number of empirical studies the RMP has spawned see Caniglia and Carmin (2005: 202–203). It goes without saying that it is not possible and not intended either to review the extensive critique of the RMP. We will only discuss those problems that seem most important to us.

2 At this point, it seems that the authors denote "social movements" as organizations and not yet as a set of opinions and cognitive beliefs of individuals – see below.

3 The authors note that this is "more of an orienting postulate than a directly testable hypothesis" (1224), but then they cite supporting evidence. Indeed, the hypothesis is testable: it can be compared at different times and across societies whether increasing or decreasing incomes lead to more or fewer resources provided to SMOs in a society.

4 The authors note correctly that their approach "has strong affinities with resource mobilization theory in sociology," but that they "concentrate upon the resources available to individuals," whereas the RMP focuses on social movement organizations (270, note 2).

5 We leave it open whether the relationship of the macro variable and cost is an empirical or analytical one. At least the macro resources must be perceived in order to become relevant for action so that there is at least an empirical component in the relationship.

6 This is also consistent with Zald's observation (1992: 335) that the RMP's "underlying psychological decision model has been a utilitarian model of cost/benefits."

7 See, e.g., Downey 2006 for another case study where the detailed behaviors of groups are described. The "strategic rationales" of the groups, outlined in this article, may be used to formulate some general hypotheses about conditions for the choice of strategies.

8 For a summary of the research see Walsh 1988. See further Walsh 1981; Walsh and Warland 1983; Walsh and Cable 1986; Walsh 1986; Walsh 1987; Cable, Walsh, and Warland 1988.

6 Political opportunity structures, protest, and social movements

1 For an overview see Meyer 2004. For an exposition of the theory see further Kitschelt 1986; Kriesi 1995; Kriesi *et al.* 1992; McAdam 1982: chapter 3; McAdam *et al.* 1996; Piven and Cloward 1979: chapter 1; Tarrow 1983, 1991a, 1991b, 1998; Tilly 1978. The latter book was also mentioned as a basic work of the resource mobilization perspective. This indicates that this and the POS perspective may be difficult to distinguish. We will discuss possible differences later in this chapter. There is meanwhile an extensive critical literature on various aspects of the POS perspective. A particularly fervent and devastating view is provided by Goodwin and Jasper 1999. This article, together with responses and other discussions of the perspective is included in Goodwin and Jasper 2004.

2 For ease of exposition, we will henceforth speak most of the time of "opportunities" or "opportunity structures" instead of *political* opportunities or opportunity structures.

3 It is worth noting that these definitions include terms that need further clarification. For example, one definition uses the unclear concept of power. What is a "significant" reduction of power? How can the "receptivity or vulnerability of the political system" be assessed?

4 It may be noted in passing that this quotation implies a macro-to-micro relationship: POSs (macro level) affect incentives (micro level).

5 I assume that the relationships between the dimensions and the probabilities are empirical and not analytical, although sometimes the formulations of the dimensions suggest analytical relationships. In Tarrow's dimensions, for example, "access" seems to imply *logically* that the likelihood of goal attainment is high, i.e. high access *means* that the likelihood of goal achievement (which means access) is high. Furthermore, it seems that a decline in the state's capacity *logically* implies that the likelihood of goal attainment increases. All this would then mean that the dimensions *define* POS. The problem then would be what the relationship between the dimensions and the general definition of POS is. In what follows, it is assumed that the relationship between the dimensions and POS is empirical.

6 See also the discussion in Jenkins, Jacobs and Agnone (2003: 280–281) about the different effects of political allies on movement support. It is interesting that the authors provide hypotheses about conditions when which effect obtains. This implies that at least sometimes dimensions have different effects on goal attainment of groups.

7 See, e.g., McAdam's causal model (1982: chapter 3), the causal model in Kriesi *et al.* 1995: XVI and XX, and in Kriesi *et al.* (1992: 22). Tarrow mentions various factors as well (1998: 71–72 and passim). See also section 8 in this chapter.

8 This is described bluntly and succinctly by Diani (1996: 1056): "Generally, these analysts produce lists of political variables that might be expected to affect protesters' behavior and chances of success. Then they explain specific episodes of mobilization by selecting from that list those dimensions that best fit the case under investigation. They account for challengers' successes by pointing out one or more facilitating conditions; they account

for their failures by stressing the absence of opportunities. Usually, however, they omit a systematic analysis of those situations in which some opportunities are clearly available while others are clearly not. This situation is problematic inasmuch as the absence of some opportunities could compensate for the presence of others."

9 See also van Dyke (2003: 23). This curve is based on Tilly 1978.

7 Collective identity and social movement activity

1 Melucci has published not only this article about his approach. See further in particular Melucci 1989 and 1995. I do not see that this later work solves any of the problems of the 1988 article that will be discussed in this chapter. Therefore, we will focus on Melucci 1988.

2 There is a vast literature on the identity perspective in general and on identity and social movement phenomena in particular. The book by Weigert, Teitge, and Teitge (1986) provides an informative overview of the identity perspective in general; for general discussions and reviews see Brewer 2001; Brubaker and Cooper 2000; Howard 2000; Huddy 2001. Reviews of the identity approach for the field of social movements are Polletta and Jasper 2001; Hunt and Benford 2004.

3 Only once in this book I would like to express my utmost frustration about all the time I have spent to set up this causal diagram – the hardest work in the whole book. I first read the text (not only the citation above) and drew a diagram. The next day I read the text again – and I changed the diagram. I don't remember how many versions of the diagram I "constructed." If Melucci could see the model, he would perhaps suggest another version. This expression of frustration should perhaps make authors who produce such vague texts aware of how strong the negative externalities are they impose on those who wish to understand what their ideas are.

4 For the following discussion of the common features of definitions of the identity concept see particularly de Weerd and Klandermans 1999; Gamson 1992; Gould (1995: 12–23); Gurin *et al.* 1999; Klandermans and de Weerd 2000; Polletta and Jasper 2001; Tajfel and Turner 1986; Taylor 1989; Taylor and Whittier 1992; Wendt 1994.

5 See, e.g., the overview of Polletta and Jasper 2001 with further references. Empirical research in the identity tradition also focuses on this proposition – see below.

6 The studies reviewed are Biggs 2006; de Weerd and Klandermans 1999; Kelly and Breinlinger 1996 (see also Kelly and Kelly 1994); Mühler and Opp 2004; Simon *et al.* 1998; Stürmer *et al.* 2003; Stürmer and Simon 2004.

7 In the analyses of the panel studies by Kelly/Breinlinger and Stürmer/Simon the lagged dependent variable is not included. It is thus an open question whether identification has still an effect if the change of the dependent variable due to the independent variables is determined, i.e. if the lagged variable is included (see Finkel 1995).

8 Similar views are held by Ferree and Miller (1985: 39); Gamson (1992: 54); Klandermans 2004: 364. This position is not only advanced by social movement scholars. See, e.g., Macy 1997 and Anthony 2005.

9 For a similar argument see already Pizzorno 1978 and the discussion in Cohen 1985.

10 For more detailed hypotheses that explain gathering information and that can be applied to explain calculation see Riker and Ordeshook (1973: 19–32).

11 It is correct that "identification" is not *explicitly* included in Olson's theory or in the theory of rational action. This has led to the conclusion that in "individual utilitarian models such as Olson's (1965), the absence of a collective identity is assumed" (Gamson 1992: 57). However, a general theory does not include all the specific conditions that may motivate an individual's behavior. These specific conditions must be determined empirically. They are, in terms of the logic of explanation (see, e.g., Hempel 1965), initial conditions. It is thus not correct that Olson's theory excludes "identification" as a possible incentive for collective action.

12 Applying Heider's POX system, the units would be P (the person), O (the organization or group) and X (protest); the U (unit) or L (liking) relations between those cognitive elements are: P likes (identifies with) the organization O; P believes that protest makes the organization better off (there is thus a U-relation between O and X), and P protests (i.e. there is a U-relation between P and X). If P would not protest (i.e. the relation between P and X is negative) there would be imbalance which is costly to an individual. Balance theory will be applied to explain social movement phenomena, including the effects of identification, in chapter 9.

13 Although Friedman and McAdam (1992) also note that "collective identities function as selective incentives motivating participation" (p. 157), without giving a detailed justification of this claim, they argue that a shared collective identity is "a public good that all can consume without contributing to its production" (166). It is not clear what exactly the public good is. To be sure, a shared collective identity might *lead* to the provision of a public good, but it *is* not a public good: the benefits or costs of identification depend on the individuals' contribution or defection. Identification is, thus, by definition, clearly a selective incentive.

8 How framing influences mobilization and protest

1 See in particular Snow and Benford 1988, 1992; Snow and Oliver 1995; Benford 1997; Benford and Snow 2000; Snow 2004. Other basic work is Gamson 1982 (see also 1992a) and Tarrow 1992. For the history of the framing concept see Noakes and Johnston (2005: 3). These authors also provide a useful summary and discussion of the approach. For this see further Polletta and Ho (2006). Thorough critical analyses are rare. See, e.g., Benford 1997; Steinberg 1998, 1999.

2 "SMO" means "social movement organization." The authors adopt the terminology of McCarthy and Zald 1977 (see chapter 5 of this book).

3 In other writings Snow and associates sometimes vary their definition. For example, in an article of 1992 Snow and Benford write that a frame "refers to an interpretive schemata that simplifies and condenses the 'world out there' by selectively punctuating and encoding objects, situations, events, experience, and sequences of actions within one's present or past environment" (137). But, again, the authors refer to Goffman and argue that this definition is equivalent to Goffman's (137). Still another version is suggested in Snow and Benford 1988 (198 – see below). We will not discuss whether all these variations of definitions offered by Snow and associates are actually equivalent to Goffman's definition. We will restrict ourselves to Snow *et al.* 1986.

4 As McAdam (1996: 339), based on Snow and Benford (1988: 198), puts it: framing refers to the "conscious strategic efforts of movement groups to fashion meaningful accounts of themselves and the issues at hand in order to motivate and legitimate their efforts."

5 A short summary of these distinctions is provided by Benford and Snow (2000: 624–625).

6 We call a norm a "value" if it is used to justify another norm.

7 Frames usually consist of several cognitive elements. Only in rare cases a "frame" is a single element such as an argument. For example, a "similarity frame" is an argument claiming that men and women are similar (McCammon *et al.* 2007).

8 A typical misunderstanding in the social movement literature is that rational choice theory is equivalent with a narrow economic model. As emphasized time and again in this book a wide version of the theory is used (see chapter 1). Steinberg (1999: 742) and other authors (see the citations in the Steinberg article) are subject to such a misunderstanding when it is argued that the assumption of framing as a "rational" process implies that "discourse is thus analyzed in terms homologous to material resources."

9 There are attempts to specify differences between frames on the one hand and other concepts such as ideology on the other. See, e.g., Benford and Snow (2000: 613 and passim); Steinberg (1998: 847–850); Oliver and Johnston (2005: 186). See also the discussion in the journal "Mobilization," vol. 5, issue 1, 2000. Oliver and Johnston (2005) are right when they note that Snow and Benford – they refer to their article of 1988 – "neither provide justification for abandoning the term 'ideology' and substituting 'frame' in this context nor explain the relation between frames and ideologies." Oliver and Johnston outline differences between these concepts (see also the discussion of this article in Johnston and Noakes 2005). Such a discussion is not very useful because the concept of ideology is used in dozens of meanings (see, e.g., Boudon 1988). There is thus not "the" meaning of ideology. Consequently, it is not possible to delineate "the" difference between framing and ideology. What could be done is to compare different concepts of ideology and the framing concept (if there is only one). Before this is undertaken one should ask why we need such a conceptual discussion. Why not first improve the theory of framing and then discuss which concepts are most fruitful for such a theory.

10 A small essay by Mao Zedong "On Contradiction" shows how many meanings "contradiction" may have if it is not used in the strict sense of formal logic.

11 To illustrate such vague definitions: Ferree (2003: 310) defines "resonance" as the "mutually affirming interaction of a frame with a discursive opportunity structure supportive of the terms of its argument." "Discursive opportunity structures" are "institutionally anchored ways of thinking that provide a gradient of relative political acceptability to specific packages of ideas" (309).

12 Examples abound where multi-factor models are proposed with the variables from other approaches, based on orienting propositions and not on informative theory. One is Cress and Snow (2000) who explain success of homeless SMOs. In doing so they "draw on various perspectives ... by assessing ways in which organizational, tactical, political mediation, and framing factors interact and combine to account for variation in the outcomes achieved by the 15 homeless SMOs we studied" (1072). Again, no theory is applied. The model by Tarrow (1998) discussed in detail in chapter 6 is also a multi-factor model that includes the idea of framing and is constructed in the same vein.

13 The authors sometimes argue that certain frames "convince" lawmakers to change the law (see, e.g., 740). But the explicit proposition is that frames "induce lawmakers to expand jury laws" (733).

9 Identity, framing, and cognitive balance: toward a new theory of identity and framing

1 Heider's original presentation of his theory is his article from 1946, a more extensive treatment is given in his book from 1958. For expositions of BT see, e.g., Abell 1968; Alessio 1990; Doreian 1970: chapters 4 and 5; Doreian (2002: 95–99); Opp 1984. See also textbooks of social psychology such as Eagly and Chaiken 1993: 133–144. For reviews, including empirical assessments and critique of the theory, see Doreian 2002, 2004; Doreian and Krackhardt 2001; Hummon and Doreian 2003; Opp 1984. A major application of BT has been social networks. See, e.g., Holland and Leinhardt 1979; Ludwig and Abell 2007; see particularly the work of P. Doreian and collaborators such as Doreian 2002; Doreian *et al.* 1996. Other interesting sociological applications are Abell 1968, 1970; Alessio 1990 discusses the relationship between balance and exchange theory; Davis 1963 and a discussion and critique of this article by Becker and Körner 1974; Hummell 1967.

2 Incidentally, this statement is a naturalistic fallacy: it is not possible to derive a normative sentence ("women should ...") from a factual statement ("women are ..."). However, this is not of relevance in this context because the beliefs of the actors are important for their behavior, even if they are false or if their derivation is false.

3 Heider does not specify how the theory can be applied to more complex cognitive systems which consist of four or more entities. A general rule to compute balance is provided by Cartwright and Harary (1956) which we follow here.

4 For the relationship of the theory of cognitive dissonance which is very similar to BT (both pertain to the family of cognitive consistency theories) and the theory of rational action see Akerlof and Dickens 1982; Gilad, Kaish, and Loeb 1987.

5 Remember the definition of balance between two elements such as p and o: balance exists if all relations between p and o are positive. If, thus, p likes o but o does not like p, then imbalance is given.

10 The dynamics of contention approach – retreat to history?

1 For details about the development of the approach see the Foreword by Doug McAdam in Goldstone (2003: xiii–xvi). The books where the approach is presented or applied are McAdam, Tarrow, and Tilly 2001; Aminzade *et al.* 2001; Goldstone 2003. A first programmatic statement is McAdam, Tarrow, and Tilly 1996. There are meanwhile several critical comments on this approach. A first "Mobilization Forum" about the latter article is published in the journal "Mobilization" 1997, vol. 2, issue 1: 87–112. A symposium on the first book by McAdam, Tarrow, and Tilly of 2001 is published in the journal "Mobilization" 2003, vol. 8, issue 1: 109–141. a good summary with further references can be found in Staggenborg and Taylor (2005: 39). An attempt to "extend and apply" the approach is Tilly 2005. The most noteworthy critical analysis of the approach, based on the first programmatic paper of 1996 that presents the approach, is the article by Lichbach (1997). He is one of the few (actually, as far as I see, the only one) in the debate who advances a "rationalist" position. See also Lichbach 2005.

2 Page numbers refer to McAdam, Tarrow, and Tilly 2001.

3 For a discussion of this causal diagram see also chapter 1, section 5 of this book.

4 A relation in the strict logical sense is an attribute that refers to (at least) two objects simultaneously. Interaction (a interacts with b, symbolically: Iab or aIb) or sympathy (a likes b, symbolically: Lab or aLb) are examples. These are binary relations (i.e. they hold between two objects). A "ternary" relation such as "a has a conflict with b over c" holds between three objects simultaneously. For details see any textbook of formal logic such as Suppes 1957 or McKay 1989.

5 This is plausible when the authors begin with "paired comparisons" such as "similarities between the Mau Mau rebellion in Kenya and the Philippine Yellow Revolution of 1986" (14).

6 This is a remarkable conversion because all three authors are well known for their theoretical contributions to the field. See, e.g., McAdam 1982 and the new introduction to the second edition (McAdam 1999); Tarrow 1998 and Tilly 1978.

7 A similar but more complex causal model is suggested by McAdam (1999: XVI). It is not clear what the differences between the models are.

8 Some contributions in Hedström and Swedberg's book (1998) also reject the application of theory and the covering law model in mechanism-based explanation. For a detailed critique see Opp 2005.

9 See also the figures on pages 317, 323, and 333 in which various causal relationships between mechanisms are shown. Each diagram consists of a system of lawful statements.

10 This figure does not include those mechanisms listed in Table 9.1 (275) because they overlap with some mechanisms discussed in previous parts of the book.

11 For the difference between "threats" and "opportunities" see Goldstone and Tilly (2001: 182–183). Whereas "opportunity" refers to the likelihood of success to achieve a group's goals by protest actions, "threat" denotes the "risks and costs" of protest.

12 The explanation of the Mau Mau revolt that is briefly summarized above includes the hypothesis that changing opportunities affect mobilization. The problems of this

proposition have been discussed in detail in chapter 6. The typical *ad hoc* argument of the authors is an illustration of one of these problems: "opportunities" are, by definition, actual or perceived chances of success; it is not clear how the authors know that the events (such as the trend toward decolonization) actually changed these chances or their perception. This is simply assumed.

13 The problems of definitions that include causal statements were discussed first in chapter 1, section 7, and illustrated when the concept of political opportunities was analyzed (chapter 6).

11 The structural-cognitive model: a synthesis of collective action, resource mobilization, political opportunity, identity, and framing perspectives

1 Sometimes different macro levels are distinguished such as the state and social movements. Depending on the explanatory problem, macro variables of both types can be included in a micro-macro explanation (see chapter 1).

2 The website "http://en.wikipedia.org/wiki/List_of_anti-globalization_demonstrations" presents a list of protests.

3 For a very short description see della Porta *et al*. (2006: 1–3).

4 There is a vast literature on globalization that will not be cited or discussed at this point. A good brief summary with further references is the entry "globalization" in Wikipedia, the free encyclopedia.

5 For a description of differences see Buckman 2004. This book gives also information about the process of globalization, the development of the anti-globalization movement, and different views of groups making up the movement. A more detailed description of various movements, from the viewpoint of an activist, is provided by Starr 2000. Reitan (2007) gives a detailed account of recent developments of the movement and provides detailed case studies of several important networks. Information about the movement in different countries is provided in della Porta 2007.

6 The exact name of the movement is "Movimento dos Trabalhadores Rurais Sem Terra."

7 This section owes much to Carter (2005) who provides a very succinct and short description of the MST. The most extensive accounts of the foundation and development of the movement are Branford and Rocha 2002, Wright and Wolford 2003. An overview of the movement is also provided in Wikipedia, entry "Landless Workers' Movement."

8 http://news.bbc.co.uk/2/hi/americas/734071.stm

9 See the article by Isabella Kenfield in the Newsletter counterpunch from June 18, 2007 (http://www.counterpunch.org/kenfield06182007.html). A good summary of the activities of the SMT is Carter 2005.

10 The following account is to a large extent based on Morris 1984. For a succinct historical account that includes also recent developments of the movement see Riches 2004.

11 For an overview of many activities up to 2007 see the website "Civil Rights Timeline. Milestones in the modern civil rights movement": http://www.infoplease.com/spot/civilrightstimeline1.html. For a more detailed account of the development of the movement see Morris 1984 and Riches 2004.

12 The description of the situation in East Germany is based on Opp 1993. See further Opp, Voss, and Gern 1995; Pfaff 2006.

12 General discussion, conclusion, and an agenda for future research

1 See Figure 11.1 in chapter 11 that summarizes the SCM. Figure 11.2 shows how the different approaches are integrated into the model.

2 More precisely, POS is *defined* as a macro change that influences the chances of success. However, in order to determine whether a POS is given this causal link, i.e. an empirical hypothesis, must be tested – see chapter 6.

Bibliography

Aarts, H., Verplanken, B. & Van Knippenberg, A., 1998. Predicting Behavior from Actions in the Past: Repeated Decision-Making or a Matter of Habit? *Journal of Applied Social Psychology,* 28, 1355–1374.

Abell, P., 1968. Structural Balance in Dynamic Structures. *Sociology,* 2, 333–352.

Abell, P., 1970. The Structural Balance of the Kinship System of Some Primitive Peoples. *In* M. Lane (ed.) *Structuralism: A Reader.* London: Cape, 359–366.

Abrams, D. & Hogg, M. (eds) 1990. *Social Identity Theory: Constructive and Critical Advances,* Berlin: Springer.

Abrams, D. & Hogg, M. A. (eds) 1999. *Social Identity and Social Cognition,* Oxford: Blackwell.

Ajzen, I., 1988. *Attitudes, Personality, and Behavior,* Milton Keynes: Open University Press.

Ajzen, I., 1991. The Theory of Planned Behavior. *Organizational Behavior and Human Decision Processes,* 50, 179–211.

Ajzen, I., 1996. The Directive Influence of Attitudes on Behavior. *In* P. M. Gollwitzer & J. A. Burgh (eds) *The Psychology of Action: Linking Motivation and Cognition to Behavior.* New York: Guilford Press, 385–403.

Ajzen, I. & Fishbein, M., 2005. The Influence of Attitudes on Behavior. *In* D. Albarizín, B.T. Johnson & M.P. Zanna (eds) *Handbook of Attitudes and Attitude Change: Basic Principles.* Mahwah, NJ: Lawrence Erlbaum, 173–221.

Ajzen, I. & Manstead, A. S. R., 2007. Changing Health-Related Behaviours. An Approach Based on the Theory of Planned Behaviour. *In* M. Hewstone, H. A. W. Schut, J. B. F. De Wit, K. V. Den Bos & M. S. Stroebe (eds) *The Scope of Social Psychology. Theory and Applications.* Hove and New York: Psychology Press, 43–64.

Akerlof, G. A. & Dickens, W. T., 1982. The Economic Consequences of Cognitive Dissonance. *American Economic Review,* 72, 307–319.

Alencar, A. I., De Oliveira Siqueira, J. & Yamamoto, M. E., 2008. Does Group Size Matter? Cheating and Cooperation in Brazilian School Children. *Evolution and Human Behavior,* 29, 42–48.

Alessio, J. C., 1990. A Synthesis and Formalization of Heiderian Balance and Social Exchange Theory. *Social Forces,* 68, 1267–1285.

Amenta, E., Bernstein, M. & Dunleavy, K., 1994. Stolen Thunder? Huey Long's 'Share Our Wealth,' Political Mediation, and the Second New Deal. *American Sociological Review,* 59, 678–702.

Amenta, E., Neal, C. & Olasky, S. J., 2005. Age for Leisure? Political Mediation and the Impact of the Pension Movement on U.S. Old-Age Policy. *American Sociological Review,* 70, 516–538.

Aminzade, R. R., Goldstone, J., McAdam, D., Perry, E. J., Sewell Jr, W. H., Tarrow, S. & Tilly, C., 2001a. *Silence and Voice in the Study of Contentious Politics*. Cambridge: Cambridge University Press.

Aminzade, R. R., Goldstone, J. A. & Perry, E. J., 2001b. Leadership Dynamics and Dynamics of Contention. *In* R. R. Aminzade, J. Goldstone, D. McAdam, E. J. Perry, W. H. Sewell Jr, S. Tarrow & C. Tilly (eds) *Silence and Voice in the Study of Contentious Politics*. Cambridge: Cambridge University Press, 126–154.

Aminzade, R. R. & McAdam, D., 2001. Emotions and Contentious Politics. *In* R. R. Aminzade, J. Goldstone, D. McAdam, E. J. Perry, W. H. Sewell Jr, S. Tarrow, & C. Tilly (eds) *Silence and Voice in the Study of Contentious Politics*. Cambridge: Cambridge University Press, 14–50.

Andreas, J., 2007. The Structure of Charismatic Mobilization: A Case Study of Rebellion During the Chinese Cultural Revolution. *American Sociological Review,* 72, 434–458.

Andrews, K.T. & Biggs, M., 2007. The Dynamics of Protest Diffusion: Movement Organizations, Social Networks, and News Media in the 1960 Sit-Ins. *American Sociological Review,* 71, 752–777.

Anthony, D., 2005. Cooperation in Microcredit Borrowing Groups: Identity, Sanctions, and Reciprocity in the Production of Collective Goods. *American Sociological Review,* 70, 496–515.

Armitage, C. J. & Conner, M., 2001. Efficacy of the Theory of Planned Behavior: A Meta-Analytic Review. *British Journal of Social Psychology,* 40, 471–499.

Axelrod, R. (ed.) 1976. *Structure of Decision,* Princeton, NJ: Princeton University Press.

Axelrod, R., 1986. An Evolutionary Approach to Norms. *American Political Science Review,* 80, 1095–1111.

Babb, S., 1996. 'A True American System of Finance': Frame Resonance in the US Labor Movement, 1866 to 1886. *American Sociological Review,* 61, 1033–52.

Barnes, S. H., Kaase, M., Allerbeck, K. R., Farah, B. G., Heunks, F., Inglehart, R., Jennings, M. K., Klingemann, D., Marsh, A. & Rosenmayr, L., 1979. *Political Action. Mass Participation in Five Western Democracies*. Beverly Hills, CA, and London: Sage.

Becker, G. S., 1976. *The Economic Approach to Human Behavior*. Chicago and London: Chicago University Press.

Becker, H. & Körner, W., 1974. Kognitives Gleichgewicht und Cliquenbildung. *Zeitschrift für Sozialpsychologie,* 5, 189–200.

Benford, R., 1993. Frame Disputes within the Nuclear Disarmament Movement. *Social Forces,* 71, 677–701.

Benford, R. & Snow, D. A., 2000. Framing Processes and Social Movements: An Overview and Assessment. *Annual Review of Sociology,* 26, 611–639.

Benford, R. D., 1997. An Insider's Critique of the Social Movement Framing Perspective. *Sociological Inquiry,* 67, 409–430.

Beyerlein, K. & Hipp, J. R., 2006. A Two-Stage Model for a Two-Stage Process: How Biographical Availability Matters for Social Movement Mobilization. *Mobilization,* 11, 219–240.

Biggs, M., 2003. Positive Feedback in Collective Mobilization: The American Strike Wave of 1886. *Theory and Society,* 32, 217–254.

Biggs, M., 2005. Strikes as Forest Fires: Chicago and Paris in the Late Nineteenth Century. *American Journal of Sociology,* 110, 1684–1714.

Biggs, M., 2006. Who Joined the Sit-Ins and Why: Southern Black Students in the 1960s. *Mobilization,* 11, 241–256.

Bonacich, P., Shure, G. H., Kahan, J. B. & Meeker, R. J., 1976. Cooperation and Group Size in the N-Person Prisoner's Dilemma. *Journal of Conflict Resolution,* 20, 687–706.

Boudon, R., 1988. *The Analysis of Ideology.* Oxford: Polity Press.

Boudon, R., 1996. The 'Cognitivist Model.' A Generalized 'Rational-Choice-Model'. *Rationality and Society,* 8, 123–150.

Boyd, R., Gintis, H., Bowles, S. & Richerson, P. J., 2003. The Evolution of Altruistic Punishment. *Proceedings of the National Academy of Sciences of the United States of America,* 100, 3531–3535.

Boykoff, J., 2006. *The Suppression of Dissent: How the State and Mass Media Squelch US American Social Movements.* New York: Routledge.

Brady, H. E., Schlozman, K. L. & Verba, S., 1999. Prospecting for Participants: Rational Expectations and the Recruitment of Political Activists. *American Political Science Review,* 93, 153–168.

Brady, H. E., Verba, S. & Schlozman, K. L., 1995. Beyond SES: A Resource Model of Political Participation. *American Political Science Review,* 89, 271–294.

Braun, N., 1995. Individual Thresholds and Social Diffusion. *Rationality & Society,* 7, 167–182.

Breen, R., 1999. Beliefs, Rational Choice and Bayesian Learning. *Rationality & Society,* 11, 463–479.

Brewer, M. B., 2001. The Many Faces of Social Identity: Implications for Political Psychology. *Political Psycholgy,* 22, 115–125.

Brubaker, R. & Cooper, F., 2000. Beyond "Identity". *Theory and Society,* 29, 1–47.

Buckman, G., 2004. *Globalization. Tame it or Scrap It?* London and New York: Zed Books.

Buechler, S. M., 1993. Beyond Resource Mobilization: Emerging Trends in Social Movement Theory. *Sociological Quarterly,* 34, 217–235.

Cable, S., Walsh, E. J. & Warland, R. H., 1988. Differential Paths to Political Activism: Comparisons of Four Mobilization Processes After the Three Mile Island Accident. *Social Forces,* 66, 951–969.

Calhoun, C., 1991. The Problem of Identity in Collective Action. *In* J. Huber (ed.) *Macro-Micro Linkages in Sociology.* Newbury Park, CA: Sage, 51–75.

Campbell, A., Gurin, G. & Miller, W. E., 1954. *The Voter Decides.* Evanston, IL: Row, Peterson and Co.

Caniglia, B. S. & Carmin, J., 2005. Scholarship on Social Movement Organizations: Classic Views and Emerging Trends. *Mobilization,* 10, 201–212.

Carter, M., 2005. The Landless Rural Workers' Movement (MST) and Democracy in Brazil. *Working Paper CBS-60–05.* Centre for Brazilian Studies at the University of Oxford.

Cartwright, D. & Harary, F., 1956. Structural Balance: A Generalization of Heider's Theory. *The Psychological Review,* 63, 277–293.

Chalmers, A. F., 1982 (2nd ed.). *What Is This Thing Called Science? An Assessment of the Nature and Status of Science and Its Methods.* St. Lucia, Qld.: University of Queensland Press.

Chamberlain, J., 1974. Provisions of Collective Goods as a Function of Group Size. *American Political Science Review,* 68, 707–16.

Chong, D., 1991. *Collective Action and the Civil Rights Movement.* Chicago: Chicago University Press.

Cialdini, R. B., 1984. *Influence. The Psychology of Persuasion.* New York: Quill William Morrow.

Clark, P. B. & Wilson, J. Q., 1961. Incentive Systems: A Theory of Organization. *Administrative Science Quarterly,* 6, 129–166.

Cohen, J., 1985. Strategy or Identity: New Theoretical Paradigms and Contemporary Social Movements. *Social Research,* 52, 663–716.

Coleman, J. S., 1990. *Foundations of Social Theory.* Cambridge, Mass., and London: Belknap Press of Harvard University Press.

Cornfield, D. B. & Fletcher, B., 1998. Institutional Constraints on Social Movement "Frame Extension": Shifts in the Legislative Agenda for the American Federation of Labor. *American Journal of Sociology,* 76, 1305–1321.

Cress, D. M. & Snow, D., 2000. The Outcomes of Homeless Mobilization: The Influence of Organization, Disruption, Political Mediation, and Framing. *American Journal of Sociology,* 105, 1063–1104.

Davenport, C., Johnston, H. & Mueller, C. (eds) 2005. *Repression and Mobilization,* Minneapolis: University of Minnesota Press.

Davies, J. C., 1969. The J-Curve of Rising and Declining Satisfaction as a Cause of some Great Revolutions and a Contained Rebellion. *In* H. D. Graham & T. R. Gurr (eds) *Violence in America: Historical and Comparative Perspectives.* Washington, DC: Praeger, 547–576.

Davis, J. A., 1963. Structural Balance, Mechanical Solidarity and Interpersonal Relations. *American Journal of Sociology,* 68, 444–462.

De Weerd, M. & Klandermans, B., 1999. Group Identification and Political Protest: Farmers' Protest in the Netherlands. *European Journal of Social Psychology,* 29, 1073–1095.

Della Porta, D. (ed.) (2007) *The Global Justice Movement. Corss-National and Transnational Perspectives,* Boulder and London: Paradigm Publishers.

Della Porta, D., Andretta, M., Mosca, L. & Reiter, H., 2006. *Globalization from Below.* Minneapolis: University of Minnesota Press.

Diani, M., 1992. The Concept of a Social Movement. *The Sociological Review,* 40, 1–25.

Diani, M., 1996. Linking Mobilization Frames and Political Opportunities: Insights from Regional Populism in Italy. *American Sociological Review,* 61, 1053–1069.

Diani, M. & McAdam, D. (eds) 2003. *Social Movements and Networks. Relational Approaches to Collective Action,* Oxford: Oxford University Press.

Doreian, P., 1970. *Mathematics and the Study of Social Relations.* London: Weidenfeld and Nicolson.

Doreian, P., 2002. Event Sequences as Generators of Social Network Evolution. *Social Networks,* 24, 93–119.

Doreian, P., 2004. Evolution of Human Signed Networks. *Metodološki zvezki,* 1, 277–293.

Doreian, P., Kapuscinski, R., Krackhardt, D. & Szczypula, J., 1996. A Brief History of Balance Through Time. *Journal of Mathematical Sociology,* 21, 113–131.

Doreian, P. & Krackhardt, D., 2001. Pre-Transitive Balance Mechanisms For Signed Networks. *Journal of Mathematical Sociology,* 25, 43–67.

Downey, D. J., 2006. Elaborating Consensus: Strategic Orientations and Rationales in Wartime Intergroup Relations. *Mobilization,* 11, 257–276.

Downey, G. L., 1986. Ideology and the Clamshell Identity: Organizational Dilemmas in the Anti-Nuclear Power Movement. *Social Problems,* 3, 357–373.

Eagly, A. H. & Chaiken, S., 1993. *The Psychology of Attitudes.* Forth Worth, TX: Harcourt.

Einwohner, R. L., 2003. Opportunity, Honor, and Action in the Warsaw Ghetto Uprising of 1943. *American Journal of Sociology,* 109, 650–675.

Eisinger, P. K., 1973. The Conditions of Protest Behavior in American Cities. *American Political Science Review,* 67, 11–28.

Ellemers, N., 1993. The Influence of Socio-Structural Variables on Idenity Management

Strategies. *In* W. Stroebe & M. Hewstone (eds) *European Review of Social Psychology, Vol. 4.* Chichester, England: Wiley, 27–57.

Ellemers, N., Spears, R. & Doosje, B. (eds) 1999. *Social Identity: Context, Commitment, Content,* Oxford: Blackwell.

Esacove, A.W., 2004. Dialogic Framing: The Framing/Counterframing of "Partial-Birth" Abortion. *Sociological Inquiry,* 74, 70–101.

Evans, J. H., 1997. Multi-Organizational Fields and Social Movement Organization Frame Content: The Religious Pro-Choice Movement. *Sociological Inquiry,* 67, 451–469.

Fazio, R. H., 1986. How Do Attitudes Guide Behavior? *In* R. M. Sorrentino & E. T. Higgins (eds) *The Handbook of Motivation and Cognition: Foundations of Social Behavior.* New York: Guilford Press, 204–243.

Fazio, R. H., 1990. Multiple Processes by Which Attitudes Guide Behavior: The Mode Model as an Integrative Framework. *In* M. P. Zanna (ed.) *Advances in Experimental Social Psychology.* San Diego, CA: Academic Press, 75–109.

Feather, N. T., 1982. *Expectations and Actions: Expectancy-Value Models in Psychology* Hillsdale, NJ: Lawrence Erlbaum.

Fehr, E. & Fischbacher, U., 2003. The Nature of Human Altruism. *Nature,* 425, 785–791.

Fehr, E. & Fischbacher, U., 2004. Third Party Punishment and Social Norms. *Evolution and Human Behavior,* 25, 63–87.

Fehr, E., Fischbacher, U. & Gächter, S., 2002. Strong Reciprocity, Human Cooperation and the Enforcement of Social Norms. *Human Nature,* 13, 1–25.

Fehr, E. & Gächter, S., 2000. Cooperation and Punishment in Public Goods Experiments. *American Economic Review,* 90, 980–994.

Fehr, E. & Gächter, S., 2002. Altruistic Punishment in Humans. *Nature,* 415, 137–140.

Ferree, M. M., 1992. The Political Context of Rationality: Rational Choice Theory and Resource Mobilization. *In* A. D. Morris & C. McClurg Mueller (eds) *Frontiers in Social Movement Theory.* New Haven, CT: Yale University Press, 29–52.

Ferree, M. M., 2003. Resonance and Radicalsm: Feminist Framing in the Abortion Debates of the United States and Germany. *American Journal of Sociology,* 109, 304–344.

Ferree, M. M. & Miller, F. D., 1985. Mobilization and Meaning: Toward an Integration of Social Psychological and Resource Perspectives on Social Movements. *Sociological Inquiry,* 55, 38–51.

Festinger, L., 1957. *A Theory of Cognitive Dissonance.* Stanford, CA: Stanford University Press.

Festinger, L., Riecken, H. W. & Schachter, S., 1956. *When Prophecy Fails: A Social and Social-psychological Study of a Modern Group that Predicted the Destruction of the World.* Minneapolis: University of Minnesota Press.

Finkel, S. E. & Muller, E. N., 1998. Rational Choice and the Dynamics of Collective Political Action. *American Political Science Review,* 92, 37–49.

Finkel, S. E., Muller, E. N. & Opp, K.-D., 1989. Personal Influence, Collective Rationality, and Mass Political Action. *American Political Science Review,* 83, 885–903.

Finkel, S. E. & Rule, J., 1986. Relative Deprivation and Related Psychological Theories of Civil Violence: A Critical Review. *Research in Social Movements, Conflicts and Change,* 9, 47–69.

Fireman, B. & Gamson, W. A., 1979. Utilitarian Logic in the Resource Mobilization Perspective. *In* M. N. Zald & J. McCarthy (eds) *The Dynamics of Social Movements.* Cambridge, MA: Winthrop, 8–44.

Fishbein, M. & Ajzen, I., 1975. *Belief, Attitude, Intention and Behavior. An Introduction to Theory and Research.* Reading, MA: Addison-Wesley.

Fleishman, J. A., 1980. Collective Action as Helping Behavior: Effects of Responsibility Diffusion on Contributions to a Public Good. *Journal of Personality and Social Psychology,* 38, 629–637.

Freeman, J., 1983. *Social Movements in the Sixties and Seventies.* New York and London: Longman.

Frey, B. S., 1999. *Economics as a Science of Human Behaviour. Towards a New Social Science Paradigm,* second extended edition. Boston: Kluwer Academic Publishers.

Friedman, D. & McAdam, D., 1992. Collective Identity and Activism. Networks, Choices, and the Life of a Social Movement. *In* A.D. Morris & C. McClurg Mueller (eds) *Frontiers of Social Movement Theory.* New Haven, CT and London: Yale University Press, 156–173.

Friedman, M., 1953. The Methodology of Positive Economics. *In* M. Friedman (ed.) *Essays in Positive Economics.* Chicago: University of Chicago Press, 3–43.

Frohlich, N., Hunt, T., Oppenheimer, J. A. & Wagner, R. H., 1975. Individual Contributions for Collective Goods. Alternative Models. *Journal of Conflict Resolution,* 19, 310–329.

Frohlich, N. & Oppenheimer, J. A., 1970. I Get By With a Little Help From My Friends. *World Politics,* 23, 104–120.

Frohlich, N., Oppenheimer, J. A. & Young, O. R., 1971. *Political Leadership and Collective Goods.* Princeton, NJ: Princeton University Press.

Gallhofer, I. N. & Saris, W., 1996. *Foreign Policy Decision-Making. A Qualitative and Quantitative Analysis of Political Argumentation.* Westport, CT: Praeger.

Gamson, W. A., 1968. *Power and Discontent.* Homewood, IL: Dorsey.

Gamson, W. A., 1975. *The Strategy of Social Protest.* Homewood, IL: Dorsey.

Gamson, W. A., 1987. Introduction. *In* M. N. Zald & J. D. McCarthy (eds) *Social Movements in an Organizational Society. Collected Essays.* New Brunswick, NJ: Transaction Books, 1–7.

Gamson, W. A., 1990. *The Strategy of Social Protest.* Belmont, CA: Wadsworth Publishing Company.

Gamson, W. A., 1992a. The Social Psychology of Collective Action. *In* A. D. Morris & C. McClurg Mueller (eds) *Frontiers in Social Movement Theory.* New Haven, CT, and London: Yale University Press, 53–76.

Gamson, W. A., 1992b. *Talking Politics.* Cambridge: Cambridge University Press.

Gamson, W. A., Fireman, B. & Rytina, S., 1982. *Encounters with Unjust Authority.* Chicago: The Dorsey Press.

Gamson, W. A. & Meyer, D.S., 1996. Framing Political Opportunity. *In* D. McAdam, J. McCarthy & M. N. Zald (eds) *Comparative Perspectives on Social Movements, Political Opportunities, and Cultural Framings.* Cambridge: Cambridge University Press, 275–290.

Gerhards, J. & Rucht, D., 1992. Mesomobilization: Organizing and Framing in Two Protest Campaigns in West Germany. *American Journal of Sociology,* 98, 555–596.

Gibson, M. L., 1991. Public Goods, Alienation, and Political Protest: The Sanctuary Movement as a Test of the Public Goods Model of Collective Rebellious Behavior. *Political Psychology,* 12, 623–651.

Gilad, B., Kaish, S. & Loeb, P. D., 1987. Cognitive Dissonance and Utility Maximization. *Journal of Economic Behavior and Organization,* 8, 61–73.

Goffman, E., 1974. *Frame Analysis. An Essay on the Organization of Experience.* New York: Harper & Row.

Goldstone, J., 1994. Is Revolution Individually Rational? Groups and Individuals in Revolutionary Collective Action. *Rationality & Society,* 6, 139–166.

Goldstone, J., 2002. Theory Development in the Study of Revolutions. *In* J. Berger & M. Zelditch Jr (eds) *New Directions in Contemporary Sociological Theory.* Lanham, MD: Rowman & Littlefield, 194–226.

Goldstone, J., Gurr, T. R. & Mosihir, F. (eds) 1991 *Revolutions in the Late 20th Century,* Boulder, CO: Westview Press.

Goldstone, J. & Tilly, C., 2001. Threat (and Opportunity): Popular Action and State Response in the Dynamics of Contentious Action. *In* R.R. Aminzade, J. Goldstone, D. McAdam, E. J. Perry, W. H. Sewell Jr, S. Tarrow & C. Tilly (eds) *Silence and Voice in the Study of Contentious Politics.* Cambridge: Cambridge University Press, 179–194.

Goldstone, J. A. (ed.) 2003 *States, Parties, and Social Movements,* Cambridge: Cambridge University Press.

Goldstone, J. A., 2004. More Movements or Fewer? Beyond Political Opportunity Structures to Relational Fields. *Theory and Society,* 33, 333–365.

Goldthorpe, J. H., 1998. Rational Action Theory for Sociology. *British Journal of Sociology,* 49, 167–192.

Goodwin, J. & Jasper, J. M., 1999. Caught in a Winding, Snarling Vine: The Structural Bias of Political Process Theory. *Sociological Forum,* 14, 27–54.

Goodwin, J. & Jasper, J. M. (eds) 2004 *Rethinking Social Movements. Structure, Meaning, and Emotion,* Lanham, MD: Rowman & Littlefield.

Gould, R. V., 1991. Multiple Networks and Mobilization in the Paris Commune, 1971. *American Sociological Review,* 56, 716–729.

Gould, R. V., 1993. Collective Action and Network Structure. *American Sociological Review,* 58, 182–196.

Gould, R. V., 1995. *Insurgent Identities: Class, Community, and Protest in Paris from 1848 to the Commune.* Chicago: Chicago University Press.

Granovetter, M., 1978. Threshold Models of Collective Behavior. *American Journal of Sociology,* 83, 1420–1443.

Gurin, P., Peng, T., Lopez, G. & Nagda, B. A., 1999. Context, Identity, and Intergroup Relations. *In* D. A. Prentice & D. T. Miller (eds) *Cultural Divides. Understanding and Overcoming Group Conflict.* New York: Russell Sage Foundation, 133–170.

Gurney, J. N. & Tierney, K., 1982. Relative Deprivation and Social Movements: A Critical Look at Twenty Years of Theory and Research. *The Sociological Quarterly,* 23, 33–47.

Gurr, T. R., 1970. *Why Men Rebel.* Princeton, NJ: Princeton University Press.

Hammond, J. L., 1999. Law and Disorder: The Brazilian Landless Farmworkers' Movement. *Bulletin of Latin American Research,* 18, 469–489.

Hardin, R., 1982. *Collective Action.* Baltimore and London: Johns Hopkins University Press.

Harmon-Jones, E. & Mills, J. (eds) 1999 *Cognitive Dissonance,* Washington, DC: American Psychological Association.

Heap, S. H., Hollis, M., Lyons, B., Sugden, R. & Weale, A., 1992. *The Theory of Choice. A Critical Guide.* Oxford: Blackwell.

Hechter, M., Friedman, D. & Appelbaum, M., 1982. A Theory of Ethnic Collective Action. *International Migration Review,* 16, 412–434.

Hechter, M. & Kanazawa, S., 1997. Sociological Rational Choice Theory. *Annual Review of Sociology,* 23, 191–214.

Heckathorn, D. D., 1989. Collective Action and the Second-Order Free-Rider Problem. *Rationality and Society,* 1, 78–100.

Heckathorn, D. D., 1993. Collective Action and Group Heterogeneity. *American Sociological Review,* 58, 329–350.

Heckathorn, D. D., 2002. Development of a Theory of Collective Action: From the Emergence of Norms to AIDS Prevention and the Analysis of Social Structure. *In* J. Berger & M. Zelditch Jr (eds) *New Directions in Contemporary Sociological Theory.* Lanham, MD: Rowman & Littlefield, 79–108.

Heckathorn, D. D., 1996. The Dynamics and Dilemmas of Collective Action. *American Sociological Review,* 61, 250–277.

Hedström, P., 2005. *Dissecting the Social. On the Principles of Analytical Sociology.* Cambridge: Cambridge University Press.

Hedström, P. & Swedberg, R. (eds) 1998. *Social Mechanisms. An Analytical Approach to Social Theory,* Cambridge: Cambridge University Press.

Heider, F., 1946. Attitudes and Cognitive Organization. *Journal of Psychology,* 21, 107–112.

Heider, F., 1958. *The Psychology of Interpersonal Relations.* New York: Wiley.

Hempel, C. G., 1952. *Fundamentals of Concept Formation in Empirical Science.* Chicago: University of Chicago Press.

Hempel, C. G., 1965. *Aspects of Scientific Explanation and other Essays in the Philosophy of Science.* New York and London: Free Press.

Hempel, C. G. & Oppenheim, P., 1948. Studies in the Logic of Explanation. *Philosophy of Science,* 15, 135–175.

Henrich, J. & Boyd, R., 2001. Why People Punish Defectors. Weak Conformist Transmission Can Stabilize Costly Enforcement of Norms in Cooperative Dilemmas. *Journal of Theoretical Biology,* 2008, 79–89.

Henrich, J., Boyd, R., Bowles, S., Camerer, C., Fehr, E. & Gintis, H. (eds) 2004. *Foundations of Human Sociality. Economic Experiments and Ethnographic Evidence from Fifteen Small-Scale Societies,* Oxford: Oxford University Press.

Henrich, J., Mcelreath, R., Barr, A., Ensminger, J., Barret, C., Bolyanatz, A., Cardenas, J. C., Gurven, M., Gwako, E., Henrich, N., Lesorogol, C., Marlowe, F., Tracer, D. & Ziker, J., 2006. Costly Punishment Across Human Societies. *Science,* 312, 1767–1770.

Hewitt, L. & McCammon, H. J., 2005. Explaining Suffrage Mobilization: Balance, Neutralization, and Range in Collective Action Frames. *In* H. Johnston & J. A. Noakes (eds) *Frames of Protest. Social Movements and the Framing Perspective.* Boston: Rowman and Littlefield, 33–52.

Hirschman, A. O., 1970. *Exit, Voice, and Loyalty. Responses to Decline in Firms, Organizations, and States.* Cambridge, MA: Harvard University Press.

Hirshleifer, J., 1985. The Expanding Domain of Economics. *American Economic Review,* 75, 53–68.

Holland, P. W. & Leinhardt, S. L. (eds) 1979. *Perspectives on Social Network Research,* New York: Academic Press.

Holtmann, E. & Killisch, W., 1989. Gemeindegebietsreferom und politische Partizipation. *Aus Politik und Zeitgeschichte. Beilage zur Wochenzeitung Das Parlament,* B30–31/89, 27–38 (eigenes Exemplar unter Partizipation).

Horne, C., 2007. Explaining Norm Enforcement. *Rationality & Society,* 19, 141–172.

Howard, J. A., 2000. Social Psychology of Identities. *Annual Review of Sociology,* 26, 367–393.

Huddy, L., 2001. From Social to Political Identity. A Critical Examination of Social Identity Theory. *Political Psychology,* 22, 127–156.

Hummell, H. J., 1967. Bewertung und Ähnlichkeit von Berufen. *Kölner Zeitschrift für Soziologie und Sozialpsychologie,* 19, 698–707.

Hummon, N. P. & Doreian, P., 2003. Some Dynamics of Social Balance Processes: Bringing Heider Back Into Balance Theory. *Social Networks*, 25, 17–49.

Hunt, S. A. & Benford, R., 2004. Collective Identity, Solidarity, and Commitment. *In* D. A. Snow, S. A. Soule & H. Kriesi (eds) *The Blackwell Companion to Social Movements*. Oxford: Blackwell, 433–457.

Inglehart, R., 1979. Value Priorities and Socioeconomic Change. *In* S. K. Barnes, Max (ed.) *Political Action. Mass Participation in Five Western Democracies*. Beverly Hills and London: Sage Publications, 305–342.

Isaac, R. M. & Walker, J. M., 1988. Group Size Effects in Public Goods Provision: The Voluntary Contributions Mechanism. *The Quarterly Journal of Economics*, 103, 177–199.

Jasper, J. M., 1997. *The Art of Moral Protest. Culture, Biography, and Creativity in Social Movements*. Chicago: The University of Chicago Press.

Jasper, J. M. & Poulsen, J. D., 1995. Recruiting Strangers and Friends: Moral Shocks and Social Networks in Animal Rights and Anti-Nuclear Protest. *Social Problems*, 42, 493–512.

Jasso, G. & Opp, K.-D., 1997. Probing the Character of Norms: A Factorial Survey Analysis of the Norms of Political Action. *American Sociological Review*, 62, 947–964.

Jenkins, J. C., 1983. Resource Mobilization Theory and the Study of Social Movements. *Annual Review of Sociology*, 9, 527–553.

Jenkins, J. C. & Form, W., 2005. Social Movememts and Social Change. *In* T. Janoski, R. Alford, A. Hicks & M. A. Schwartz (eds) *The Handbook of Political Sociology. States, Civil Societes, and Globalization*. Cambridge: Cambridge University Press, 331–348.

Jenkins, J. C., Jacobs, D. & Agnone, J., 2003. Political Opportunities and African-American Protest, 1948–1997. *American Journal of Sociology*, 109, 277–303.

Johnston, H., 2005. Comparative Frame Analysis. *In* H. Johnston & J. A. Noakes (eds) *Frames of Protest. Social Movements and the Framing Perspective*. Boston: Rowman and Littlefield, 237–260.

Johnston, H. & Noakes, J. A. (eds) 2005 *Frames of Protest. Social Movements and the Framing Perspective*, Boston: Rowman and Littlefield.

Karklins, R. & Petersen, R., 1993. Decision Calculus of Protesters and Regimes: Eastern Europe 1989. *Journal of Politics*, 55, 588–614.

Kelly, C. & Breinlinger, S., 1996. *The Social Psychology of Collective Action: Identity, Injustice and Gender*. London: Taylor & Francis.

Kelly, C. & Kelly, J., 1994. Who Gets Involved in Collective Action? Social Psychological Determinants of Individual Participation in Trade Unions. *Human Relations*, 47, 63–89.

Kenny, P., 2001. Framing, Political Opportunities, and Civic Mobiliziation in the Eastern European Revolutions: A Case Study for Poland's Freedom and Peace Movement. *Mobilization*, 6, 193–210.

Kerbo, H. R., 1982. Movements of Crisis and Movements of Affluence. A Critique of Deprivation and Resource Mobilizatin Theories. *Journal of Conflict Resolution*, 26.

Khawaja, M., 1994. Resource Mobilization, Hardship, and Popular Collective Action in the West Bank. *Social Forces*, 73, 191–220.

Kimura, K., 1989. Large Groups and a Tendency Toward Failure: A Critique of M. Olson's Model of Collective Action. *Journal of Mathematical Sociology*, 14, 263–271.

Kitschelt, H., 1986. Political Opportunity Structures and Political Protest: Anti-Nuclear Movements in Four Democracies. *British Journal of Political Science*, 16, 57–85.

Kitschelt, H., 1991. Resource Mobilization Theory: A Critique. *In* D. Rucht (ed.) *Research on Social Movements. The State of the Art in Western Europe and the USA.* Frankfurt am Main and Boulder, CO: Westview Press, 323–347.

Kitts, J. A., 2000. Mobilizing in Black Boxes: Social Networks and Participation in Social Movement Organizations. *Mobilization,* 5, 241–257.

Klandermans, B., 1984. Mobilization and Participation: Social Psychological Expansions of Resource Mobilization Theory. *American Sociological Review,* 49, 583–600.

Klandermans, B., 1992. The Social Construction of Protest and Multiorganizational Fields. *In* A. D. Morris & C. McClurg Muleler (eds) *Frontiers in Social Movement Theory.* New Haven, CT, and London: Yale University Press, 77–103.

Klandermans, B., 1997. *The Social Psychology of Protest.* Cambridge, MA: Blackwell.

Klandermans, B., 2002. How Group Identification Helps to Overcome the Dilemma of Collective Action. *American Behavioral Scientist,* 45, 887–900.

Klandermans, B., 2004. The Demand and Supply of Participation: Social-Psychological Correlates of Participatoin in Social Movements. *In* D. A. Snow, S. A. Soule & H. Kriesi (eds) *The Blackwell Companion to Social Movements.* Oxford: Blackwell, 360–379.

Klandermans, B. & De Weerd, M., 2000. Group Identification and Political Protest. *In* S. Stryker, T. J. Owens & R. W. White (eds) *Self, Identity, and Social Movements.* Minneapolis: University of Minnesota Press, 68–90.

Klandermans, B., De Weerd, M., Subecedo, J.-M. & Costa, M., 1999. Injustice and Adversarial Frames in a Supranational Political Context: Farmers' Protest in the Netherlands and Spain. *In* D. Della Porta, H. Kriesi & D. Rucht (eds) *Social Movements in a Globalizing World.* New York: St. Martin's Press, 134–147.

Koopmans, R., 1995. *Democracy from Below. New Social Movements and the Political System in West Germany.* Boulder, CO: Westview Press.

Koopmans, R., 2005. The Missing Link Between Structure and Agency: Outline of an Evolutionary Approach to Social Movements. *Mobilization,* 10, 19–33.

Koopmans, R. & Statham, P., 1999. Ethnic and Civic Conceptions of Nationhood and the Differential Success of the Extrme Right in Germany and Italy. *In* M. Giugni, D. McAdam & C. Tilly (eds) *How Social Movements Matter.* Minneapolis: University of Minnesota Press, 225–251.

Kopstein, J. & Lichbach, M. (eds) 2005 (2nd. ed.) *Comparative Politics. Interests, Identities, and Institutions in a Changing Global Order,* Cambridge: Cambridge University Press.

Kornhauser, W., 1959. *The Politics of Mass Society.* New York: Free Press.

Kriesi, H., 1995. The Political Opportunity Structure of New Social Movements: Its Impact on Their Mobilization. *In* J. C. Jenkins & B. Klandermans (eds) *The Politics of Social Protest. Comparative Perspectives on States and Social Movements.* Minneapolis: University of Minnesota Press, 167–198.

Kriesi, H., Koopmans, R., Duyvendak, J. W. & Giugni, M. G., 1992. New Social Movements and Political Opportunities in Western Europe. *European Journal of Political Research,* 22, 219–244.

Kriesi, H., Koopmans, R., Duyvendank, W. & Giugni, M. G., 1995. *New Social Movements in Western Europe.* Minneapolis: University of Minnesota Press.

Kuran, T., 1995. *Private Truths, Public Lies: The Social Consequences of Preference Falsification.* Cambridge, MA: Harvard University Press.

Kurzman, C., 1996. Structural Opportunity and Perceived Opportunity in Social Movement Theory: The Iranian Revolution of 1979. *American Sociological Review,* 61, 153–170.

Kurzman, C., 1998. Organizational Opportunity and Social Movement Mobilization: A Comparative Analysis of Four Religious Movements. *Mobilization,* 3, 23–49.

Laitin, D. D., 1998. *Identity in Formation: The Russian-Speaking Population in the Near Abroad.* Ithaca, NY: Cornell University Press.

Law, K. S. & Walsh, E. J., 1983. The Interaction of Grievances and Structures in Social Movement Analysis: The Case of JUST. *The Sociological Quarterly,* 24, 123–136.

Leighley, J. E., 1995. Attitudes, Opportunities and Incentives: A Field Essay on Political Participation. *Political Research Quarterly,* 48, 181–209.

Leites, C. & Wolf, N., 1970. *Rebellion and Authority* Chicago: Markham.

Lichbach, M., 1997. Contentious Maps of Contentious Politics. *Mobilization,* 2, 87–98.

Lichbach, M., 2005. How to Organize Your Mechanisms: Research Program, Stylized Facts, and Historical Narratives. *In* C. Davenport, H. Johnston & C. Mueller (eds) *Repression and Mobilization.* Minneapolis: University of Minnesota Press, 227–243.

Lichbach, M. I., 1995. *The Rebel's Dilemma.* Ann Arbor: University of Michigan Press.

Lichbach, M. I., 1996. *The Cooperator's Dilemma.* Ann Arbor: University of Michigan Press.

Linares, F., 2004. Hawks, Zealots and Hypocrites, but Not Free Riders: The Logics of Cooperation in Llano Del Beal. *Rationality & Society,* 16, 437–476.

Lipsky, M., 1968. Protest as a Political Resource. *American Political Science Review,* 62, 1144–1158.

Little, D., 1991. *Varieties of Social Explanation. An Introduction to the Philosophy of Social Science.* Boulder, CO: Westview Press.

Lofland, J., 1989. Consensus Movments: City Twinning and Derailed Dissent in the American Eighties. *Research in Social Movements, Conflict and Change,* 11, 163–196.

Lofland, J., 1996. *Social Movement Organizations: Guide to Research on Insurgent Realities.* New York: Aldine De Gruyter.

Lohmann, S., 1993. A Signaling Model of Informative and Manipulative Political Action. *American Political Science Review,* 87, 319–333.

Lohmann, S., 1994. Dynamics of Informational Cascades: the Monday Demonstrations in Leipzig, East Germany, 1989–91. *World Politics,* 47, 42–101.

Ludwig, M. & Abell, P., 2007. An Evolutionary Model of Social Networks. *European Physical Journal B,* 58, 97–105.

Macy, M. W., 1990. Learning Theory and the Logic of Critical Mass. *American Sociological Review,* 55, 809–826.

Macy, M. W., 1991. Chains of Cooperation: Threshold Effects in Collective Action. *American Sociological Review,* 56, 730–747.

Macy, M. W., 1997. Identity, Interest and Emergent Rationality: An Evolutionary Synthesis. *Rationality & Society,* 9, 427–449.

Marks, G. & McAdam, D., 1999. On the Relationship of Political Opportunities to the Form of Collective Action: the Case of the European Union. *In* D. Della Porta, H. Kriesi & D. Rucht (eds) *Social Movements in a Globalizing World.* New York: St. Martin's Press, 97–111.

Marwell, G. & Ames, R. E., 1979. Experiments on the Provision of Public Goods. I. Resources, Interest, Group Size, and the Free-Rider Problem. *American Journal of Sociology,* 84, 1335–1360.

Marwell, G. & Oliver, P., 1984. Collective Action Theory and Social Movements Research. *Research in Social Movements, Conflict and Change,* 7, 1–28.

Marwell, G. & Oliver, P., 1993. *The Critical Mass in Collective Action. A Micro-Social Theory.* New York: Cambridge University Press.

Marwell, G., Oliver, P. & Prahl, R., 1988. Social Networks and Collective Action: A Theory of the Critical Mass. III. *American Journal of Sociology,* 94, 502–534.

Mäs, M., 2005. *Regionalismus, Nationalismus und Ausländerfeindlichkeit.* Wiesbaden: VS Verlag für Sozialwissenschaften.

Matsueda, R. L., Kreager, D. A. & Huizinga, D., 2006. Deterring Delinquents: A Rational Choice Model of Theft and Violence. *American Sociological Review,* 71, 95–122.

McAdam, D., 1982. *Political Process and the Development of Black Insurgency 1930–1970.* Chicago and London: University of Chicago Press.

McAdam, D., 1986. Recruitment to High-Risk Activism: The Case of Freedom Summer. *American Journal of Sociology,* 92, 64–90.

McAdam, D., 1988a. *Freedom Summer.* Oxford: Oxford University Press.

McAdam, D., 1988b. Micromobilization Contexts and Recruitment to Activism. *In* B. Klandermans, H. Kriesi & S. Tarrow (eds) *International Social Movement Research.* Greenwich, CT: Jai Press, 125–154.

McAdam, D., 1994. Culture and Social Movements. *In* E. Laraña, H. Johnston & J. R. Gusfield (eds) *New Social Movements. From Ideology to Identity.* Philadelphia: Temple University Press, 36–57.

McAdam, D., 1995. "Initiator" and "Spin–Off" Movements: Diffusion Processes in Protest Cycles. *In* M. Traugott (ed.) *Repertoires and Cycles of Collective Action.* Durham, NC: Duke University Press, 217–239.

McAdam, D., 1996. The Framing Function of Movement Tactics: Strategic Dramaturgy in the Civil Rights Movement. *In* D. McAdam, J. McCarthy & M. N. Zald (eds) *Comparative Perspectives on Social Movements. Political Opportunities, Mobilizing Structures, and Cultural Framings.* Cambridge: Cambridge University Press, 338–355.

McAdam, D., 1999 (2nd ed.). *Political Process and the Development of Black Insurgency 1930–1970.* Chicago and London: University of Chicago Press.

McAdam, D., 2001. Harmonizing the Voices: thematic Continuity across the Chapters. *In* R.R. Aminzade, J. Goldstone, D. McAdam, E. J. Perry, W. H. Sewell Jr, S. Tarrow & C. Tilly (eds) *Silence and Voice in the Study of Contentious Politics.* Cambridge: Cambridge University Press, 222–240.

McAdam, D., 2004. Revisiting the U.S. Civil Rights Movement: Toward a More Synthetic Understanding of the Origins of Contention. *In* J. Goodwin & J. M. Jasper (eds) *Rethinking Social Movements. Structure, Meaning, and Emotion.* Lanham, MD: Rowman & Littlefield, 201–232.

McAdam, D., McCarthy, J. & Zald, M. N., 1988. Social Movements. *In* N. Smelser (ed.) *The Handbook of Sociology.* Beverly Hills, CA: Sage, 695–737.

McAdam, D., McCarthy, J. & Zald, M. N. (eds) 1996a. *Comparative Perspectives on Social Movements. Political Opportunities, Mobilizing Structures, and Cultural Framings,* Cambridge: Cambridge University Press.

McAdam, D. & Paulsen, R., 1993. Social Ties and Activism: Towards a Specification of the Relationship. *American Journal of Sociology,* 99, 640–667.

McAdam, D., Tarrow, S. & Tilly, C., 1996b. To Map Contentious Politics. *Mobilization,* 1, 17–34.

McAdam, D., Tarrow, S. & Tilly, C., 2001. *Dynamics of Contention.* Cambridge: Cambridge University Press.

McCammon, H. J., Campbell, K. E., Granberg, E. M. & Mowery, C., 2001. How Movements Win: Gendered Opportunity Structures and U.S. Women's Suffrage Movements, 1866 to 1919. *American Sociological Review,* 66, 49–70.

McCammon, H. J., Muse, C. S., Newman, H. D. & Terrell, T. M., 2007. Movement Framing and Discursive Opportunity Structures: The Political Successes of the U.S. Women's Jury Movements. *American Sociological Review,* 72, 725–749.

McCarthy, J. D., 1986. Prolife and Prochoice Movement Mobilization: Infrastructure Deficits and New Technologies. *In* M. N. Zald & J. D. McCarthy (eds) *Social Movements and Resource Mobilization in Organizational Society: Collected Essays.* New Brunswick, NJ: Transaction Books, 49–67.

McCarthy, J. D. & Wolfson, M., 1996. Resource Mobilization by Local Social Movement Organizations: Agency, Strategy, and Organizations in the Movement against Drinking and Driving. *American Sociological Review,* 61, 1070–1088.

McCarthy, J. D., Wolfson, M., Baker, D. P. & Mosakowski, E., 1988. The Founding of Social Movement Organizations. Local Citizens' Groups Opposing Drunken Driving. *In* G. R. Carroll (ed.) *Ecological Models of Organizations.* Cambridge, MA: Ballinger, 71–84.

McCarthy, J. D. & Zald, M. N., 1973. *The Trend of Social Movements in America: Professionalization and Resource Mobilization.* Morristown, NJ: General Learning Corporation.

McCarthy, J. D. & Zald, M. N., 1977. Resource Mobilization and Social Movements. *American Journal of Sociology,* 82, 1212–1241.

McCarthy, J. D. & Zald, M. N., 2002. The Enduring Vitality of the Resource Mobilization Theory of Social Movements. *In* J. Turner (ed.) *Handbook of Sociological Theory.* New York: Kluwer Academic/Plenum Publishers, 533–565.

Mckay, T. J., 1989. *Modern Formal Logic.* New York: Macmillan.

Mcveigh, R., Myers, D. J. & Sikkink, D., 2004. Corn, Klansmen, and Coolidge: Structure and Framing in Social Movements. *Social Forces,* 83, 653–690.

Melucci, A., 1988. Getting Involved: Identity and Mobilization in Social Movements. *In* B. Klandermans, H. Kriesi & S. Tarrow (eds) *International Social Movement Research, Volume 1.* Greenwich, CT: JAI Press, 329–348.

Melucci, A., 1989. *Nomads of the Present: Social Movements and Individual Needs in Contemporary Society.* Philadelphia: Temple University Press.

Melucci, A., 1995. The Process of Collective Identity. *In* H. Johnston & B. Klandermans (eds) *Social Movements and Culture.* Minnesota: University of Minnesota Press, 41–63.

Merton, R. K., 1957. *Social Theory and Social Structure,* 2nd ed. Glencoe, IL: Free Press.

Meyer, D. S., 2004. Protest and Political Opportunities. *Annual Review of Sociology,* 30, 125–145.

Meyer, D. S. & Minkoff, D.C., 2004. Conceptualizing Political Opportunity. *Social Forces,* 82, 1457–1492.

Milbrath, L. W. & Goel, M. L., 1977 (2nd. ed.). *Political Participation. How and Why Do People Get Involved in Politics?* Boston: Rand McNally.

Minkoff, D. C. & McCarthy, J. D., 2005. Reinvigorating the Study of Organizational Processes in Social Movements. *Mobilization,* 10, 289–308.

Moe, T. M., 1980. *The Organization of Interests. Incentives and the Internal Dynamics of Political Interest Groups.* Chicago and London: University of Chicago Press.

Moore, W. H., 1995. Rational Rebels: Overcoming the Free-Rider Problem. *Political Research Quarterly,* 48, 417–454.

Morris, A. D., 1984. *The Origins of the Civil Rights Movement. Black Communities Organizing for Change.* New York: Free Press.

Morrow, J. D., 1994. *Game Theory for Political Scientists* Princeton, NJ: Princeton University Press.

Mühler, K. & Opp, K.-D., 2004. *Region und Nation. Zu den Ursachen und Wirkungen regionaler und überregionaler Identifikation.* Wiesbaden: VS Verlag für Sozialwissenschaften.

Muller, E. N., 1972. A Test of a Partial Theory of Potential For Political Violence. *American Political Science Review,* 66, 928–959.

Muller, E. N., 1979. *Aggressive Political Participation.* Princeton, NJ: Princeton University Press.

Muller, E. N., 1980. The Psychology of Political Protest. *In* T. R. Gurr (ed.) *Handbook of Political Conflict.* New York: The Free Press, 69–99.

Muller, E. N., 1985. Income Inequality, Regime Repressiveness, and Political Violence. *American Sociological Review,* 50, 47–61.

Muller, E. N. & Jukam, T. O., 1983. Discontent and Aggressive Political Participation. *British Journal of Political Science,* 13, 159–179.

Muller, E. N. & Opp, K.-D., 1986. Rational Choice and Rebellious Collective Action. *American Political Science Review,* 80, 471–489.

Muller, E. N. & Weede, E., 1990. Cross-National Variation in Political Violence. A Rational Action Approach. *Journal of Conflict Resolution,* 34, 624–651.

Mummendey, A., Klink, A., Mielke, R., Wenzel, M. & Blanz, M., 1999. Socio-Structural Characteristics of Intergroup Relations and Identity Management Strategies: Results from a Field Study in East Germany. *European Journal of Social Psychology,* 29, 259–285.

Nepstad, S. E. & Bob, C., 2006. When Do Leaders Matter? Hypotheses on Leadership Dynamics in Social Movements. *Mobilization,* 11, 1–22.

Nepstad, S. E. & Smith, C., 1999. Rethinking Recruitment to High-Risk/Cost Activism: The Case of Nicaragua Exchange. *Mobilization,* 4, 25–40.

Noakes, J. A. & Johnston, H., 2005. Frames of Protest: A Road Map to a Perspective. *In* H. Johnston & J. A. Noakes (eds) *Frames of Protest. Social Movements and the Framing Perspective.* Boston: Rowman and Littlefield, 1–29.

Noonan, R. K., 1995. Women Against the State: Political Opportunities and Collective Action Frames in Chile's Transition to Democracy. *Sociological Forum,* 10, 81–111.

North, D. C., 1981. *Structure and Change in Economic History.* New York: W. W. Norton & Company.

North, D. C. & Thomas, R. P., 1973. The Rise of the Western World. A New Economic History. Cambridge: Cambridge University Press.

Oberschall, A., 1973. *Social Conflict and Social Movements.* Englewood Cliffs, NJ: Prentice Hall.

Oberschall, A., 1979. Protracted Conflict. *In* M. N. Zald & J. D. McCarthy (eds) *The Dynamics of Social Movements.* Cambridge, MA: Winthrop, 45–70.

Oberschall, A., 1980. Loosely Structured Collective Conflict: A Theory and an Application. *Research in Social Movements, Conflict and Change,* 3, 45–68.

Oberschall, A., 1993. *Social Movements: Ideologies, Interests, and Identities.* New Brunswick, NJ: Transaction Books.

Oberschall, A., 1994. Rational Choice in Collective Protests. *Rationality & Society,* 6, 79–100.

Oegema, D. & Klandermans, B., 1994. Why Social Movement Sympathizers Don't Participate: Erosion and Nonconversion of Support. *American Sociological Review,* 59, 703–722.

Oliver, P., 1980. Rewards and Punishments as Selective Incentives for Collective Action. *American Journal of Sociology,* 85, 1356–1375.

Oliver, P., 1993. Formal Models of Collective Action. *Annual Review of Sociology,* 19, 271–300.

Oliver, P. & Johnston, H., 2005. What a Good Idea! Ideologies and Frames in Social

Movement Research. *In* H. Johnston & J. A. Noakes (eds) *Frames of Protest. Social Movements and the Framing Perspective.* Boston: Rowman and Littlefield, 185–203.

Oliver, P. & Marwell, G., 1988. The Paradox of Group Size in Collective Action. *American Sociological Review,* 53, 1–8.

Olson, M., 1965. *The Logic of Collective Action* Cambridge, MA: Harvard University Press.

Olson, M., 1982. *The Rise and Decline of Nations. Economic Strength, Stagflation, and Social Rigidities.* New Haven, CT, and London: Yale University Press.

Olson, M., 1986. A Theory of Social Movements, Social Classes, and Castes. *In* S. Lindenberg, J. S. Coleman & S. Nowak (eds) *Approaches to Social Theory.* New York: Russell Sage Foundation, 317–344.

Olson, M., 1990. The Logic of Collective Action in Soviet-Type Societies. *Journal of Soviet Nationalities,* 1, 8–27.

Opp, K.-D., 1970. Theories of the Middle Range as a Strategy for the Construction of a General Sociological Theory. A Critique of a Sociological Dogma. *Quality and Quantity,* 4, 243–253.

Opp, K.-D., 1984. Balance Theory: Progress and Stagnation of a Social Psychological Theory. *Philosophy of the Social Sciences,* 14, 27–49.

Opp, K.-D., 1986. Soft Incentives and Collective Action. Participation in the Anti-Nuclear Movement. *British Journal of Political Science,* 16, 87–112.

Opp, K.-D., 1988a. Community Integration and Incentives for Political Protest. *In* B. Klandermans, H. Kriesi & S. Tarrow (eds) *From Structure to Action: Comparing Social Movement Research Across Cultures.* Greenwich, CT: Jai Press.

Opp, K.-D., 1988b. Grievances and Participation in Social Movements. *American Sociological Review,* 53, 853–864.

Opp, K.-D., 1989a. Integration into Voluntary Associations and Incentives for Political Protest. *In* B. Klandermans, H. Kriesi & S. Tarrow (eds) *Organizing for Change: Social Movement Organizations in Europe and the United States.* Greenwich, CT: JAI Press, 345–362.

Opp, K.-D., 1989b. *The Rationality of Political Protest. A Comparative Analysis of Rational Choice Theory.* Boulder, CO: Westview Press.

Opp, K.-D., 1990. Postmaterialism, Collective Action, and Political Protest. *American Journal of Political Science,* 34, 212–235.

Opp, K.-D., 1993. Spontaneous Revolutions. The Case of East Germany in 1989. *In* H.D. Kurz (ed.) *United Germany and the New Europe.* Cheltenham: Edward Elgar, 11–30.

Opp, K.-D., 1994. Repression and Revolutionary Action. East Germany in 1989. *Rationality and Society,* 6, 101–138.

Opp, K.-D., 1999. Contending Conceptions of the Theory of Rational Action. *Journal of Theoretical Politics,* 11, 171–202.

Opp, K.-D., 2000. Adverse Living Conditions, Grievances, and Political Protest after Communism. The Example of East Germany. *Social Forces,* 79, 29–65.

Opp, K.-D., 2001. Social Networks and the Emergence of Protest Norms. *In* M. Hechter & K.-D. Opp (eds) *Social Norms.* New York: Russell Sage Foundation, 234–273.

Opp, K.-D., 2005. Explanations by Mechanisms in the Social Sciences. Problems, Advantages and Alternatives. *Mind & Society,* 4, 163–178.

Opp, K.-D. & Gern, C., 1993. Dissident Groups, Personal Networks, and Spontaneous Cooperation: The East German Revolution of 1989. *American Sociological Review,* 58, 659–680.

Opp, K.-D. & Roehl, W., 1990. Repression, Micromobilization, and Political Protest. *Social Forces*, 69, 521–548.

Opp, K.-D., Voss, P. & Gern, C., 1995. *The Origins of a Spontaneous Revolution. East Germany 1989*. Ann Arbor: Michigan University Press.

Passy, F., 2001. Socialization, Connection, and the Structure/Agency Gap: A Specification of the Impact of Networks on Participation in Social Movements. *Mobilization*, 6, 173–192.

Perrow, C., 1979. The Sixties Observed. *In* M. N. Zald & J. D. McCarthy (eds) *The Dynamics of Social Movements*. Cambridge, MA: Winthrop, 192–211.

Pfaff, S., 2006. *Exit-Voice Dynamics and the Collapse of East Germany: The Crisis of Leninism and the Revolution of 1989*. Durham, NC: Duke University Press.

Pichardo, N. A., 1988. Resource Mobilization: An Analysis of Conflicting Theoretical Variations. *Sociological Quarterly*, 29, 97–110.

Piven, F. F. & Cloward, R. A., 1979. *Poor People's Movements. Why They Succeed, How They Fail*. New York: Vintage Books.

Piven, F. F. & Cloward, R. A., 1991. Collective Protest: A Critique of Resource Mobilization Theory. *International Journal of Politics, Culture and Society*, 4, 435–458.

Piven, F. F. & Cloward, R. A., 1992. Normalizing Collective Protest (NOTE: Identical to: Collective Protest: A Critque of Resource Mobilization Theory, 1991). *In* A. Morris & C. McClurg Mueller (eds) *Frontiers in Social Movement Theory*. New Haven, CT, and London: Yale University Press, 301–325.

Pizzorno, A., 1978. Political Exchange and Collective Identity in Industrial Conflict. *In* C. Crouch & A. Pizzorno (eds) *The Resurgence of Class Conflict in Western Europe since 1968*. New York: Holmes and Meier, Nicht angegeben.

Polletta, F., 1998. "It was like a fever." Narrative and Identity in Social Protest. *Social Problems*, 45, 137–159.

Polletta, F., 2005. How Participatory Democracy Became White: Culture and Organizational Choce. *Mobilization*, 10, 271–288.

Polletta, F. & Ho, M. K., 2006. Frames and Their Consequences. *In* R. E. Goodin & C. Tilly (eds) *The Oxford Handbook of Contextual Political Analysis*. Oxford: Oxford University Press, 187–209.

Polletta, F. & Jasper, J. M., 2001. Collective Identity and Social Movements. *Annual Review of Sociology*, 27, 283–305.

Popkin, S., 1988. Political Entrepreneurs and Peasant Movements in Vietnam. *In* M. Taylor (ed.) *Rationality and Revolution*. Cambridge: Cambridge University Press, 9–62.

Popper, K. R., 1959. *The Logic of Scientific Discovery*. New York: Basic Books.

Price, M. E., Cosmides, L. & Tooby, J., 2002. Punitive Sentiment as an Anti-Free Rider Psychological Device. *Evolution and Human Behavior*, 23, 203–231.

Priest, G., 2000. *Logic. A Very Short Introduction*. Oxford: Oxford University Press.

Prosch, B. & Abraham, M., 1991. Die Revolution in der DDR. Eine strukturell-individualistische Erklärungsskizze. *Kölner Zeitschrift für Soziologie und Sozialpsychologie*, 43, 291–301.

Reicher, S. D., 1984. The St. Paul's Riot: An Explanation of the Limits of Crowd Action in Terms of a Social Identity Model. *European Journal of Social Psychology*, 14, 1–21.

Reicher, S. D., 1996. "The Battle of Westminster": Developing the Social Identity Model of Crowd Behaviour in Order to Explain the Initiation and Development of Collective Conflict. *European Journal of Social Psychology*, 26, 115–134.

Reitan, R., 2007. *Global Activism*. London and New York: Routledge.

Reynolds, P. D., 2007 (first 1971). *A Primer in Theory Construction*. Boston: Allyn and Bacon.

Riches, W. T. M., 2004 (2nd ed.). *The Civil Rights Movement. Struggle and Resistance*. New York: Palgrave Macmillan.

Riker, W. H. & Ordeshook, P. C., 1973. *An Introduction to Positive Political Theory*. Englewood Cliffs, NJ: Prentice Hall.

Rosenthal, N. & Schwartz, M., 1989. Spontaneity and Democracy in Social Movements. *In* B. Klandermans (ed.) *International Social Movement Research, Volume 2*. Greenwich, CT: JAI Press, 33–60.

Rucht, D., 1994. *Modernisierung und neue soziale Bewegungen*. Frankfurt: Campus.

Salert, B., 1976. *Revolutions and Revolutionaries. Four Theories*. New York: Elsevier.

Sandler, T., 1992. *Collective Action. Theory and Applications*. Ann Arbor: Michigan University Press.

Sandler, T., 2001. *Economic Concepts for the Social Sciences*. Cambridge: Cambridge University Press.

Schelling, T. C., 1978. *Micromotives and Macrobehavior*. New York and London: W.W. Morton and Company.

Schussman, A. & Soule, S. A., 2005. Process and Protest: Accounting for Individual Protest Participation. *Social Forces,* 84, 1083–1108.

Simon, B., Loewy, M., Stürmer, S., Weber, U., Freytag, P., Habig, C., Kampmeier, C. & Spahlinger, P., 1998. Collective Identification and Social Movement Participation. *Journal of Personality and Social Psychology,* 74, 646–658.

Simon, H. A., 1979. Rational Decision Making in Business Organizations. *American Economic Review,* 69, 493–513.

Simon, H. A., 1983. *Reason in Human Affairs*. Stanford, CA: Stanford University Press.

Skocpol, T., 1995. Contribution to "The Role of Theory in Comparative Politics: A Symposium". *World Politics,* 48, 37–46.

Smelser, N. J., 1963. *Theory of Collective Behavior*. New York: Free Press.

Snow, D., 2004. Framing Processes, Ideology, and Discursive Fields. *In* D. A. Snow, S. A. Soule & H. Kriesi (eds) *The Blackwell Companion to Social Movements*. Oxford: Blackwell, 380–412.

Snow, D. & Benford, R., 1988. Ideology, Frame Resonance, and Participant Mobilization. *International Social Movement Research,* 1, 197–218.

Snow, D. & Benford, R., 1992. Master Frames and Cycles of Protest. *In* A. Morris & C. McClurg Mueller (eds) *Frontiers of Social Movement Theory*. New Haven, CT: Yale University Press.

Snow, D. & Oliver, P., 1995. Social Movements and Collective Behavior: Social Psychological Dimensions and Considerations. *In* K. S. Cook, G. A. Fine & J. House (eds) *Sociological Perspectives on Social Psychology*. Boston: Allyn and Bacon, 571–599.

Snow, D., Rochford, B., Worden, S. & Benford, R., 1986. Frame Alignment Processes, Micromobilization, and Movement Participation. *American Sociological Review,* 51, 464–481.

Snow, D., Zurcher, L. & Ekland-Olson, S., 1980. Social Networks and Social Movements: A Microstructural Approach to Differential Recruitment. *American Sociological Review,* 45, 787–801.

Snyder, D. & Kelly, W. R., 1979. Strategies for Investigating Violence and Social Change: Illustrations from Analyses of Racial Disorders and Implications for Mobilization Research. *In* M. N. Zald & J. D. McCarthy (eds) *The Dynamics of Social Movements*.

Resource Mobilization, Social Control, and Tactics. Cambridge, MA: Winthrop, 212–237.

Staggenborg, S., 1986. Coalition Work in the Pro-Choice Movement: Organizational and Environmental Opportunities and Obstacles. *Social Problems,* 33, 374–390.

Staggenborg, S. & Taylor, V., 2005. Whatever Happened to the Women's Movement? *Mobilization,* 10, 37–52.

Steinberg, M. W., 1998. Tilting the Frame: Considerations on Collective Action Framing from a Discursive Turn. *Theory and Society,* 27, 845–872.

Steinberg, M. W., 1999. The Talk and Back Talk of Collective Action: A Dialogic Analysis of Repertoires of Discourse among Nineteenth-Century English Cotton Spinners. *American Journal of Sociology,* 105, 736–780.

Stürmer, S. & Simon, B., 2004. The Role of Collective Identification in Social Movement Participation: A Panel Study in the Context of the German Gay Movement. *Personality and Social Psychology Bulletin,* 30, 263–277.

Stürmer, S., Simon, B., Loewy, M. & Jörger, H., 2003. The Dual-Pathway Model of Social Movement Participation: The Case of the Fat Acceptance Movement. *Social Psychology Quarterly,* 66, 71–82.

Suppes, P., 1957. *Introduction to Logic.* Toronto: D. van Nostrand Company.

Tajfel, H., 1978. Social Categorization, Social Identity, and Social Comparison. *In* H. Tajfel (ed.) *Differentiation Between Groups: Studies in the Social Psychology of Intergroup Relations.* New York: Academic Press, 61–76.

Tajfel, H., 1981. *Human Groups and Social Categories. Studies in Social Psychology.* Cambridge: Cambridge University Press.

Tajfel, H. & Turner, J., 1979. An Integrative Theory of Intergroup Conflict. *In* W. G. Austin & S. Worchel (eds) *The Social Psychology of Intergroup Relations.* Monterey, CA: Brooks/Cole, 33–48.

Tajfel, H. & Turner, J. C., 1986. The Social Identity Theory of Intergroup Behavior. *In* S. Worchel & W. Austin (eds) *Psychology of Intergroup Relations.* Chicago: Nelson-Hall, 7–24.

Tarrow, S., 1983. *Struggling to Reform: Social Movements and Policy Change During Cycles of Protest.* Cornell University.

Tarrow, S., 1991a. *Struggle, Politics, and Reform: Collective Action, Social Movements, and Cycles of Protest.* Ithaca, NY: Cornell University Press.

Tarrow, S., 1991b. Understanding Political Change in Eastern Europe. *PS: Political Science and Politics,* 12–20.

Tarrow, S., 1992. Mentalities, Political Cultures, and Collective Action Frames: Constructing Meaning through Action. *In* A. D. Morris & C. McClurg Mueller (eds) *Frontiers in Social Movement Theory.* New Haven, CT: Yale University Press, 174–202.

Tarrow, S., 1994 (1st ed.). *Power in Movement. Social Movements, Collective Action and Politics.* Cambridge: Cambridge University Press.

Tarrow, S., 1996. States and Opportunities: The Political Structuring of Social Movements. *In* D. McAdam, J. McCarthy & M. N. Zald (eds) *Comparative Perspectives on Social Movements, Political Opportunities, and Cultural Framings.* Cambridge: Cambridge University Press, 41–61.

Tarrow, S., 1998 (2nd ed.). *Power in Movement. Social Movements, Collective Action and Politics* Cambridge: Cambridge University Press.

Tarrow, S., 2001. Silence and Voice in the Study of Contentious Politics: Introduction. *In* R. R. Aminzade, J. Goldstone, D. McAdam, E. J. Perry, W. H. Sewell Jr, S. Tarrow &

C. Tilly (eds) *Silence and Voice in the Study of Contentious Politics*. Cambridge: Cambridge University Press, 1–13.

Taylor, M., 1988. Rationality and Revolutionary Collective Action. *In* M. Taylor (ed.) *Rationality and Revolution*. Cambridge: Cambridge University Press, 63–97.

Taylor, V., 1989. Social Movement Continuity: The Women's Movement in Abeyance. *American Sociological Review,* 54, 761–775.

Taylor, V. & Whittier, N. E., 1992. Collective Identity in Social Movement Communities: Lesbian Feminist Mobilization. *In* A. D. Morris & C. McClurg Mueller (eds) *Frontiers in Social Movement Theory*. New Haven, CT: Yale University Press, 104–129.

Teske, N., 1997. *Political Activists in America: The Identity Construction Model of Political Participation*. Cambridge: Cambridge University Press.

Tillock, H. & Morrison, D. E., 1979. Group Size and Contributions to Collective Action: An Examination of Olson's Theory Using Data from Zero Population Growth Inc. *Research in Social Movements, Conflicts and Change,* 2, 131–158.

Tilly, C., 1978. *From Mobilization to Revolution*. New York: Random House.

Tilly, C., 1979. Repertoires of Contention in America and Britain, 1750–1830. *In* M. N. Zald & J. D. McCarthy (eds) *The Dynamics of Social Movements. Resource Mobilization, Social Control, and Tactics*. Cambridge, MA: Winthrop, 126–155.

Tilly, C., 1997. Kings in the Beggars' Raiment. *Mobilization,* 2, 107–111.

Tilly, C., 2005. Repression, Mobilization, and Explanation. *In* C. Davenport, H. Johnston & C. Mueller (eds) *Repression and Mobilization*. Minneapolis: University of Minnesota Press, 211–226.

Toch, H., 1965. *The Social Psychology of Social Movements*. Indianapolis, IN: Bobbs-Merrill.

Turner, R. H., 1969. The Public Perception of Protest. *American Sociological Review,* 34, 815–831.

Turner, R. H., 1981. Collective Behavior and Resource Mobilization as Approaches to Social Movements: Issues and Continuities. *Research in Social Movements, Conflict and Change,* 4, 1–24.

Turner, R. N. & Killian, L., 1972. *Collective Behavior*. Englewood Cliffs, NJ: Prentice Hall.

Udéhn, L., 1993. Twenty-five Years with *The Logic of Collective Action. Acta Sociologica,* 36, 239–261.

Useem, B., 1980. Solidarity Model, Breakdown Model, and the Boston Anti-Busing Movement. *American Sociological Review,* 45, 357–369.

Van Dyke, N., 2003. Crossing Movement Boundaries: Factors That Facilitate Coalition Protest by American College Students, 1930–1990. *Social Problems,* 5049, 226–250.

Varese, F. & Yaish, M., 2000. The Importance of Being Asked: The Rescue of Jews in Nazi Europe. *Rationality and Society,* 12, 307–334.

Veltmeyer, H. & Petras, J., 2002. The Social Dynamics of Brazil's Rural Landless Workers' Movement: Ten Hypotheses on Successful Leadership. *Canadian Review of Sociology and Anthropology,* 39, 79–96.

Verba, S., Schlozman, K. L. & Brady, H. E., 1995. *Voice and Equality. Civic Voluntarism in American Politics*. Cambridge, MA: Harvard University Press.

Voss, K., 1996. The Collapse of a Social Movement: The Interplay of Mobilizing Structures, Framing and Political Opportunities in the Knights of Labor. *In* D. McAdam, J. McCarthy & M. N. Zald (eds) *Comparative Perspectives on Social Movements, Political Opportunities, and Cultural Framings*. Cambridge: Cambridge University Press, 227–258.

Voss, T. & Abraham, M., 2000. Rational Choice Theory in Sociology: A Survey. *In* S. R. Quah & A. Sales (eds) *The International Handbook of Sociology*. London: Sage Publications, 50–83.

Walsh, E. J., 1978. Mobilization Theory Vis-À-Vis a Mobilization Process: The Case of the United Farm Workers' Movement. *Research in Social Movements, Conflict and Change*, 1, 155–175.

Walsh, E. J., 1981. Resource Mobilization and Citizen Protest in Communities Around Three Mile Island. *Social Problems*, 29, 1–21.

Walsh, E. J., 1986. The Role of Target Vulnerabilities in High-Techology Protest Movements: The Nuclear Establishment at Three Mile Island. *Sociological Forum*, 1, 199–218.

Walsh, E. J., 1987. Challenging Offical Risk Assessments via Protest Mobilization: The TMI Case. *In* B. B. Johnson & V. T. Covello (eds) *The Social and Cultural Constructin of Risk*. Dordrecht: D. Reidel, 85–101.

Walsh, E. J., 1988. *Democracy in the Shadows. Citizen Mobilization in the Wake of the Accident at Three Mile Island*. New York: Greenwood Press.

Walsh, E. J. & Cable, S., 1986. Litigation and Citizen Protest After the Three Mile Island Accident. *Research in Political Sociology*, 2, 293–316.

Walsh, E. J. & Warland, R. H., 1983. Social Movement Involvement in the Wake of a Nuclear Accident: Activists and Free Riders in the TMI Area. *American Sociological Review*, 48, 764–780.

Weigert, A. J., Teitge, J. S. & Teitge, D. W., 1986. *Society and Identity. Toward a Sociological Psychology*. Cambridge: Cambridge University Press.

Wendt, A., 1994. Collective Identity Formation and the International State. *American Political Science Review*, 88, 384–398.

White, J. W., 1988. Rational Rioters: Leaders, Followers, and Popular Protest in Early Japan. *Politics and Society*, 16, 1–34.

Whitely, P. F., 1995. Rational Choice and Political Participation-Evaluating the Debate. *Political Research Quarterly*, 48, 211–233.

Wilson, T. D., 2002. *Strangers to Ourselves. Discovering the Adaptive Unconscious*. Cambridge, MA: Belknap Press.

Wiltfang, G. & McAdam, D., 1991. Distinguishing Cost and Risk in Sanctuary Activism. *Social Forces*, 69, 987–1010.

Wood, E. J., 2000. *Forging Democracy from Below: Insurgent Transitions in South Africa and El Salvador*. Cambridge: Cambridge University Press.

Wood, E. J., 2003. *Insurgent Collective Action and Civil War in El Salvador*. Cambridge: Cambridge University Press.

Zald, M. N., 1991. The Continuing Vitality of Resource Mobilization Theory. Response to Herbert Kitschelt's Critique. *In* D. Rucht (ed.) *Research on Social Movements. The State of the Art in Western Europe and the USA*. Frankfurt am Main and Boulder, CO, 348–354.

Zald, M. N., 1992. Looking Backward to Look Forward. Reflections on the Past and Future of the Resource Mobilization Research Program. *In* A. D. Morris & C. McClurg-Mueller (eds) *Frontiers in Social Movement Theory*. New Haven, CT: Yale University Press, 326–348.

Zald, M. N. & Ash, R., 1966. Social Movement Organizations: Growth, Decay and Change. *Social Forces*, 44, 327–341.

Zald, M. N. & Berger, M. A., 1978. Social Movements in Organizations: Coup d'Etat, Insurgency, and Mass Movement. *American Journal of Sociology*, 83, 823–861.

Zald, M. N. & McCarthy, J., 1980. Social Movement Industries: Cooperation and Competition Among Movement Organizations. *Research in Social Movements, Conflict and Change,* 3, 1–20.

Zald, M. N. & McCarthy, J., 2002. The Resource Mobilization Research Program: Progress, Challenge, and Transformation. *In* J. Berger & M. Zelditch Jr (eds) *New Directions in Contemporary Sociological Theory.* Lanham, MD: Rowman and Littlefield, 147–176.

Zald, M. N. & McCarthy, J. D., 1979. *The Dynamics of Social Movements. Resource Mobilization, Social Control, and Tactics.* Cambridge, MA: Winthrop.

Zald, M. N. & McCarthy, J. D., 1987. *Social Movements in an Organizational Society. Collected Essays.* New Brunswick, NJ: Transaction Books.

Index